# Dictionary of
# Asia Pacific Business Terms

## TAN CHWEE HUAT
*Faculty of Business Administration*
*National University of Singapore*

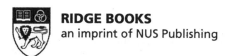

**RIDGE BOOKS**
an imprint of NUS Publishing

© 2004    Singapore University Press
NUS Publishing
Yusof Ishak House
31 Lower Kent Ridge Road
Singapore 119078

Fax: (65) 6774-0652
E-mail: supbooks@nus.edu.sg
Website: http://www.nus.edu.sg/npu

ISBN 9971-69-275-9 (Paper)

Typeset by: Scientifik Graphics (Singapore) Pte Ltd
Printed in Singapore

# PREFACE

The world of business uses numerous acronyms and abbreviations, and has its unique terminology. This reference volume covers the Asia Pacific business world from Myanmar to Japan, and Mongolia to Indonesia, as well as the South Asia sub-continent including Bangladesh, Bhutan, India, Nepal, Pakistan and Sri Lanka. Business terms used in Australia, New Zealand and the South Pacific countries, as well as some American terms common to the business community, are also included.

The collection in this volume also includes terms related to the United Nations, International Monetary Fund, the World Bank and other major international organizations. It gives capsule entries on the key players and concepts in the various countries and institutions. It provides a one-stop reference source for library users. It is also a useful desk book for academics, students, bankers, financiers and other business people, as well as secretaries and administrators.

Most of the terms are specific to the Asia Pacific. They are not found in standard business, banking or finance dictionaries.

# LEXICON

# LEXICON

**A Shares (China)**
These are domestic shares of Chinese companies denominated and traded in RMB by local Mainland persons.

**Accession**
This is a process by which a country becomes a member of an international organization e.g. World Trade Organization.

**Acer**   *www.global.acer.com*
Acer started in 1976 in Taiwan under the name Multitech. It is among the world's top ten branded PC vendors. It has marketing and service operations in more than 100 countries. It offers a wide range of IT products and services. It has been listed among the World's 100 Best Managed Companies and among Asia's Most Admired Companies.

**Acer's Aspire Academy Singapore**
Acer's Aspire Academy Singapore was formed in 2000 with the merger of Acer's Aspire Academy Taiwan and local Internet company 1to80.com. The merger combined 1to80.com's expertise in online learning with the academy's strength in classroom teaching. Courses included the Asian Executive Development Network and the Global Executive Development Series developed by the University of Michigan and the Thunderbird Graduate School of International Management in the US.

**ACI Singapore — The Financial Markets Association**   *www.acisin.com*
Formed in 1973, this association was known as the Forex Association of Singapore before July 1998. It promotes the educational and professional interests of the forex industry. It is affiliated to ACI — The Financial Markets Association, the global umbrella body of national associations. The Paris-based organization has 24,000 members in 80 countries.

**Administrative Punishment Law (China)**
In China, the Administrative Punishment Law came into effect on 1 October 1996. It set out procedures that administrative authorities must follow in imposing administrative punishment. Such punishment can only be imposed on the basis of published regulations.

3

**Agency for International Development (US)**
The Agency for International Development (AID) is a US government agency that administers foreign assistance programs in developing countries.

**Agrarian Services Centre (Sri Lanka)**
In Sri Lanka, Agrarian Services Centres (ASCs) were set up in the 1970s at the district level to coordinate the supply of agricultural inputs and services at the grassroots level.

**Agreement on Textile and Clothing**
In 1994, the Agreement on Textile and Clothing (ATC) replaced the former Multi Fiber Agreement (MFA). This followed the evolution of WTO from GATT after the Uruguay Round of meetings.

**Agri-bank**
See Vietnam Bank for Agriculture and Rural Development; and Vietnam Bank for Agriculture.

**Agri-Bio Park (Singapore)**
In Singapore, the Agri-Bio Park is a 10-hectare industrial park set up by the Agri-Food and Veterinary Authority (AVA) to attract agri-biotechnology companies. These companies deal with aquaculture, crop and livestock production, micro-propagation and tissue culture, genetic engineering and animal vaccines.

**Agricultural Bank of China**   *www.abchina.com*
The Agricultural Bank of China (ABC) was set up in 1979 to finance farming and the production and distribution of agricultural products.

**Agricultural Development Bank of Nepal**
The Agricultural Development Bank of Nepal (known as the Cooperatives Bank before 1967) was set up by the government in 1963. It provides loans for agricultural production and agro-business activities.

**Agricultural Development Bank of Pakistan**
The Agricultural Development Bank of Pakistan (ADBP) was formed in 1961 as a result of merging the Agricultural Development Finance Corporation (formed in 1951) and the Agricultural Development Bank (formed in 1957). It provides credit to the agricultural sector. Its capital is subscribed mainly by the Federal government (95%) and the provincial governments.

**Agricultural Refinance Development Corporation**
See National Bank for Agriculture and Rural Development (India).

**Agri-Food and Veterinary Authority (Singapore)** *www.ava.gov.sg*
In Singapore, the Agri-Food and Veterinary Authority (AVA) was formed on 1 April 2000, when the Primary Production Department in the Ministry of National Development was restructured into a new statutory board.

**AGTEX**
Long Binh Industrial Park (Vietnam).

**Air India** *www.airindia.com*
Air India is India's national flag carrier. It started in 1933 as Tata Airlines which was converted to a public company and renamed Air India in 1946. In the 1950s, Indian Airlines was formed with the merger of eight domestic airlines while Air India International was established to operate overseas services. The word "international" was dropped and from 1 March 1994, the airline has been functioning as Air India Ltd. It has a worldwide network of 44 destinations. (See also: Indian Airlines)

**Airport and Aviation Services Limited (Sri Lanka)**
In Sri Lanka, the government-owned company Airport and Aviation Services Limited (AAS) was formed in 1983 to succeed the Airport Authority and to develop and maintain all civil airports in Sri Lanka.

**Airport Core Program (Hong Kong)**
See Hong Kong International Airport.

**Airport Logistics Park of Singapore**
The Airport Logistics Park of Singapore (ALPS) is developed by the Civil Aviation Authority of Singapore (CAAS) and JTC Corporation. The 26-hectare park is located next to Changi Airport and within the free trade zone.

**Airport Authority of Thailand** *www.airportthai.or.th*
The Airport Authority of Thailand (AAT) operates airports. There are 28 commercial airports in Thailand, five of which are managed by AAT. These are international airports in Bangkok, Chiang Mai, Hat Yai, Phuket and Chiang Rai. The others are under the administration of the Department of Aviation, Ministry of Transport and Communications. (See also: New Bangkok International Airport)

**Airports Authority of India**   *www.civilaviation.nic.in*
The Airports Authority of India (AAI) was formed in 1995. It manages five international airports and 87 domestic airports.

**Airports of Thailand PCL**   *www.airportthai.or.th*
See Airport Authority of Thailand.

**All Ordinaries Share Price Index (Australia)**
This index (All Ords) is made up of the weighted share prices of about 500 Australian companies. Established by the Australian Exchange (ASX) at 500 points in January 1980, it measures the overall performance of the Australian share market. The companies are weighted according to their size in terms of market capitalization.

**Allahabad Bank (India)**   *www.allahabadbank.com*
In India, the Allahabad Bank is the oldest public sector bank with branches all over the country. It has served customers for about 140 years.

**Allied Bank of Pakistan**   *www.abl.com.pk*
The Allied Bank of Pakistan started in 1942 as the Australasia Bank at Lahore. It was the first Muslim bank to be established on the territory that became Pakistan in 1947. On 1 January 1974, all scheduled banks were nationalized, including Australasia Bank. Three small provincial banks were merged into Australasia Bank and the new entity was renamed the Allied Bank of Pakistan Ltd. In 1991, through the Employees Stock Ownership Plan (ESOP), Allied Bank became the world's first bank to be owned and managed by its employees.

**Allied Banking Corporation (Philippines)**
Allied Banking Corporation is listed on the Philippine Stock Exchange. It started in 1977 after the acquisition of General Bank & Trust Company. During the initial years, the bank catered mainly to the financial needs of local Chinese merchants. The bank is part of the Lucio Tan Group of Companies, which is a large conglomerate in the Philippines. After obtaining the expanded commercial banking licence in 1981, the bank diversified into merchant banking. Its major banking-related subsidiaries include: Allied Bank Philippines (UK) Plc, Allied Leasing & Finance Corp and First Allied Savings Bank.

**PT Alter Abadi (Indonesia)**
This is Indonesia's leading kaolin producer. Kaolin, or china clay, is used as raw material in many consumer products such as paper, ceramics and paint.

The company mines its kaolin from concession areas of over 2,400 hectares in South Sumatra and is one of the largest concession holders in Indonesia.

**Amata City project (Vietnam)**
Amata City is a Thai-Vietnamese joint venture located in Dong Nai province in Vietnam. It is next to Highway No. 1 and 25 kilometres northeast of Ho Chi Minh City. It is developed by Thai company Bang Pakong Industrial Park PCL and Sonadezi, the Vietnamese state developer of industrial estates in Dong Nai province. The industrial zone covers 700 hectares and provides infrastructure for 200 factories that employ 25,000 workers.

**American Chamber of Commerce of the Philippines** *www.amchamphilippines.com*
The American Chamber of Commerce of the Philippines (AmCham) was founded in 1902 and incorporated in 1920 under Philippine laws. It is a private independent and non-profit association affiliated with the Chamber of Commerce of the United States (COCUSA) and the Asia Pacific Council of American Chambers (APCAC). It maintains links with other foreign chambers in Manila and Philippine business groups. Its network in the US includes the Philippine-American Chamber of Commerce in New York, US-RP Business Committee, Asia Society and the US-ASEAN Business Council.

**American Depository Receipt**
This depository receipt enables American investors to trade shares from other countries.

**American Stock Exchange (AMEX)**
This is a stock exchange in New York for trading the shares of small and medium companies. In contrast, the New York Stock Exchange trades in shares of large companies.

**Ankatan Bersenjata Republik Indonesia (ABRI)**
Indonesian Armed Forces.

**Anukret**
Sub-decree (Cambodia).

**ANZ Banking Group** *www.anz.com/nz*
Australia and New Zealand Banking Group (ANZ) is the second largest Australia-based bank and is among the world's 100 largest banks. It offers a full range of financial services in Australia and New Zealand. It has offices in Fiji, Solomon Islands, Tonga, Vanuatu and other Pacific island countries. It has a wide international network trading as ANZ and ANZ Grindlays.

**APEC Business Advisory Council**   *www.abaconline.org*
The Asia Pacific Economic Cooperation (APEC) Business Advisory Council
(ABAC) was initiated by APEC Leaders at the APEC Summit in Osaka in
November 1995. It was formed in May 1996 with three CEOs from each of
the 18 APEC members. Its main objective is to advise APEC Leaders on
specific business priorities. There is one standing committee on Review of the
APEC Action Plan. Specific task forces are then formed to focus on finance,
trade and investment, technology and other issues. The reports of these task
forces and other committees are published in an annual report to be discussed
at the APEC Leaders' Meeting.

**APEC Centre for Technology Exchange and Training for SMEs**
*www.actetsme.org*
The APEC Centre for Technology Exchange and Training for SMEs
(ACTETSME) promotes technology exchange and training for small and
medium enterprises in the APEC region. It is located in the Science &
Technology Park at Laguna, Philippines.

**Apparel Export Promotion Council (India)**
In India, the Apparel Export Promotion Council (AEPC) is a non-profit
company owned by the Ministry of Commerce. It provides services to promote
apparel exports.

**Approved Boutique Fund Manager Scheme (Singapore)**
In Singapore, the Approved Boutique Fund Manager (ABFM) scheme was
introduced in 1999. It promotes the growth of local fund management
professionals and adds diversity to the Singapore fund management industry.

**Approved Cyber Trader Scheme (Singapore)**
In Singapore, the Approved Cyber Trader (ACT) scheme was introduced in
1999 to promote Singapore as a regional e-commerce hub. ACT companies
enjoy a concession tax incentive on offshore income derived from transactions
over the Internet.

**Approved International Fair (Singapore)**
In Singapore, the Approved International Fair (AIF) status is granted by the
International Enterprise Singapore (known as Trade Development Board or
TDB before 2002). It encourages exhibitors to develop Singapore as an
international exhibition city.

**Approved International Shipping Enterprise Scheme (Singapore)**
In Singapore, the Approved International shipping Enterprise Scheme is administered by the International Enterprise (known as Trade Development Board or TDB before 2002) to promote Singapore as an international maritime centre. A company with AIS status gets tax exemption on income from the operation of its ships in international waters.

**Approved International Trader Scheme (Singapore)**
In Singapore, the Approved International Trader (AIT) scheme is administered by the International Enterprise (formerly known as Trade Development Board or TDB before 2002) to promote Singapore as a global trading centre. A company with AIT status is taxed at a concession rate of 10% on income derived from offshore international trading activities in approved commodities.

**Approved Marine Insurer (Singapore)**
In Singapore, the Approved Marine Insurer (AMI) status was introduced in February 2000 by the Monetary Authority of Singapore. Companies with AMI status are exempted from the tax on underwriting profits, as well as certain income derived from investing premium income and shareholders' funds in relation to marine insurance business.

**Approved Oil Trader Scheme (Singapore)**
In Singapore, the Approved Oil Trader (AOT) scheme is administered by International Enterprise (known as Trade Development Board or TDB before 2002) to promote Singapore as an international oil trading centre. A company with AOT status is taxed at a concession rate of 10% on income derived from international trading activities in approved oil products.

**Approved Securities Company (Singapore)**
In Singapore, a securities company that has been granted the Approved Securities Company (ASC) status by the government enjoys concession tax rates.

**Approved Shipping Logistics Scheme (Singapore)**
In Singapore, the Approved Shipping Logistics (ASL) scheme was introduced by IE Singapore (formerly Trade and Development Board) to encourage companies in the maritime industry to engage in ship agency, ship management and logistics activities.

**APSARA**
In Cambodia, the APSARA Authority was established in 1995 as a public legal entity with administrative and financial autonomy. Its mission is to develop

tourism and protect the Seam Reap Angkor area. It is governed by an Administration Council with the First and Second Prime Ministers as Co-Presidents. Other council members include ministers from related ministries and the Seam Reap Governor.

### Arab-Malaysian Unit Trust Berhad (AMUT)
In Malaysia, AMUT is a joint venture between the Arab-Malaysian Banking Group and Australia's investment bank Mcquarie Bank.

### Asahi Bank (Japan)   *www.daiwabank.co.jp*
In March 2002, Asahi Bank joined Daiwa Banking Holdings which has changed its name to Resona Holdings. Asahi Bank and Daiwa Bank have merged to become Resonal Bank. Its operations in the Saitama prefecture have been separated to form the Saitama Resona Bank. (See also: Daiwa Bank Holdings, Resona Holdings)

### ASB Bank (New Zealand)   *www.asbbank.co.nz*
In New Zealand, the ASB Bank started as the Auckland Savings Bank in 1847. Over the decades, it expanded beyond savings to provide a full range of financial services. It was renamed ASB Bank in 1987. The Commonwealth Bank of Australia (CBA) bought 75% of ASB Bank shares in 1989. The bank began operating on a truly national basis when it amalgamated with its wholly owned subsidiary Westland Bank. The enlarged bank has about 130 branches throughout New Zealand.

### ASCO Training Institute (Thailand)
See Association of Securities Companies.

### ASEAN Bankers Association   *www.aseanbankers.org*
The ASEAN Bankers Association (ABA) was formed in 1976 with five members (Indonesia, Malaysia, Philippines, Singapore and Thailand). The number of members increased when more associations from other ASEAN countries joined — Brunei in 1983, Vietnam in 1995 and Cambodia in 1999. Its main objective is to promote the development of the financial system and banking profession in the ASEAN countries.

### ASEAN Common Effective Preferential Tariff (CEPT)
In ASEAN, the CEPT was launched in 1993. The scheme provides for tariff cuts and other measures to liberalize intra-ASEAN trade.

## ASEAN-EC Management Centre

The ASEAN-EC Management Centre (AEMC) is located in Brunei. Its formation was the result of an inter-regional dialogue focusing on economic cooperation program for ASEAN countries and the European Union. AEMC addresses current management issues and problems in comparative, regional and inter-regional perspectives.

## ASEAN Economic Ministers

ASEAN Economic Ministers' (AEM) meeting was institutionalized at the 1977 Kuala Lumpur ASEAN Summit. The AEM meeting is held annually and reports to the ASEAN Heads of Government during the ASEAN Summit.

## ASEAN Fund Limited    *www.aseanbankers.org*

The ASEAN Fund (ASEAN Fund Limited or AFL) was launched by the ASEAN Bankers' Association in 1988. It is a US$150 million fund listed on the Singapore Exchange. It invests in equities of companies in Indonesia, Malaysia, Philippines, Singapore and Thailand for long-term capital appreciation. (See also: ASEAN Bankers Association, ASEAN Supreme Fund)

## ASEAN Industrial Cooperation (AICO) Arrangement

An AICO arrangement is a cooperative arrangement consisting of at least two participating companies from two ASEAN countries. The companies must fulfill these criteria: incorporated and operating in any ASEAN country, have a minimum of 30% national equity, and undertake resource sharing industrial complementation or industrial cooperation activities.

## ASEAN Labour Ministers' Meeting

The ASEAN Labour Ministers' Meeting (ALMM) is an annual meeting for ASEAN Labour Ministers to discuss issues of common concerns, including technical cooperation and matters relating to the International Labour Organization (ILO). The meeting is usually preceded by the Senior Officials' Meeting (SLOM).

## ASEAN Ministerial Meeting

The ASEAN Ministerial Meeting (AMM) was established by the 1967 Bangkok Declaration. It is responsible for the formulation of policy guidelines and coordination of ASEAN activities. ASEAN Foreign Ministers meet annually during the AMM. However, the AMM could include other relevant ministers as and when necessary.

**ASEAN National Secretariat**
Each ASEAN country has a National Secretariat in the Foreign Ministry that organizes and implements ASEAN-related activities at the country level.

**ASEAN Regional Forum**
The ASEAN Regional Forum (ARF) is a major component of the regional security architecture where countries inside and outside the Asian Pacific (including all the major powers) discuss important security issues. The ARF consists of Brunei, Cambodia, Indonesia, Laos, Malaysia, Myanmar, Philippines, Singapore, Thailand, Vietnam, Australia, Canada, China, European Union, India, Japan, South Korea, Mongolia, New Zealand, Papua New Guinea, Russia and USA.

**ASEAN Secretariat**
The ASEAN Secretariat was set up by an Agreement signed by the ASEAN Foreign Ministers during the 1976 Bali Summit. Its objective is to enhance coordination and implementation of policies, projects and activities of the various ASEAN bodies. (See also: ASEAN National Secretariat)

**ASEAN Secretary General**
The Secretary General of ASEAN is appointed on merit by the ASEAN Heads of Government with the recommendations of the ASEAN Ministerial Meeting. The person is accorded ministerial status with the mandate to initiate, advise, coordinate and implement ASEAN activities.

**ASEAN Summit**
The highest authority of ASEAN is the meeting of the Heads of Government, the ASEAN Summit. The Heads of Government meet formally every three years and informally at least once in between to set directions for ASEAN activities.

**ASEAN Supreme Fund**   *www.aseanbankers.org*
The ASEAN Supreme Fund (ASEAN Supreme Fund Limited or ASL) was launched in 1996 by the ASEAN Bankers Association. It is a US$100 million fund listed on the exchanges in Singapore and Osaka. It invests in equity and equity-related securities of companies in ASEAN countries. (See also: ASEAN Bankers Association, ASEAN Fund)

**Asia Business Fellowship Program (Singapore)**
In Singapore, the Asia Business Fellowship Program was started by the Ministry of Trade and Industry (MTI) in 2001. The aim was to build a group of future

business leaders who had knowledge and links to the Asian region. Over five years, MTI would sponsor 100 students each year for MBA and business-related graduate studies in universities in China, India and other countries in the region. These Asia Business Fellows would be required to serve Singapore enterprises in their internationalization drive. For executives in charge of business development, MTI would co-sponsor an in-market immersion program, so that these executives could be placed in companies in the region to broaden their exposure.

### Asia-Europe Meeting
The idea of having an Asia-Europe Meeting (Asem) was mooted by Singapore Prime Minister Goh Chok Tong in 1996 to bring Europe and Asia closer. Its three main objectives are political dialogue, economic cooperation and cultural interaction. The first summit was held in Bangkok, the second in London and the third in Seoul.

### Asia Forest Network    *www.mekonginfo.org*
The Asia Forest Network (AFN) was formed in 1987. It is a non-profit corporation registered both in the Philippines and the US. It supports communities to protect sustainable use of Asia's forests. It comprises a coalition of planners, policy-makers, government foresters and NGOs in South and Southeast Asia.

### Asia Pacific Association for Business Administration    *www.apaba.org.tw*
In Taiwan, the Asia Pacific Association for Business Administration (APABA) was formed in 1995. It promotes experience exchange among its members on business management in the Asia Pacific region. It reinforces the international competitive advantage of Taiwan industries with its ideal of "rooting industries in Taiwan and operating in the Asia Pacific region".

### Asia Pacific Economic Cooperation    *www.apecsec.org.sg*
The Asia Pacific Economic Cooperation (APEC) forum was set up in 1989. It is a grouping of 21 economies comprising both developed and developing economies on both sides of the Pacific Ocean. APEC operates on consensus reached through collective and individual action plans. It is the primary international organization for promoting trade and economic cooperation among member economies. It provides a forum for ministerial discussion on economic issues. Member economies include Australia, Brunei, Canada, Chile, China, Hong Kong, Indonesia, Japan, Korea, Malaysia, Mexico, New Zealand, Papua New Guinea, Peru, Philippines, Russia, Singapore, Chinese Taipei, Thailand, United States and Vietnam. The Secretariat is in Singapore.

## Asia Pacific Resources International Limited (APRIL)

APRIL is a Singapore-registered company that is listed on the New York Stock Exchange. It is owned by Indonesian businessman Sukanto Tanoto who is also the chairman of Raja Garuda Mas (RGM) Group. In 1997, APRIL had a strategic alliance with Finland's UPM-Kymmene to expand its paper and pulp plants in the Riau province in Indonesia — PT Riau Pulp and Paper and PT Riau Andalan Kertas. APRIL also has a paper mill in Suzhou, China.

## Asia Pacific Risk and Insurance Association (APRIA)

*www.scicollege.org.sg/apria.htm*

APRIA was formed in 1997 to encourage academics and practitioners in the Asia-Pacific region to do joint research for the benefit of the insurance industry. The Secretariat is the Singapore College of Insurance.

## Asian Currency Unit (ACU)

In Singapore, the ACU is a unit within a bank which has been granted such a licence by the Monetary Authority of Singapore (MAS) to deal in the Asian Dollar Market. The unit maintains separate accounting records for its transactions. This is to ensure that the flow of funds to and from the Asian Dollar Market will not disrupt domestic monetary management. The first ACU was started in 1968 by the Singapore branch of the Bank of America. The bank was granted permission by the Singapore Government to set up a currency unit similar to its Eurocurrency Unit in London. The objective was to attract Asian non-resident deposits to fund the bank's Asian lending activities. Since then, many other banks have been granted ACU licences. The ACU is supervised by the MAS and is subject to Singapore banking law. However, it is exempted from some provisions of the Banking Act.

## Asian Development Bank   *www.adb.org*

The Asian Development Bank (ADB) was formed in 1966. It is a multilateral finance institution owned by 61 member countries. Its main objective is to reduce poverty in Asia and the Pacific. It promotes economic development and cooperation among member countries. The headquarters is located in Manila, Philippines. The ADB has 23 other offices around the world. It has about 2,000 employees from about 50 countries.

## Asian Dollar Bond

An Asian dollar bond is an international bond denominated in US dollars.

## Asian Dollar Market

The Asian Dollar Market is the Asian counterpart of the Eurodollar market.

It is a financial market in Asia where banks accept deposits of major currencies (US$, yen, mark, sterling pound, Swiss franc) outside their countries of issue. These funds are lent out for investment in Asia. The market is so called because the most important currency traded is the US dollar. Participants in the market include financial institutions, government agencies, multinational corporations and international organizations. Financial institutions in Singapore are given special ACU licences (Asian Currency Unit) by the Monetary Authority of Singapore to trade in the Asian Dollar Market. These ACUs are eligible for tax incentives offered by the Singapore Government.

**Asian Dollars**
These are US dollars circulating in Asian financial markets.

**Asian Institute of International Financial Law (Hong Kong)**
The Asian Institute of International Financial Law (AIIFL) at the University of Hong Kong Faculty of Law was set up in 1999 in cooperation with the HKU's School of Business & Management and the Department of Economics.

**Asian Wall Street Journal**
This financial newspaper is widely read by investors in Asia. It is the Asian edition of the Wall Street Journal in the United States.

**Asiatrust Bank**   *www.asiatrustbank.com*
The Asiatrust Bank started in 1960 as the Quezon City Development Bank. It was organized under the Private Development Banks Act with support from the Development Bank of the Philippines by way of counterpart equity investment and loan rediscounting facilities. In 1982, the bank changed its name to Asiatrust Bank and introduced new products and services. In 1988, the Bank launched its own credit card, the Asiatrust Bank VISA Card, through a tie-up with Equitable Card Network Inc. In 1991, the Bank installed its first automated teller machine called the "Cash Station" and became the 12th member of the Megalink, a consortium of banks that operates a nationwide network of ATMs. In 1990, the bank joined partnership with the Asian Development Bank (ADB) which invested in 15% of Asiatrust's equity. In 1993, the ASEAN Strategic Capital Limited, a Singapore-based regional investment company became a shareholder in Asiatrust with a 12% equity stake.

**Askari Commercial Bank (Pakistan)**   *www.askari.com*
In Pakistan, the Askari Commercial Bank has a network of 36 outlets with 1,200 employees throughout the country. It has total assets of Rs51 billion

and equity base of Rs 2.6 billion. In 2001, it won the "Best Bank in Pakistan" award given by the Global Finance magazine. It also won the Euromoney and Asiamoney awards in 1994, 1995 and 1996.

**Asosiasi Lembaga Pembiayaan Pembangunan Indonnesia (ALPPIA)**
See Indonesian Association of Development Financing Institutions.

**Asset Management Company (Malaysia)**
In Malaysia, the Asset Management Company (AMC) was set up in 1998 by the government to take over non-performing loans (NPLs) in the financial system. It relieved banks of the tedious loan recovery process, allowing them to concentrate on their core business of lending to productive sectors. It would buy the NPLs of financial institutions at market prices, revive and sell them.

**Asset Management Corporation (Thailand)** *www.bot.or.th/govnr/public/news/be.htm*
In Thailand, the Asset Management Corporation was set up in 1997 under the Emergency Decree as part of the financial sector restructuring program. This state agency administered the assets of 58 finance companies whose operations were suspended by the Finance Minister on 26 June 1997 (16 companies) and on 5 August 1997 (42 companies). Its initial capital of 1 billion baht was subscribed by the Thai Government and the shareholder was the Ministry of Finance. (See also: Financial Sector Restructuring Authority — Thailand)

**Associated Chinese Chambers of Commerce and Industry of Malaysia (ACCCIM)**
In Malaysia, the ACCCIM is the central organization of the Chinese chambers of commerce with 17 constituent chambers located in the 13 states of the country. Founded in 1947, it is an autonomous private sector organization that represents more than 20,000 Chinese Malaysian companies, individuals and trade associations. It promotes cooperation among the various chambers and arbitrates disputes among members. It presents recommendations of the Malaysian Chinese business community on the nation's economic development and disseminates information relating to the economy. It maintains rapport with the government and its agencies on matters affecting the economy. At the national level, ACCCIM is a member of the National Chamber of Commerce & Industry of Malaysia (NCCIM) which is an apex organization with four other private sector organizations namely: the Malay Chamber of Commerce Malaysia, the Associated Indian Chamber of Commerce & Industry of Malaysia, the Malaysian International Chamber of Commerce & Industry and the Federation of Malaysian Manufacturers.

**Association of Banks in Cambodia**
In Cambodia, all approved financial institutions under the new Law on Banking and Financial Institutions are members of the Association of Banks in Cambodia (ABC). As of 2002, there were 23 approved financial institutions.

**Association of Investment Management Companies (Thailand)**
In Thailand, the Association of Investment Management Companies (AIMC) was formed in 1994. It promotes investment management company standards and protects investors' interest.

**Association of Management Corporations in Singapore**
The Association of Management Corporations in Singapore (AMCIS) was formed in January 2002. Its aim is to give management corporations (MCs) stronger leverage when bargaining with service providers, as well as to share information in the management of properties and to provide feedback to the authorities. The services it offers include a property management portal (www.amcis-enabledhomes.com) as well as auditing, legal, elevator and air-conditioning services.

**Association of National Numbering Agencies** *www.anna-web.com*
The Association of National Numbering Agenciess (ANNA) was founded in 1992 in Brussels to promote the ISO 6166 standard and to distribute ISINs (International Securities Identification Numbers) among its members and the global financial community. ANNA operates the Global ISIN Access Mechanism (GIAM) for the international identification of securities. It also implements the ISO 10962 (Classification for Financial Instruments).

**Association of Pacific Rim Universities**
The Association of Pacific Rim Universities (APRU) started in 1997. It is a group of 34 universities in the Pacific Rim. It includes Stanford, Caltech, USC, UC Berkeley and UCLA (US), British Columbia (Canada), Peking, Tsinghua, Fudan and Hong Kong University of Science & Technology (China), Tokyo and Kyoto (Japan), National Taiwan, Seoul National, Australian National, Sydney, Auckland and National University of Singapore. Its objective is to promote collaboration among member universities. APRU is modelled after the prestigious Association of American Universities (AAU). For 2002–3, its Secretariat was located at the National University of Singapore.

**Association of Securities Analysts of the Philippines** *www.asap.com.ph*
The Association of Securities Analysts of the Philippines (ASAP) was formed in 1996. Its objective is to advance the professional growth of securities analysts.

**Association of Securities Companies (Thailand)**   *www.asco.or.th*
In Thailand, the Association of Securities Companies (ASCO) started in 1973
as the Thai Finance and Securities Trading Association and was later renamed
the Thai Finance and Securities Association. The ASCO represents the securities industry in dealing with regulatory agencies as well as supports securities-
related businesses of member companies. ASCO Training Institute provides
training for traders and financial advisors. It prepares them for qualification
examinations.

**Association of Southeast Asian Nations**   *www.aseansec.org*
The Association of Southeast Asian Nations (ASEAN) was formed on 8 August
1967 in Bangkok, Thailand with the signing of the Bangkok Declaration.
The five original member countries were Indonesia, Malaysia, Philippines,
Singapore and Thailand. Brunei joined in 1984 and Vietnam in 1995. Since
then, other Southeast Asian countries have been admitted as members:
Cambodia, Laos and Myanmar. The main objectives of ASEAN are to promote
economic, social and cultural development of the region through cooperative
programs; to safeguard stability of the region against big power rivalry; and
to serve as a forum for the resolution of intra-regional differences. The
secretariat is located in Jakarta.

**Association of Valuers & Property Consultants in Private Practice
Malaysia**   *www.peps.com.my*
The Association of Valuers & Property Consultants in Private Practice Malaysia
(Persatuan Penilai Dan Perunding Harta Swasta Malaysia, or PEPS) was
founded in 1984. Its members are valuers, property managers and estate agents
registered under the Valuers, Appraisers & Estate Agents Act. PEPS is a
principal member of the International Real Estate Federation.

**Assurances Generales du Lao (AGL)**
AGL is an insurance joint venture between the Government of Lao and
Assurances Generales de France. It started in 1992 and was granted a monopoly
by the government on condition that it provided a full range of insurance
services including fire insurance cover for factories.

**PT Astra International**
In Indonesia, Astra is the largest automotive maker. It is also the agent for cars
including Toyota, Daihatsu, Peugot, BMW, Isuzu and Nissan. Astra also
operates in other sectors including plywood, agribusiness, heavy equipment,
electronics and financial services. It is a major shareholder of PT Bank
Universal.

**Asuransi Ekspor Indonesia (ASEI)**
ASEI is an Indonesian state-owned company that provides export insurance and export credit guarantee.

**Asuransi Kredit Indonesia (Askrindo)**
Askrindo is an Indonesian credit insurance company that provides credit guarantee cover to banks for financing small and medium industries.

**ASX Derivatives (ASXD) Options Market (Australia)**
The ASXD Options Market (formerly known as the Australian Options Market) started in 1976. It is part of the Australian Stock Exchange (ASX) and is the sixth largest options market in the world. It trades options on more than 50 of Australia's and New Zealand's companies and three indices, including the All-Ordinaries Index. The ASXD is an open outcry, quote-driven market where market-makers create liquidity. The open outcry system is supplemented by DATS (Derivatives Automated Trading System).

**ATA carnet**
ATA means Admission Temporair/Temporary Admission (French/English). An ATA carnet is an international customs document that is used temporarily for duty-free admission of certain goods into some countries.

**AUSTRACLEAR**
AUSTRACLEAR is used for the registering and trading of money market securities in Australia. It is owned and operated by major participants in the money market.

**Australia-Fiji Business Council**   *www.afbc.org.au*
The Australia-Fiji Business Council (AFBC) was formed in 1986. It provides a framework for the private sector to communicate with the Australian and Fiji governments at the highest level to solve trade and investment issues.

**Australian Accounting Standards Board**   *www.aasb.com*
See Financial Reporting Council.

**Australian Financial Institutions Commission**
The Australian Financial Institutions Commission (AFIC) was formed in 1992 to supervise credit unions, building societies and friendly societies. In 1999, its powers were transferred to the Australian Prudential Regulation Authority. (See also: Australian Prudential Regulation Authority)

**Australian Financial Markets Association**
The Australian Financial Markets Association (AFMA) is the national association representing about 200 organizations that participate in the Australian over-the-counter (OTC) wholesale financial markets. AFMA was formed in 1986 to streamline market practices and establish trading standards in OTC markets. These markets cover transactions in financial securities facilitated outside an exchange and include trading in foreign exchange, interest rate products, financial derivatives, repurchase agreements, commodities, equity and electricity derivatives.

**Australian and New Zealand Banking Group**
The Australian and New Zealand Bank (ANZ) was formed by merging the Bank of Australia and the Union Bank of Australia. It took over the National Mutual Royal Bank in 1990 and the Town and Country Bank in 1991. It is the largest Australian international bank with offices in more than 50 countries.

**Australian Institute of International Affairs**   *www.aiia.asn.au*
The Australian Institute of International Affairs (AIIA) started in 1933. It is the only nationwide organization of its kind in Australia. It is an independent non-profit organization that promotes interest and understanding of international affairs in Australia. It provides a forum for discussion but does not seek to formulate or promote its own institutional views.

**Australian Institute of Bankers**
The Australian Institute of Bankers (AIB) is now known as the Australian Institute of Banking and Finance (AIBF).

**Australian Office of Financial Management (AOFM)**   *www.aofm.gov.au*
The AOFM was established in 1999 under the Financial Management and Accountability Act. It is responsible for the Commonwealth of Australia's debt management. It administers the following acts: Commonwealth Inscribed Stock Act, Financial Management Act, Loans Redemption and Conversion Act, Loans Securities Act, and Treasury Bills Act.

**Australian Options Market**
See ASX Derivatives (ASXD) Options Market.

**Australian Payments Clearing Association**
The Australian Payments Clearing Association (APCA) was set up in 1992 to reform the national payments clearing system. It is owned by financial institutions and the Reserve Bank of Australia.

**Australian Prudential Regulation Authority (APRA)** *www.apra.gov.au*
In 1997, the Final Report of the Financial System Inquiry (Wallis Inquiry) made several recommendations to reform financial regulation in Australia. In 1998, the task of supervising the banking sector was transferred from the Reserve Bank of Australia (central bank) to the newly formed Australian Prudential Regulation Authority (APRA). The integrated body has also taken over the supervisory responsibility of the Insurance and Superannuation Commission and the Australian Financial Institutions Commission. The main objectives of APRA are to establish prudential standards, operate in a flexible and accountable manner, and apply best practices, risk-based techniques to the supervision of financial institutions. (See also: Council of Financial Regulators)

**Australian Research Council** *www.deetya.gov.au/divisions/hed/highered/research*
The Australian Research Council (ARC) allocates funds for approved research program to be carried out at various Australian universities.

**Australian Securities and Investments Commission (ASIC)** *www.asic.gov.au*
The ASIC is an independent government body that administers the Corporations Laws and consumer protection law for investments, life and general insurance, superannuation and banking throughout Australia. Its objective is to reduce fraud and unfair practices in financial markets. The Corporations Law also confers powers on ASIC in its role of market supervision. These include powers to review compliance reports submitted by exchanges and suspend trading securities. Under the ASIC Act, the ASIC has powers of investigation, inspection of books and information gathering. (See also: Council of Financial Regulators)

**Australian Science, Technology & Engineering Council (ASTEC)**
*www.astec.gov.au*
ASTEC is an independent body that evaluates Australia's science policy. Through analysis and public debate of scientific policy, it ensures the best use of government fund and creates public awareness in science.

**Australian Transaction Reports and Analysis Centre**
Under the Financial Transaction Reports Act, certain "cash dealers" are required to report significant cash transactions to the Australian Transaction Reports and Analysis Centre (AUSTRAC).

**Australian Wine and Brandy Corporation**
The Australian Wine and Brandy Corporation (AWBC) is based in Adelaide.

It promotes Australian wine and ensures export quality control. It licenses exporters and issues certificates of compliance with export regulation.

**Australian Wine Foundation**   *www.winetitles.com.au* (Australian Wine online)
The Australian Wine Foundation (AWF) formulated the Strategy 2025 Plan to promote the wine industry and increase its international competitiveness.

**Authorized Institution (Hong Kong)**
In Hong Kong, there are three types of deposit-taking institutions: licensed banks, restricted licence banks and deposit-taking companies. Under the Banking Ordinance, these are collectively known as authorized institutions (AIs).

**Authorized Trading Centre (Singapore)**
After the massive floatation of Singapore Telecom shares in 1993, the number of shareholders in Singapore increased significantly. In order to cope with the large volume of trade, the Singapore Exchange set up Authorized Trading Centres (ATCs). To buy and sell shares at ATCs, investors do not need a trading account. What they need are a CDP (Central Depository) securities account to hold their shares and an ATM (automatic teller machine) card to pay for their shares. ATCs are located at stock-broking companies and at some branches of local banks.

**Automated Trading System for the Stock Exchange of Thailand (ASSET)**
ASSET is a computerized trading system introduced at the Stock Exchange of Thailand in 1991. The system automatically matches transactions with immediate confirmation to the buying and selling brokers.

**Aviva Limited (Singapore)**
This is the new name for Insurance Corporation of Singapore (ICS) with effect from 1 August 2002.

**B Shares (China)**
B shares are issued by Mainland Chinese companies. They are priced and traded in foreign currencies, e.g. US dollars in Shanghai Stock Exchange and Hong Kong dollars in Shenzhen Stock Exchange. When the B share market was launched in 1992, it was restricted to foreign investors. With effect from 19 February 2001, it has been opened to Chinese investors.

**Ba Ria Serece Port (Vietnam)**
In Vietnam, this is the first privately owned Vietnam-European joint venture seaport. It is located at Phu My village, about 40 kilometres from Vung Tau along the Thi Vai River. It can accommodate vessels up to 40,000 dwt. The Vietnamese partners are: ASTC of Ba Ria Vung Tau, Bitex, VIGECAM, and the Asian Commercial Joint Stock Bank. The European partners are SCPA and Sogenma of France and Norsk Hydro of Norway.

**Bach Ho Oilfield**
Bach Ho (White Tiger) oilfield is located in Vietnam. The contract was awarded to VietSovPetro, a joint venture between Vietnam and Russia.

**Bach Mai Hanoi International Medical Centre**
This is the first joint venture hospital in Vietnam. It is developed by Vietnam's Bach Mai Hospital and Australia's Indochina Medical Company Pty. Ltd.

**Bad Cheque Blacklisting**
See Biro Maklumat Cek.

**Bad Debt Workout Team (Satuan Tugas Khusus or STK)**
In 1994, in order to tackle problem loans, Bank Indonesia (BI) identified a group of banks with severe loan difficulties. It required each of them to form a bad debt workout team (STK) to be headed by a member of its board of directors. The STK would work on the loan problem and report monthly to BI. The STK was temporary and would be dissolved once the bad debt problem was under control.

**Badan Koordinasi Penanaman Modal (BKPM) (Indonesia)**
See Investment Coordinating Board.

**Badan Pemeriksa Keuangan (Indonesia)**
This is the Supreme Audit Board in Indonesia. It controls the accountability of public finance, has investigation powers and is independent of the Executive. It reports to the Dewan Perwakilan Rakyat. (See also: Dewan Perwakilan Rakyat)

**Badan Penyehatan Perbankan Nasional (BPPN) (Indonesia)**
See Indonesian Bank Restructuring Agency.

**Badan Urusan Logistik (BULOG) (Indonesia)**
See Board of Logistic Affairs.

**Badan Usaha Malik Negara (BUMN) (Indonesia)**
This is a state-owned enterprise in Indonesia. (See also: Indonesian state-owned enterprise)

**Badla System (India)**
In the Bombay Stock Exchange (BSE), the badla system is a speculative carry-over trading system. It allows investors to carry over the transaction of a particular stock to the next settlement cycle without cash settlement in the current cycle. The system provides liquidity to the stock market.

**Baht**
Currency of Thailand (1 baht = 100 satangs).

**BAHTNET**
In Thailand, BAHTNET is a Real Time Gross Settlement (RTGS) system introduced in 1995. It is used by banks, finance companies, other financial institutions and some government departments. It provides inter-bank fund transfer, third party fund transfer, account inquiry and other electronic services.

**Bakrie Group (Indonesia)**
In Indonesia, the Bakrie Group is one of the largest companies. It started in 1942 as a commodity trading company by Achmad Bakrie in Lampung in South Sumatra. Bakrie is a blue chip company on the Jakarta Stock Exchange. It has diversified into petrochemicals, finance, construction and telecommunications. Bakrie is a major shareholder in PT Telkom. The chairman is Mr Aburizal Bakrie, the son of the founder. He has employed many professional managers including president director Tanri Abeng who has helped to expand the company overseas including Australia, China, Tajikistan, Singapore and Vietnam.

**Bali Urban Infrastructure Project (BUIP) (Indonesia)**
In Indonesia, BUIP was a US$ 115 million project funded by the World Bank. BUIP developed highways, city transportation management, clean water installation, waste water disposal system and flood control facility.

**BancNet Inc (Philippines)**    *www.bancnet.net*
In the Philippines, BancNet Inc started in 1990. It is the largest ATM network in the country. It offered bill payment facilities in 1993 and point-of-sale arrangement in 1994. It became an Internet service provider in 1997 and introduced Electronic Data Interchange (EDI) facilities in 1999. It launched the first inter-bank fund transfer through the ATM in 2001.

**Banco Espanol-Filipino de Isabel (Philippines)**
This is now known as the Bank of the Philippine Islands. Set up in 1851, it was the first commercial bank in the Philippines and in Southeast Asia. (See also: Bank of the Philippine Islands)

**Bangko Sentral ng Pilipinas**   *www.bsp.gov.ph*
Bangko Sentral ng Pilipinas (BSP) is the central bank of the Philippines. It started in 1993 as part of the restructuring of the old Central Bank of the Philippines (CBP), which was originally set up in 1949. The restructuring was necessary because of substantial deficits in the CBP's operations before 1993 that were incurred in connection with:
(a) certain quasi-fiscal activities conducted by the CBP consistent with government policies at the time (i.e. foreign exchange forward cover contracts and swaps entered into by the CBP with certain banks and government-owned and -controlled corporations or GOCCs) and the CBP's assumption of foreign exchange liabilities of certain GOCCs and private sector companies during the Philippines' foreign exchange crisis in 1980s;
(b) development banking by the CBP;
(c) the CBP's conduct of open market operations and incurrence of high interest expenses on the CBP's domestic securities issued in connection with such operations.

Under the New Central Bank Act, the BSP was granted autonomy from other sectors of the government. The BSP no longer undertakes quasi-fiscal activities and is not permitted to engage in development banking.

**Bangkok Bank**   *www.bangkokbank.com*
Bangkok Bank started in 1944. Since then, it has been the leading bank in Thailand with about 600 domestic branches. It is also one of the largest banks in Southeast Asia with branches in major Asian cities as well as in the United Kingdom and United States. Its Special Asset Management Unit has been the model for troubled debt restructuring in Thailand.

**Bangkok Declaration**
The Bangkok Declaration was signed on 8 August 1967 by Indonesia, Malaysia, Philippines, Singapore and Thailand. The Declaration established the Association of Southeast Asian Nations, or ASEAN. The Declaration united the ASEAN member countries in a joint effort to promote economic cooperation and the welfare of the people in the region. It also set out guidelines for ASEAN's activities and defined the aims of the organization.

**Bangkok Metropolitan Bank**   *www.bmb.co.th*
Bangkok Metropolitan Bank (BMB) started in 1950 as the 12th commercial bank in Thailand. Its founders were Phraya Tonavanik Montri, Ng Zi Liang and Udane Tejapaibul. In 1993, BMB became a Public Company Limited (PCL) and its capital was increased to 10 billion baht. During the 1997–98 financial crisis, BMB and numerous other banks ran into difficulty and were intervened by the Bank of Thailand (BOT, central bank). With effect from 1 April 2002, BMB merged with Siam City Bank (SCIB) and all assets were transferred to SCIB.

**Bangkok International Banking Facility (BIBF)**
In Thailand, the BIBF was introduced in 1992. Banks with BIBF licences can set up offshore banking units (OBUs) to attract foreign capital to finance economic development. Incentives are provided for OBUs. Income is taxed at 10% instead of the normal 30%. Municipal taxes and stamp duties are waived.

**Bangkok Stock Dealing Centre**   *www.bsdc.or.th*
The Bangkok Stock Dealing Centre (BSDC) was set up in 1995 in accordance with the Securities Act. It is Thailand's second market besides the Stock Exchange of Thailand (SET). It had 74 finance and securities companies as its founding members. It is a self-regulatory organization and non-profit organization supervised by the Securities and Exchange Commission. BSDC provides a market for small and medium enterprises to raise funds. Computerized trading takes place in six different boards. The boards have different rules and trade in different securities. They are main board, dealing board, big lot board, foreign board, odd lot board and private placement board.

**Bangladesh Bank**   *www.bangladesh-bank.org*
The Bangladesh Bank, the central bank started in 1971. It manages the monetary and credit system to stabilize domestic monetary value. It regulates the issue of the currency and keeps the reserves. It supervises financial institutions under the Bank Company Act and Financial Institutions Act.

**Bangladesh Export Processing Zones Authority (BEPZA)**
*www.bangladesh-epz.com*
In Bangladesh, the BEPZA was established by an Act of Parliament in 1980. It develops and manages export processing zones. The Chittagong EPZ was set up in 1983 and the Dhaka EPZ in 1993. (See also: Chittagong EPZ, Dhaka EPZ)

**Bangladesh Sericulture Board**

Bangladesh Sericulture Board (BSB) started in 1977 under the Ministry of Textiles. It produces and distributes mulberry saplings, silkworm eggs and provides technical services to silk growers through its extension network. Through its Bangladesh Sericulture Research & Training Institute (BSRTI), it maintains a germplasm centre and undertakes research on mulberry trees and silkworm varieties.

**Bangladesh Sericulture Research & Training Institute**

See Bangladesh Sericulture Board.

**Bangladesh Silk Foundation**

The Bangladesh Silk Foundation (BSF) started in 1997 as an autonomous financially sustainable organization. Its objective is to enhance productivity and income of small silk producers.

**Bangladesh Small and Cottage Industries Corporation**

The Bangladesh Small and Cottage Industries Corporation (BSCIC) was set up by an Act of Parliament in 1957. It provides assistance to small and cottage industries.

**Bank for Agriculture and Agricultural Cooperatives**   *www.baac.or.th*

In Thailand, the BAAC was set up in 1966 by the government as a state enterprise under the Ministry of Finance. It provides credit directly to individual farmers and farmer institutions.

**Bank for Foreign Trade of Vietnam (Vietcombank)**

This is one of the three state-owned commercial banks in Vietnam. It was set up in 1963 and has about 20 branches in Vietnam. It is authorized to deal in foreign exchange and international banking business. It is estimated that about 80% of Vietnam's foreign trade pass through Vietcombank. It has a subsidiary Vietnam Finance Co Limited in Hong Kong. It has a joint venture bank with Korea's Daewoo Securities and Korea First Bank.

**Bank for International Settlements**   *www.bis.org*

The Bank for International Settlements (BIS) is an international organization that fosters cooperation among central banks and other agencies in pursuit of monetary and financial stability. It serves as a bank for central banks.

**Bank for International Settlements Guidelines**

In 1988, in a move to increase the financial soundness of the global banking system, the Bank of International Settlements (BIS, generally regarded as the central bank of all central banks) introduced guidelines that required international banks to have capital equivalent to at least 8% of their risk-weighted assets by the end of 1992. Of the capital, at least 4% must be Tier 1 capital, which includes shareholders' funds and minority interests. Tier 2 capital comprises subordinated debt, loan-loss provisions, and 45% of unrealized profits on securities holdings.

### Bank for Investment and Development of Vietnam (BIDV)

In Vietnam, BIDV was formerly the Bank for Construction and Development. It finances mainly infrastructure and commercial projects for the government and state-owned enterprises. VID Public Bank is its joint venture bank with the Public Bank Berhad from Malaysia.

### Bank Indonesia   *www.bi.go.id*

Bank Indonesia (BI) started in 1953 as the central bank. It resulted from nationalizing De Javasche Bank, a Dutch bank that started in 1828. On 17 May 1999, a new Central Bank Act was introduced to confer BI the status of an independent state institution and freedom from interference from the government or external parties. Its main tasks are to formulate and implement monetary policy; to regulate and ensure a smooth payment system, and to supervise the banking system. BI also formulates exchange rate policy, manages international reserves and acts as lender of last resort.

### Bank Indonesia Certificate

Bank Indonesia Certificate or Sertifikat Bank Indonesia (SBI) is a discount financial instruments issued by Bank Indonesia (Central Bank) for short term investment by banks.

### Bank Islam Malaysia Berhad (BIMB)

BIMB is Malaysia's first Islamic bank set up in 1983. Its activities are based on Islamic banking principles. In 1996, as part of its expansion, BIMB set up a Syariah-based Consumer Financing Centre which focused on retail banking such as motor vehicle financing, education financing and personal finance.

### Bank Negara Malaysia   *www.bnm.gov.my*

Bank Negara Malaysia (BNM), the central bank was set up in 1959. Its objectives include: act as a banker and financial adviser to the government, promote monetary stability and a sound financial structure, issue currency and keep reserves safeguarding the value of the currency. BNM also regulates and supervises the financial system.

**Bank of Asia (Thailand)**   *www.boa.co.th*
In Thailand, the Bank of Asia for Industry and Commerce was founded in
1939 by former Prime Minister Dr Pridi Bhanomyong. The name was later
shortened to Bank of Asia (BOA). It was listed on the stock exchange in 1978
and was registered as a public company limited (PCL) in 1992. It has a network
of about 120 branches. In 1998, Dutch bank ABN AMRO became the major
shareholder of BOA.

**Bank of Ayudhya (Thailand)**   *www.bay.co.th*
In Thailand, the Bank of Ayudhya (BAY) started in 1945 in Ayudhya, the
ancient capital. Its head office was later moved to Bangkok. In 1970, the bank
was granted the Royal Appointment Emblem (Garuda) in recognition of the
good performance undertaken for the country. It was listed on the Stock
Exchange of Thailand in 1977. It was registered as a public company limited
(PCL) in 1993 with capital of 8 billion baht. BAY is the fifth largest domestic
commercial in Thailand in terms of assets. It has about 420 branches, including
three overseas branches in Hong Kong, Vientiane and Cayman Islands.

**Bank of Baroda (India)**   *www.bankofbaroda.com*
In India, the Bank of Baroda (BOB) was set up in 1908. It has 2,600 branches
with 46,000 employees. Its 38 overseas offices include Botswana, Guyana,
Hong Kong, Kenya and Uganda.

**Bank of Bhutan**
The Bank of Bhutan (BOB) is the only commercial bank in Bhutan. Apart
from its main office in Phuntsholing, it has 23 branches. The major shareholder
is the Royal Government, with the remaining 25% held by the State Bank
of India, with which BOB has an institutional relationship.

**Bank of China**   *www.bank-of-china.com*
The Bank of China (BOC) started in 1912. It is the leading international bank
in China with offices in major financial centres in the world. It provides a full
range of financial services. Since 1949, BOC had served as the only foreign
exchange and foreign trade-related specialized bank. After the 1994 financial
reform, BOC became a state-owned commercial bank, joining ranks with three
major banks to be the pillars of the financial industry. BOC became a note-
issuing bank in Hong Kong and Macau in 1994 and 1995 respectively. BOC
was ranked the "Best Bank in China" by Euromoney for eight times between
1992 and 2001. It has been among the Fortune Global 500 list for 12
consecutive years.

**Bank of Communications**    *www.bankcomm.com*

In China, the Bank of Communications (BOCOM) was set up in 1908. It was one of the four largest banks and the earliest banknote issuers in China early last century. After 1949, the bank's domestic business was incorporated into that of the People's Bank of China and People's Construction Bank of China while its Hong Kong branch continued its operation. As the pilot bank for state financial reform, BOCOM was reorganized by the State Council. In 1987, it became the first joint-stock commercial bank in China. The bank was rated the "best bank in China" by Euromoney and Global Finance magazines respectively in 1998 and 1999. The bank has branches in Hong Kong, New York, Singapore and Tokyo. It has representative offices in London and Frankfurt.

**Bank of India**    *www.bankofindia.com*

The Bank of India was founded in 1906 by a group of businessmen from Mumbai. It was under private ownership and control until July 1969 when it was nationalized with 13 other banks. It has more than 2,500 branches and offices in ten countries. The bank had its first public issue in 1997. It has about 403,000 shareholders.

**Bank of Japan**    *www.boj.or.jp*

Bank of Japan is the central bank. Its mission is to maintain price stability and to ensure stability of the financial system. It issues and manages bank notes. It controls the volume of money in the economy and interest rates on a daily basis through money market operations. It provides settlement services and acts as the lender of last resort. The Institute for Monetary and Economic Studies (IMES) was founded in 1982 within the Bank of Japan to conduct research on monetary issues.

**Bank of Lao PDR (BOL)**

BOL is the central bank of Laos. Its main function is to maintain monetary control and to promote the development of financial markets. The main objective of monetary control is to reduce inflationary rate while recognizing the need for continued credit growth to finance the development needs of the country. The objective is achieved through high interest rate structure (to absorb excess liquidity and encourage savings) and using monetary policy instruments such as reserve requirement ratio, credit and discount window, and the issue of treasury bills.

**Bank of New Zealand**    *www.bnz.co.nz*

The Bank of New Zealand is the oldest bank in New Zealand. It is a member of the National Australia Bank (NAB) group, one of the world's largest banking groups. NAB is listed on the stock exchanges in Australia, London, New York, Tokyo and New Zealand.

**Bank of Papua New Guinea**   *www.bankpng.gov.pg*
The Bank of Papua New Guinea was set up in 1973. As the central bank, it formulates and implements monetary policies, supervises financial institutions, and promotes an efficient payments system.

**Bank of Punjab (Pakistan)**   *www.punjabbank.com*
In Pakistan, the Bank of Punjab was established in 1989 and was given the status of a scheduled bank in 1994. Its major shareholder is the Government of Punjab. It has a network of about 250 branches throughout the country and provides a wide range of commercial banking services.

**Bank of Punjab (India)**   *www.bankofpunjab.com*
In India, the Bank of Punjab was founded in 1995. It now has a wide network of branches across the country focussing on retail banking. As a tribute to its late founder, it has set up a state-of-the-art Dr Inderjit Singh Institute of Banking and Insurance Management at Gurgaon, New Delhi.

**Bank of South Pacific**   *www.bsp.com.pg*
The Bank of South Pacific (BSP) started in Port Moresby in 1957 as a branch of the National Bank of Australia. In 1974, it was incorporated as the Bank of South Pacific, a wholly owned subsidiary of the Australian parent bank. In the 1980s, shares were issued to the public in Papua New Guinea (PNG). In 1993, the nationally owned company National Investment Holdings Ltd acquired 100% of the shareholding and changed its name to BSP Holdings Ltd. In 1998, BSP Holdings went into voluntary liquidation and its shareholders now hold shares in Bank of South Pacific Limited. Some of the major shareholders are PNG Privatization Commission (25%), Motor Vehicles Insurance Ltd (12%), Public Officers Superannuation Fund Board (10%), National Provident Fund Board (10%). In April 2002, BSP acquired the Papua New Guinea Banking Corporation.

**Bank of Taiwan**   *www.bot.com.tw*
The Bank of Taiwan was set up in 1946. It is a government-owned bank under the Ministry of Finance. It has about 1,100 domestic and ten overseas branches with 7,000 employees. In 2000, it was ranked by the Banker Magazine as 105th in the world and first in Taiwan by Tier 1 capital. By shareholders' equity, it was ranked 75th in the world by Euromoney.

**Bank of Thailand**    *www.bot.or.th*

The Bank of Thailand (BOT) is the central bank of Thailand. It started in 1942. Before that, it was known as the Thai National Banking Bureau within the Ministry of Finance. BOT formulates monetary policy, provides banking facilities to the government, supervises financial institutions and develops the financial system. It issues bank notes and manages the country's assets and liabilities. It also provides payment systems for the financial infrastructure with compliance to international standards.

**Bank of the People of Cambodia**

See National Bank of Cambodia.

**Bank of the Philippine Islands (BPI)**    *www.bpi.com.ph*

Bank of the Philippine Islands started in 1851 as El Banco Espanol Filipino de Isabel II in honour of the reigning queen of Spain. It is the oldest bank in the Philippines and in Southeast Asia. In 1969, BPI became the financial flagship of the Ayala group of companies that had been associated with the bank since the beginning. In 1974, BPI consolidated with the Peoples Bank and Trust Company.

In 1981, it acquired the Commercial Bank and Trust Company. This was followed by the buy-out of the Ayala Investment and Development Corporation. In 1982, it was granted a licence by the Central Bank to operate as an expanded commercial bank or universal bank. In the years that followed, BPI made several acquisitions: Makati Leasing and Finance Corporation in 1982, Family Bank and Trust Company in 1985, and Citytrust Banking Corporation in 1996.

In 2000, the insurance companies of the Ayala Group were placed under BPI and collectively called Ayala Inscos to serve as the bank's insurance group. These included FGU Insurance Corporation, Universal Reinsurance Corporation, Ayala Life Assurance, Ayala Health Care and Ayala Plans. BPI thus became the first bancassurance company in the Philippines.

In 2000, BPI merged with the Far East Bank and Trust Company to become the largest local bank with a network of 700 branches. It has also introduced an Internet bank, BPI Direct Savings Bank. BPI has numerous subsidiaries including BPI Capital Corporation, BPI Family Bank, BPI Investment Management Inc and BPI Leasing Corporation. Its diversified affiliates such as Ayala Land, Ayala Corporation and others are in real estate, food, information technology, telecommunications and other industries.

**Bank of Tokyo — Mitsubishi** *www.btm.co.jp*
The Bank of Tokyo — Mitsubishi is a member of the Mitsubishi Tokyo Financial Group (MTFG). It has a global network covering Asia, Africa, the Americas, Europe, Middle East and Oceania. (See also: Mitsubishi Tokyo Financial Group)

**Bank of Tonga**
The Bank of Tonga is owned jointly by the government, Bank of Hawaii International, Bank of New Zealand and the WestPac Banking Corporation. It provides a full range of commercial banking services.

**Bank Pembangunan Daerah (BPD) (Indonesia)**
This is an Indonesian state-owned regional development bank that provides medium and long term loans for development projects.

**Bank Perkreditan Rakyat (BPR) (Indonesia)**
This is an Indonesian rural credit bank such as a market bank, employee bank, village bank and paddy bank. It accepts savings and extends loans to traders in market places and villages. The operation of this type of bank is limited to the villages.

**Bank Simpanan Nasional (Malaysia)** *www.bsn.com.my*
In Malaysia, Bank Simpanan Nasional (BSN) or National Savings Bank started in 1974. It is a statutory board under the Ministry of Finance. It promotes and mobilizes savings, particularly from the small savers. It uses the funds to finance economic development of the nation. Savings in BSN are fully guaranteed by the government.

**Bank Tabungan Negara (BTN) (Indonesia)**
This is an Indonesian state-owned savings bank. It collects savings such as the National Development Savings Scheme (Tabungan Pembangunan Nasional or Tabanas), Time Insurance Savings Scheme (Tabungan Asuransi Berjanka or Taska) and savings for the down payment in house ownership credit scheme.

**Bank Thai** *www.bankthai.co.th*
In Thailand, Bank Thai was set up in 1998 as a government commercial bank with the Financial Institutions Development Fund as the major shareholder. Its mission is to be a bank operated by Thais and for Thais with professional management team under a code of good governance. It has a network of about 80 branches nationwide.

**Bankard Inc (Philippines)**   *www.bankard.com*
Bancard Inc is listed on the Philippine Stock Exchange. It was started by the PCIBank in 1981 as the Philippine Commercial Credit Card Inc (PCCCI) to offer domestic credit card service. In 1991, PCIBank was granted a licence by MasterCard International to issue credit cards in the Philippines. PCIBank then signed an agreement with Bankard Inc designating the latter to manage its PCIBank MasterCard international credit card operations. On 8 July 1992, PCCCI changed its name to Bankard Inc.

**Bankers Association of the Philippines**   *www.bap.org.ph*
The Bankers Association of the Philippines (BAP) was formed in 1949. Its forerunners, the Association of Manila Banks formed to take up foreign exchange operations, and the Manila Clearing House organized to handle the clearing of checks, were both disbanded with the establishment of the Central Bank. In 1964, BAP was incorporated into a corporate organization registered with the Securities and Exchange Commission. As a non-stock, non-profit organization, the BAP provides a venue for member banks to discuss issues that affect commercial banking.

**Bankers' Equity Limited (Pakistan)**
In Pakistan, the Bankers' Equity Limited (BEL) was set up in 1979 to provide industrial financing to the private sector. It is owned by the State Bank of Pakistan and the nationalized commercial banks.

**Banking and Financial Institutions Act (Malaysia)**
In Malaysia, the BAFIA came into force in 1989. It licenses and regulates banks, finance companies, merchant banks, discount houses and moneybrokers. It also regulates credit and charge card companies, building societies, factoring, leasing companies and development finance institutions.

**Bankruptcy Law in Indonesia**
In July 1998, the Indonesian Government introduced a new Bankruptcy Law to replace an outdated bankruptcy law passed in 1905. Under the new law, a person or institution with debts owed to two or more creditors can be declared bankrupt by a court order if there is a default on at least one of the debts. All bankruptcy matters are dealt with in a new commercial court. A creditor or a government prosecutor can petition the Court to declare the debtor a bankrupt. For a debtor bank, the petition must come from the central bank, Bank Indonesia. For public listed companies, the petition must come from the Bapepam (the Capital Market Supervisory Board). The Court must set a hearing date within 48 hours after the petition is registered, hold the

hearing within 20 days and make a ruling within 30 days. Eight days after the Court's ruling, the parties may appeal to the Supreme Court which will make its ruling within 30 days after the appeal has been registered. The new law allows a plaintiff or government prosecutor to apply to the Court to seize the debtor's assets. The Court may appoint a receiver to manage the debtor's business or oversee payments to the creditors.

**Banks in Nepal**
There are 13 commercial banks, 7 development banks, 44 finance companies, 29 cooperative societies and 30 non-government organizations performing limited banking transactions. The two largest banks are Nepal Bank Ltd and Rastriya Banijya Bank. Others are Nepal Arab Bank, Himalayan Bank, Nepal Bangladesh Bank and Everest Bank.

**Bao Minh**
Bao Minh was formerly a branch of Vietnam's State Insurance Company (Bao Viet) in Ho Chi Minh City. In 1995, it was granted autonomy to become a separate insurance company.

**Barings Crisis**
In February 1995, the financial world was shocked when the well-known British Barings PLC suddenly went bankrupt. Its Singapore-based futures trader Nicholas Leeson made US$1.3 billion losses on the Nikkei 225 futures contracts and on Japanese long bonds. Barings was eventually bought over by Dutch banking group, ING in March 1995.

**Bases Conversion Development Authority (Philippines)**
In the Philippines, under the Bases Conversion Act, the Bases Conversion Development Authority (BCDA) is empowered to convert former US military lands to the private sector for development. Private companies may be involved as joint venture partner with BCDA. The Subic Bay Metropolitan Authority (SBMA) is an affiliate agency of BCDA. Clark Development Corporation is a subsidiary of BCDA. (See also: Subic Bay Freeport, Clark Special Economic Zone)

**Basle Accord**
This was an international bank agreement decided in Basle, Switzerland. It required all banks with international operations to maintain a capital adequacy ratio (CAR) of at least 8% of their risk-weighted assets.

**Basle Committee on Banking Supervision**   *www.bis.org/publ/index.htm*
The Basle Committee on Banking Supervision (BCBS) was set up in 1974 by the G-10 central banks. It formulates supervisory standards and recommends best practices in banking. In addition to the G-10 countries, 9 central banks from Asia, Latin America, Middle East and Europe were admitted to membership in 1996.

The Committee has three main tasks: (a) discuss how to handle specific supervisory problems, (b) coordinate supervisory responsibility of banks' foreign establishments, (c) enhance standards of supervision especially in relation to solvency. In 1997, the BCBS established some "Core Principles for Effective Banking Supervision". These included: sound macroeconomic policies, well-developed public infrastructure, market discipline, procedures for resolution of problems in banks, and mechanisms to provide systemic protection. In 1999, it issued a paper on a new capital adequacy framework. The paper proposed minimum capital requirements, supervisory review of capital adequacy and enhanced public disclosure as the three pillars of the framework. (See also: CAMEL, CAMELS, CAMELOT)

**Basle Convention**
The Basle Convention was adopted in 1989 by a United Nations sponsored conference in Basle, Switzerland. It restricts trade in hazardous waste.

**Becamex**
See Song Be Export Import Trading Company.

**Beema Samiti (Insurance Board) (Nepal)**
The Beema Samiti (Insurance Board) of Nepal was set up in 1968. It licenses insurers, agents and brokers. It formulates policies to protect the interests of the insured. It arbitrates in disputes between insurers and policyholders.

**Berhad**
Malay word meaning limited. It denotes a limited liability company in Malaysia. It is sometimes shortened as bhd. (See also: Sendirian Berhad)

**Bernama (Berita Nasional Malaysia)**
Malaysia's national news agency.

**Beta Mekong Fund**
This is a closed-end investment fund listed on the Dublin Stock Exchange. It is managed by Indochina Asset Management Limited.

**Beta Vietnam Fund**
A closed-end investment fund listed on the Dublin Stock Exchange. It is managed by Indochina Asset Management Limited.

**Bharatiya Reserve Bank Note Mudran Private Limited (India)**
The Bharatiya Reserve Bank Note Mudran Private Limited (BRBNMPL) is a fully owned subsidiary of the Reserve Bank of Bank. (See also: Reserve Bank of India)

**Bhd**
Short form for the Malay word "berhad" (limited). (See also: Berhad, Sendirian Berhad)

**BHP Billiton**    *www. bhpbilliton.com*
BHP Billiton is of the world's largest diversified resources companies. It was formed from a merger of BHP (incorporated in 1885 in Australia) and Billiton (started in 1860 in Netherlands). Headquartered in Melbourne, it has offices in London, Johannesburg (South Africa) and Houston (US). With operations in three key resource regions of Africa, Australia and Latin America, the company also has presence in the markets of North America, Asia and Europe. In 2002, it was ranked 281 among the Fortune 500 companies.

**Bhutan Chamber of Commerce and Industry**
The Bhutan Chamber of Commerce and Industry is a private sector organization to safeguard the interests of the private sector.

**Bhutan Development Finance Corporation**
The Bhutan Development Finance Corporation was set up in 1988 to finance small and medium industries.

**Big Blue**
Informal name for IBM.

**Big Board**
Informal name for New York Stock Exchange.

**Big Four Japanese Securities Houses**
The Big Four Japanese Securities Houses referred to Daiwa, Nikko, Nomura and Yamaichi. (See also: Daiwa Securities, Nikko Securities, Nomura Securities)

**PT Bimantara Citra**
This is an Indonesian conglomerate with diversified operations in infrastructure, telecommunications, media and automotive industries. Its television broadcasting unit PT Rajawali Citra Televisi Indonesia (RCTI) is a leading TV station and controls a major market share in TV advertising.

**BioInformatics Institute (Singapore)**
See Biomedical Research Council.

**Biomedical Research Council** *www.a-star.edu.sg*
The Biomedical Research Council (BMRC) oversees and supports public biomedical R&D. Its main objective is to stimulate research for improving human health. BMRC is the centre for a cluster of public research institutes: BioInformatics Institute (BII), Bioprocessing Technology Centre (BTC), Genome Institute of Singapore (GIS), Institute of Bioengineering (IBE) and the merged Institute of Molecular and Cell Biology and Institute of Molecular Agrobiology (IMA).

**Bioethics Advisory Committee (Singapore)**
In Singapore, the Bioethics Advisory Committee (BAC) was set up in 2000 to develop principles governing the legal, ethical and social implications of human biology research, and to promote public understanding of life sciences.

**Bioprocessing Centre (Singapore)**
See Biomedical Research Council.

**BIOTEC (Thailand)** *www.biotec.or.th*
In Thailand, BIOTEC was set up in 1983 as the National Centre for Genetic Engineering and Biotechnology (NCGEB) under the Ministry of Science, Technology and Energy. In 1991, when the National Science & Technology Development Agency (NSTDA) was formed, BIOTEC became one of its centres, operating outside the civil service. Its objective is to induce research and application of biotechnology in both private and public institutions. Some of the programs include the Shrimp Biotechnology Program, the Rice Genome Project and the Thailand Tropical Diseases Research Program.

**Biro Maklumat Cek**
This is a bureau within Bank Negara Malaysia (central bank) set up to monitor bad cheques. Under its rules, any person who issues a bad cheque (i.e. without sufficient fund in the account) three times within 12 months is blacklisted. The bank account will be closed and the customer is prohibited to operate any bank account in Malaysia for six months.

**Biyagama Export Processing Zone (Sri Lanka)**
The Biyagama Export Processing Zone was set up in 1985 as the second EPZ in Sri Lanka. The 180-hectare zone is about 24 kilometres north of Colombo Port.

**Blue Dragon Oilfield**
Blue Dragon oilfield is located in Vietnam. The exploration contract was awarded to Mobil, Japan Petroleum Exploration Company, Indonesian Petroleum, Nissho Iwai, Petro Vietnam and Russia's Zarubezhneft.

**Board for Financial Supervision (India)**
In India, the Board for Financial Supervision (BFS) was formed in 1994. It is an autonomous unit within the Reserve Bank of India.

**Board for Industrial and Financial Reconstruction (India)**
See Sick Industrial Companies Act.

**Board of Audit of Japan**   *www.jbaudit.go.jp*
The Board of Audit of Japan is a constitutional organization independent of the Cabinet. It audits state accounts and those of public organizations. It also monitors the propriety of public finance.

**Board of Commissioners of Currency of Singapore (BCCS)**
In Singapore, the BCCS or Currency Board was formed in 1967. Its history may be traced back to 1899 when Singapore was part of the Straits Settlements (which comprised Penang, Malacca and Singapore). In 1952, it was known as the Board of Commissioners of Currency, Malaya and British Borneo. The BCCS came into existence after Singapore became independent in 1965. Its main function was to issue and redeem currency notes. In January 2002, the Singapore Government announced that BCCS would merge with MAS by 31 March 2003. However, there would be no change in the way the currency issue is managed. The Currency Act will be retained, and the Singapore currency will continue to be fully backed by gold and foreign assets.

**Board of Investment (Pakistan)**   *www.boipak.gov.pk*
In Pakistan, the Board of Investment promotes investment opportunities to local, foreign and overseas Pakistani investors. It is the contact point for investors and all government agencies on investment matters.

**Board of Investment (Sri Lanka)**
In Sri Lanka, the Board of Investment (BOI) is a statutory authority that approves, administers and facilitates foreign investment. It was formed in 1992 with the merger of the Greater Colombo Economic Council (GCEC) and the

Foreign Investment Advisory Council (FIAC). It also manages the export processing zones in Katunayake, Biyagama, Koggala and Kandy. (See also: Greater Colombo Economic Commission)

**Board of Investment (Thailand)** *www.boi.go.th*
In Thailand, the Board of Investment (BOI) provides one-stop services to investors. Its objectives are to reduce investment risks and to improve rate of return on investment. The BOI offers tax incentives such as tax holidays or tariff exemptions. It also offers non-tax privileges such as guarantees and protection.

**Board of Investments (Philippines)** *www.boi.gov.ph*
In the Philippines, the Board of Investments (BOI) is attached to Department of Trade and Industry (DTI). It is the main government agency to promote investments in the Philippines. It is divided into 4 operating groups: investment promotion, technical services, industrial development and project assessment. Its One-Stop Action Centre offers investors what they need to know about investing in the Philippines. Its annual Investment Priorities Plan indicates the preferred areas needed for economic development. It has offices in London, Bonn, San Francisco and Tokyo.

**Board of Logistic Affairs (Indonesia)** *Badan Urusan Logistik or BULOG*
This is an Indonesian government agency that conducts market operation by releasing and buying stocks to stabilize prices of main commodities such as rice and sugar.

**BOJNET (Japan)**
BOJNET is a centralized fund transfer and securities settlement system used by the Bank of Japan.

**Bombay Stock Exchange** *www.bseindia.com*
In India, the Bombay Stock Exchange (BSE) (or The Stock Exchange, Mumbai) is the oldest and largest stock exchange. It is owned by its broker members. Its management structure has changed significantly since 1993 when the Securities and Exchange Board of India (SEBI) imposed control on all exchanges under the Securities Contracts (Regulation) Act. BSE faces competition from the National Stock Exchange (NSE) which started trading in 1994 with encouragement from the government and SEBI.

The BSE publishes four stock price indices: BSE Sensitive Index, BSE-100 Index, BSE-200 and DOLLEX. The BSE Sensitive Index is also known as the

BSE Sensex or the BSE-30 Index. It is the most widely quoted index in India. It is market capitalization-weighted index composed of 30 stocks with the base April 1979 = 100. It accounts for about 30% of the total market capitalization of the exchange.

The BSE-100 Index, formerly known as the BSE National Index, started in January 1989. It is a market value weighted index composed of 100 stocks and accounts for about 43% of the market capitalization of the market. The BSE-200 Index started in May 1994. It is a market value weighted index composed of 200 stocks and accounts for about 55% of the market capitalization of the market. DOLLEX is the US dollar version of the BSE-200 Index to facilitate investment evaluation in US dollar terms for foreign investors.

### Bombay Stock Exchange On-Line Trading System
The Bombay Stock Exchange On-Line Trading System (BOLT) was introduced in 1995 to replace the open outcry system. BOLT is an automated order-match system with price-time priority.

### Bond Trading in China
Bonds are traded on the Shanghai and Shenzhen stock exchanges. They are also traded on the nationwide computer-based, over-the-counter market using the Securities Trading Automated Quotation System (STAQS). All bonds are settled and cleared through the exchanges' computerized system or through the China Government Securities Depository Trust and Clearing Co Ltd.

### Borobudur Temple
This is a famous ancient Indonesian temple located in Central Java. It is on the World Heritage List on the basis of satisfying cultural criteria. After renovation, it has become a popular tourist destination.

### Bougainville Development Corporation
In Papua New Guinea, the Bougainville Development Corporation (BDC) enters into joint ventures, serving as management bureau for its subsidiaries in activities such as transport, restaurant and steel company. The main shareholder of BDC is the Bougainville Royalty Trust which is controlled by the provincial government.

### Bretton Woods Agreement
The Bretton Woods Agreement was adopted in 1944 at an international conference of 44 nations at Bretton Woods, New Hampshire, United States.

As a result of this agreement, the International Monetary Fund (IMF) and the World Bank (International Bank for Reconstruction and Development) were created. (See also: International Monetary Fund, World Bank)

**Brunei Agricultural Research Centre**   *www.agriculture.gov.bn*
The Brunei Agricultural Research Centre started in 1928 as the Kilanas Agricultural Station. It provides appropriate technology to support commercial agricultural activities towards sustainable food production.

**Brunei Currency Board**   *www.finance.gov.bn*
The Brunei Currency Board is a statutory body in the Ministry of Finance. It ensures that financial policies are carried out to achieve stability in the financial system. It also encourages development in the financial sector.

**Brunei Industrial Development Authority**   *www.bina.gov.bn*
The Brunei Industrial Development Authority promotes and manages industrial sites. It processes applications from investors who plan to operate in these sites.

**Brunei LNG Sdn Bhd**
See Brunei Shell Petroleum Company.

**Brunei Shell Petroleum Company**   *www.shell.com.bn*
The main activity of Brunei Shell Petroleum (BSP) Company is to explore and produce crude oil and natural gas from onshore and offshore fields. Its concession area covers about 7,000 square kilometres offshore and about 2,000 square kilometres onshore. Brunei LNG Sdn Bhd (BLNG) was set up in 1969. Its main activity is the liquefaction of natural gas purchased from BSP. It is owned by the Brunei Government (50%), Shell Group (25%) and Mitsubishi Corporation (25%). The Brunei Shell Tankers (BST) Sdn Bhd delivers LNG to Brunei's overseas market. It is owned jointly by the Brunei Government and Shell. Brunei Shell Marketing Company (BSM) Sdn Bhd distributes oil derivatives within Brunei. It is owned jointly by the Brunei Government and Shell.

**Brunei Shell Marketing Company Sdn Bhd**
See Brunei Shell Petroleum Company.

**Brunei Shell Tankers Sdn Bhd**
See Brunei Shell Petroleum Company.

**BSE Indices**
See Bombay Stock Exchange.

**BSP Holdings Limited (PNG)**
See Bank of South Pacific.

**Building and Construction Authority (BCA)**
In Singapore, the BCA is a statutory board under the Ministry of National Development. It was formed on 1 April 1999 after the merger of the Construction Industry Development Board and the Building Control Division (of the former Public Works Department). It ensures that the industry deliver safe and quality buildings using the most cost effective methods.

**Bull and Bear Bonds**
"Bull and Bear" bonds are high-risk high-return index-linked bonds. The redemption price is linked to an index, such as the Nikkei Dow Index of stocks in Japan.

**Bulldog Bonds**
These are Sterling-denominated bonds issued in the United Kingdom by foreign companies. It is the United Kingdom equivalent of the samurai and Yankee bonds.

**Bundesbank**
Central bank of Germany.

**Bureau of Indian Standards**   *www.bis.org.in*
The Bureau of Indian Standards (BIS) is the national standards body of India. It deals with all matters related to standardization, certification and quality.

**Bureau of Internal Revenue (Philippines)**   *www.bir.gov.ph*
In the Philippines, the Bureau of Internal Revenue in the Department of Finance assess and collects all national internal revenue taxes, fees and charges. It also enforces related forfeitures, penalties and fines.

**Bureau of Monetary Affairs (Taiwan)**   *www.mof.gov.tw*
In Taiwan, before July 1991, in the Ministry of Finance, the Bureau of Monetary Affairs (BMA) was known as the Department of Monetary Affairs. Its main responsibility is the supervision of banks and other financial institutions.

**Bureau of Product Standards (Philippines)**
In the Philippines, the Bureau of Product Standards (BPS) of the Department

of Trade and Industry has a product certification scheme under which a manufacturer obtains a licence to use the Philippine Standard (PS) Mark for its capability to make safe and quality products.

**Bureau of Trade Regulation and Consumer Protection (Philippines)**
In the Philippines, a sole proprietorship must register with the Bureau of Trade Regulation and Consumer Protection of the Department of Trade and Industry. A corporation or a partnership must register with the Securities and Exchange Commission.

**Bureau of Treasury (Philippines)**   *www.treasury.gov.ph*
In the Philippines, the Bureau of the Treasury (BTr) assists the Department of Finance in formulating policies on borrowing, investment and capital market development. It manages cash resources of the government, public debt and government securities. It also administers the Securities Stabilization Fund and manages contributions to the Bond Sinking Fund.

**PT Bursa Efek Jakarta (Indonesia)**
In Indonesia, Bursa Efek Jakarta (BEJ) or Jakarta Stock Exchange Inc is the company that manages the Jakarta Stock Exchange. It was transferred to the private sector in 1992. It is owned by about 200 brokerage firms that constitute the membership and are the shareholders of the exchange.

**PT Bursa Efek Surabaya**
See Surabaya Stock Exchange.

**PT Bursa Paralel Indonesia**
This was the Indonesian over-the-counter market set up in 1991. It merged with the Surabaya Stock Exchange in 1995.

**Bursa Saham Kuala Lumpur**
See Kuala Lumpur Stock Exchange.

**Business and Investment Development Committee (Fiji)**
In Fiji, the Business and Investment Development Committee is the main agency to approve investments.

**Business.Connect**
In Singapore, Business.Connect was launched by SPRING Singapore (formerly known as the Productivity and Standards Board or PSB) in 1997

to help local enterprises build alliance with foreign partners. The program involves both outbound missions — where Singapore delegates visit foreign countries, as well as inbound missions — where foreign businesses visit Singapore. Collaboration comes in various forms. They include mutual transfer of technology, joint ventures, consultancy services, joint marketing and licensing distribution, as well as setting up joint manufacturing in a third country.

### Business Cooperation Contract (BCC) (Vietnam)

In Vietnam, BCC is an investment contract whereby a foreign partner signs a contract with a Vietnamese partner to do business, and share the costs and the profit. No legal entity is formed, liability of either party is not limited to the investment contributed.

### Business Headquarters Program (Singapore)

In Singapore, the Business Headquarters (BHQ) program was introduced in 1994 by the Economic Development Board (EDB) to attract foreign companies to use Singapore as a base to expand their services to the region. Such services include product development, logistics, merchandising, customer support, financial management and procurement. It is an extension of the Operational Headquarters (OHQ) program that the EDB introduced in 1986 to encourage companies to use Singapore as their headquarters to manage subsidiaries in the region.

### Business Times–Singapore Regional Index (BT-SRI)

BT-SRI is a stock index launched by the Singapore Exchange and the Singapore Press Holdings in 1996. The value-weighted index is constructed using the Paasche formula, which immunizes the index level from any changes in the capitalization of the component stocks.

### Cagamas Bonds (Malaysia)

In Malaysia, these are securitized mortgaged-backed bonds issued by the national mortgage corporation, Cagamas Berhad.

### PT Cahaya Kalbar

This is a leading cocoa and edible oil producer in Indonesia.

### CALABARZON Region

In the Philippines, the CALABARZON region includes the provinces Cavite, Laguna, Batangas, Rizal and Quezon.

**Cambodia Brewery Ltd**
Cambodia Brewery Ltd (CBL) is a joint venture between Asia Pacific Brewery of Singapore and Progress Import and Export Company of Cambodia. It is located in Kandal province, 15 kilometres east of the capital Phnom Penh. The brewery was opened in 1996. CBL has about 45% market share for its two main brands, Tiger Beer and ABC Stout.

**Cambodia Commercial Bank**
This is a joint venture bank set up by the National Bank of Cambodia and the Siam Commercial Bank.

**Cambodia Development Resource Institute**   *www.cdri.org.kh*
The Cambodia Development Resource Institute (CDRI) started in 1990 as an independent organization to analyze socio-economic development issues. The Centre for Peace and Development (previously Centre for Conflict Resolution) is part of the institute. CDRI depends on funds donated by international organizations such as the Asian Development Bank, World Bank and International Development Research Centre.

**Cambodia Finance Bank**
This is a joint venture bank set up in 1992 by the National Bank of Cambodia and a Thai-Cambodia group.

**Cambodia Gold and Trust Corporation**
This is an official corporation authorized by the National Bank of Cambodia to deal in gold bars.

**Cambodia International Airlines**
This was a Thai-owned Cambodian airline. In 1994, with the inauguration of national carrier Royal Air Cambodge, it ceased operations. (See also: Royal Air Cambodge)

**Cambodian Export Promotion Agency**
The Cambodian Export Promotion Agency (CEPA) became the Export Promotion Department in the Ministry of Commerce in 1997.

**Cambodian Import and Export Inspection and Fraud Repression Department (CAMCONTROL)**   *www.comcontrol.gov.kh*
CAMCONTROL was set up in 1997 within the Ministry of Commerce. It analyzes quality of food and consumption products, inspects imports and exports. It supervises and certifies compliance with standards on quality, safety and trademark.

**Cambodian Institute for Cooperation and Peace** *www.cicp.org.kh*
The Cambodian Institute for Cooperation and Peace (CICP) was founded in 1994. It is an independent research institute which promotes dialogue between government officials, national and international organizations, scholars and the private sector on economic development issues. It is affiliated to the regional association ASEAN-ISIS (ASEAN Institutes of Strategic and International Studies).

**Cambodian Investment Board** *www.cambodiainvestment.gov.kh*
The Cambodian Investment Board is one of the two boards under the Council for the Development of Cambodia (CDC). It provides information to investors and processes application for investment incentives. (See also: Council for the Development of Cambodia)

**Cambodian National Insurance Company**
Cambodian National Insurance Company (CAMINCO) is a government-owned company which deals mainly with marine cargo insurance. Another firm, Indochine Insurance Union provides a wide range of insurance cover including fire, theft, motor vehicle and health insurance.

**Cambodian Rehabilitation and Development Board**
See Council for the Development of Cambodia.

**Cambridge Energy Research Associates**
This is a leading international consultancy firm focusing on energy industries.

**Camintel**
Camintel is a telecommunications joint venture between Cambodia's Ministry of Posts and Telecommunications and Indonesian company PT Indosat.

**Campbell Inquiry (Australia)**
In 1979, the Australian Financial System Inquiry (chaired by Sir Keith Campbell) was set up to recommend changes to the regulatory structure of the financial system to promote efficiency and stability. It emphasized deregulation but recommended the strengthening of regulations enforcing prudential standards. (See also: Martin Inquiry, Wallis Inquiry)

**Canadia Bank (Cambodia)** *www.camnet.com.kh/canadia*
In Cambodia, the Canadia Bank started in 1991 as the Canadia Gold and Trust Corporation Ltd, a joint venture between overseas Cambodians and the National Bank of Cambodia. In 1993, it changed its name to Canadia Bank

and registered as a commercial bank. It has several branches within Cambodia and numerous international correspondent banks.

**Canara Bank (India)**    *www.canarabankindia.com*
In India, the Canara Bank started as the Canara Bank Hindu Permanent Fund in 1906. It became the Canara Bank Ltd in 1910. It has about 2,400 branches in 22 states in India. It has operations in London, Hong Kong, Moscow and Dubai.

**Capital Adequacy Ratio**
Under the Basle Accord, all banks with international operations must maintain a capital adequacy ratio (CAR) of at least 8% of their risk-weighted assets. (See also: Bank for International Settlements, Basle Accord)

**Capital Issues (Control) Act (India)**
In India, the Capital Issues (Control) Act was repealed in 1992. Securities transactions are governed by the Securities & Exchange Board of India Act and the Securities Contracts (Regulation) Act.

**Capital Market Development Program (Pakistan)**
In Pakistan, the Capital Market Development Program (CMDP) was introduced by the government in collaboration with the Asian Development Bank in the late 1990s. The objectives were to increase mobilization of long term resources, and to make the capital market diversified and competitive. As part of the reform, the Corporate Law Authority (CLA) (from the Department of Finance) was restructured as an autonomous Securities and Exchange Commission. The governing boards of the three stock exchanges were also restructured to include outside directors.

**Capital Markets Development Authority (Fiji)**    *www.cmda.com.fj*
In Fiji, the CMDA regulates and develops the capital markets. It licenses securities exchanges, central depositories, and securities institutions and professionals.

**Capital Market Law (Indonesia)**
In Indonesia, the Capital Market Law (No. 8/1995) came into effect in January 1996. It has replaced the 1952 Emergency Law to provide a comprehensive legal framework to develop Indonesia's capital market. Its main objective is to create an orderly, fair and efficient capital market. It ensures that the interests of investors are protected. It empowers the Capital Market Supervisory Agency (BAPEPAM) to investigate any person or institution suspected of violating the Capital Market Law. (See also: Capital Market Supervisory Agency)

## Capital Market Society of Indonesia

The Capital Market Society of Indonesia (CMS) is a non-profit private sector organization launched in 1996. It promotes the Indonesian capital market by providing information and education support. It organizes seminars, training sessions and research. It conducts courses and helps individuals in obtaining licences for BAPEPAM, the market watchdog.

## Capital Market Services Licence (Singapore)

In Singapore, under the Securities and Futures Act (SFA) a person who conducts business in securities must hold a Capital Market Services (CMS) licence.

## Capital Market Supervisory Agency (BAPEPAM)

BAPEPAM (Badan Pengawas Pasar Modal) supervises, regulates and monitors capital market activities in Indonesia to ensure that these activities are conducted in an orderly, fair and efficient manner so that the interests of investors are protected. BAPEPAM has the authority to investigate any person or institution suspected of violating the Capital Market Law.

## Carnet

This is a customs document that allows the holder to carry or send merchandise temporarily into some foreign countries for display or demonstration without paying duties. ATA carnet means Admission Temporair/Temporary Admission carnet.

## Cedel

Based in Luxembourg, Cedel is a clearing system to settle international financial instruments such as bonds. (See also: Asian bonds; Euroclear)

## Central Bank of China (Taiwan)   *www.cbc.gov.tw*

In Taiwan, the Central Bank of China (CBC) is both a government bank and an agency under the Executive Yuan. Its main objectives are to promote financial stability, guide sound banking practices, maintain stability of the currency and to foster economic development. It regulates money and credit, foreign exchange, issues currency and acts as financial agent of the government.

## Central Bank of Myanmar (CBM)

The aim of the Central Bank of Myanmar is to preserve the internal and external value of the Kyat. It formulates and implements monetary policy to foster monetary, credit and financial conditions conducive to an orderly, balanced and sustained economic development.

### Central Bank of Myanmar Law
The Central Bank of Myanmar Law was enacted in 1990 to replace the old Bank Law of 1975. It confers upon the Central Bank of Myanmar powers to operate with relative independence and to exercise supervisory and regulatory authority over financial institutions both state-owned and private banks.

### Central Bank of Solomon Islands
The Central Bank of Solomon Islands was established in 1983. It is the successor of the former Solomon Islands Monetary Authority. It supervises and inspects commercial banks and other institutions to ensure compliance with the laws. It also administers a Small Loan Guarantee Scheme for loans given to citizens by commercial banks.

### Central Bank of Sri Lanka Bank
The Central Bank of Sri Lanka Bank (CBSL) was set up in 1950 under the Monetary Law Act as the apex institution in the financial system. The old Currency Board has been replaced by the Monetary Board which manages the bank. The CBSL is in charge of monetary policy, exchange rate management and banking supervision.

### Central Bank of the Philippines
The Central Bank of the Philippines was set up in 1949. It was restructured and renamed Bangko Sentral ng Pilipinas in 1993. (See also: Bangko Sentral ng Pilipinas)

### Central Bank of Vanuatu
The Central Bank of Vanuatu acts as the clearing house for the commercial banks. It issues guidelines to banks with respect to loans. It guarantees the local currency, the Vatu which replaced the New Hebrides franc in 1981. The Vatu is linked to the Special Drawing Rights, a reserve fund created by the International Monetary Fund.

### Central Board of Direct Taxes (India)
In India, the Central Board of Direct Taxes (CBDT) is constituted by the Central Government under the Central Board of Revenue Act. It holds overall control over all other income tax authorities. It also exercises power under the Income Tax Act. It acts as the appellate authority on income tax matters.

### Central Board of Revenue (Pakistan)   *www.cbr.gov.pk*
In Pakistan, the Central Board of Revenue is responsible for the collection of various taxes such as direct taxes, customs, sales tax and central excise. Direct taxes include income tax, wealth tax and capital value tax.

**Central Carpet Industries Association** *www.nepalcarpet.org*
In Nepal, the Central Carpet Industries Association (CCIA) is a non-government organization formed in 1990. Its objective is to promote organized effort in the industry. It maintains a sustained supply of raw materials, ensures quality of carpets and stabilizes the market prices.

**Central Depository Company of Pakistan** *www.cdcpakistan.com*
The Central Depository Company of Pakistan Ltd (CDC) was formed in 1993 to operate the Central Depository System (CDS) on behalf of the financial services industry. CDS is an electronic book entry system to record and transfer securities.

**Central Credit Information Services (Thailand)** *www.centralinfo.co.th*
In Thailand, the Central Credit Information Services Co Ltd is a credit bureau that provides credit information on businesses and individual consumers. Its credit reports are used by financial institutions to verify the credit-worthiness of their borrowers. Its shareholders include major banks such as Bangkok Bank, Krung Thai Bank, Siam Commercial Bank and Thai Farmers Bank. It is a member of the Consumer Data Industry Association. (See also: Consumer Data Industry Association)

**Central Deposit Insurance Corporation (Taiwan)** *www.cdic.gov.tw*
In Taiwan, the Central Deposit Insurance Corporation (CDIC) started in 1958 as the sole agent in charge of deposit insurance. Its objective is to safeguard the interest of depositors in financial institutions. Its board of directors consists of members who are appointed by the Ministry of Finance and the Central Bank. Insured financial institutions include banks, trust and investment companies, credit cooperative associations and others. However, participation by institutions is voluntary and about 40% of them have participated.

**Central Depository Private Ltd (Singapore)**
At the Singapore Exchange, the Central Depository Private Ltd (CDP) is a wholly owned subsidiary of the Exchange. CDP operates as a central nominee and all securities at the CDP are registered in its name. However, it has no rights to the registered securities as it only holds the securities on behalf of investors.

**Central Institute for Economic Management (Vietnam)** *www.ciem.org.vn*
In Vietnam, the Central Institute for Economic Management (CIEM) in the Ministry of Planning and Investment was established in 1978. It participates in the formulation of economic policies and translates them into policy

documents, decrees or laws for consideration by the National Assembly. The CIEM cooperates with the Stockholm School of Economics and the Institute of Southeast Asian Studies (ISEAS) in Singapore.

### Central Provident Fund (CPF)    *www.cpf.gov.sg*
In Singapore, the CPF was introduced in 1955. It is a compulsory savings scheme to which both the employees and their employers make monthly contributions. Since 1992, self-employed persons are also required to contribute to their CPF Medisave accounts. The objective of the CPF scheme is to make funds available to employees when they reach retirement age or when they are physically or mentally unable to work. CPF members are allowed to use their savings to buy properties, shares and for other approved purposes.

### Central Registration Hong Kong Limited    *www.centralregistration.com* or *www.computershare.com*
The Central Registration Hong Kong Limited merged with the Hong Kong Registrars Limited. It has been renamed Computershare Hong Kong Investors Services Limited with effect from 10 June 2002. The parent company Computershare is one of the world's leading financial services and technology providers. (See also: Computershare Hong Kong Investor Services Limited)

### Central Reinsurance Corporation (Taiwan)    *www.crc.com.tw*
In Taiwan, the Central Reinsurance Corporation (Central Re) is the successor of the National Reinsurance Fund that was set up in 1956 and incorporated in 1968. As the national reinsurer, Central Re assists domestic insurers in arranging reinsurance.

### Central Steering Board for State-owned Enterprises (CSBSOE)
This is the central equitization board in Vietnam. Its members comprise cabinet ministers. It drafts regulations for state-owned enterprises to abide when they are equitized (privatized).

### Central Trading & Development Corporation
Central Trading & Development Corporation (CT&D) from Taiwan is the developer of Tan Thuan Export Processing Zone, in Ho Chin Minh City, Vietnam. (See also: Tan Thuan Export Processing Zone)

### Central Trust of China (Taiwan)    *www.ctoc.com.tw*
In Taiwan, the state-owned Central Trust of China (CTC) was formed in 1935 as a subsidiary organization within the Central Bank of China. Its objective was to facilitate public savings to promote public enterprises. Later, its

operations were expanded to include trust, custody, procurement and insurance. In 1947, the CTC became an independent unit in the banking system under a new charter introduced by the government. In 1949, CTC moved to Taiwan with the government. Initially, it handled procurement of equipment and supplies for the government. It introduced the Military Servicemen's Insurance (MSI) program in 1950 and the Government Employees' Insurance (GEI) program in 1958. With the implementation of National Health Insurance (NHI) in 1995, the administration of medical benefits was transferred to the Bureau of National Health Insurance while CTC still implements the enrolment and cash benefits. CTC now provides a wide range of services including procurement, international banking, foreign trade, life insurance and others.

**Centre for Applied Research in Education (Brunei)**
See Universiti Brunei Darussalam.

**Centre for Conflict Resolution (Cambodia)**
See Cambodia Development Resource Institute.

**Centre for Financial Engineering (Singapore)**   *http://cfe.nus.edu.sg*
In Singapore, the Centre for Financial Engineering (CFE) was set up jointly by the Institute of High Performing Computing (IHPC) and the Business School at the National University of Singapore in 1998 to produce frontier research in the field of financial engineering. CFE administers the MSc degree program in Financial Engineering. It conducts training with ACI-Singapore in areas such as risk management, bond analytics and asset securitization.

**Centre for International Forestry Research**   *www.cifor.cgiar.org*
The Centre for International Forestry Research (CIFOR) is one of the 16 centres supported by the Consultative Group on International Agricultural Research (CGIAR). It is an international research institutes to conserve forests and improve the livelihood of people in the tropics. CIFOR employs 150 staff at its headquarters in Bogor, Indonesia and its regional offices in Brazil, Cameroon and Zimbabwe. It works in more than 30 countries and has links with 300 researchers in 50 institutions worldwide. CIFOR receives contributions from over 50 governments and funding agencies. (See also: Consultative Group for International Agriculture Research)

**Centre for Micro Finance**   *www.cmfnepal.org*
In Nepal, the Centre for Micro Finance (CMF) was set up in 1998. It is an autonomous wholly-owned Nepali agency which provides technical assistance

and training to strengthen the micro-finance sector. Funds for the micro-finance sector come from commercial banks, the Agricultural Development Bank of Nepal, the Small Farmers' Development Program and savings and credit cooperatives. The CMF has established networking with similar organizations in other countries. (See also: Savings and credit cooperatives, Small Farmers' Development Program)

**Centre for Peace and Development**
See Cambodia Development Resource Institute.

**Centre for Strategic Studies**    *www.vuw.ac.nz/css*
In New Zealand, the Centre for Strategic Studies was set up in 1993. It is an independent national think-tank to sustain awareness and understanding within New Zealand about strategic issues in the external environment.

**Centre for Strategic and International Studies**    *www.csis.or.id*
In Indonesia, the Centre for Strategic and International Studies (CSIS) was formed in 1971. It is a private non-profit research organization that undertakes policy-oriented studies on domestic and international affairs.

**Centre for the Administration of Duty Exemptions and Drawbacks (Indonesia)**
This centre (Pusat Pengelolaan Pembebasan dan Pengembalian Bea Masuk or P4BM) was set up by the Department of Finance as part of the 6 May 1986 reform package to promote non-oil exports.

**PT Centris Multi Persada Pratama (CMPP) (Indonesia)**
This is one of the largest taxi companies in Indonesia.

**Ceylon Fisheries Corporation**
In Sri Lanka, the Ceylon Fisheries Corporation (CFC) was set up in 1964 to promote the production and marketing of fish.

**Ceylon Fisheries Harbours Corporation**
In Sri Lanka, the Ceylon Fisheries Harbours Corporation (CFHC) was set up in 1972 to build and manage facilities such as fishing harbours.

**Ceylon Institute of Scientific and Industrial Research**
In Sri Lanka, the Ceylon Institute of Scientific and Industrial Research (CISIR) was set up in 1955 to provide technical facilities to the industrial sector.

# LEXICON

# Ceylon Petroleum Corporation
# Ceylon Petroleum Corporation
I# Ceylon Petroleum Corporation
In Sri Lanka, the Ceylon Petroleum Corporation (CPC) was set up in 1961. It abolished the monopoly held by foreign companies. The CPC was empowered to import, export, supply and refine petroleum products, and to explore for oil.

# Ceylon Transport Board
See Peoplised Bus Companies.

# Chaebol
A Chaebol is a Korean conglomerate usually started and controlled by a family group (e.g. Daewoo, Samsung, Hyundai).

# Chartered Financial Analyst (Singapore)
The Singapore chapter of the International Society of Financial Analysts was formed in 1987. It is affiliated to the Institute of Chartered Financial Analysts (ICFA) in the USA. The primary mission of ICFA, established in 1962, is to enhance professional standards of those involved in investment decision-making. It administers the Chartered Financial Analyst (CFA) examination.

# Chek Lap Kok Airport
See Hong Kong International Airport.

# Chemical Construction Installation Company (CCIC)
Vietnam's Chemical Construction Installation Company is a state-owned enterprise. It undertakes planning and feasibility studies, survey and site investigation, engineering design, preparation of tender document, site supervision and construction as well as project management for turnkey projects.

# Chennai
New name for Madras.

# CHESS Depository Interests (CDI)
CHESS Depository Interests (CDI) is the general term for two products, CHESS Units of Foreign Securities (CUFs) and Depository Interests (DIs). Both types of CDI are electronic depository receipts issued over different security types. CUFs are the only equity component of the product and apply to foreign securities only. DIs are the debt component and apply to both foreign and domestic securities. (ASX website glossary)

CHESS Units of Foreign Securities (CUFs)
See CHESS Depository Interests (CDI).

Chiang Mai Initiative (CMI)
In May 2000, at their meeting in Chiang Mai, Thailand, the finance ministers of ASEAN + 3 (China, Japan and South Korea) agreed to strengthen economic cooperation among East Asian countries. Participants also agreed to commit swap arrangements that will help each other handle any foreign exchange predicament.

Chiao Tung Bank (Taiwan)    www.ctnbank.com.tw
The Chiao Tung Bank (formerly Bank of Communications) started in 1907 to provide funds for transportation services. In 1949, it moved to Taiwan. The Bank of Communications Act was amended in 1979 and the bank was reorganized as a development bank to provide credit for industrial, mining, transportation and public utility enterprises. In 1991, the Act was further amended and the bank extended its business to the service industry. In 1996, the bank was listed on the Taiwan Stock Exchange and in September 1999, the bank was privatized.

China Association of Banks
The China Association of Banks (CAB) was formed in May 2000. It is self-regulatory organization set up by banks, including foreign and joint venture banks in China.

China Banking Corporation (Philippines)    www.chinabank.com
China Banking Corporation is listed on the Philippine Stock Exchange. It started operations in 1920. It was the first bank in the Philippines to have on-line computerised operations and telephone banking, known as Tellerphone. Its subsidiaries include ASEAN Finance Corporation Ltd, CBC Finance Inc and CBC Venture Capital Corporation.

China Construction Bank    www.ccb.com.cn
China Construction Bank started in 1954 to implement China's first Five-year National Economic Plan. Its main role was to manage key construction projects. It is one of China's big four state-owned commercial banks. It focuses on medium and long term lending. It has operations throughout China as well as in international financial centres. In 2001, it was ranked 29 among the world top banks by The Banker magazine.

**China Council for Promotion of International Trade**
The China Council for Promotion of International Trade (CCPIT) was formed
in 1952. It organizes trade fairs and international exhibitions.

**China Everbright Bank**   *www.cebbank.com*
China Everbright Bank started in 1992. It is part of the Everbright Group.
In 2001, The Banker magazine ranked it 210th among the top 1,000 banks
in the world.

**China Everbright International Trust and Investment Corporation**
China Everbright International Trust and Investment Corporation (CEITIC)
was formed in 1991 after the merger of Everbright Finance Company and
China Industry Commerce Trust and Investment Corporation. It arranges lease
financing, equity investment and loans. It also takes deposits in Chinese and
foreign currencies and issues securities.

**China External Trade Development Centre (Taiwan)**  *www.taiwantrade.com.tw*
In Taiwan, the China External Trade Development Centre (CETRA) was
founded in 1970. It is non-profit trade organization sponsored by the
government, industrial and commercial associations to promote foreign trade.
It assists Taiwan businesses to reinforce their competitiveness in the foreign
market.

**China Foreign Exchange Trading System (CFETS)**
In 1994, the China Foreign Exchange Trading System was introduced to
replace the old Foreign Exchange Adjustment Centre. Foreign exchange
transactions are monitored by the People's Bank of China (PBOC) and the
State Administration for Exchange Control (SAEC).

**China Industry Commerce Trust and Investment Corporation**
See China Everbright International Trust and Investment Corporation
(CEITIC).

**China Insurance Company**
See People's Insurance Company of China.

**China Insurance Regulatory Commission**   *www.circ.gov.cn*
The China Insurance Regulatory Commission was set up on 18 November
1998 as a unit within the State Council with the power to regulate insurance
business in China.

**China International Trust and Investment Corporation**   *www.citic.com.cn*
China International Trust and Investment Corporation (CITIC) was set up in 1979 by Rong Yiren, former Vice President of China. Its formation was initiated and approved by Deng Xiaoping, chief architect of China's reform. It has grown into a large conglomerate with 38 subsidiaries, including those in Hong Kong, US, Canada, Australia and New Zealand. It has representative offices in Tokyo, New York and Frankfurt. Its core business ranges from finance, investment and services. In 2001, its assets totalled RMB433 billion and its after-tax profit amounted to RMB2.4 billion. In 1987, CITIC's bank department was incorporated as CITIC Industrial Bank. (See also: CITIC Industrial Bank, CITIC Securities Co Ltd)

**China Investment Bank**
China Investment Bank (CIB) operates under the authority of the Ministry of Finance and under the direct supervision of the People's Construction Bank of China (PCBC). It is not a bank. Its primary function is to administer funds from international agencies such as the World Bank and some overseas commercial bank lenders. It lends, but only to state-approved priority projects. Because of its limited role, the CIB is not a source of funding for foreign businesses.

**China National Chartering Corporation**
China National Chartering Corporation (SINOCHART) is a national corporation which charters foreign vessels and books shipping space for Chinese import and export cargoes.

**China National Foreign Trade Transportation Corporation**
China National Foreign Trade Transportation Corporation (SINOTRAN) is a national corporation which arranges customs clearance for import and export cargoes, handles domestic transportation of imports and exports, and arranges for insurance.

**China Ocean Shipping Company**
China Ocean Shipping Company (COSCO)is a national corporation which books shipping space, cargo transshipment, and operates China's flag vessels and controls Chinese ships operating under foreign flags.

**China Securities Investment Corporation (Taiwan)**
See Chinatrust Commercial Bank.

**China Securities Regulatory Commission**   *www.csrc.gov.cn*
The State Council Securities Commission (SCSC) and the China Securities
Regulatory Commission (CSRC) were set up in October 1992. The SCSC is
China's authority responsible for centralized market regulation. The CSRC is
SCSC's executive branch responsible for supervising and regulating the
securities markets. In 1998, under the State Council Reform Plan, SCSC and
CSRC were merged as one unit directly under the State Council. The basic
functions of CSRC are to supervise the securities markets and to formulate
policies related to securities markets.

**China-Singapore Suzhou Industrial Park Development Corporation**
The China-Singapore Suzhou Industrial Park Development Corporation
(CSSD) is a joint venture between China and Singapore to develop the Suzhou
Industrial Park. In 1999, Singapore reduced its stake from 65% to 30% and
China increased its stake to 65%.

**China Venturetech Investment Corporation**
China Venturetech Investment Corporation (CVIC, Venturetech) was set up
in 1985. It is a venture capital company owned by several ministries in China.
It raises capital for high-tech development, application and marketing. It
specializes in small and medium start-up especially in biotechnology,
information technology and material science.

**China Zhengzhou Commodity Exchange**
The China Zhengzhou Commodity Exchange (CZCE) is responsible for grain
and oilseed trading.

**Chinatrust Commercial Bank (Taiwan)**   *www.chinatrust.com.tw*
In Taiwan, the Chinatrust Commercial Bank (CTCB) started as the China
Securities Investment Corporation (CSIC) in 1966. It was re-organized and
in 1992, it was renamed the Chinatrust Commercial Bank. It has a network
of about 35 branches and 100 ATMs. It was among the first to introduce 24-
hour automatic service banking centre and telephone banking. It has more than
30 overseas offices in major cities in the world.

**Chinese Securities Association (Taiwan)**   *www.csa.org.tw*
Chinese Securities Association (CSA) started in 1956 as the Taipei Securities
Business Association (TSBA) which was re-organized as the Taipei Brokers
Association (TBA) in 1962, renamed Taipei Securities Brokers Association in
1963, and renamed Taipei Securities Dealers Associatin (TSDA) in 1969. The
TSDA was upgraded to a national association and renamed the Chinese

Securities Association (CSA) in 1998. The main objectives are to promote securities market development and to protect the interest of members and investors. CSA has about 400 members representing 240 securities firms.

**Chittagong Export Processing Zone**  *www.epbbd.com*
The Chittagong Export Processing Zone is one of the two EPZs in Bangladesh. It is located about 6 kilometres from the business centre, 3 kilometres from the port, and 7 kilometres from the airport. It occupies an area of about 250 hectares. (See also: Dhaka Export Processing Zone)

**Chittagong Stock Exchange**  *www.csebd.com/cse*
The Chittagong Stock Exchange (CSE) is one of two exchanges in Bangladesh. It was established in 1995 and operates a Computerized Automated Trading System. The other exchange is the Dhaka Stock Exchange. Both exchanges are self-regulated, private sector entities whose rules must be approved by the Securities Exchange Commission. Dual listing is permitted on both exchanges.

**Ciputra Group**
This is one of leading property developers in Indonesia.

**CITIC Industrial Bank**  *www.citicb.com.cn*
CITIC Bank is a subsidiary of the conglomerate, China International Trust and Investment Corporation (CITIC). It was founded in 1987 and was one of the new commercial banks that were set up as a result of China's economic reform and opening up to the outside world. For example, in 1987, the bank worked with Prudential Securities to offer the first aircraft leasing in China. In 1992, it cooperated with American Express to start the first foreign currency ATM in China. With Lehman Brothers, it offered $200 Dragon Bond for Ford Auto. This was the first time that a Chinese bank participated in foreign corporate bond issue. (See also: China International Trust and Investment Corporation)

**CITIC Prudential Life Insurance Co Ltd**  *www.citic-prudential.com.cn*
CITIC Prudential Life Insurance Co Ltd is the first Sino-British joint venture to operate life insurance business in China. It is jointly owned by the CITIC group and Prudential Corporation of United Kingdom. (See also: China International Trust and Investment Corporation)

**CITIC Securities Co Ltd**  *www.citics.com*
In China, CITIC Securities Co. Ltd (CITICS) was incorporated in 1995. It is one of the first tier of securities companies approved to carry out

comprehensive securities business nationwide. With headquarters in Shenzhen, it has 32 outlets in major cities in China. It is part of the CITIC group. (See also: China International Trust and Investment Corporation)

**PT Citra Marga Nusaphala Persada**
This is a major toll road operator company in Indonesia.

**City Banks (Japan)**
This is a general term for large Japanese commercial banks located in the cities.

**Civil Aviation Authority (Pakistan)**
In Pakistan, the Civil Aviation Authority (CAA) promotes and regulates civil aviation activities and develop infrastructure for air service.

**Civil Aviation Authority of Singapore (CAAS)**  *www.caas.gov.sg*
The CAAS was established in 1984 to develop civil aviation in Singapore. It is responsible for all aspects of civil aviation, including the development and operation of airports such as Changi Airport. The CAAS provides consultancy services on airport development. Its projects include Baiyun Airport at Guangzhou in China, Zamboanga Airport in the Philippines, Nadi Airport in Fiji and Karachi Airport in Pakistan.

**Civil Code of the Socialist Republic of Vietnam**
Vietnam's Civil Code was adopted by the National Assembly on 28 October 1995. It was promulgated on 9 November 1995 and came into effect on 1 July 1996. The Civil Code is the most important legislation since 1975. It has gone through numerous drafts and took legislators fourteen years before a final version was accepted. The Code covers a wide scope and attempts to "ensure the legal rights and interests of individuals and organizations, the interests of the State and the interests of the public, to ensure legal safety and equality in civil relations ... and to promote economic development".

**Clark Special Economic Zone**
Clark Special Economic Zone (CSEZ) in the Philippines has been converted from the former US Clark Air Base. It is about a two-hour drive from Manila. It is managed by the Bases Conversion and Development Authority (BCDA). Investors enjoy special incentives similar to those given to investors in the Subic Bay Freeport Zone. (See also: Subic Bay Freeport Zone)

**Clean Water Program (PROKASIH)**
The PROKASIH program was launched in 1989 to improve the water quality

of Indonesia's river systems through the "polluter pays" principle. The program had four phases: preparation of a systematic water pollution control package; mobilization of institutions and management resources; improvement of the quality of activities and institutional capabilities; and development in terms of intensification and expansion activities. The program covered more than 50 rivers in 17 provinces. Each provincial governor is responsible for program implementation within the province.

### Clearing House Automated Payment System (CHAPS)
CHAPS is a payment system available nationwide in Britain. It is operated by settlement banks which communicate through computers. Payments sent through the system are guaranteed and cleared on the same day.

### Clearing House Electronic Sub-register System (CHESS)
Clearing House Electronic Sub-register System provides the central register for electronic transfer of share ownership in the Australian Stock Exchange (ASX).

### Clearing House Interbank Payment System (CHIPS)
CHIPS is a computerized network used in the United States for the transfer of international payments. Members may be "settling" or "non-settling". A non-settling member maintains an account with a settling member to effect settlement on its behalf.

### Clothing Industry Training Institute (Sri Lanka)
In Sri Lanka, the Clothing Industry Training Institute (CITI) was set up in 1984 under the Ministry of Handlooms and Textile Industries to train specialised manpower for the clothing industry.

### Cluster Development Fund (Singapore)
In Singapore, the objective of this $200 million fund is to support the IT industry by encouraging projects under the IT2000 Plan. The fund is used to provide seed money or as co-investment with industry in IT services and products.

### Coconut Cultivation Board
See Coconut Development Authority (Sri Lanka).

### Coconut Development Authority (Sri Lanka)
In Sri Lanka, the Coconut Development Authority (CDA) was set up in 1971. It is the apex body which plans, coordinates and monitors the work of other functional boards including the Coconut Cultivation Board (CCB), Coconut

Research Institute (CRI), Coconut Processing Board and the Coconut Marketing Board.

### Coconut Marketing Board
See Coconut Development Authority (Sri Lanka).

### Coconut Processing Board
See Coconut Development Authority (Sri Lanka).

### Coconut Research Institute
See Coconut Development Authority (Sri Lanka).

### Colombo Brokers' Association
See Colombo Stock Exchange.

### Coles Myer (Australia) *www.colesmyer.com*
Coles Myer started in 1900. It is Australia's largest retailer. With more than 2,000 stores and 160,000 employees in Australia and New Zealand, it operates the following retail brands: Coles, Myer, Grace Bros. Megamart, Kmart, Target, Liquorland, Officeworks and e.colesmyer. In 2002, it was ranked 406 among the Fortune 500 global companies.

### Colombo Consumer Price Index
In Sri Lanka, the Colombo Consumer Price Index (CCPI) is computed monthly by the Department of Census and Statistics (DCS) with weights derived from the average expenditure patterns of 455 working class households as observed in the Colombo Family Survey 1949/50. The expenditure was re-valued at 1952 prices and the index is computed using 1952 as the base period. Retail price data for the computation of the index are collected from seven markets within the Colombo municipal area. (See also: Great Colombo Consumer Price Index, GCPI)

### Colombo Securities Exchange Ltd
See Colombo Stock Exchange.

### Colombo Share Brokers' Association
See Colombo Stock Exchange.

### Colombo Stock Exchange (Sri Lanka)
In Sri Lanka, the share market started in 1896 under the administration of the Colombo Share Brokers' Association that was renamed the Colombo

Brokers' Association in 1904. It set up a public trading floor in 1984. A second trading floor was set up by another group, the Stock Brokers' Association. In 1985, the two trading floors merged to form the Colombo Securities Exchange Ltd which was renamed the Colombo Stock Exchange (CSE) in 1990. An over-the-counter board system was introduced in 1996. The open outcry system was replaced by an automated screen trading system in 1997.

### Colonial Limited (Australia)   *www.colonial.com.fj*
Colonial Limited started in 1873 in Melbourne, Australia. It is one of the oldest, largest and most diversified financial services group. It has operations in Australia, New Zealand, Fiji, United Kingdom, and many Asian countries. In 1996, it demutualized and changed its structure from a mutual society to a shareholder-owned company. In 1997, its shares were listed on the Australian and New Zealand stock exchanges.

### Colonial National Bank (Fiji)   *www.colonial.com.fj*
In Fiji, the Colonial National Bank provides a wide range of financial services through its own branches and post offices across the islands.

### Commerce International Merchant Bankers Berhad (Malaysia)
In Malaysia, the Commerce International Merchant Bankers Berhad (CIMB) is a investment banking arm of the Commerce Group. It offers a wide range of financing, trading and risk management services. The CIMB group comprises CIMB, CIMB Securities Sdn Bhd and CIMB Futures Sdn Bhd.

### Commercial & Industrial Security Corporation (Singapore)
In Singapore, the Commercial & Industrial Security Corporation (CISCO) was formed in 1972. It is a statutory board under the Ministry of Home Affairs. It is an auxiliary police force providing security services on a commercial basis for the public and private sectors. It designs, installs and maintains security systems, central alarm monitoring and computer data storage. It escorts cash and valuables and guards banks and financial institutions.

### Commercial Law of Vietnam
The Commercial Law came into effect on 1 January 1998. It governs the formation of contracts, agency bidding, branches, and representative offices, sales promotion, commercial advertising, commercial paper, remedies and commercial disputes.

### COMMEX Malaysia
See Commodity and Monetary Exchange of Malaysia.

**Commission of Peoplisation (Sri Lanka)**
See Presidential Commission on Privatization (Sri Lanka).

**Commissioner for Administrative Complaints (HK)**
In Hong Kong, the role of the Commissioner for Administrative Complaints
(CAC) is to consider complaints from persons who claim to have been injured
by the unjust administrative action taken by the government.

**Committee for Quality Assurance in Higher Education (Australia)**
In Australia, the Committee for Quality Assurance in Higher Education
(CQAHE) was set in 1993 to ensure quality in higher education institutions.
It provides recommendations on research, teaching and community service.

**Committee on Banking Regulation and Supervisory Practices (Cooke
Committee)**
The Committee on Banking Regulation and Supervisory Practices (CBRSP)
is a committee of bank supervisors under the Bank for International
Settlements. It ensures that all banks are supervised according to some broad
principles. It is also called the Cooke Committee after its first chairman.

**Committee on Global Financial System**
The Committee on Global Financial System was formerly known as the Euro-
Currency Standing Committee. It is an international forum for regular
exchange of views among central bankers. It is responsible for developing and
overseeing the implementation of BIS statistics on banking, derivatives and
foreign exchange market activities.

**Committee on Payment and Settlement Systems**    *www.bis.org/publ.index.htm*
The Committee on Payment and Settlement Systems (CPSS) is set up by the
G-10 central banks to provide a forum for issues related to payment and
settlement systems. It sets out core principles for the design and operation of
systemically important payment systems.

**Committee to Review Arrangements for Institutional Credit for
Agriculture and Rural Development**
See National Bank for Agriculture and Rural Development (India).

**Commodities and Monetary Exchange of Malaysia**    *www.klce.com.my*
In December 1998, the Kuala Lumpur Commodities Exchange (KLCE)
changed its name to the Commodities and Monetary Exchange of Malaysia
(or COMMEX Malaysia) and merged with its subsidiary Malaysian Monetary

Exchange (MME). (See also: Kuala Lumpur Commodities Exchange KLCE, Kuala Lumpur Options and Financial Futures Exchange KLOFFE and Malaysian Monetary Exchange MME)

### Commodities Trading Act (Malaysia)
See Futures Industry (Amendment & Consolidation) Act 1997 — Malaysia.

### Commodities Trading Commission (Malaysia)
In Malaysia, the Commodities Trading Commission (CTC) merged with the Securities Commission in 1998 as a result of the Futures Industry (Amendment & Consolidation) Act 1997 which came into effect on 16 April 1998 and repealed the Commodities Trading Act 1985. The Act brought the regulation of the commodity futures market under the ambit of the Futures Industry Act 1993, thus rationalizing the regulation of the futures market in Malaysia. It also authorizes the merger of the Commodities Trading Commission (CTC) with the Securities Commission.

### Commodity Exchange of New York
The Commodity Exchange of New York (COMEX) was founded in 1933. It is the third commodity exchange in the world. It trades mainly metals and is best known for gold and silver futures trading.

### Commonwealth Bank of Australia    *www.commbank.com.au*
The Commonwealth Bank of Australia was founded in 1911. It is one of the leading provided of integrated financial services in Australia. The Commonwealth Bank Group is one of the top five capitalized stocks on the Australian Stock Exchange and is included in the Morgan Stanley Capital Global Index.

### Commonwealth Government Securities
The Commonwealth of Australia issues debt securities to the public in the form of Treasury bonds, Treasury indexed bonds and Treasury notes. These are collectively known as Commonwealth Government Securities.

### Commonwealth Ministerial Action Group
The Commonwealth Ministerial Action Group (CMAG) is the Common-wealth body in charge of upholding the political principles to which member nations subscribe.

### Commonwealth of Independent States
The Commonwealth of Independent States (CIS) is a group of 11 former Soviet Union republics: Armenia, Azerbaijan, Belarus, Kazakhstan, Kirgizistan,

Moldova, Russia, Tajikistan, Turkmenistan, Ukraine and Uzbekistan. Georgia and the Baltic states did not join.

### Commonwealth Science & Industrial Research Organization (Australia)
*www.csiro.au*
In Australia, the Commonwealth Science & Industrial Research Organization (CSIRO) is the largest research organization in Australia with 34 divisions located across the country. It does a wide range of research projects commissioned by the government and industry.

### Communications Authority of Thailand    *www.cat.or.th*
The Communications Authority of Thailand (CAT) is a state enterprise set up in 1977 under the Ministry of Transport and Communications. It operates postal and telecommunications services in Thailand. It is also the owner of Thailand's telecommunication infrastructure and investor in submarine and satellite network.

### Company Announcements Office (Australia)
Companies listed on the Australian Stock Exchange (ASX) must submit periodic reports to its Company Announcements Office.

### Company Registration Authority (China)
In China, the Company Registration Authority (CRA) grants registration to a company and issues business licences.

### Computer Assisted Order Routing and Execution System (Japan)
At the Tokyo Stock Exchange, shares are traded through the Computed Assisted Order Routing and Execution System (CORES). It is an automated trading system introduced in 1982.

### Computershare Hong Kong Investor Services Limited
*www.centralregistration.com* or *www.computershare.com*
The Central Registration Hong Kong Limited merged with the Hong Kong Registrars Limited. It has been renamed Computershare Hong Kong Investor Services Limited with effect from 10 June 2002. The parent company Computershare is one of the world's leading financial services and technology providers.

### Confederation of Asia Pacific Chambers of Commerce and Industry
*www.mongolchamber.mn/cacci/brief.htm*
The Confederation of Asia Pacific Chambers of Commerce and Industry (CACCI) was formed in 1966. It is a regional organization comprising apex

chambers of commerce and business associations. It promotes intra-regional trade and investment and represents 3 million business enterprises in Asia Pacific.

### Confederation of Asia Pacific Employers   *www.cape-emp.org*
The Confederation of Asia Pacific Employers (CAPE) was formed in 2001 by employers' organizations that participated in the 5th Asia Pacific High Level Employers' Conference held in Singapore in 2000. The objective is to make the Asia Pacific region an attractive and better place to do business in, as well as to promote social and economic development for its people. Membership is open to national employers' organizations in the Asia Pacific region, i.e. area covered by the International Labour Organization's Regional Office for Asia and the Pacific, located in Bangkok, which share the common objectives with CAPE. The confederation will coordinate and strengthen cooperation with the International Organization of Employers. (See also: International Organization of Employers)

### Consolidated Daily Report of Condition (CDRC) (Philippines)
The Consolidated Daily Report of Condition enables the Central Bank of the Philippines to determine whether or not a bank is complying with the required capital-to-risk assets ratio and with the required reserves on deposits. (See also: Consolidated Statement of Condition)

### Consolidated Insurance Company Inc (Philippines)
Consolidated Insurance Company Inc is listed on the Philippine Stock Exchange. It provides non-life insurance coverage for fire, marine, motor car, casualty and bonds.

### Consolidated Statement of Condition (Philippines)
The Consolidated Statement of Condition (CSOC) and the Consolidated Statement of Income and Expense (CSIE) enable the Central Bank of the Philippines to monitor banks' asset quality and to establish trends and generate relevant balance sheet and operating ratios of every bank for comparison with other banks. (See also: Consolidated Daily Report of Condition)

### Construction Planning and Research Unit (Brunei)   *www.mod.gov.bn*
In Brunei, the Construction Planning and Research Unit (CPRU) in the Ministry of Development promotes construction quality through conformity assessment and certification of qualified persons and construction materials. It is a correspondent member of the International Standards Organization (ISO) and subscribes to other standards bodies.

**Consultative Group on International Agricultural Research** *www.cgiar.org*
The Consultative Group on International Agricultural Research (CGIAR) was formed in 1971 when the first meeting at the World Bank was attended by 18 governments and organizations. Its mission is to contribute, through its research, to promoting sustainable agriculture for food security in the developing countries. Since then, membership has expanded to 58. The number of CGIAR centres has increased to 16. These centres are autonomous institutions, each with its charter, international board of trustees, director and staff. The centres in Asia are the Centre for International Forestry Research in Bogor (Indonesia), the ICLARM World Fish Centre in Penang (Malaysia), International Crops Research Institute for the Semi-Arid Tropics (ICRISAT) in Patancheru (Andhra Pradesh, India) and the International Rice Research Institute in Los Banos (Philippines). (See also: Centre for International Forestry Research, ICLARM World Fish Centre, International Rice Research Institute)

**Consumer Data Industry Association** *www.cdiaonline.org*
The Consumer Data Industry Association was founded in 1906. It is an international trade association which represents consumer information companies that provide credit and mortgage reports, check fraud and verification services.

**Consumer Goods Safety Ordinance (CGSO) (Hong Kong)**
In Hong Kong, the Consumer Goods Safety Ordinance (CGSO) was one of four pieces of consumer protection legislation introduced in 1994. It ensures that goods supplied for private use or consumption are safe and for incidental purposes. It empowers the Commissioner of Customs and Excise to control the safety of consumer goods. (See also: Hong Kong Consumer Protection Laws)

**Consumer Protection in Hong Kong**
See Hong Kong Consumer Protection Laws.

**Consumers Association of Singapore**
The Consumers Association of Singapore (CASE) is a non-profit organization founded in 1971 by the National Trades Union Congress (NTUC). Its objectives are to inform, educate and protect consumers. It publishes informational brochures, organizes seminars and campaigns and conducts surveys. It helps to bridge the gap between buyers and sellers by resolving consumer-trader issues.

**Contact Singapore** *www.contactsingapore.org.sg*
Contact Singapore is a one-stop information centre to assist Singaporeans

overseas to stay in touch with development in Singapore. It has overseas offices in Boston, Chicago, Hong Kong, London, Perth, San Francisco, Shanghai, Sydney and Toronto. It runs the Singapore Employment Advisory and Recruitment Channel (SEARCH) program to help match the skills of students and professionals with the manpower needs of employers in Singapore.

### Contracts for the International Sale of Goods (CISG) Convention
The United Nations Convention on Contracts for the International Sale of Goods convention (CISG Convention) was based on the work of the United Nations Commission on International Trade Law (UNCITRAL) and was adopted in Vienna on 11 April 1980. It covers uniform rules for international sales contracts.

### Controller of Capital Issues (India)
In India, after independence in 1974, the government controlled access to the capital markets through the Office of the Controller of Capital Issues (CCI). As part of the financial reform, the CCI was abolished in May 1992. The Securities and Exchange Board of India (SEBI) is now responsible for regulating new domestic issues.

### Convertible Rupee Account
In Sri Lanka, the Convertible Rupee Account (CRA) was introduced in 1971 to allow non-traditional exporters to keep part of their export earnings in CRAs and allowed them to use them to finance restricted imports and for other purposes including those otherwise subject to foreign exchange control.

### Cooperation Internationale en Recherche Agronomique pour le Development (CIRAD)
CIRAD was formed after merging two French international research institutes: International Coconut Research Institute (IRHO) and International Coffee Research Institute (IRCC).

### Cooperative Credit Purchasing Company (Japan)
In Japan, the Cooperative Credit Purchasing Company (CCPC) was set up in 1993 to take over the non-performing loans of banks.

### Cooperative Export Import Enterprise (Myanmar)
In Myanmar, the Cooperative Export Import Enterprise was set up in 1994 to promote cooperative exports. It collects, analyzes and disseminates market information and identifies potential markets.

## Copyright Agreement between US and Vietnam

The Copyright Agreement between the US and Vietnam Governments on the Establishment of Copyright Relations was signed on 27 June 1997 during US Secretary of State Madeline Albright's visit to Vietnam. The Copyright Agreement provides a legal basis for protecting the copyrightable works of American companies and individuals in Vietnam and the copyrights of Vietnamese in the US. It is expected to improve prospects for increased transfer of technology to Vietnam.

## Copyright Tribunal (Singapore)

In Singapore, the Copyright Tribunal was set up in 1987. It settles disputes between copyright owners and users of copyright materials. It has jurisdiction in two areas: grant compulsory licences to ensure that the copyright holder's monopoly is not abused, and to settle royalty rates in cases of statutory compulsory licence.

## Corporate Debt Restructuring Advisory Committee  *www.bot.or.th*

In Thailand, in response to the financial crisis, the Corporate Debt Restructuring Advisory Committee (CDRAC) was set up in 1998 as a special unit within the central bank, Bank of Thailand. It is chaired by the bank's governor and has representatives from the Thai Bankers Association, Foreign Banks Association, Federation of Thai Industries, Board of Trade of Thailand and other related organizations. It is responsible for mapping out debt restructuring measures to support negotiations between the private sector and financial institutions.

## Corporate Debt Restructuring Committee (Malaysia)

In Malaysia, during the financial crisis, the Corporate Debt Restructuring Committee was set up to help viable Malaysian companies from being forced into liquidation.

## Corporate Law Authority (Pakistan)

In Pakistan, the Corporate Law Authority (CLA) was a department in the Ministry of Finance. It administered corporate law until 1981. Its functions have been taken over by the Securities and Exchange Commission.

## Corporate Law Economic Reform Program

See Financial Reporting Council (Australia).

## Council for Economic Planning and Development (Taiwan)

*www.cepd.gov.tw*

In Taiwan, the Council for Economic Planning and Development (CEPD) serves in an advisory capacity to the Executive Yuan (Cabinet). It drafts national economic development plans, evaluate project proposals, and coordinates economic policy-making activities.

**Council for the Development of Cambodia**    *www.cambodiainvestment.gov.kh*
The Council for the Development of Cambodia (CDC) was formed in 1994 under the Law on Foreign Investment. It is the highest government decision-making body for private and public sector investment. It is chaired by the Prime Minister and its members are ministers from related agencies. The CDC is in charge of two boards: (a) Cambodian Rehabilitation and Development Board (CRDB) and (b) Cambodian Investment Board (CIB). The CRDB manages aids from donor countries and UN agencies. The CIB monitors private sector investments.

**Council of Financial Regulators (Australia)**
In Australia, the Council of Financial Regulators was set up in 1998 to replace the Council of Financial Supervisors and to coordinate Australia's financial regulatory agencies. It is chaired by Reserve Bank of Australia (central bank). Its members include the Australian Prudential Regulatory Authority (APRA) and the Australian Securities and Investments Commission (ASIC). (See also: Australian Prudential Regulatory Authority, and Australian Securities and Investments Commission)

**Council of Scientific and Industrial Research (India)**
In India, the Council of Scientific and Industrial Research (CSIR) was set up in 1942. It promotes, guides and coordinates scientific and industrial research. It has developed numerous specialized R&D institutions. It has a network of 40 laboratories and 80 field centres across India. It has about 25,000 staff, of which 6,000 are scientists, including 3,000 PhD holders.

**Credit Information Bureau (Sri Lanka)**
In Sri Lanka, the Credit Information Bureau was set up in 1990 under the Credit Information Bureau Act. In 1995, the Act was amended to allow merchant banks and other institutions to have access to the Bureau.

**Credit Information Bureau Inc (Philippines)**
In the Philippines, the Credit Information Bureau Inc (CIBI) is a non-stock and non-profit corporation providing credit rating services. For example, it provides credit rating for corporate papers (CPs). All CP issues require CIBI ratings before they are presented to the Securities and Exchange Commission for approval. CIBI rates both short term and long term commercial papers. The ratings are based on the corporate borrower's revenue, assets, net worth,

net income, current ratio and debt-to-equity ratio. For short term papers, CIB 1 is the best grade while CIB 6 is the lowest. For long term CPs, the top of the scale of 9 is CIB Aaa while the lowest is CIB C.

## Credit Information Centre (Vietnam)
In Vietnam, the State Bank has set up a Credit Information Centre to provide institutional lenders with information on the creditworthiness of borrowers. Such reports are available on a confidential basis.

## Credit Information Services Limited (Hong Kong)   *www.cishk.com*
In Hong Kong, Credit Information Services Limited (CIS) is a privately owned credit reference agency. It started in the early 1980s when finance houses were incurring losses from fraudulent collateral financing. CIS was started by twelve finance houses in the vehicle and equipment leasing business. These companies collected and shared credit information thus setting up the first credit database in Hong Kong. During later years, shareholders of CIS expanded to include banks and credit card companies. By the end of 2001, the database had more than one million records contributed by about 100 members. Usage averaged 530,000 records per month. In 1999, Trans Union International Inc and Dun & Bradstreet were invited to join as shareholders. (See also: Dun & Bradstreet, Trans Union International Corporation)

## Crore
10 million (India).

## Cyberview (Malaysia)
In Malaysia, Cyberview Sdn Bhd is the developer of the 2,800-hectare flagship zone in Cyberjaya. One of its major stakeholders is the Multimedia Development Corporation.

## Dai Hung Oilfield (Vietnam)
Dai Hung (Big Bear) oilfield is located in Vietnam. It is owned by an international consortium including Australia's BHP, Japan's Sumitomo, France's Total, Malaysia's Petronas and Petro Vietnam.

## Daimyo Bond
Daimyo bonds are similar to Samurai bonds except that settlement is through Euroclear or Cedel systems instead of in Japan. The first Daimyo bonds were issued by the World Bank in 1987. They were followed by the Inter-American Development Bank and African Development Bank in 1988. (See also: Samurai bonds)

**Daiwa Bank Holdings (Japan)**  *www.daiwabank.co.jp*
Daiwa Bank Holdings was formed in December 2001 after the merger of Daiwa Bank, Kinki Osaka Bank and Nara Bank. In March 2001, Asahi Bank joined Daiwa Bank Holdings. Since then, the group has undergone some reorganization. It is now known as Resona Holdings. Daiwa Bank and Asahi Bank have merged to become Resona Bank. Operations of the Asahi Bank in Saitama prefecture are separated from Asahi Bank to form Saitama Resona Bank. (See also: Resona Holdings)

**Daiwa Securities Group (Japan)**  *www.ir.daiwa.co.jp*
In Japan, Daiwa Securities started in 1902 as the Fujimoto Bill Broker. In 1942, the name was changed to Fujimoto Securities. In 1943, it merged with Nippon Trust Bank to form Daiwa Securities. In 1999, it became the first listed company to adopt a holding company structure as Daiwa Securities Group. The group includes Daiwa Securities, Daiwa Securities SMBC, Daiwa Asset Management and numerous overseas companies. In 2001, it introduced the Daiwa Securities Brand Mark. It also established Daiwa Securities Media Networks for broadcasting business.

**Dalian Commodity Exchange (China)**
In China, the Dalian Commodity Exchange (DCE) trades spot and futures contracts for barley, soybean and soybean meal.

**Dana Islam**
Islamic unit trust.

**Dana Moneter Internasional (Indonesia)**
International Monetary Fund.

**Danaharta**  *www.danaharta.com.my*
In Malaysia, Pengurusan Danaharta Nasional Berhad was set up by the National Economic Action Council under the National Economic Recovery Plan. Its task is to remove non-performing loans (NPLs) from the banking system so as to allow banks to get back to the business of lending to viable borrowers without being unduly distracted by managing NPLs. (See also: Danamodal)

**Danamodal (Malaysia)**  *www.bnm.gov.my/danamodal*
Danamodal Nasional Berhad was set up to revitalize Malaysia's financial services industry. It serves as an interim funding vehicle for banks that are unable to raise capital directly. It ensures that the recapitalization process is

commercially driven and that investment decisions are made according to market-based principles. Its operations are supervised by Bank Negara, the central bank. (See also: Danaharta)

**Dasar Ekonomi Baru (Malaysia)**
New Economic Policy.

**Dasar Pendidikan Kebaangsaan (Malaysia)**
National Education Policy.

**Dasar Penswastaan (Malaysia)**
Privatization Policy.

**Dasar Perindustrian Negara (Malaysia)**
National Industrialization Policy.

**Dasar Persyarikatan Malaysia**
See Malaysia Incorporated Policy.

**Data Storage Institute (Singapore)**
See Science and Engineering Research Council.

**PT Davomas Abadi (Indonesia)**
This is Indonesia's largest producer of cocoa butter and cocoa powder. Its main customers are multinational manufacturers of chocolate products.

**PT Daya Guna Samudra (Indonesia)**
This is one of Indonesia's largest integrated fishing companies. It was founded in 1978 by Burhan Uray and is part of the diversified Djajanti Group. It is the largest fishing vessel operator in the Arafura Sea, one of its licensed fishing areas. It also operates cold storage facilities for frozen fish, a shrimp processing and fishmeal plant on the island of Benjina. Its operations are mainly for the export market. Its shares were offered for public subscription in 1996 and are traded on the Jakarta Stock Exchange.

**DBS Group Holdings Limited (Singapore)** *www.dbs.com*
In Singapore, DBS Group Holdings Limited is the holding company of DBS Bank. In terms of market capitalization, it is among the largest companies listed on the Singapore Exchange. DBS Bank started in 1968 as a development finance institution. Since then, it has diversified into a full service bank. It has more than 100 branches in Singapore and has branches or offices in major cities in Asia,

UK and US. In 1998, it acquired the government-owned POSBank. In 2001, it acquired 60% stake in stockbroking company Vickers Ballas.

**DBS Thai Danu Bank**   *www.dbs.co.th*
DBS Thai Danu Bank (DTDB) started in 1948 as Thai Danu Bank. Its major shareholder is the Development Bank of Singapore.

**DCB-RHB Mudharabah Fund (Malaysia)**
This is an Islamic-based unit trust launched in 1996 by DCB-RHB Unit Trust Management in Malaysia.

**Dena Bank (India)**   *www.denabank.com*
In India, the Dena Bank (India) was founded in 1938 as the Devkaran Nanjee Banking Company Ltd. In 1939, it became a public company and changed its name to Dena Bank. In 1969, it was among the 14 banks that were nationalized. It is now a public sector bank.

**Department of Finance (Philippines)**   *www.dof.gov.ph*
In the Philippines, the Department of Finance (DOF) formulates and administers fiscal policies, manages financial resources of the government and supervises the revenue operations of local government units. It manages all public sector debt, both domestic and foreign. It rationalizes, privatizes and is accountable for corporations and assets owned by the government.

**Department of Monetary Affairs (Taiwan)**
In Taiwan, in July 1991, the Department of Monetary Affairs (DMA) in the Ministry of Finance was upgraded to the Bureau of Monetary Affairs (BMA). (See also: Bureau of Monetary Affairs)

**Department of Trade and Industry (Philippines)**   *www.dti.gov.ph*
In the Philippines, the Department of Trade and Industry (DTI) is the government agency which champions consumers and business. As consumer champion, it promotes consumer choice, enforces trade law and forges alliance with consumer groups to strengthen consumer power. As business champion, it encourages businesses to grow and compete locally and globally. It provides services to companies seeking to invest in the Philippines.

**Deposit Insurance and Credit Guarantee Corporation of India**
The Deposit Insurance and Credit Guarantee Corporation of India (DICGC) is a wholly-owned subsidiary of the Reserve Bank of India. (See also: Reserve Bank of India)

**Depository Interests**
See CHESS Depository Interests (CDI).

**Derivatives Automated Trading System (DATS)**
See ASX Derivatives (ASXD) Options Market.

**Development Bank of Japan** *www.dbj.go.jp*
The Development Bank of Japan (DBJ) was set up in 1999 as the successor to the Japan Development Bank and the Hokkaido-Tohoku Development Finance Public Corporation. The financial functions of the Japan Regional Development Corporation and the Japan Environment Corporation were also transferred to DBJ. The bank provides long term finance to projects as a supplement to the financial services provided by ordinary financial institutions.

**Development Bank of Singapore** *www.dbs.com*
The Development Bank of Singapore (DBS Bank) was set up in 1968 by the Singapore Government to take over the industrial financing function of the Economic Development Board which was formed to spearhead Singapore's industrialization plan. As stated in its first annual report, the original objective was to provide industrial financing and to assist in setting up new industries. In the 1980s, the bank began to diversify as a commercial bank.

Its major shareholder is the Singapore Government which owns substantial equity through its holding companies such as Temasek Holdings. DBS shares are listed on the Singapore Exchange under DBS Group Holdings. In the 1990s, DBS expanded internationally by acquiring Wing Lung Bank in Hong Kong, PT DBS Buana Tat Lee Bank in Indonesia, Thai Danu Bank and TSD Leasing Ltd in Thailand. In 1998, DBS bought the Post Office Savings Bank from the Singapore Government. It is one of the Big Three local banks in Singapore and has offices in many Asian countries, UK and US.

**Development Bank of Solomon Islands**
The Development Bank of Solomon Islands (DBSI) was established in 1977. It is a government statutory body that provides finance for agriculture and other development projects.

**Development Bank of the Philippines**
The Development Bank of the Philippines (DBP) was set up in 1946 under the name of Rehabilitation Finance Corporation. It provided credit facilities to rehabilitate and develop agriculture and industry and to reconstruct war-damaged properties. Its activities have expanded and it now allocates government funds to all sectors of the economy.

## Development Bank of Vanuatu

The Development Bank of Vanuatu (DVB) was set up in 1983 as a statutory body to succeed the Development Bank of New Hebrides which was formed in 1979. Its objective is to promote economic development of the natural resources in Vanuatu.

## Dewan Penunjang Ekspor (DPE) (Indonesia)

See Export Support Board.

## Dewan Pertimbangan Agung (DPA) (Indonesia)

This is Indonesia's Supreme Advisory Council. It assists the President, who chooses its members from political parties, functional groups and prominent persons.

## Dewan Perwakilan Rakyat (Indonesia)

This is Indonesia's House of Representatives. It is the legislative branch of the State. It has 500 members: 100 nominated by the President (from the Armed Forces, reduced to 75 in 1997), and 400 directly elected. The Dewan approves all statutes and debates on government policies.

## Dhaka Export Processing Zone  *www.epbbd.com*

The Dhaka Export Processing Zone is one of the two EPZs in Bangladesh. The 58-hectare zone is located at Savar, about 35 kilometres from Dhaka city centre, 25 kilometres from Zia International Airport. (See also: Chittagong Export Processing Zone)

## Dhaka Stock Exchange  *www.dsebd.org*

In Bangladesh, the Dhaka Stock Exchange (DSE) started in April 1954 as the East Pakistan Stock Exchange and was renamed the Dhaka Stock Exchange in 1962. DSE is one of two exchanges in Bangladesh. It was established in 1954 and operates a Computerised Automated Trading System. The other exchange is the Chittagong Stock Exchange. Both exchanges are self-regulated, private sector entities whose rules must be approved by the Securities Exchange Commission. Dual listing is permitted on both exchanges.

## Dien Nam-Dien Ngoc Industrial Park (Vietnam)

In Vietnam, Dien Nam-Dien Ngoc Industrial Park is located 20 kilometres south of Danang city. The 145-hectare park is designed to attract foreign investment in non-polluting hi-tech industries. About 180 factories are expected to be built, employing 42,000 workers including 8,000 office workers, 15,000 technicians and 20,000 manual workers.

**Diet**
Japanese Parliament.

**Dinh Vu Economic Zone (Vietnam)**
In Vietnam, this economic zone is developed by an international group in cooperation with Hai Phong City authorities. The group includes US insurance company American International Group (AIG), Thailand-based Asia Infrastructure Development Co. Ltd. and Antwerp-based International Port Engineering & Management (IPEM). DVEZ is located on the Dinh Vu Peninsula in Hai Phong near the Tonkin Gulf.

**Directorate General of Posts and Telecommunications (Vietnam)**
In Vietnam, the Directorate General of Posts and Telecommunications (DGPT) is the ministerial body responsible for the provision and regulation of telecom services. Vietnam Posts and Communications (VNPT) is its business arm.

**Disclosure and Accounting Standards Committee (Singapore)**
In Singapore, the Disclosure and Accounting Standards Committee (DASC) was set up in 2000 by the government to review the corporate regulatory framework, disclosure and accounting standards and corporate governance.

**Discount Finance House of India**
The Discount Finance House of India (DFHI) was set up by the Reserve Bank of India (RBI, central bank) in 1988 to develop a secondary market for short term money market instruments. It buys and sells T-bills issued by RBI auctions, commercial bills, certificates of deposit and commercial papers.

**Doktoranda (Dra) (Indonesian)**
A female graduate in any profession (except engineering and law). (See also: Insinyur for engineer, Sarjana Hukum for law)

**Doktorandus (Drs) (Indonesian)**
A male graduate in any profession (except engineering and law). (See also: Insinyur for engineer, Sarjana Hukum for law)

**DOSRI Rule (Philippines)**
In the Philippines, the DOSRI Rule limits how much a bank can lend to its directors, officers, stockholders and related interests (DOSRI).

**Dow Jones Industrial Average (DJIA)**
DJIA is the share price index of shares traded on the New York Stock Exchange.

The DJIA is a price-weighted average of 30 actively traded stocks. It is named after Charles Dow and Eddie Jones who first teamed up in 1882 to report stock market news in New York. Charles Dow was also the first editor of the Wall Street Journal.

### DSE All Share Price Index (Bangladesh)
In Bangladesh, at the Dhaka Stock Exchange, the DSE All Share Price Index is a market capitalization weighted index comprising all listed companies.

### DTC Association     *www.dtca.org.hk*
The DTC Association (Hong Kong Association of Restricted Licence Banks and Deposit-taking Companies) was set up in 1981. Its members are the restricted licence banks (RLB) and the deposit-taking companies (DTC). There are about 45 RLBs and 60 DTCs. These institutions function the same way as banks and are supervised by the Hong Kong Monetary Authority (HKMA) under the same Banking Ordinance. The DTC Association and the Hong Kong Association of Banks (HKAB) are the two organizations that the authorities regularly consult on proposed changes to the industry. In July 1997, the DTC Association, HKAB and the HKMA jointly issued a Code of Banking Practice Guidelines on the following: (a) Annualize Percentage Rates & Borrowing Charges, (b) Local Property Fraud and (c) Banking for the Blind.

### Dun & Bradstreet
Dun & Bradstreet is a leading international company providing information management services. It has about 350 offices in 40 countries. It provides solutions to business in the area of customer and supplier base management.

### Duty Drawback Office (Bangladesh)
In Bangladesh, duties paid on exported products are refunded through the Duty Drawback Office (DEDO) of the National Board of Revenue.

### Dwifungsi (Indonesian)
The term means dual function. It is used by Indonesian armed forces to describe their dual role of both security and socio-political functions.

### EAGA Development Strategy (EDS)
The objectives of the EAGA (East ASEAN Growth Area) Development Strategy (EDS) are to maximize individual country gains from comparative advantage, to exploit their complementarities and to use shared natural resources, technology and information. EAGA includes Brunei Darussalam, Indonesia, Malaysia and Philippines.

**Early Stage Fund (ESF)**
In Singapore, the ESF is part of the US$1 billion Technology Investment Fund (TIF). Statutory board A*STAR (formerly known as the National Science & Technology Board) uses this amount to co-invest with the private sector in specific programs to seed and develop ideas at the embryonic stage in order to stimulate the creation of high growth companies based in Singapore.

**East ASEAN Business Council**  *www.brunet.bn/org/bimpeabc*
The East ASEAN Business Council (EABC) was formed on 19 November 1994 in Davao, Mindanao (Philippines) at the First East ASEAN Business Convention and Exhibits. Its objective is to catalyze the private sector to cooperate in economic activities and to increase trade, tourism and investment in the region. Its Brunei-based Secretariat was set up in 1996. (See also: East ASEAN Growth Area)

**East ASEAN Growth Area**
The East ASEAN Growth Area (EAGA) comprises the Brunei Darussalam, Indonesia (Kalimantan, Sulawesi, Maluku and Irian Jaya), Malaysia (Sabah, Sarawak and Labuan) and Philippines (Mindanao and Palawan).

**East Asian and Oceanian Stock Exchanges Federation (EAOSEF)**
*http://eaosef.com*
The East Asian and Oceanian Stock Exchanges Federation (EAOSEF) started in 1982 as an informal organization called the East Asian Stock Exchanges Conference (EASEC). Its objectives were to promote friendship and to exchange information among members. In 1990, it was enlarged to include stock exchanges from the Oceanic region. It also adopted a constitution to become an international federation of stock exchanges called EAOSEF. In 1998, its charter was revised to change the basis of its membership from a country-based to an exchange-based system that it has today. Currently, EAOSEF comprises 15 stock exchanges.

**East Asian Institute (Singapore)**
The East Asian Institute (EAI) at the National University of Singapore was formerly known as Institute of East Asian Political Economy, which itself was renamed from the Institute of East Asian Philosophies (IEAP). The EAI conducts research on social and economic issues of East Asian countries.

**Eastern Federal Union Assurance (Pakistan)**
See State Life Insurance Corporation.

**Economic and Social Commission for Asia and the Pacific**    *www.unescap.org*
The regional arm of the United Nations Secretariat for the Asia and the Pacific
is the Economic and Social Commission for Asia and the Pacific (ESCAP).
It is located in the United Nations Building in Bangkok, Thailand. It promotes
economic and social development through regional cooperation and integration. It serves as the main within the UN system for the ESCAP region.

**Economic Committee — Recommendations (Singapore)**
During the 1970s and early 1980s, the Singapore economy had continuous high
growth despite the oil crisis and world recession. In 1985, growth slowed down
significantly and the Singapore economy had its first major recession with a
negative growth rate. The government set up a special Economic Committee
chaired by Brigadier-General Lee Hsien Loong, the then Minister of State for
Trade and Industry to examine Singapore's economic problems, to identify new
growth areas and to define new economic strategies. The Committee gave a wide
range of recommendations dealing with all aspects of the economy. For the
financial sector, it identified seven areas of growth: risk management, fund
management, capital markets, unlisted securities market, financial and
commodity futures, financing third-country trading and reinsurance.

**Economic Cooperation Organization**
The Economic Cooperation Organization (ECO) is a new economic grouping
of ten countries in the South, Central and West Asia. At its inception in 1985,
there were only three member countries: Iran, Pakistan and Turkey. Since then,
several other countries have joined the group. They include: Afghanistan,
Azerbaijian, Kazakhistan, Kyrghistan, Tajikistan, Turkmenistan and
Uzbekistan. The objective is to reduce trade barriers and promote industrial
collaboration and investment in the region.

**Economic Court (Vietnam)**
In Vietnam, the Economic Court was set up in 1993 as a division of the
People's Court system. It decides on disputes relating to commercial contracts.
These are contracts between two legal entities (a company, a state-owned
enterprise, a licensed foreign enterprise), or between a legal entity and an
individual with business registration. It also decides on disputes between a
company and its owners. Other disputes dealt by the Court include the
purchase and sales of shares and stocks.

**Economic Development Board (Singapore)**    *www.sedb.com.sg*
In Singapore, the Economic Development Board started in 1961. It formulates
and implements economic and industrial development strategies. Its mission
is to develop Singapore into a global hub for knowledge-driven industries.

## Economic Law and Improved Procurement System (Indonesia)

ELIPS is a government project to reform economic laws in Indonesia. One of its tasks is to draft new arbitration laws jointly with the Ministry of Finance. The UNCITRAL Arbitration Rules have been used as a primary source for the new international arbitration law proposed by ELIPS.

## Economic Restructuring Shares (Singapore) *www.cpf.gov.sg*

In January 2003, the Singapore Government gave Economic Restructuring Shares (ERS) to its citizens to offset the increase in Goods and Services Tax (GST) which was raised from 3% to 5%. It was part of the GST Assistance Package, which also included HDB rental and conservancy rebates, hospital GST subsidy and school GST subsidy. The amount of ERS depends on the annual value of homes owned by the recipients. Owners of property with annual value up to $10,000 would get $1,200 worth of ERS. They include most of the HDB flat owners. They would receive $400 each year from 2003 to 2005. The amount would be enough to cover the GST increase for about 5 years. Singaporeans owning more valuable properties receive only $600 over the 3-year period. Active National Servicemen (NSmen) would receive an additional $200 while inactive NSmen would get only $100 more. ERS may be exchanged for cash at any time.

## Economic Stabilization Program (Philippines)

The Economic Stabilization Program was a program agreed between the Philippines and the International Monetary Fund in 1992. It would provide the Philippines with foreign funds on the condition that it adhered to IMF guidelines to introduce tightening measures to narrow its deficits. It would instil macroeconomic discipline in the management of the economy.

## EFTA-Singapore Free Trade Agreement

The EFTA-Singapore Free Trade Agreement (ESFTA) was signed on 26 June 2002 between Singapore and four EFTA countries: Switzerland, Liechtenstein, Norway and Iceland. The agreement took effect on 1 January 2003. The agreement covers trade and goods and services, investment, competition, government procurement and intellectual property. (Singapore government press release on 26 June 2002)

## e-Government Action Plan (Singapore)

In Singapore, the First e-Government Action Plan (eGAP I) was launched in June 2000. Its objective was to get as many government services online as possible. By 2003, about 1,600 public services are provided online. Examples are registering a business, filing income tax, applying for a new passport. In July 2003, the Second e-Government Action Plan was launched.

The government would invest $1.3 billion over three years to upgrade infrastructure, develop capabilities and improve electronic public service.

**Eigyo Tokkin Fund (Japan)**
In Japan, eigyo tokkin are funds specially designed by securities companies offering institutional investors specified rates of return.

**Eldistra (Indonesia)**
See Electronic Long Distance Trading System.

**Electronic Long Distance Trading System (Eldistra) (Indonesia)**
Eldistra is a trading system used at the Surabaya Stock Exchange in Indonesia. (See also: Surabaya Stock Exchange)

**Electronic Road Pricing (Singapore)**
In Singapore, the Electronic Road Pricing (ERP) was introduced in 1998. It replaced the Area Licensing Scheme (ALS) and the manual Road Pricing System (RPS). Under the RPS system, motorists are charged every time they drive past an ERP gantry during specific hours. Charges are deducted from a stored-value Smartcard inserted into the electronic device (called the in-vehicle unit) installed on the dash board. Charges are higher during peak hours. Charges also vary according to the location of the gantry.

**Electronic Trade Related Services (ETRS)**
These services enable trade documents to be transmitted electronically. The documents include purchase orders, packing lists, invoices, letters of credit and shipping documents.

**EMAS (Malaysia)**
See Exchange Main Board Share Index (Malaysia).

**EMAS Index (Malaysia)**
This is the main board all-shares price index at the Kuala Lumpur Stock Exchange.

**Emergency (Essential Powers) Act, 1979 Essential (Protection of Depositors) Regulations 1986 (Malaysia)**
This Act gives Bank Negara Malaysia (Central Bank) the power to investigate the affairs of any person it suspects or has reason to believe is a deposit-taker. It empowers the Bank freeze the properties of the deposit-taker and other persons associated with the deposit-taker, assume control over the deposit-

taker, and to appoint receivers and managers. The Act also enumerates the powers of the managers, provisions on priority of payment and cost.

## Employees' Provident Fund (Sri Lanka)

In Sri Lanka, the Employees' Provident Fund (EPF) was set up in 1958 under the Employees' Provident Fund Act. It provides retirement benefits to workers in the public sector.

## Employees' Provident Fund (Malaysia)    *www.kwsp.gov.my*

In Malaysia, the Employees' Provident Fund (EPF) started in 1951. It is a National Social Security Organization that provides old-age benefits for its members upon retirement. It has about 10 million members. The rate of contribution is 23% of the employee's wages of which 11% is from the employee's monthly wage while 12% is contributed by the employer.

## Employees' Provident Fund Corporation (Nepal)

In Nepal, Employees' Provident Fund Corporation was established in 1963. It draws its resources from contributions from employers and employees.

## Employees' Provident Fund Organization (India)    *www.epfindia.com*

In India, the Employees' Provident Fund was introduced under the Employees' Provident Fund and Miscellaneous Provisions Act in 1952. The EPF Organization administers three schemes: Employees' Provident Fund Scheme, Employees' Deposit Linked Insurance Scheme and the Employees' Pension Scheme. The Central Board of Trustees is a tripartite body consisting of representatives from the Central Government, State Governments, employers and employees.

## Employees' Trust Fund (Sri Lanka)

In Sri Lanka, the Employees' Trust Fund (ETF) was set up in 1982 under the Employees' Trust Fund Act.

## Energy Market Authority    *www.ema.gov.sg*

The Energy Market Authority of Singapore (EMA) was set up on 1 April 2001 under the Ministry of Trade and Industry. It regulates the electricity and gas industry.

## Enterprise des Telecommunications Lao (ETL)

ETL is Laos' national telecommunication carrier. It was formerly part of the Enterprise des Post et Telecommunications Lao (EPTL). In 1996, ETL signed a master contract with Thailand's Shinawatra International for the provision of telecommunication service in Laos.

**Enterprise for ASEAN Initiative**
The Enterprise for ASEAN Initiative is a US initiative launched at APEC 2002 meeting by President George W. Bush with leaders from ASEAN. The EAI sets forth a roadmap to promote increased investment, economic growth, and free trade between the US and ASEAN countries.

**Entrepot Produksi Tujuan Ekspor (EPTE) Zone (Indonesia)**
Special export production zone in Indonesia.

**Entrepreneur Skills Development Centre (ESDC) (Malaysia)**
The ESDC is located in Kuala Lumpur, Malaysia. It is a centre within the Federation of Malaysian Manufacturers and is recognized by Malaysia's Human Resource Development Fund. Employers can claim part of their costs of sending their employees to be trained at the ESDC. (See also: Federation of Malaysian Manufacturers)

**Environment Compliance Certificate (Philippines)**
See Environmental Impact Statement (Philippines).

**Environmental Impact Statement (Philippines)**
In the Philippines, under the EIS (Environmental Impact Statement) system, all government agencies, government corporations and private companies are required to prepare an environmental impact assessment for any project that affects the quality of the environment. The assessment is needed in order to obtain an Environment Compliance Certificate (ECC). The Environmental Management Bureau is the government agency responsible to review the completeness of the Environment Impact Statement.

**Environmental Management Bureau**
See Environmental Impact Statement (Philippines).

**Equitable Banking Corporation (Philippines)**    *www.Equitablepci.com*
Equitable Bank was established in 1950 and was the first commercial bank to be licensed by the Bangko Sentral ng Pilipinas. The bank's initial focus was to provide banking services to the Chinese-Filipino community. It has since diversified its services with a network of 107 branches nationwide. Its major banking-related subsidiaries include EBC Investments Inc, Equitable Savings Bank, Equitable Finance Ltd and EBC Insurance Brokerage Inc.

**Equitize**
In Vietnam, this term means privatize.

## Equity Participation Fund (Pakistan)

In Pakistan, the Equity Participation Fund (EPF) was set up in 1970 to assist the growth of small and medium industries in the less developed areas of the country.

## Euro

A new common currency used by member countries of the European Union.

## Eurobonds

International bonds floated in the Eurodollar Market. (See also: Asian dollar bond)

## Euroclear clearing system

Based in Brussels, Euroclear was formed in 1972. It is a clearing system to settle international financial instruments such as Asian dollar bonds, Eurodollar bonds, certificates of deposit and other securities. It acts as the safekeeping centre for the securities.

## Euro-Currency Standing Committee

See Committee on Global Financial System.

## Eurodollar market

The Eurodollar market refers to the financial market in Europe where institutions accept deposits of major currencies outside their countries of origin. The market is so called because the most popular currency traded is the US dollar.

## European Bank for Reconstruction and Development

The European Bank for Reconstruction and Development was formed in 1991. It has about 60 member countries which include many from the Central and Eastern Europe and the former Soviet Union. It assists countries to implement economic reforms. The activities include promoting a market-oriented economy, strengthening financial and legal systems and developing infrastructure to support the private sector.

## European Community

See European Union.

## European Free Trade Association

European Free Trade Association (EFTA) includes Austria, Finland, Iceland, Liechtenstein, Norway, Sweden and Switzerland.

**European Monetary System**
The European Monetary System (EMS) was established in 1979. It was designed to reduce volatility of exchange rates among member states and thus provide greater unification of goods and services in the European Community.

**European Union**
The European Community (EC) was a regional organization formed in 1958 after the Treaty of Rome. The objective was to allow free movement of goods, people, services and capital among member countries. The original members were Belgium, France, West Germany, Italy, Luxembourg and Netherlands. Several other countries joined later: Denmark, Ireland and United Kingdom (1973), Greece (1981), Spain and Portugal (1986). The group is now known as European Union (EU). There is an European Parliament. A common currency, the Euro, is used in member countries. (See also: Treaty of Rome)

**Everbright Bank (China)**
See China Everbright Bank.

**Everbright Finance Company (China)**
See China Everbright International Trust and Investment Corporation (CEITIC).

**Exchange Banks' Association (Hong Kong)**
See Hong Kong Association of Banks.

**Exchange Control Act (Malaysia)**
In Malaysia, the Exchange Control Act restricts dealings in gold and foreign currencies, payments to and from residents, issuance of securities outside Malaysia, imports and exports and settlements. The Act also empowers the Controller for Foreign Exchange to grant permissions and consent on the foregoing and to enforce the provisions of the Act.

**Exchange Fund (Hong Kong)**
In Hong Kong, the Exchange Fund is managed by the Hong Kong Monetary Authority. It issues and redeems Certificates of Indebtedness that give authority to the note-issuing banks to issue banknotes. The amount of banknotes that each bank is allowed to issue depends on the amount of Certificate of Indebtedness that it holds. In 1990, Exchange Fund Bills of 91, 182 and 364-day were introduced. In 1995, notes of 2, 3, 5, 7 and 10-year maturities were introduced. The Exchange Fund Ordinance empowers the Financial Secretary to control the Fund in consultation with the Exchange Fund Advisory Committee.

**Exchange Fund Investment Limited (Hong Kong)** *www.info.gov.hk/hkma*
In Hong Kong, the Exchange Fund Investment Limited (EFIL) was formed in October 1998 by the government to manage the Hang Seng Index constituent stocks acquired for the account of the Exchange Fund in August 1998. EFIL also manages the portfolio of Hong Kong equities transferred from the Land Fund to the Exchange Fund in November 1998. EFIL is registered as an Investor Advisor under the Securities Ordinance and is subject to regulation by the Securities and Futures Commission.

**Exchange Main Board Share Index (EMAS) (Malaysia)**
In Malaysia, EMAS is an index showing the share price performance of main board companies on the Kuala Lumpur Stock Exchange. (See also: Kuala Lumpur Composite Index)

**Exchange Traded Fund (ETF)**
Open ended listed investment fund that combines some of the characteristics of shares and managed funds. (ASX website glossary)

**Exchange Traded Options (ETO)**
These are options which are bought and sold on the options market operated by the ASX. (ASX website glossary)

**Export Credit Guarantee Corporation of India** *www.ecgcindia.com*
The Export Credit Guarantee Corporation of India was set up in 1957 by the government to strengthen export promotion by providing credit risk insurance cover to exporters.

**Export Development Board (Sri Lanka)**
In Sri Lanka, the Export Development Board (EDB) was set up in 1979 to promote exports. It prepares the National Export Development Plan and provides a wide range of incentives and assists exporters in product development and export marketing.

**Export Import Bank of India** *www.eximbankindia.com*
The Export Import Bank of India started operations in 1982. It is wholly owned by the government. It finances and promotes India's foreign trade. It is the main organization to coordinate other institutions engaged in financing exports and imports. It has overseas offices in Budapest, Johannesburg, Milan, Singapore and Washington DC.

**Export Import Bank of Thailand**     *www.exim.go.th*
The Export Import Bank of Thailand started its operations in 1994. It is owned by the government under the Ministry of Finance. It engages in financial activities customary to commercial banks, except for accepting deposit from the public.

**Export-Import Bank (Taiwan)**     *www.eximbank.com.tw*
In Taiwan, the Export–Import Bank started in 1979. It finances import and export trade and offers export credit insurance and other services.

**Export processing zone (Vietnam)**
In Vietnam, export processing zone (EPZ) was introduced in 1991 to provide foreign investors with special tax and regulatory incentives. The major EPZs are: Tan Thuan EPZ (set up in 1991 near HCMC), Linh Trung (1992, near HCMC), Haiphong (1993, Hai Phong), Da Nang (1993, Da Nang) and Can Tho (1993, Can Tho). (See also: industrial zone, Tan Thuan Export Processing Zone).

**Export Processing Zone Authority (Philippines)**
In the Philippines, its Export Processing Zone Authority (EPZA) is now known as the Philippine Economic Zone Authority. (See Philippine Economic Zone Authority)

**Export Processing Zones Authority (Pakistan)**     *www.epza.com.pk*
In Pakistan, the Export Processing Zones Authority (EPZA) was set up in 1980 to plan, develop and operate export processing zones. It is an autonomous body under the Ministry of Industries and Production. The Karachi EPZ is the first to be developed. Two new EPZs have been set up. The zone in Sialkot (Punjab) has a potential for sports goods, surgical goods and cutlery. The Risalpur zone is located in the Frontier Province. (See also: Karachi Export Processing Zone)

**Export Promotion Board (Nepal)**     *www.yomari.com/epb*
In Nepal, the Export Promotion Board (Nepal) is a division within the Ministry of Industry, Commerce and Supplies. It promotes trade with other countries by providing information on policies on trade, investment, taxation and other related resources.

**Export Promotion Bureau (Bangladesh)**     *www.epbbd.com*
In Bangladesh, the Export Promotion Bureau provides investors with information on industrial and trade policies, investment incentives and related matters.

**Export Promotion Bureau (Pakistan)**   *www.epb.gov.pk*
In Pakistan, the Export Promotion Bureau (EPB) was set up in 1963. It is a department within the Ministry of Commerce and is the main government agency to promote exports. In 1997, it set up a Export Facilitation Committee to resolve problems faced by exporters. It is representatives from all exporter associations as well as related government departments.

**Export Support Board (Indonesia)**
In Indonesia, the Export Support Board or Dewan Penunjang Ekspor (DPE) was set up in 1986 under the Department of Trade to provide services to small and medium exporters.

**Fannie Mae Securities**
This is an informal name for securities issued by the US Federal National Mortgage Association (FNMA, hence Fannie Mae). The main business of this independent agency is to buy mortgages from banks and insurance companies, and to help these lenders in home financing. (See also: Ginnie Mae)

**Far East Bank & Trust Company (Philippines)**
Far East Bank & Trust Company (FEBTC) was incorporated in 1960. It was one of the largest and diversified universal banks in the Philippines. In 2000, it merged with Bank of the Philippine Islands. (See also: Bank of the Philippines Islands)

**Fed, The**
Short form for Federal Reserve System in the United States.

**Federal National Mortgage Association (FNMA)**
See Fannie Mae securities.

**Federal Reserve System**
This is the central banking system of the United States. Its main functions are to regulate money supply, determine the legal reserve of member banks, oversee the mint, effect transfer of fund, facilitate the clearance and collection of cheques and examine member banks. The system consists of 12 Federal Reserve Banks, national and state banks. The Federal Reserve Board is a 7-member governing body of the Federal Reserve System. These governors are appointed by the US President.

### Federation Internationale des Bourses de Valueurs (FIBV)
(International Federation of Stock Exchanges)   *www.fibv.com*
In 2001, FIBV changed its name to World Federation of Exchanges. (See World Federation of Exchanges)

### Federation of Bangladesh Chambers of Commerce and Industries (FBCCI)   *www.fbcci.org*
In Bangladesh, the FBCCI was established in 1973. It is the apex representative organization safeguarding the interest of the private sector in trade and industry. It also consults and advises the government in formulating commercial, industrial and fiscal policies.

### Federation of Euro-Asian Stock Exchanges (FEAS)   *www.feas.org*
The FEAS was established in 1995 at the initiation of the Istanbul Stock Exchange. The founding members were 12 stock exchanges in emerging markets in Europe and Asia at different stages of development. As of 1998, there were 22 member exchanges.

### Federation of Malaysian Manufacturers   *www.fmm.org.my*
The Federation of Malaysian Manufacturers (FMM) was established in 1968. It is the premier economic organization representing over 2,200 companies. FMM is officially recognized as the voice of the Malaysian manufacturing industry. Its main aim is to increase the international competitiveness of Malaysian manufacturers. FMM plays an active role in government policy formulation by making recommendations on key national economic issues. FMM is the authorized body to issue certificates of origin in accordance with the International Convention for Simplification of Customs Facilities. The Malaysian Product Numbering System is managed by the FMM that also provides bar coding facilities to subscribers. The FMM Entrepreneur & Skills Development Centre provides training to enhance the productivity of workers in the manufacturing sector. Its SMI Resource Centre assists small and medium industries through consultancy services.

### Federation of Malaysian Unit Trust Managers (FMUTM)
The FMUTM is an association that represents 28 unit trust management companies in Malaysia.

### Federation of Nepalese Chambers of Commerce and Industry (FNCCI)
*www.fncci.org*
In Nepal, the FNCCI was set up in 1965 to promote business and industry. It is an umbrella organization whose membership comprises district chambers,

associations and private sector undertakings. It represents the business community at the national and international levels.

**Federation of Pakistan Chambers of Commerce & Industry (FPCCI)**
*www.fpcci.com*
In Pakistan, the FPCCI was incorporated in 1960 as the apex body for chambers and associations of commerce and industry. It represents the private business community and presents its views to the government. It promotes trade and seeks cooperation with chambers of commerce in other countries.

**Fiji Development Bank** *www.fijidevelopmentbank.com*
The Fiji Development Bank was set up by the government in 1967. It promotes and develops natural resources, transport and other industries in Fiji. It assists by providing medium and long term loans. It also provides equity participation, guarantee and underwriting.

**Fiji Islands Bureau of Statistics** *www.statsfiji.gov.fj*
The Fiji Islands Bureau of Statistics is the official national statistical agency.

**Fiji National Provident Fund (FNPF)** *www.fnpf.com.fj*
In Fiji, the FNPF was set up in 1966. It is a social security savings scheme supported by employers, employees and the government. It provides financial security for workers when they retire. It also allows pre-retirement withdrawal by member for home ownership, healthcare and education.

**Fiji National Training Council (FNTC)** *www.fntc.ac.fj*
In Fiji, the FNTC was set up in 1973. It is a statutory institution under the Ministry of Labour and Industrial Relations. It provides, facilitates and regulates training in Fiji. It has numerous industrial training boards each specializing in an industry such as construction, engineering, tourism and productivity.

**Fiji Trade and Investment Board (FTIB)** *www.ftib.org.fj*
In Fiji, the FTIB was formed under the Economic Development Board Act in 1980. It is a statutory organization that promotes exports, investment and facilitates economic development.

**Filipino Fund Inc**
Filipino Fund Inc is listed on the Philippine Stock Exchange. It is a closed-end investment company incorporated in 1991. Its focus is on long term capital appreciation through investment in high-growth Philippine listed companies.

The investment manager of the fund is BPI Investment Management Inc, a wholly-owned subsidiary of the Bank of the Philippine Islands. (See also: Bank of the Philippine Islands)

### Finance and Treasury Centre (FTC) Scheme

The FTC scheme was introduced by the Monetary Authority of Singapore in 1993 to attract international companies to locate their treasuries in Singapore. It provides a concessionary tax rate of 10% and other tax benefits for income derived from treasury activities.

### Financial Action Task Force on Money Laundering

The OECD's Financial Action Task Force (FATF) on Money Laundering was set up by the G-7 Summit in Paris in 1989. It has issued a set of 40 recommendations to combat money laundering.

The FATF has 26 members. It focuses on three main tasks:
(a) monitor members' progress in applying measures to counter money laundering;
(b) review money laundering techniques and counter measures and their implications for the 40 recommendations;
(c) promote the adoption of the FATF Recommendations by non-member countries.

### Financial Advisors Act (Singapore)

In Singapore, the Financial Advisors Act (FAA) came into effect in October 2002. It governs financial advisory services in respect of investment products, including securities, futures and life insurance.

### Financial Holding Company

A financial holding company is a company that owns a bank or financial institution. In some countries, it is a legal requirement for banks to separate their financial and non-financial operations.

### Financial Holding Company (Singapore)

The Monetary Authority of Singapore requires local banking groups to separate their financial and non-financial activities. All financial activities have to be grouped either under the bank or under a financial holding company (FHC). The non-financial activities must be separated from the banking group and divested. They can be sold to third parties or to shareholders of the bank, so that these shareholders own them directly, and not through the bank.

**Financial Information Services Co Ltd (Taiwan)** *www.fisc.com.tw*
In Taiwan, the Financial Information Services Co Ltd (FISC) was set up in 1998 as the successor to the Financial Information Service Centre in the Ministry of Finance. Its services include the following: operating inter-bank information system, clearing inter-bank business, disaster recovery services of inter-bank information system.

**Financial Institutions Development Fund (Thailand)** *www.bot.or.th*
In Thailand, the Financial Institutions Development Fund (FIDF) was set up in 1988 through the enactment of an Emergency Decree regulating the Bank of Thailand (BOT). Its objective is to relax BOT's limitation in implementing financial measure to rehabilitate financial institutions in order to maintain stability in the financial system.

**Financial Institutions of Myanmar Law**
Under the old Bank Law of 1975, only state-owned banks were allowed to operate in Myanmar. In 1990, the Financial Institutions of Myanmar Law was enacted to allow the setting up of private financial institutions, subject to the approval from the Central Bank of Myanmar.

**Financial Institutions Reform and Expansion (India)**
The Financial Institutions Reform and Expansion project is a joint effort of the Government of India and the USAID. In 1997, it proposed to the Securities and Exchange Board of India (SEBI) to set up the Indian Association of Securities Intermediaries, a self-regulatory organization of sub-brokers to bring sub-brokers into the formal capital market system.

**Financial Package for SMIs (PAKSI)**
In Malaysia, PAKSI or Financial Package for SMIs (small and medium industries) provides SMIs with soft loans for projects and working capital.

**Financial Reconstruction Commission (Japan)**
In Japan, the Financial Reconstruction Commission (FRC) was set up in 1998 under the Financial Reconstruction Law. Its objective was to create a strong and competitive financial system in Japan. It was responsible for disposing failed institutions and restoring others through capital injection. The FRC had the power to appoint financial administrators or temporarily nationalize banks such as Long Term Credit Bank of Japan, Nippon Credit Bank and others. In January 2001, with the reorganization of the government ministries, the commission was abolished. Some of its tasks have been taken over by the Financial Services Agency that was reorganized from the former Financial Supervisory Agency. (See also: Financial Services Agency)

### Financial Reporting Act (Malaysia)

In Malaysia, the Financial Reporting Act was introduced in 1997. It establishes a financial reporting framework that consists of the Malaysian Accounting Standards Board (MASB) and the Financial Reporting Foundation (FRF). Under the Act, the FRF oversees the MASB that is an independent body responsible for developing accounting and reporting standards in Malaysia.

### Financial Reporting Council

In Australia, the Corporate Law Economic Reform Program was introduced in January 2000 to establish new standard setting arrangements. The institutional arrangement for accounting standard setting involves the Financial Reporting Council (FRC) that oversees the Australian Accounting Standards Board (AASB) in charge of setting standards for the private and public sectors. This has replaced an earlier arrangement which the AASB had with the accounting profession's Public Sector Accounting Standards Board.

The FRC includes representatives from the business community, professional accounting bodies, governments and regulatory agencies. It advises the government on accounting standard setting process and the development of international accounting standards. It determines the broad direction of the AASB and provides advice and feedback. However, it does influence the AASB's technical deliberations and the content of particular accounting standards.

### Financial Reporting Foundation (Malaysia)

See Financial Reporting Act.

### Financial Sector Assessment Program

The Financial Sector Assessment Program (FSAP) is a joint program introduced by IMF and World Bank in May 1999. It aims to increase the effectiveness of efforts to promote the soundness of financial systems in member countries.

### Financial Sector Restructuring Authority (Thailand)    *www.fra.or.th*

The Financial Sector Restructuring Authority (FRA) in Thailand was set up on 24 October 1997 under the Emergency Decree on Financial Sector Restructuring BE 2540 (1997) as part of the financial sector restructuring program. As an independent body, it was formed to oversee the rehabilitation of 58 finance companies whose operations were suspended by the Finance Minister on 26 June 1997 (16 companies) and on 5 August 1997 (42 companies) and to safeguard the interest of depositors and investors. The administration of the purchase of the assets of these companies was done by the Asset Management Corporation that was set up in October 1997. (See also: Asset Management Corporation — Thailand)

**Financial Sector Restructuring for Economic Recovery**
As part of the financial reform, the government in Thailand announced its Financial Sector Restructuring for Economic Recovery (FRER) package in August 1998. The package consisted of numerous measures to dispose of the assets of closed finance companies and to strengthen the financial system. (See also: Financial Sector Restructuring Authority)

**Financial Services Agency (Japan)** *www.fsa.go.jp*
In Japan, the Financial Supervisory Agency was set up in June 1998 within the Prime Minister's Office to inspect and supervise private sector financial institutions and for surveillance of securities transactions. In December 1998, the FSA became an organization under the newly-established Financial Reconstruction Commission in the Prime Minister's Office. In July 2000, the Financial Supervisory Agency was reorganized to become the Financial Services Agency (FSA). In January 2001, with the reorganization of the central government ministries, the Financial Reconstruction Commission was abolished and FSA was placed under the Cabinet Office. The FSA has taken over the task of disposing failed financial institutions.

**Financial Services and the Treasury Bureau** *www.info.gov.hk/fstb*
In Hong Kong, the Financial Services and the Treasury Bureau comprises the Financial Services Branch and the Treasury Branch. The former maintains Hong Kong's status as a financial centre by providing an appropriate economic and legal environment for an open, fair and efficient market. The Treasury is responsible for overall resource planning and drawing public expenditure guidelines.

**Financial Stability Forum** *www.fsforum.org/standards*
The Financial Stability Forum (FSF) was set up in 1999. It brings together 25 national regulatory authorities from 11 countries. It coordinates the efforts of these organizations to promote international financial stability and reduce systemic risk. Its Compendium of Standards provides a common reference for accepted economic and financial standards. The Compendium highlights 12 key standards for sound financial systems.

**Financial Structure of Myanmar**
The financial structure of Myanmar includes the Central Bank of Myanmar, four state-owned banks, domestic private banks, representative offices of foreign banks, a state-owned finance company and a state-owned insurance company.

**Financial Supervisory Agency (Japan)**
See Financial Services Agency.

**Financial System Planning Bureau (Japan)**    *www.mof.gov.jp*
In Japan, the Financial System Planning Bureau (FSP Bureau) in the Ministry of Finance is in charge of planning the development of the Japanese financial system. It shares responsibility of supervising securities markets with the Financial Supervisory Agency (FSA) but does not supervise individual banks and other private financial institutions. In 2000, it became part of the new Financial Authority.

**Financial Times**
This is London's leading financial daily newspaper. The Financial Times – Stock Exchange Index (FT-SE 100, or "Footsie 100") is widely used by investors to observe share prices of 100 largest companies traded on the London Stock Exchange.

**First Abacus Financial Holdings Inc (Philippines)**
The First Abacus Financial Holdings Inc is listed on the Philippine Stock Exchange. The company, formerly known as Seven Seas Oil Exploration and Resources Inc was incorporated with the purpose of oil exploration. It has diversified and acquired equity interests in real estate, restaurant and family entertainment through the Philippine Racing Club Inc and Fun Time Pizza, USA. In 1996, with the acquisition of a 100% equity stake in Abacus Capital & Investments Corporation, it changed its name to First Abacus Financial Holdings Inc. The company's financial services include underwriting, stock broking and investment banking.

**First Bangkok City Bank**
In Thailand, the First Bangkok City Bank was set up in 1934 as the Tan Peng Choon Bank. It was an extension of a trading company and provided a channel for overseas Chinese in Thailand to remit money to China. After World War II, the bank expanded its activities to serve the banking needs in Thailand. In 1960, the name was changed to Thai Development Bank. In 1977, the name was changed again to First Bangkok City Bank to avoid the misunderstanding that it was government-related as the name "development" might have implied. It was listed on Stock Exchange of Thailand in 1987. It offered a whole range of banking services. It was affected by the 1997 financial crisis and absorbed by the Krung Thai Bank.

**First Cavite Industrial Estate**
In the Philippines, the First Cavite Industrial Estate (FCIE) was set up in 1990. It is a joint venture of three partners: Philippine's National Development Corporation, Japan's Marubeni and Japan International Development Organization (JAIDO). FCIE is located in Barangay Langkaan, Dasmirinas, Cavite which is about 45 kilometres from Manila.

**First Women's Bank (Pakistan)**
In Pakistan, the First Women's Bank (FWB) was set up in 1990 with capital provided by Habib Bank, Muslim Commercial Bank, National Bank of Pakistan, United Bank, Allied Bank and the Ministry of Women's Development. Most of the borrowers are small businesses run by women. In Islamic banking, husbands and wives may not have joint bank accounts and it is difficult for women to obtain conventional credit.

**Fixed Delivery & Settlement System**
The Fixed Delivery & Settlement System (FDSS) is used in some stock exchanges. For example, in the Kuala Lumpur Stock Exchange, it is based on a T+5 rolling settlement. Under a fixed rolling settlement system, all trades are scheduled for settlement the same number of days after the trade date. It allows trades to settle on all business days of the week. For example, in a T+5 rolling settlement, Monday trades are settled by the following Monday (five business days hence).

**Fixed Income Money Market and Derivatives Association of India (FIMMDA)** *www.fimmda.org*
In India, the FIMMDA represents market players and assists in developing the bond, money and derivatives markets. It is the main interface with regulators on issues related to these markets.

**Flexible Accelerated Security Transfer (Australia)**
Flexible Accelerated Security Transfer (FAST) is an electronic transfer and registration system used in Australia.

**Food and Agriculture Organization** *www.fao.org*
The Food and Agriculture Organization (FAO) was founded in 1945. It is one of the largest specialized agencies in the United National system. Its objectives are to raise the level of nutrition, the standard of living and to improve agricultural productivity of rural populations. FAO has 183 member countries.

**Footsie**
This is the informal name for Financial Times – Stock Exchange (FT-SE) Index. (See Financial Times)

**Foreign Banks' Association**   *www.fba.or.th*
In Thailand, the Foreign Banks' Association was formed in 1996. It represents foreign banks with the Bank of Thailand (central bank) and other regulatory bodies on issues of concern to foreign banks.

**Foreign Currency Banking Unit (FCBU) (Sri Lanka)**
In Sri Lanka, the FCBU was introduced in 1979. The objective was to develop offshore market. Exporters were allowed to borrow from FCBUs to finance their orders.

**Foreign Exchange Adjustment Centre (FEAC)**
In the 1980s, enterprises in China that were involved in foreign trade were permitted to buy back some of their foreign exchange earnings based on a "retention quota". Foreign Exchange Adjustment Centres (FEACs) were set up to facilitate the trade of these quotas. They were also known as swap centres. In 1994, the foreign exchange retention quotas were abolished. They were replaced by the China Foreign Exchange Trading System. (See also: China Foreign Exchange Trading System)

**Foreign Exchange Certificate (China)**
In China, the Foreign Exchange Certificate (FEC) was introduced in 1980 as a special currency to be used by foreigners. It was abolished on 1 January 1994.

**Foreign Exchange Certificate (Myanmar)**
The Central Bank of Myanmar issues Foreign Exchange Certificates (FECs) in denominations of 1 unit, 5 units and 10 units (equivalent to US$1, US$5 and US$10 respectively) for the convenience of tourists and foreign currency account holders. The FECs are exchangeable with US dollars.

**Foreign Exchange Control (Myanmar)**
Foreign exchange control is administered by Central Bank of Myanmar in accordance to instruction from the Ministry of Finance and Revenue. Travellers may bring in foreign currency up to US$2,000 without any declaration.

**Foreign Exchange Entitlement Certificate Scheme (Sri Lanka)**
In Sri Lanka, the Foreign Exchange Entitlement Certificate Scheme (FEECS) was introduced in 1968. It was a system with dual exchange rates. There was

an official exchange rate for essential imports and non-traditional exports. There was another higher rate that applied to all other imports and exports. The scheme continued until 1977.

**Foreign Exchange in Vietnam**
See Foreign Exchange Trading Centre.

**Foreign Exchange Management Act**
In India, the Foreign Exchange Management Act was passed in 1999 to liberalize the foreign exchange market. It has replaced the Foreign Exchange Regulation Act.

**Foreign Exchange Trading Centre (FETC) (Vietnam)**
FETCs were set up by the State Bank of Vietnam in Hanoi and Ho Chi Minh City to channel foreign exchange through the banking system. Participants in the FETCs include Vietnamese commercial banks with foreign exchange licences, major licensed trading companies including joint venture with foreign companies. The FETC is run by a Board of Management with representatives from the State Bank and commercial banks. It helps to set the official exchange rate of VND and the US dollar. It provides an organized market where buyers and sellers of foreign exchange can meet to strike deals with one another.

At the start of each session, the FETC obtains bids from buyers and sellers. Negotiations take place with the supervision of the Board of Management to strike a rate that then applies to all deals done in that session. The closing rate at each session then becomes the official market exchange rate. Between the closed session and the following session, all banks are required to sell at a rate within 0.5% of the fixed rate and buy at the fixed rate.

**Foreign Institutional Investor (India)**
In India, the Foreign Institutional Investor (FII) concept was introduced in 1992 to attract foreign investors. It is one of the three categories of foreign investors that are allowed to invest directly in Indian securities. The other two categories are Non-resident Indian and Overseas Corporate Body. They may make portfolio investment in listed and unlisted companies.

**Foreign Investment and Technology Transfer Act (Nepal)**
In Nepal, the Foreign Investment and Technology Transfer Act was introduced in 1992 and amended in 1996. Its objective is to encourage foreign investment and the transfer of technology.

### Foreign Investment Board (Solomon Islands)

In the Solomon Islands, the Foreign Investment Board approves foreign investments and technology agreements. Its chairman is the Prime Minister.

### Foreign Investment Commission (Myanmar)

See Myanmar Investment Commission.

### Foreign Investment Department (FID) (Vietnam)

In Vietnam, the FID is a department within the Ministry of Planning and Investment (MPI). It advises foreign investors on current legislation, introduces projects wanted by the government, receives investment documents (such as application, company charter, feasibility study report, contract between the foreign investor and its Vietnamese partner), prepares opinion for the Office of Project Evaluation in Hanoi and delivers the licence to the investor. (See also: Ministry of Planning and Investment)

### Foreign Investment Law (Myanmar)

In Myanmar, the Foreign Investment Law was enacted in 1988 to provide incentives for the inflow of direct foreign investment. The important features of this Law include non-nationalization, tax holiday of up to three years and 100% foreign ownership. The law also guarantees the repatriation in foreign currency the rightful entitlement of the foreign investor. Foreign investors may incorporate enterprise on a 100% ownership basis.

### Foreign Investment Negative List (Philippines)

In the Philippines, the Foreign Investment Negative List (or Negative List) is a list of areas of economic activity whose foreign ownership is limited to a maximum of 40% of the capital. This list is published by the National Economic Development Authority (NEDA).

### Foreign Investment Review Board (Australia)    www.treasury.gov.au/firb

In Australia, the Foreign Investment Review Board (FIRB) was set up in 1976 to approve and monitor foreign direct investment proposals.

### Foreign Ownership of Local Banks (Singapore)

In Singapore, foreign ownership of local banks was liberalized in 1990. The ceiling on foreign shareholding of Singapore-incorporated banks was raised from 20 to 40%. Within the higher 40% limit, however, a sub-limit of 5% was imposed on the holdings of any single or related group of foreign shareholders the maturity of the commitment.

**Foreign Service Corporation (Vietnam)**
In Vietnam, this is a state-owned company that assists foreign companies to recruit local staff.

**Forest Research Institute of Malaysia (FRIM)** *www.frim.gov.my*
The Forest Research Institute of Malaysia started in 1929 as the Forest Research Institute, a branch within the Forest Department. In 1985, under the Malaysian Forestry Research and Development Act, the institute became a statutory body and was renamed Forest Research Institute of Malaysia (FRIM) under the Malaysian Forestry Research and Development Board (MFRDB). The main objective of FRIM is to develop appropriate technology for the conservation, management, development and use of forest resources.

**Fort Bonifacio Development Corporation (Philippines)**
In the Philippines, Fort Bonifacio Development Corporation (FBDC) is a joint venture between the Bases Conversion Development Corporation and Bonifacio Land Corporation to convert former military camps within Metro Manila for civilian use.

**Forum for East Asia Latin American Cooperation**
The inaugural meeting of the Forum for East Asia Latin American Cooperation (FEALAC) was hosted by Chile in March 2001. The objective of the forum is to strengthen political, economic and cultural links between East Asia and Latin America. The second ministerial meeting was held in Manila 2003.

**Franchising and Licensing Association of Singapore**
The Franchising and Licensing Association of Singapore started in 1993 as the Singapore International Franchise Association. Its present name was adopted in July 2003. The association has been working closely with government agencies such as SPRING and IE Singapore as well as international bodies to develop the franchise industry in Singapore. As of 2003, there were more than 350 franchises with 2,600 franchisees in Singapore.

**Fuh Hwa Securities Finance Company (Taiwan)**
In Taiwan, Fuh Hwa Securities Finance Company was set up in 1980 to specialize in providing margin finance for the purchase and short sale of securities. It was a monopoly until 1990 when the Securities and Exchange Act was amended to allow other securities firms to provide margin financing and stock loan business.

**Full Licence Bank (Singapore)**
In Singapore, a local or foreign bank with a full licence from the Monetary Authority of Singapore may transact the whole range of banking activities, both personal and corporate.

**Fund for Food (Malaysia)**
The RM 700 million fund was set up in 1993 by Bank Negara Malaysia (Central Bank) to provide low interest term loans to promote investment in primary food production and distribution (including fisheries, animal husbandry, vegetables and fruits). Participating financial institutions include commercial banks, Tier 1 finance companies, Bank Pertanian, Bank Pembangunan, Bank Industri and Bank Islam Malaysia. Malaysian companies, Malaysian citizens, small and medium primary food production projects are eligible to apply for such loans through the financial institutions.

**Fund for Receiving and Developing the System of Financial Institutions (Thailand)**
This is a fund of which all financial institutions in Thailand must become members and contribute up to 0.5% of their year-end deposits. The fund may be used to help any financial difficulty in order to maintain the economic stability of Thailand.

**Fund for Small and Medium Scale Industries (Malaysia)**
In Malaysia, the RM1.5 billion fund was set up in 1998 to promote small and medium industries (SMI) in manufacturing, agro-based and supporting services. Participating financial institutions include commercial banks, finance companies, Bank Pertanian, Bank Pembangunan, Bank Industri, Bank Islam Malaysia and Malaysian Industrial Development Finance Berhad. SMIs must fulfill the following conditions. Their shareholders' fund must not exceed RM10 million. They must be Malaysian-owned companies (at least 51% ownership) registered under the Companies Act 1965, the Cooperative Societies Act 1996. Entrepreneurs must be registered under the Registrar of Business and are citizens residing in Malaysia.

**Futures Industry (Amendment & Consolidation) Act 1997 (Malaysia)**
In Malaysia, the Futures Industry (Amendment & Consolidation) Act 1997 came into effect on 16 April 1998 and repealed the Commodities Trading Act 1985. It brought the regulation of the commodity futures market under the ambit of the Futures Industry Act 1993, thus rationalizing the regulation of the futures market in Malaysia. It also authorizes the merger of the Commodities Trading Commission (CTC) with the Securities Commission.

## G-7 Nations
United States, Japan, Germany, France, United Kingdom, Italy, Canada.

## G-10 Nations
The G-10 is made up of 11 industrial countries: Belgium, Canada, France, Germany, Italy, Japan, Netherlands, Sweden, Switzerland, United Kingdom and United States. Switzerland was the 11th member.

## PT Gadjah Tunggal (Indonesia)
This is an Indonesian conglomerate with diversified business operations including tyre manufacturing.

## Gajah Mada University (Indonesia)
This leading Indonesian university is located at Yogyakarta. It was ranked 49th among the best Asian universities by Asiaweek magazine in 1998.

## Geisha Bonds
Geisha bonds are privately placed bonds issued by foreigners in Japan and denominated in foreign currencies (usually in US dollars). Publicly offered bonds are known as Shogun bonds.

## General Agreement on Tariffs and Trade (GATT)
The GATT was signed in 1948 by 23 nations to solve trade conflicts. It became an important organization for international trade negotiations. Its objective was to expand world trade to promote economic development of the world. It was renamed the World Trade Organization after the Uruguay Round of talks which ended in 1993. (See also: Tokyo Round, Uruguay Round and World Trade Organization)

## General Department of Rubber (GDR) (Vietnam)
Vietnam's General Department of Rubber controls 18 plantations and processing units. Examples are Dong Nai, Phu Rieng, Binh Long, Loc Ninh and Tay Ninh rubber companies.

## Genome Institute of Singapore
See Biomedical Research Council.

## Ginnie Mae
This is an informal name for the US Government National Mortgage Association (GNMA, hence Ginnie Mae), an agency of the US Department of Housing and Urban Development. (See also: Fannie Mae)

**Gintic Institute of Manufacturing Technology (Singapore)**
See Science and Engineering Research Council.

**Global Development Learning Network**   *www.gdln.org*
The objective of the Global Development Learning Network (GDLN) is to provide cost effective interactive learning activities throughout the developing world. It is a partnership of public, private and non-government organizations. It provides quality programs drawn from public and private sources, including the World Bank Group. It uses the World Bank Telecommunications Network to broadcast its programs. There are three kinds of program: courses and seminars, development dialogues and web-based programs. (See also: World Bank Institute)

**Golden Tiger Resources**
This is an Australian-Canadian mining company exploring manganese resources in Na Tum in northern Vietnam. It is one of the first companies to have its licence renewed under the new Vietnamese Mining Law. Formerly called Leader Resources, Golden Tiger shares are listed on the Australian Stock Exchange in Perth and Vancouver Stock Exchange.

**Golkar (Indonesia)**
See Golongan Karya (functional groups).

**Golongan Karya (Golkar)**
Golkar (functional groups) was set up by a group of military and civilian leaders to offset the influence of the Indonesian Communist Party, which was subsequently banned after being blamed for an abortive coup bid in 1965. The political upheavals that followed the abortive coup led to the ascent of General Suharto as president. Golkar, which literally means functional groups, has been the dominant socio-political force during President Suharto's 30-year administration. It claims a membership of 36 million out of the 200 million people in the country.

**Goods and Services Tax (GST) (Singapore)**
In Singapore, the GST was introduced on 1 April 1994 to broaden the revenue base and to shift the government reliance from direct taxes to indirect taxes. The GST rate is 3%. Businesses whose turnover exceeds $1 million per year are required to register for GST. These registered traders will collect GST on their sale of goods and services. GST is also chargeable on goods imported into Singapore.

### Government Agent of the District (Sri Lanka)

In Sri Lanka, under the Kachcheri district administrative system, the Government Agent (GA) is a senior civil servant who heads a district office. He represents the central government and also has planning and development administration responsibilities. In a large district, the GA may have support staff of several hundred, both office and field officials. He is also involved in social and religious activities in an ex-officio capacity.

### Government Employees Provident Fund (Bhutan)

In Bhutan, the Government Employees Provident Fund (GEPF) is managed on behalf of the government by the Royal Insurance Corporation of Bhutan (RICB). It represents a portfolio of investments based on joint contribution by civil servants and the government.

### Government Housing Bank (Thailand)     *www.ghb.co.th*

In Thailand, the Government Housing Bank (GHB) was set up in 1953. It is a housing financial institution owned by the Ministry of Finance. It provides loans to persons of moderate income to buy their homes. However, it operates on a commercial basis without government subsidy. Its sources of fund include deposits (current, savings and time deposits), long term borrowing from the Government Savings Bank and the Bank of Thailand, and the issue of bonds guaranteed by the Ministry of Finance. The GHB has about 1,500 employees working in 130 branches nationwide. Of these branches, 23 are in Bangkok while the others are in the provinces.

### Government Investment Corporation

In Singapore, the Government Investment Corporation (GIC) was formed in 1981 when the Monetary Authority of Singapore (MAS) was reorganized. Funds previously managed by the MAS were transferred to GIC. Through offices in international financial centres, it invests in global equity, fixed income and foreign exchange markets. Through subsidiaries such as GIC Real Estate Private Ltd and GIC Special Investment Private Limited, it also invests in real estate and private equity.

### Government Investment Act 1983 (Malaysia)

This Act confers on the Minister power to receive investment money for a fixed period and to pay dividend thereon. The Act also appoints the central bank as the agent of the government and allows the issue of the investment by way of scripless book-entry.

**Government National Mortgage Association (GNMA)**
See Ginnie Mae.

**Government Savings Bank (Thailand)**    *www.gsb.or.th*
In Thailand, the Government Savings Bank started as the Savings Office in 1913 under the Royal Treasury Department. It was later transferred to the Post and Telegraph Department. In 1947, the Government Savings Bank (GSB) replaced the Savings Office. The GSB is a non-profit organization state enterprise guaranteed by the government and supervised by the Ministry of Finance. Through its 570 branches, it mobilizes small savings and invests these funds in government securities. It encourages savings through the sale of popular saving certificates with a lottery feature.

**Government Shareholding Agency (Solomon Islands)**
In the Solomon Islands, the Government Shareholding Agency (GSA) was set up in 1977. It is the government's arm to manage its commercial investments.

**Grameen Bank Approach (Bangladesh)**
The Grameen Bank approach first started in Bangladesh. The bank provides small loans and savings services to village women who manage small business. It has more than 2.3 million borrowers of whom 94% were women. It provides micro credit for more than 39,000 villages. Average loan is about US$160 and repayment rate is 95%. Loans are given to groups of five. All loans are cut off if one defaults. These borrowers meet weekly to make loan repayment and to discuss business plans. These loans have helped many families to pull out poverty and eliminated exploitation by moneylenders. The scheme has caused fundamental change in the family relationship of the members as women begin to play an active role in household management and budget. The Grameen success has become a model for many other developing countries.

**PT Great River Indonesia**
This is one of Indonesia's largest apparel makers.

**GreTai Securities Market (Taiwan)**    *www.gretai.org.tw*
In Taiwan, the GreTai Securities Market (GTSM) started in 1994 as an over-the-counter market. In 1995, it opened business to foreign investment. In 1999, the Securities and Futures Commission (SFC) lifted restriction on margin trading and approved this type of trade for 105 GTSM-listed stocks. In 2000, GTSM introduced the TIGER (Taiwan Innovative Growing Enterpreneurs) Board and also launched the Electronic Bond Trading System

(EBTS). In January 2002, GTSM opened another new market for unlisted stocks called "Emerging Stock". (See also: Over-the-counter Securities Exchange)

### Greater Colombo Consumer Price Index

In Sri Lanka, the Greater Colombo Consumer Price Index (GCPI) was introduced in 1989 with the weights based on the household expenditure of the lowest four expenditure deciles in the Greater Colombo Area revealed in the Labour Force and Socio Economic Survey of 1985/86. These expenditure patterns, which were re-valued at the January–June 1989 prices, are used as the base of the GCPI. The item coverage of the GCPI is wider than the Colombo Consumer Price Index (CCPI), as is the geographic coverage, as price collection is undertaken in 14 markets, including seven markets in the Colombo Municipality and seven other markets in the Greater Colombo Area. (See also: Colombo Consumer Price Index)

### Greater Colombo Economic Commission

In Sri Lanka, the Greater Colombo Economic Commission (GCEC) was set up in 1978 to approve investment in the export processing zones. In 1992, it merged with the Foreign Investment Advisory Committee to form the Board of Investment. (See also: Board of Investment)

### Greater Mekong Sub-region

The Greater Mekong Sub-region (GMS) includes six countries which share the Mekong River: Cambodia, China (Yunnan Province), Laos, Myanmar, Thailand and Vietnam. Several international aid agencies are involved in development activities in GMS. They include the Asian Development Bank (ADB), Australian International Development Assistance Bureau (AIDAB), Canadian International Development Agency (CIDA), Economic and Social Commission for Asia and the Pacific (ESCAP), International Development and Research Centre (IDRC), and Swedish International Development Agency (SIDA). Projects include transport, energy, natural resources, investment and tourism.

### Green Trade Company (Cambodia)   *www.moc.gov.kh*

In Cambodia, the Green Trade Company (GTC) was set up in 1998 after the merger of three state-owned companies: Cambodia Food Company, Material & Equipment Company and Agricultural Product Company. GTC is state-owned company under the technical supervision of the Ministry of Commerce and financial supervision of the Ministry of Economy and Finance. GTC buys and sells commodities and foodstuff to maintain market prices of agricultural products. It also manages food reserves for emergency needs of the government.

### Gross Problematic Assets (GPA)

This is an indicator used by international rating agency Standard & Poor's to measure stress in a financial system. Problematic assets include overdue loans, restructured assets (where the original terms have been altered), foreclosed assets, and non-performing assets sold to special purpose vehicles. GPA ranges are estimates of the potential level of problematic assets in the financial system in a reasonable worst-case economic recession or slowdown, expressed as a percentage of domestic credit to the private sector and non-financial public enterprises.

### Growth Enterprise Market     *www.hkgem.com*

The Growth Enterprise Market (GEM) is an alternative stock market operated by the Hong Kong Exchange and Clearing Ltd (HKEx). It provides a fund raising venue for "high growth high risk" companies in the technology industries in Hong Kong.

### PT Gudang Garam (Indonesia)

This is Indonesia's largest cigarette maker. It is one of the blue chip companies on the Jakarta Stock Exchange.

### H-shares (China)

These are foreign shares issued by companies incorporated in Mainland China. They are primarily listed in Hong Kong and traded in Hong Kong dollars. H-shares listed in Hong Kong have to comply with the Hong Kong Stock Exchange Listing Rules. For example, accounts must comply with Hong Kong or international standards. Articles of association must contain provisions that reflect the different nature of domestic shares and foreign shares (including H shares) and the different rights of their respective holders. Investor protection provisions equivalent to those in the laws of Hong Kong must be written into its constitutional documents.

### Habib Bank AG Zurich     *www.habibbank.com*

Habib Bank AG Zurich was incorporated in Switzerland in 1967. It has an international network of 35 branches and provides a wide range of banking services.

### Habitat

United Nations Centre for Human Settlements.

### Haiphong Industrial Zone

In Vietnam, Haiphong Industrial Zone is developed by a consortium that includes US-based financial group AIG, Belgian port engineering firm IPEM,

and Thailand's Asia Infrastructure Development Company. The US$1 billion
project includes a deep seaport on the Dinh Vu peninsula.

**Hang Seng Bank**   *www.hangseng.com*
Hang Seng Bank was founded in 1933. It is the second largest listed bank in
Hong Kong. As a strong capitalized commercial bank focusing on Hong Kong
and Mainland China, it provides a wide range of financial products and
services. It is a principal member of the HSBC Group that is among the world's
largest financial service organizations. The bank is quoted on SEAQ in the
United Kingdom, and offers US investors a sponsored-level American Depository Receipt program.

**Hang Seng Index**   *www.hsi.com.hk*
This is a widely followed index for shares traded on the Hong Kong Stock
Exchange. It tracks the price movement of 33 companies. There are four sub-
indices: financial, property, utilities and commerce & industry. It is weighted
by market capitalization and thus influenced by large companies such as
Cheung Kong, Hong Kong Bank, Hong Kong Land and Hang Seng Bank.

**Hang Seng Composite Index Series**   *www.hsi.com.hk*
The Hang Seng Composite Index Series was launched on 3 October 2001.
It provides a comprehensive benchmark of the performance of the Hong Kong
stock market. Comprising the top 200 listed companies in terms of market
capitalization, the series is composed of two distinct series: the geographical
series and the industry series.

**Hang Seng Freefloat Index Series**   *www.hsi.com.hk*
The Hang Seng Freefloat Index Series was launched on 23 September 2002.
It is a variant of the Hang Seng Composite Index Series adjusted for the
liquidity of constituent stocks. It is aimed at meeting investors' demand for
an alternate market benchmark that takes into account the long term strategic
holdings not readily available for trading in the market.

**Hanoi Hilton**
This was the name given by American prisoners of war (POWs) to the
infamous Hoa Lo (The Oven) Prison in Hanoi. It was demolished in 1995.
On that site stands the Hanoi Towers, a 13-storey office building which was
opened in 1997.

**Hanoi International Technology Centre (HITC)**
HITC is located at Tu Liem, 8 kilometres west of Hanoi's city centre. It was

developed by the Schmidt Group. In 1995, HITC took in its first tenants that included Siemens, Toyota and Danzas.

**Hanoi Towers**
See Hanoi Hilton.

**Hanoi University of Technology**   *www.hut.edu.vn*
The Hanoi University of Technology (HUT) was established in 1956. The campus occupies an area of 35 hectares. There are 24 faculties and institutes. It has about 40,000 undergraduate and 1,000 postgraduate students in about 60 different specialized fields of study.

**Harakiri swap (Japan)**
This is a swap transaction in which the Japanese bank or broker has no spread. (Harakiri: Japanese ancient ritual suicide)

**Harrisons and Crosfield Holding**
See London Sumatra Indonesia.

**Haryana State Cooperative Apex Bank (HARCOBANK)**   *www.harcobank.nic.in*
In India, the Haryana State Cooperative Apex Bank (HARCOBANK) provides finance to farmers, rural artisans and entrepreneurs. At the state level, it has 13 branches at Chandigarth and Panchkula. At the district level, there are 19 Central Cooperative Banks (CCB) with 336 branches throughout the State of Haryana. It has more than 2,000 Patwar Circles (PACs) (mini-banks) catering to 2.5 million members living in the rural areas. Its Staff Training College at Panchkula provides training to grassroots and middle level managers of the CCBs and the PACs.

**HCMC-Vung Tau Ferry Service**
HCMC-Vung Tau Ferry Service operates a hydrofoil ferry service linking Ho Chi Minh City with Vung Tau. The service started in 1996 and is a joint venture between Vietnam's Proshipser Co Ltd (under Saigon Port Authority and Coast Guard) and Singapore's Sembawang Maritime Company. The ferry service has cut the journey to half an hour from the two-and-a-half hours by road.

**Health Corporation of Singapore**
The Health Corporation of Singapore (HCS) is the holding company of several public hospitals in Singapore.

**Health Promotion Board (Singapore)**
In Singapore, the Health Promotion Board (HPB) is a new statutory board
set up in April 2001 to promote a healthy lifestyle in Singapore.

**Health Sciences Authority (Singapore)**
In Singapore, the Health Sciences Authority (HSA) is a statutory board set
up in April 2001 to regulate healthcare products.

**Heaven and Hell Bonds (Japan)**
"Heaven and Hell" bonds are high-risk high-return foreign exchange index-
linked bonds. They were invented by Nomura of Japan in 1985 for IBM Credit
Corporation.

**PT Hero Supermarket (Indonesia)**
This is one of the largest supermarket chains in Indonesia. It has 65
supermarkets, 20 convenience stores under the "Star Mart" name and
numerous speciality stores like Toys City and Shop-in. Most of the outlets are
in the Greater Jakarta area.

**Hexagon**
This is a banking system developed by the HSBC Group. It provides an
integrated solution to meet customers' global banking needs. Transactions may
be performed electronically anytime, anywhere with a PC and a modem link.

**Higher Education Contribution Scheme (Australia)**
In Australia, the Higher Education Contribution Scheme (HECS) was introduced in 1989. Under the scheme, students pay part of their university
education cost through interest-free loans. They may defer repayment until
they start to work.

**Himalayan Bank Limited (Nepal)**   *www.hbl.com.np*
In Nepal, the Himalayan Bank Limited (HBL) started in 1992 by Nepalese
businessmen in partnership with the Employees Provident Fund and Habib
Bank. It provides a wide range of commercial, industrial and merchant banking
services.

**Hindu Undivided Family (India)**
In India, in this form of business, the male head of the family is the manager
and all other members of the family (such as nephews, sons or brothers) are
beneficiaries.

### HKFE Clearing Corporation Limited (HKCC)

In Hong Kong, the HKCC is a clearing house wholly-owned by the Hong Kong Futures Exchange (HKFE). It clears and registers transactions on the exchange's markets. Its board of directors ensures that operational procedures are consistent with the exchange's market and risk management policies. The board comprises a minimum of six directors which include: the chairman of the exchange; the Chief Executive Officer of the exchange; two members of the clearing house, or representatives of such members; and one independent director, unconnected with any exchange or clearing house member. The HKCC is obliged to meet counter-party liabilities when a member defaults on its settlement obligations. The maximum extent of the Clearing House's liabilities as counter-party is: the amount of margin collected by and on deposit with the clearing house pursuant to its rules; and the value of the Reserve Fund. The HKCC has a reserve fund to meet its counter-party liabilities. The fund comprises the following components: members' cash deposits, insurance, bank guarantees, interest income, member's additional deposits; and resources appropriated by the clearing house from time to time out of its general revenue. (See also: Hong Kong Futures Exchange)

### PT HM Sampoerna (Indonesia)

This is one of the large cigarette producers in Indonesia.

### Ho Chi Minh City International Exhibition and Convention Centre (HIECC)

In Vietnam, HIECC is the first international convention centre. It is located half way between Ho Chi Minh City centre and the Tan Son Ngat International Airport. It is a joint venture between Tan Binh Sports Complex run by Ho Chi Minh People's Committee and Singapore-based Intertrade.

### Home Development Finance Corporation (Sri Lanka)

In Sri Lanka, the Home Development Finance Corporation (HDFC) was set up in 1984 to provide funds at reasonable rates for housing construction and to implement government policy on housing.

### Home Mutual Development Fund (Philippines)

In the Philippines, the Home Mutual Development Fund is a provident fund for employees of private and government agencies. It collects contributions from members and provides housing and consumer loans to members.

### Hong Kong Association of Banks

The Hong Kong Association of Banks (HKAB) replaced the Exchange Banks'

Association in 1981. The statutory body has three permanent committee members: Hongkong and Shanghai Banking Corporation, Standard Chartered Bank and the Bank of China. Other members are the licensed banks in Hong Kong. The HKAB submits views and recommendations to the government on policies related to the banking sector. In the past, the HKAB was authorized to fix the maximum interest rates for Hong Kong dollar deposits of less than HK$500,000 and with a maturity of less than 15 months. Since October 1994, retail deposit interest rates have been deregulated.

### Hong Kong Bank
See Hongkong and Shanghai Banking Corporation (HSBC).

### Hong Kong Banking Ordinance
The Banking Ordinance of Hong Kong provides a legal framework for banking supervision in Hong Kong. Under Section 7(1) of the Ordinance, the main function of the Hong Kong Monetary Authority (HKMA) is to promote stability and effective working of the banking system. The regulatory framework is in line with international standards, especially those recommended by the Basle Committee on Banking Supervision. The objective is to preserve stability of the banking system and to provide flexibility for financial institutions to take commercial decisions.

The HKMA follows international practice as embodied in the principles of the revised Concordat issued by the Basle Committee. The Minimum Standards of the Basle Committee in July 1992 have also been incorporated into the authorization criteria for overseas applicants for banking licences.

Institutions are required to maintain adequate liquidity and capital adequacy ratios, to submit periodic returns to the HKMA on the required financial information, to adhere to limits on loans to any one customer or to directors and employees, and to seek approval for the appointment of directors and senior management, and for changes in control. However, branches of foreign banks are not required to hold capital in Hong Kong and are not subject to capital ratio requirements or to capital-based limits on large exposures. (See also: Hong Kong Monetary Authority)

### Hong Kong Consumer Protection Laws
In Hong Kong, four consumer protection laws were passed in 1994. They were: Consumer Goods Safety Ordinance (CGSO), the Sale of Goods Ordinance (SOGO), the Supply of Service (Implied Terms) Ordinance (SOSITO) and the Unconscionable Contracts Ordinance (UCO).

**Hong Kong Exchanges and Clearing Ltd (HKEx)**   *www.hkex.com.hk*
In 2000, the Stock Exchange of Hong Kong Ltd and Hong Kong Futures Exchange Ltd were demutualized. With Hong Kong Securities Clearing Company Ltd, the three companies merged to become the Hong Kong Exchanges and Clearing Ltd (HKEx). The HKEx is the second largest in Asia and 10th largest in the world. Its cash market deals in a wide range of equities and bond products as well as exchange traded funds. Its derivatives market operates futures and options products.

**Hong Kong Futures Exchange**
The Hong Kong Futures Exchange merged with the Stock Exchange of Hong Kong and the Hong Kong Securities Clearing to form the Hong Kong Exchanges and Clearing Ltd (HKEx) in 2000. (See also: Hong Kong Exchanges and Clearing Ltd)

**Hong Kong Institute for Monetary Research**   *www.hkimr.org*
The Hong Kong Institute for Monetary Research (HKIMR) was set up in 1999. It conducts research in monetary policy, banking and finance areas that are of strategic importance to Hong Kong and Asia. It is affiliated to the Hong Kong Monetary Authority and is funded by grants from the Exchange Fund.

**Hong Kong Institute of Bankers**   *www.hkib.org*
The Hong Kong Institute of Bankers was formed in 1963 to provide education and training. Its professional development programs and various examinations assist bank employees to advance in their banking career.

**Hong Kong Interbank Clearing Limited (HKICL)**
HKICL is owned jointly by the Hong Kong Monetary Authority and the Hong Kong Association of Banks. It was formed in 1995 to take over the clearing functions provided by the former Management Bank of the Clearing House and the Hongkong and Shanghai Banking Corporation. It provides interbank clearing and settlement services to all banks in Hong Kong.

**Hong Kong International Airport**
The Hong Kong International Airport (HKIA) was opened in July 1998. The 1,250-hectare airport replaces the old Kai Tak Airport. The HKIA is built on reclaimed land on Chek Lap Kok Island which is linked to the city via train, bridges, tunnels and expressways. In 1989, Sir David Wilson, then the governor of Hong Kong, announced the Airport Core Program (ACP) to construct a new airport at Chek Lap Kok as part of an ambitious development strategy. The ACP consisted of ten integrated infrastructure projects costing

US$20 billion. In 1991, the New Airport Projects Coordination Office (NAPCO) was formed to provide overall program management services in coordinating all ten projects. It worked closely with all government departments and private sector agencies involved in the projects. HKIA has a 500,000-square metre passenger terminal, one of the largest in the world. It is about eight times larger than Kai Tak Airport. It was designed by renowned British architect firm Foster and Partners.

**Hong Kong Investment Fund Association**   *www.hkif.org.hk*
The Hong Kong Investment Fund Association (HKIFA) was formed in 1986 as an industry organization to promote Hong Kong as a major fund management centre in Asia. Its members include unit trusts, mutual funds, provident funds, retirement schemes and closed-end investment companies.

**Hong Kong Monetary Authority (HKMA)**   *www.info.gov.hk/hkma*
The Hong Kong Monetary Authority (HKMA) was set up in 1993 with the merger of the Office of the Exchange Fund and the Office of the Commissioner of Banking. The objective was to ensure that the central banking functions could be performed with professionalism and continuity, in the lead up to 1997 and beyond, in a manner that would command the confidence of the people of Hong Kong and the international financial community. The HKMA maintains exchange rate stability within the linked exchange rate system through management of the Exchange Fund, monetary operations and other means. The linked exchange rate system adopted since 17 October 1983 is a currency board arrangement. Its core feature is the full backing of domestic currency notes by a foreign currency at a fixed exchange rate of US$1 to HK$7.80. In the foreign exchange market, the Hong Kong dollar exchange rate is determined by supply and demand. The exchange rate of the Hong Kong dollar has remained remarkably stable since 1983 because of strong official reserves. These reserves form part of the Exchange Fund that is managed by the HKMA. The HKMA adopts a prudent investment strategy to ensure that the investment management process of the Fund keeps pace with international best practices. (See also: Hong Kong Banking Ordinance)

**Hong Kong Mortgage Corporation (HKMC)**   *www.hkmc.com.hk*
Hong Kong Mortgage Corporation was formed in March 1997 to develop Hong Kong's secondary mortgage market. It is fully owned by the government through the Exchange Fund.

**Hong Kong Note Printing Limited**
In 1996, the Hong Kong government bought the banknote printing plant of

De La Rue and renamed it Hong Kong Note Printing Limited (HKNPL). The chairman of the company is the Chief Executive of the Hong Kong Monetary Authority (HKMA). Hong Kong currency notes are issued by these three banks: Hongkong and Shanghai Banking Corporation, Standard Chartered Bank and the Bank of China. In 1997, the HKMA sold 15% of the shareholding to China Bank Note Printing and Minting Corporation.

**Hong Kong Registrars Limited**    *www.computershare.com*
The Hong Kong Registrars Limited merged with the Central Registration Hong Kong Limited. With effect from 10 June 2002, it has been renamed Computershare Hong Kong Investor Services Limited. The parent company Computershare is one of the world's leading financial services and technology providers for the global securities industry.

**Hong Kong Securities Clearing Company**    *www.hkex.com.hk*
Hong Kong Securities Clearing Company Limited was formed in 1989. It created the Central Clearing and Settlement System (CCASS) which started operations in 1992. Share settlement is on a continuous net settlement basis by electronic book entry to participants' accounts with CCASS. Transactions are settled on the second trading day (T+2) following the transaction. The company is a subsidiary of the Hong Kong Exchanges and Clearing Limited. (See also: Hong Kong Exchanges and Clearing Limited)

**Hong Kong Securities Institute**
The Hong Kong Securities Institute (HKSI) was formed in December 1997. It is a professional body for practitioners in the securities, fund management and investment business. It is sponsored by the Hong Kong Securities and Futures Commission, and has the support of the Stock Exchange of Hong Kong, the Hong Kong Futures Exchange and the industry. Its mission is to set professional standards for practitioners in Hong Kong's financial services industry. (See also: Hong Kong Futures Exchange, Hong Kong Securities and Futures Commission, and Stock Exchange of Hong Kong)

**Hong Kong Stock Exchange**
See Stock Exchange of Hong Kong.

**Hongkong and Shanghai Banking Corporation (HSBC)**
The Hongkong and Shanghai Banking Corporation (HSBC or Hong Kong Bank) has been associated with the economy of Hong Kong for more than a century. It is one of the three currency note issuing banks (the other two are Standard Chartered and Bank of China). In the past, the bank provided

cheque clearing facilities on behalf of the Hong Kong Association of Banks and acted as lender of last resort. In December 1990, a holding company HSBC Holdings Plc was set up and registered as a non-resident company incorporated in the United Kingdom. The Hong Kong Bank is a wholly-owned subsidiary of HSBC Holdings and maintains its headquarters and management in Hong Kong.

### PT Hotel Sahid International

This is a leading Indonesian hotel chain with 11 hotels and subsidiary companies managing apartments.

### House Building Finance Corporation

In Pakistan, the House Building Finance Corporation (HBFC) was set up in 1952 to finance the construction of houses. After amendments in the Housing Building Finance Corporation Act in 1973, it is able to extend facilities to the rural area.

### Housing & Development Board (Singapore)

In Singapore, the Housing and Development Board (HDB) started in 1960 as a statutory board under the Ministry of National Development to provide low-cost public housing. It builds up, rents and sells flats. About 88% of the Singapore population lives in HDB flats. The HDB manages about 600,000 flats and about 40,000 commercial and industrial properties. The HDB has won several international awards for good design, construction quality and workmanship. It provides consulting services to governments of other countries.

### Hsinchu Science-based Industrial Park (Taiwan)   *www.sipa.gov.tw*

In Taiwan, the Hsinchu Science-based Industrial Park (HSIP) was set up in 1980 to create an environment for high-tech R&D activities. The 600-hectare park is located about 70 kilometres south of Taipei. It is surrounded by famous research institutes such as the Industrial Technology Research Institute, National Tsing Hua University and National Chao Tung University. It is regarded as the Silicon Valley of Taiwan. About 300 high-tech companies are located in the park and employ about 100,000 workers.

### Hua Nan Commercial Bank (Taiwan)   *www.hncb.com.tw*

In Taiwan, the Hua Nan Commercial Bank was formally established in 1947. However, its history may be traced back to the K.K. Hua Nan Bank that was founded in 1919. It provides a wide range of domestic and international banking services. It has overseas offices in major financial centres. In 2000, it was 168th by Tier-1 capital in the worldwide ranking by *The Banker* magazine.

**HSBC Group**   *www.asiapacific.hsbc.com*
The HSBC Group is one of the world's largest financial institutions. It began as the Hongkong and Shanghai Banking Corporation (HSBC) in Hong Kong in March 1865 and in Shanghai in April the same year. Its Chinese name "Wayfoong" means "abundance of remittances" or "focus of wealth". The bank is the founding member of the HSBC Group and is the flagship in the Asia Pacific. The group has 7,000 offices and 32 million customers in 81 countries. It owns 62% of Hang Seng Bank, the second largest bank in Hong Kong. (See also: Hang Seng Bank)

**HSI Services Limited**   *www.hsi.com.hk*
HSI Services Limited is a wholly-owned subsidiary of Hang Seng Bank.

**Ichibu (Japan)**
This is the first section of the stock exchange in Tokyo, Nagoya and Osaka exchanges.

**ICLARM World Fish Centre**   *www.worldfishcenter.org*
The ICLARM World Fish Centre (official name: International Centre for Living Aquatic Resources Management) is an international research organization. Its mission is to contribute to food security by raising and sustaining the productivity of fisheries and aquaculture systems. It has joint projects with national governments and non-government organizations. The centre has its headquarters in Penang (Malaysia) and offices in Bangladesh, Cameroon, Egypt, Malawi, Philippines, Solomon Islands and Vietnam. In 1999, it joined the Consultative Group for International Agricultural Research. (See also: Consultative Group for International Agricultural Research).

**IDBI Bank (India)**   *www.idbibank.com*
The IDBI Bank was set up in 1994 after the Reserve Bank of India (central bank) issued guidelines for the entry of new private sector banks in 1993. Its initial capital of Rs 1,000 million was contributed by the Industrial Development of India or IDBI (80%) and the Small Industries Development Bank of India or SIDBI (20%). In 1999, the bank raised its capital to 1,400 million with a public issue. As a commercial bank, it provides a wide range of retail and corporate services. It has formed a strategic alliance with TATA AIG General Insurance Company to sell insurance products. (See also: Industrial Development Bank of India)

**Immigration and Checkpoints Authority (Singapore)** *http://app.ica.gov.sg*
The Immigration and Checkpoints Authority (ICA) is a government agency under the Ministry of Home Affairs. It was formed on 1 April 2003 as a result of merging the former Singapore Immigration & Registration (SIR) and the enforcement work performed by the Customs and Excise Department (CED) at the various checkpoints.

**PT Indah Kiat**
This is Indonesia's largest paper and pulp producer. It is part of the Sinar Mas Group.

**Indian Airlines** *www.indian-airlines.nic.in*
Indian Airlines was formed in 1953. It is fully owned by the government and has staff strength of 22,000. Its annual turnover, together with that of its subsidiary Alliance Air, is about Rs 4,000 crores (or US$ 1 billion). Its network covers 75 destinations including 16 abroad, carrying about 7.5 million passengers annually.

**Independent Consumer and Competition Commission**
In Papua New Guinea, the Independent Consumer and Competition Commission (ICCC) was set up in 2002. It is an independent economic regulator that monitors and regulates market behaviour, controls prices and protects consumers.

**Indian Bank** *www.indianbank.com*
Indian Bank was set up in 1907 as part of the Swadeshi movement. It is owned by the government and has 1,400 branches with 22,400 employees. It has overseas branches in Colombo and Singapore.

**Indian Banks' Association** *www.iba.org.in* or *www.indianbanksassociation.org*
The Indian Banks' Association (IBA) was formed in 1946 with 22 members. It now has about 200 members that are banks in the public and private sectors, foreign banks, cooperative banks, development financial institutions, merchant banks, mutual funds, housing finance corporations and others. Its main objective is to promote sound banking principles and practices.

**Indian Chamber of Commerce**
The Indian Chamber of Commerce (ICC) started in 1874 as the Bengal Chamber of Commerce in Calcutta. Its main role is to promote business by providing its members with information on economic policy. It maintains constant dialogue with the central and state governments.

**Indian Overseas Bank**   *www.iob.com*
The Indian Overseas Bank (IOB) was set up in 1937. By 1947, it had 38 branches in India and seven overseas branches. In 1969, it was among the 14 banks that were nationalized. In 1999, it was the first bank to be awarded the ISO 9001 certificate. It has about 1,500 domestic and six international branches. In 2000, it raised capital from the public and reduced the government's shareholding to 75%. Its shares are listed on the stock exchanges in Madras, Mumbai as well as the National Stock Exchange.

**Indian Stock Index Futures**
Indian Stock Index Futures was launched on the Singapore Exchange derivatives market (SGX-DT) on 25 September 2000. The contract is based on the S&P CNX Nitty Index that is owned by the India Index Services & Products Ltd (IISPL), a subsidiary of the National Stock Exchange of India Ltd (NSE). The SGX S&P CNX Nitty Index is a market capitalization weighted index that comprises 50 component stocks representing some 48% of the total market capitalization of the Indian bourse. The index is traded in US dollars, with a contract size equivalent to US$20 multiplied by the index.

**Indira Gandhi Institute of Development Research (India)**   *www.igidr.ac.in*
The Indira Gandhi Institute of Development Research (IGIDR) was set up by the Reserve Bank of India in 1987 to carry out research on development issues. In 1990, it became a full fledged teaching and research institute when it introduced a PhD program in development issues.

**PT Indocement Tunggal Prakarsa**
This is Indonesia's leading cement producer.

**PT Indofood Sukses Makmur**
This is Indonesia's largest instant noodle producer with about 85% of the market share. Some of its brands include Indomie, Sarimi, Top Mie and Pop Mie. Indofood has a wide distribution network which includes PT Intranusa Citra, Indomarco Adhi Prima, PT Tristara Makmur, PT Cemako Mandiri Corp, PT Cereko Reksa Corp and PT Putra Daya Usahatama. In 1995, Indofood purchased PT Bogasari, Indonesia's largest flour mill. Indofood is the food flagship of the Salim Group.

**PT Indomobil**
This is the automotive division of the Salim Group in Indonesia. It has numerous automotive plants including Nissan assembly plant, Dunlop tire manufacturing plant and other components plants.

## Indonesia Australia Business Council

The IABC was set up in 1989 as a body to represent private sector interest in commercial relations between Indonesia and Australia. The formation of IABC was the result of merging DKSPIA (Dewan Kerja Sama Pengusaha Indonesia Australia) and AUSTCHAM (Australian Chamber of Commerce in Indonesia), two business groups that had operated in Indonesia for over 15 years, with support from the business members of IKAMA (Australian Alumni Association of Indonesia). The IABC is affiliated with KADIN (Indonesian Chamber of Commerce & Industry).

## Indonesia Malaysia Thailand Growth Triangle

The IMT-GT consists of two Indonesian provinces of North Sumatra and Daerah Istimewa Aceh, four northern Malaysian states (Kedah, Penang, Perak and Perlis) and five provinces of southern Thailand (Narathiwat, Pattani, Satun, Songkhla and Yala).

## PT Indonesian Asahan Aluminium (INALUM)

This is Indonesia's only aluminium producer. It has melting facility in Kuala Tanjung, and a water-generated power plant in Paritohan (North Sumatra).

## Indonesian Association of Development Financing Institutions
## (Asosiasi Lembaga Pembiayaan Pembangunan Indonesia or ALPPIA)

ALPPIA provides training and holds seminars on long term development finance.

## Indonesian Bank Restructuring Agency (IBRA)   *www.bppn.go.id*

The Indonesian Bank Restructuring Agency (IBRA) or Badan Penyehatan Perbankan Nasional (BPPN) was set up in 1998 by Presidential Decree No. 27 of 1998. It is an independent body reporting to the Ministry of Finance. Its main mission is to improve the banking sector to an internationally accepted standard. It has set up the Asset Management Company to focus on debt recovery for banks that have failed.

## Indonesian Capital Market Supervisory Agency (BAPEPAM)

*www.bapepam.go.id*

In Indonesia, capital market activities are supervised by the Capital Market Supervisory Agency (BAPEPAM).

## Indonesian Central Securities Depository
## Kustodian Sentral Efek Indonesia (KSEI)   *www.ksei.co.id*

The Indonesian Central Securities Depository started in December 1997. It is a non-profit organization and a company privately owned by 11 custodian banks, 31 market participants, 5 registrars, 2 stock exchanges and a clearing guarantee institution. In 1998, KSEI was granted a licence from the Capital Market Supervisory Agency (BAPEPAM) as a depository and settlement institution. It implemented the Book Entry Settlement System in July 2000.

### Indonesian Civil Servants Corps
### (Korps Pegawai Republik Indonesia KORPRI)

KORPRI was set up by Presidential Decree on 29 November 1971. Its objective was to re-order the then compartmentalized civil servants according to their respective political and ideological aspirations. KORPRI is based on the state philosophy Pancasila and the 1945 Constitution.

### Indonesian Clearing and Guarantee Corporation
### (PT Kliring Penjaminan Efek Indonesia, KPEI)   *www.kpei.co.id*

In Indonesia, KPEI provides clearing service and guarantees securities settlement at the Jakarta Stock Exchange. Its shareholders are Jakarta Stock Exchange Limited (90%) and Surabaya Stock Exchange (10%).

### Indonesian Debt Restructuring Agency   *www.indra.go.id*

The Indonesian Debt Restructuring Agency (INDRA) is a trust organization set up by the Indonesian Government and administered by the Bank Indonesia, the central bank. INDRA provides exchange rate protection to private debtors that agree with their foreign creditors to restructure their external debt.

### Indonesian Environmental Impact Assessment Agency (BAPEDAL)

Among BAPEDAL's primary areas of focus is AMDAL (environment Impact Assessment). Under the anti-pollution statute in 1987, AMDAL is required for all new industrial construction and for existing facilities that produce hazardous or toxic waste. BAPEDAL has compiled a list of pollutants for factories. These factories are then categorized into gold, green, blue, red and black.

### PT Indonesian Satellite Corporation (Indosat)

Indosat is one of the largest Indonesian international telecommunication companies in which the government has a major shareholding. It has numerous subsidiaries and affiliated companies including:
- PT Indosat Multi Media (IMM)
- PT Sisindosat Lintasbuana
- PT Aplikasa Lintasarta
- PT Bangtelindo
- PT Satelit Palapa Indonesia (Satelindo)

- PT Indoprima Mikroselindo (Primasat)
- Acasia Communications Sdn Bhd
- PT Multi Media Asia Indonesia (MMAI)
- ASEAN Telecom Holding Sdn Bhd (ATH)
- PT Indokomsat Lintas Dunia
- PT Indosel

## Indonesian School of Mortgage Banking
The Indonesian School of Mortgage Banking was set up in 1997 by Yayasan Dharma Tirta in cooperation with Bank Papan, Mortgage Banker Association of America and Financial Analysis Development Institute of Indonesia.

## Indonesian State-owned Enterprise
An Indonesian state-owned enterprise is basically a company owned by the government but has the flexibility of a private enterprise. During the transition from the "Old Order" administration of President Sukarno to the "New Order" administration of President Suharto, many state-owned enterprises were trans-formed from state corporations (Perusahaan Negara, or PN) into one of the three new categories: government agency (Perusahaan Jawatan, or Perjan), public corporation (Perusahaan Umum, or Perum), or limited liability company (Perseroan Terbatas, or PT).

## Indovina Bank (IVB)
In Vietnam, IVB was licensed in 1990 as the first joint venture bank. Its partners are the Industrial and Commercial Bank of Vietnam (Incombank) and PT Bank Dagang Nasional Indonesia. It has offices in Hanoi, Ho Chi Minh City and Hai Phong City.

## Industri Pesawat Terbang Nusantara (IPTN)
State-owned Nusantara Aircraft Industry.

## Industrial and Commercial Bank of China    *www.icbc.com.cn*
The Industrial and Commercial Bank of China (ICBC) is the largest commercial bank in China. Its total assets exceed RMB 4 trillion. It provides a full range of financial services. In 2000, it was awarded "Bank of the Year in China" by *The Banker* and awarded the "Best Domestic Bank in China" by Euromoney. In *The Banker's* 2001 ranking, ICBC was 7th among the top 1000 banks in terms of Tier-1 capital.

## Industrial and Commercial Bank of Vietnam (Incombank)
Incombank is one of the three state-owned commercial banks in Vietnam. Its

clients are mainly from the industrial and commercial sectors. It has a joint venture bank with Bank Dagang Nasional from Indonesia.

**Industrial Credit and Investment Corporation of India**  *www.icicibank.com*
The Industrial Credit and Investment Corporation of India (ICICI) is jointly owned by Indian and foreign entities. It provides medium term loans. It provides underwriting services and subscribes to equity, debentures and loan guarantees. It provides a wide range of corporate and personal financial services.

**Industrial Development Bank of India**  *www.idbi.com*
The Industrial Development Bank of India (IDBI) was set up in 1964 as a fully-owned subsidiary of the Reserve Bank of India. In 1976, ownership was transferred to the Government of India. In 1982, its International Finance Division was transferred to the newly established government-owned Export Import Bank of India. IDBI set up the Small Industries Development Bank of India as a wholly-owned subsidiary to cater to the needs of the small scale sector. In 1993, it set up the IDBI Capital Market Services Limited as a stockbroking company. When the commercial banking was opened to the private sector, IDBI set up the IDBI Bank Limited in 1994. Through a public offer, IDBI raised Rs 20 billion in 1995, and the government stake was reduced to about 72%. In 2000, it set up the IDBI Intech Limited as a subsidiary for IT related activities. In 2001, subsidiary IDBI Trusteeship Services Limited was set up to provide services to subscribers and issuers of debentures. (See also: IDBI Bank, Small Industries Development Bank of India)

**Industrial Development Bank of Pakistan**  *www.idbp.com.pk*
The Industrial Development Bank of Pakistan (IDBP) is the oldest development financial institution in Pakistan. It is owned by the Federal Government (57%), State Bank of Pakistan (36%), provincial governments and public sector companies. In development banking, it provides medium and long term loans and guarantees. It also provides commercial and merchant banking services.

**Industrial Development Board (Sri Lanka)**
In Sri Lanka, the Industrial Development Board (IDB) was set up in 1969 to promote and develop small and medium industries.

**Industrial Estate Authority of Thailand**  *www.ieat.go.th*
The Industrial Estate Authority of Thailand (IEAT) is a state enterprise attached to the Ministry of Industry. It implements the government's industrial development policy. It develops and manages the state's industrial estates. It also jointly manages industrial estates with private developers.

### Industrial Finance Corporation of India

The Industrial Finance Corporation of India (IFCI) is owned by the Industrial Development Bank of India (IDBI) and commercial banks. In 1994, it raised about Rs 5.2 billion through a public share issue. It provides medium and long term loans and underwrites equity and debentures.

### Industrial Finance Corporation of Thailand  *www.ifct.co.th*

The Industrial Finance Corporation of Thailand (IFCT) was set up in 1959 to provide medium and long term loans for the expansion and modernization of industrial enterprises in the private sector. The IFCT has been operating as a development finance company. With effect from 1992, the IFCT has been authorized to carry out activities related to the development of the capital market in Thailand.

### Industrial Investment Bank of India (IIBI)  *www.iibiltd.com*

The Industrial Investment Bank of India Ltd (IIBI) was formed in 1997 by converting the Industrial Reconstruction Bank of India. It is the only all-India financial institution fully owned by the government. It provides short, medium and long term loans as well as investment in capital market instruments.

### Industrial Linkage Program (Malaysia)  *www.jaring.my/smidec/ilp.htm*

Malaysia's Industrial Linkage Program (ILP) is a cluster-based industrial development program under the Second Industrial Master Plan (Second IMP) (1996–2005). The objective is to nurture local SMIs into reliable suppliers of components to larger companies. The priority areas include electrical and electronic industry, transport equipment industry and machinery groups.

### Industrial Zone (IZ)

In 1994, Vietnam adopted Decree CP-193 *Promulgating the Regulations on Industrial Zones.* Since then, several industrial zones have been set up. They have been successful in attracting foreign investments in manufacturing for the local and export markets.

The concept of industrial zone was introduced as an alternative to the export processing zone (EPZ) which was introduced in 1991 to provide special tax and regulatory incentives to investors. The industrial zone provides investors the flexibility to sell their products into the domestic markets as well as the export market. On 24 October 1995, Ministry of Planning and Investment Circular No. 2374/UB-KCX provides *Guidance on the Conversion of Export Processing Zones into Industrial Zones and the Adjustment of Investment Licences of Foreign Investment Enterprises Operating under the Regulations on Export*

*Processing Zones.* This circular has enables foreign investors in the EPZs to reorganize and sell their products in the local as well as export markets. (See also: export processing zone)

### Infocomm Development Authority (IDA) (Singapore)   *www.ida.gov.sg*

In Singapore, the IDA was formed on 1 December 1999 as a result of merging National Computer Board (NCB) and the Telecommunication Authority of Singapore (TAS). Its mission is to develop Singapore into a global information and communications technology (ICT) centre. Its objectives include:

– positioning Singapore as vital node in the regional and global information infrastructure
– promoting and developing the ICT industry
– encouraging companies to adopt ICT as a competitive tool
– developing electronic commerce related supporting services
– attracting and development manpower to make Singapore the ICT talent capital
– keeping policy and regulatory framework transparent, pro-business and pro-consumer
– building a critical mass of ICT users
– harnessing ICT to enhance quality of life
– enabling the Singapore Government to be a leading and exemplary user of ICT.

### Infocomm Master Plan 21 (Singapore)

The Infocomm Master Plan 21 is a blueprint to turn Singapore into an infocomm hub. The plan has a three-prong approach: set up a nurturing backdrop, draw and retain foreign talent, and make Singapore known for e-learning in the region.

### Information Technology Agreement (ITA)

The ITA was endorsed by 28 countries at the World Trade Organization (WTO) Inaugural Ministerial Conference held in Singapore in December 1996. Tariffs were eliminated on most IT products by the year 2000.

### Infrastructure Development Finance Company (India)

In India, the Infrastructure Development Finance Company (IDFC) is a financial institution where the Reserve Bank of India (central bank) has a minority stake. (See also: Reserve Bank of India)

### Infrastructure Development Fund (Malaysia)

In Malaysia, the RM 5 billion Infrastructure Development Fund was set up in June 1998. The fund was raised through domestic and foreign bond issues. It helped to revive deferred infrastructure projects to boost the Malaysian economy. The projects included monorail, sewerage and highway projects.

## Inland Revenue Board of Malaysia

The Inland Revenue Board of Malaysia was formerly the Department of Inland Revenue. It became a statutory board in 1996. It is a major revenue-collecting agency of the Ministry of Finance. It administers the Income Tax Act, Petroleum (Income Tax) Act, Real Property Gains Tax Act, Promotion of Investment Act, Stamp Act, Labuan Offshore Business Activity Act and others.

## Insinyur (Ir)

An engineering graduate in Indonesia.

## Institute for Communications Research (Singapore)

See Science and Engineering Research Council.

## Institute for Defence Studies and Analysis   *www.idsa-india.org*

In India, the Institute for Defence Studies and Analysis (IDSA) was set up in 1965. It conducts independent research and analysis on strategic and security issues.

## Institute for Development and Research in Banking Technology (India)

*www.idrbt.com*

The Institute for Development and Research in Banking Technology (IDRBT) was set up by the Reserve Bank of India as an autonomous research centre. Its projects include financial network and application architecture, payments system and security technology, data mining, data warehousing and risk management.

## Institute for Monetary and Economic Studies (Japan)   *www.imes.boj.or.jp*

The Institute for Monetary and Economic Studies started in 1982. It is a research organization within the Bank of Japan. It conducts a wide range of studies on the theoretical, institutional and historical aspects of monetary and economic issues. (See also: Bank of Japan)

## Institute of Bioengineering (Singapore)

See Biomedical Research Council.

## Institute of Chartered Accountants of Nepal   *www.ican.org.np*

The Institute of Chartered Accountants of Nepal (ICAN) was formed in 1997 under the Nepal Chartered Accountants Act. There are two classes of members: Chartered Accountant and Registered Auditor. The Nepal Chartered Accountant Regulations Act came into effect in 1999.

**Institute of Chartered Accountants of Pakistan**   *www.icap.org.pk*
The Institute of Chartered Accountants of Pakistan (ICAP) was set up in 1961. Its mission is to promote professional and ethical standards in the accountancy profession.

**Institute of Chemical and Engineering Sciences (Singapore)**
See Science and Engineering Research Council.

**Institute of Developing Economies (Japan)**
In Japan, the Institute of Developing Economies (IDE) is the largest economic research organization. In 1998, it merged with the Japan External Trade Organization (JETRO), resulting in a new organization with comprehensive capabilities in trade and investment as well as in economic research. (See also: Japan External Trade Organization)

**Institute of Fiscal and Monetary Policy (Japan)**
The Institute of Fiscal and Monetary Policy (IFMP) is the research division of Ministry of Finance, Japan.

**Institute of High Performance Computing (Singapore)**
See Science and Engineering Research Council.

**Institute of Materials Research and Engineering (Singapore)**
The Institute of Materials Research and Engineering (IMRE) was set up in 1996 at the National University of Singapore. Its research supports key industry clusters, especially electronics, chemicals and engineering. (See also: Science and Engineering Research Council)

**Institute of Microelectronics (Singapore)**
The Institute of Microelectronics (IME) at the National University of Singapore collaborates with electronics companies in joint R&D projects such as advanced packaging methodologies and process development, multi-chip module and high-density interconnection. (See also: Science and Engineering Research Council)

**Institute of Molecular Agrobiology (Singapore)**
See Science and Engineering Research Council.

**Institute of Molecular and Cell Biology (Singapore)**
See Science and Engineering Research Council.

**Institute of Pacific Studies (Fiji)**
The Institute of Pacific Studies is located at the University of the South Pacific in Suva, Fiji. It is an autonomous body providing research, training and consulting services.

**Institute of Policy Studies (Singapore)** *www.ips.org.sg*
In Singapore, the Institute of Policy Studies (IPS) is a public policy think-tank set up in 1987. It promotes interest in public policy issues in Singapore. It conducts research on public policies and publishes such findings.

**Institute of Policy Studies (Sri Lanka)**
In Sri Lanka, the Institute of Policy Studies (IPS) is a statutory organization under the Ministry of Finance. It conducts research on economic policies. Topics include economic liberalization and stabilization, privatization and distributional equity.

**Institute of Research for Economic and Commerce** *www.moc.gov.la/erit.html*
In Lao PDR, the Institute of Research for Economic and Commerce is under the Ministry of Commerce. It conducts research on policies on trade and the economy. It drafts rules and regulations on trade for decision-makers.

**Institute of Security and International Studies** *www.isisthailand.polsci.chula.ac.th*
In Thailand, the Institute of Security and International Studies (ISIS) was founded in 1981 as the Southeast Asian Studies Program of the Faculty of Political Science, Chulalongkorn University. It conducts independent academic research on international and security issues.

**Institute of Southeast Asian Studies** *www.iseas.edu.sg*
In Singapore, the Institute of Southeast Asian Studies (ISEAS) was set up in 1968. It is an autonomous regional research centre for scholars and specialists concerned with modern Southeast Asian affairs.

**Institute of Strategic and International Studies** *www.jaring.my.isis*
In Malaysia, the Institute of Strategic and International Studies (ISIS) was set up in 1983. It is an autonomous non-profit organization. It conducts independent policy research on strategic issues including defence, security and foreign affairs, national and international economic affairs.

## Institute of Technical Education (Singapore)

In Singapore, the Institute of Technical Education (ITE) was set up in 1992 as a post-secondary institution. It was known as the Vocational and Industrial Board (VITB) before 1992 and the Adult Education Board (AEB) in the 1960s. The ITE is the national institution for providing pre-employment technical training for secondary school leavers and continuing education and training for working adults. For school leavers, full time institutional training and apprenticeship programs are offered. For working adults, skill training and continuing education programs are offered.

## Institutional Investors, Mergers & Acquisitions, Research & Publication Department (India)

The Institutional Investors, Mergers & Acquisitions, Research & Publication Department (IIMARP) is a department within the Securities and Exchange Board of India.

## Insurance Act 1996 (Malaysia)

This Act deals with the licensing of insurers, insurance brokers, adjusters and reinsurers. It also deals with setting up of subsidiary and offices, establishment of insurance fund, direction and control of defaulting insurers, the control on management of licensee, accounts of licensee, examination and investigation powers of the central bank, winding-up, transfer of business of licensee.

## Insurance Business in Vietnam

In 1993, Vietnam opened up its insurance sector to foreign insurance companies, breaking the monopoly enjoyed by the state-owned insurance company BAO VIET. Government Decree 100-CP allows private enterprises and foreign insurers to apply for insurance business licence. There are four types of insurance business: insurance companies, National Reinsurance of Vietnam, insurance brokering organizations and insurance agents. There are four types of insurance companies: mutual insurance companies, joint venture insurance companies, branches of foreign insurance companies and wholly-owned foreign insurance companies.

## Insurance Business Law (Myanmar)

In Myanmar, the Insurance Business Law was passed in 1996. It paves the way for opening up the insurance industry to the private sector. The Insurance Business Supervisory Board was formed in 1996. It has representatives from Myanmar Insurance, Central Bank of Myanmar, Office of the Attorney General and Directorate of Investment and company Administration. Currently, the licence to operate insurance business is restricted to nationals only and in the following classes of insurance: life, fire, motor, cash-in-safe and fidelity insurance.

### Insurance Corporation of Sri Lanka
The Insurance Corporation of Sri Lanka (ICSL) was set up in 1961 under the Insurance Corporation Act. It had a monopoly in insurance until 1985 when the government opened up the industry to the private sector.

### Insurance Regulatory and Development Act (India)
In India, the Insurance Regulatory and Development Act (IRDA) was passed in December 1999. It promotes private sector participation in the insurance sector and permits foreign equity stake in domestic private insurance companies up to a maximum of 26% of paid up capital.

### Integrated Information System for Small Enterprise Development (SI-PUK Indonesia)
### (Sistem Informasi – Terpadu Pengembangan Usaha Kechil)
SI-PUK is a set of internet-based information systems designed by Bank of Indonesia (Central Bank) to support financial institutions providing loans to small enterprises. It consists of the following sub-systems:
(a) Information system of Baseline Economic Survey (SIB or Sistem Informasi Baseline Economic Survey);
(b) Information system of export-oriented agroindustry (SIABE or Sistem Informasi Agroindustri Berbasis Ekspor);
(c) Information system of Lending Model for small enterprises (SI-LMUK or Sistem Informasi Pola Pembisyanan/Lending Model Usaha Kechil);
(d) Decision support system for investment (SPKUI or Sistem Penunjang Keputusan Untuk Investasi);
(e) Information system for credit procedure (SI-PMK or Sistem Informasi Prosedur Memperoleh Kredit).

### Intellectual Property Office of Singapore
The Registry of Trade Marks and Patents was renamed the Intellectual Property Office of Singapore (IPOS) on 9 September 1999. In addition to registering trademarks and granting patents, it regulates trademark, patent and copyright. It monitors development in intellectual property, and reviews current laws, such as the Copyright Act. In April 2001, IPOS became a statutory board to spearhead a national effort to build intellectual property (IP) as a strategic and competitive resource. It seeks closer links with IP centres in other countries and work with international agencies.

## PT Intercallin (Indonesia)

See PT International Chemical Industry Company Ltd.

## Interest Equalization Tax (US)

In the US, the Interest Equalization Tax (IET) was introduced in 1965 to discourage foreign institutions from raising funds in the US to improve balance of payments. It was abolished in 1974.

## International Accounting Standards Committee    *www.iasc.org.uk*

The International Accounting Standards Committee (IASC) is a private body formed in 1973. It harmonizes accounting principles around the world. It has 153 member bodies from 122 countries.

## International Air Transport Association    *www.iata.org*

Founded in 1919, the International Air Transport Association (IATA) is a Canada-based association representing about 270 airlines in the world. Its mission is to ensure members' aircraft can operate safely and efficiently within clearly defined rules.

## International Association of Insurance Supervisors    *www.iaisweb.org*

The International Association of Insurance Supervisors (IAIS) was founded in 1994. It sets internationally endorsed principles and standards that are essential for effective insurance supervision. Its members include insurance supervisors from more than 100 countries. IAIS is supported by a secretariat at the Bank of International Settlements. The Association's address is at the Bank for International Settlements, CH-4002, Basel, Switzerland.

## International Auditing Practices Committee

See International Federation of Accountants, IFAC.

## International Bank for Reconstruction and Development (IBRD)

*www.worldbank.org*

The IBRD (also known as the World Bank) is part of the World Bank Group. It was established in 1945. The main objective is to provide or guarantee loans to member nations for development projects. Examples of such projects are electric power, roads, ports, telecommunications, education, tourism and family planning. The IBRD has two affiliate institutions: the International Finance Corporation and the International Development Association. (See also: Bretton Woods Agreement, World Bank Group)

### International Beverages Company (IBC)

IBC is a joint venture between Vietnam's soft drink manufacturer SP Co and Singapore's Macandrey Company. It manufactures local soft drinks such as Tribeco, SP Cola, Festi Cola and Hoa Binh cream soda. It has a joint venture with Pepsi International. It also bottles foreign soft drinks such as Schweppes and orange soda Crush.

### International Business Park (Singapore)

In Singapore, the International Business Park is located at Jurong East. It is ideal for companies that wish to integrate their business and production activities in one location. Companies have a choice of taking up prepared land sites to build their own facilities or move into The Synergy, a ready-built facility at IBP.

### International Campaign to Ban Landmines   *www.icbl.org*

The International Campaign to Ban Landmines (ICBL) was started in 1992 by six organizations from several countries. It now has a network of more than 1,000 groups from 60 countries. It calls for an international ban on the production and use of anti-personnel landmines. In 1997, the ICBL and its coordinator Jody Williams received the Nobel Peace Prize.

### International Centre for Integrated Mountain Development (Nepal)

*www.icimod.org.sg*

In 1974, the idea for such a centre was launched at an international workshop on mountain environment organized by the German Foundation for International Development in Munich. In 1975, a regional meeting of UNESCO recommended the setting up of the centre and welcomed the offer by Nepal to host such an institution. In 1981, an agreement between Nepal and UNESCO was signed. In 1983, the first Board of Directors meeting was held. The basic objectives of ICIMOD are to promote the development of an economically and environmentally sound mountain ecosystem and to improve the living standards of mountain populations, especially in the Hindu Kush Himalayan region.

### International Centre for Living Aquatic Resources Management

*www.worldfishcentre.org*

The International Centre for Living Aquatic Resources Management is now known as the ICLARM-World Fish Centre. (See ICLARM World Fish Centre).

### International Centre for Settlement of Investment Disputes
*www.worldbank.org*
The International Centre for Settlement of Investment Disputes (ICSID) is a World Bank organization. It provides facilities to conciliate and arbitrate disputes between foreign investors and their host countries.

### International Chamber of Commerce
The International Chamber of Commerce was founded in 1919. It is a non-government organization that promotes world trade and investment through consultation with inter-governmental bodies. It offers services such as the ATA Carnet system to the international business community.

### PT International Chemical Industry Company Ltd (Intercallin)
This is Indonesia's largest dry cell maker. It was established in 1968 and is part of the ABC Group. Its products are sold under the brand name "ABC".

### International Commercial Bank of China (Taiwan)    *www.icbc.com.tw*
The International Commercial Bank of China (ICBC) was founded in 1912 as The Bank of China through the reorganization of the Ta Ching Bank and its predecessor the Hupu Bank which was set up in 1904 during the Ching Dynasty. It served as the central bank until the government set up the Central Bank of China in 1928. Thereafter the bank gave up its central banking role and developed into an international exchange bank. The bank acquired the name International Commercial Bank of China in 1971. With its head office in Taipei, ICBC has a network of about 65 domestic branches and 25 foreign offices in major financial centres in the world.

### International Committee on the Reconstruction of Cambodia (ICORC)
The ICORC comprises representatives from donor countries. They met in Paris in 1993, in Tokyo in 1994 and again in Paris in 1995. These meetings resulted in US$1.6 billion in contribution from 40 donor countries and international organizations such as the Asian Development Bank, World Bank and International Monetary Fund.

### International Corporate Governance Network    *www.icgn.org*
The International Corporate Governance Network (ICGN) started in 1995 in Washington DC in the United States. The first meeting was attended by representatives from the AFL-CIO (US), Association of British Insurers, Australian Investment Managers' Association, World Federation of Investment Clubs and others. During the following years, many European institutions joined ICGN. They included: Association Francaise de la Gestion Financiere, Barclays Global Investors, Deutsche Boerse, European Association of Securities

Dealers, European Federation of Investment Funds, Paris Bourse, Unicerdito Italiano and the European Association of Employed Shareholders. In 2000, ICGN Conference was held in New York, in 2001 it was in Tokyo and in 2002 it was in Milan. The 2003 conference will be in Amsterdam. The ICGN Secretariat is administered by the Institute of Chartered Secretaries & Administrators (ICSA) in London.

**International Court of Justice**  *www.icj-cji.org*

The International Court of Justice (ICJ) was set up in 1945 to be the judicial organ of the United Nations. It sits in The Hague in the Netherlands and acts as a world court. It settles in accordance with international law the legal disputes submitted to it by States. It also gives legal advice to international agencies. The court is composed of 15 judges elected to 9-year terms of office by the United Nations General Assembly and the Security Council.

**International Crops Research Institute for Semi-Arid Tropics**
*www.icrisat.org*

The International Crops Research Institute for Semi-Arid Tropics (ICRISAT) was set up in 1972. It is one of the 16 centres supported by the Consultative Group for International Agricultural Research. Its mission is to improve the livelihood of 300 million poor living in semi-arid tropics across the world. ICRISAT is located at Patancheru (near Hyderabad, India). (See also: Consultative Group for International Agricultural Research)

**International Development Association**  *www.worldbank.org/ida*

The International Development Association (IDA) is an affiliate of the World Bank. It helps poor countries reduce poverty by providing interest-free loans for long repayment periods. IDA helps to build the human capital, policies, institutions, and physical infrastructure that these countries need to achieve sustained growth.

**International Development Research Centre**  *www.idrc.ca*

The International Development Research Centre (IDRC) was started in 1970 by the Canadian government. It helps developing countries find solutions to social, economic and environmental problems through research. To achieve its objectives, IDRC funds the work of scientists working in universities, private enterprise, government and non-profit organizations in developing countries. It has a 21-member international board of governors to oversee its activities. It employs 360 staff in its headquarters in Ottawa and six regional offices: Egypt (Cairo), India (New Delhi), Kenya (Nairobi), Senegal (Dakar), Singapore and Uruguay (Montevideo).

International Enterprise (Singapore)    *www.iesingapore.gov.sg*
In Singapore, the International Enterprise (known as Trade Development
Board before 2002) plays an important role in achieving Singapore's vision to
be the premier services hub in Asia. It explores new markets and business niches
for Singapore's exports and expanding avenues of supplies, and makes
Singapore a more attractive base for international traders.

International Federation of Accountants    *www.ifac.org*
The International Federation of Accountants (IFAC) is a private organization
and has 153 member bodies from 113 countries. Through its International
Auditing Practices Committee (IAPC), it has formulated the International
Standards on Auditing (ISA) and Auditing Practices Statements.

International Finance Corporation (IFC)    *www.worldbank.org*
The International Finance Corporation (IFC) was set up in 1956. It is part
of the World Bank Group. It promotes private sector investments, both foreign
and domestic, in developing member countries. Its investment and advisory
services are designed to reduce poverty and improve people's lives in an
environmentally and socially responsible manner. (See also: World Bank
Group)

International Group of Department Stores (IGDS)
The IGDS was established in 1946 as a non-profit organization whose
members range from medium to big retailers across the world. In 1992, the
Indonesian retailer Matahari joined the IGDS and was the only Indonesian
retailer that became a member in the group.

International Labour Organization    *www.ilo.org*
The International Labour Organization (ILO) was set up in 1919. The
Geneva-based organization became a United Nations specialized agency in
1946. It promotes social justice and internationally recognized human and
labour rights. The ILO formulates international labour standards in the form
of conventions and recommendations setting minimum standards of basic
labour rights: freedom of association, the right to organize, collective
bargaining, abolition of forced labour, equality of opportunity and treatment,
and other standards regulating conditions across the entire spectrum of work
related issues. It provides technical assistance labour-related issues.

International Maritime Organization    *www.imo.org*
The International Maritime Organization (IMO) was set up in 1948 as the
Inter-governmental Maritime Consultative Organization (IMCO). The

present name was adopted in 1982. It is a United Nations specialized agency responsible for improving maritime safety and preventing pollution from ships.

**International Monetary and Financial Committee (IMFC)**
The International Monetary and Financial Committee (IMFC) is the highest decision making in the International Monetary Fund (IMF). It was transformed from the previous Interim Committee in September 1999. At its first meeting in April 2000, it formulated several principles for managing Fund lending in times of crisis. These included streamlining and consolidating existing facilities, shortening the maturity of loans, charging progressively higher rates of interest in the event of either of weak implementation of IMF conditions or repeated use of IMF resources.

The IMF operated six assistance facilities:
(1) traditional standby, (2) high interest Supplemental Reserve Facility (SRF) introduced in 1998, (3) Contingency Credit Line (CCL) announced in 1998, (4) Extended Fund Facility (EFF) introduced in 1975 for long term loans to developing countries, (5) Poverty Reduction and Growth Fund (PRGF), (6) Compensatory and Contingency Financing Facility (CCFF) which makes low interest loans to countries experiencing exogenous shocks.

Four facilities (contingency element of the CCFF, the Currency Stabilization Fund, the Buffer Stock Financing Facility and support for commercial bank debt reduction plan) were eliminated at the April 2000 meeting of the IMFC.

**International Monetary Fund (IMF)**    *www.imf.org*
After World War II there was chaos in the international monetary system. In 1994, at the Bretton Woods conference, the formation of the IMF was proposed. The IMF was formed in 1947 to restore orderly exchange practices. Member nations may borrow from the IMF to solve their balance of payments deficit. The main objectives of the IMF are to:
(a) Promote international monetary cooperation through a permanent institution which provides the machinery for consultation and collaboration on international monetary problems;
(b) Facilitate the expansion and balanced growth of international trade and to contribute to the promotion and maintenance of high levels of employment and real income and to the development of economic policy;
(c) Promote exchange stability, to maintain orderly exchange arrangements among members, and to avoid competitive exchange depreciation;
(d) Assist in the establishment of a multilateral system of payments in respect

of current transactions between members and in the elimination of foreign exchange restrictions which hamper the growth of world trade;

(e) Give confidence to members by making the Fund's resources available to them under adequate safeguards, thus providing them with opportunity to correct maladjustments in their balance of payments without resorting to measures destructive of national or international prosperity.

In the April 2000 meeting of the International Monetary and Financial Committee, governors of IMF (24 ministers and central bank governors representing the 182 members of IMF) encouraged the development of standards in areas of direct concern to the IMF — data dissemination, transparency of fiscal, monetary and financial policies, and banking supervision. The IMF has spearheaded the Code of Good Practices on Fiscal Transparency, the Code of Good Practices on Transparency in Monetary and Financial Policies, the Special Data Dissemination Standards, and the General Data Dissemination Standard. The IMF and the Basel Committee on Banking Supervision have jointly created the Basel Core Principles. (See also: Basel Committee on Banking Supervision, International Monetary and Financial Committee)

### International Natural Rubber Organization
The main objective of International Natural Rubber Organization (INRO) is to stabilize world natural rubber prices.

### International Organization of Employers    *www.ioe-emp.org*
The International Organization of Employers was formed in 1920. It is the only organization at the international level that represents the interests of business in the labour and social policy fields. It consists of 135 national employer organizations from 131 countries. It promotes and defends the interests of employers in international forums, particularly in the International Labour Organization (ILO). It acts as the secretariat to the Employers' Group at the ILO International Labour Conference, the ILO Governing Body and all other ILO-related meetings. (See also: Confederation of Asia Pacific Employers)

### International Organization of Securities Commissions (IOSCO)
*www.iosco.org*
Membership of the IOSCO is open to a securities commission or a similar government body. Members agree to cooperate to promote high standards of regulation in order to maintain just, efficient and sound markets; to exchange information on their respective experience; to unite their efforts to establish standards and effective surveillance of international securities transactions.

IOSCO has four Regional Standing Committees, which meet to discuss specific regional problems of the members: Africa–Middle East, Asia–Pacific, European and Inter-American regional committees. The IOSCO secretariat is located in Montreal. Since 1974, IOSCO members have been meeting every year to discuss issues related to world securities and futures markets. The 1998 annual conference was held in Nairobi (Kenya), 1999 in Lisboa (Portugal) and 2000 in Sydney (Australia).

**International Research, Consulting and Training Centre for Foreign Economic Relations (Vietnam)**
In Vietnam, the ICTC was set up in 1993 under the Ministry of Trade. It promotes trade and investment in Vietnam. Its consulting arm works with foreign companies and offers services such as setting up representative offices, conducting market surveys and feasibility studies, short-listing joint venture partners, organizing business tours, promoting and organizing exhibitions and trade fairs. Its training centre conducts courses in foreign trade practices.

**International Researchers Club (Singapore)**   *www.ihpc.nus.edu/irc*
In Singapore, the International Researchers Club (IRC) was formed in 2001 with the support of the National Science & Technology Board (now known as A*STAR). The main focus is to help integrate foreign researchers into the Singapore society, through the organization of educational, social and recreational activities for its members and their families. Foreign researchers join as ordinary members while Singapore researchers join as associate members.

**International Rice Research Institute**   *www.irri.or*
The International Rice Research Institute (IRRI) was set up in 1960 by the Ford and Rockefeller foundations in cooperation with the government of the Philippines. It is a non-profit agricultural and training centre with offices in more than ten countries. Its objective is to find sustainable ways to improve the well being of rice farmers and consumers while protecting the environment. The IRRI research headquarters has laboratories and training facilities on a 250-hectare experimental farm on the campus of the University of the Philippines Los Banos, about 60 kilometres from Manila.

**International Securities Market Association**
International Securities Market Association (ISMA) is a Zurich-based self-regulatory organization and trade association for the international securities market. It oversees the functioning of the market by enforcing a code that covers trading, settlement and good practice. It has a series of recommendations

for member firms to comply. Its members are mostly banks and securities companies located in major financial centres in the world.

### International Shipping Service Centre (ISSC) (China)
The ISSC is set up by the Shanghai Shipping Exchange to simplify cargo inspection and cut costs. (See also: Shanghai Shipping Exchange)

### International Society of Financial Analysts
The Singapore Chapter of the International Society of Financial Analysts (ISFA) was formed in 1987. It serves as a forum for fund management professionals to exchange views on developments in the industry. It also aims to raise the professionalism of local financial analysts and fund managers. The Singapore Chapter of ISFA is affiliated to the Institute of Chartered Financial Analysts (ICFA) in the United States. The primary mission of the ICFA, established in 1962, is to enhance professional and ethical standards of those involved in the investment decision-making process through the adoption of a program of studies leading to the Chartered Financial Analyst (CFA) designation.

### International Standards on Auditing (ISA)
See International Federation of Accountants.

### International Standards Organization    *www.iso.org*
The International Standards Organization (ISO) was formed in 1947. The Geneva-based organization is a world-wide federation of national bodies with about 100 member countries. It sets quality standards for various products. Adoption of ISO standards has become the prerequisite for international business. The ISO is located at 1 rue de Varembe, CH-1211 Geneva, Switzerland.

### International Trade Centre    *www.intracen.org*
The International Trade Centre UNCTAD/WTO (ITC) was created in 1964 by the General Agreement on Tariffs and Trade (GATT). Since 1968 it has been operated jointly by GATT (now the World Trade Organization or WTO) and the United Nations Conference on Trade and Development (UNCTAD). As an executing agency of the United Nations Development Program (UNDP), the ITC is responsible for implementing UNDP-financed projects in developing countries related to trade promotion.

### International Trade Organization
See General Agreement on Tariffs and Trade.

### Investment Advisory Centre of Pakistan

The Investment Advisory Centre of Pakistan (IACP) was set up in 1963 by the government. The Karachi-based organization provides industrial and management consultancy.

### Investment Coordinating Board (Indonesia)

An Indonesian government agency that supervises domestic and foreign private investments.

### Investment Corporation of Pakistan

The Investment Corporation of Pakistan (ICP) was set up in 1966 to broaden the base of investment and to develop the capital market. It underwrites new issues of securities and debenture.

### Investment Credit Scheme (Indonesia)

The Investment Credit Scheme (Kredit Investasi) is supported by Bank Indonesia (Central Bank) to provide funds for industrialization. Under the scheme, medium and long term credits are provided to entrepreneurs to expand and modernize their operations.

### Investment Management Association of Singapore (IMAS)

The IMAS was registered in 1997. Its objectives are to promote professionalism in the investment management industry. Its Code of Ethics and Standards of Professional Conduct serves as a benchmark for practitioners. The IMAS participated in formulating the licensing examination for Investment Representatives which came into effect in December 1999.

### Investments Priority Plan (Philippines)

Under its Investments Priority Plan (IPP), the Philippine government provides fiscal and non-fiscal incentives under the Omnibus Investments Code to promote priority areas and activities in support of exports, infrastructure development and social reforms.

### IPE Brent Crude Oil Futures

In 1995, SIMEX (now SGX-DT) launched the world's first mutual offset energy contract in Brent crude oil futures. The mutual offset agreement is with London's International Petroleum Exchange (IPE). Under the arrangement, each Brent crude oil futures contract, worth 1,000 barrels of crude oil, can be bought or sold on either exchange during the 18 hours of combined trading on the two exchanges.

Pioneered by IPE, Brent crude is a cash-settled contract based on North Sea oil. Brent crude is used as a price benchmark for about 65% of the world's oil. In terms of trading volume, Brent crude futures is the world's second largest after light sweet crude futures traded on the New York Mercantile Exchange. As of June 1995, trading volume of Brent crude futures was about 40 million barrels a day. Major traders of Brent crude futures at SGX-DT are investment banks, oil refineries and independent oil companies in Singapore and other Asian countries.

### Islamabad Stock Exchange (Pakistan)   *www.ise.com.pk*
In Pakistan, the Islamabad Stock Exchange (G) Limited (ISE) was incorporated as a company limited by guarantee in 1989. It caters to the needs of the northern part of Pakistan. It has about 100 members, one-third of who are corporate bodies. There are about 300 listed securities traded through the automated system ISECTS. The ISE has introduced a reform package recommended by the Asian Development Bank through the government. As a result, the government board has been restructured and an Investors Protection Fund has been planned.

### Islamic Banking Act 1983 (Malaysia)
In Malaysia, this Act provides for the licensing and regulation of Islamic banking business. The Act has provisions on the financial requirement, ownership, control and management of Islamic banks, restrictions on their business, powers of supervision and control over Islamic banks.

### ISO 9000 Standard   *www.iso.org*
The ISO 9000 standard is about quality management. It enhances customer satisfaction by meeting quality requirements.

### ISO 14000 Standard   *www.iso.org*
The ISO 14000 standard is about environment management. A company that meets this standard minimizes harmful effect on the environment caused by its activities and continually improves its environmental performance.

### Jabatan Telekom Brunei
Jabatan Telekom Brunei (JTB) was formed in 1952. It is one of the six departments in the Ministry of Communication and offers domestic and international telecommunications services in voice, message and data communications.

## Jabotabek (Indonesia)
Greater Jakarta Area (covering Jakarta, Bogor, Tanerang and Bekasi).

## Jakarta Automated Trading System (JATS)
In 1995, the manual trading system at the Jakarta Stock Exchange (JSX) was replaced by the Jakarta Automated Trading System (JATS) to increase efficiency. JATS handles 50,000 transactions daily as compared to only 3,800 under the manual system. It is also an integrated system that connects trading, clearing, settlement, depository and broker accounting systems.

## Jakarta Initiative Task Force (Indonesia)    *www.jitk.or.id*
In 1998, as part of the overall financial restructuring strategy, the Indonesian Government formed the Jakarta Initiative Task Force (JITF) to serve as a mediator and facilitator of specific restructuring cases, particularly those involving foreign lenders.

## Jakarta Stock Exchange    *www.jsx.co.id*
The Jakarta Stock Exchange (JSX) became a privately owned and operated stock exchange in 1992. Its roots may be traced back to 1912 when the first stock exchange was set up. In 1995, the Jakarta Automated Trading System (JATS) was introduced to replace the manual system. In July 2000, scripless trading was introduced. In 2002, remote trading was initiated to increase market access and efficiency. (See also: Surabaya Stock Exchange)

## Jaminan Peneliharaan Kesehatan Masyarakat (Indonesia) (Guaranteed Health Maintenance for the People)
This health scheme was introduced in 1992 by the Indonesian government for its own employees. In 1997, a law was passed to allow the private sector to apply for licences to develop and manage insurance plans for their own employees. Employees protected by managed care policies can only seek covered medical treatment from clinics and hospitals under contract wth the employing company. In 1998, six of largest Indonesian companies launched their own managed care schemes. They were Bakrie, Astra, Pertamina, Bank Niaga, Lippo and Astek.

## Jamsostek
Jamsostek is Indonesia's social security insurance scheme introduced in 1993. It is governed by the Social Security Law of 1992 and supervised by the Ministry of Manpower. It provides wider benefits than the previous workers' compensation scheme. It includes death, disablement, retirement benefits and work-related accidents insurance and health insurance for workers and their

families. It is funded by compulsory contributions ranging from 7% to 11% of wages.

### Japan ASEAN Comprehensive Economic Partnership (JACEP)

This partnership was proposed by Japanese Prime Minister Koizumi in 2002 when he visited Southeast Asia. The framework is being worked out by economic ministers from the respective countries. The partnership would cover numerous sectors such as trade, investment, science and technology, human resource development, tourism and agriculture.

### Japan Bank for International Cooperation   *www.jbic.go.jp*

The purpose of Japan Bank for International Cooperation (JBIC) is to undertake lending and other financial operations to promote Japanese exports, imports or other Japanese economic activities overseas. It assists in economic and social development in developing areas in accordance with the principle that it shall not compete with commercial financial institutions. It has representative offices in major cities in the world.

### Japan Bond Research Institute

One of the bond rating companies in Japan.

### Japan Business Federation

See Nippon Keidanren.

### Japan Economic Foundation   *www.jef.or.jp*

Japan Economic Foundation was set up to promote understanding abroad of the state of Japan's economy, industry and trade in machine goods, and to explain Japan trade policies.

### Japan External Trade Organization (JETRO)   *www.jetro.go.jp*

The Japan External Trade Organization (popularly known as JETRO) was set up by the government in 1958 as a national organization to implement trade policy. It conducts a wide range of programs to promote trade and investment particularly for small and medium enterprises. With headquarters in Tokyo, JETRO has 36 offices in Japan and another 80 offices in 60 countries. In 1998, it merged with the Institute of Developing Economies (IDE), Japan's largest research organization, resulting in a new organization with comprehensive capabilities in trade and investment as well as in economic research.

### Japan Finance Corporation for Municipal Enterprises   *www.jfm.go.jp*

Japan Finance Corporation for Municipal Enterprises (JFM) is a government financial institution. It provides low cost long term finance for projects undertaken by municipal enterprises, local governments and public corporation set up by local governments. JFM funds are raised through bond issues guaranteed by the Japanese Government.

### Japan Finance Corporation for Small Business    *www.jfs.go.sp*
Japan Finance Corporation for Small Business (JFS) is a government financial institution. It provides funds to help the growth of small businesses while supplementing private financial institutions. For example, JFS provides long term (up to 20 years), fixed rate, low interest stable financing which is difficult to obtain private financial institutions.

### Japan Institute of International Affairs    *www.jiia.or.jp*
The Japan Institute of International Affairs (JIIA) was founded in 1959 through the initiative of former Prime Minister Shigeru Yoshida. It is a private, non-profit independent research organization. It fosters the study of international politics, economics and law.

### Japan International Cooperation Agency    *www.jica.go.jp*
The Japan International Cooperation Agency (JICA) was formed in 1974 to administer Japan's official development assistance programs. Under Japan's Official Development Assistance Program, JICA is in charge of bilateral grants while the Overseas Economic Cooperation Fund (OECF) is in charge of bilateral loans. (See also: Japan's Official Development Assistance)

### Japan Regional Development Corporation    *www.region.go.jp*
Japan Regional Development Corporation started in 1974 under the Japan Regional Development Corporation Act. It carries out activities to encourage people and industry to relocate to local areas from metropolitan areas. It contributes to the development of affluent and comfortable regional communities.

### Japan Securities Clearing Corporation
Japan Securities Clearing Corporation (JSCC) is a wholly-owned subsidiary of the Tokyo Stock Exchange with which securities companies and other financial institutions have accounts. The JSCC also provides stock certificate custodian services for Japanese shares listed on foreign stock exchanges.

### Japan Securities Dealers Association
In the 1950s, there were more than a thousand securities companies in Japan, with 33 regional securities associations. In 1973, these associations merged to

form the Japan Securities Dealers Association. It is a self-regulatory organization and plays an active role in the development of regulations and matters relating to the securities industry. In Japan, over-the-counter (OTC) stocks must be registered with JSDA which provides the rules of fair practice for OTC stock transactions. OTC stocks are traded on a computerized on-line trading JASDAQ system.

### Japan Securities Depository Centre
The Japan Securities Depository Centre (JASDEC) was set up in 1985 as the central securities depository institution under the supervision of the Ministry of Finance. It is a custody agent as well as a clearing agent for Tokyo Stock Exchange.

### Japan Singapore Economic Partnership Agreement
The Japan Singapore Economic Partnership Agreement (JSEPA) is a Free Trade Agreement signed between Japan and Singapore. Under this agreement, about 98% of bilateral trade has been liberalized. About 94% of Singapore's exports enter Japan duty-free. One major benefit from JSEPA is the mutual recognition agreement which dispenses with the need to test Singapore's electronic products in Japan once they have been tested by a recognized body in Singapore. JSEPA ensures that investors enjoy the same treatment from the host country as that of companies of the host country.

### Japanese Bankers Association    www.zenginkyo.or.jp
The Japanese Bankers Association (JBS) was formed in 1945 by the regionally based bankers association nationwide. In 1999, JBA allowed individual banks to join as direct members. It has about 140 full members (banks), 47 associate members (banks) and 72 special members (bankers associations). In addition to JBA, there are several other banking associations such as the Regional Banker Association of Japan, the Second Association of Japanese Banks and the Trust Companies Association of Japan.

### Japan's Official Development Assistance
Japan's Official Development Assistance (ODA) began in 1954 when it joined the Colombo Plan, an organization set up in 1950 to assist Asian countries in their socio-economic development. There are three categories of ODA: (a) bilateral grants, (b) bilateral loans and (c) contribution to multilateral donor organization. Grants are undertaken by the Japan International Cooperation Agency (JICA).Loans are managed by Overseas Economic Cooperation Fund (OECF).

**JCB Corporation**
JCB (Japan Credit Bureau) is the largest credit card company in Japan.

**JETRO**
See Japan External Trade Organization.

**Joint Financial Intelligence Unit** *www.info.gov.hk/police/jfiu*
In Hong Kong, the Joint Financial Intelligence Unit was set up in 1989 to receive reports about suspicious financial activity made under the provisions of the Drug Trafficking (Recovery of Proceeds) Ordinance (DTROP) and the Organized and Serious Crimes Ordinance (OSCO). The unit is jointly run by the Police Force and the Customs and Excise Department. It does not investigate suspicious transactions. Its role is to receive reports and pass them to the appropriate investigative unit such as the Narcotics Bureau or the Organized Crime & Triad Bureau. In Hong Kong, the Joint Financial Intelligence Unit was set up in 1989 to receive reports about suspicious financial activity made under the provisions of the Drug Trafficking (Recovery of Proceeds) Ordinance (DTROP) and the Organized and Serious Crimes Ordinance (OSCO). The unit is jointly run by the Police Force and the Customs and Excise Department. It does not investigate suspicious transactions. Its role is to receive reports and pass them to the appropriate investigative unit such as the Narcotics Bureau or the Organized Crime & Triad Bureau.

**Jollibee Foods Corporation (Philippines)**
Jollibee Foods Corporation is the largest Philippine fast-food chain with 208 domestic outlets and 24 outlets overseas. It has opened new branches in Brunei, Dubai, Hong Kong, Kuwait, Papua New Guinea, Xiamen (China), Saipan, United States and Vietnam. It is developing the Donut Magic concept in Saudi Arabia, Bahrain and Vietnam. It was recognized as the Philippines' most innovative corporation responding to customer needs by the *Far Eastern Economic Review*. Jollibee was cited by *Forbes* magazine as one of the world's 200 best small companies.

**JSX LQ 45 Index (Indonesia)**
The Jakarta Stock Exchange LQ45 Index was introduced in 1997. It consists of 45 stocks that are of high market value and liquidity. The aggregate market value of these stocks accounts for more than 70% of the total market capitalization on the JSX. It accounts for about 72% of the total value of transaction in the market. The index thus reflects the changes in the market value of all stocks that are actively traded. The LQ45 is meant to complement the existing Composite Index.

**Jurong Town Corporation (JTC) (Singapore)**    *www.jtc.gov.sg*
In Singapore, the JTC was set up as a statutory board in 1968 to develop and manage industrial estates to support Singapore's industrialization plan. It now manages 30 industrial estates and provides facilities to about 4,600 companies. The largest is the Jurong Industrial Estate which is a large scale integrated industrial real estate.

**Kabushiki Kaisa (KK)**
Japanese joint stock company.

**Kabutocho**
Tokyo's financial district.

**Kabuya**
Japanese slang for stockbroker.

**Kai Tak Airport (Hong Kong)**
Hong Kong's Kai Tak International Airport was opened in 1930. Before its closure in 1998, it was the world's third business airport for international passengers and busiest for international freight. Kai Tak was constrained by its urban location. Flights were subject to an overnight curfew. About 60 airlines operated from Kai Tak, which had only one runway. In a typical day, over 420 aircraft arrived or departed or one every two minutes at peak period. On 5 July 1998, it was replaced with the new Hong Kong International Airport (HKIA) located at Chek Lap Kok. (See also: Chek Lap Kok Airport)

**Kamikaze Pricing**
This is a slang term for predatory pricing by a Japanese institution to gain market share.

**Kaohsiung Export Processing Zone**
In Taiwan, Kaohsiung Export Processing Zone (KEPZ) was set up in 1966. It is located in the southern port of Kaohsiung County.

**Karachi Electric Supply Corporation**
Karachi Electric Supply Corporation (KESC) has the licence to generate, transmit and distribute power in Karachi and its suburban areas. It is undergoing the process of being privatization after the UBS Securities (Pakistan) Ltd was appointed as financial advisor in 1998.

**Karachi Export Processing Zone** *www.epza.com.pk*
In Pakistan, the Karachi Export Processing Zone (KEPZ) is the first EPZ developed by the Export Processing Zones Authority (EPZA). It is located 10 kilometres from the container Port of Qasim and the Karachi International Airport. It provides a wide range of incentives for investors. They include 100% ownership and repatriation of capital and profits, duty free import of machinery and equipment. (See also: Export Processing Zones Authority)

**Karachi Port**
Karachi Port is the main port in Pakistan handling most of its dry and liquid cargo. Port Quasim is located south of Karachi and is the second deep seaport of Pakistan.

**Karachi Stock Exchange** *www.kse.com.pk*
In Pakistan, the Karachi Stock Exchange started in 1947 and was converted to a company limited by guarantee in 1949. It is the oldest and the largest among the three exchanges. The other two are Lahore Exchange (1970) and Islamabad Exchange (1992). It has about 200 members. There are 88 corporate members of whom eight are publicly quoted companies. KSE has about 750 listed securities. Since the 1980s, steps have been taken to increase the attractiveness of the market. Foreign exchange regulations have been liberalized and the market is open to foreign investors.

**Katunayake Export Processing Zone (Sri Lanka)**
The Katunayake Investment Processing Zone (KIPZ) was set up in 1978 as the first EPZ in Sri Lanka. The 200-hectare zone is located near Katunayake International Airport and about 30 kilometres from Colombo Port.

**Keidanren** *www.keidanren.org.jp*
In Japan, Keidanren (Japanese Federation of Economic Organizations) was formed in 1946 to help to reconstruct the war-devastated Japanese economy. In May 2002, it merged with the Nikkeiren (Japan Federation of Employers' Organization) to form the Nippon Keidanren (Japan Business Federation). (See also: Nippon Keidanren)

**Keiretsu (Japan)**
This is a group of Japanese companies, usually centred round a bank and with interlocked cross shareholding. Examples are conglomerates such as Mitsui, Mitsubishi, Sumitomo and Sanwa.

**Keisan Tanshin (Japan)**
This is a quick report of three or four pages of financial highlights of a company.

**Kepres (Indonesia)**
Presidential Instruction.

**Khazanah Bonds**
In Malaysia, these bonds are issued by Khazanah Nasional Berhad, the wholly-owned subsidiary of the Ministry of Finance primarily for benchmarking purposes.

**Kina**
This is the currency of Papua New Guinea.

**Kina Securities Limited (Papua New Guinea)**   *www.kina.com.pg*
Kina Securities Limited is a leading stock broking firm in Papua New Guinea. It provides floating, underwriting and placement services for new and existing ventures. It is one of largest fund managers in PNG.

**Kingai Fund (Japan)**
In Japan, kingai (kingaishin) funds are fund trusts managed by trust banks for institutional investors such as banks, life insurance companies and trading companies.

**Kip**
Currency of Lao PDR.

**Kiwi Bonds**
Kiwi bonds were first issued in 1985 to provide a default-free retail instrument. They have maturities of 6 months, 1, 2 and 4 years. Interest is payable quarterly or compounded quarterly and paid on maturity. The minimum investment is NZ$1,000 and in multiples of NZ$100 thereafter. No single bondholder is permitted to hold more than NZ$250,000 of any one issue. The interest rates on Kiwi bonds are set at a margin below that of government bonds of similar maturity. Kiwi bonds have been a relatively popular retail investment with investors typically holding to maturity.

**PT Kliring Penjaminan Efek Indonesia, KPEI**   *www.kpei.co.id*
See Indonesian Clearing and Guarantee Corporation.

## KLSE Bernama Real-time Information Services Sdn Bhd (KULBER) (Malaysia)

In Malaysia, KULBER was incorporated in 1986. It is a joint venture between Securities Clearing Automated Network Services Sdn Bhd (SCANS) and the national news agency Pertubuhan Berita Nasional Malaysia (BERNAMA). KULBER provides information about the Kuala Lumpur Stock Exchange (KLSE) to local and foreign information vendors. Information includes buy and sell quotes, closing prices, volumes and indices. (See also: Securities Clearing Automated Network Services Sdn Bhd, SCANS).

## KLSE Composite Index(Malaysia)

This is a market weighted index for stocks listed on the Kuala Lumpur Stock Exchange.

## Koggala Export Processing Zone (Sri Lanka)

The Koggala Export Processing Zone (KgEPZ) was set up in 1991 as the third EPZ in Sri Lanka. The 180-hectare zone is located in the Southern Province and is about 16 kilometres from the Port of Galle. It is served by a highway, railway and a domestic airstrip.

## Kokusai Denshin Denwa (KDD)

In Japan, Kokusai Denshin Denwa Company (KDD) was formed in 1953 but traces its history up to its predecessors in 1871. For almost a century, it was Japan's sole supplier of international telecommunications services.

## Konsortium Perkapalan Berhad (KPB)(Malaysia)

In Malaysia, KPB was set up in 1982 to undertake container haulage with a modest fleet of 15 prime movers and 60 trailers. In the early days, its operations were confined to the northern region with Penang as its hub. In 1989, when the Malaysian government removed geographical restriction on hauliers, KPB expanded its operations to Port Klang (central Malaysia) and Pasir Gudang (southern Malaysia). KPB is listed on the Kuala Lumpur Stock Exchange. It is now Malaysia's second largest shipping company and biggest container haulier. The other major company is MISC.

## Koperasi Unit Desa (KUD) (Indonesia)

KUD is a village unit cooperative established by Indonesian farmers. It distributes farm inputs, provides credit to farmers and markets farm products.

## Korps Pegawai Republik Indonesia (KORPRI)

See Indonesian Civil Servants Corps.

## KOSGORO (Indonesia)
This is a mass organization affiliated with Golkar.

## Kostrad (Indonesia)
Army Strategic Command.

## PT Krakatau Steel (Indonesia)
This is a major Indonesian steel producer. It has many subsidiaries including PT Krakatau Engineering Corporation which is involved in engineering and construction management.

## Kram (Cambodia)
Law.

## Kredit Investasi (Indonesia)
See Investment Credit Scheme.

## Kredit Investasi Kechil (KIK) (Indonesia)
Indonesian investment credit scheme designed to finance the medium and long term needs of small entrepreneurs.

## Kredit Usaha Kecil (KUK) (Indonesia)
## (Small scale credit program)
This is an Indonesian financing program under which banks are required to channel a specified percentage of their loans to small businesses.

## Kredit Usaha Tani (KUT) (Indonesia)
This is an Indonesian credit scheme to finance the needs of farmers and smallholders especially for food crops.

## Kret (Cambodia)
Decree.

## Krung Thai Bank    www.ktb.co.th
Krung Thai Bank (KTB) started in 1966 after the merger of the Agriculture Bank and Provincial Bank. As the Ministry of Finance is its main shareholder, the "wayupak bird" which is the official seal of the Ministry has been adopted as the bank's logo. In 1987, the KTB was entrusted by the government to administer the "4 April Project" in succession of the Bank of Thailand (Central Bank) to solve financial problems faced by some Thai financial institutions and tool over the Sayam Bank.

In 1989, KTB was listed on the Stock Exchange of Thailand. In 1994, it was registered as a public company limited. In 1995, it was granted the status of "Group 1 State Enterprises". KTB has about 500 domestic branches and 12 foreign offices.

## KSO
KSO is an Indonesian acronym for Joint Operation Scheme. It is a scheme whereby the government award rights to operators to provide domestic telephone services jointly with Telkom. KSO contractors operate outside Jakarta and East Java.

## Kuala Belalong Field Studies Centre (Brunei)
See Universiti Brunei Darussalam.

## Kuala Lumpur Commodity Exchange
The KLCE was set up in 1980. In 1985, under the Malaysian Commodities Trading Act, KLCE was restructured and an independent Commodities Trading Commission was formed to supervise and regulate commodity futures trading in Malaysia. The KLCE traded in crude palm oil futures, RBD palm olein and crude palm kernel oil futures, cocoa futures, and SMR20 rubber futures and tin futures. In 1996, KLCE set up a wholly-owned subsidiary, the Malaysian Monetary Exchange (MME), a financial futures market which traded in the 3-month KLIBOR financial futures. In 1998, KLCE and MME merged to become the Commodity and Monetary Exchange of Malaysia (COMMEX). (See also: COMMEX Malaysia, Kuala Lumpur Options and Financial Futures Exchange and Malaysian Monetary Exchange)

## Kuala Lumpur Composite Index (KLCI)
KLCI refers to the share price performance of 100 component stocks on the main board of the Kuala Lumpur Stock Exchange.

## Kuala Lumpur Inter-bank Offer Rate
KLIBOR is the rate quoted by banks in the Kuala Lumpur inter-bank market where the participants are banks and other financial institutions.

## Kuala Lumpur International Airport (KLIA)
In Malaysia, KLIA was opened in 1998. The 10,000-hectare airport is located at Sepang, about 70 kilometres south of Kuala Lumpur. It has replaced the old airport at Subang. The first phase of the RM 9-billion KLIA can handle 25 million passengers a year while the capacity of Subang was only 16 million.

**Kuala Lumpur Options and Financial Futures Exchange (KLOFFE)**
KLOFFE was set up as Malaysia's first financial futures market. It traded in the KLCE composite index (KLCI) stock index futures, and stock index options. In 1996, Malaysia set up a second financial futures market, the Malaysian Monetary Exchange (MME) to trade in the 3-month KLIBOR financial future. In January 1999, KLOFFE was acquired by the KLSE. (See also: Malaysian Monetary Exchange)

**Kuala Lumpur Stock Exchange**
The KLSE was set up in 1983 when the Stock Exchange of Malaysia and Singapore was split up into two exchanges, the other one being the Stock Exchange of Singapore. The operations are governed by the Securities Industry Act which was implemented by Registrar of Companies until 1993 when such functions were taken over by the newly formed Securities Commission. Similarly, the Capital Issues Committee (CIC) used to supervise the issue of shares and other securities by companies applying for listing on the exchange.

**Kustodian Sentral Efek Indonesia (KSEI)**  *www.ksei.co.id*
See Indonesian Central Securities Depository.

**L3 Regulation**
See Legal lending limit regulations.

**Laboratories for Information Technology**
See Science and Engineering Research Council (Singapore).

**Labour Banks in Japan**  *www.rokin.or.jp*
In Japan, the first two labour banks were founded in 1950 in Okayama and Hyogo prefectures. Labour banks are financial cooperatives which are formed from worker-based organizations. They operate according to the Labour Bank Law. Their objective is to raise the living standards of workers by promoting the activities of labour unions and consumer cooperatives. In 1998, there were 41 labour banks. Several mergers have taken place and by 2002, they have been reorganized into 13 banks. Labour banks are managed by the Financial Services Agency and the Ministry of Labour. In addition, the Rokinren Bank, a financial institution is responsible for the fund management of labour banks. The National Association of Labour Banks is one of the central administrative organs.

**Labour Standards Law  (Taiwan)**
In Taiwan, the Labour Standards Law was introduced in 1984. It sets standards for major industries. These are standards on working hours, overtime pay, and other terms and conditions of employment.

**Labuan Offshore Financial Services Authority**
In Malaysia, the Labuan Offshore Financial Services Authority (LOFSA) is a statutory agency set up in 1996 to supervise the financial services industry in the Labuan International Offshore Financial Centre. It administers the Offshore Banking Act, the Offshore Insurance Act, Labuan Companies Act, Labuan Trust Companies Act, Labuan Offshore Limited Partnerships Act, Labuan Offshore Securities Industry Act and others.

**Laguna International Industrial Park**
In the Philippines, the Laguna International Industrial Park (LIIP) is located in the Barrios of Ganado and Mamplasan, Municipality of Binan, Laguna. It is about 12 kilometres from Manila.

**Laguna Lake Development Authority (Philippines)**
In the Philippines, the Laguna Lake Development Authority is the leading agency which promotes the development and balanced growth in the Laguna de Bay basin. The area includes parts of Manila, Quezon, Pasay, Taguig, Pateros, Marikina, Caloocan and Muntinlupa.

**Lahore Stock Exchange (Pakistan)**   *www.lse.brain.net.com.pk*
The Lahore Stock Exchange started in 1970. It has 150 members and about 600 companies are listed on the exchange. It is one of three exchanges in Pakistan. The others are Karachi and Islamabad exchanges.

**Lakh (India)**
100,000.

**Land Bank of Taiwan**   *www.landbank.com.tw*
The Land Bank of Taiwan started in 1946. It is a wholly-owned government bank which specializes in providing credit for real estate and agriculture.

**Land Bank of the Philippines**
The Land Bank of the Philippines (LBP) provides financial support for agrarian reform in the Philippines. Its charter is contained in the Code of Agrarian Reforms. It collects deposits and grants loans to farmers' associations for the production, marketing of crops and commodities.

**Land Transport Authority (Singapore)**   *www.lta.gov.sg*
In Singapore, the Land Transport Authority (LTA) is a statutory board under the Ministry of Transport. It plans, develops and manages Singapore's land transport system.

## Lang Co Tourist Complex

Lang Co is a seaside town located along Highway One between Danang and Hue in Vietnam. A US$750 million mega tourism project is being developed by a 50-year joint venture between Hue's Huong Giang Tourist Co and Japan's Fujiken Group. When completed, the tourist resort is expected to host one million tourists annually.

## Lao Trade Promotion Centre    *www.moc.gov.la/ltpcprofile.html*

The Lao Trade Promotion Centre (LTPC) was set up in 2001 under the Ministry of Commerce. It assists Lao manufacturers and exporters to produce and market their products.

## Laos — Banking Reform

In March 1988, the Council of Ministers passed Decree No. 11 on the Reform of the Lao Banking System. The objective was to move away from state planning and control. As a result, the various branches of the State Bank became autonomous commercial banks. These were: Bank Sethathilath, Bank Nakhoneluang, and Foreign Commercial Bank of Lao PDR (Banque pour le Commerce Exterrior Lao).

The State Bank was renamed the Bank of Lao PDR (BOL) to function as the central bank. It has been empowered to license, supervise and regulate financial services. It also keeps the national reserves. The Foreign Commercial Bank acts as the nation's main foreign exchange bank. In 1989, a state-private joint venture bank was set up. After Bangkok Bank opened a branch in Vientiane in 1993, several other foreign banks were also allowed to open branches.

## Laos — Foreign Exchange Control

Before the introduction of banking reform in Lao PDR, the Foreign Commercial Bank of Lao PDR (Banque pour le Commerce Exterrior Lao) had a monopoly over foreign exchange transactions. Under the Foreign Exchange Decree, all foreign exchange transactions must be carried out through institutions authorized by the Bank of the Lao PDR. These institutions include commercial banks and foreign exchange dealers. They are required to submit periodic reports to the BOL.

## Law on Cooperatives (Vietnam)

In Vietnam, the Law on Cooperatives was introduced in 1996 to regularize the establishment, organization and operations of cooperatives.

## Law on Credit Institutions (Vietnam)

In 1997, Vietnam's National Assembly adopted the Law on Credit Institutions. Important provisions included the following areas: banking licences, board of management, internal control, loan security, credit risk, mandatory liquidity and capital adequacy ratio, bankruptcy.

## Law on the Promotion and Management of Foreign Investment (Laos)

In Laos, this law was passed in 1994 to replace the Foreign Investment Law of 1988. For a joint venture with local partners, the foreign investor must contribute at least 30% equity capital. Property and investments are fully protected by law. There is no requisition, confiscation or nationalization, except for "public purpose", in which case they will get prompt, adequate and effective compensation.

## L-Star 1 and L-Star 2 (Laos)

These are two multimedia satellites owned by Laostar, a joint venture by the Laotian Government and Asian Broadcasting and Communication Network. Each satellite is equipped with band transponders to provide multimedia telecommunications including direct TV broadcast that will serve Southeast Asia. The launch service was provided by Arianespace.

## Lazard Vietnam Fund

This is a closed-end investment fund listed on the Dublin Stock Exchange.

## Leaprodexim

See Vietnam National Leather and Footwear Corporation.

## Legal Adjustments and Reforms for Globalising the Economy

In India, the Legal Adjustments and Reforms for Globalising the Economy (LARGE) was a research project initiated by 1993 by the Ministry of Finance and the United Nations Development Program (UNDP). It involved the National Law School of India in Bangalore and the objective was to examine economic legislation in India to make it more market friendly.

## Legal lending limit (L3) regulation

This is an Indonesian banking regulation. It is the maximum amount of credit that is to be provided to a bank's owners or its business subsidiaries. According to new regulations that took effect from 1997, a bank is only allowed to provide credit to its own group at a maximum of 10% of its equity.

**Lembaga Getak Malaysia**
See Malaysian Rubber Board.

**Lembaga Urusan dan Tabung Haji (LUTH)**
See Pilgrims Management and Fund Board.

**Lemhannas**
**(National Resilience Institute)**
Indonesian national defence college administered under the Department of Defence and Security.

**Liberalized Exchange Rate Management System (India)**
In India, the Liberalized Exchange Rate Management System (LERMS) was introduced in March 1992. It was a dual exchange rate system with an official and a market rate. The market rate was applied to 60% of all current account transactions, the remaining 40% was converted at the official rate. The exchange rate was reunified at the free market rate from March 1993.

**Lien Khuong Airport (Vietnam)**
In Vietnam, this airport serves the Central Highland's resort of Dalat.

**Life Insurance Corporation of India**   *www.licindia.com*
The Life Insurance Corporation (LIC) of India provides a wide range of life insurance products. Its subsidiaries include: LIC International, LIC (Nepal), LIC Housing Finance and LIC Mutual Fund.

**Life Underwriters' Association of Singapore**
The Life Underwriters' Association of Singapore (LUA) was formerly known as the Singapore Insurance Agents' Association which was formed in 1969. The new name was adopted in 1978 to reflect its representation of only life insurance agents. This was also to enable the association to maintain closer ties with life underwriter associations in other countries.

**Lifelong Learning Fund (Singapore)**
In Singapore, the $5 billion Lifelong Learning Fund was set up in August 2000. It signals the government's strong emphasis on Lifelong Learning. It provides resources to support training programs for workers. The Lifelong Learning Fund supports initiatives by community groups provide learning opportunities for the community. The Ministry of Manpower manages this fund as part of its overall Manpower 21 plan.

**Lippo Group (Indonesia)**
This is an Indonesian conglomerate which includes Lippobank, Lippo
Securities, Lippo Life, Lippoland Development and others. The founding
shareholders were from the Riady family.

**Lippo Karawaci (Indonesia)**
Lippo Karawaci is a new 2,400-hectare residential, office and retail community
located at Tangerang, West of Jakarta. Development started in 1992 by PT Lippo
Karawaci, the property division of the Lippo Group. There are more than 3,300
residential units including house, shophouses and apartments to cater to different
lifestyles. The modern shopping centre includes Lippo Supermall which attracts
some 700,000 shoppers a week with 230 shops, restaurants, cinemas and an
amusement centre with a roller coaster. More than 6,000 employees work in the
business park which provides offices for the Lippo Group and other well-known
companies such as PT Matahari and PT Dynaplast.

Education centres include the Pelita Harapan school with 1,200 pupils and
Pelita Harapan University which started in 1994 with cooperation from
institutions from western countries. There is also a 65-hectare golf course. The
Imperial Country Club has a full range of facilities including tennis, squash
courts, fitness centre, sauna, whirlpool and swimming pool. The Siloan
Gleneagles Hospital has 350 beds.

**Lippobank (Indonesia)**
Lippobank is the banking arm of Lippo Group. It is one of Indonesia's largest
retail commercial banks with more than 300 branches in about 100 cities. It
has joint ventures with foreign partners including Banque Nationale de Paris,
Tokai Bank, Daiwa bank and Bankers Trust. It also has merchant bank
operations in Sydney, Bangkok, Kuala Lumpur, Hanoi and Ho Chi Minh City.

**Liquid Asset Requirement (Malaysia)**
In Malaysia, banks and other financial institutions are required by Bank Negara
(Central Bank) to maintain a sum equivalent to the Liquid Asset Ratio which
is a specified percentage of their eligible liabilities.

**Loan (Local) Ordinance, 1959 (Malaysia)**
In Malaysia, this is the ordinance that authorizes the raising of loans by the
government for the purposes of the Development Fund. The Act appoints the
central bank as the agent of the government and enables the raising of the loans
by way of scripless book-entry.

**Local Initiative Facility for the Urban Environment (LIFE)**
Under the United Nation Development Program (UNDP), the LIFE initiative involves 12 pilot countries promoting dialogue between local governments, non-government organizations (NGOs) and low income residents to improve urban environment.

**London Inter-bank Offer Rate**
LIBOR is the rate quoted by banks in the Eurocurrency Unit inter-bank deposit market.

**London Sumatra Indonesia (Lonsum)**
Lonsum is a large Indonesian plantation company with a history of about 100 years. The company was bought over by Indonesian businessmen from Britain's Harrisons & Crosfield. It operates 19 plantations (15 in Sumatra, the others in Java and Bali) with an area of more than 70,000 hectares.

**Lok Sabha (India)**
House of the People (Indian Parliament).

**Long Binh Industrial Park (Vietnam)**
This industrial park is located in Long Binh District, Dong Nai Province in Vietnam. It is developed by AGTEX (an affiliate of Vietnam's Ministry of Defence) and Japan's Nissho Iwai. Of the 100 hectares, 50 will be used as an export processing zone and the other 50 will be an industrial zone. Long Binh is about 30 kilometres northeast of Ho Chi Minh City, near Highway One and other national routes.

**Low Exercise Price Option (LEPO) (Australia)**
An All Ords LEPO is a European call option over the Australian Stock Exchange (ASX) All Ordinaries (All Ords) Share Price Index with a 1 point strike price.

**LQ45 Index (Indonesia)**
This is the stock index used in the Jakarta Stock Exchange. It consists of 45 stocks of high market value and good liquidity listed on the exchange.

**Mactan Export Process Zone (Philippines)**
In the Philippines, the Mactan Export Process Zone (MEPZ) was established in 1979 as a self-contained industrial estate for exported-oriented industries. It is located on Mactan Island, about 14 kilometres from Cebu city. It provides a wide range of investment incentives including tax-free imports of equipment and materials, tax holidays, no limitation on foreign ownership.

**Majelis Permusyswaratan Rakyat (MPR)**
MPR or People's Consultative Assembly consists of 1000 members drawn from a broad cross-section of the community, including all members of the Parliament. The President is elected by the Assembly for five years. The MPR approves the guidelines of the state policy and can amend the Constitution.

**Mahkamah Agung (Indonesia)**
This is the Supreme Court of Indonesia. It is the judicial branch of the State.

**Majlis Tindakan Ekonomi Negara (Malaysia)**
See National Economic Action Council.

**Malay Chamber of Commerce Malaysia (MCCM)**
In Malaysia, the MCCM was founded in 1957 under the name Associated Malay Chambers of Commerce of Malaya. In 1974, it was renamed Malay Chamber of Commerce and Industry of Malaysia. Its present name was adopted in 1992. The Chamber has branches in every state of Peninsular Malaysia. Membership is open to individuals, companies and organizations involved in businesses or industries which are fully owned by Malays. The MCCM provides a wide range of services to members to promote their business. It represents members in government bodies and agencies or special committees relevant to trade, industry and commerce. It issues certificate of origin to Malaysian goods for export. It is an affiliate of the National Chambers of Commerce and Industries of Malaysia.

**Malaysia Airlines**    *www.malaysia-airlines.com*
Malaysia Airlines System (MAS) started in 1947 with a five-seater aircraft. It now has a fleet of more than 100 aircraft and flies to more than 100 destinations across six continents.

**Malaysia Airports Berhad**
This is a wholly-owned government company incorporated in 1992. It manages all airports in Malaysia including five international airports (KLIA at Sepang, Penang, Langkawi, Kota Kinabalu and Kuching), 14 domestic airports and 18 short take-off and landing airports.

**Malaysia Banking Mediation Bureau**
The Malaysia Banking Mediation Bureau was set up in 1997 by the banking industry to provide dispute resolving services to customers. The Bureau has the power to make awards up to RM 25,000 and such award is binding on the bank or finance company.

### Malaysia External Trade Development Corporation (MATRADE)
*www.matrade.gov.my*

MATRADE was set up in 1993 as the external trade promotion arm of Malaysia's Ministry of International Trade and Industry (MITI). It promotes the export of Malaysian goods and services. It plans and implements trade promotion activities locally and abroad.

### Malaysia Incorporated Policy
The Malaysia Incorporated Policy (Dasar Syarikatan Malaysia) was introduced in 1983. The objective was to strengthen cooperation between the private and public sectors in order to achieve national objectives.

### Malaysian Industrial Development Authority     *www.mida.gov.my*
The Malaysian Industrial Development Authority (MIDA) is the main government agency to promote and coordinate industrial development. It is the first point of contact for investors who intend to set up manufacturing and related services. It makes recommendations to the Ministry of International Trade and Industry policies and strategies on industrial promotion and development.

### Malaysia Monetary Exchange (MME)
Malaysia Monetary Exchange (MME) was formerly known as the Kuala Lumpur Futures Market. It was incorporated in 1992 as a wholly-owned subsidiary of the Kuala Lumpur Commodity Exchange (KLCE). The MME traded in 3-month KLIBOR futures contract that was based on a Ringgit interbank time deposit in the Kuala Lumpur Wholesale Money Market having a principal value of RM1 million with a 3-month or 2 serial months maturity.

In December 1998, the Kuala Lumpur Commodity Exchange (KLCE) changed its name to the Commodity and Monetary Exchange of Malaysia (or COMMEX Malaysia) and merged with its subsidiary Malaysian Monetary Exchange (MME). (See also: Kuala Lumpur Commodity Exchange, Kuala Lumpur Options and Financial Futures Exchange; Malaysian Derivatives Clearing House)

### Malaysian Accounting Board
See Financial Reporting Act 1997 (Malaysia).

### Malaysian Administrative Modernization and Management Planning Unit (MAMPU)
In Malaysia, this is the planning unit in the Prime Minister's Department.

**Malaysian Agricultural Research and Development Institute** *www.mardi.my*
The Malaysian Agricultural Research and Development Institute (MARDI) was set up in 1969. Its main functions are to conduct research on the production, utilization and processing of all crops (except rubber and oil palm) and livestock. It is also a centre for the collection and dissemination of information on agriculture.

**Malaysian American Electronics Industries Association (MAEI)**
In Malaysia, MAEI companies include American companies such as Motorola and Texas Instruments.

**Malaysian Associated Indian Chamber of Commerce and Industry (MAICCI)**
In Malaysia, the MAICCI was formed in 1951 and was known as the Associated Indian Chambers of Commerce & Industry (AICCI). It represents the Malaysian Indian business community and comprises state members from Kuala Lumpur, Selangor, Penang, Perak, Negeri Sembilan, Malacca, Johore, Kelantan and Pahang Indian chambers. It promotes cooperation among various Indian Chambers of Commerce and Industry in the States of Malaysia and coordinate their activities. It makes representations to the federal or state government on matters affecting the interests of its members. It is an affiliate of the National Chamber of Commerce and Industry of Malaysia (NCCIM).

**Malaysian Central Depository (MCD)**
MCD is a subsidiary of Kuala Lumpur Stock Exchange set up in 1990 to provide central clearing and settlement of securities. The Securities Industry (Central Depository) Act 1991 authorized the setting up of a Central Depository and provided the legal framework and safeguards for users in the Central Depository System (CDS).

The MCD operate a Central Depository System for shares, bonds, debentures and other securities. Investors use CDS for safekeeping of shares. Stockbroking companies are appointed Authorized Depository Agents (ADAs) to provide CDS services to investors. All individual and corporate investors must open CDS accounts with ADAs to trade in securities. Financial institutions (banks, finance companies, insurance companies, unit trusts) and other institutional investors participate in CDS as Authorized Direct Members.

**Malaysian Exchange of Securities Dealing and Automated Quotation (MESDAQ)** *www.mesdaq.com.my*
MESDAQ was set up in 1997. It is a Malaysian stock exchange that specializes

in growth companies especially those with technology-based operations. Its board of directors formulates policies and issues guidelines for the operations of the exchange.

## Malaysian Derivatives Clearing House Berhad (MDCH)

The MDCH was a clearing house for trade transacted at the Malaysian Monetary Exchange (MME). In 1998, the Futures Industry (Amendment & Consolidation) Act 1997 came into force and repealed the Commodities Trading Act 1985. It rationalized the regulation of the futures market in Malaysia and authorized the merger of the Commodities Trading Commission (CTC) with the Securities Commission. The MDCH also merged with the Malaysian Futures Clearing Corporation (MFCC). (See also: Malaysian Monetary Exchange)

## Malaysian Futures Clearing Corporation (MFCC)

In 1998, the Futures Industry (Amendment & Consolidation) Act 1997 came into force and repealed the Commodities Trading Act 1985. It rationalized the regulation of the futures market in Malaysia and authorized the merger of the Commodities Trading Commission (CTC) with the Securities Commission. The Malaysian Derivatives Clearing House also merged with the Malaysian Futures Clearing Corporation.

## Malaysian Futures & Options Registered Representative Course

The MFORR course is designed for persons who are interested to register as futures broker's representatives, futures fund manager's representatives, futures trading advisers and their representatives in Malaysia. In addition to knowledge on futures and options, the course covers rules, regulations, trading procedures and operations of the Kuala Lumpur Options and Financial Futures Exchange (KLOFFE) and Malaysia Commodities & Monetary Exchange.

## Malaysian Institute of Economic Research (MIER)

In Malaysia, the MIER is a government-backed economic think-tank. One of its activities is to make forecast of economic growth.

## Malaysian Institute of Microelectronic Systems    *www.mimos.my*

The Malaysian Institute of Microelectronic Systems (MIMOS) is a research organization for the information communication technology (ICT). It also advises the government on policies and strategies on the development of ICT.

## Malaysian International Chamber of Commerce and Industry (MICCI)

The MICCI started in 1837 as the Penang Chamber of Commerce &

Agriculture. Its first committee included Arab, Indian and Chinese merchants as well as Europeans. This international mix has continued since then. The MICCI serves businesses which have international interests, whether they are foreign or locally based. It has more than 400 member companies from 26 different nationalities. It is a member of the National Chamber of Commerce and Industry of Malaysia together with the Malay, Chinese and Indian chambers of commerce and the Federation of Malaysian Manufacturers. (See also: National Chamber of Commerce and Industry of Malaysia)

## Malaysian National Focal Point

The Malaysian National Focal Point (MNFP) was set up in 1992 as a unit in the Ministry of International Trade and Industry. It compiles and disseminates online information about government policies, programs, incentives and facilities for investment, trade, technology and industry in Malaysia. Its database contains information on the country profile of Malaysia and a directory listing of important business contacts in Malaysia.

## Malaysian National Insurance Sdn Bhd

This is Malaysia's largest local insurance company.

## Malaysian Palm Oil Promotion Council (MPOPC)    *www.mpopc.org.my*

The MPOPC was incorporated in 1990 to take over the activities of the Palm Oil Promotion Fund Committee. Its objective is to promote the marketability of Malaysian palm oil in the world.

## Malaysian Rating Corporation Bhd

This company started in 1996. It is Malaysia's second rating agency. (See also: Rating Agency Malaysia Berhad)

## Malaysian Rubber Board    *www.lgm.gov.my*

The Malaysian Rubber Board (MRB) or Lembaga Getah Malaysia (LGM), was formed in 1998 as a result of merging three agencies: RRIM (Rubber Research Institute of Malaysia), MRRDB (Malaysian Rubber Research and Development Board) and MRELB. It is a government agency under the Ministry of Primary Industries. Its objective is to assist in the development and modernization of the Malaysian rubber industry in all aspects from cultivation, extraction, processing of rubber as well as the manufacturing and marketing of rubber products.

## Malaysian Rubber Research and Development Board

See Malaysian Rubber Board.

### Malaysian Share Registration Services Sdn Bhd (MSRS)

The MSRS was incorporated in 1996 to provide the services of a share registrar. Formerly known as SCANS Registration Services Sdn Bhd, it changed to the present name in March 1998. MSRS uses a share registry system called SCANS Electronic Registration and Transfer Services or SERTS. The system is linked to the Central Depository System (CDS), which is operated by the Malaysian Central Depository Sdn Bhd (MCD). MSRS is owned by SCANS (51%) and MIDFCCS (49%) and has a share capital of RM10 million. (See also: SCANS Electronic Registration and Transfer Services, or SERTS)

### Malaysian Timber Council

The Malaysian Timber Council was set up in 1992. Its objective is to promote the development of timber-based industry and the marketing of timber products. It is governed by a board of trustees appointed by the Minister of Primary Industries. Council members include representatives from the various timber-related associations, government ministries and agencies.

### Malaysian Trade Allocation and Confirmation System

This is a system that records and confirms trades transacted at the Malaysian Monetary Exchange. (See also: Malaysian Monetary Exchange)

### Management System Certification Institute (Thailand)   *www.masci.or.th*

In Thailand, the Management System Certification Institute (MASCI) was set up in 1998 by the Ministry of Industry. It is an independent organization under the Industrial Development Foundation. It is a certification body which functions according to international standards. MASCI issues certificates for ISO 9000, ISO 14000 and TIS18000 systems. MASCI has taken over the certification functions of the Thai Industrial Standards Institute that remains an accreditation agency under the Ministry of Industry. (See also: Thai Industrial Standards Institute)

### Manila International Futures Exchange (MIFE)

The MIFE was incorporated in 1984. It trades in financial and commodity futures contracts. In 1990, MIFE launched an interest rate contract based on the Central Bank 91-day Treasury bill. In 1991, currency contracts were introduced.

### Manila Reference Rate

The MRR 90 or 90-day Manila Reference Rate is based on the weighted average of the interest rate on promissory notes and time deposits with a 90-day maturity.

## Manila Stock Exchange (MSE)

Manila Stock Exchange (MSE) was set up on 8 August 1927 by five American businessmen: Eric Little, Gordon Mackay, John Russell, Frank Wakefield and W.P.G. Elliot. Originally located in downtown Manila, it transferred to Pasig in 1992. When the Makati Stock Exchange started in 1965, the two exchanges operated side by side, trading in the same securities. In 1992, the two exchanges unified to form the Philippine Stock Exchange. Trading on the new exchange began on 25 March 1994. (See also: Makati Stock Exchange, Philippine Stock Exchange)

## Makati Stock Exchange (MkSE)

The Makati Stock Exchange (MkSE) was organized on 27 May 1963 by five businessmen: Hermenegildo Reyes, Bernard Gaberman, Eduardo Ortigas, Aristeo Lat and Miguel Campos. Due to problems caused by those who opposed its creation, MkSE's operations started only on 16 November 1965. It was located in Makati, the financial district of Metropolitan Manila. It operated side by side with the Manila Stock Exchange, trading in the same securities. In 1992, the two exchanges unified to form the Philippine Stock Exchange. Trading on the new exchange began on 25 March 1994. (See also: Manila Stock Exchange, Philippine Stock Exchange)

## Maldives Tourism Promotion Board    *www.visitmaldives.com*

The objective of Maldives Tourism Promotion Board is to promote the Maldives as a premium destination in South Asia.

## Maritime and Port Authority of Singapore (MPA)

The MPA is a statutory board under the Ministry of Communications and Information Technology. It was formed in 1996 to replace the former Port of Singapore Authority (PSA) which has been corporatized into PSA Corporation Ltd. MPA is responsible for all port and maritime affairs of Singapore. Its mission is to promote Singapore as a premier port and international maritime centre.

## Market for Alternative Investment (Thailand)    *www.set.or.th/mia*

In the stock market in Thailand, the Market for Alternative Investment (MAI) started in 1999. It is an alternative fund raising channel for small and medium enterprises. Its listing requirements called Section 2 Hi-Growth are more flexible in terms of capital, financial standing and track record than the first section on the Stock Exchange of Thailand.

## Martin Inquiry (Australia)

In 1983, when the Labour Government came into power in Australia, it formed the Martin Inquiry (chaired by V. E. Martin) to assess the importance of the banking system and the effectiveness of competition in the banking sector and the impact of barriers to competition. (See also: Campbell Inquiry, Napier Inquiry, Wallis Inquiry)

## Mass Rapid Transit Corporation Singapore Limited (MRTC)

The MRTC was set up in 1983 to construct the MRT system in Singapore. Between 1983 and 1990, MRTC completed the construction of the 67-kilometre MRT system including 67 stations and 3 depots. In 1996, the 16-km Woodlands Line was completed with 6 elevated stations and an underground bus interchange. Singapore MRT Limited (SMRT) operates the MRT system under a licence granted by the MRTC for an initial period of 10 years. SMRT's associate company Transit Link has integrated Singapore's MRT-Bus systems, enabling commuters to use the Transit Link farecard, a common stored-value ticket, on MRT trains as well as buses.

## PT Matahari Putra Prima

This is one of the largest department store chains in Indonesia with about 80 outlets in major cities. One of its owners is the Lippo Group.

## PT Matsushita Gobel Battery Industry (MGBI)

MGBI is one of Indonesia's largest dry cell makers. It is a Japanese joint venture and is a subsidiary of Gobel Group, Indonesia's largest electronics enterprise. Its products are sold under the brand names of Eveready and Energizer.

## MEDCO (Indonesia)

MEDCO is one of the largest local Indonesian oil exploring companies. The company has been operating since 1984 and has invested US$16 million in drilling projects. MEDCO came into being with the buyout by Ariffin Panigoro of two foreign oil companies: Stanvac and Tessoro. MEDCO is pumping 6,500 barrels of oil per day from its well. It is estimated that MEDCO's wells have reserves of 20 million barrels.

## MediaCorp Group (Singapore)    *www.corporate.mediacorpsingapore.com*

In Singapore, the MediaCorp Group comprises MediaCorp TV, MediaCorp News, MediaCorp Radio, MediaCorp Press, MediaCorp Publishing, MediaCorp Studios and MediaCorp Technologies.

**Media Development Authority (Singapore)**  *www.mda.gov.sg*
The Media Development Authority (MDA) was formed on 1 January 2003
as a result of merging the Singapore Broadcasting Authority (SBA), the Films
and Publications Department and the Singapore Film Commission.

**Medisave account**
In Singapore, Medisave is the national health care savings scheme whereby
Central Provident Fund (CPF) members set aside part of their savings in the
Medisave Account to meet their personal or immediate family's hospitalization
expenses.

**Medishield scheme**
In Singapore, the Medishield scheme was introduced in 1990. It is a low-cost
medical insurance scheme for Central Provident Fund (CPF) members and
their dependants. It helps to meet the cost of prolonged hospitalization and
medical expenses.

**Medium Term Philippine Development Plan (MTPDP)**
This is a development plan which sets specific targets for the economy, e.g.
the MTPDP (1993–98) set these targets: an average of 7.5% GNP growth,
a per capita GNP increase from US$826 in 1992 to US$1,270 by 1998, export
increase by 18.8% annually, reduction of poverty incidence from 41.0% in
1990 to 30% by 1998.

**Mekong Project Development Facility (MPDF)**
The MPDF is a project that supports small and medium businesses in the
Mekong region. It is managed by the International Finance Corporation, the
private lending arm of the World Bank.

**Melayu Islam Beraja (Brunei)**
Melayu Islam Beraja (MIB, or Malay Islamic Monarchy) is the national
philosophy of Brunei Darussalam.

**Membaca, Menulis dan Mengira (3M)**
In Malaysia, these terms mean reading, writing and arithmetic (3R).

**Metro Pacific Corporation (Philippines)**
Metro Pacific is listed on the Philippine Stock Exchange. It is the investment
holding company in the Philippines of the Hong Kong-based First Pacific
Company Limited. (See also: PDCP Development Bank Inc [Philippines])

**Metrojaya (Malaysia)**
This is Malaysia's leading retailer. In addition to numerous supermarkets, it runs the Cosmart hypermarket chain in major cities such as Kuala Lumpur, Penang and Seremban.

**Metropolitan Bank and Trust Company (Philippines)** *www.sequel.net/metrobank*
Metropolitan Bank and Trust Company is listed on the Philippine Stock Exchange. It has about 340 branches in the Philippine and has overseas branches in Guam, Kaoshiung, New York, Seoul, Taichung, Tainan, Taipei, Tokyo, and representative offices in Beijing, Hong Kong, London and Shanghai. The bank's overseas branch network has enabled it to process remittances from Filipino overseas contract workers. Its major banking-related subsidiaries include: First Metro Investment Corp, First Metro Leasing & Finance Corp, Unibancard Corp, Metropolitan Bank (Bahamas) Ltd, First Metro International Investment Co. Ltd, Asia Money Link Corporation, MB Remittance Centre (Hong Kong) and MBTC International Finance Ltd.

**Metropolitan Insurance Company Inc (Philippines)**
Metropolitan Insurance Company Inc is listed on the Philippine Stock Exchange. It provides non-life insurance coverage for fire, marine, motor car, casualty and bonds.

**PT MGBI**
See PT Matsushita Gobel Battery Industry.

**Micro Enterprise Development Program (Nepal)**   *www.medep.org.np*
In Nepal, the objective of the Micro Enterprise Development Program (MEDEP) is to assist the development of micro enterprises that will provide employment for low income families in rural areas.

**Mikuni & Co (Japan)**
This is one of the bond rating companies in Japan.

**Military Electronics Telecommunications Corporation (METC)**
In Vietnam, METC is a state-owned enterprise under the Ministry of Defence. Formerly known as Sigelco, it has a joint venture "Viettel" with New Tel, the telecom interest of New York-based Goldman Sachs.

**Mineral Resources Department (Fiji)**   *www.mrd.gov.fj*
The Mineral Resources Department is the national geological survey and mining organization of Fiji. It provides information and assists investors in the mining sector.

### Mineral Resources Development Corporation (PNG)
In Papua New Guinea, the Mineral Resources Development Corporation (MRDC) was set up in 1975 to manage certain land matters in regard to the Ok Tedi project. In 1996, MRDC was partially privatized with the creation of Orogen Minerals Limited, with the state retaining 51% shareholding in Orogen.

### Minimum Corporate Income Tax (Philippines)
In the Philippines, the Minimum Corporate Income Tax (MCIT) was introduced under the Tax Reform Act in 1997. Beginning on the fourth taxable year from the time that the corporation started operations, a MCIT of 2% of the gross income is imposed when the MCIT is greater than the regularly computed tax. Any excess of the MCIT over the normal income tax can be carried forward and credited against the normal income tax for three succeeding taxable years.

### Minimum Sum Scheme (Singapore)
In Singapore, under the Central Provident Fund (CPF), the Minimum Sum Scheme came into effect in 1987. The objective is to ensure that CPF members will have a minimum sum to live on after age 60.

### Ministry of Aeronautics and Astronautics (China)
In China, the Ministry of Aeronautics and Astronautics has been divided into two semi-autonomous corporations: China National Aviation Industry Corporation (CNAIC) and China National Space Industry Corporation (CNSIC).

### Ministry of Finance (Japan)   *www.mof.go.jp*
In Japan, with the reorganization of the central government, the Ministry of Finance changed its Japanese name to "Zaimusho" in 2001. Its main tasks are to manage government assets, liabilities and national treasury, to maintain confidence in the national currency, and to ensure proper declaration and payment of taxes and customs duties.

### Ministry of Foreign Economic Relations and Trade (China)
In China, the Ministry of Foreign Economic Relations and Trade (MOFERT) is now known as the Ministry of Foreign Trade and Economic Cooperation (MOFTEC).

### Ministry of Foreign Trade and Economic Cooperation (China)
In China, the Ministry of Foreign Trade and Economic Cooperation (MOFTEC) (former Ministry of Foreign Economic Relations and Trade or MOFERT) formulates and implements China's foreign trade policy.

## Ministry of Planning and Investment (MPI)

In Vietnam, the MPI was formed in 1995 as a result of merging several development agencies including the State Committee for Cooperation and Investment (SCCI) and the State Planning Committee (SPC). Since its formation, the MPI has been liberalizing the economy to attract foreign investment. MPI has five departments dealing with foreign investments: Foreign Investment Department (FID), Project Monitor Department, Monitoring Department for Industrial Parks and Export Processing Zones, Foreign Investment Legislation Department and Office of Project Evaluation (OPE).

## Mitsubishi Securities    *www.mitsubishi-sec.co.jp*

Mitsubishi Securities Co Ltd was formed on 1 September 2002 as a result of merging Kokusai Securities, Tokyo-Mitsubishi Securities, Tokyo-Mitsubishi Personal Securities and Issei Securities. It is part of the Mitsubishi Tokyo Financial Group. (See also: Mitsubishi Tokyo Financial Group)

## Mitsubishi Tokyo Financial Group    *www.mtfg.co.jp*

The Mitsubishi Tokyo Financial Group Inc was established on 2 April 2001. It is a holding company that oversees the operations of its member companies and subsidiaries. These include Bank of Tokyo-Mitsubishi and Mitsubishi Trust & Banking Corporation. The former Nippon Trust Bank and Tokyo Trust Bank have been integrated into the restructured Mitsubishi Trust & Banking Corporation. In September 2002, a new company Mitsubishi Securities Co Ltd was added to the group after merging several other securities companies. (See also: Mitsubishi Securities)

## Mizuho Bank (Japan)    *www.mizuhobank.co.jp*

Mizuho Bank was formed in April 2002 after the merger of Dai-Ichi Bank, Fuji Bank and the Industrial Bank of Japan. It is part of the Mizuho Financial Group. It specializes in consumer bank while its sister bank Mizuho Corporate Bank focuses on corporate banking. (See also: Mizuho Corporate Bank, Mizuho Financial Group)

## Mizuho Corporate Bank    *www.mizuhocbk.co.jp*

Mizuho Corporate Bank (MHCB) was formed in April 2002 after the merger of Dai-Ichi Kangyo Bank, Fuji Bank and the Industrial Bank of Japan. It provides a wide range of corporate financial services. It is part of the Mizuho Financial Group. It specializes in corporate banking while its sister bank, Mizuho Bank focuses on consumer banking. (See also: Mizuho Bank, Mizuho Financial Group)

**Mizuho Financial Group**   *www.mizuho-sc.com*
In Japan, the Mizuho Financial Group (MHFG) was formed on 20 September 2000 as a result of integrating the Dai-Ichi Kangyo Bank Group, Fuji Bank Group and the Industrial Bank of Japan Group. In April 2002, Mizuho Securities was formed after merging the securities subsidiaries of these three banks. Under the umbrella of Mizuho Holdings Inc, Mizuho Securities, the three banks and Mizuho Trust & Banking now form the 5 pillars of the Mizuho Financial Group.

**Mizuho Securities**
See Mizuho Financial Group.

**Monetary Authority of Singapore**   *www.mas.gov.sg*
The Monetary Authority of Singapore (MAS) was set up as a statutory board in 1971. It performs all the functions of a central bank except that of issuing currency which is done by the Board of Commissioners of Currency. Its Board of Directors is chaired by the Minister for Finance. As the central bank of Singapore, the MAS promotes the stable growth of the economy in general, and of the financial services sector in particular.

**Mong Cai Special Economic Zone (Vietnam)**
Mong Cai is Vietnam's first Special Economic Zone. Located in the province of Quang Ninh, Mong Cai is a town on the border with China's southern province of Yunnan. Investors will enjoy discounts on rent and other incentives such as tax breaks or exemption.

**Monopolies and Restrictive Trade Practices Act (India)**
In India, the Monopolies and Restrictive Trade Practices Act was introduced in 1969. Its objective is to prevent concentration of economic power and to prohibit monopolistic, restrictive and unfair trade practices.

**MSCI-Hong Kong Index**
MSCI-Hong Kong Index futures contract was first traded on SIMEX on 31 March 1993. The MSCI-HK index is widely used to measure the performance of the Hong Kong stock market. It is a broad-based representation of 36 stocks, as compared to Hang Seng's 33 stocks. Like the Hang Seng Index, it is market capitalization weighted. It is adjusted regularly to maintain its representativeness of the Hong Kong bourse.

**Mufukat**
Common unanimous decision (Indonesia).

## Multi Fiber Agreement (MFA)

In 1994, the Multi Fiber Agreement was replaced by the Agreement on Textiles and Clothing (See Agreement on Textiles and Clothing or ATC).

## Multilateral Investment Guarantee Agency    *www.worldbank.org*

The Multilateral Investment Guarantee Agency (MIGA) is part of the World Bank Group. It promotes foreign direct investment by providing political risk insurance (guarantee) to investors and lenders, and by providing skills and resources to help emerging economies attract and retain this investment.

## Multimedia Development Corporation (Malaysia)

The MDC is a Malaysian government-owned company that promotes the development of the Multimedia Super Corridor. It attracts foreign companies and facilitates knowledge transfer and wealth creation. It provides information on the MSC, assists in seeking licence approvals and introduces companies to potential local partners and financiers.

## Multimedia Super Corridor Research and Development Grant Scheme (MGS)

In Malaysia, the objective of the scheme is to encourage R&D in multimedia products and services to be used in the Multimedia Super Corridor. It helps local companies or joint ventures to develop multimedia technology and application. The applicant must be at least 51% Malaysian-owned.

## Mumbai

New name for Bombay.

## Muslim Commercial Bank (Pakistan)    *www.mcb.com.pk*

In Pakistan, the Muslim Commercial Bank (MCB) was set up about 50 years ago. It has about 1,000 branches in the country and overseas operations in Sri Lanka and Bahrain. It provides a wide range of corporate, commercial and consumer banking services. It has the largest ATM network in Pakistan, with 100 machines in 15 cities. Its rupee travellers' cheque has been the market leader for several years.

## PT Mustika Ratu

This is an Indonesian traditional herb and cosmetic producer. The company exports about 25% of its products. Its largest overseas market is Malaysia. In 1997, it opened a trading house Wisma Mustika Ratu in Malaysia.

**Musyawarah**
Mutual deliberation.

**Mutual offset system**
This is a system of substitution between two participating exchanges whereby a trade executed on one exchange may be used to offset a position on the other exchange. For example, SGX-DT (formerly SIMEX) has a mutual offset arrangement with Chicago Mercantile Exchange's (CME) International Monetary Market (IMM) for several of its financial futures contracts. SIMEX also has a mutual offset agreement with London's International Petroleum Exchange (IPE) for Brent crude oil futures contract.

**Myanmar Agricultural and Rural Development Bank (MARDB)**
The MARDB was set up under the Myanmar Agricultural and Rural Bank Law. It took over the functions of the Myanmar Agricultural Bank which was established under the 1975 Banking Law. The MARDB supports the development of agricultural livestock and rural socio-economic enterprises. In 1993, it introduced the Rural Savings Scheme to encourage savings among the farmers and to develop a rural banking system.

**Myanmar Economic Bank**
Myanmar Economic Bank is the largest state-owned commercial bank for domestic banking in Myanmar. It has a nationwide network of more than 300 branches. Its total deposit is about seven times of all the other 15 domestic banks. It acts as an agent of the Central Bank in treasury matters. It handles state fund accounts and replenishes local cash requirement throughout the country.

**Myanmar Electric Power Enterprise**
Myanmar Electric Power Enterprise (MEPE)is a state-owned enterprise under the Ministry of Energy. It plans, designs, constructs, maintains and operates electric supply facilities and sells electricity throughout Myanmar.

**Myanmar Five Star Line**
Myanmar Five Star Line (MFSL) is a state-owned shipping line. It operates coastal and overseas transport services with a fleet of about 20 vessels. It has no direct service to US and Canada. It has a transshipment agreement with Japan's Nippon Yusen Kaisha Line (NYK). MFSL serves the Myanmar-Japan sector while NYK serves Japan and US-Canada sector.

## Myanmar Foreign Trade Bank
It was established in 1976 in Yangon. It has a network of 124 foreign banks in 58 countries. It focuses mainly on foreign trade and foreign currency transactions.

## Myanmar Insurance Corporation
The Myanmar Insurance Corporation is the sole state-owned insurance company in Myanmar. It provides a wide range of insurance cover.

It has granted permission to open representative offices by several foreign companies including Yasuda Fire and Marine, Mitsui Fire and Marine and Overseas Union Insurance. It also has a reinsurance program with international re-insurers. The Myanmar Insurance Law was enacted in 1993 to facilitate coverage of insurance business.

## Myanmar Investment and Commercial Bank (MICB)
The MICB was set up in 1989 to specialize in commercial lending and investment banking. It serves mainly foreign and local private corporations and individuals. It has a worldwide network of more than 120 correspondent banks.

## Myanmar Investment Commission
In Myanmar, the Foreign Investment Commission (FIC) was formed to administer the Foreign Investment Law. In 1994, the Myanmar Citizens Investment Law was introduced and the FIC was renamed the Myanmar Investment Commission (MIC). The MIC promotes foreign investment and approves proposals.

## Myanmar Mines Authorities (MMA)
The MMA organizes annual gem emporiums where the state-owned Myanmar Gems Enterprise and local merchants market their gems, jade and jewelry. The events also attract gems merchants from other countries. The emporiums have been held every year since 1962.

## Myanmar Oil and Gas Enterprise (MOGE)
The MOGE is jointly developing Yadana oilfield with America's Unocal, France's Total, and Thailand Petroleum Authority. A 350-kilometre pipeline is being constructed from Myanmar's offshore Yadana oilfield to Thailand where the gas will be sold.

**Myanmar Securities Exchange Centre**
The Myanmar Securities Exchange Centre is a joint venture between the Myanmar Economic Bank and the Daiwa Research Institute of Japan. Its main objective is to set up a stock exchange. In 1997, it issued the shares of Union of Myanmar Forest Products Joint Venture for subscription by Myanmar citizens.

**Myanmar Small Loans Enterprise**
This is a state-owned finance company in Myanmar dealing in small loans.

**Nagoya Stock Exchange**   *www.nse.or.jp*
Nagoya Stock Exchange is the successor to the Nagoya Stock Exchange Co Ltd which was founded in 1886. It was established in 1949 as a corporation with securities companies as members. The NSE provides a market for the trading of numerous securities. Domestic stocks are divided into 440 first section issues and 140 second section issues. In 1999, a Growth Company Market section was introduced. Trades are executed by a computer system.

**Nakadachi Member (Japan)**
See Saitori member.

**Nakornthon Bank (Thailand)**
Nakornthon Bank was known as Wang Lee Bank until 1965. Founded in 1933, it is the second oldest bank in Thailand. In 1973, it expanded into worldwide banking, and entered into a joint venture with Citibank that helped to improve its management system. In 1983, the bank was listed on the Stock Exchange of Thailand. It was the first bank to issue the multi-function global ATM/ debit card in Thailand. It has numerous branches in Bangkok as well in the provinces.

**Nantze Export Processing Zone (Taiwan)**
In Taiwan, Nantze Export Processing Zone was set up in 1969. It is located near Kaoshiung.

**Napier Inquiry (Australia)**
In Australia, the first financial system inquiry was the Royal Commission on Monetary and Banking Systems chaired by Justice Napier in 1935. Its objective was to recommend changes to ensure stability of the financial system after the Great Depression showed that economic conditions could be affected by changes in the financial market. It recommended that the financial system should be subject to intervention to avoid instability and facilitate the operation of monetary policy. Banks should be licensed and the government

should control monetary policy. (See also: Campbell Inquiry, Martin Inquiry, Wallis Inquiry)

## Narasimha Committee (India)

In India, the Narasimha Committee was appointed by the government to recommend changes in the banking system. Some of the recommendations included the following:

- Increase of capital of banks through public issue of shares;
- Reduce the statutory liquidity ratio and restrict its use as an instrument to finance fiscal deficit;
- Remove government involvement in banking and reduce the role of the Reserve Bank of India to that of a regulatory body;
- Streamline interest rate structure, and remove cross subsidization;
- Permit foreign banks to open branches;
- Allow formation of private banks with participation from foreign banks.

## National Aquatic Resources Agency (Sri Lanka)

In Sri Lanka, the National Aquatic Resources Agency (NARA) was set up in 1982. Its main objective is to conduct fisheries research. It assists the Ministry to identify, assess, develop and manage Sri Lanka's marine resources.

## National Archives of Cambodia  *www.camnet.com.kh/archives.cambodia*

The National Archives of Cambodia (NAC) is a department of the Council of Ministers. It preserves documents with legal and historical value. It makes these documents accessible to the Cambodian administration, organizations and individual researchers.

## National Association of Labour Banks

See Labour Banks in Japan.

## National Australia Bank  *www.national.com.au*

In 1955, the National Bank merged with the Colonial Bank of Australasia and absorbed the Queensland National Bank and Ballarat Banking Co Ltd. In 1981, it merged with the Commercial Banking Co of Sydney to form the National Australia Bank (NAB). In 2002, it was ranked 303 among the Fortune 500 global companies.

## National Bank for Agriculture and Rural Development (India)
*www.nabard.org*

In India, the National Bank for Agriculture and Rural Development (NABARD) was set up in 1982 as recommended by the government's Committee to Review Arrangements for Institutional Credit for Agriculture and Rural Development (CRAFICARD). It took over the functions of the Agricultural Credit Department (ACD) and Rural Planning and Credit Cell (RPCC) of the Reserve Bank of India (central bank) and Agricultural Refinance Development Corporation (ARDC).

NABARD is an apex institution that deals with all matters concerning policy, planning and operations of credit for agriculture and other economic activities in the rural areas of India. Its refinance is available to state land development banks, state cooperative banks, regional rural banks, commercial banks and other institutions approved by the RBI. It is a wholly-owned subsidiary of the Reserve Bank of India. (See also: Reserve Bank of India)

### National Bank of Cambodia
Formerly known as the Bank of the People of Cambodia, the National Bank of Cambodia (NBC) is the central bank of Cambodia. It is supervised by the Council of Ministers and has the status of a ministry. It approves, supervises and regulates all financial institutions in Cambodia. It fixes foreign exchange rates and interest rates for the purpose of the purchase and discounting of commercial papers. It has the power to intervene in the financial markets to stabilize the national currency.

### National Bank of Pakistan   www.nbp.com.pk
The National Bank of Pakistan provides a wide range of banking services. It has about 1,500 local branches and 24 international offices. Its subsidiary National Discounting Services Ltd is the trustee to the National Investment Trust (NIT) and sells and repurchases NIT unit certificates.

### National Bank of Vanuatu
The National Bank of Vanuatu (NBV) was set up in 1991 to take over the assets of the Vanuatu Cooperative Savings Bank Ltd (VCSBL). Its objective is to be a viable domestic bank.

### National Board of Revenue (Bangladesh)   www.nbr-bd.org
In Bangladesh, the National Board of Revenue (NBR) was established in 1972. It is the central authority for tax administration in Bangladesh. It is under the Internal Resources Division of the Ministry of Finance. Its main responsibility is to collect domestic revenue for the government.

### National Broadcasting Commission (Papua New Guinea)
In PNG, the National Broadcasting Commission (NBC) provides broadcasting

services through two main radio networks: KALANG and KARAI stations. English is the main language in broadcasting.

**National Centre for Scientific and Technological Information and Documentation (Vietnam)**    *www.vista.gov.vn*
In Vietnam, the National Centre for Scientific and Technological Information and Documentation (NACESTID) was formed in 1990 with the merger of the Central Library for Science and Technology (founded in 1960) and the Central Institute for Scientific and Technical Information (founded in 1972). Under the Ministry of Science, Technology and Environment, NACESTID manages and coordinates scientific and technological information. It also formulates S&T plans and policies.

**National Chamber of Commerce and Industry Malaysia (NCCIM)**
The NCCIM started in 1962 as the United Chambers of Commerce of Malaya. In 1974, it was reorganized under the present name. It is an apex organization comprising the five main private sector bodies which represent the business interests of the Malay, Chinese and Indian communities, international investors and the Malaysian manufacturers.

Its constituent members include:
- Malay Chamber of Commerce Malaysia (MCCM)
- Associated Chinese Chambers of Commerce (ACCCIM)
- Malaysian Associated Indian Chamber of Commerce and Industry (MAICCI)
- Malaysian International Chamber of Commerce & Industry (MICCI)
- Federation of Malaysian Manufacturers (FMM).

In addition to its wide range of trade-related activities, the NCCIM participates in dialogue with the various government ministries on trade and investment matters.

**National Clearing Company of Pakistan Limited**    *www.nccpl.com.pk*
The National Clearing Company of Pakistan Limited (NCCPL) has been set up by the three stock exchanges in Pakistan. It was one of the conditions under the Asian Development Bank's Capital Market Development Program. It has replaced individual clearing houses operated by the three exchanges. Its objective is to improve the efficiency of the settlement process, reduce systemic risk of the current clearance and settlement practices. It will operate the National Clearing and Settlement System (NCSS). The capital of company is subscribed by the Karachi Stock Exchange (40%), Lahore Stock Exchange (20%), Islamabad Stock Exchange (10%) and the remainder by financial institutions.

## National Committee on Culture and Information (Cambodia)
*www.moi-coci.gov.kh*
In Cambodia, the National Committee on Culture and Information (NCOCI) was established in 2000. The chairman is the Ministry of Information while the vice chairman is the Ministry of Culture and Fine Arts. Other relevant ministries are also represented in the committee.

## National Computer Board (Singapore)
In Singapore, the NCB was set up in 1981 to promote the use of information technology (IT) and to develop the IT industry. NCB spearheaded IT2000, a master plan that sought to transform Singapore into an intelligent island. In 1999, the NCB merged with the Telecommunications Authority of Singapore (TAS) to form the Infocomm Development Authority (IDA) of Singapore. (See also: Infocomm Development Authority)

## National Cost of Quality (NCOQ) Program (Singapore)
In Singapore, the NCOQ program was launched by SPRING Singapore (Productivity Standards and Innovation Board, formerly the Productivity and Standards Board or PSB) in 1998. Its objective is to help companies reduce wastage and costs. A company first goes through the training stage to inculcate a cost-conscious mindset in every employee. The next stage is data collection and analysis. This helps to determine wastage and inefficiency. In the third stage of action planning, work teams are formed to measure and reduce unnecessary costs. In the final stage of implementation, a system is implemented to eliminate costs arising from poor quality practices. (*Singapore Enterprise*, April 2001)

## National Database and Registration Authority (Pakistan)    *www.nadra.gov.pk*
In Pakistan, the National Database and Registration Authority (NADRA) was formed in March 2000 with the merger of the National Database Organization and the Directorate General of Registration. Its objective is to introduce a computerized system of registration for the entire population. One of its projects is to issue state-of-the-art National Identity Cards (NICs) to all adult citizens of Pakistan.

## National Design Centre (Sri Lanka)
In Sri Lanka, the National Design Centre was set up in 1984. It assists cottage industries to improve designs, develop new production and marketing methods.

### National Development Bank (Sri Lanka)
In Sri Lanka, the National Development Bank was set up in 1979 under the National Development Bank Act to provide long term funds for development.

### National Development Finance Corporation (Pakistan)
In Pakistan, the National Development Finance Corporation (NDFC) was set up in 1973 to provide financial assistance to public sector enterprises.

### National Economic Action Council (Malaysia)    www.neac.gov.my
In Malaysia, the National Economic Action Council (NEAC) was set up in January 1998 by the government as a consultant to the cabinet on economic problems. The NEAC was chaired by the Prime Minister. Its members included economic ministers, representatives from various fields in the private sector and selected organizations. Its main objectives were:
– to ensure that the country did not enter into an economic recession as a result of the decline in the value of the ringgit and the fall in the share market;
– to restore public and investor confidence, particularly that of foreign investors with regard to the economy;
– to revive the national economy and make it competitive globally;
– to strengthen the economic base of the country to achieve a developed nation status through economic growth.

### National Economic and Development Authority (Philippines)
www.neda.gov.ph
In the Philippines, the National Economic and Development Authority (NEDA) is the highest social and economic development planning and policy coordinating body in the Philippines. Its board is chaired by the President. Members include Secretaries from the various government departments. Assisting the NEDA Board are five cabinet-level inter-agency committees:

1. *Development Budget Coordination Committee (DBCC)*
   The DBCC recommends to the Board matters related to government expenditures for economic and social development, national defence, and government debt service.

2. *Infrastructure Committee (InfraCom)*
   The InfraCom advises the Board on matters concerning infrastructure development, including highways, airports, seaports and shore protection; railways; power generation and others.

3. *Investment Coordination Committee (ICC)*
   The ICC evaluates the fiscal, monetary and balance of payments implications of major national projects, and recommends the timetable of their implementation.

4. *Social Development Committee (SDC)*
   The SDC advises the Board on matters concerning social development, including education, manpower, health and nutrition, population and family planning, housing, human settlements, and the delivery of other social services. It coordinates the activities of government agencies concerned with social development.

5. *Committee on Tariff and Related Matters (CTRM)*
   The CTRM advises the Board on tariff and related matters and on the effects on the country of various international developments. It coordinates agency positions and recommends national positions for international economic negotiations.

## National Economic and Social Development Board (Thailand)

*www.nesdb.go.th*

In Thailand, the National Economic Development Board was set up in 1959 as recommended by the World Bank. In 1972 the name was changed to National Economic and Social Development Board (NESDB) to emphasize the importance of social development. The NESDB is a central planning authority of Thailand. It is responsible for formulating National Economic and Social Development Plans. Since its inception, NESDB has completed seven Development Plans.

## National Economic Consultative Council (Malaysia)

In Malaysia, the National Economic Consultative Council (NECC) was formed in 1989 to review the post-1990 (post NEP) policy framework.

## National Economic Council (Pakistan)

In Pakistan, the National Economic Council (NEC) is the supreme economic policy-making body. It is chaired by the President and all Federal Ministers in charge of development ministries and provincial governors are members.

## National Economic Recovery Plan (Malaysia)

Malaysia's National Economic Recovery Plan (NERP) was formulated as a response to the 1998 financial crisis. It had six major objectives:

1. Stabilize the ringgit;
2. restore market confidence;
3. maintain financial market stability;
4. strengthen economic fundamentals;
5. continue the equity and socio-economic agenda;
6. restore adversely affected sectors.

### National Economics University (Vietnam)

Vietnam's National Economics University (NEU) is located in Hanoi. It organized the first government-approved MBA program in Vietnamese language in 1996.

### National Electronic Commerce Committee (Malaysia)    *www.e.com.ec/necc*

In Malaysia, the National Electronic Commerce Committee (NECC) started in 1998 with the Multimedia Development Corporation as the secretariat. Its main role was to establish the objectives and a framework of e-commerce and to establish a National Strategic Plan that included the charter for e-commerce development.

### National Electronics and Computer Technology Centre (Thailand)

*www.nectec.or.th*

In Thailand, the National Electronics and Computer Technology Centre (NECTEC) is an organization under the National Science and Technology Development Agency (NSTDA). It is responsible for the development of information technology in Thailand. Its mission is to ensure Thailand's competitiveness in electronics and computer and the use of IT to stimulate economic and social impact.

### National Engineering Research and Development Centre (Sri Lanka)

In Sri Lanka, the National Engineering Research and Development Centre (NERD) was set up in 1974 to conduct applied R&D and to commercialize the results.

### National Environment Action Plan (Maldives)    *www.presidencymaldives.gov.mv*

In the Maldives, the government's environmental protection policy of the Maldives is stated in its National Environment Action Plan (NEAP). The main aim is to protect and preserve the environment. NEAP-I was formulated in 1989 to address environmental planning and management needs. NEAP-II was announced in 1999.

### National Exchange for Automated Trading (India)

The National Exchange for Automated Trading (NEAT) is a screen-based computerized trading system used in the National Stock Exchange in India. (See also: National Stock Exchange)

### National Federation of Workers and Consumers Insurance Cooperatives (Japan)   *www.zenrosai.or.jp*

In Japan, the National Federation of Workers and Consumers Insurance (Zenrosai) first started in 1957. It is a cooperative insurer and non-profit organization offering insurance services to its members. It has about 14 million members. The Zenrosai Group comprises three major organizations: Zenrosai (National Federation of Workers and Consumers Insurance Cooperatives), Zenrosai Saikyosairen (Zenrosai Reinsurance Federation) and Zenrosai Kyokai (Zenrosai Federation for Workers' Welfare and Cooperative Insurance).

### National Fisheries Authority (Papua New Guinea)   *www.fisheries.gov.pg*

In PNG, under the Fisheries Management Act of 1998, the National Fisheries Authority (NFA) is responsible for the management and development of the fisheries sector. It recommends the granting of fishing licences. It implements monitoring, control and surveillance schemes. It also operates the National Fisheries College (NFC or Fiscol) which provides training in fisheries and seafood.

### National Fisheries College (Papua New Guinea)

See National Fisheries Authority.

### National Guarantee Fund (Australia)

In Australia, the National Guarantee Fund (NGF) is a compensation fund available to meet certain types of claims arising from dealings with ASX participating organizations. The governing legislation sets out the categories of claims that can be made. Clients of ASX participating organizations can make claims in certain circumstances for compensation of reportable sales and purchases of quoted securities entered on ASX's equities market, for loss resulting from unauthorized transfer of certain securities, or for property entrusted to an ASX participating organization which has become insolvent.

### National Health Insurance (Taiwan)   *www.nhi.gov.tw*

In Taiwan, the National Health Insurance (NHI) program was introduced in 1995 to consolidate several existing programs. Administered by the Bureau of National Health Insurance, it is a compulsory social insurance program to provide health care and social rehabilitation. By 2000, about 21 million persons have enrolled in NHI representing a coverage rate of about 96%.

### National Housing Authority (Thailand)
In Thailand, the National Housing Authority (NHA) was set up in 1972 by the government to embark on a large-scale public housing program. It works closely with the Government Housing Bank (owned by the Ministry of Finance) which provides low interest mortgage loans to low income households. (See also: Government Housing Bank)

### National Housing Bank (India)
In India, the National Housing Bank (NHB) is a fully-owned subsidiary of the Reserve Bank of India. (See also: Reserve Bank of India)

### National Housing Corporation (Vanuatu)
In Vanuatu, the National Housing Corporation (NHC) was set up in 1984 to provide low cost housing.

### National Housing Development Authority (Sri Lanka)
In Sri Lanka, the National Housing Development Authority (NHDA) was set up in 1979 to provide funds at reasonable rates for housing construction and to implement government policy on housing.

### National Industrial Relations Commission (Pakistan)
In Pakistan, the National Industrial Relations Commission (NIRC) was set up in 1972 under the Industrial Relations Ordinance. It promotes the formation and registration in industry-wide trade unions. The NIRC has the power to punish and to prevent unfair labour practices.

### National Infocomm Award (Singapore)
In Singapore, the National Infocomm Award (NIA) is organized by the Infocomm Development Authority (IDA). The aim is to promote and recognize innovative development of infocomm technology by companies in Singapore. There are two categories: (a) the most innovative use of infocomm technology, (b) the most innovative infocomm product or service.

### National Information Communications Technology Development Authority (Cambodia)   *www.nida.gov.kh*
In Cambodia, NIDA was set up in August 2000. It formulates and implements IT policy. Its role is both a regulator and promoter to ensure an integrated approach.

**National Institute of Financial Management (India)**   *www.nifm.org*
In India, the National Institute of Financial Management (NIFM) provides training, research and consulting in finance and related areas. It offers numerous management development programs as well as MBA (finance).

**National Institute of Fisheries Training (Sri Lanka)**
In Sri Lanka, the National Institute of Fisheries Training (NIFT) was set up under the Ministry of Fisheries to provide training in fisheries.

**National Institute of Plantation Management (Sri Lanka)**
In Sri Lanka, the National Institute of Plantation Management (NIPM) under the Ministry of Plantation Industries, provides training to the agricultural sector.

**National Institute of Public Health (Cambodia)**   *www.camnet.com.kh/nphri*
In Cambodia, the National Institute of Public Health (NIPH) is a research institute within the Ministry of Health. It provides health service management training. It collects national health statistics for decision-makers to analyze and implement strategies.

**National Institute of Statistics (Cambodia)**   *www.nis.gov.kh*
In Cambodia, the National Institute of Statistics (NIS) is part of the Ministry of Planning. It compiles statistics provided by decentralized offices. It also collects primary data through household surveys and population census.

**National Insurance Academy (India)**   *www.niapune.com*
In India, the National Insurance Academy (NIA) at Pune provides training to the insurance industry.

**National Insurance Company Limited (India)**   *www.nationalinsuranceindia.net*
Formed in 1906, the National Insurance Company Limited (NICL) is the oldest insurance company in India. It is a public sector general insurance company with headquarters in Kolkata. It has nearly 1,000 offices with 19,000 employees. It has branches in Nepal and Hong Kong.

**National Insurance Corporation (Pakistan)**
In Pakistan, National Co-insurance Scheme (NCS) was introduced by the government in 1955. It provided insurance to the public sector. It was managed by the Pakistan Insurance Corporation. In 1972, NCS was converted to the National Insurance Corporation (NIC).

### National Insurance Corporation (Sri Lanka)

In Sri Lanka, the National Insurance Corporation was set up in 1979 under the Insurance (Special Provision) Act.

### National Integrated Protected Areas System Act (Philippines)

In the Philippines, the National Integrated Protected Areas System (NIPAS) Act provides for the establishment and management of a national integrated protected area system and defines its scope and coverage. For example, environmentally critical areas include all areas declared by law as national parks, watershed reserves, wildlife preserves and sanctuaries.

### National Investment Scheme (Papua New Guinea)

In PNG, the National Investment Scheme (NIS) assists business groups to start new large commercial projects. It provides funds for feasibility study, and unsecured loans to complement commercial funds.

### National Investment Trust (Pakistan)

In Pakistan, the National Investment Trust (NIT) was set up in 1962. It is the only mutual fund in Pakistan. It mobilizes domestic savings through the sale of its units and invests the funds in shares and debentures. It is an open-ended mutual fund that supports new entrants to the equity market. It retains the option to purchase 15% of all new public share issues from the issuers. The Trust has a large portfolio of shares and has appointed at least one director on the boards of many companies.

### National Law School of India University   *www.nls.ac.in*

The National Law School of India University (NLSIU) was established in 1987 at Bangalore in the State of Karnataka. It has several research centres such as the Centre for Intellectual Property Law, Research and Advocacy (CIPRA), and Centre for Environmental Law, Education, Research and Advocacy (CEERA).

### National Listing Committee (Australia)

At the Australian Stock Exchange (ASX), its National Listing Committee (NLC) has the powers to admit companies to the Official List and to grant official quotation of securities.

### National Livestock Development Board (Sri Lanka)

In Sri Lanka, the National Livestock Development Board (NLDB) was set up in 1973. Its objective is to breed livestock and to issue breeding materials to farmers. It also provides training and demonstration facilities to livestock smallholders.

### National Private Bank Association (Indonesia)

Perhimpunan Bank-Bank Umum Nasional Swasta (or PERBANAS) was formed in 1952 and has about 165 members.

### National Provident Fund (Papua New Guinea)

In PNG, the NasFund was launched in 31 May 2002 to revitalize the National Provident Fund (NPF).

### National Provident Fund (Solomon Islands)

In the Solomon Islands, the National Provident Fund (NPF) was set up in 1976. It is a compulsory savings scheme with contribution from employers and employees.

### National Research Council of Thailand    *www.nrct.net*

The National Research Council of Thailand (NRCT) was formed under the National Research Council Act of 1959 as the national body on research related matters. The council is also assigned to give the Prime Minister comments on research issues. The NRCT is chaired by the Prime Minister.

### National Savings Bank (Sri Lanka)

In Sri Lanka, the National Savings Bank was set up in 1972 under the National Savings Bank Act. It amalgamated the Post Office Savings Bank, the Ceylon Savings Bank and the Savings Certificates Movement.

### National Savings Organization (Pakistan)

In Pakistan, the history of the National Savings Organization (NSO) dates back to 1873 when the Government Savings Act was passed. It now has a network of 12 Regional Directorates of National Savings (RDNS) with numerous National Savings Centres in the country. It encourages savings with various savings accounts and saving certificates.

### National Science Council (Taiwan)    *www.nsc.gov.tw*

In Taiwan, the National Science Council (NSC) promotes science and technology (S&T) development. It plans, evaluates and reviews S&T programs. It provides financial support to research and education institutions. It develops science-based industrial parks such as those located at Hsinchu and Tainan. The NSC has established several specialized laboratories such as the Synchrotron Radiation Research Centre, National Centre for High-performance Computing, National Centre for Research on Earthquake Engineering, and the National Nano Device Laboratories. Its Science and Technology Information Centre (STIC) distributes information on science and technology.

**National Securities Clearing Corporation Limited (India)**   *www.nseindia.com*
In India, the National Securities Clearing Corporation Limited (NSCCL) was formed in 1995. It is the wholly-owned subsidiary of National Stock Exchange (NSE). It clears and settles securities traded on the exchange. It guarantees settlement obligations through the Settlement Guarantee Fund which is contributed by trading members.

**National Securities Depository Limited (India)**
In India, the National Securities Depository Ltd (NSDL) was registered with the Securities and Exchange Board in 1996. It was the first depository in India. It was promoted by the National Stock Exchange, the Unit Trust of India and Industrial Development Bank of India.

**National Science & Technology Board (Singapore)**
In Singapore,the National Science and Technology Board (NSTB) was set up in 1991. It is the driving force behind Singapore's R&D effort toward higher value, knowledge-intensive economic activities. In 2002, it was renamed A*STAR (Agency for Science Technology and Research).

**National Stock Exchange (India)**   *www.nseindia.com*
In India, the National Stock Exchange Ltd (NSE) was formed in 1992 with encouragement from the government and upon the recommendation of the Study Group on Establishment of New Stock Exchanges. It is funded by major financial institutions as a tax-paying company unlike other stock exchanges in India. It started trading in the wholesale debt market (WDM) in June 1994, in the capital market in September 1994, and in the derivatives segment in June 2000. The WDM covers money market instruments such as government securities, T-bills, PSU bonds, CPs and CDs. The capital market deals in equities and debentures.

**National Tariff Commission (Pakistan)**   *www.ntc.gov.pk*
In Pakistan, the National Tariff Commission (NTC) was formed in 1990. It is an autonomous agency within the Ministry of Commerce. It makes recommendations to the federal government on tariff protection to the domestic industries. It also advises the government on international trade negotiations, trade and investment policies.

**National Trust Council (Singapore)**   *www.trustsg.org*
In Singapore, the National Trust Council (NTC) was formed in 2001. It helps businesses and consumers increase trust and in electronic commerce. It promotes the National Trust Mark Program. It develops a risk management

framework to reduce fraud in EC transactions as well as to promote good business practices. The NTC has developed the TrustSg program to build confidence among consumers and businesses. The TrustSg program is an approved certification scheme to accredit organizations such as trade associations, chambers or businesses whose members are bound by an online Code of Practice to promote good business practices. (See also: National Trust Mark, TrustSg program)

**Nepal Incentive and Convention Association** *www.nica.org.np*
The Nepal Incentive and Convention Association is a non-profit organization formed in 1999 to promote MICE (meetings, incentives, conference and exhibitions) tourism. It was established by the Department of Tourism, hoteliers, tour operators, airlines and conference organizers.

**Nepal Industrial & Commercial Bank Limited** *www.nicbank.com.np*
The Nepal Industrial & Commercial Bank Limited (NIC Bank) was the first bank to be established under the Commercial Bank Act. It was promoted by a group of prominent Nepali entrepreneurs and leading industrial houses that included the state-owned Rastriya Banijya Bank (RBB). The promoters own 65% shareholding that includes 5% holding by the RBB. The remaining 35% shares have been subscribed by the public. It provides a full range of com-mercial banking services. In April 2002, the bank was conferred the honour of "Commercially Important Person" by the Finance Minister for being among the top 10 taxpayers in the country.

**Nepal Industrial Development Corporation**
The Nepal Industrial Development Corporation (NIDC) was established to grant medium and long term loans to industries that commercial banks were reluctant to make.

**Nepal Rastra Bank** *www.nrb.org.np*
The Nepal Rastra Bank (NRB) was set up in 1956 under the Rastra Bank Act. As the central bank of Nepal, it supervises commercial banks, development banks, finance companies, cooperative societies and non-government organi-zations which provide banking services.

**Nepal Stock Exchange** *www.nepalstock.com*
In Nepal, securities trading began in 1937 with the floatation of the shares of Biratnagar Jute Mills and the Nepal Bank. In 1976, the Securities Exchange Centre (SEC) was formed to promote the capital market. In 1993, the SEC was converted into the Nepal Stock Exchange Limited (NEPSE). The

shareholders are the government, Nepal Rastra Bank (central bank), Nepal Industrial Development Corporation and members of the exchange. There are about 30 member brokers and 2 market makers. About 120 companies are listed on the exchange that adopts the open outcry system on the trading floor.

**Nepal Tourism Board**   *www.welcomenepal.com*
The Nepal Tourism Board (NTB) is a national organization established as a partnership between the government and the private sector tourism industry. It promotes Nepal as a tourism destination.

**Network China (Singapore)**
Singapore's Network China was launched in 2001. Since then, about 800 Singapore-based companies have joined the network. It will work closely with the Singapore Chamber of Commerce and Industry (SingCham) in Beijing to assist Singapore companies both in Singapore and China. (See also: Singapore Chamber of Commerce and Industry)

**Network for Electronic Transfers (Singapore)**
In Singapore, the Network for Electronic Transfer Private Limited (NETS) was set up in 1985 by major local banks. It is a joint venture company that operates the electronic fund transfer at point-of-sale (EFTPOS) system for these banks.

**New Airport Projects Co-ordination Office (NAPCO)**
See Hong Kong International Airport.

**New Bangkok International Airport Co Limited**   *www.suvarnabhumiairport.com*
In Thailand, the New Bangkok International Airport Co Limited was formed in 1996 as a privately managed and state-owned company under the Ministry of Transport and Communications. Its main shareholders are the Airport Authority of Thailand (91.5%) and Ministry of Finance (8.5%). It is responsible for constructing and operating Suvarnabhumi Airport.

**New Company Law (Indonesia)**
In Indonesia, the New Company Law (NCL or Law on Limited Liability Companies) came into effect in March 1996. It contains 129 articles dealing with issues on formation, dissolution, liability, capitalization, management and control.

**New Economic Mechanism (Laos)**
In Laos, the New Economic Mechanism (NEM) was launched in 1986 to transform the economy from a centrally planned economy to a market economy.

### New Entrepreneurs Fund (Malaysia)
### (Tabung Usahawan Baru)
In Malaysia, the RM 1.25 billion fund was set up in 1989 to stimulate the growth of small and medium bumiputera enterprises. Participating financial institutions included commercial banks, Bank Pembangunan Malaysia Berhad, Bank Industri Malaysia Berhad and Malaysian Industrial Development Finance Berhad.

### New Jubilee Insurance (Pakistan)
See State Life Insurance Corporation.

### New Light of Myanmar
The New Light of Myanmar is the only English newspaper in Myanmar.

### New Singapore Shares
On 1 November 2001, the Singapore Government gave New Singapore Shares (NSS) to its citizens. The number of shares depended on the person's monthly income and type of housing. It ranged from 200 shares for persons with high income to 1,400 shares for low-income earners living in 1–3 room HDB flats. The shares are worth $1 per share. They are neither transferable nor tradeable. Within the first 12 months (before 1 November 2002), shareholders may cash in up to half of their shares. After that, they may cash their shares without limit. NSS will earn annual dividends (guaranteed minimum of 3%) for five years from 2002 to 2007. The dividends will be in the form of bonus shares. On 1 March 2007, the government will redeem all NSS at $1 per share in cash.

### Ngultrum (NU)
Currency of Bhutan (1 Ngultrum = 100 Chetrums, US$1 = 48NU).

### Nguoi lao dong
Labourer, a Vietnamese weekly newspaper.

### Nhan Dan
The People, a Vietnamese newspaper.

### Nihon Keizai Shimbun
Nihon Keizai Shimbun (Japan Economic News) is a leading financial daily newspaper in Japan. Its stock indices (Nikkei 225, Nikkei 300) are widely followed by investors.

**Nikkei 225 Average Futures**
The Nikkei 225 Average Futures started trading in Japan on 3 September 1988.

**Nikkei 225 Futures Options**
The Nikkei 225 Futures Options was first traded on SIMEX (now SGX-DT) in 1992. This was SIMEX's first futures options contract to be based on a stock index. The underlying commodity of the Nikkei futures options contract is the SIMEX Nikkei 225 futures contracts.

**Nikkei 225 Options**
The Nikkei 225 Options was introduced in 1999.

**Nikkei 225 Stock Average Index Futures**
The Nikkei 225 Stock Average Index Futures was first traded on SIMEX (now SGX-DT) in 1986. The Chicago Mercantile Exchange (CME) had secured the rights to trade the Nikkei Index in the US and Asia outside Japan from Nihon Keizai Shimbun and had sub-licensed it to SIMEX.

The Nikkei Stock Average is the best known index covering the Japanese stock market. Published since 1949, the index is calculated and managed by Nihon Keizai Shimbun Inc., a newspaper information and communication group. The average is based on 225 stocks and accounts for 21% of the First Section of the Tokyo Stock Exchange. It represents about 50% of the market value and 60% of the turnover. (See also: Nikkei 300 Index)

**Nikkei 300 Index**
In 1994, SIMEX (now SGX-DT) became the first non-Japanese exchange to get licensing rights from the Nihon Keizai Shimbun to trade futures and options contracts based on the newly-created Japanese stock index, the Nikkei 300.

The Nikkei 300 is a market capitalization-weighted index consisting of 300 representative stocks listed on the Tokyo Stock Exchange. In contrast, the Nikkei 225 is a price-weighted index comprising 225 representative stocks. The Nikkei 300 is traded alongside SIMEX's existing Nikkei 225 and offers investors a wider choice of instruments for managing their portfolios.

**Nikkeiren**
In Japan, Nikkeiren was formed in 1948 as an umbrella organization of industrial and regional employers' associations to build a sound labour management relationship in Japan. (See also: Nippon Keidanren)

**Nikkeiren International Cooperation Centre**   *www.nicc.or.jp*
In Japan, the Nikkeiren International Cooperation Centre (NICC) was formed in 1989 as an organization in the Nikkeiren secretariat. It provides technical assistance to strengthen employers' organizations in developing countries. For example, its Asian Personnel Managers Training Program provides opportunity for Asian managers to study Japanese approaches to business management, with particular emphasis on personnel management.

**Nikko Cordial Corporation (Japan)**   *www.nikko.co.jp*
Nikko was incorporated in April 1944 after the merger of Kawashimaya Securities and Nomura Securities. In October 2001, Nikko transformed into a holding company structure and was renamed Nikko Cordial Corporation. The group includes Nikko Cordial Securities, Nikko Asset Management and others.

**Nikko Cordial Securities Inc (Japan)**   *www.nikko.co.jp/SEC*
Nikko Cordial Securities Inc is the new name for Nikko Securities Co Ltd with effect from October 2001. It is one of the leading securities houses in Japan. It has overseas offices in major cities Asia, Europe and North America.

**Nippon Keidanren (Japan Business Federation)**   *www.keidanren.or.jp*
Japan Business Federation was formed in May 2002 with the merger of Keidanren (Japan Federation of Economic Organizations) and Nikkeiren (Japan Federation of Employers' Associations). As of June 2002, its membership of 1,540 was comprised of 1,232 companies (including 70 foreign), 127 industrial associations and 47 regional employers' associations. Keidanren was formed in 1946 to help to reconstruct the war-devastated Japanese economy. Nikkeiren was formed in 1948 as an umbrella organization of industrial and regional employers' associations to build a sound labour management relationship in Japan.

**NTT Communications**   *www.ntt.com*
In Japan, the NTT Communications Corporation (NTT Com) is a Tokyo-based subsidiary of Nippon Telegraph and Telephone Corporation. It provides international services for voice, video and data communication reaching more than 200 countries. Its mission is to be a global IP solution company.

**Noi Bai Airport (Vietnam)**
In Vietnam, this is the international airport in Hanoi. After an upgrading program costing US$72 million, Noi Bai can receive 4 million passengers and 40,000 tonnes of goods annually.

**Nomura Holdings (Japan)**   *www.nomuraholdings.com*
Nomura Group is a leading financial services group in Japan and has worldwide operations. It provides a wide range of financial services and products.

**Nomura Securities (Japan)**   *www.nomuraholdings.com*
Nomura Securities Co Ltd (NSC) started in 1925 as a spin-off from the securities department of Osaka Nomura Bank. It is one of the largest securities houses in Japan. It is a wholly-owned subsidiary of Nomura Holdings Inc which forms part of the Nomura Group. (See also: Nomura Holdings)

**Non-Resident Foreign Currency Account (Sri Lanka)**
In Sri Lanka, exchange controls were liberalized in 1978. Commercial banks were allowed to open Non-Resident Foreign Currency (NRFC) Account for non-resident Sri Lankans who had foreign exchange earnings from abroad and for foreign nationals.

**Non-Resident Indian**
In India, the Non-Resident Indian (NRI) is one of the 3 categories of foreign investors which are allowed to invest directly in Indian securities. The other two categories are Foreign Institutional Investor and Overseas Corporate Body. They may make portfolio investment in listed and unlisted companies.

**Non-Voting Depository Receipt (Thailand)**   *www.set.or.th/nvdr*
In the Stock Exchange of Thailand (SET), the Non-Voting Depository Receipt (NVDR) is a new trading instrument issued by the NVDR Company Limited, a wholly-owned subsidiary of the SET. The purpose of NVDR is not only to stimulate trading in the Thai stock market, but also to help eliminate foreign investment barriers such as the foreign investment limits. NVDR investors will receive all financial benefits of ordinary shareholders, i.e. dividends, rights issues and warrants. The only difference is the voting right. (See also: Thai NVDR Company Limited)

**Norinchukin Bank (Japan)**
In Japan, the Norinchukin Bank was established in 1923 as a special corporation with limited liability based on the Norin-chuo-kinko Law. In 1986, it was converted to a private corporation. It is the central financial institution for cooperatives serving the agriculture, forestry and fishery industries. The financing for these industries is carried out through cooperatives based on the spirit of mutual support and with government protection and aid.

### North American Free Trade Agreement (NAFTA)

The North American Free Trade Agreement (NAFTA) started on 1 January 1994. It involves Canada, Mexico and United States. It removes trade barriers to promote fair competition and increase investment.

### North Eastern Development Finance Corporation   *www.nedfi.com*

In India, the North Eastern Development Finance Corporation Limited (NEDFi) was incorporated in 1995 to finance development in the North Eastern states of India. It has been promoted by financial institutions such as Industrial Development Bank of India, ICICI Ltd, Industrial Finance Corporation of India, Small Industries Development Bank of India, Life Insurance Corporation, General Insurance Corporation, Unit Trust of India and the State Bank of India.

### North-South Trade

North-South Trade involves the North (developed countries) and the South (developing countries).

### NUS College in Bio Valley (Singapore)

The NUS College in Bio Valley (NCBV) was set up in January 2003 by the National University of Singapore (NUS) in partnership with the University of Pennsylvania (Penn) in the US. NCBV students spend one year of internship with start-up companies while starting part time at the Penn's School of Engineering and Applied Science. NCBV was the second overseas college set up by NUS after the first one at Silicon Valley. These overseas college programs provide NUS students the opportunity to gain first hand experience of innovation and entrepreneurship through internship abroad.

### O Cach Industrial Zone

In Vietnam this is an industrial zone located in Gia Lam. It is a fully owned foreign project developed by Koland from South Korea. The 100-hectare zone has facilities for 120 small and medium companies producing electronics, textiles and chemicals.

### Office of the Commissioner of Insurance (Hong Kong)   *www.info.gov/hk/oci*

In Hong Kong, the Office of the Commissioner of Insurance (OCI) was set up in 1990. It administers the Insurance Companies Ordinance. Its objective is to protect the interest of insurance policy holders and to promote the stability of the insurance industry.

### Office of Employment Advocate (Australia)

In Australia, the Office of Employment Advocate (OEA) is a new statutory office set up under the Workplace Relations Act. It advises employers and employees about their rights and duties. It assesses and approves Australian Workplace Agreements (AWAs).

## Offshore Banking Unit (Philippines)

In the Philippines, the offshore banking system was established by a Presidential Decree in 1976. An offshore banking unit (OBU) may be a branch, subsidiary or affiliate of a bank that is authorized by the Central Bank as a separate accounting unit to transact offshore banking business in the Philippines. An OBU may transact in any currency other than the Philippine peso.

## Offshore Financial Centre (Vanuatu)

In Vanuatu, the Offshore Financial Centre (OFC) was established in 1971. Many financial organizations operate in the OFC. These include banks, insurance companies, trust companies, accounting firms and shipping companies. They are attracted by the tax-free status of exempt and international companies.

## Okurasho (Japan)

Japan's Ministry of Finance.

## Omnibus Investments Code (Philippines)

In the Philippines, the Omnibus Investments Code of 1987 integrates the basic laws on investment and harmonizes the provisions. It provides a comprehensive range of fiscal and non-fiscal incentives to investors. It provides for the creation of a Council for Investments in Trade, Tourism, Agriculture, Natural Resources, Transportation, Communications and Services. It serves as a one-stop facility to provide investors with information on investment opportunities and procedures.

## Ong Teng Cheong Institute of Labour Studies (Singapore)

The Ong Teng Cheong Institute of Labour Studies was known as Singapore Institute of Labour Studies, or SILS, before 2002. It is affiliated to the National Trades Union Congress (NTUC). It is responsible for labour education. It trains union leaders to manage their organization, how to represent interest of the workers, and to establish good employment relations at the workplace. It conducts courses leading to the award of diplomas in employment relations. The institute conducts research on issues related to employment relations.

## Open Academy (Singapore)  *www.ipamonline.com*

In Singapore, the Open Academy (OA) was launched by the Institute of Public Administration and Management (IPAM) at the Civil Service College in June

2001. OA aims to bring just-in-time learning to public officers through a virtual learning hub. OA also harnesses technology for distance learning. Through distance learning, the public service can establish links with other institutions and public services around the world. (See also: Civil Service College)

## Open Economic Zone (China)
In China, in 1985 the government designated three delta areas and two peninsulas as open economic development zones. These zones enjoy flexibility in foreign trade and investment. The deltas are: (a) Yangtze Delta (Suzhou, Wuxi and Changzhou in Jiangsu province, and Jiaxing and Huzhou in Zhejiang province), (b) Southern Fujian Delta (Xiamen, Zhangzhou, Quanzhou and numerous counties), (c) Zhujiang or Pearl River Delta (Panyu, Zengcheng counties, Foshan, Zhongshan, Jiangmen and several cities and counties). The two peninsulas are in the northeast: (a) Shandong peninsula (including Qindao, Jinan, Yantai, Weihai and several others), (b) Liaodong peninsula (Dalian, Shenyang, Anshan, Panjin, Yingkou, Liaoyang and others).

## Organda (Indonesia)
Organization of Transportation Companies in Indonesia.

## Organization of Petroleum Exporting Countries (OPEC)
OPEC includes Algeria, Indonesia, Iran, Kuwait, Libya, Nigeria, Qatar, Saudi Arabia, United Arab Emirates and Venezuela. Non-OPEC countries include Brunei, Egypt, Norway, Oman and Russia.

## Oriental Bank of Commerce (India)   www.obcindia.com
In India, the Oriental Bank of Commerce (OBC) was established in 1943. It is one of the strongest public sector banks in India, with capital and reserves of Rs 1549 crores. In 2001, its capital adequacy ratio was 11.8% as against a norm of 9% prescribed by the Reserve Bank of India. Its non-performing assets of 3.6% were among the lowest in the banking industry.

## Osaka Securities Exchange (Japan)   www.ose.or.jp
Osaka Securities Exchange (OSE) started in 1878 as the Osaka Stock Exchange together with the Tokyo Stock Exchange. In 1943, all stock exchanges were merged into the Japan Securities Exchange. This was dissolved in 1947. The Securities and Exchange Law established the present Osaka Securities Exchange on 1 April 1949. OSE provides a marketplace for transacting a wide range of securities, and securities-related futures and options. In 1997, the trading floor for stocks was closed and shifted to a

completely computer assisted system. In March 2001, OSE merged with Kyoto Stock Exchange. In April, OSE was demutualized. The exchange converted its entity into a joint stock corporation. One of the major exchanges in Japan, it is a market for trading a wide range of securities including domestic and foreign stocks, bonds, futures and options.

### Over-the-counter Securities Exchange (Taiwan)

In Taiwan, the Over-the-counter Securities Exchange was set up in 1994. It was previously known as the OTC Business Centre and belonged to the Taipei Securities Dealers Association. Trading may take place through negotiated pricing at the dealer's office or through the Exchange's computerized matching system. The OTC market is now known as Gre Tai Securities Market. (See also: Gre Tai Securities Market)

### Over-the-counter Trading

Over-the-counter (OTC) trading takes places outside the normal stock exchange.

### Oversea-Chinese Banking Corporation (Singapore)        *www.ocbc.com*

In Singapore, the Oversea-Chinese Banking Corporation (OCBC Bank) started in 1932 after the merger of three banks: Chinese Commercial Bank (founded in 1912), Ho Hong Bank (1917) and Oversea-Chinese Bank (1919). Over the decades, it has developed into one of the Big Three local banks in Singapore. In August 2002, it acquired Keppel Capital Holdings Limited which fully owned Keppel TatLee Bank, Keppel Securities, and Keppel TatLee Finance. OCBC has offices in 14 countries including Australia, China, Hong Kong SAR, Japan, Malaysia, UK and USA.

### Overseas Corporate Body (India)

In India, an Overseas Corporate Body (OCB) is one that is at least 60% owned by individuals of Indian nationality or origin resident outside India. It may be a company, partnership, society or other body corporate. It may be a trust in which at least 60% of the beneficial interest is irrevocably held by such persons provided that such ownership interest should be actually held by them and not in the capacity as nominees. The OCB is one of the three categories of foreign investors that are allowed to invest directly in Indian securities. The other two categories are Non-resident Indian and Foreign Institutional Investor. They may make portfolio investment in listed and unlisted companies.

### Overseas Private Investment Corporation (US)
The Overseas Private Investment Corporation (OPIC) is a US agency under the International Development Cooperation Agency. It promotes US private investment in developing countries.

### Overseas Union Bank (Singapore)   *www.uobgroup.com*
In Singapore, the Overseas Union Bank (OUB) became a wholly-owned subsidiary and merged into the United Overseas Bank (UOB) in January 2002. The OUB Malaysia also merged with UOB Malaysia.

### P3GI (Indonesia)
Research Centre of Indonesian Sugarcane Plantations.

### Pacific Basin Economic Council   *www.phec.org*
The Pacific Basin Economic Council was founded in 1967. It is an association of senior businessmen in the Pacific Basin. Its objective is to expand trade and investment through fostering open markets. Its multinational membership includes more than 1,000 companies from 20 economies.

### Pacific Economic Cooperation Council
The PECC was set up in 1980 as an international organization consisting primarily of members drawn from the public, academic and private sectors with the objective of bringing into fruition the Pacific Basin Cooperation Concept advocated by the late Japanese Prime Minister Masayoshi Ohira. PECC holds a general meeting every 18 months. By 1997, PECC had 22 member economies from the Asia Pacific region. PECC enjoys the status of official observer at the APEC ministerial meetings.

### Pacific Northwest International Trade Association   *www.pnita.org*
The Pacific Northwest International Trade Association (PNITA) was founded in 1982. It is a private non-profit trade association that promotes international trade throughout the Pacific Northwest region. It represents businesses in the states of Washington, Oregon and Idaho in the United States.

### Paddy Lands Act
In Sri Lanka, the Paddy Lands Act (PLA) was introduced in 1958 to give protection to tenant paddy farmers.

### Paket Februari or Pakfeb (Indonesia)
This was a banking reform package introduced by Bank Indonesia in February 1991. It was designed to improve bank supervision. Its provisions included

decrees on ownership and management of new banks. It also required all banks to maintain the internationally-adopted standard of 8% capital adequacy ratio (CAR) as recommended by the Bank for International Settlements.

### Paket Mei or Pakmei (Indonesia)

This was a banking reform package introduced by Bank Indonesia in May 1993. It covered capital adequacy, lending limits and provision of loan losses. One important aspect was the revision of the legal lending limits that restricted lending to individuals and groups. The previous restriction of group lending to 50% was reduced to 20%, with implementation to be completed within four years up to 31 March 1997.

### Paket Desember (Indonesia)

This was a banking reform package introduced in Indonesia in 1988 to liberalize the financial system. It provided incentives for the entry of joint ventures in leasing, factoring, venture capital and securities trading. Further reform packages were introduced in 1991 and 1993. For example, the package in 1991 included measures to improve bank supervision and capital adequacy for the banks. These reforms resulted in the introduction of a new banking act in 1992 that replaced the act of 1967. (See also: Paket Februari, Pake Mei and Paket Oktober)

### Paket Oktober (Indonesia)

This was a reform package introduced in Indonesia in October 1988 to liberalize the restrictive regulatory financial framework. (See also: Paket Februari, Paket Mei, Paket Desember)

### Pakistan Credit Rating Agency    *www.pacra.com.pk*

The Pakistan Credit Rating Agency (PACRA) was set up in 1994 as a joint venture among IBCA (international credit rating agency), International Finance Corporation (IFC) and the Lahore Stock Exchange. It is now an affiliate of Fitch Ratings after IBCA merged with the American Fitch Investors Services. PACRA provides a full range of credit rating services including corporate entities and fixed income instruments.

### Pakistan Industrial Credit and Investment Corporation    *www.picic.com*

The Pakistan Industrial Credit and Investment Corporation (PICIC) was set up in 1957 with assistance from the World Bank. It provides medium and long credit to the private industrial sector. It also participates in the capital market through purchase and underwriting of shares.

### Pakistan National Shipping Corporation

Pakistan National Shipping Corporation is the national flag carrier. It serves as the link between major trading partners and to influence on freight rates charged by the Conferences and other liners operating to Pakistan.

### Pakistan Software Export Board  *www.pseb.org.pk*

The Pakistan Software Export Board was set up by the government in 1995 to nurture the local software industry. It provides a link between local and foreign IT companies. The IT parks at Islamabad, Karachi and Lahore provide one-stop facilities for software houses.

### Pakistan Telecommunication Authority  *www.pta.gov.pk*

The Pakistan Telecommunication Authority (PTA) was formed in 1996. It regulates the establishment, operation and maintenance of telecommunications services.

### Pakistan Tourism Development Corporation  *www.tourism.gov.pk*

The Pakistan Tourism Development Corporation (PTDC) was set up in 1970. Its objective is develop tourism infrastructure and encourage the private sector to play an active role in tourism development. It has several subsidiaries including PTDC Motels (Pvt) Ltd, Associated Hotels of Pakistan Ltd and Pakistan Tours Ltd.

### Pakistan Trade Office  *www.paktrade.org*

The Pakistan Trade Office (Pak Trade) is operated by the Ministry of Commerce. It provides information on trade and investment opportunities in Pakistan.

### PAKSI

See Financial Package for SMIs.

### Palm Oil Institute of Malaysia  *www.porim.gov.my*

The Palm Oil Institute of Malaysia (PORIM) was set up in 1979 to conduct research on oil palm and its products. Its objectives are to expand current uses of palm oil products and to find new uses, and to improve quality of the products. It also promotes the use of palm oil products.

### Palm Oil Registration and Licensing Authority (Malaysia)  *www.porla.gov.my*

In Malaysia, the objective of the Palm Oil Registration and Licensing Authority (PORLA) provides services and assistance to the industry. The objective is to enhance the position of the palm oil industry as the leading supplier to the world oils and fats market.

## Pancasila (Indonesia)

Pancasila is Indonesia's national ideology of five principles of monotheism, humanitarianism, Indonesian unity, sovereignty and social justice (i.e. belief in one supreme God, just and civilized humanity, nationalism, democracy and social justice).

## Panin Group (Indonesia)

In Indonesia, the Panin group is a financial conglomerate with diversified activities. Its affiliates include Panin Bank, Panin Life and Panin Insurance. It offers a wide range of banking services, insurance and multi-finance products. Panin's international joint venture partners include the Dai-Ichi Kangyo Bank, ANZ Banking group, International Finance Corporation, Nippon Credit Bank, Credit Lyonnais, AMP Society, SEAVI and Schroders.

## Papua New Guinea Agricultural Bank

The Papua New Guinea Agricultural Bank started in 1967 and was formerly known as the Papua New Guinea Development Bank. It promotes economic development especially in the rural areas through the granting of loans.

## Papua New Guinea and Australia Trade and Commercial Relations Agreement (PATCRA)

PATCRA is a bilateral trade agreement to foster trade and investment between the two countries.

## Papua New Guinea Banking Corporation   *www.pngbank.com.pg*

The Papua New Guinea Banking Corporation (PNGBC) started in 1974. It was the largest commercial bank in the PNG with 84 branches and agencies throughout the country. In April 2002, it was acquired by the Bank of South Pacific. (See also: Bank of South Pacific)

## Papua New Guinea Investment Corporation

The Papua New Guinea Investment Corporation was set up in 1972. Its objective is to acquire foreign-owned large companies and sell them to local groups such as cooperatives through a mutual fund.

## Pawan Hans Helicopters Limited (India)   *www.pawanhans.com*

In India, the Pawan Hans Helicopters Limited (PHHL) was incorporated in 1985. It is the largest helicopter operator in India. The government has 78.5% shareholding in the company.

## Payments Registration and Electronic Settlement System (Australia)

In Australia, the Payments Registration and Electronic Settlement System

(PRESS) is a centralized system which controls credit, settlement and queuing of payments. It has been developed by the APCA (Australian Payments Clearing Association) and Reserve Bank of Australia.

### PCI Leasing and Finance Inc (Philippines)
In the Philippines, the PCI Leasing and Finance Inc is listed on the Philippine Stock Exchange. It is a wholly-owned subsidiary of listed Philippine Commercial International Bank (PCI Bank) and focuses on leasing and financing. Its leasing products include direct leases, sale and leaseback arrangements and dollar-denominated leases. Its financing products include commercial and consumer loans, instalment paper purchases, receivables discounting and factoring. (See also: Philippine Commercial International Bank)

### PDCP Development Bank Inc (Philippines)
PDCP Bank, formerly called Private Development Corporation of the Philippines (PDCP), is a development bank established in 1963 as a development finance institution cum investment house. It was set up with the assistance of the World Bank and the USAID and the sponsorship of the Philippine government. In 1992, it was converted into a thrift bank. In 1996, it acquired the First Philippine International Bank (FirstBank). In 1998, it received approval to operate as a commercial bank. It has a network of 77 branches nationwide. Its subsidiaries include PDCP Insurance Brokers Inc. Among its shareholders is Metro Pacific Corporation — also a listed company, which is the investment holding company in the Philippines of the Hong Kong-based First Pacific Company Limited.

### PDI bonds
Past Due Interest bonds.

### Pelabuhan Indonesia
Indonesian Port Authority.

### Pemberitahuan Ekspor Barang Tertentu (PEBT) (Indonesia)
Certificate of export for special products.

### Penanaman Modal Asing (PMA)
Foreign joint venture in Indonesia.

### Penang Chamber of Commerce & Agriculture
In Malaysia, the Penang Chamber of Commerce & Agriculture was formed in 1837. Its members included Arab, Chinese, European and Indian merchants. It was the predecessor of the Malaysian International Chamber of

Commerce and Industry. (See also: Malaysian International Chamber of Commerce and Industry)

### Pension institutions (Indonesia)
As of 1996, there were 262 pension institutions comprising 239 employer pension funds (DPPK) and 22 financial institution pension funds (DPLK). About 80% of their assets came mainly from their members' and employers' regular instalments. Investments by pension funds are mainly on fixed-income instruments such as bonds and deposits.

### People-mover Rapid Transit (Malaysia)
In Malaysia, People-mover Rapid Transit (PRT) is a light rail system in the capital city Kuala Lumpur. The main portion stretches from Jalan Tun Razak and Brickfields. It cuts across Golden Triangle area and forms part of the KL Linear City project along the Klang River.

### People's Bank (Sri Lanka)
In Sri Lanka, the People's Bank was set up in 1961 under the People's Bank Act. It is a state-owned commercial bank.

### People's Bank of China
The People's Bank of China (PBC/PBOC) was set up in 1948 as the central bank of China. Within the context of a planned economy, its main role was to give out funds allocated by the State Planning Commission to state-owned enterprises. In the 1980s, the government reduced its intervention and allowed PBOC more autonomy in financial matters. The central bank now plays an important role in transforming the banking system into a market-driven sector. It supervises and controls the financial industry through regulations.

### People's Bank of the Union of Burma
The People's Bank of the Union of Burma was set up as a result of merging all the nationalized banks. It acted as the central bank of Burma. In 1975, its name was changed to Union Bank of Burma. (See also: Central Bank of Myanmar)

### People's Insurance Company of China
Before 1988, People's Insurance Company of China (PICC) was the state insurance monopoly, it resumed offering insurance products in 1979 after being out of business since 1958, when insurance was deemed inappropriate to a socialist system. PICC now offers a wide range of insurance products. It has two subsidiaries: China Insurance Company (CIC) and the Tai Ping

Insurance Company (TPIC) that deal specifically in international business mostly trade and shipping.

**People's Unit Trust (Papua New Guinea)**   *www.pm.gov.pg*
In PNG, the People's Unit Trust (PUT) was launched on 6 June 2002 to enable citizens to participate in the benefits of privatization. The government has privatized several national institutions, including the Orogen Minerals, Papua New Guinea Banking Corporation and the National Provident Fund. Investment in the PUT is initially restricted to PNG citizens, superannuation funds and institutions, plus selected international aid and donor agencies. For the short term, the Independent Public Business Corporation (IPBC) is the trustee and manager. PUT will eventually be listed on the Port Moresby Stock Exchange.

**Peoplised Bus Companies (Sri Lanka)**
In Sri Lanka, during the late 1950s, the Ceylon Transport Board (CTB) was the sole authority to operate passenger bus service in the country. In 1978, its functions were decentralized by creating nine Regional Transport Boards (RTBs) and the Sri Lanka Central Transport Board (SLCTB). In 1979, the government allowed private bus companies to provide passenger services in parallel with the SLCTB. Starting from 1990, bus depots under the SLCTB were converted into independent companies to form Peoplised Bus Companies. These companies were later clustered into Regional Bus Companies.

**Perbadanan Kemajuan Negeri Selangor (Malaysia)**
Selangor State Development Corporation (Malaysia).

**Perhimpunan Bank-Bank Umum Nasional Swasta (Perbanas)**
See National Private Bank Association.

**PT Peringkat Efek Indonesia (PEFINDO)**
This is Indonesia's first securities credit rating agency set up in 1994. Its main function is to rate bonds and other debt instruments. It provides investors with information about the ability of companies to pay their loans and interest.

**Persahaan Dagang (PD) (Indonesia)**
Trading enterprise in Indonesia.

**Persahaan Persaorangan (PP)**
Sole proprietorship in Indonesia.

### Persatuan Penilai Dan Perunding Harta Swasta Malaysia (PEPS)
*www.peps.com.my*
See Association of Valuers & Property Consultants in Private Practice Malaysia.

### Perum Pengembangan Keuangan Koperasi (Perum PKK)
Perum PKK is an Indonesian state-owned corporation that covers risk on credit extended by banks to cooperatives.

### Perumka
Perumka is Indonesia's state railway company. After undergoing management restructuring in the early 1990s, Perumka turned losses into profits. In 1991, it lost Rp 92.2 billion. Its profits totalled RP 6.41 billion in 1994, Rp 11.87 billion in 1995, and Rp 17.89 billion in 1996. Much of its profits have come from new commercial trains that have better facilities and cater to executive class. These include Argo Bromo (Jakarta-Surabaya), Argo Gede (Jakarta-Bandung), Bima (Jakarta-Surabaya), Mutiara (Jakarta-Surabaya) and Parahiyangan (Jakarta-Bandung). It has also expanded its cargo trains called Antaboga from Jakarta and Surabaya.

### Perusahaan Inti Rakyat (PIR)
PIR is a scheme in Indonesia to develop smallholders by assigning more agricultural estates and providing guidance in cultivating, processing and marketing products. The scheme is carried out in plantations, poultry farms and fisheries.

### Perusahaan Jawatan (Perjan)
Government agency in Indonesia. (See also: Indonesian state-owned enterprise)

### Perusahaan Negara (PN)
State corporation in Indonesia. (See also: Indonesian state-owned enterprise)

### Perusahaan Pertambangan Minyak dan Gas Bumi Negera (PERTAMINA)
State-owned Indonesian petroleum and natural gas company.

### Perusahaan Listrik Negara (PLN)
PLN is Indonesia's state-owned electric company. In 1995, it set up a subsidiary PT Pembangkit Listrik Jawa Bali (PJB) which now operates the Surabaya coal-fired plant and the Saguling hydro-power plant in West Java, the Tambak Lorok steam power plant in Central Java, and steam and gas power plants in Bali. In 1996, PJB made profits totalling Rp 350 billion and was the largest contributor to PLN's earnings.

**Perusahaan Umum (Perum)**
Public corporation in Indonesia. (See also: Indonesian state-owned enterprise)

**Petrolimex**
This is Vietnam's National Petroleum Import Export Corporation. It has a US$4.4 million joint venture with Japan's Nissho Iwai and Tayca Corporation to produce raw materials for detergent.

**Petronas (Malaysia)**
In Malaysia, Petronas (Petrolium Nasional) is the national oil company. It has 25 fully-owned and 13 partly-owned subsidiaries, e.g. Petronas Gas Berhad (publicly listed in 1995), Petronas Penapisan (Terengganu) Sdn Bhd and Petronas Penapisan (Melaka) Sdn Bhd.

**Petronas Gas Berhad**
In Malaysia, Petronas Gas is a subsidiary of Petronas which has a monopoly over gas processing and distribution in Malaysia. When Petronas Gas shares were floated on the Kuala Lumpur Stock Exchange in 1995, the 117 million shares at RM 5.80 each attracted more than 645,000 applications for about 990 million shares worth RM 5.25 billion, with an over-subscription rate of about 8 times.

**PetroVietnam Insurance Company (Vietnam)**
In Vietnam, this insurance company specializes in the oil and gas industry.

**Philippine Amanah Bank**
The Philippine Amanah Bank (PAB) was formed by a Presidential Decree in 1973 to provide banking facilities to the Muslim community in Mindanao.

**Philippine Association of Securities Brokers and Dealers Inc (PASBDI)**
The Philippine Association of Securities Brokers and Dealers Inc (PASBDI) serves as the voice of the securities industry and protects the interest of its members. Its board of governors includes representatives from the Philippine Stock Exchange, Investment House Association of the Philippines (IHAP), Association of Independent Brokers and Dealers Inc (AIBD) and the public sector.

**Philippine Association of Stock Transfer and Registry Agencies Inc (PASTRA)**
PASTRA was registered with the Securities and Exchange Commission (SEC) in 1978. Its main objective is to safeguard the interests of its members, their clients and the investing public. Through the association, members can

collectively assist, petition and cooperate with regulatory agencies such as the SEC and the Philippine Stock Exchange.

### Philippine Bank of Communications   *www.pbcom.com.ph*
The Philippine Bank of Communications started operations in 1939. It was listed on the stock exchange in 1988. It acquired the Consumer Savings Bank in 2001, thus becoming one of the highly capitalized commercial banks with PHP 8 billion. It provides a wide range of financial services and credit facilities.

### Philippine Banking Corporation
Philippine Banking Corporation is listed on the Philippines Stock Exchange. It started in 1935 as a mutual savings bank and loan association in Tanauan, Batangas. A few years later, it was converted into a commercial bank. It now provides a wide range of banking services. Its subsidiaries include Philbancor Venture Capital Corporation and the PBC Capital Investment Corporation.

### Philippine Central Depository   *www.pcd.com.ph*
The Philippine Central Depository (PCD) was set up in 1996. It is a private company owned by major capital market participants: Philippine Stock Exchange (PSE, 32%), Bankers Association of the Philippines (32%), Financial Executives Institute of the Philippines (10%), Development Bank of the Philippines (10%), Investment House Association of the Philippines (7%), Social Security System (5%) and Citibank (5%).

PCD participants include PSE-trading participants, custodian banks, government and corporate financial institutions, insurance companies, commercial banks, and other institutional investors. PCD uses the book-entry system to record ownership and movement of securities among its participants. Securities are held in trust by PCD Nominee Corporation (PCNC), a wholly-oowned subsidiary of PCD. The PCD also provides registry and clearing and settlement services to issuers of fixed income securities such as bonds, commercial papers, NCDs and other negotiable instruments.

### Philippine Chamber of Commerce and Industry   *www.philcham.com*
The Philippine Chamber of Commerce and Industry (PCCI) was formed in 1978 as a result of merging the Chamber of Commerce of the Philippines (CCP, formed in 1903) and the Philippine Chamber of Industry (PCI). It is a non-stock, non-profit and non-government organization of business enterprises, local chambers and industry associations representing various sectors of business. It is recognized as the sole official representative of the entire private business community.

**Philippine Commercial International Bank**   *www.pcib.com*
PCI Bank is listed on the Philippine Stock Exchange. It provides a broad range of banking services in the Philippines through its extensive branch network. Its banking-related major subsidiaries include: PCI Capital Corporation, PCIB Savings Bank Inc, PCI Leasing & Finance Inc, PCIB CIGNA Life Insurance Corporation. (See also: Bankard Inc Philippines, PCI Leasing and Finance Inc)

**Philippine Deposit Insurance Corporation (PDIC)**   *www.pdic.gov.ph*
The PDIC was formed in 1963. It is a government-owned and controlled corporation that provides depositor protection and ensures settlement of depositor claims. Deposits are insured up to PHP 100,000. All banks are required to become members of PDIC.

**Philippine Dispute Resolution Centre Inc**
The Philippine Dispute Resolution Centre Inc (PDRCI) is a non-profit organization which promotes the use of arbitration and other modes of alternative dispute resolution to settle domestic and international disputes. It provides commercial arbitration, referral and information services.

**Philippine Economic Zone Authority**
The Philippine Economic Zone Authority (PEZA) (formerly known as the Export Processing Zone Authority or EPZA) manages the country's four export processing zones. It also manages privately owned development sites that have been designated as special economic zones.

**Philippine Export & Foreign Loan Guarantee Corporation (Philguarantee)**
Philguarantee is a government agency that provides guarantee cover to Filipino exporters on their loans obtained from domestic and foreign sources. It thus enhances the credit-worthiness of these exporters and enables them to obtain funds.

**Philippine National Bank**   *www.philnabank.com*
The Philippine National Bank (PNB), formerly controlled by the government was privatized in 1995 with the private sector owning 51% of the bank. It is the largest Philippine bank in terms of assets. It provides a full range of financial services through a network of 320 branches. PNB also provides banking services to the Philippine Government and government corporations. Its major banking-related subsidiaries include: Century Bank, PNB Credit Card Corp, PNB General Insurers Co. Inc, PNB International Finance Ltd, PNB Remittance Centres Inc, PNB Securities Inc, PNB Venture Capital Corp, RPB Venture Capital Corp, PNB Corp Guam and PNB Italy S.p.A.

**Philippine Overseas Employment Administration**   *www.poea.gov.ph*
The Philippine Overseas Employment Administration (POEA) was formed in 1982. It is the government agency responsible for promoting overseas employment of Filipino workers. In 1987, POEA was reorganized to include expanded functions such as strengthening the worker protection and regulatory components of the overseas employment program.

In 1995, Republic Act 8042 defined specific policy thrusts for POEA. Among others, these included: guarantee of migrant workers rights, stricter rules on illegal recruitment activities, repatriation of workers, reintegration program, shared government information systems on migration and assistance to overseas Filipino workers and their families. The POEA also conducts Pre-Employment Orientation Seminars (PEOS) and Pre-Departure Orientation Seminar (PEOS) for workers before their departure for overseas employment.

**Philippine Savings Bank**   *www.psbank.com.ph*
The Philippine Savings Bank is listed on the Philippine Stock Exchange. Its main thrust of operation is the retail sector and the small and medium clientele. For example, its "Negosyo Na" working capital loan is a credit facility for small and medium enterprises.

**Philippine-SEC Institute Foundation Inc**   *www.sec.gov.ph*
The Philippine-SEC Institute Foundation Inc (PhilSEC) was incorporated in 1992. It organizes training programs and develops professional standards among securities market participants.

**Philippine Stock Exchange**   *www.pse.com.ph*
The Philippine Stock Exchange (PSE) was incorporated on 14 July 1992 after unifying the Manila Stock Exchange (MSE) and Makati Stock Exchange (MkSE). The MSE was set up in 1927 while the MkSE started operations in 1965. Although the two exchanges operated as separate entities, they were basically trading the same listed issues. With persuasion from President Fidel Ramos administration, the PSE was set up to unify the two exchanges in order to develop a more efficient capital market. The Securities and Exchange Commission granted the PSE its licence to operate as a securities exchange on 4 March 1994. It simultaneously cancelled the licences of the MSE and MkSE. On 25 March 1994, the one price-one market exchange was achieved through the successful link-up of the two existing trading floors. From then on, the PSE has been the sole exchange in the Philippines. In 2002, the exchange finally moved to a new building at Taguig, Metro Manila to bring

under one roof its two separate and competing trading floors. (See also: Manila Stock Exchange, Makati Stock Exchange)

### Philippine Stock Exchange Foundation Inc

The Philippine Stock Exchange Foundation Inc (PSEFI) was incorporated in 1995. It is a private non-stock, non-profit, qualified donee institution. Its main objectives are to develop the Philippine capital market, promote social development and preserve Philippine arts and culture. The PSEFI is a member of the League of Corporate Foundation and the Philippine Business for Social Progress.

### Philippine Trust Company

The Philippine Trust Company is a bank listed on the Philippine Stock Exchange. It offers a full range of banking services through branches located at key business centres in the Philippines. Philtrust Finance Limited is its subsidiary in Hong Kong.

### PHIVIDEC Industrial Authority

In the Philippines, the PHIVIDEC Industrial Authority (PIA) was formed in 1974. The PHIVIDEC Industrial Estate (PIE) is located in Misamis Oriental Province in Mindanao. It encourages industrial development in the rural areas.

### Phu Bai Airport (Vietnam)

This is the airport at Hue city in Vietnam. After renovation, it was reopened in 1996.

### Phu My Port (Vietnam)

Phu My Port is located in Ba Ria-Vung Tau province about 70 km east of Ho Chi Minh City. It is Vietnam's first deep-water port capable of handling ships of up to 40,000 dwt. It started operations in 1996. It is also Vietnam's first joint venture port. The partners are Agricultural Technique Service Company of Ba Ria-Vung Tau, Import and Export and Production Company of Binh Tay of HCM City, Vietnam Corporation of Agricultural Material, Asia Commercial Joint Stock Bank, Commerce Society of Potassium and Nitrate of France, the Maritime General Corporation of France and Norsk Hydro Company of Norway.

### Piawan Brunei Darussalam   *www.mod.gov.bn*

In Brunei, the Piawan Brunei Darussalam (PBD) Standards are formulated by the Ministry of Development to maintain high quality and consistency for material and workmanship in the construction industry.

## Pips

In foreign exchange trading, the last decimal places of a price quotation are called pips (1/100th of 1%).

## Planters' Development Bank (Philippines)

Planters' Development Bank is listed on the Philippine Stock Exchange. It is a privately-owned development bank which is also involved in commercial banking. It has had about 40 years of experience in financing rural small and medium enterprises. It is active in the lending programs funded by the government and multilateral institutions channelled through the Development Bank of the Philippines and the Land Bank of the Philippines. Its affiliates include Filrice Incorporated, PDB Leasing Corporation and PDB Insurance Agency Inc.

## PNG Harbours Limited

In Papua New Guinea, under the privatization policy in 2001, the PNG Harbours Limited was formed to take over the assets and staff of the Harbours Board. The new pre-privatization company is under the control of the Privatization Commission. The Harbours Board would retain its regulatory functions until a new regulatory Maritime Safety Authority is created by legislation.

## PNG Power

In Papua New Guinea, PNG Power was formed in 2002 to take over the functions of the Electricity Commission (Elcom). Shares of the wholly-owned state company are held by the Minister for Privatization and Corporatization as trustee for the State.

## PT Polysindo Eka Perkasa (Indonesia)

This is the flagship company of the Texmaco Group which is one of largest integrated polyester producers in Indonesia. It is located at Kaliwungu and Karawang in West Java. (See also: Texmaco Group)

## Port Development Board (Hong Kong)

In 1998, Hong Kong's Port Development Board was renamed Hong Kong Port Maritime Board. Its functions have been increased to include all aspects of the port and to promote it as an international shipping centre.

## Port Moresby Stock Exchange   www.pomsox.com.pg

The Port Moresby Stock Exchange (POMSoX) started trading in 1999. POMSoX is closely aligned to the Australian Stock Exchange (ASX) which has licensed its Business and Listing Rules to POMSoX. Major stockbrokers include Capital Stockbrokers Limited and Kina Securities Limited.

**Port of Singapore Authority**
The Port of Singapore Authority (PSA) was formed in 1964 to develop Singapore into a global shipping centre offering a wide range of marine services such as pilotage, tugs, bunkers, cargo and container handling and warehousing. In October 1997, as a result of corporatization, the regulatory functions of PSA were taken over by the new statutory board Maritime and Port Authority. Its commercial operations are now managed by the PSA Corporation.

**Post Office Savings Bank (Singapore)**
In Singapore, the Post Office Savings Bank (POSB) was opened in 1877. For decades, it remained one of the oldest financial institutions in Singapore. In 1998, the government sold it to the DBS Bank.

**Postal and Telecommunication Corporation (Papua New Guinea)**
In PNG, the Postal and Telecommunication Corporation is a government corporation and provides all forms of communication systems.

**Postal Savings System (Taiwan)**
In Taiwan, the Postal Savings System (PSS) has the largest branch network with about 1,600 branches and 1,500 ATMs throughout the island. It has about 16% share of the deposit market.

**Power Gas (Singapore)**   *www.spower.com.sg/power_gas.htm*
In Singapore, Power Gas Limited is one of the oldest companies. It was set up in 1861 as the Singapore Gas Company and became part of the Public Utilities Board in 1963. In 1995, Power Gas was incorporated as a wholly-owned subsidiary of Singapore Power. In January 2002, Power Gas transferred its businesses in gas import, production and retailing to Gas Supply Pte Ltd and City Gas Pte Ltd. With that, Power Gas is now the sole gas transporter and gas system operator in Singapore. (See also: Singapore Power)

**Prakas (Cambodia)**
Ministerial regulation or order.

**Pre-departure Orientation Seminar (Philippines)**
In the Philippines, workers departing for overseas employment are required to undergo a pre-departure orientation seminar. (See also: Philippine Overseas Employment Administration)

**Presidency Bank of Bengal (Myanmar)**
This was the first bank to be set up in Burma (now Myanmar) in 1865 under the British rule.

**Presidential Commission on Privatization (Sri Lanka)**
In Sri Lanka, the Presidential Commission on Privatization (PSP) was appointed in 1987 to study and prepare a general framework to implement the privatization program. It was later renamed the Commission of Peoplization. In 1989, the Public Investment Management Board (PIMB) was formed to undertake the privatization program for the Commission. In 1990, the PIMB was renamed the Public Investment and Management Company (PIMC) and empowered to prepare public enterprises for privatization and to manage such enterprises until their divestiture.

**Pribumi (Indonesia)**
Ethnic Indonesian.

**Prime Commercial Bank Ltd (Pakistan)**   *www.primebank.com.pk*
The Prime Commercial Bank Ltd was started in 1992 by a group of Pakistani banking professionals who teamed up with shareholders of the National Commercial Bank from Saudi Arabia. It has a network of 23 branches and provides a wide range of commercial, consumer and corporate banking services.

**Prime Minister's Science, Engineering and Innovation Council (Australia)**
*www.dist.gov.au/science/PMSEIC/PMSEIC.html*
In Australia, PMSEIC is a national level advisory body that encourages the scientific community leaders and major users of science and technology to raise issues with the Prime Minister and other ministers.

**Private Development Bank (Philippines)**
Private development banks in the Philippines accept savings and time deposits. They use the funds to provide medium and long term loans to finance industry and agriculture. They may act as correspondent and collection agents and rediscount papers with any bank.

**Private Development Corporation of the Philippines (PDCP)**
See PDCP Development Bank Inc (Philippines).

**Privatization Commission (Bangladesh)**   *www.bangladeshonline.com/pb.re2.htm*
In Bangladesh, the Privatization Commission was set up in 1993. It is responsible for privatizing state-owned enterprises.

**Privatization Commission (Pakistan)**   *www.privatization.gov.pk*
In Pakistan, the Privatization Commission (PC) was formed to implement the
government's privatization policy. In November 2000, a Ministry of
Privatization was formed and the chairman of the Commission was appointed
Minister. There is also a Cabinet Committee on Privatization that formulates
privatization policy for approval by the Cabinet.

**Production Credit for Rural Women (Nepal)**
In Nepal, the Production Credit for Rural Women (PCRW) scheme was
introduced in 1982. It aimed to increase the income of rural women and family
welfare by providing low interest loans for farm production and social purposes.

**Productivity and Standards Board (Singapore)**
In Singapore, the Productivity and Standards Board (PSB) was formed in 1996
as a result of merging the National Productivity Board and Singapore Institute
of Standards and Industrial Research (SISIR). Its mission is to raise
productivity in order to enhance economic growth for a better quality of life
in Singapore. It works closely with other government agencies, employer
groups and the National Trades Union Congress. In 2001, the PSB privatized
its training, consulting, technology application, tests and certification
functions. It now focuses on statutory functions while revenue generating
services are provided by two new companies PSB Corporation Private Ltd and
PSB Certification Private Ltd. These two companies are subsidiaries of PSB
Holdings Private Limited that is owned by PSB the statutory board. In 2002,
PSB was renamed SPRING Singapore (Standards, Productivity and Innovation
through Growth).

**Profit and Loss Sharing**
In Islamic banking, the profit and loss sharing (PLS) system involves the bank
paying depositors a rate that is based on actual earnings realized by the bank
on those deposited funds.

**Program for Pollution Control, Evaluation and Rating (PROPER)**
In Indonesia, this program was introduced in 1995 to promote compliance
with existing pollution regulations. The colour rating ranged from gold for
excellent to black for very poor.

**Projek Lebuhraya Utara-Selatan (PLUS) (Malaysia)**
In Malaysia, PLUS is a toll road operating company owned by United
Engineers Malaysia.

## Proprietary Limited (Pty Ltd) Company
Private limited liability company in Australia or South Africa.

## Prudential Bank (Philippines)    www.prudentialbank.com
Prudential Bank is listed on the Philippine Stock Exchange. It offers a wide range of banking products and services. It also has investments in Prudential Venture Capital Corp and AEA Development Corporation. In 1987, the Prudential Bank and Bank of Tokyo jointly acquired Pilipinas Bank.

## PSA Corporation (Singapore)
In Singapore, PSA Corporation (PSA Corp) was corporatized from the former Port of Singapore Authority (PSA) on 1 October 1997. The regulatory functions of PSA are performed by the new statutory board Maritime and Port Authority of Singapore (MPA). PSA Corp operates four container terminals at Tanjong Pagar, Keppel, Brani and Pasir Panjang.

## PSB Corporation (Singapore)
In Singapore, the PSB Corporation Private Ltd was formed on 1 April 2001 when the former Productivity & Standards Board (PSB) privatized its training, consultancy and certification functions. It provides one-stop integrated solution to help companies achieve business excellence through three Ps: people, products and processes.

## Public Bank Berhad (Malaysia)    www.publicbank.com.my
Public Bank Berhad was set up in 1966. It is Malaysia's third largest bank. As of 31 December 1995, its paid-up capital was about RM 620 million and its profits totalled RM 595 million. Its group assets totalled RM 33 billion and shareholders' funds were over RM 2 billion. It had a network of more than 150 branches in Malaysia, Hong Kong, Sri Lanka and Laos. It also has offices in Cambodia, Vietnam, New Zealand, Australia, China and Myanmar. It had more than 5,000 employees.

## Public Calling Office (Philippines)
In the Philippines, a public calling office (PCO) is a telephone station that provides long distance telephone service to a particular area. It has access to the whole PLDT (Philippine Long Distance Telephone) and international networks.

## Public Enterprise Reform Commission (Sri Lanka)
In Sri Lanka, the Public Enterprise Reform Commission (PERC) was set up in 1995 to manage the privatization program. It has representatives from the

public and private sectors. It reviews the privatization program, proposes assets for privatization and regulates privatized industries. The objectives of PERC include: improving the competitive position and efficiency of the Sri Lanka economy, attracting technology and expertise, developing and democratizing management, motivating the private sector and generating state revenue and other benefits.

### Public Information Services Office (PISO)
In 1993, BAPEPAM (Indonesia's Capital Market Supervisory Agency) set up PISO to make capital market information easily accessible to investors. Services include information on listed companies, stock exchanges, clearing settlement, depository institutions, investment funds, securities companies, custodians, securities administration agencies and trust agents.

### Public Investment Management Board (Sri Lanka)
See Presidential Commission on Privatization.

### Public Investment and Management Company (Sri Lanka)
See Presidential Commission on Privatization.

### Public Key Infrastructure Forum (Singapore)
In Singapore, the Public Key Infrastructure (PKI) forum was formed in March 2001 shortly after the formation of the National Trust Council. It is an industry-led and government-supported initiative. The forum, comprising 19 infocomm industry players, serves as the key channel for industry and government collaboration to spur PKI adoption in the local e-commerce environment (*Singapore Enterprise*, April 2001). The aim of the forum is to develop a secure, trustworthy and safe environment for electronic commerce. PKI is recognized as a mature solution that addresses key elements of security: authentication, non-repudiation, confidentiality and integrity. (See also: National Trust Council)

### Public Sector Accounting Standards Board (Australia)
See Financial Reporting Council.

### Public Sector Reform Advisory Group (Papua New Guinea)
In PNG, the Public Sector Reform Advisory Group (PSRAG) was launched on 17 April 2002. It comprises eminent citizens selected by the government from the community to assist in implementing the public sector reform program.

## Public Sector Undertakings (India)

In India, Public Sector Undertakings (PSUs) are companies owned by the central government (about 200) or state governments (about 600). The important ones include the Oil and Natural Gas Corporation (ONGC), the Steel Authority of India (SAIL) and Coal India. Under the Sick Industrial Companies Act, PSUs may be referred to the Board of Industrial and Financial Reconstruction.

## Public Service 21 (Singapore)

The Public Service for the 21st Century or PS21 program was launched in 1995. Its objectives were:
- To nurture an attitude of service excellence in meeting the needs of the public with high standards of quality, courtesy and responsiveness;
- To foster an environment which induces and welcomes continuous change for greater efficiency and effectiveness by employing modern management tools and techniques while paying attention to the morale and welfare of public service officers.

## Public Utilities Board (Singapore)

In Singapore, the Public Utilities Board (PUB) was set up in 1963 as a statutory board to supply electricity, water and piped gas. In 1995, PUB's electricity and piped gas divisions were corporatized and restructured into five subsidiaries under Singapore Power Ltd. The PUB continues as the national water authority and has taken on the additional role of regulator of the privatized electricity and piped gas industries. As the regulator for electricity and piped gas, the PUB protects consumer interest on pricing, performance standards, reliability and safety of supply. It also advises the government on matters relating to electricity and piped gas. Seven companies have been licensed to produce, transmit and supply electricity and piped gas. They are: Power Senoko Ltd, Power Seraya Ltd, Power Grid Limited, Power Supply Limited, Power Gas Limited, Tuas Power Limited and SembCorp Cogen Private Limited.

## Public Works Department (Sri Lanka)

See Road Development Authority.

## Punjab National Bank (India)    *www.pnbindia.com*

In India, the Punjab National Bank was started in 1895. It was the first bank to be set up solely with Indian capital. In 1969, it was among the 14 banks to be nationalized. It offers a wide range of banking services with the largest branch network of 3,900 branches in India. In 2000, it was ranked 515 among the largest banks in the world by Banker's Almanac, London.

**Pusat Pengelolaan Pembebasan dan Pengembalian Bea Masuk (P4BM) (Indonesia)**
See Centre for the Administration of Duty Exemptions and Drawbacks.

**PT Putra Surya Multidana**
This is a large Indonesian consumer finance company that focuses on financing motorcycle and light commercial vehicle sales. It is part of the diversified Putra Surya Perkasa Group which has interests in banking, manufacturing and property.

**Quezon City Development Bank (Philippines)**
Old name of Asia Trust Bank. (See: Asia Trust Bank)

**Radanasin Bank (Thailand)**    *www.uob-radanasin.co.th*
See UOB Radanasin Bank.

**Raja Chelliah Committee on Tax Reform (India)**
In India, the Raja Chelliah Committee was set up in 1994 to review the tax system. The government has implemented many of its recommendations to simplify procedures and rationalize the rate structure. These included reduction in customs and excise duties, corporate tax and simplifying income tax filing procedures.

**Rajya Sabha (India)**
Council of States.

**PT Ramayana Lestari Sentosa (Indonesia)**
This is one of the largest retailers in Indonesia. Founded in 1983, Ramayana operates a chain of supermarkets and department stores. It has about 60 outlets, mostly under the Ramayana name and several under the name of Robinson. Most outlets are located in Java, except one in Batam and one in Bali.

**Rastriya Banijya Bank (Nepal)**
In Nepal, the Rastriya Banijya Bank (RBB) is a wholly-owned state bank. It has a 5% shareholding in the Nepal Industrial & Commercial Bank Limited (NIC Bank).

**RATE**
RATE stands for risk, assessment, tools of supervision and evaluation. It is a supervisory structure prescribed by the Bank of England. (See also: CAMEL, CAMELS, CAMELOT)

**Rating Agency Malaysia Berhad**
Incorporated in 1990, RAM is one of the two rating agencies in Malaysia. The other agency is Malaysian Rating Corporation Berhad that was launched in 1996. The major shareholders of RAM are IBCA (UK) and the Asian Development Bank. Other shareholders include local banks, merchant banks and other financial institutions. Ratings undertaken by RAM include specific corporate ratings as well as rating of securities that are of interest to investors.

**Real Estate and Housing Developers' Association Malaysia**   *www.rehda.com*
In Malaysia, the Real Estate and Housing Developers' Association (REHDA) started in 1970 as the Housing Developers' Association to represent property developers in the private sector. The present name was adopted on 13 October 2000. It has about 800 members who are responsible for some 80% of real estate built in the country. REHDA members are developers of all property categories, from trading housing projects to theme parks and industrial estates.

**Real Estate Developers' Association of Singapore**   *www.redas.com*
The Real Estate Developers' Association of Singapore (REDAS) started in 1959 as the Singapore Land and Housing Developers' Association. The present name was adopted in 1977. Its objective is to promote real estate development and investment locally and worldwide. It represents the private sector real estate developers. It promotes integrity and professionalism among its members.

**Red chips**
These are shares of Chinese companies listed in Hong Kong through the acquisition of local companies.

**Refrigeration and Electrical Engineering Corporation (REE)**
In Vietnam, this was the first state-owned company in Ho Chi Minh City to be equitized (privatized).

**Regional Development Bank (Sri Lanka)**
See Regional Rural Development Bank.

**Regional Directorates of National Savings (Pakistan)**
See National Savings Organization.

**Regional Rural Development Bank (Sri Lanka)**
In Sri Lanka, Regional Rural Development Banks were introduced in 1985 under the Regional Rural Development Bank Act. They were set up with capital provided by the Central Bank. They mobilized savings from the rural sector and

ensured that the funds were used in the same sector. Their activities were confined to the district where they were located. They have been amalgamated to form Regional Development Banks (Rdbs) that will operate on a provincial basis.

**Reksadana (Indonesia)**
Pension mutual funds in Indonesia.

**Report on Observance of Standards and Codes (IMF)**
*www.imf.org/external/np/rosc*
The IMF Report on Observance of Standards and Codes (ROSC) includes assessment of core standards (data, fiscal code, monetary and financial code, and Basel core principle on banking) and non-core standards (securities market regulation, insurance market regulation, payment system, deposit insurance system, accounting, audit and bankruptcy code.

**Research Institute of Investment Analysts Malaysia (RIIAM)**
*www.klse-ris.com.my*
RIIAM was incorporated in 1985 as a company limited by guarantee. It is affiliated to the Kuala Lumpur Stock Exchange (KLSE). It conducts research and courses for the financial community. Its membership is open to people in the securities industry. In 1994, RIIAM launched a Diploma in Investment Analysis jointly with Australia's Royal Melbourne Institute of Technology. RIIAM is a member of the Asian Securities Analysts Federation which is part of the International Council of Investment Analysts. The KLSE–RIIAM Information System (or KLSE-RIS) is a service available on the website: www.klse-ris.com.my

**Reserve Bank Information and Transfer System (RITS) (Australia)**
In Australia, Commonwealth Government Securities (CSGs) are cleared through the RITS that is regulated by the Reserve Bank of Australia. RITS members include banks, investment houses, insurance companies, pension and superannuation funds and nominee companies.

**Reserve Bank of Australia** *www.rba.gov.au*
The Reserve Bank of Australia (RBA) is a statutory authority established by the Reserve Bank Act that gives it specific powers. As a result of the reform in the Australian financial sector, RBA has two boards. The Reserve Bank Board is responsible for the bank's monetary and banking policy and other matters while the Payments System Board is responsible for the bank's payments system policy.

The RBA is responsible for monetary policy management and the maintenance of financial system stability. It is also responsible for the safety and efficiency of the payments system. In carrying these responsibilities, the RBA participates in the financial markets and the payments system.

The RBA is responsible for the printing and issuing of Australian currency notes. It also provides banking and registry services to some Federal and State Government customers.

**Reserve Bank of Fiji**    *www.reservebank.gov.fj*
In Fiji, the Reserve Bank is the central bank. It regulates the issue of currency and promotes monetary stability.

**Reserve Bank of India**    *www.rbi.org.in*
The Reserve Bank of India (RBI) started in 1935 as a private institution with shares held by investors, until its nationalization in 1949. It is the central bank with head office in Mumbai (Bombay). It regulates, supervises and inspects banks, credit institutions and finance companies under the Reserve Bank of India Act and the Banking Regulation Act. It also manages monetary policy and exchange rate policy.

RBI has 22 regional offices, mostly in state capitals. Its fully owned subsidiaries are: National Housing Bank (NHB), National Bank for Agriculture and Rural Development (NABARD), Deposit Insurance and Credit Guarantee Corporation of India (DICGC), Bharatiya Reserve Bank Note Mudran Private Limited (BRBNMPL). It has a majority stake in the State Bank of India. It has minority stakes in Infrastructure Development Finance Company (IDFC), Securities Trading Corporation of India (STCI) and Discount & Finance House of India (DFHI).

**Reserve Bank of New Zealand**    *www.rbnz.govt.nz*
The Reserve Bank of New Zealand was established in 1934. As the central bank, it operates monetary policy to maintain price stability, promotes the maintenance of a sound financial system and meets the currency needs of the public.

**Reserve Currency**
A foreign currency held by a country as part of its reserve funds and with which it makes international payments.

**Reserve Fund**
In some countries, banks and other financial institutions are usually required by the central bank to maintain a reserve fund to which they must transfer a specified percentage of their annual net profits.

**Resident Foreign Currency Account**
In Sri Lanka, in 1991 commercial banks were allowed to open Resident Foreign Currency (RFC) accounts. It permitted Sri Lankan residents who received foreign currency to maintain foreign currency accounts.

**Resident Non-National Foreign Currency Account**
In Sri Lanka, the Resident Non-National Foreign Currency (RNNFC) scheme was introduced in 1980. It permitted non-national residents in Sri Lanka to maintain foreign currency accounts.

**Resona Holdings Inc (Japan)**   *www.resona-hd.co.jp*
Resona Holdings Inc is the new name for Daiwa Holdings with effect from October 2002. Daiwa Bank and Asahi Bank will merge to become Resona Bank. The operations of Asahi Bank in Saitama prefecture will become Saitama Resona Bank. Other subsidiaries have also been renamed. Kinki Osaka Bank will become Osaka Resona Bank, and Nara Bank will become Nara Resona Bank. Daiwa Trust & Banking and Asahi Trust will merge to become Resona Trust & Banking. (See also: Daiwa Holdings)

**Restricted Licence Bank (Singapore)**
In Singapore, the first restricted licence was granted by the Monetary Authority of Singapore to a foreign bank in 1971. Under the bank liberalization program, restricted banks have been renamed wholesale banks.

**Resurgent India Bond**
The one-time Resurgent India Bond was issued in 1998–99 to finance deficit. It raised $4.2 billion despite the turmoil in the international market.

**Reuters**
International financial news agency founded in 1851.

**RHB Islamic Index (Malaysia)**
In Malaysia, this stock index tracks Syariah-approved companies traded on the main board of the Kuala Lumpur Stock Exchange. These companies include Telekom Malaysia Bhd, Tenaga Nasional Bhd, Petronas Gas Bhd and others.

**Rice Research Development Institute (Sri Lanka)**
In Sri Lanka, the Rice Research Development Institute (RRDI) at Batalagoda was set up in 1952. Its objective is to develop high yielding rice varieties to replace the local varieties.

## Riel
Currency of Cambodia.

## Rights in Land (Indonesia)
In Indonesia, rights in land are stated in the Basic Agrarian Law (BAL). There are 11 rights, of which 5 are relevant to investors:
- Hak Milik (right to own land)
- Hak Guna Usaha (right to cultivate land)
- Hak Guna Bangunan (right to build on the land)
- Hak Pakai (right to use land)
- Hak Sewa Untuk Bangunan (right of lease for building).

There are other rights not covered by BAL. Examples are Hak Kuasa Pertam Bangan (mining rights) and Hak Pengusahaan Hutan (forest exploitation rights).

## Rizal Commercial Banking Corporation (Philippines)   *www.rcbc.com*
Rizal Commercial Banking Corporation (RCBC) is listed on the Philippine Stock Exchange. It started in 1960 as a development bank. In 1963, it acquired a commercial bank licence, and in 1989 a universal banking licence. Through its 160 branches, it serves a diversified market which includes corporate to retail banking. It has a strong Filipino-Chinese and Japanese market niche. As of 1997, RCBC had assets amounting to PHP 106 billion and net worth of PHP 11.5 billion. Its major banking-related subsidiaries include: RCBC California International Inc, RCBC Capital Corporation, RCBC International Finance Ltd, and RCBC Savings Bank.

## Road Development Authority (Sri Lanka)
In Sri Lanka, during the early years of independence, the Public Works Department (PWD) was responsible for the construction and maintenance of public roads. In the 1970s, the PWD was abolished. Its functions were taken over by the Department of Highways and in 1986 by the Road Development Authority (RDA).

## ROCA Rating System
The ROCA rating system is used by the US Federal Reserve Board to assess the condition of a US branch within the whole foreign banking organization (ROCA: risk management, operational controls, compliance and asset quality). (See also: CAMEL rating system: capital, asset, management, earnings and liquidity)

## Rokinren Bank (Japan)
See Labour Banks, Shinkin Banks.

## Rotating Savings and Credit Association (Nepal)   *www.cmfnepal.org*
In Nepal, rotating savings and credit associations (ROSCAs) are traditional savings and credit associations. They are known locally as Dhukuti or similar terms. They tend to be non-registered, but quite formally structured in terms of membership rights and obligations. (See also: Savings and Credit Cooperatives)

## Royal Air Cambodge (RAC)
RAC is the national carrier of Cambodia. It is a joint venture between the Cambodian government and Malaysian Air Service.

## Royal Insurance Corporation of Bhutan
The Royal Insurance Corporation of Bhutan (RICB) was set up in 1975. It provides both life and general insurance. The government is the majority shareholder but there are also private sector shareholders.

## Royal Monetary Authority (Bhutan)
In Bhutan, the Royal Monetary Authority (RMA) is the central bank.

## Royal Nepal Academy of Science & Technology   *www.ronast.org.np*
The Royal Nepal Academy of Science & Technology (RONAST) was founded in 1982. Its objectives are to promote science and technology as well as to facilitate the transfer of appropriate technologies.

## Royal Securities Exchange of Bhutan
The Royal Securities Exchange of Bhutan started in 1993. It has four members and 13 companies are listed on the exchange. Equities, bonds and bills are traded on the exchange. Transactions are settled by book entry system.

## Royal University of Fine Arts (Cambodia)   *www.moi-coci.gov.kh*
In Cambodia, the Royal University of Fine Arts trains artists, musicians, architects, archeologists and other cultural specialists. It is under the Ministry of Culture and Fine Arts which was established in 1997.

## Rubber Association of Singapore
The Rubber Association of Singapore (RAS) was set up in 1967 by virtue of the Rubber Industry Act and the Rubber Dealers Act. Its main objective was to promote and regulate the rubber industry in Singapore. It set official prices

for all grades and types of natural rubber. These prices were widely used for the settlement of contracts by producers and customers. The RAS provided clearing house facilities and endorsed certificates of origin and commercial documents relating to the rubber trade. It also licensed rubber packers, shippers and manufacturers of technically specified rubber. When the RAS Commodity Exchange was formed in 1992, it took over the functions of the RAS. In 1994, the RAS Commodity Exchange was renamed the Singapore Commodity Exchange (SICOM) in 1994.

**Rubber Research Institute of Malaysia**
See Malaysian Rubber Board.

**Rufiyaa**
Currency of the Maldives (US$1 = 12 MRf).

**Rules of Origin**
In international trade negotiation, the Rules of Origin (ROO) determine the type of product eligible for preferential tariff treatment.

**Rural banks in Indonesia**
See Bank Perkreditan Rakyat.

**Rural Banks (Philippines)**
Rural banks in the Philippines provide credit to small farmers and merchants. They can only be owned by Filipino citizens. With the permission from the Central Bank, some are allowed to collect deposits, open current accounts, act as collection agents or act as trustees for farmers' estates. They may also invest in the equities of companies engaged in related businesses.

**Rural Energy Development Program (Nepal)**    *www.redp.org.np*
In Nepal, the Rural Energy Development Program (REDP) is a joint project of the government and UNDP. It aims to improve rural livelihood through the promotion of rural energy systems.

**Rural Savings Scheme (Myanmar)**
The Rural Savings Scheme in Myanmar was introduced in 1993 to encourage the saving habit of farmers.

**SAARC Agricultural Information Centre**    *www.siac-dhaka.org* or *www.saarc-sec.org*
The SAARC Agricultural Information Centre (SAIC) started in Dhaka in 1988 as the first regional institution of SAARC. Its objective is to share information

mutually for the advancement of agriculture and ecology of SAARC member countries.

### SAARC Chamber of Commerce and Industry  *www.saarcnet.org*
The SAARC Chamber of Commerce & Industry (SCCI) was set up in 1992 with headquarters in Pakistan. It is the apex organization of all the national chambers of commerce and industry from the SAARC countries (SAARC: South Asia Association for Regional Cooperation). Its objective is to promote cooperation among member countries to achieve the SAARC Economic Union by 2008.

SAARCNET is a web-based information service set by SCCI to strengthen business linkages in the region.

### SAARC Human Resources Development Centre  *www.saarc-sec.org*
The SAARC Human Resources Development Centre (SHRDC) was set up in Islamabad to undertake research, training and dissemination of information on human resources development issues.

### SAARC Meteorological Research Centre  *www.saarc-sec.org*
The SAARC Meteorological Research Centre (SMRC) in Dhaka was inaugurated in January 1995. It focuses on research aspects of weather forecasting and monitoring. It is developing a networking system among member countries.

### Saham Dwi Warna (Indonesia)
This is a golden share in a public company that gives the shareholder (usually the government) a veto right in major decisions.

### Saigon Motors Company (SAMCO)
SAMCO is a 20-year joint venture of Inchcape Vietnam Ltd and Vietnamese company Sacoxu. It repairs, maintains and distributes vehicles.

### Saigon Post and Telecommunications Services (SPTS)
The Saigon Post and Telecommunications Services (SPTS) is a telecom services company, providing its subscribers the use of Vietnam's national telecom network. It also imports, exports, installs and maintains telecom equipment.

### Saigon Postal Corporation
In Vietnam, the Saigon Postal Corporation (PSC) was formed as a joint stock company in 1996 to provide competing services to the VNPT (Vietnam National Post and Telecommunications Corporation).

## Saigon Trade Centre

Saigon Trade Centre is located in Ho Chi Minh City. The 33-storey 128-metre tower is the tallest building in Vietnam. The US$55 million project is a joint venture between Luks Industrial Company from Hong Kong and Lam Vien Company under Vietnam's Ministry of Defence.

## Saitori Member (Japan)

In Japan, at the Tokyo Stock Exchange (TSE), saitori members are stock exchange officials whose income is derived from the amount of trade they handle each day. Their commission rate depends on the average price of shares. The TSE membership prevents them from taking orders from the public or from dealing for their personal accounts. They are allocated a certain number of listed issues to handle and may exercise their discretion as to how to match the orders. At the Osaka Stock Exchange, they are known as nakadachi members.

## Sale of Goods Ordinance (Hong Kong)

In Hong Kong, the Sale of Goods (Amendment) Ordinance (SOGO) was one of four pieces of consumer protection legislation introduced in 1994. It ensures that goods must be of saleable quality. They must be reasonably fit for a common purpose, with the appropriate standard of appearance and finish, free from defects, safe and durable. (See also: Hong Kong Consumer Protection Laws)

## Salim Group (Indonesia)

Salim Group is one of the largest Indonesian conglomerates, owned by Liem Sioe Liong (Sudomo Salim). One of its divisions is PT Indomobil that has numerous automotive plants including Nissan assembly plant, Dunlop tire manufacturing plant and other components plants. Salim's food flagship company PT Indofood Sukses Makmur is a leading instant noodle producer in Indonesia. (See also: PT Indofood Sukses Makmur)

## Samurai bonds

These are Yen-denominated bonds issued in Japan by a foreign borrower. The first Samurai bond was issued by the Asian Development Bank in 1970. Three subsequent issues were by the World Bank in 1971 and another by the Asian Development Bank in 1971. These issues were mainly subscribed by financial institutions and were listed on the Tokyo and Osaka stock exchanges. Following the supranational institutions, sovereign governments began to issue Samurai bonds. They included Australia and Canada in 1972. The first non-government issuer was Sears Overseas Finance in 1979, guaranteed by Sears

Roebuck. Other subsequent issuers included the European Investment Bank and Inter-American Development Bank.

## San Miguel Corporation (Philippines)  *www.sanmiguel.com.ph*

San Miguel Corporation (SMC) was founded in 1890. It is the largest Philippine beverage and food conglomerate listed on the Philippine Stock Exchange. It has expanded into other Asia Pacific countries through joint ventures, licensing and exports.

In 1998, it combined its soft drinks interests with those of Coca-Cola Amatil Ltd of Australia in a transaction valued at US$2.7 billion. It has entered into a licensing agreement with the American brewer Miller Brewing Co to produce and distribute Miller Genuine Draft in the Philippines.

San Miguel has expanded its distribution network in China with sales offices in 16 cities. Through its subsidiary company San Miguel Foods International, it bought over 49% of the feeds and poultry business of PT Dharmala Agrifood (a subsidiary of the Dharmala Group, one of Indonesia's top ten companies). The company has also diversified into property development through San Miguel Properties Philippines Inc (SMPPI). It has numerous subsidiaries including San Miguel International Ltd, San Miguel Foods Inc, SMC Juice Inc.

## Sarachor (Cambodia)

Ministerial circular.

## Satellite Dealer (India)

In India, Satellite Dealers (SDs) are second tier dealers in trading and distributing government securities, in contrast with Primary Dealers (PDs). In 1997, about ten financial institutions were given approval by the Reserve Bank of India to be registered as Satellite Dealers. They would set up separate units dedicated to the securities business and in particular, the government securities market.

## Save the Children through Credit Program (Sri Lanka)

In Sri Lanka, Save the Children through Credit (SAVECRED) program is a poverty alleviation program introduced in 1989 by the Redd Barna institution. Based on Grameen Bank approach, it not only provides small credit and savings facilities to micro-enterprises (managed mostly by village women and their families) but also focuses on development through discussion among loanee members. (See also: Grameen Bank Approach)

**Savings and Credit Cooperatives (Nepal)**  *www.cmfnepal.org*
In Nepal, Savings and Credit Cooperatives (SACCOs) are member owned, controlled and capitalized organizations which provide financial services to their members. There are more than 700 SACCOs registered with the Cooperative Department and half of these are members of the national federation of cooperatives. (See also: Rotating Savings and Credit Association)

**Savings and Loan Association (Philippines)**
In the Philippines, savings and loan associations accept saving deposits from members and grant small personal loans and long term loans for home building.

**Savings and Mortgage Bank (Philippines)**
In the Philippines, savings and mortgage banks collect savings from depositors and invest them in loans secured by bonds, real estate mortgages and long term loans for home building.

**SBI Capital Markets (SBICAP) (India)**  *www.sbicaps.com*
In India, the SBI Capital Markets Ltd was formed in 1986. It was a wholly-owned subsidiary of the State Bank of India until 1997 when shares were issued to the Asian Development Bank which hold about 14% of the capital. As an investment bank, SBICAP provides a full range of financial services.

**SBI Gilts Limited (India)**  *www.sbigilts.com*
In India, the SBI Gilts Limited is an accredited Primary Dealer in the government securities market.

**SCAN Electronic Registration and Transfer Services (SERTS) (Malaysia)**
In Malaysia, SERTS is an integrated electronic share registry system used by the Malaysian Share Registration Services Sdn Bhd to serve its clients many of which are companies listed on the Kuala Lumpur Stock Exchange (KLSE). The system is electronically linked to the Central Depository System (CDS) at the KLSE. The SERTS-CDS linkage improves the performance of company registrars and benefits company shareholders. (See also: Malaysian Share Registration Services Sdn Bhd, or MSRS; Securities Clearing Automated Network Services Sdn Bhd, or SCANS)

**Science and Engineering Research Council (Singapore)**
In Singapore, the Science and Engineering Research Council (SERC) is the centre for a cluster of public research institutes: Data Storage Institute (DSI), Gintic Institute of Manufacturing Technology, Institute of Chemical and

Engineering Sciences (ICES), Institute for Communications Research (ICR), Institute of High Performance Computing (IHPC), Institute of Materials Research and Engineering (IMRE), Institute of Microelectronics (IME) and Laboratories for Information Technology (LIT). Its main objectives is to support research in key disciplines through the research institutes.

## Securities Analysts Association (Thailand)  *www.saa-thai.org.th*
In Thailand, the Securities Analysts Association (SAA) is a professional organization representing financial analysts. It promotes the standards of investment decision-making through the education of financial analysts. Its main program leads to the designation of Certified Investment and Securities Analyst (CISA) which is recognized by the Securities and Exchange Commission.

## Securities and Exchange Board of India  *www.sebi.gov.in*
The Securities and Exchange Board of India (SEBI) was set up by the Indian government in 1988. Its powers to regulate the capital market were limited until the Securities and Exchange Board of India Act was passed in 1992. The Act governs all stock exchanges and securities transactions. The SEBI head office is in Mumbai and three regional offices are located in New Delhi, Calcutta and Madras.

## Securities and Exchange Commission (Bangladesh)  *www.secbd.org*
In Bangladesh, the Securities and Exchange Commission was set up in 1993 as a statutory body under the Ministry of Finance. It supervises the securities and capital markets. It also regulates the two stock exchanges at Dhaka and Chittagong. (See also: Dhaka Stock Exchange and Chittagong Stock Exchange)

## Securities and Exchange Commission (Philippines)  *www.sec.gov.ph*
In the Philippines, the Securities and Exchange Commission (SEC) was established in 1936. It was reorganized in 1975 and was given additional powers as a quasi-judicial body. It was reorganized again in December 2000. Its main role is to regulate the securities industry. It has four core functions: capital markets, company registration, enforcement and support services. It derives its power from Presidential Decree, the Revised Securities Act, Corporation and Partnership Laws, Investment Company Act and Investment Houses Law.

## Securities and Exchange Commission (Taiwan)
In Taiwan, the Securities and Exchange Commission (SEC) was formed in 1960 under the Ministry of Economic Affairs. It formulated rules about

securities transactions. The Taiwan Stock Exchange started trading in 1962. The SEC supervised the securities market and the exchange when the Securities and Exchange Law was passed in 1968. The SEC was then transferred to the Ministry of Finance. When the Futures Trading Law was introduced in 1997, the SEC changed its name to the Securities and Futures Commission. (See also: Securities and Futures Commission)

**Securities and Exchange Commission (Thailand)**   *www.sec.or.th*
In Thailand, the Securities Exchange Commission was set up in 1992 to supervise all institutions related to the capital and securities markets.

**Securities and Exchange Commission of Pakistan**   *www.secp.gov.pk*
The Securities and Exchange Commission (SEC) of Pakistan was set up in 1999 to succeed the Corporate Law Authority (CLA) that had been administering corporate law since 1981. It is an independent regulator to promote an efficient and transparent capital market and to enforce corporate governance standards in line with international practices.

**Securities and Exchange Council (Japan)**
In Japan, the Securities and Exchange Council of Japan was established in 1952. It comprises 16 business representatives appointed by the Ministry of Finance to serve on a part-time basis. It acts as an advisor to the MOF on policy related to the securities industry.

**Securities and Futures Commission (Taiwan)**   *www.sfc.gov.tw*
In Taiwan, the Securities and Futures Commission (SEF) was known as the Securities and Exchange Commission (SEC) before March 1997. When the Futures Trading Law was passed in 1997, the new name was adopted to reflect its new role. The SFC is responsible for developing, regulating and supervising the capital, securities and futures market. (See also: Securities and Exchange Commission)

**Securities and Futures Institute (Taiwan)**   *www.sfi.org.tw*
In Taiwan, the Securities and Futures Institute (SFI) promotes surveys and research studies on the securities and futures industry.

**Securities and Exchange Surveillance Commission (Japan)**   *www.fsa.go.jp/sesc*
In Japan, the Securities and Exchange Surveillance Commission (SESC) was formed on 20 July 1992 upon the recommendation of an Advisory Committee to the Prime Minister. The recommendation was made after a series of financial scandals involving major securities houses were discovered in 1991. The SESC

is an independent organization attached to the Financial Services Agency (FSA) which was renamed from the former Financial Supervisory Agency. Within the SESC, its Compliance Inspections Office inspects securities houses, stock exchanges and financial futures brokers. Its Market Surveillance Group conducts daily surveillance and can require information from securities houses. The Enforcement Division investigates securities crimes such as insider trading, market manipulation and falsified financial statements.

### Securities and Futures Act (Singapore)
In Singapore, the Securities and Futures Act (SFA) came into effect on October 2002. Activities regulated under the act include dealing in securities, futures, foreign exchange, fund management, custodial services for securities and others. A person who conducts any of these regulated activities must hold a Capital Market Services (CMS) licence.

### Securities and Futures Commission of Hong Kong  *www.hksfc.org.hk*
The Securities and Futures Commission of Hong Kong (SFCHK) oversees the operations of the Stock Exchange of Hong Kong, the Hong Kong Futures Exchange and their clearing houses to ensure the sound functioning of their systems. It also administers the two statutory Investor Compensation Funds.

It has five executive directors and five non-executive directors. There are four operating divisions: (a) The Supervision of Markets Division, (b) The Corporate Finance Division, (c) The Intermediaries and Investment Products Division, (d) The Enforcement Division. (See also: Stock Exchange of Hong Kong, the Hong Kong Futures Exchange)

### Securities Clearing Automated Network Services Sdn Bhd (SCANS) (Malaysia)
In Malaysia, SCANS was incorporated in 1983. It is the clearing house appointed by the Kuala Lumpur Stock Exchange (KLSE). It provides clearing and settlement facilities for contracts done by KLSE members. SCANS is wholly owned by the KLSE. It provides share registration services through its subsidiary, Malaysian Share Registration Services Sdn Bhd. Another subsidiary, KLSE-BERNAMA Real-Time Information Services Sdn Bhd (KULBER) provides information to local and foreign information vendors. (See also: KLSE-BERNAMA Real-Time Information Services Sdn Bhd (KULBER); Malaysian Share Registration Services Sdn Bhd)

### Securities Clearing Corporation of the Philippines
The Securities Clearing Corporation of the Philippines (SCCP) is a private

institution that serves as a clearance and settlement agency for trades transacted in the Philippine Stock Exchange (PSE). It is owned by the PSE (51%) and commercial banks (49%). It guarantees the settlement of trades in the event of trading participant default. It administers the Clearing and Trade Guarantee Fund.

**Securities Commission (Malaysia)**   *www.sc.com.my*
In Malaysia, the Securities Commission (SC) was set up on 1 March 1993. It is the central authority to regulate and develop the capital market.

**Securities Exchange Centre (Nepal)**
In Nepal, the Securities Marketing Centre was set up in 1976 to develop a stock exchange. In 1984, it was replaced by the new Securities Exchange Centre (SEC) which was converted into the Nepal Stock Exchange (NEPSE) in 1993. (See also: Nepal Stock Exchange)

**Securities Exchange Commission (Sri Lanka)**
In Sri Lanka, the Securities Exchange Commission (SEC) was set up in 1991. It issues licences and ensures the proper conduct of the stock market and to protect investor interests. It formulates rules for the operation of the stock exchange and unit trusts.

**Securities Exchange of Thailand**
The Securities Exchange of Thailand (SET) was set up in 1975 for the listing and trading of securities. It was reorganized in 1992. It is now known as the Stock Exchange of Thailand. (See also: Stock Exchange of Thailand)

**Securities Industry Act (Malaysia)**
Securities Industry Act governs the establishment of stock markets. It empowers the Securities Commission to approve the rules of a stock exchange or clearing house. The Commission has the power to prohibit the trading in particular securities. The Act also controls the issue of licences for dealers, investment advisors and fund managers.

**Securities Industry Development Centre (Malaysia)**   *www.sc.com.my/html/sidc*
In Malaysia, the Securities Industry Development Centre is a department within the Research and Development Division of the Securities Commission. It undertakes and disseminates non-proprietary research relevant to the needs of industry. (See also: Securities Commission)

**Securities Investment and Trust Enterprise (Taiwan)**
In Taiwan, securities investment and trust enterprises (SITEs) were created by

legislation introduced by the Securities and Futures Commission in August 1983. They are domestic mutual fund companies offering open-end as well as closed-end equity and bond funds.

### Securities Investment Trust & Consulting Association (Taiwan)

*www.sitca.org.tw*

In Taiwan, the Securities Investment Trust & Consulting Association (SITCA) was reorganized in 1998 from the Securities Investment Trust & Advisory Association of Taipei that was set up in 1990. It is a self-regulatory organization that ensures its members meet the requirements of the securities market and support the administrative operations of government agencies. It enforces a code of conduct and settles disputes between members and their clients.

### Securities Investors Protection Fund Inc (Philippines)

In the Philippines, the Securities Investors Protection Fund Inc (SIPFI) is a non-stock non-profit corporation. It protects investors against losses in the case of failure, insolvency, or fraud of a member-broker or dealer. All brokers or dealers licensed by the Securities and Exchange Commission are members of the SIPFI.

### Securities Trading Corporation of India

The Securities Trading Corporation of India (STCI) is a financial institution where the Reserve Bank of India (central bank) has a minority stake. (See also: Reserve Bank of India)

### Security Bank Corporation (Philippines)

Security Bank Corporation is listed on the Philippine Stock Exchange. It obtained its universal banking licence in 1994. It provides a full range of financial services. Its subsidiaries are engaged in credit card, leasing, forex brokerage, investment banking, fund management and non-life insurance services. They include SB Capital Investment Corporation, SB Forex Inc, Security Diners International Corporation and Security Finance Inc.

### PT Sekar Bumi (Indonesia)

This is an Indonesian company that deals with shrimp processing, frozen food distribution and cashew nut processing.

### Selangor Science Park-1 (Malaysia)

In Malaysia, the Selangor Science Park-1 (SPP-1) is a 480-acre science park in Subang and provides R&D facilities for entrepreneurs. The project is developed by the Selangor State Development Corporation (PKNS or

Perbadanan Kemajuan Negeri Selangor) with assistance from the Malaysian Technology Development Corporation Sdn Bhd (MTDC) and Standards and Industrial Research Institute of Malaysia (SIRIM).

### Semaun Holdings Sdn Bhd (Brunei)    *www.semaun.gov.bn*
In Brunei, Semaun Holdings Sdn Bhd was formed in 1994 as a private limited company. It is wholly owned by the government under the Ministry of Industry and Primary Resources. Its mission is to spearhead industrial and commercial development through investment in key industrial sectors in Brunei. It also invests overseas through strategic partnership with local companies.

### Sempati Air (Indonesia)
This is a private Indonesian airline. As of 1997, it had 25 aircraft including seven B737s and four A300s.

### Senior Labour Officials' Meeting
See ASEAN Labour Ministers' Meeting.

### Sepang Airport (Malaysia)
See Kuala Lumpur International Airport.

### SESDAQ (Singapore)
SESDAQ (Stock Exchange of Singapore Dealing and Automated Quotation System) is the second board set up by the Singapore Exchange to provide a market for small and medium enterprises which would not otherwise be eligible for admission to main board. The admission criteria are less stringent than those of the main board.

### SESKOAD (Indonesia)
Army's Staff and Command College.

### SGX-ASX Link (Singapore)
The SGX-ASX Link was launched in 2001. It allows for the trading, settlement and holding of SGX and ASX-quoted securities by investors in both the Singapore Exchange and Australian stock exchanges.

### SGX-ST (Singapore)
See Singapore Exchange – Securities Trading.

### SGX SESDAQ (Singapore)
This is the second board of SGX-ST (former Stock Exchange of Singapore). It lists and trades the shares of small and medium companies.

**Shanghai Commodity Exchange**
See Shanghai Futures Exchange.

**Shanghai Futures Exchange (SFE)**
In China, the SFE was formed when the Shanghai Metal Exchange and the Shanghai Commodity Exchange merged in 1999. It trades in aluminium, copper, lead, nickel, tin, zinc, plywood and rubber.

**Shanghai Metal Exchange**
See Shanghai Futures Exchange.

**Shanghai Securities Central Clearing and Registration Corporation**
This is a subsidiary of the Shanghai Securities Exchange (SHH). It is responsible for the central depository, as well as registration and clearing of SHH securities.

**Shanghai Stock Exchange**   *www.sse.com.cn*
The Shanghai Stock Exchange (SHSE) was opened on 19 December 1990. The SHSE and the Shenzhen Stock Exchange are the two major securities exchanges in China. The SHSE uses a computerized trading system that automatically matches the closest offer and bid and has a capacity of 5,000 deals per second. Its wholly-owned subsidiary, the Shanghai Securities Central Registration and Settlement Company is responsible for central registration, custody and settlement. (See also: Shenzhen Stock Exchange)

**Shanghai Shipping Exchange**
In China, the Shanghai Shipping Exchange (SSE) was set up in 1996. It conducts contracts for the carriage of goods by sea, stevedore and warehouse services, chartering of ships, ship sales and purchase and other types of shipping-related transactions approved by the Ministry of Communications. The SSE is developing an International Shipping Service Centre to simplify cargo inspection. The SSE also acts as a mediator between government and corporations. It has been authorized to implement the International Container Freight Rate Filing System that requires all shipping companies to file rates with the exchange.

**Share Depository Centre (Thailand)**
In Thailand, the Share Depository Centre (SDC) was set up in 1988. Its main tasks are to clear and settle securities traded at the Stock Exchange of Thailand.

**Share Investment External Rupee Account (Sri Lanka)**
In Sri Lanka, foreign investors are allowed to bring in funds for investment

and to repatriate profits and sale proceeds freely through the Share Investment External Rupee Account (SIERA).

## Share Ownership Top-Up Scheme (Singapore)

In 1993, the Singapore Government introduced the CPF Share Ownership Top-up Scheme (SOTUS) to help its people to own shares. A cash grant of $200 was given to Singaporeans who had contributed at least $500 in their CPF account during the qualifying period form 1 March 1993 to 31 August 1993. Members who put in less than $500 received a pro-rated grant from the government. The $200 cash grant and the voluntary CPF contributions could be used to buy Singapore Telecom shares which were floated in October 1993. As a result of the first SOTUS, 1.26 million Singaporeans received $242 million in government contribution and it led to some 1.48 million CPF members to subscribe for Telecom shares.

In 1994, the government implemented the second SOTUS. It paid $300 into the CPF account of each Singaporean member aged 21 and above, provided he had contributed at least $750 into the account between 1 March 1994 and 31 August 1995. The second SOTUS is meant to help Singaporeans to build up enough CPF savings to subscribe for shares when the next statutory board is privatized.

## Shari'ah Supervisory Board (SSB) (Indonesia)

In Indonesia, the Shari'ah Supervisory Board oversees the operations of Indonesian Islamic banks.

## Shenzhen Securities Clearing Corporation (China)

This is a subsidiary of the Shenzhen Securities Exchange (SHZ). It is responsible for the depository as well as registration and clearing of SHZ securities.

## Shenzhen Stock Exchange (China)   www.sse.org.cn

In China, the Shenzhen Stock Exchange (SZSE) was set up on 1 December 1990. It operates an electronic trading system that automatically matches offers and bids. It exercises a 10% price cap for both rise and fall margins within the day to control fluctuations in share prices. It has an automatic real time market monitoring system. Its wholly-owned subsidiary, Shenzhen Securities Settlement Company manages registration, custody and settlement. The SZSE and the Shanghai Stock Exchange are the two major securities exchanges in China. (See also: Shanghai Stock Exchange)

**Shibosai Bonds (Japan)**
In Japan, Shibosai bonds are privately placed yen-denominated bonds issued by supranational institutions, sovereign states and government agencies.

**Shinkin Banks (Japan)**
In Japan, shinkin banks are specialized banks which operate according to the 1951 Shinkin Bank Law (revised in 1981). They are non-profit making cooperatives. Their members are local residents and small businesses. Each shinkin bank is a member of the Zenshinren Bank which acts as the national federation of shinkin banks. (See also: Shokochukin Bank)

**Shintaku Ginko (Japan)**
Trust Bank (Japan).

**Shogun Bonds (Japan)**
Shogun bonds are publicly offered bonds issued by foreigners in Japan and denominated in foreign currencies (usually in US dollars). Privately placed bonds are known as Geisha bonds.

**Shokochukin Bank (Japan)**
In Japan, the Shokochukin Bank is a specialized bank set up under the Shokochukin Bank Law of 1936. It finances cooperatives and small businesses. A revision of the Law allows it to provide some securities-related services.

**Siam City Bank (Thailand)**  *www.scib.co.th*
Siam City Bank provides a wide range of retail, corporate and other banking services. It has more than 200 branches in Thailand. It has branches in Phnom Penh and Cayman Island and representative offices in Yangon and Shantou.

**Siam Commercial Bank (Thailand)**  *www.scb.co.th*
Siam Commercial Bank is the oldest commercial bank in Thailand. Its business started in 1904 under the name of The Book Club. It became a commercial bank in 1906. It was selected as the Best Domestic Commercial Bank in Thailand by Asia Money in 2002. The selection was based on the bank's performance since the 1997 crisis and its recapitalization.

**Sick Industrial Companies Act (India)**  *www.bifr.nic.in*
In India, the Sick Industrial Companies Act (SICA) was enacted in 1985. Its objective is to determine sickness and expedite the revival of potentially viable units or closure of non-viable units. The SICA applies to both public and private industrial undertakings. Under the SICA, two quasi-judicial bodies: the Board

of Industrial and Financial Reconstruction (BIFR) and the Appellate Authority for Industrial and Financial Restructuring (AAIFR) were constituted in 1987.

### Sinar Mas Group (Indonesia)

In Indonesia, Sinar Mar Group is a diversified conglomerate. Its affiliated companies include PT Sinar Mas Asuransi, PT Sinar Mas Multiartha and many others.

### Singapore Accounting Standards (SAS)

The SAS are based on International Accounting Standards issued by the International Accounting Standards Committee.

### Singapore Accreditation Council (SAC)

The SAC was set up in 1996 as a result of a Memorandum of Understanding signed by the Ministry of Trade & Industry and the Singapore Confederation of Industries (SCI). In April 2002, the SAC was transferred from SCI to SPRING Singapore (formerly known as the Productivity & Standards Board). The main objective of SAC is to carry out independent accreditation of conformity of assessment bodies and personnel. Its accreditation is an endorsement of the independence, integrity and technical competence of such bodies and personnel in offering their services nationally and internationally. It certifies ISO-9000, QS-9000 and other international standards.

The SAC is a signatory to the multilateral recognition agreements of the Asia Pacific Laboratory Accreditation Cooperation, the European Cooperation for Accreditation, the International Laboratory Accreditation Cooperation, the Pacific Accreditation Cooperation and the International Accreditation Forum. In March 2002, the SAC signed a Mutual Recognition Agreement with the International Auditor and Training Certification Association for its Auditor Registration Scheme. In August 2002, SAC signed a cooperation agreement with the College of American Pathologists. This would enhance the credibility of SAC's Laboratory Accreditation Scheme in the field of medical testing.

The Singapore Accreditation Council – Singapore Laboratory Accreditation Scheme (SAC-SINGLAS) is a voluntary scheme that offers accreditation to laboratories in the following fields: calibration and measurement, chemical and biological testing, civil engineering testing, electrical testing, mechanical testing, non-destructive testing, environmental testing and medical testing.

### Singapore Australia Free Trade Agreement

The Singapore Australia Free Trade Agreement (SAFTA) came into force on 28 July 2003. It would promote greater integration of the two economies and create opportunities for cooperation.

**Singapore Banking Corporation (Cambodia)** *www.camnet.com.kh/sbcbank*
In Cambodia, the Singapore Banking Corporation (SBC) was incorporated in
1993. As a consumer bank, it provides a wide range of retail products and services.

**Singapore Broadcasting Authority**
See Media Development Authority.

**Singapore Business Federation**
The Singapore Business Federation (SBF) was formed in April 2002 as a result
of restructuring the Singapore Federation of Chambers of Commerce and
Industry (SFCCI). It serves as the apex chamber of commerce and industry
in Singapore. It will represent Singapore in multilateral forums such as ABAC,
ASEM, ASEAN-CCI, ICC as well as bilateral business councils set up between
Singapore and other countries.

**Singapore Commodity Exchange** *www.sicom.com.sg*
In 1994, the RAS Commodity Exchange (RASCE) was renamed the Singapore
Commodity Exchange (SICOM). SICOM trades in the following contracts:
RSS1 (ribbed smoke sheet grade 1), RSS3 (ribbed smoked sheet grade 3, RSS3
index), TSR 20 (technically specified rubber grade 20), coffee (Singapore
Robusta standard grade). SICOM provides a centralized and regulated marketplace for commodity trading. Its computerized trading network provides an
efficient price system to ensure the best bids and offers are available to all
participants. All contracts are cleared with its clearing house.

**Singapore Confederation of Chambers of Commerce and Industry**
See Singapore Business Federation.

**Singapore Confederation of Industries (SCI)** *www.sci.org.sg*
Founded in 1932, the SCI was known as the Singapore Manufacturers
Association (SMA) before 1996. It represents a wide range of industries locally
and abroad. The Singapore Accreditation Council (SAC) was set up as a
division within the SCI in 1996. It helps Singapore companies attain world
class quality standards. (See also: Singapore Accreditation Council)

**Singapore Exchange (SGX)** *www.singaporeexchange.com*
The Singapore Exchange (SGX) was formed in 1999 as a result of merging
the Stock Exchange of Singapore (SES) and the Singapore International
Monetary Exchange (SIMEX). For trading purposes, it has two main
subsidiaries: SGX–Securities Trading (for equities and bonds) and SGX–
Derivatives Trading (for derivatives). (See also: SGX–Derivatives Trading and
SGX–Securities Trading)

### Singapore Exchange–Derivatives Trading (SGX-DT)

SGX-DT was formerly known as the Singapore International Monetary Exchange (SIMEX) which was formed in 1983. It trades in a wide range of financial futures and options contracts.

### Singapore Exchange–Securities Trading (SGX-ST)

The SGX-ST (known as Stock Exchange of Singapore or SES before 1999) was set up on 24 May 1973 after the split of the joint Stock Exchange of Malaysia and Singapore. SES started full operation as a separate exchange on 4 June 1973. However, many of the 300-odd companies were co-listed on the Kuala Lumpur Stock Exchange (KLSE) and their prices moved in tandem due to arbitraging. In 1987, SES introduced a second board known as SESDAQ (Stock Exchange of Singapore Dealing and Automated Quotation). It enables smaller Singapore companies with growth prospects to raise funds in the capital market.

In 1989, the KLSE delisted about 180 Malaysian companies from the SES main board. As a result, the amount of capitalization of the exchange was affected. In order to overcome the reduced depth and breadth of the exchange, SES introduced an over-the-counter market known as CLOB International to facilitate trading of Malaysian shares. Later, companies from Hong Kong and Philippines were also added to the list. Trading of Malaysian shares on CLOB International ceased when the Malaysian Government imposed capital controls in 1998.

### Singapore Human Resources Institute (SHRI)

The SHRI, formerly known as the Singapore Institute of Human Resource Management and Singapore Institute of Personnel Management was founded in 1965. Its main objective is to promote effective HR practices in Singapore. In 1971, a Code of Professional Ethics was adopted to encourage members to maintain high professional standards. The SHRI conducts courses leading to the award of certificates and diplomas in human resource management, compensation management and applied psychology. It also offers degree program jointly with universities from UK and Australia.

### Singapore Immigration and Registration

See Immigration and Checkpoints Authority (Singapore).

### Singapore Initiative in New Energy Technology

Singapore Initiative in New Energy Technology (SINERGY) serves as a collaboration platform to fund R&D and test-bedding activities in clean energy technology.

**Singapore Institute of Directors**
The Singapore Institute of Directors (SID) was formed in 1998 following a private sector initiative to raise the level of corporate governance in Singapore. The role of SID is to promote the highest professional and ethical standards in company directorship. It acts as a forum for the exchange of information on issues relating to corporate governance and directorship in Singapore.

**Singapore Institute of Labour Studies**
See Ong Teng Cheong Institute of Labour Studies.

**Singapore Inter-bank Offer Rate**
The Singapore Inter-bank Offer Rate (SIBOR) is the rate quoted by the banks in the ACU inter-bank deposit market.

**Singapore International Arbitration Centre**
The Singapore International Arbitration Centre (SIAC) was set up in 1990 as a non-profit public company limited by guarantee. It provides facilities for the conduct of commercial arbitration and conciliation.

**Singapore International Chamber of Commerce** *www.sicc.org.sg*
The Singapore International Chamber of Commerce (SICC) was formed in 1837. It is one of the oldest business organizations in Singapore. Its membership is open to companies of all nationalities if they have a place of business in Singapore. It has about 1,000 members, from 50 different countries. About one-third of them are Singapore companies while American, British and Japanese companies form the other three large groups. The SICC represents multinational investment interest in Singapore. It is represented in numerous statutory boards. It is a member of the newly formed Singapore Business Federation (known as Singapore Federation of Chambers of Commerce and Industry, SFCCI before 2000). It also works closely with national business groups in Singapore such as the American Chamber of Commerce, British Chamber of Commerce, German Business Association and Japanese Chamber of Commerce. (See also: Singapore Business Federation)

**Singapore International Foundation** *www.sif.org.sg*
The Singapore International Foundation (SIF) is a non-profit, non-government organization (NGO) set up in 1991. Its mission is to enable Singaporeans everywhere to think globally, be responsible world citizens and to foster global friendship. SIF is funded by contribution from public and private sectors in Singapore. It has six core programs: Singapore Volunteers Overseas (SVO), Youth Expedition Project, Humanitarian Relief Program

(HRP), Friends of Singapore, Overseas Singaporeans and isc@SIF. For example, in June 2003, under the HRP's "Operation H20 to Sri Lanka", in partnership with Sri Lankan NGO Sarvodaya Shramandara Movement, medical and engineering volunteers provided specialist assistance to Sri Lanka flood victims.

### Singapore International Monetary Exchange (SIMEX)
See Singapore Exchange – Derivatives Trading.

### Singapore Land Authority    *www.sla.gov.sg*
The Singapore Land Authority (SLA) is a statutory board formed in June 2001. It comprises the former Land Office, Singapore Land Registry, Survey Department and Land Systems Support Unit.

### Singapore-Myanmar Joint Ministerial Working Committee
The Singapore-Myanmar Joint Ministerial Working Committee was formed in 1996 to promote bilateral economic relations. Since then, several cooperation programs have been implemented. These include projects in agribusiness, tourism, transport and trade.

### Singapore National Employers Federation    *www.snef.org.sg*
The Singapore National Employers Federation (SNEF) was formed in 1980 after the merger of Singapore Employers Federation and National Employers Council. Its main objective is to help employers to achieve excellence in employment practices and to increase their competitiveness in the world market. It promotes tripartite partnership with the government and the unions. It represents employers' interest in numerous national tripartite committees such as the National Wages Council and the National Productivity and Quality Council.

### Singapore Network Information Centre
The Singapore Network Information Centre (SGNIC) is a wholly-owned company of the National Computer Board (now Infocomm Development Authority). It administers domain name registration and regulations that determine the type of domain names that are allowed. Under the Domain Name Agreement, there is a registration fee and an annual maintenance fee for domain names registered by a company or organization.

### Singapore ONE
Singapore ONE ("One Network for Everyone") is a key component of the IT2000 Plan launched in 1997. It is a high speed, high capacity, multimedia

broadband network that allows a wide range of commercial and government services such as video conferencing, electronic libraries to be delivered directly to the office or home. Singapore ONE aims to link every home, workplace and school through an islandwide high speed, high capacity broadband network. It is spearheaded by government agencies such as the Infocomm Development Authority, A*STAR, Telecommunication Authority of Singapore, Economic Development Board and Singapore Broadcasting Authority.

### Singapore Post
Singapore Post Limited started as the Singapore Postal Services Department. It was incorporated in March 1992. It was listed on the Singapore Exchange on 13 May 2003. It is the dominant provider of domestic and international postal services in Singapore.

### Singapore Power   *www.spower.com.sg*
Singapore Power Limited was incorporated on 1 October 1995 to take over the electricity and gas operations from the Public Utilities Board (PUB). It is one of the largest companies in Singapore. In 2002, it had 4,120 employees and its net profit was $412 million. Its ownership in Senoko Power and Power Seraya was transferred to Temasek Holdings. The energy management unit of its subsidiary Power Grid was transferred to the Energy Market Authority on 1 April 2001. This was part of the government's plan to separate ownership of power generation from that of transmission and distribution. The subsidiaries of Singapore Power include Power Grid, Power Gas, Power Supply, Singapore Power International, SP Telecommunications, Development Resources, Power Automation, SP Systems, SP Capital, SP Resources and Singapore District Cooling.

### Singapore Regional Index Fund
This is a unit trust fund launched by six local banks (DBS, Keppel, OCBC, OUB, Tat Lee and UOB) in 1996. It is an open-ended unit trust fund that invests in the 38 component stocks of the Business Times Singapore Regional Index (BT-SRI).

### Singapore Telecommunications   *www.singtel.com*
Singapore Telecommunications Ltd (SingTel, or Singapore Telecom) was corporatized on 1 April 1992. It is licensed to provide telecommunications services in Singapore. It was listed on the Singapore Exchange in 1993. SingTel is one of the largest companies in Asia with subsidiaries dealing in mobile phone services, publishing, telecom equipment and others. The company has extensive interest in submarine cable and satellite systems. In Australia, its

wholly-owned subsidiary, SingTel Optus is a leader in integrated communication.

### Singapore-Thailand Enhanced Economic Relationship (STEER)

In February 2002, when Thai Prime Minister Thaksin and Singapore Prime Minister Goh Chok Tong met in Bangkok, they agreed to deepen economic cooperation through the Singapore-Thailand Enhanced Economic Relationship (STEER) scheme. STEER will enable cooperation between the two countries in many areas, including agriculture and food, the automotive industry, finance, tourism and transport.

### Singapore-Thailand Enhanced Program (STEP)

This program enables Singapore and Thailand to leverage on each other's strengths and harness the synergies that exist between the two countries for mutual advantage. One of the key instruments to realize STEP is the Thailand-Singapore Civil Service Exchange Program (CSEP) whereby the two countries will cooperate in education, trade, information technology, telecommunications, tourism, productivity services and industrial parks.

### Singapore Tourism Board (STB)

In 1997, the Singapore Tourist Promotion Board (STPB) was renamed Singapore Tourism Board (STB). The new name reflects STB's wider role, not just in promoting visitors to Singapore, but also in developing Singapore into a regional tourism hub. The Tourism 21 has been launched as the blueprint to develop Singapore as the tourism capital in the 21st century.

### Singapore-United States Business Council (SUBC)

The SUBC was formed in 1996 to promote trade and investment between Singapore and United States as well as joint ventures in other countries. It comprises 6 American and 8 Singapore chief executives and is chaired by Deputy Prime Minister Tony Tan. The council meets every 18 months. In May 1998, it had its second meeting and the theme was economic crisis in the region.

### Singapore Volunteers Overseas (SVO) Program

The SVO program is administered by the Singapore International Foundation. It provides Singapore professionals an opportunity to share their skills in developing countries. Since the SVO was set up in 1991, it has sent more than 150 volunteers to Botswana, Ghana, Indonesia, Laos, Myanmar, Nepal, Philippines, Sri Lanka and Vietnam. (See also: Singapore International Foundation)

## SingCham (Singapore)

SingCham (Singapore Chamber of Commerce and Industry) was launched in Beijing on 22 August 2002. Its objective is to promote Singapore's business interests, and to expand economic relations between Singapore and China. It will work closely with Network China to assist Singapore companies both in Singapore and China. (See also: Network China)

## Sistem Informasi Agroindustri Berbasis Ekspor (SIABE) (Indonesia)

Export Oriented Agroindustry Information System. (See also: Integrated Information System for Small Enterprise Development)

## Sistem Informasi Baseline Economic Survey SIB (Indonesia)

Information System for Baseline Economic Survey. (See also: Integrated Information System for Small Enterprise Development)

## Sistem Informasi Pola Perbiayan /Lending Model Usaha Kechil (SI-LMUK) (Indonesia)

Lending Model Information System. (See also: Integrated Information System for Small Enterprise Development)

## Sistem Informasi Prosedur Memperoleh Kredit (SI-PMK) (Indonesia)

Information System for Credit Procedure. (See also: Integrated Information System for Small Enterprise Development)

## Sistem Penunjang Keputusan Untuk Investasi (SPKUI) (Indonesia)

Decision Support System for the Financial Aspect of Lending Model. (See also: Integrated Information System for Small Enterprise Development)

## Sistem Transit Aliran Ringan (STAR)

In Malaysia, this is the Light Rail Transit system in Kuala Lumpur, the national capital.

## Skills Development Fund

In Singapore, the Skills Development Fund (SDF) was set up in 1979. It is used to subsidize a wide range of training programs to upgrade the skills of workers. The fund comes from the Skills Development Levy imposed on employers.

## Skills Redevelopment Program (Singapore)

In Singapore, the Skills Redevelopment Program (SRP) is a national scheme to encourage employability of workers. It has $140 million to re-train 100,000 workers over 5 years.

**Skim Khas Perumahan Kos Rendah dan Sederhana (Malaysia)**
See Special Scheme for Low and Medium Cost Houses.

**Skim Perbankan Tanpa Faedah (Malaysia)**
Interest Free Banking Scheme.

**Small and Medium Enterprises Development Authority**   *www.smeda.org*
In Pakistan, the Small and Medium Enterprises Development Authority
(SMEDA) is the apex policy formulation body for SMEs. It assists them with
technical and marketing support.

**Small and Medium Finance Office (Thailand)**
In Thailand, the Small and Medium Finance Office provides low interest loans
and technical assistance to small industrial enterprises including cottage and
handicraft industries.

**Small and Medium Industries Development Corporation (SMIDEC)**
Malaysia's SMIDEC was set up in 1996 as a specialized agency to provide
advisory services, guidance and assistance to small and medium industries in
Malaysia.

**Small Business Finance Corporation (Pakistan)**
In Pakistan, the Small Business Finance Corporation (SBFC) was set up in
1972 by the government. It provides soft loans to small businesses, individuals
and cottage industries. It also funds the Youth Investment Promotion Society
(YIPS).

**Small Claims Tribunal (Singapore)**
In Singapore, the Small Claims Tribunal (SMT) was set up in 1985 to settle
small claim disputes in a quick and inexpensive way. It deals with disputes
arising from contract for the sale of goods or services. The value of the claim
should not be more than $10,000. The proceedings are held in private and
in an informal manner. Parties are not allowed to be represented by lawyers
or agents.

**Small Farmers' Development Program (Nepal)**
In Nepal, the Small Farmers' Development Program (SFDP) was adopted in
1975 as part of the FAO-UNDP rural development program. It has been
implemented by the Agricultural Development Bank of Nepal and caters to
low-income farmers.

**Small Industries Development Bank of India**   *www.sidbi.com*
The Small Industries Development Bank of India (SIDBI) was set up in 1990 as a subsidiary of the Industrial Development Bank of India (IDBI) to specialize in financing small industries. It also holds equity in the IDBI Bank which is the commercial bank subsidiary of IDBI. (See also: Industrial Development Bank of India)

**Small Industry Credit Guarantee Corporation (Thailand)**   *www.sicgc.or.th*
In Thailand, the Small Industry Credit Guarantee Corporation started in 1992. It provided credit guarantee to small industries so that they can obtain credit from financial institutions.

**SME21 Plan (Singapore)**
In Singapore, the SME 21 Plan is a 10-year strategic plan to build the capabilities of small and medium enterprises (SMEs) to enhance their competitiveness.

**Social Security System (Philippines)**   *www.sss.gov.ph*
In the Philippines, the Social Security System (SSS) was implemented in 1957. It administers social security protection to workers in the private sector. The Government Service Insurance System (GSIS) protects workers in the public sector. The SSS administers two programs: Social Security (SS) Program and the Employees' Compensation (EC) Program. The SS Program provides replacement income for workers in times of death, disability, sickness, maternity and old age. The EC Program provides compensation to the worker when the illness, death or accident occurs during work-related activities.

**Sofitel Cambodiana**
Sofitel Cambodiana is the largest hotel in Cambodia. The 4-star hotel was opened in 1990 and has been managed by France's Accor group. Sofitel is a French hotel chain.

**Solid Bank (Philippines)**   *www.solidbank.com.ph*
Solidbank is listed on the Philippine Stock Exchange. It was set up in 1963. Over the past decade, the bank has accelerated its automation program with most of its branches converted to the on-line systems. Its homebanking and Interactive Voice Response System or Solidphone enables clients to transact banking over the telephone. It has also introduced several new products to broaden its customer base. They include the Fun Savers Club for children, the Save and Shop and the three types of Common Trust Funds (Solid Value, Growth, and Premium), Auto and Home-Perfect loans. Its major subsidiaries include Solid Insurance Brokers Inc and Solid Philippines Venture Capital Corp.

## Solomon Islands Airways Limited

The Solomon Islands Airways Limited (SOLAIR) is majority-owned by the government. It provides most of the domestic air services.

## SOLTEL (Solomon Islands)

In the Solomon Islands, SOLTEL is a joint venture between the government and Cable & Wireless Company. It provides telephone and cable links with other countries through modern satellite communication system.

## Soneri Bank (Pakistan)    *www.soneri.com*

In Pakistan, the Soneri Bank started in Lahore in April 1992, followed by a branch in Karachi in May 1992. The bank has 39 branches providing the whole range of corporate and retail banking services.

## Song Be Export Import Trading Company (Becamex)

In Vietnam, this state-owned company is jointly developing the Vietnam Singapore Industrial Park in Song Be Province. (See also: Vietnam Singapore Industrial Park)

## South Asia Preferential Trade Agreement    *www.saarc-sec.org*

The South Asia Preferential Trade Agreement (SAPTA) came into effect on 7 December 1995. At the end of the first round of negotiations, tariff concessions for 226 product categories were agreed upon on a product by product basis.

## South Asian Association for Regional Cooperation    *www.saarc-sec.org*

The South Asian Association for Regional Cooperation (SAARC) was formed on 8 December 1985 to promote regional cooperation among South Asian countries. It included Bangladesh, Bhutan, India, Maldives, Nepal, Pakistan and Sri Lanka. It enables the people of South Asia to work together in a spirit of friendship, trust and understanding. It promotes economic and social development in member states. The Secretariat was set up in Kathmandu in 1987. Its role is to coordinate SAARC activities and serves as a channel of communication with other international organizations. Members agreed to liberalize trade by lowering or removing tariffs and non-tariff barriers and other direct measures to promote mutual trade. Several steps have been taken, including the South Asia Preferential Trade Agreement (SAPTA) which took effect in December 1995. It plans to create a South Asia Free Trade Area (SAFTA).

**South Asian Federation of Exchanges**   *www.safe-asia.org*
The South Asian Federation of Exchanges (SAFE) was formed in 2000 by a group of nine South Asian exchanges. It is a forum to promote capital market development in South Asia. Members work towards common standards and best business practices. Members include exchanges from Bangladesh, Bhutan, India, Mauritius, Nepal, Pakistan and Sri Lanka.

**South Pacific Regional Trade and Economic Cooperation Agreement**
The South Pacific Regional Trade and Economic Cooperation Agreement (SPARTECA), provides for duty-free and unrestricted access for many products from Fiji to Australia and New Zealand.

**South Pacific Stock Exchange (Fiji)**   *www.cmda.com.fj/spse.shtml*
The South Pacific Stock Exchange is the only stock exchange in Fiji. There are 15 companies listed on the SPSE. Trading takes place three times a week: Monday, Tuesday and Thursday. Securities traded include government and statutory authority bonds, treasury bills, corporate bonds, Reserve Bank of Fiji notes and tradeable term deposits.

**Southeast Asian Ministers of Education Organization**   *www.seameo.org*
The Southeast Asian Ministers of Education Organization (SEAMEO) was established on 30 November 1965 as a chartered international organization. Its main purpose is to promote cooperation in education, science and culture in Southeast Asia.

Its secretariat is located in Bangkok. It has set up numerous specialized centres located in member countries. Examples are:
- SEAMEO BIOTROP (Regional Centre for Tropical Biology) in Bogor (Indonesia)
- SEAMEO CHAT (Regional Centre for History and Tradition) in Yangon (Myanmar)
- SEAMEO INNOTECH (Regional Centre for Education Innovation and Technology) in Manila (Philippines)
- SEAMEO RECSAM (Regional Centre for Science and Mathematics) in Penang (Malaysia)
- SEAMEO RELC (Regional Language Centre) in Singapore
- SEAMEO RETRAC (Regional Training Centre) in Ho Chi Minh City (Vietnam)
- SEAMEO SEAMOLEC (Regional Opening Learning Centre) in Jakarta (Indonesia)

- SEAMEO RIHED (Regional Centre for Higher Education) in Bangkok (Thailand)
- SEAMEO SEARCA (Regional Centre for Graduate Study and Research in Agriculture) in Los Banos (Philippines)
- SEAMEO SPAFA (Regional Centre for Archaeology and Fine Arts) in Bangkok (Thailand)
- SEAMEO TROPMED Network (Regional Tropical Medicine and Public Health Network) with four regional centres (Indonesia, Malaysia, Philippines and Thailand)
- SEAMEO VOCTECH (Regional Centre for Vocational and Technical Education) in Brunei Darussalam.

### Southern Steel Sheet Corporation Bonds
Southern Steel Sheet Corporation is a joint venture between Vietnam's Southern Steel Company, Nomura of Japan and Federal Ironworks of Malaysia. In 1996, the joint venture was given permission by the Ministry of Finance to issue 6,000 bonds each valued at US$100 to its employees to raise capital for future projects. The bonds have a 25-year tenure that is the same as that of the joint venture.

### Special Administration Region (SAR) of Hong Kong
As agreed in the Sino-British Joint Declaration, the British government returned Hong Kong to China on 1 July 1997. Hong Kong Special Administration Region (SAR) is administered under a special "one country two systems" arrangement for 50 years.

### Special Drawing Rights
Special Drawing Rights (SDRs) are reserve assets of member countries of the International Monetary Fund that they may draw based on a quota. The value of SDR is based on a currency basket comprising US dollar, mark, yen, pound and franc.

### Special Economic Zone (China)
In China, Special Economic Zones (SEZs) have been set up in Hainan, Shantou, Shenzhen, Xiamen and Zhuhai. Foreign investors and overseas Chinese may invest in manufacturing activities and are entitled to special investment incentives.

### Special Scheme for Low and Medium Cost Houses (Malaysia)
### (Skim Khas Perumahan Kos Rendah dan Sederhana)
The special scheme was a RM 2.0 billion revolving credit facility set up by

Bank Negara Malaysia in 1998. It provided bridging finance to developers for building houses costing RM 150,000 and below. Participating financial institutions included commercial banks, finance companies and Bank Islam Malaysia Berhad.

### Special Government Bank (Philippines)

In the Philippines, special government banks are government-controlled banks set up by special laws to provide credit for specific projects to promote economic development. Examples are the Development Bank of the Philippines, the Land Bank of the Philippines and the Philippine Amanah Bank.

### Special Standard for Application of Banking Accounting in Indonesia (Standar Khusus Akuntansi Perbankan Indonesia or SKAPI)

These are accounting guidelines developed by the Bank Indonesia and the Indonesian Accountants Association in order to meet international standards.

### SPH MediaWorks (Singapore)

SPH MediaWorks is the broadcasting arm of Singapore Press Holdings Ltd (SPH). It started in May 2001. Its formation was the result of liberalizing the media industry by the government. SPH was given a licence to run two TV channels (Channel U in Mandarin and Channel i, in English). MediaCorp was given a licence to publish newspapers. (See also: MediaCorp)

### Spratly Islands

The Spratly Islands is a group of 51 islands located in the South China Sea. Over the past decade, they have become an issue of territorial claims by Brunei, China, Malaysia, Philippines and Taiwan.

### SPRING Singapore

SPRING Singapore (Standard, Productivity and Innovation for Growth) was known as the Productivity and Standards Board before 2002. (See also: Productivity and Standards Board)

### Sri Lanka Bureau of Foreign Employment

The Sri Lanka Bureau of Foreign Employment (SLBFE) was set up in 1985 as an agency to recruit and train female workers for overseas employment and to protect the welfare of these workers.

### Sri Lanka Business Development Centre

The Sri Lanka Business Development Centre (SLBDC) is a semi-government body which promotes entrepreneurship and provides training to small and medium enterprises.

## Sri Lanka Export Credit Insurance Corporation

The Sri Lanka Export Credit Insurance Corporation (SLECIC) was set up in 1979 under the Export Credit Insurance Corporation Act. It provides insurance cover against non-payment of goods due to commercial and non-commercial risk for all types of exports.

## Sri Lanka Institute of Cooperative Management

The Sri Lanka Institute of Cooperative Management (SLICM) under the Ministry of Cooperatives, provides training to employees in the cooperative sector.

## Sri Lanka Institute of Development Administration

The Sri Lanka Institute of Development Administration (SLIDA) is based in Colombo. It provides training in areas related to development administration. It publishes the *Journal of Development Administration*. Its monographs include the Handbook on Training for Public Service in Sri Lanka.

## Sri Lanka Interbank Payment System

The Sri Lanka Interbank Payment System (SLIPS) was introduced in 1993. Companies use it for salary payments and the public uses it to pay bills from suppliers of services.

## Sri Lanka Ports Authority

The Sri Lanka Ports Authority (SLPA) was formed in 1979 by merging the Colombo Port Commission, Port Tally and Protective Services Corporation and the Port Cargo Services Corporation.

## Sri Lanka Railway

The Sri Lanka Railway (SLR) was founded in 1864. It is responsible for the railway network in the country.

## Sri Lanka State Plantations Corporation

The Sri Lanka State Plantations Corporation (SLSPC) was set up in 1958. It was formerly known as the Colombo State Plantations Corporation.

## Sri Lanka Sugar Corporation

The Sri Lanka Sugar Corporation was set up in 1967. It was incorporated as the Sri Lanka Sugar Company Limited in 1989.

**Sri Lanka Tea Board**
The Sri Lanka Tea Board (SLTB) was set up in 1976 to promote and develop the tea industry. The Tea Promotion Board (TPB) and the Tea Commissioner's Division come under the purview of SLTB.

**Standar Khusus Akuntansi Perbankan Indonesia**
See Special Standard for Application of Banking Accounting in Indonesia.

**Standard and Poor's (S&P)**
This is an international financial rating agency well known for its S&P 500 Index which tracks 500 major US companies.

**Standard Chartered**   *www.standardchartered.com*
Standard Chartered PLC started about 150 years ago. It is a world-class international bank with 32,000 employees in 55 countries. It is listed on the London Stock Exchange. It provides a full range of financial services around the world.

**Standard Chartered Nakornthon Bank (Thailand)**
*www.standardcharterednakornthon.co.th*
In Thailand, Nakornthon Bank started in 1933. It was originally called Wanglee Chan Bank. In 1985, it changed its name to Nakornthon. In 1999, Standard Chartered acquired a 75% shareholding in the bank and renamed it Standard Chartered Nakornthon Bank. (See also: Standard Chartered – Thailand)

**Standard Chartered – Singapore**   *www.standardchartered.com.sg*
In Singapore, Standard Chartered opened its first branch in 1859. It has a network of 20 branches with 2,000 employees. In 1999, it was among the first four foreign banks to receive a Qualifying Full Bank (QFB) licence.

**Standard Chartered – Thailand**   *www.standardchartered.com/th*
In Thailand, Standard Chartered was established in 1894. In the early days, much of its business was for the purchase of bills drawn against shipments of rice to Hong Kong and the Straits Settlements. Over the years, it has developed into a premier commercial in Thailand. In 1999, the group acquired, Nakornthon Bank, a Thai bank with a network of 67 branches. The bank has been renamed Standard Chartered Nakornthon Bank. (See also: Standard Chartered Nakornthon Bank)

### State Administration for Exchange Control (China)
In China, all loans made by foreign banks must be registered with the State Administration for Exchange Control (SAEC), a unit within the People's Bank of China (central bank). A loan may be declared void if it does not meet policy requirements, with the bank being held liable for unrecovered funds.

### State Administration for Industry and Commerce (China)
In China, the State Administration for Industry and Commerce (SIAC) is responsible for the registration of business. Foreign businesses must register with the local or provincial Administration for Industry and Commerce after receiving foreign investment approval from the Ministry of Foreign Trade and Economic Cooperation (MOFTEC).

### State Bank of India     *www.sbi.co.in*
The State Bank of India (SBI) started in 1806 as the Bank of Calcutta. Over the decade, the name was changed several times. In 1921, it was known as the Imperial Bank of India after the merger of Bank of Bengal, Bank of Madras and Bank of Bombay. In 1955, it was acquired by the Reserve Bank of India (central bank) and was renamed State Bank of India.

SBI is the largest commercial bank with more than 9,000 branches and 215,000 employees. In 1994, SBI was the first public sector bank to increase its capital by raising Rs 22,104 million through the issue of shares that are traded on the major stock exchanges in India. The Reserve Bank of India remains the main shareholder (about 60%) while the other shares are held by financial institutions, mutual funds, companies and individuals. It has 52 foreign offices in 34 countries.

### State Bank of Pakistan     *www.sbp.org.pk*
The State Bank of Pakistan (SBP) was set up on 1 July 1948. As the central bank, it promotes monetary and financial stability and foster a sound and dynamic financial system to achieve sustained economic growth.

### State Committee for Cooperation and Investment (SCCI)
In Vietnam, the SCCI is now part of the Ministry of Planning and Investment (MPI). See Ministry of Planning and Investment approve regional corporate bonds before they are submitted to the PBOC and SDPC.

### State Council Securities Commission (China)
See China Securities Regulatory Commission.

## State Development and Planning Commission (SDPC)

In China, the SDPC is responsible for approving the debt offered by state investment companies and provides an annual securities issuing plan. Corporate bonds must be approved by the SDPC and the People's Bank of China.

## State Economic Development Corporation (Malaysia)

In Malaysia, in the late 1960s and early 1970s, the federal government decentralized many of its economic activities to the state governments by setting up state economic development corporations. These corporations had to fulfil the objectives of the New Economic Policy (NEP) by incorporating more than 1,000 government-owned companies under the monitoring of the various agencies that in turn undertook the massive public projects. These projects created jobs that subsequently improved the standard of living of the people.

## State Electric Company (Maldives)    www.stelco.com.mv

In the Maldives, the State Electric Company was founded in 1949. It is the state-owned company responsible for the generation and supply of electricity.

## State Life Insurance Corporation (Pakistan)

In Pakistan, all life insurance companies were nationalized in 1972. The State Life Insurance Corporation was formed to manage the 35 companies among which Easter Federal Union (EFU) was the largest. With the recent liberalization program, many insurance companies have been given licences to start life insurance business. They include Eastern Federal Union Assurance, New Jubilee Insurance, Metropolitan Life, American Life and Commercial Union.

## State Mortgage and Investment Bank (Sri Lanka)

In Sri Lanka, the State Mortgage and Investment Bank (SMIB) was set up in 1975 under the State Mortgage and Investment Law. It combined the Ceylon State Mortgage Bank and the Agriculture and Industrial Credit Corporation. It provides long term housing loans at reasonable rates.

## State Securities Committee (Vietnam)

In Vietnam, the State Securities Committee (SSC) was set up in 1996 to develop a stock market. It drafted the securities law to be approved by the National Assembly.

## State Trading Corporation of Bhutan

The State Trading Corporation of Bhutan (STCB) was set up in 1968. It is a government procurement agency and also deals in scarce items such as specialized steel and industrial raw materials.

**State Trading Organization (Maldives)**    *www.stomaldives.com*
In the Maldives, the State Trading Organization was formed in 1964. It undertakes trading and commercial activities on behalf of the government.

**Statutory Reserve Deposit**
In Vanuatu, deposit banks are required to maintain a 10% Statutory Reserve Deposit (SRD) on Vanu deposits.

**PT Steady Safe (Indonesia)**
This is a major Indonesian transportation company with a fleet of 4,000 taxis and 1,200 buses. It also operates ferries between Java and Sumatra islands.

**Stock Borrowing and Lending (SBL) Arrangements (Malaysia)**
In Malaysia, these arrangements were introduced by the Securities Commission in 1997 to allow for regulated short selling and hedging activities to develop the derivatives market. During the 1998 financial crisis, these arrangements were suspended.

**Stock Exchange Automated Quotation**
The Stock Exchange Automated Quotation (SEAQ) is a screen-based quote dissemination system used in the UK. There is also a quotation system for international equities known as SEAQ International.

**Stock Exchange Executive Council (China)**
In China, the Stock Exchange Executive Council (SEEC) is a non-governmental research, consulting and coordination organization set up in 1989. Its member firms consist of China's large investment and trust corporations, securities firms and other non-bank financial institutions. The objectives of SEEC are to promote China's securities market and to develop a centrally regulated national securities exchange system.

**Stock Exchange of Hong Kong**
The Stock Exchange of Hong Kong merged with the Hong Kong Futures Exchange and the Hong Kong Securities Clearing to form the Hong Kong Exchanges and Clearing Ltd (HKEx) in 2000. (See also: Hong Kong Exchanges and Clearing Ltd)

**Stock Exchange of Mauritius**    *www.semdex.com*
The Stock Exchange of Mauritius (SEM) started in 1989 with five listed companies. In 2003, there were 39 listed companies with market capitalization of about US$1,656 million.

## Stock Exchange of Singapore

The Stock Exchange of Singapore (SES) was incorporated in 1973 when the joint Stock Exchange of Malaysia and Singapore split into two exchanges: Stock Exchange of Singapore and the Kuala Lumpur Stock Exchange. In 1999, as a result of demutualization and merger with the Singapore International Monetary Exchange SIMEX, it is now known as the Singapore Exchange – Securities Trading. (See Singapore Exchange – Securities Trading)

## Stock Exchange of Singapore Dealing and Automated Quotation

The Stock Exchange of Singapore Dealing and Automated Quotation system (SESDAQ) was set up in 1987. This second board gives small and medium enterprises an opportunity to tap the equity market and to have their shares traded. Listing requirements are less stringent than those of the main board.

## Stock Exchange of Thailand  *www.set.or.th*

The Stock Exchange of Thailand (SET) was formerly known as the Securities Exchange of Thailand. It was set up in 1974 and trading was computerized in 1991. It was reorganized in 1992 as a non-profit organization to serve as a secondary market for transacting securities. It is self-regulated with powers to enforce standards and rules against unfair practices. It is supervised by the Securities Exchange Commission.

## Stock Exchanges in China

There are five exchanges in China: Shanghai Securities Exchange (SHH), Shenzhen Stock Exchange (SHZ), China Zhengzhou Commodity Exchange (CZCE), Dalian Commodity Exchange (DCE) and Shanghai Futures Exchange (SFE). They are regulated by the China Securities Regulatory Commission (CSRC).

Stocks are divided into many categories in China. In the Shanghai and Shenzhen Securities Exchanges, they are categorized into the following types:

(a) State Share: shares held by the government and converted to equity when state-owned enterprises went public. State shares account for 50% of total shares of listed firms although they cannot be traded on the exchange.

(b) Legal person share: basically the same as state shares except that the shares are converted from the original investment of another SOE rather than the government. These account for about 8% to 10% of total shares. These shares also cannot be traded on the exchanges.

(c) Employee share: shares issued to employees as part of an employee-ownership plan. They account for about 3%–4% of total shares. Without approval, they cannot be traded on the exchanges.

(d) A-shares: shares traded on exchanges and quoted in RMB. They account for about 30% of total shares.

(e) B-shares: Stocks traded on exchanges but quoted in foreign currencies. B shares are quoted in US$ and HK$ in Shanghai and Shenzhen respectively. They account for about 7%–8% of total shares. It is estimated that Chinese nationals already account for 80% of the trading volume in this market despite regulations restricting ownership. The official ban on Chinese nationals buying B-shares was lifted on 19 February 2001.

In addition, there are another two types of stocks related to but not traded in China:

(a) H-shares: Chinese companies listed in Hong Kong through an IPO issue.

(b) Red chips: Chinese companies listed in Hong Kong through the acquisition of local companies.

### Stock Exchanges in India

There are 22 stock exchanges in India including major exchanges in Mumbai: Bombay Stock Exchange (BSE) and National Stock Exchange (NSE). The others are at Ahmedabad, Bangalore, Baroda, Bhubaneswar, Calcutta, Cochin, Coimbotore, Delhi, Gauhati, Hyderabad, Indore, Jaipur, Kanpur, Ludhiana, Madras (Chennai), Mangalore, Patna, Pune and Rajkot. (See also: Bombay Stock Exchange, National Stock Exchange)

### Stock Exchanges in Japan  *www.tse.or.jp*

In Japan, the history of securities trading dates back to 1878 when the Tokyo Stock Exchange Co Ltd was formed. In 1943, under the Japan Securities Exchange Law, 11 stock exchanges throughout Japan were unified under the Japan Securities Exchange. This was dissolved in 1947. Under the new Securities and Exchange Law, in April 1949, three stock exchanges were established in Tokyo, Osaka and Nagoya. In July, five additional exchanges were set up in Kyoto, Kobe (dissolved in 1967), Hiroshima (merged into Tokyo Stock Exchange in 2000), Fukuoka and Niigata (merged with Tokyo Stock Exchange in 2000). The Sapporo Securities Exchange was formed in 1950. Today, there are five stock exchanges in Japan.

### Subic Bay Freeport (Philippines)

In the Philippines, the Subic Bay Freeport (SBF) zone was established under the Bases Conversion Act as a self-sustaining industrial, commercial and financial investment centre. As a former US naval base, SBF has excellent infrastructure facilities. Investors are entitled to special incentives including exemption from tax, full foreign ownership and full repatriation of profits.

### Sugar Cane Research Institute (Sri Lanka)

In Sri Lanka, the Sugar Cane Research Institute (SRI) was set up in 1984 by the government. Its objective is to develop high yielding varieties of sugar cane.

### Sukarno-Hatta Airport (Indonesia)

Jakarta international airport.

### Superannuation Guarantee Charge (Australia)

In Australia, the objective of the Superannuation Guarantee Charge (SGC) is to make individuals fund their own retirement through a system of compulsory savings.

### Supply of Service (Implied Terms) Ordinance (Hong Kong)

In Hong Kong, the Supply of Service (Implied Terms) Ordinance (SOSITO) was one of four pieces of consumer protection legislation introduced in 1994. It sets out the terms implied into contracts for the supply of services where a supplier must carry out the service with reasonable care and skill. (See also: Hong Kong Consumer Protection Laws)

### Surabaya Stock Exchange (Indonesia)

**Bursar Efek Surabaya (BES)**    *www.bes.co.id*

The Surabaya Stock Exchange (SSX) started in 1989. It introduced the electronic long distance trading called ELDISTRA. In 1993, it opened an operational office in Jakarta. In 1995, it merged with the Indonesian Parallel Stock Exchange. In August 2001, SSX launched trading of LQ45 futures. In August 2002, it introduced online trading through the Internet. (See also: Jakarta Stock Exchange)

### Surat Berharga Pasar Uang (SBPU) (Indonesia)

These are short term Indonesian money market instruments comprising mainly promissory notes issued by Indonesian banks and non-bank financial institutions.

### Suruhanjaya Sekuriti (Malaysia)

See Securities Commission (Malaysia).

### Sushi Bond

Sushi bonds are foreign currency bonds issued by Japanese companies in the Eurobond market. They are different from Euroyen bonds that are denominated in yen.

## Sustainable Human Development

The Sustainable Human Development (SHD) approach as formulated by the United Nation includes poverty elimination, advancing the position of women, creating opportunities for productive employment and protecting the environment.

## Suvarnabhumi Airport (Thailand)    *www.suvarnabhumiairport.com*

The New Bangkok International Airport Co Limited (NBIA) was formed in 1996 as a privately managed state-owned company to construct and operate Suvarnabhumi Airport. Its main shareholders are the Airport Authority of Thailand (91%) and Ministry of Finance (8.5%). The company is attached to the Ministry of Transport and Communications.

## Syariah Advisory Council (Malaysia)

In Malaysia, the Syariah Advisory Council advises the Securities Commission on matters related to instruments and institutions necessary for developing an Islamic capital market.

## Sydney Futures Exchange

The Sydney Futures Exchange (SFE) started trading in 1960 as the Sydney Greasy Wool Futures Exchange. By 1964, it had become the world's leading wool future exchange. Today, SFE is one of the largest financial futures exchanges in the Asia Pacific region.

## Sydney Organizing Committee for the Olympic Games

*www.sydney.olympic.org*

The Sydney Organizing Committee for the Olympic Games (SOCOG) was set up by the New South Wales Government (Australia) to stage the 2000 Olympic Games in Sydney.

## Syndicate Bank (India)    *www.syndicatebank.com*

In India, the Syndicate Bank started in 1925 as the Canara Industrial and Banking Syndicate Ltd which changed to its present name in 1964. It was nationalized in 1969 and is owned by the government which holds 73.5% of the shares. It has about 1,700 branches with 30,000 employees. In 2001, it was ranked 10th in India and 803rd in the world by Banker's Almanac.

## Systemic risk

This is the type of risk when the failure of one participant in the system to meet its obligation will cause other participants to be unable to meet their obligations.

## Tabung Haji (Malaysia)

This is an Islamic institutional fund in Malaysia. It invests in Syariah-approved stocks on the Kuala Lumpur Stock Exchange.

## Tabung Industri Kechil dan Sederhana (Malaysia)

See Fund for Small and Medium Scale Industries.

## Tabung Usahawan Baru (Malaysia)

See New Entrepreneurs Fund.

## Tabung Untuk Makanan (Malaysia)

See Fund for Food.

## Tai Ping Insurance Company (China)

See People's Insurance Company of China.

## Taichung Export Processing Zone

In Taiwan, Taichung Export Processing Zone was set up in 1969. It is located in Taichung County (Central Taiwan).

## Tainan Science-based Industrial Park

*www.amozart.tnsipa.gov.tw* or *www.tnsipa.gov.tw*

In Taiwan, the Tainan Science-based Industrial Park (TSIP) is located about 12 kilometres northeast of Tainan City. TSIP will be developed in three phases. Construction started in 1996 and is expected to last 15 years. The first and second phases will cover about 650 hectares. An additional 2,000 hectares surrounding TSIP will be developed by the Tainan County Government into the Tainan Science Park City Special Zone.

## Taipei Futures Dealers Association

Taipei Futures Dealers Association was formed in April 1997. Its members are licensed futures brokers in Taipei.

## Taipei Securities Dealers Association

The Taipei Securities Dealers Association (TSDA) was formed in 1969. It replaced the Taipei Securities Business Association which started in 1956 and renamed Taipei Brokers Association in 1963 and later Taipei Securities Brokers Association. In 1998, TSDA was upgraded to a national association and renamed the Chinese Securities Association (CSA). (See also: Chinese Securities Association)

### Taipei Securities Investment Trust and Advisory Association

The Taipei Securities Investment Trust and Advisory Association was set up in 1990. It has been reorganized as Securities Investment Trust & Consulting Association (SITCA) in 1998. (See also: Securities Investment Trust & Consulting Association)

### Taipei World Trade Centre    *www.twtc.org.ta*

The Taipei World Trade Centre (TWTC) was initiated in 1986 by the China External Trade Development Council (CETRA). It provides exhibition space, conference facilities, offices and hotels for international business.

### TAIPEIBANK    *www.taipeibank.com.tw*

In Taiwan, the TAIPEIBANK started in 1969 with capital from the Taipei City Government. It was formerly known as the City Bank of Taipei. The name TAIPEIBANK was adopted in 1993 and its shares were listed on the Taiwan Stock Exchange in 1997. The bank was privatized in 1999 when the Taipei City Government released its shares.

### Taiwan Business Bank    *www.tbb.com.tw*

Taiwan Business Bank was formed after the merger and reorganization of several companies and savings institutions over the past five decades. It provides financing to small and medium businesses. In 1976, it was reorganized as the Taiwan Small to Medium Business Bank Co Ltd. It is the first bank in Taiwan to provide an individualized one-to-one service website on the Internet. It has 120 branches in Taiwan and abroad.

### Taiwan Chamber of Commerce    *www.tcoc.com.tw*

The Taiwan Chamber of Commerce was founded in 1946. It is the sole official organization representing 21 county and city chambers of commerce and 82 provincial trade associations. It unifies the business community to support government economic policy. It provides a wide range of services including the issue of certificate of origin and sharing domestic and foreign trade information. One of its unique services is to promote the abacus and is approved by the government to handle abacus-related activities.

### Taiwan Cooperative Bank    *www.tch-bank.com.tw*

Taiwan Cooperative Bank (TCB) was set up in 1946 and was closely associated with the cooperative system. It was previously known as the Cooperative Bank of Taiwan. The present name was adopted in 1989 when it set up an international department. TCB provides financial assistance through farmers' and fishermen's associations and cooperative organizations. The bank is 60% owned by the Ministry of Finance. The other owners are farmers' and fishermen's associations, and credit cooperatives. TCB has about 140 branches all over the island. It has jointly invested with the Bank of Taiwan, Land Bank of Taiwan and Taiwan Business Bank to set up the United Taiwan Bank in Brussels (Belgium). It also has overseas operations in Manila and Hong Kong.

**Taiwan Futures Exchange**  *www.taifex.com.tw*
The Taiwan Futures Exchange (TAIFEX) started in 1998. Its products include: TAIEX futures, TSE electronic sector index futures, TSE banking and insurance sector index futures, Mini-TAIEX futures and TAIEX options.

**Taiwan Institute of Economic Research**  *www.tier.org.tw*
The Taiwan Institute of Economic Research was set up in 1976. It is a private independent institute researching on domestic and foreign macroeconomics and industrial economics. It provides consultancy services to government and businesses.

**Taiwan International Mercantile Exchange**
Taiwan International Mercantile Exchange (TAIMEX) was formed on 9 September 1997.

**Taiwan Ratings Corporation**  *www.taiwanratings.com*
Taiwan Ratings Corporation (TRC) was set up in 1997. It is a joint venture between Standard and Poor's and several Taiwan institutions including the Taiwan Stock Exchange. It is an independent credit rating organization to Taiwan's financial markets. Its ratings related to the Taiwan financial markets are prefixed with "tw". For example, long term credit ratings range from the highest "twAAA" to the lowest "twD".

**Taiwan Securities Analysts Association**
The Taiwan Securities Analysts Association collects and publishes data for securities analysis. It promotes research and survey methodologies of securities analysis.

**Taiwan Securities Central Depository Co Ltd**  *www.tscd.com.tw*
The Taiwan Securities Central Depository Co Ltd (TSDC) started in 1990 and set up links with all securities firms in Taiwan. The main shareholder is the Taiwan Stock Exchange (TSE) while others are securities firms and financial institutions. The TSDC is licensed by the Securities and Futures Commission and provides book-entry settlement of securities and custodial services for TSE as well as OTC-listed securities.

### Taiwan Stock Exchange Corporation   *www.tse.com.tw*

The Taiwan Stock Exchange Corporation (TSEC) started trading in 1962. Since 1993, trading has been done by the Fully Automated Securities Trading (FAST) system. Its central depository and book entry system provides efficient settlement and custodian services. TSEC has adopted several measures to enhance price integrity and market transparency.

### Takaful Act 1984 (Malaysia)

This Act regulates takaful business in Malaysia. "Takaful" means a scheme based on brotherhood, solidarity and mutual assistance. It provides for mutual financial assistance to the participants in case of need whereby the participants mutually agree to contribute for that purpose.

### PT Tambang Timah (Indonesia)

This is an Indonesian state-owned tin mining company listed on the stock exchange. It is the country's largest tin producer. Its operations are mainly on Bangka Island, off the east coast of Sumatra.

Over the past decade, by increasing its output steadily, Tambang Timah has made Indonesia one of the world's largest tin producers. There are three tin producers in Indonesia. The other two are PT Koba Tin (25% owned by Tambang Timah) and PT Gunung Kikara Mining.

### Tan Duc Vocational Training School (Vietnam)

This school in Vietnam is managed by an Australian company. It conducts business courses in Ho Chi Minh City. Courses range from telephone skills for secretaries, to negotiating skills for senior managers.

### Tan Thuan Export Processing Zone (Vietnam)

Tan Thuan Export Processing Zone (TTZ) is the first EPZ in Vietnam. It is located near Ho Chi Minh City, next to the HCMC port area. The US$90 million project is 30% owned by the Ho Chi Minh City People's Committee and 70% by Taiwanese developer Central Trading & Development Corporation (CTDC).

The 300-hectare zone is located on a peninsula bordered on the north, east and west sides by the Saigon River and south-west by Provincial Road 15. TTZ has attracted mainly labour-intensive light industries from Taiwan and Japan such as textiles, plastics, electronics, and furniture. The EPZ provides full infrastructure support including water supply, electricity, telecommunications, transport, banks, shops and warehouses. The TTZ has a full service support centre which expedites investment licence procedures.

**Tariff and Customs Code of the Philippines**
The Tariff and Customs Code of the Philippines (TCCP) is the basic law that governs customs matters. There are 21 general commodity classifications, which are further sub-classified. The rates of customs duty vary for each classification and sub-classification.

**Tau**
The price change of a foreign exchange option for 1% change in the implied volatility. (See also: delta, gamma, rho, theta, vega)

**Taxes in Vietnam**
The direct business taxes in Vietnam include the business income tax, turnover tax, profit remittance tax, personal income tax, contractor tax, royalty tax, land and housing taxes.

**Tea Promotion Bureau (Sri Lanka)**
In Sri Lanka, the Tea Promotion Bureau (TPB) was set up in 1932. Its objective is to promote the tea industry.

**Tea Research Institute (Sri Lanka)**
In Sri Lanka, the Tea Research Institute (TRI) was set up in 1925 to solve pest and disease problems affecting tea plants.

**Tea Small Holding Development Authority (Sri Lanka)**
In Sri Lanka, the Tea Small Holding Development Authority (TSHDA) was set up in 1975. Its objective is to increase the productivity of smallholders in the tea industry.

**Technical Education Skills Development Authority (Philippines)**
In the Philippines, the Technical Education Skills Development Authority (TESDA) was set up to provide technical education and skills to support Philippine development goals. It is governed by a board with representatives from the government and the private sector.

**PT Telekomindo Selular Mitra Raya (Telesera) (Indonesia)**
This is an Indonesian cellular phone operator owned by PT Rajawali Wira Bhakti Utama, Telkom Pensioner Funds Foundation, Kartika Eka Paksi Foundation, Tri Daya Foundation, Telkom Employee Cooperatives and Telekomindo Employee Cooperative.

**Telesera (Indonesia)**
See PT Telekomindo Selular Mitra Raya.

**Televisi Pendidikan Indonesia**
Televisi Pendidikan Indonesia (TPI) is one of the five privately-owned television stations in Indonesia.

**PT Telkom (Indonesia)**
**(Telekomunikasi Indonesia)**
In 1990, PT Telkom was transformed from a government agency into a limited liability company. Since then, the company has adopted a profit-oriented policy to compete in the world telecommunication market.

**Telstra (Australia)**   *www.telstra.com.au*
In 2002, Telstra (Australia) was ranked 411 among the Fortune 500 global companies.

**Templeton Vietnam Opportunities Fund**
This is a closed-end investment fund listed on the New York Stock Exchange.

**Tenaga Nasional Berhad (Malaysia)**
This is Malaysia's privatized national power company. It was listed on the exchange in 1992.

**Texmaco Group (Indonesia)**
In Indonesia, the Texmaco is the largest fully integrated polyester producer. It is among the top 15 in the world. The Texmaco Group operates 12 manufacturing units and employs about 20,000 people. Its flagship company PT Polysindo Eka Perkasa is located in Kaliwungu and Karawang in West Java. Two other major companies are PT Texmaco Jaya (weaving and finishing operations) and PT Texmaco Perkasa Engineering (which makes spinning, weaving, finishing machines and components). (See also: PT Polysindo Eka Perkasa)

**PT Texmaco Perkasa Engineering (Indonesia)**
This company is a member of the Texmaco Group. It started as a small factory producing spare parts for the Texmaco Group. Since then, it has expanded into precision textile machinery, heavy engineering and fabrication, machine tools and automotive components. It has one of the largest foundries in Indonesia. Its fabrication unit houses the only clean room in Southeast Asia with titanium fabrication capabilities — one of only five in the world. (See also: Texmaco Group)

### Textile Training and Services Institute (Sri Lanka)
In Sri Lanka, the Textile Training and Services Institute (TTSI) is a autonomous statutory body which provides training and consulting services to the textile industry.

### Thai Airways International   *www.thaiair.com*
Thai Airways International (THAI) started as the Thai Airways Company (TAC) in 1951 when the government purchased shares in three small private airlines and combined their fleets to create a national airline. Rapid growth followed with service reaching remote provinces of Thailand. In 1960, it formed an alliance with Scandinavian Airlines System (SAS) and Thai Airways International was born. Since then, THAI has extended its routes to numerous regional and international destinations. In 1995, it joined Lufthansa and United Airlines to form a global alliance.

### Thai Appraisal Foundation   *www.thaiappraisal.org.th*
Thai Appraisal Foundation is a non-profit organization administered by the Ministries of Interior and Education. Its objective is to foster high standards of professional practice in the fields of property valuation or appraisal and urban land studies. It is also a forum for discussing issues affecting appraisers in Thailand.

### Thai Bond Dealing Centre   *www.thaibdd.or.th*
The Thai Bond Dealing Centre (Thai BDC) was set up in 1998. It is Thailand's first and only organized secondary market for bonds. Its history goes back to 1994 when the Bond Dealers Club (BDC) was formed within the Association of Securities Companies (ASCO) to trade in bonds. In 1998, the BDC was transformed into a full bond exchange and renamed Thai BDC.

### Thai Farmers Bank   *www.gototfb.*com
Thai Farmers Bank started in 1945 and was listed on the Stock Exchange of Thailand in 1976. It is the third largest commercial bank in Thailand. It provides a full range of consumer, commercial and corporate banking services. It has a network of about 530 branches including those in Hong Kong, Los Angeles, Vientiane, Phnom Penh, Cayman Island and Shenzhen. It has offices in London, New York, Beijing, Shanghai and Kunming.

### Thai-German Institute   *www.tgi.or.th*
In Thailand, the Thai-German Institute is the largest and most advanced independent training centre for industrial technologies. With German-backed quality principles, state-of-the-art equipment and highly-trained staff, the institute offers training for Thailand's technicians and engineers.

**Thai Industrial Standards Institute**    *www.tisi.go.th*
The Thai Industrial Standards Institute (TISI) was set up in 1969 in the Ministry of Industry as the national standards body of Thailand. Its mission is to establish the national policy and master plan in standardization to be in line with international practice with participation by the private and public sectors.

**Thai Military Bank**    *www.tmb.co.th*
The Thai Military Bank started in 1957 to serve military personnel. In 1964, its operations were expanded to serve corporate and private clients. In 1973, it became a commercial and operated on the same basis as other banks. In 1983, it was listed on the Stock Exchange of Thailand. In 1994, it was registered as a public company. It has overseas branches in Ho Chi Minh City and Vientiane and representative offices in Beijing and He Fei.

**Thai NVDR Company Limited**    *www.set.or.th/nvdr*
The Thai NVDR Company Limited was set up in October 2000. It is a wholly-owned subsidiary of the Stock Exchange of Thailand (SET). Its main business is to issue Non-Voting Depository Receipts (NVDRs) to investors and to use the proceeds to invest in the Invested Securities.   The Thailand Securities Depository Co Limited (TSD) acts as the registrar and depository centre for both underlying securities and the NVDRs.

**Thai Rating and Information Service (TRIS)**    *www.tris.tnet.co.th*
TRIS is Thailand's first credit rating agency. It was set up in 1993 with sponsorship from Thai financial institutions. It provides credit rating services and disseminates the results and other related information about the Thai bond market for the benefit of investors. TRIS is a founding member of AFCRS, ASEAN Forum of Credit Rating Agencies.

The shareholders of TRIS comprise four major groups: commercial banks (22%), finance companies (22%), securities companies (22%) and other institutions (34%). The last group includes life insurance companies, investment management companies, Ministry of Finance, Stock Exchange of Thailand, Asian Development Bank, Government Savings Bank and Industrial Finance Corporation of Thailand. No single shareholder owns more than 5% of TRIS. This is to ensure that TRIS is free from any outside influence.

**Thai Real Estate Business School**    *www.trebs.ac.th*
The Thai Real Estate Business School conducts courses related to real estate management, valuation, surveying and property development.

### Thai-Singapore-21 (TS-21) Industrial Estate

In Thailand, this industrial estate at the eastern seaboard was initiated in 1997 in Bangkok by Singapore Prime Minister Goh Chok Tong and Thai premier Chavalit Yongchaiyudh. It was a joint venture between Thailand's Eastern Sugar Group and JTC International, the international arm of Singapore's Jurong Town Corporation. The project was affected by the economic crisis and was delayed.

### Thai Valuers Association    *www.tva.or.th*

The Thai Valuers Association started informally as the "Independent Valuers Club". It is an independent professional organization for individual valuers as well as corporate members. It aims to develop the property valuating profession according to international standards.

### Thailand Development Research Institute    *www.info.tdri.or.th*

The Thailand Development Research Institute (TDRI) started in 1984 as a non-profit, non-government organization to do policy research and to disseminate results to the public and private sectors. It provides technical and policy analysis that supports the formulation of policies with long term implications for sustaining social and economic development in Thailand. The TDRI is funded by its users, local and foreign donors. During the early years, its supporters included the National Economic and Social Development Board, the Department of Technical and Economic Cooperation, the Canadian International Development Agency (CIDA) and the US Agency for International Development (USAID). The research programs of TDRI include human resources and social development, international economic relations, macroeconomic policy, natural resources and environment, science and technology development and sector economics.

### Thailand Productivity Institute    *www.ftpi.or.th*

Thailand Productivity Institute (FTPI) was set up in 1995. It is an independent agency overseen by representatives from government and business community. Its main objective is to increase productivity and competitiveness of Thai industries. It provides consulting services and training on productivity, ISO 9000 and ISO 14000.

### Thailand Securities Depository    *www.tsd.co.th*

The Thailand Securities Depository Co Limited (TSD) started in 1995. It is a subsidiary of the Stock Exchange of Thailand (SET). It provides services such as: securities depository, securities clearing and settlement, as well as securities registration.

**Thailand Securities Institute**   *www.tsi-thailand.org*
The Thailand Securities Institute (TSI) was set up by the Stock Exchange of Thailand in 2000. As an education and training centre for industry practitioners, it provides programs to update participants on new developments, professional know-how and ethical conduct.

**Thanlyin Kyauktan (Myanmar)**
This is Myanmar's largest development zone. The 40 sq km zone is located 14 kilometres southeast of Yangon city.

**The Enterprise Challenge (Singapore)**
In Singapore, The Enterprise Challenge (TEC) was set up in March 2000 under the Public Service 21 (PS21) program. It is a $10 million fund to sponsor innovative proposals to improve the Public Service. (See also: Public Service 21)

**Third Country Training Program (TCTP)**
In 1996, the World Bank signed its first TCTP with Singapore to provide training for third countries. In a typical TCTP arrangement, Singapore would sign an agreement with countries (e.g. Australia, Canada, Japan) or regional bodies (Asian Development Bank) or international organizations (e.g. Commonwealth Secretariat, UNDP) to provide training in Singapore for participants from developing countries.

**Tick**
In futures trading, the smallest possible price fluctuation upwards or downwards is a tick.

**Tier-1 Capital**
This refers to paid-up capital, non-cumulative perpetual preference shares, share premium, statutory reserve fund, general reserve fund, retained profits, surplus or loss arising from sale of fixed and long term investments as well as minority interest (consistent with the components of Tier-1 capital) and after deducting goodwill.

**Tier-2 Capital**
This refers to hybrid capital instruments, minority interest arising from preference shares, subordinated term debt, revaluation reserves and general provisions for bad debts.

**PT Timor Putra Nasional (Indonesia)**
In 1996, the Indonesian Government granted this company tariff and tax exemptions to produce a "Indonesian-made" car for the domestic market.

**Tokkin Fund (Japan)**
In Japan, tokkin funds (tokutei kinsen shintaku) are specified money trusts set up by companies or financial institutions to provide a means by which the capital appreciation on their investment can be converted into a dividend.

**Tokyo Round**
This was the seventh round of multilateral negotiation about GATT. It started in 1973 and ended in 1979. Among many other agreements, participating countries (99) agreed to reduce tariffs on thousands of products. This was implemented over a period of eight years ending 31 December 1986.(See also: Uruguay Round)

**Tokyo Stock Exchange** *www.tse.or.jp*
In its present form, the Tokyo Stock Exchange (TSE) was established on 1 April 1949. It is one of the five exchanges in Japan. It is one of the world's largest and most liquid markets. It has a market capitalization of 280 trillion yen (US$2.3 trillion) and a daily trading volume of 700 billion yen (US$5.8 billion). On 1 November 2001, TSE was demutualized and a new company Tokyo Stock Exchange Inc was formed. (See also: Stock Exchanges in Japan)

**Tonga Development Bank**
Tonga Development Bank is a quasi government body. It is a development financial institution that provides development finance especially to farmers, fishermen and commercial ventures.

Funds come from the government and concession loans from the Asian Development Bank, European Development Bank and other international sources.

**TOPIX (Japan)** *www.tse.or.jp*
TOPIX is a stock price index introduced in the Tokyo Stock Exchange (TSE) in 1969. It includes all companies (about 1,500) listed in first section of the exchange. It is a weighted index, the market price of each component stock is multiplied by the number of shares listed. It is computed and published every 60 seconds via TSE's market information system. TSE also publishes sub-indices for each of the 33 industry groups and 3 indices for large, medium and small companies.

**Tourism New South Wales (Australia)**    *www.tourism.nsw.gov.au*
In Australia, Tourism New South Wales (TNSW) is the New South Wales government tourism marketing and policy agency.

**Township Labour Office (Myanmar)**
In Myanmar, any enterprise employing five or more workers has to recruit through the Township Labour Office (TLO).

**Tracker Fund of Hong Kong**
In August 1998, the Hong Kong Government acquired a substantial portfolio of Hong Kong shares during a market operation. In October 1998, the Exchange Fund Investment Limited (EFIL) was set up to advise the government how to dispose of this portfolio in an orderly manner. In disposing these shares, the government chose a stock neutral solution with minimal disruption to the market. In November 1999, the Tracker Fund of Hong Kong (TraHK) was launched as part of the disposal program. TraHK was an Exchange Traded Fund that met the government requirements.

State Street Global Advisors Asia Ltd was appointed as the Fund Manager and State Street Bank and Trust Company was appointed as the Trustee of TraHK. With an issue size of HK$33.3 billion, TraHK's Initial Public Offer was the largest in Asia ex-Japan at the time of launch. By July 2002, about HK$135 billion in Hang Seng Index constituent stocks had been returned to the market through TraHK's unique tap mechanism.

**Trade Affiliated Member (Philippines)**
A Trade Affiliated Member (TAM) is a member of the Manila International Futures Exchange (MIFE). It is a corporation that is interested in one particular contract by virtue of its business. It has to trade through a full member as it is not a member of the Clearing House, and has no floor trading rights.

**Trade Policy Review Body**
See Trade Policy Review Mechanism.

**Trade Policy Review Mechanism**
The Trade Policy Review Mechanism (TPRM) was first set up on a trial basis in 1989 by GATT. It became a permanent feature of World Trade Organization under the Marrakesh Agreement that established the WTO in 1995. The TPRM enables the WTO to review trade policies of each member on a regular basis and report on those policies. The four largest trading entities in terms of world market share are reviewed every two years. The 16 next largest trading

entities are reviewed every four years and other members every six years. The reviews are conducted by the Trade Policy Review Body (TPRB) based on two documents: a policy statement by the member under review and a comprehensive report by the WTO Secretariat. The reports and the minutes of the review are published following the TRPB meeting.

**Trade Promotion Centre (Nepal)** *www.tpcnepal.org.np*
In Nepal, the Trade Promotion Centre (TPC) was set up in 1971. It is a non-profit organization to promote export trade.

**Training Expertise & Assistance Management Program (Singapore)**
In Singapore, through the Training Expertise & Assistance Management (TEAM) program, large companies act as mentors to provide training and development to SMEs, such as their suppliers and business partners. This program was introduced by the SPRING Singapore (Productivity Standards and Innovation Board) in 2001. It provides support to defray the cost of setting up a training program by the mentors.

**Trans-ASEAN Gas Pipeline (TAGP)**
The TAGP was conceived out of the 2nd ASEAN Informal Summit in December 1997, when the ASEAN Heads of State adopted the ASEAN Vision 2020. The vision called for cooperation to establish connecting arrangements for electricity and natural gas within ASEAN through the ASEAN Power Grid and the TAGP.

The ASEAN Council on Petroleum (ASCOPE) was tasked to lead the TAGP project to enhance greater energy security in the ASEAN region. ASCOPE established a TAGP Task Force in November 1998 to review and formulate a master plan of the TAGP. The master plan, which was completed in April 2001, identified seven possible TAGP interconnections for full integration of the pipeline network in the ASEAN region. In July 2002, ASEAN Energy Ministers signed a MOU on TAGP. The project would enable member countries to source natural gas from fellow ASEAN members. This would encourage ASEAN member countries to source for natural gas internally as well as enhance the security of supply within the region.

**Trans Union International**
Trans Union International Inc is an international credit information company with operations in Asia, Africa, Europe, Latin America and US. Its services include credit reports, risk scoring models, fraud detection and search tools. Its US database contains 1.7 billion records that are updated monthly on 200

million customers. In 1999, Trans Union was invited to join Credit Information Services Ltd in Hong Kong as a major stakeholder. (See also: Credit Information Services Limited)

**Treasury Bills Act (Malaysia)**
In Malaysia, this Act provides for issue of Treasury Bills. The Act among other things appoints the central bank as the agent of the government and permits the issue by way of scripless book-entry.

**Treaty of Rome**
The Treaty of Rome in 1957 created the European Community (EC) with free movement of goods, people, services and capital. The EC expanded to become the European Union. (See also: European Community)

**Thrift Banks (Philippines)**
In the Philippines, thrift banks include savings and mortgage banks, savings and loan associations and private development banks.

**TTHK Company (Cambodia)**
TTHK is Toyota Motor's first retail outlet and service centre in Cambodia. The joint venture started in 1995 and is owned by Toyota Tsusho of Japan (41%), Toyota Tsusho of Singapore (10%), Australia's Henry Walker Group (24.5%) and Cambodia's Kong Nuong Import Export Co (24.5%).

**Tugrik**
Currency of Mongolia (1 tug = 100 mongos).

**Tumen Economic Development Area**
The Tumen Economic Development Area (TEDA) includes Vostoguy, Nahotka, Vladivostock in the former Soviet Union, and parts of Jilin Province in China.

**Tumen River Economic Zone**
The Tumen River Economic Zone covers the area from Zurogine in the former Soviet Union and Rajin in North Korea.

**UCO Bank (India)**    *www.ucobank.com*
In India, UCO Bank is a 60-year-old bank wholly owned by the Government of India. Its head office is in Calcutta and it has 35 regional offices in the country.

### Unconscionable Contracts Ordinance (Hong Kong)

In Hong Kong, the Unconscionable Contracts Ordinance (UCO) was one of four pieces of consumer protection legislation introduced in 1994. It empowers the courts to give relief to consumers who are affected by unconscionable contracts. (See also: Hong Kong Consumer Protection Laws)

### Uniform Consumer Credit Code (Australia)

In Australia, the Uniform Consumer Credit Code (UCCC) was introduced in 1996. It provides laws which apply uniformly and equally to all forms of consumer lending and to all lenders throughout Australia.

### Uniform Customs and Practice (UCP)

The UCP is an international code of rules on documentary credits. Its full title is the Uniform Customs and Practice for Documentary Credits (UCPDC). It was first developed by the International Chamber of Commerce in Paris. It has been updated regularly.

### Union Bank of Burma

In 1967, the People's Bank of the Union of Burma was set up as a result of merging all the nationalized banks. It acted as the central bank of Burma. In 1975, its name was changed to Union Bank of Burma. (See also: Central Bank of Myanmar)

### Union Bank of India   *www.unionbankofindia.com*

The Union Bank of India was incorporated in 1919. At the time of nationalization in 1969, it had 240 branches in 28 states. As of 2001, it had 2,050 branches.

### Union Bank of the Philippines

The Union Bank of the Philippines is listed on the Philippine Stock Exchange. It was among the first government institutions that were privatized. It started as the Union Savings and Mortgage Bank through capital provided by Land Bank and Social Security System (SSS) and advances from then Central Bank of the Philippines. In 1982, it was granted a commercial bank licence.

The bank started its privatization in 1988 when Land Bank sold its 39% ownership to Aboitiz Group of Companies. The second phase followed through the sale of SSS' shares amounting to 30% of the shares. The third phase took place in 1992 when the SSS sold another 13.3% through a secondary offering. The bank offers a wide range of products and services to both corporate and individual clients. Some services are provided through subsidiaries such as UBP Capital Corporation, Crosby UBP Securities Inc and UBP Insurance Brokerage Inc and Union Bank Currency Brokers Inc.

## Unit Trust of Bhutan
The Unit Trust of Bhutan (UTB) was set up in 1980 by the Government Employees Provident Fund (GEPF) and the Royal Insurance Corporation of Bhutan. Its objective is to encourage savings and investment by Bhutanese.

## Unit Trust of India     *www.unittrustofindia.com*
The Unit Trust of India (UTI) was set up in 1964 by an Act of Parliament. It is the largest mutual fund in India.

## United Bank Limited (Pakistan)     *www.ubl.com.pk*
In Pakistan, the United Bank Limited was set up in 1959. It is one of the largest nationalized bank with 9,000 employees working in 1,200 domestic and 19 overseas branches. It has assets of Rs 155 billion. It provides a wide range of consumer and corporate banking services.

## United Bank of India     *www.unitedbankofindia.com*
The United Bank of India (UBI) was formed in 1950 with the merger of four banks: Comilla Banking Corporation (formed in 1914), Bengal Central Bank (1918), Comilla Union Bank (1922) and Hooghly Bank (1932). It was one of the 14 major banks that were nationalized in 1969. After nationalization, it expanded its network. It is now the Lead Bank in the states of Assam, Manipur, Tripura and West Bengal. UBI is known as the "Tea Bank" and has been the largest lender to the tea industry.

## United Nations     *www.un.org*
The United Nations was formed on 24 October 1945. Its purposes are to maintain international peace and security, to develop friendly relations among nations, to cooperate in solving international economic, social, cultural and humanitarian problems. It promotes respect for human rights and fundamental freedoms. It is a centre for harmonizing the actions of nations in attaining these goals. The six main organs within the UN are General Assembly, Security Council, Economic and Social Council, Trusteeship Council, International Court of Justice and the Secretariat.

## United Nations Children's Fund     *www.unicef.org*
The United Nations Children's Fund (UNICEF) was created in 1946 by the UN General Assembly to help children after World War II in Europe. It was first known as the UN International Children's Emergency Fund. In 1953, it

became a permanent part of the UN system. Its task is to help poor children in developing countries. Its name was shortened to UN Children's Fund but the acronym UNICEF was retained. UNICEF carries out its work through seven regional offices and 126 country offices covering more than 160 countries.

**United Nations Commission on International Trade Law**   *www.uncitral.org*
The United Nations Commission on International Trade Law (UNCITRAL) is a legal body within the UN system in the field of international trade law. It coordinates the work of organizations in this field and encourages cooperation among them. It promotes wider participation in existing international conventions and wider acceptance of existing model and uniform laws. It promotes ways and means of ensuring a uniform interpretation and application of international conventions and uniform laws.

**United Nations Conference on Trade and Development (UNCTAD)**
*www.unctad.org*
UNCTAD was formed in 1964 under the UN General Assembly. It aims at the development-friendly integration of developing countries into the world economy. It is a forum for inter-governmental discussion supported by discussion with experts. It undertakes research, policy analysis and data collection to provide inputs for the discussion of experts and government representatives.

**United Nations Development Program**   *www.undp.org*
United Nations Development Program (UNDP) is the UN's global development network. It has offices in 166 countries working with them on their own solutions to global and national development challenges. In each country office, the UNDP resident representative serves as the coordinator of development activities for the United Nations system. This coordination ensures the most effective use of UN and international aid resources. UNDP assists in development challenges such as poverty reduction, crisis prevention and recovery, energy and environment, and preventing the spread of HIV/AIDS.

**United Nations Educational, Scientific and Cultural Organization**
*www.unesco.org*
The United Nations Educational, Scientific and Cultural Organization (UNESCO) started in 1945. It has its headquarters in Paris and 73 field offices in different parts of the world. The main objective is to contribute to peace and security in the world by promoting collaboration among nations through education, science, culture and communication.

United Nations Industrial Development Organization (UNIDO)
*www.unido.org*
UNIDO was formed in 1966 and became a specialized agency of the United
Nations in 1985. It promotes industrial development in the developing world
in cooperation with 169 member states. Its head office is in Vienna. It has
35 country and regional offices. As a technical cooperation agency, UNIDO
designs and implements programs to support the industrial development
efforts of its clients.

United Nations Institute for Training and Research   *www.unitar.org*
The United Nations Institute for Training and Research (UNITAR) started
in 1965 as an autonomous body within the United Nations. Its objective is
to enhance the effectiveness of the organization through training and research.
It conducts training in multilateral diplomacy and international cooperation
for diplomats accredited to the UN as well as national officials involved in UN-
related work. It also carried out a wide range of programs in social and
economic development. It develops training materials including distance
learning packages, workbooks, software and videos. UNITAR is supported by
voluntary contributions from governments, foundations and other sources.

United Nations University   *www.unu.edu*
The United Nations University is an organ of the United Nations set up by
the General Assembly in 1972. It is an international community of scholars
engaged in research related to the global problems of human survival,
development and welfare. It operates through a worldwide network of research
centres, with its planning headquarters in Tokyo.

United Overseas Bank (Singapore)   *www.uobgroup.com*
In Singapore, the United Overseas Bank (UOB) started in 1935 as the United
Chinese Bank. In 1965, it changed its name to United Overseas Bank when
it set up its first overseas branch in Hong Kong. Over the decades, UOB has
developed into one of the Big Three local banks in Singapore by acquiring
several local banks: Chung Khiaw Bank (in 1971), Lee Wah Bank (1973), Far
Eastern Bank (1984), Industrial & Commercial Bank (1987) and Overseas
Union Bank (2001). It has a network of 270 offices in Australia, Asia, Europe
and North America.

United States Information Agency (USIA)
USIA (also known as United States Information Service, USIS in some
countries) is a government agency providing cultural programs overseas
including the Voice of America.

## United States – Singapore Free Trade Agreement
The US-Singapore Free Trade Agreement (USSFTA) was signed on 6 May 2003 in Washington by US President George W. Bush and Singapore Prime Minister Goh Chok Tong. It came into force in January 2004. The USSFTA will increase the flow of trade, investment, talent, ideas and technology across the Pacific.

## United States Trade Representative
The United States Trade Representative is a cabinet official who is the chief advisor to the US President on international trade policy.

## Universiti Brunei Darussalam   *www.ubd.edu.bn*
The Universiti Brunei Darussalam (UBD) started its first intake of students in 1985 with 176 students. In 1986, the Sultan Hassanail Bolkiah Institute of Education was integrated with the university. UBD has more than 300 academic staff and about 3,000 students in seven faculties: arts and social sciences, business economics and policies studies, Islamic studies, science, education, Brunei studies and medicine. UBD has two research centres. The Kuala Belalong Field Studies Centre was set up in 1991. It is located deep in the Ulu Temburong National Park for research on rain forests. The Centre for Applied Research in Education coordinates research projects between UDBS, Ministry of Education and the schools.

## UOB Radanasin Bank (Thailand)   *www.uob-radanasin.co.th*
UOB Radanasin Bank was established in 1999. It is a member of the Singapore-based United Overseas Bank (UOB) group. In 1999, the UOB bought 75% of the bank from the Bank of Thailand. Before this, Radanasin Bank was a government-owned bank under the purview of the Financial Institution Development Fund. The bank has about 1,200 employees working in its network of 36 branches of which 27 are located in Bangkok.

## Urban Bank Inc (Philippines)   *www.urbanvirtualbank.com*
The Urban Bank Inc is listed on the Philippine Stock Exchange. It has evolved from a development bank in 1980 to a universal bank in 1994. It provides a wide range of services. In 1995, the bank obtained an approval from the Securities and Exchange Commission to form a Special Purpose Trust Fund on the registration and sale of Asset-Backed Securities, thus making it one of the three institutions and the first Philippine bank to be so authorized. In 1998, Urban Bank's Virtual Banking Development Laboratory was awarded an ISO 9001 Certification for the development and serving of office and banking software. It was the first Philippine bank to be ISO certified by

Certification International, an ISO-accredited certifying body based in England. Among its major banking-related subsidiaries are: Urbancorp Finance Inc, Urbancorp Investments Inc, Urbancorp Insurance Brokers Inc and Urbancorp Securities Inc.

## Urban Redevelopment Authority (Singapore)    *www.ura.gov.sg*

In Singapore, the Urban Redevelopment Authority (URA) is the national planning and conservation authority. It prepares concept plans, development plans and grants planning approvals to guide the physical development of Singapore. It is also the government's land sales, property and car park management agent.

## Uruguay Round

The Uruguay Round was the eighth round of multilateral negotiations of GATT. The 7-year talk started in 1987 and ended in 1993 involving 117 member countries. There were many agreements regarding reduction of tariffs and other trade-related matters. GATT would be expanded and renamed the World Trade Organization or WTO. (See also: Tokyo Round)

## US-ASEAN Business Council    *www.us-asean.org*

The US-ASEAN Business Council is the premier national private organization in the United States representing private sector interests in ASEAN. Its main objective is to promote trade, investment and technology cooperation. The council provides visibility for member companies and access to government and private sector decision-makers at the highest levels.

## US-Singapore Business Partnership Program

The US-Singapore Business Partnership Program between the US Chamber of Commerce and International Enterprise Singapore (formerly known as Trade Development Board) provides a gateway for US companies into Singapore and the Asia Pacific market. The USpartner Singapore Portal is the first initiative under the partnership program. Through the portal, American and Singapore companies will find it easier to discover each other and forge partnerships.

## USpartner Singapore

The USpartner Singapore program was developed by SPRING Singapore (Standards Productivity and Innovation Board) and the US Chamber of Commerce in 2001. It is a program for Singapore SMEs and US companies to explore business opportunities. It provides Internet-based business matching service. Profiles and collaborative interests of companies are electronically captured and matched. It also arranges business partnering events such as business missions.

**UTI Bank (India)**   *www.utibank.com*
In India, UTI Bank was formed in 1994 with its registered office in Ahmedabad and head office in Mumbai. It was among the first to be set up after the government allowed new private banks to be established. It was promoted by the Unit Trust of India (the largest mutual fund in India, with 42% shareholding), Life Insurance Corporation of India, General Insurance Corporation and its four subsidiaries (National Insurance Company Ltd, New India Assurance Company, Oriental Insurance Company and United Insurance Company).

**Value Added Tax**
Value added tax is a consumption tax. It is based on the value at each point of the production and distribution process.

**Vantage Equities Inc (Philippines)**
Vantage Equities Inc is a financial service company listed on the Philippine Stock Exchange. It started as Palawan Oil & Gas Exploration Inc. In 1996, the company acquired 100% of Vantage Securities Corporation (formerly AGJ Securities Corporation) and 65% of PMI, a fund management company. In 1997, the company's name was changed to Vantage Equities Inc.

**Vanuatu Financial Services Commission**
The Vanuatu Financial Services Commission (VFSC) was established in 1993 as an independent statutory body under the Vanuatu Financial Services Commission Act to replace the Registrar of Companies. It provides services for the supervision of financial services. Its revenue comes from fees for services it provides under the Acts it administers such as the Companies Act, Banking Act, Insurance Act, Stamp Duties Act, Business Names Act and others.

**Vanuatu National Provident Fund**
The Vanuatu National Provident Fund (VNPF) started in 1987 and collected 6% of all wage payments: 3% from the employer and 3% from the employee.

**Vatu**
Currency of Vanuatu (1 VT = 100 centimes).

**Venture Investment Support for Start-ups (VISS)**
In Singapore, under VISS, the National Science & Technology Board (NSTB, renamed A*STAR in 2002) co-invests in early stage promising and strategic companies which are based or linked to Singapore. A*STAR invests with a minimum leverage factor of $1 VISS investment for $2 of private investment.

### Vereenigde Oostindische Compagnie (VOC)
Dutch East India Company.

### VID Public Bank
VID Public Bank is a 50-50 joint venture bank between the Bank for Investment and Development of Vietnam and Public Bank Berhad of Malaysia. It has offices in Hanoi, HCMC, Danang and Haiphong.

### Viet Kieu
Overseas Vietnamese.

### Vietcombank
See Bank for Foreign Trade Bank of Vietnam.

### Vietindebank
See Bank for Investment and Development of Vietnam.

### Vietnam Academic Research and Education Network (VARNET)
VARNET has been created by Vietnam's Institute of Information Technology (IOIT) to exchange academic information with other academic institutions. The IOIT operates under the National Centre for Natural Science Research.

### Vietnam Airlines (VNA)
Although Vietnam Airlines (VNA) started more than four decades ago, it was only in the mid-1990s that it began to expand its operations. For example, in 1976, VNA had a fleet of 5 aircraft and served only one international route to Beijing. In 1997, it expanded to 22 aircraft and served 21 international and 16 domestic destinations. Its fleet included 4 Boeing B676s, 10 Airbus A320s, 6 Aerospatiales ATR72, and 2 Fokker F70s. VNA is connected to global ticket distribution networks including Abacus, Amadeus, Sabre and Infini.

### Vietnam Bank for Agriculture (Agribank)
It was set up in 1990. It is now known as the Vietnam Bank for Agriculture and Rural Development. (See also: Vietnam Bank for Agriculture and Rural Development)

### Vietnam Bank for Agriculture and Rural Development (VBARD or Agribank)
Vietnam Bank for Agriculture and Rural Development (VBARD or Agribank) was set up in 1996 to succeed the Vietnam Bank for Agriculture which was set up in 1990. It is one of the three state-owned commercial banks in

Vietnam. It concentrates on the agricultural sector. It has the largest domestic network and undertakes agriculture-related foreign trade transactions.

According to its 1996 Annual Report, Agribank's statutory capital was VDN 2,200 billion and had 21,000 employees working in 2,564 branches. The bank had business relationship with 7 million farmer households, 3,300 state enterprises, 8,000 production cooperatives and 1,000 limited companies with outstanding loans of VDN 17,574 billion.

### Vietnam Confederation of Labour
This is a state-sponsored trade union in Vietnam.

### Vietnam Development Information Centre  *www.vdic.org.vn*
The Vietnam Development Information Centre (VDIC) is a joint project of the World Bank and development assistance agencies.

### Vietnam Economic Association
The Vietnam Economic Association is a non-government organization. In 1996, it was authorized by the government to start an Open University for business and management in Hanoi. By the end of 1996, more than 2,000 persons had registered for the entrance examination, far exceeding the planned capacity of 800. The association publishes the monthly *Vietnam Economic Times* in English.

### Vietnam Enterprise Investments
This is a closed-end investment fund listed on the Irish Stock Exchange.

### Vietnam Frontier Fund
This is a closed-end investment fund listed on the Irish Stock Exchange.

### Vietnam Information Network for Science and Technology Advance (VISTA Network)  *www.vista.gov.vn*
The Vietnam Information Network for Science and Technology Advance (VISTA Network) is the biggest databank on science and technology in Vietnam. It is managed by the National Centre for Science and Technological Information and Documentation (NACESTID) under the Ministry of Science, Technology and Environment.

### Vietnam International Arbitration Centre (VIAC)
The VIAC settles disputes that arise from foreign trade contracts.

**Vietnam International Assurance Company (VIA)**
This is a joint venture insurance company whose partners are Vietnam's state insurance company Bao Viet (51%), London's Commercial Union (24.5%), and Japan's Tokio Marine & Fire Insurance Co (24.5%). VIA offers general insurance, life insurance and reinsurance to domestic and foreign investors. (See also: Insurance business in Vietnam)

**Vietnam International Leasing Company (VILC)**
VILC is the first company to be granted a leasing licence by the State Bank of Vietnam. It is a 5-party joint venture involving Korean Industrial Leasing Co (32%), Vietnam Industrial and Commercial Bank (19%), Nippon Credit Bank (17%), Banque Francaise du Commerce Exterieur (17%) and International Finance Co (15%).

**Vietnam Law on Oil and Gas**
Vietnam issued its first Law on Oil and Gas on 6 July 1993. However, details were specified in Decree 84/CP passed on 17 December 1996. The Decree covers the exploration, investigation, mining, and mining development of oil and gas, including the processing, purchasing, storing and transporting of the mineral.

**Vietnam – Law, Ordinance, Decree and Regulation**
In Vietnam, laws are passed by the National Assembly and are highest form of legal documents. Ordinances are passed by the Standing Committee of the National Assembly when the Assembly is not in session. Decrees are passed by the government and implement the laws and ordinances. Decrees are accompanied by regulations that provide the details.

**Vietnam Management Initiative**
Vietnam Management Initiative (VMI) was a project started in 1996 at Vietnam's National Economic University in Hanoi. It introduced concepts of market economics to Vietnamese officials and managers.

**Vietnam National Coffee Corporation (Vinacafe)**
Vinacafe is the largest economic organization specializing in the production, processing, export and import of coffee and related products and activities.

**Vietnam National Leather and Footwear Corporation (Leaprodexim)**
This is a state-owned enterprise set up under the Ministry of Light Industry in 1987. It organizes production, export-import operations and services related to leather and footwear industries.

### Vietnam National Maritime Bureau (Vinamarine)
This is Vietnam's state organization that oversees the maritime industry.

### Vietnam Steel Corporation (VSC)
This is a state-owned steel company that manages 14 mills and factories, three trading and service enterprises and several foreign joint ventures.

### Vietnam National Milk Company (Vinamilk)
Vinamilk is one of Vietnam's successful consumer goods companies. It produces about 65 products including fresh milk, condensed milk, powdered milk, yogurt and ice cream. It has a market share of 80%. This is expected to decrease when the government allows international milk producers to enter the market.

### Vietnam Posts and Telecommunications Corporation (VNPT)
Vietnam Posts and Telecommunications Corporation is the business arm of the Directorate General of Posts and Telecommunications (DGPT). (See also: Directorate General of Posts and Telecommunications)

### Vietnam Ocean Shipping Company (VOSCO)
Vietnam Ocean Shipping Company is a state-owned shipping company. It owns, manages and operates ocean going fleet of different types of vessels from 4,500 to 20,000 dwt.

### Vietnam Science Technology and Education Net  *www.moste.gov.vn/stenet*
Vietnam Science Technology and Education Net (SSTE-net) is a project supported by Swedish International Development Agency (SIDA). It aims to set up ICT services, data communication network, supportive service organization and end-user training for the science technology and education sector in Vietnam. Delft University has been contracted to assist in the project.

### Vietnam Singapore Technical Training Centre (VSTTC)
The VSTTC was set up in 1997. It is located in the Vietnam Singapore Industrial Park. It trains Vietnamese workers in a wide range of technical skills.

### Vietnam Singapore Industrial Park (VSIP)
VSIP is an industrial park located in Song Be Province, about 17 kilometres north of Ho Chi Minh City. The 500-hectare park is jointly developed by Vietnam's state-owned company Song Be Export Import Trading Company (Becamex) and a group of Singapore companies led by government-linked Sembawang Group. They include Sembawang Industrial, Sembawang

Engineering, Jurong Town Corporation, Temasek Holdings, UOL Overseas Investments, KPM Group, LKN Construction and MC Development Asia. During the first phase, 500 hectares will be developed for infrastructure to support ready-built factories to attract investors. The park offers one-stop service to simplify the application process for investors to set up operations. Foreign companies from France, Japan, Malaysia, Singapore, Switzerland, United States and others are expected to employ about 10,000 workers producing electronic goods, food products and supporting services.

**Vietnamese Reinsurance Company (VINARE)**
In Vietnam, VINARE was the first reinsurance company which started operations in 1995. In Vietnam, an insurance company is allowed to re-insure with another insurance company provided that it must re-insure part of the liability with VINARE.

**VietSovPetro**
This is a Vietnam Soviet petroleum joint venture set up in 1981. Its main activity is exploring oil at the White Tiger (Bach Ho) field in the Cuu Long basin. Production began in 1986.

**Vijaya Bank (India)**   *www.vijayabank.com*
In India, the Vijaya Bank was founded in 1931 in Mangalore, Karnataka to promote banking among the farming community. It was nationalized in 1980. It has a network of 840 branches in 28 states and 4 union territories. In 1995, it set up a subsidiary Vibank Housing Finance Limited to finance the housing sector.

**Vision 2020 Task Force (Maldives)**   *www.presidencymaldives.gov.mv*
In the Maldives, the President established the Vision 2020 Task Force in August 1999. The functions of the Task Force included organizing consultations and eliciting public opinion in the formulation of long term strategies of national development.

**Vung Tau (Vietnam)**
This Vietnamese town is located 120 kilometres south of Ho Chi Minh City. It has prospered because of oil exploring activities, especially those of the Vietnam-Soviet joint venture Vietsovpetro. It is also popular among local tourists.

**Voice Response Unit**
A Voice Response Unit (VRU) in a telephone call centre handles simple

customer requests such as balance inquiry and fund transfer without personal assistance. Customers give instruction and respond by pressing specific keys on the phone keypad.

**Wall Street**
Name of the street in New York where the New York Stock Exchange (NYSE) is located. In general, the term may also mean the American financial community including the NYSE and all the financial institutions.

**Wallis Inquiry (Australia)**
In Australia, the Wallis Inquiry was set up in 1996 to review the success of earlier inquiries: Campbell Inquiry (1979) and Martin Inquiry (1983). It reviewed the process of deregulation and recommended the removal of most of the regulatory barriers. (See also: Campbell Inquiry, Martin Inquiry)

**Ways and Means Advances (India)**
In India, Ways and Means Advances were given by Reserve Bank to the central and state governments to bridge temporary mismatch in their receipts and payments and to improve their cash and debt management.

**Wealth Management Institute (Singapore)**  *www.wmi.com.sg*
Wealth Management Institute (WMI) was launched in September 2003 with the support of Government Investment Corporation (GIC), Temasek Holdings and fund management companies. With the Singapore Management University and Swiss Banking School, the WMI offers an MSc in Wealth Management.

**Westpac Banking Corporation (Australia)**  *www.westpac.com.au*
In Australia, Westpac Banking Corporation was formed in 1982 with the merger of the Bank of New South Wales and the Commercial Bank of Australia (CBA).

**WestpacTrust (Australia)**  *www.westpactrust.co.nz*
In Australia, WestpacTrust started in 1861 as a branch of the Bank of New South Wales (BNSW) in New Zealand. In 1912, the Commonwealth Bank of Australia (CBA) extended its operations to New Zealand. In 1982, BNSW and CBA merged to form Westpac. In 1996, Westpac and Trust Bank New Zealand merged to form WestpacTrust, creating New Zealand's largest bank with 1.3 million customers.

**Wholesale Debt Market (India)**
In India, a wholesale debt market (WDM) is where fixed income instruments

such as government bonds, treasury bills, commercial papers and corporate instruments are traded among institutional investors. (See also: National Stock Exchange of India)

**Woolworths (Australia)**   *www.woolworthslimited.com.au*
In 2002, Woolsworths (Australia) was ranked 442 among the Fortune 500 global companies.

**Workforce Development Agency (Singapore)**   *www.wda.gov.sg*
The Workforce Development Agency (WDA) was set up in September 2003. It is a new statutory board responsible for building a lifelong education and training system for workers in Singapore. Its objective is to enhance the employability and competitiveness of employees and job seekers.

**World Bank Group**   *www.worldbank.org*
The World Bank was founded in 1944 as a result of the Bretton Woods Agreement. It is owned by more than 184 member countries. These countries are represented by a board of governors and a Washington-based board of directors. Member countries are shareholders who carry ultimate decision-making powers. The group comprises the International Bank of Reconstruction and Development (IBRD, better known as World Bank), International Development Agency (IDA), International Finance Corporation (IFC), Multilateral Investment Guarantee Agency (MIGA) and the International Centre for Settlement of Investment Disputes (ICSID). (See also: International Bank for Reconstruction and Development, International Development Agency, International Finance Corporation)

**World Bank Institute**   *www.worldbank.org/wbi*
The World Bank Institute (WBI) was formed to help share World Bank's expertise and that of its member countries with policy makers and decision-makers in the developing world. It designs and delivers course and seminars aimed at reducing poverty and promoting economic growth. Its Global Development Learning Network links training centres around the world and promotes the exchange of information. (See also: Global Development Learning Network, World Bank Group)

**World Federation of Exchanges**   *www.world-exchanges.org*
In the 1930s, there was a need for international cooperation among stock exchanges. The Paris-based International Chamber of Commerce initiated the formation of International Bureau of Stock Exchanges, which existed until World War II. In 1957, representatives of several European bourses met in Paris

to foster informal cooperation. In 1961, the Federation Internationale des Bourses de Valeurs (FIBV) was formed in London. Since then, the activities of members have expanded to include derivative markets, clearing houses, settlement agencies and other financial services. In 2001, FIBV changed its name to World Federation of Exchanges. It is the trade organization for regulated securities and derivative markets, settlement institutions and related clearing houses. Its main purpose is to facilitate the representation and the development of organized and regulated markets.

## World Health Organization  *www.who.int*

The World Health Organization (WHO) was formed in 1948. It is a United Nations specialized agency for health. Its objective is the attainment by all peoples of the highest possible level of health. Health is defined in the WHO Constitution as a state of complete physical, mental and social well-being and not merely the absence of disease. WHO is governed by 191 member states through the World Health Assembly. The main tasks of the Assembly are to approve the WHO program and the budget for the following biennium and to decide on major policy issues.

## World Intellectual Property Organization  *www.wipo.int*

The World Intellectual Property Organization (WIPO) is a specialized agency of the United Nations. It promotes the use and protection of intellectual property. It administers 23 international treaties dealing with different aspects of intellectual property. It has 179 nations as its member states. Its headquarters are in Geneva.

## World Tourism Organization  *www.world-tourism.org*

The World Tourism Organization was set up in 1925 in the Hague as the International Union of Official Tourist Publicity Organizations. After World War II, it was renamed the International Union for Official Tourism Organizations (IUOTO) and moved to Geneva. In 1967, IUOTO was transformed into an inter-governmental organization to deal on a worldwide basis with all matters concerning tourism and to cooperate with other organizations, particularly those within the United Nations system such as the International Civil Aviation Organization. In 1975, IUOTO was renamed World Tourism Organization (WTO) and its first General Assembly was held in Madrid where the Spanish Government provided a building for its new headquarters. In 1976, WTO became an executing agency of the United Nations Development Program (UNDP). The membership of WTO includes 138 countries and more than 350 affiliates representing local government, private sector, tourism associations and education institutions.

## World Trade Organization (WTO)   *www.wto.org*

In January 1995, as a result of the Uruguay Round negotiations, the WTO was set up to succeed GATT (General Agreement on Tariffs and Trade). Its main functions are to administer WTO trade agreements, handle trade disputes and monitor national trade policies. WTO is also a forum for trade negotiations. It provides technical assistance and training for developing countries. It has about 145 member countries. (See also: General Agreement on Tariffs and Trade)

## WTO Inaugural Ministerial Conference

Singapore hosted the inaugural WTO (World Trade Organization) Ministerial Conference from 9 to 13 December 1997. It was the largest and highest profile international conference ever held in Singapore. There were about 4,500 participants, including 2,338 delegates from 123 member nations, 51 observer governments and 41 observer organizations, 1,604 press representatives, 236 non-governmental organization members and 124 members of the WTO Secretary.

The conference achieved some significant results. The adoption of a Ministerial Declaration, containing a substantive future work program for the WTO, helped ensure that the momentum of global trade liberalization would be maintained.

## Yield to maturity

This is the measure of the expected total return from bonds when held to maturity. The calculation takes into account the appreciation of par from the current market price when bought at a discount or depreciation when bought at a premium.

## Yondai Shoken (Japan)

Big Four Japanese securities houses: Daiwa, Nikko, Nomura and Yamaichi.

## Zaibatsu (Japan)

Japanese corporate group.

## Zenshinren Bank (Japan)

See Shinkin banks.

# ABBREVIATIONS

# ABBREVIATIONS

| | |
|---|---|
| AA | Articles of Association |
| AAANZ | Accounting Association of Australia and New Zealand |
| AAAS | American Academy of Asian Studies |
| AAB | Asian arrangement to borrow |
| AAB | Authorized agent bank |
| AABL | Associated Australian Banks in London |
| AACSB | Association to Advance Collegiate Schools of Business |
| AADCP | ASEAN Australia Development Cooperation |
| AAECP | ASEAN Australia Economic Cooperation Program |
| AAF | ASEAN Automotive Federation |
| AAGR | Average annual growth rate |
| AAH | Academy of Accounting Historians |
| AAI | Airports Authority of India |
| AAIA | Associate of the Association of International Accountants |
| AAII | Associate of the Australian Insurance Institute |
| AAIIBP | Al-Amanah Islamic Investment Bank of the Philippines |
| AALCC | Asian African Legal Consultative Committee |
| AALS | Approved Aircraft Leasing Scheme (Singapore) |
| AAMO | Asian Association of Management Organizations |
| AAMS | Australian Aerial Medical Services |
| AANA | Australian Association of National Advertisers |
| AAPRC | Audit Administration of the People's Republic of China |
| AAR | Against all risks (insurance) |
| AAR | Authority for Advance Ruling (India) |
| AARD | Agency for Agricultural Research and Development (Indonesia) |
| AARRO | Afro-Asian Rural Reconstruction Organization |
| AAS | Airport and Aviation Services Limited (Sri Lanka) |
| AAS | Australian Academy of Sciences |
| AAS | Automobile Association of Singapore |
| AASA | Associate of the Australian Society of Accountants |
| AASB | Australian Accounting Standards Board |
| AASC | Auditing and Accounting Services Company |
| AASC | Australian Accounting Standards Committee |
| AASSRC | Association of Asian Social Science Research Councils |
| AAT | Airport Authority of Thailand |
| AB | Aktiebolag (limited liability company in Finland, Sweden) |
| ABA | ASEAN Bankers' Acceptance |
| ABA | ASEAN Bankers Association |

| | |
|---|---|
| ABA | Australian Bankers Association |
| ABAC | APEC Business Advisory Council |
| ABACUS | Automated Business and Control United Systems |
| ABARE | Australian Bureau of Agricultural and Resource Economics |
| ABB | Agricultural Bank of Vietnam |
| ABB | Asea Brown Boveri |
| ABB | Australian Barley Board |
| ABC | Agricultural Bank of China |
| ABC | ASEAN Banking Council |
| ABC | Asia Broadcast Centre |
| ABC | Asia Business Centre |
| ABC | Asian Badminton Confederation |
| ABC | Association of Banks in Cambodia |
| ABC | Australian Broadcasting Corporation |
| ABC | Automated Banking Consortium |
| ABDA | PT Asuransi Bina Dharma Arta (Indonesia) |
| ABEI | Anshan Bureau of Electronic Industry (China) |
| ABEP | Anshan Broadcasting Equipment Plant (China) |
| ABF | ASEAN Business Forum |
| ABF | Asian Business Fellowship program |
| ABFM | Approved Boutique Fund Management scheme |
| ABI | Approved Bond Intermediary (Singapore) |
| ABIA | Associate of the Bankers' Institute of Australasia |
| ABIO | Australian Banking Industry Ombudsman scheme |
| ABM | Automated batch mixing |
| ABN | Algemene Bank Nederland |
| ABN | Asian Business News Network |
| ABRI | Angkatan Bersenjata Republik Indonesia (Indonesian Armed Forces) |
| ABS | Asset-backed securities |
| ABS | Association of Banks in Singapore |
| ABS | Australian Bureau of Statistics |
| ABTA | Australian British Trade Association |
| ABTAC | Australian Book Trade Advisory Committee |
| ABTUC | All Burma Trade Union Congress |
| ABU | Asia Pacific Broadcasting Union |
| ABU | Asian Broadcasting Union |
| A/C | Account |
| ACA | Associate of the Institute of Chartered Accountants |
| ACA | Association of Certified Accountants |
| ACAI | Association of Custodial Agencies of India |
| ACASTD | Advisory Committee on the Application of Science and Technology to Development (UN) |
| ACAT | ASEAN Centre for Appropriate Technology |

| | |
|---|---|
| ACATETSME | APEC Centre for Technology Exchange and Training for Small and Medium Enterprises |
| ACC | Account |
| ACC | Administrative Committee on Coordination (UN) |
| ACC | ASEAN Consultative Committee |
| ACC | Asian Coconut Community |
| ACC | Associated Cement Company (India) |
| ACCA | Associate of the Association of Certified Accountants |
| ACCA | Association of Chartered Certified Accountants |
| ACCC | Agricultural Coordination Committee of the Cabinet (Pakistan) |
| ACCC | Australian Competition and Consumer Commission |
| ACCFTU | All Ceylon Federation of Free Trade Unions (Sri Lanka) |
| ACCI | Australian Chamber of Commerce and Industry |
| ACCSM | ASEAN Conference on Civil Servant Matters |
| ACCSQ | ASEAN Consultative Committee for Standards and Quality |
| ACCT | American Chamber of Commerce in Taiwan |
| ACCTC | ASEAN Centre for Combating Transnational Crime |
| ACE | Almanac of China's Economy |
| ACE | American Commodity Exchange |
| ACE | AMEX Commodities Exchange |
| ACE | ASEAN Confederation of Employers |
| ACEDAC | ASEAN Centre for Development of Agriculture Cooperatives |
| ACEF | Asian Cultural Exchange Foundation |
| ACEID | Asian Centre of Educational Innovation for Development |
| ACESA | Australian Commonwealth Engineering Standards Association |
| ACF | ASEAN Cultural Fund |
| ACFERT | Almanac of China's Foreign Economic Relations and Trade |
| ACFIC | All China Federation of Industry and Commerce |
| ACFSC | Australian Corporations and Financial Services Commission |
| ACFTU | All China Federation of Trade Unions |
| ACG | Asia-Pacific Central Securities Depository Group |
| ACH | Automated Clearing House |
| ACHA | Australian Clearing House Association |
| ACI | Airports Council International |
| ACI | Asahi Chemical Industry Company Limited |
| ACI | Australian Consolidated Industries Limited |
| ACIAR | Australian Centre for International Agricultural Research |
| ACID | Asian Council of Industrial Development |
| ACII | Associate of the Chartered Insurance Institute |
| ACIT | International Academy of Tourism |
| ACLEDA | Association of Cambodian Local Economic Development Agencies |
| ACM | Asian Common Market |
| ACMA | Associate of the Institute of Cost and Management Accountants |
| ACMM | Associate of Conservatorium of Music, Melbourne |

| ACMRR | Advisory Committee on Marine Resources Research (UN) |
| ACO | Authorized Code Owner |
| ACOH | Advisory Committee on Operational Hydrology (UN) |
| ACOMR | Advisory Committee on Oceanic Meteorological Research (UN) |
| ACORD | Auckland Committee on Racism and Discrimination |
| ACP | African Caribbean and Pacific Countries |
| ACP | Airport Core Program (Hong Kong) |
| ACP | Asian Caribbean and Pacific region |
| ACPA | American China Policy Association |
| ACR | Annual confidential report |
| ACS | Audit, compliance and surveillance |
| ACS | Australian Computer Society |
| ACT | Action Committee on Tariffs |
| ACT | Approved Cyber Trader scheme (Singapore) |
| ACT | Australian Capital Territory |
| ACTID | Action Committee on Tariff and Industrial Development |
| ACTIVE | All Companies Together in Various Exercises (Singapore) |
| ACTRSWD | Asian Centre for Training and Research in Social Welfare and Development |
| ACTS | Adult Cooperative Training Scheme (Singapore) |
| ACT(S) | Association of Corporate Treasurers (Singapore) |
| ACTT | ASEAN Crisis Team for Tourism |
| ACTU | Australian Council of Trade Unions |
| ACU | ASEAN Clearing Union |
| ACU | ASEAN Cooperation Unit |
| ACU | Asian Currency Unit |
| ACV | Actual cash value |
| AD | Anti-dumping |
| ADA | Authorized Depository Agent |
| ADAB | Australian Development Assistance Bureau |
| ADB | Agricultural Development Bank |
| ADB | Asian Development Bank |
| ADBC | Agricultural Development Bank of China |
| ADBN | Agricultural Development Bank of Nepal |
| ADBP | Agricultural Development Bank of Pakistan |
| ADBV | Agricultural Development Bank of Vietnam |
| ADC | Advanced developing country |
| ADC | Analogue to digital converter |
| ADCOS | Australian Development Cooperation Scholarship |
| ADF | Approved deposit fund |
| ADF | Asian Development Fund |
| ADFA | Australian Defence Force Academy |
| ADFC | Agricultural Development Finance Company (India) |
| ADFIAP | Association of Development Finance Institutions of Asia and the Pacific |

| | |
|---|---|
| ADI | Asian Development Institute |
| ADLE | Additional deduction for labour expense |
| ADM | Asian dollar market |
| ADM | Authorized direct member (Malaysia) |
| ADP | Annual Development Plan (Bangladesh) |
| ADPC | Asian Disaster Preparedness Centre |
| ADR | Additional drawing right |
| ADR | Alternative dispute resolution |
| ADR | American depository receipt |
| ADS | Annual dividend statement |
| ADS | Australian Development Scholarship |
| ADS | PT Asian Development Securities (Indonesia) |
| ADSS | Australian Defence Science Service |
| ADV | Advance |
| ADX | Average Directional Index |
| ADSL | Asymmetric digital subscriber line technology |
| AEA | Apparel Exporters Association (Sri Lanka) |
| AEBF | Asia-Europe Business Forum |
| AEC | Asian Economic Cooperation |
| AEC | Atomic Energy Commission |
| AECF | Asia-Europe Cooperation Framework |
| AEDC | Asia's Emerging Dragon Corporation |
| AEDF | Asian Economic Development Fund |
| AEEMTRC | ASEAN-EC Energy Management Training and Research Centre |
| AEESCA | Association for Engineering Education in South and Central Asia |
| AEESEA | Association for Engineering Education in South East Asia |
| AEETC | Asia-Europe Environmental Technology Centre |
| AEFGC | Asia-Europe Forum of Governors of Cities |
| AEGDM | ASEAN Expert Group on Disaster Management |
| AEGE | ASEAN Expert Group on Environment |
| AEI | Association of Indonesian Securities Issuers |
| AEITTP | Asia-Europe Information Technology and Telecommunications Program |
| AEIS | Association of Electronic Industries in Singapore |
| AEM | ASEAN Economic Ministers |
| AEMC | ASEAN-EC Management Centre |
| AEMM | ASEAN Economic Ministers Meeting |
| AEMM | Asia-Europe Ministerial Meeting |
| AEMEC | ASEAN Economic Ministers on Energy Cooperation |
| AEMM | ASEAN-EU Ministerial Meeting |
| AENRIC | ASEAN Environmental and Natural Resources Information Centre |
| AEP | Alien Employment Permit (Philippines) |
| AEPC | Apparel Export Promotion Council (India) |
| AERB | Atomic Energy Regulatory Board (India) |

| | |
|---|---|
| AES | Asian Environmental Society |
| AESIP | Aboriginal Education Strategic Initiative Program (Australia) |
| AESMEC | Asia-Europe Small and Medium Enterprises Conference |
| AEU | Asian Electronics Union |
| AEVG | Asia-Europe Vision Group |
| AEW | Airborne Early Warning system |
| AFA | ASEAN Federation of Accountants |
| AFB | Approved foreign broker |
| AFBC | Australia-Fiji Business Council |
| AFBD | Association of Futures Brokers and Dealers |
| AFC | ASEAN Finance Corporation |
| AFCI | Association of Finance Companies (Thailand) |
| AFCUL | Australian Federation of Credit Unions Ltd |
| AFDC | Agricultural and Fishery Development Corporation (Korea) |
| AFE | Almanac of Fujian's Economy (China) |
| AFEB | Authorized foreign exchange bank |
| AFES | Association of Financial Engineering (Singapore) |
| AFF | ASEAN Fisheries Federation |
| AFFM | Australian Financial Futures Market |
| AFHB | ASEAN Food Handling Bureau |
| AFI | Rules on the Administration of Financial Institutions (China) |
| AFIC | Asian Finance and Investment Corporation |
| AFIC | Australian Financial Institutions Commission |
| AFL | ASEAN Fund Limited |
| AFL-CIO | American Federation of Labour – Congress of Industrial Organizations (United States) |
| AFMA | ASEAN Federation of Mining Associations |
| AFMA | Australian Financial Markets Association |
| AFMM | ASEAN Foreign Ministers Meeting |
| AFN | Asia Forest Network |
| AFPFL | Anti-Fascist People's Freedom League |
| AFPPD | Asian Forum of Parliamentarians on Population and Development |
| AFRASEC | Afro-Asian Organization for Economic Cooperation |
| AFS | Automation Feasibility Study Scheme |
| AFT | Automatic fund transfer |
| AFTA | ASEAN Free Trade Area |
| AFTA | Asian Free Trade Agreement |
| AFTAK | Association of Foreign Trading Agents of Korea |
| AFR | Australian Financial Review |
| AFTEX | ASEAN Federation of Textile Industries |
| AG | Aktiengesellschaft (Public limited liability company in Austria, Germany, Switzerland) |
| AG | Attorney General |
| AG | Auditor General |
| AGFI | Agriculture and fisheries |

| | |
|---|---|
| AGI | Adjusted gross income |
| AGL | Assurances Generales du Lao |
| AGM | Annual general meeting |
| AGPS | Australian Government Publishing Service |
| Agrexport | Vietnam National Agricultural Produce Export-Import Corporation |
| Agribank | Vietnam Bank for Agriculture and Rural Development |
| AGSM | Australian Graduate School of Management |
| AHC | Ad hoc committee |
| AHCC | Asian Highway Coordinating Committee |
| AHGM | ASEAN Heads of Government Meeting |
| AHMSP | Animal Health Monitoring and Surveillance Project (Vanuatu) |
| AHP | Asian Highway Project |
| AHTN | ASEAN Harmonized Tariff Nomenclature |
| AI | Air India |
| AI | Association of Industry (Macau) |
| AI | Authorized institution |
| AIA | American International Assurance |
| AIA | ASEAN Investment Agreement |
| AIA | ASEAN Investment Area |
| AIA | Association for Insurance Advancement (Singapore) |
| AIB | Academy of International Business |
| AIB | Australian Institute of Bankers |
| AIBC | ASEAN India Business Council |
| AIBD | Asia Pacific Institute for Broadcasting Development |
| AIBD | Association of International Bond Dealers |
| AIBF | Australian Institute of Banking and Finance |
| AIC | Administration for Industry and Commerce (China) |
| AIC | ASEAN Industrial Complementation Scheme |
| AICO | ASEAN Industrial Cooperation Scheme |
| AICPA | American Institute of Certified Public Accountants |
| AID | Agency for International Development (US) |
| AIDA | Australia-Indonesia Development Area |
| AIDA | Australian Industries Development Corporation |
| AIDB | All India Development Bank |
| AIDC | Asian Industrial Development Council |
| AIDC | Australian Industries Development Council |
| AIDS | Acquired immune deficiency syndrome |
| AIDAB | Australian International Development Assistance Bureau |
| AIDIA | Associate of the Industrial Design Institute of Australia |
| AIEDP | Asian Institute for Economic Development and Planning |
| AIEF | Australian International Education Foundation |
| AIEPE | Agri-industrial Export Processing Estate (Philippines) |
| AIESEC | International Association of Students in Economics and Management |

| | |
|---|---|
| AIF | Approved International Fairs status (Singapore) |
| AIFI | All India Financial Institution |
| AIFM | ASEAN Institute of Forest Management |
| AII | Air India International |
| AII | Australian Insurance Institute |
| AIIA | Associate of the Indian Institute of Architects |
| AIIA | Australian Institute of International Affairs |
| AIICH | Regulations on the Administration of Individual Industrial and Commercial Households |
| AIIM | All India Institute of Medicine |
| AIJSCC | ASEAN India Joint Sectoral Cooperation Committee |
| AIJV | ASEAN Industrial Joint Venture |
| AIL | Approved Issuer Levy (New Zealand) |
| AIM | Asian Institute of Management |
| AIM | Australian Institute of Management |
| AIM | Alternative investment market |
| AIM | Amanah Ikhtiar Malaysia |
| AIM | Automated information machine |
| AIMA | All India Management Association |
| AIMC | Association of Investment Management (Thailand) |
| AIMCO | Association of Internal Management Consultants |
| AIMM | Australian Institute of Mining and Metallurgy |
| AIMPE | Australian Institute of Marine and Power Engineers |
| AIMR | Association for Investment Management and Research |
| AINDT | Australian Institute for Non-destructive Testing |
| AINSE | Australian Institute of Nuclear Science and Engineering |
| AIOD | ASEAN and International Organization Department |
| AIP | Agency Investment Program |
| AIP | Annual investment plan |
| AIP | ASEAN Industrial Project |
| AIPF | All India Pharmacists' Federation |
| AIPU | All India Pharmacists' Union |
| AIR | All India Radio |
| AIRC | Australian Industrial Relations Commission |
| AIS | Approved Investment Scheme (Singapore) |
| AIS | Approved International Shipping Enterprise Scheme (Singapore) |
| AIS | Australian Iron and Steel Limited |
| AIT | American Institute in Taiwan |
| AIT | Approved International Trader Scheme (Singapore) |
| AIT | Asian Institute of Technology |
| AIT | Asian Institute of Tourism |
| AITUC | All India Trade Union Congress |
| AIU | Association of Indonesia Underwriters |
| AJDF | ASEAN-Japan Development Fund |
| AKF | Account keeping fee |

| | |
|---|---|
| AKKI | Indonesian Credit Card Association |
| ALGOL | Algorithmic language |
| ALL | Administrative Litigation Law (China) |
| ALM | Asset liability management |
| ALM | Association of Lloyd's Members |
| ALMA | Alliance of the Poor against Demolition (Philippines) |
| ALPPIA | Asosiasi Lembaga Pembiayaan Pembangunan Indonesia (Indonesian Association of Development Financial Institutions) |
| ALS | Area Licensing Scheme (Singapore) |
| ALS | ASEAN Liner Service |
| ALS | Automation Leasing Scheme (Singapore) |
| AMAF | ASEAN Ministerial Meeting on Agriculture and Forestry |
| AMBDC | ASEAN Mekong Basin Development Cooperation |
| AmbH | Aktien mit beschrankter Haftung (Limited liability company in Germany) |
| AMBI | Association of Merchant Bankers of India |
| AMC | Asset Management Committee |
| AMC | Asset Management Company |
| AMC | Asset Management Corporation |
| AMC | Association of Management Consultants |
| AMCHAM | American Chamber of Commerce |
| AMCIS | Association of Management Corporations in Singapore |
| AMCM | Autoridade Monetaria e Cambial de Macau (Monetary Authority of Macau) |
| Amcorp | Arab-Malaysian Corporation |
| AMCR | Average Monthly Crime Rate |
| AMD | Advanced Medical Directive (Singapore) |
| AMDAL | Analysis of Environmental Impact (Indonesia) |
| AMDC | ASEAN Mekong Development Cooperation |
| AME | Australian Multimedia Enterprise |
| AMEICC | AEM-MITI Economic and Industrial Cooperation Committee |
| AMETIAP | Association of Maritime Education and Training Institutions in the Asia Pacific |
| AMEX | American Stock Exchange |
| AMF | Asian Monetary Fund |
| AMFI | Association of Mutual Funds of India |
| AMI | Approved Maritime Insurer |
| AMIB | Agricultural Machinery Industry Bureau (China) |
| AMIC | Asian Mass Communications Research and Information Centre |
| AMIC | Asian Media Information and Communication Centre |
| AMIRA | Australian Mineral Industries Research Association |
| AMLA | Administration of Muslim Law Act (Singapore) |
| AMM | Annual Ministerial Meeting |
| AMM | ASEAN Ministerial Meeting |
| AMMB | Arab-Malaysian Merchant Bank Berhad |

| | |
|---|---|
| AMME | ASEAN Ministerial Meeting on the Environment |
| AMNZIE | Associate Member of the New Zealand Institution of Engineers |
| AMP | Association of Muslim Professionals (Singapore) |
| AMRO | Amsterdam-Rotterdam Bank |
| AMS | Aggregate Measure of Support |
| AMS | Automatic Order Matching and Execution System |
| AMU | Asset Management Unit |
| AMU | Asian Monetary Unit |
| AMUT | Arab-Malaysian Unit Trusts Berhad |
| AMV | Aggregate market value |
| ANA | All Nippon Airways |
| ANA | Australian National Airways |
| ANA | Australian Natives' Association |
| ANC | Australian Newspapers Council |
| ANCSA | Indonesia National Service Administration |
| ANDAL | Environment Impact Statement (Indonesia) |
| ANI | Australian National Industries Limited |
| ANIE | Asian New Industrializing Economy |
| ANL | Australian National Library |
| ANN | Asian Pacific News Network |
| ANNA | Association of National Numbering Agencies |
| ANRPC | Association of Natural Rubber Producing Countries |
| ANTA | Australian National Travel Association |
| ANTC | Australian National Television Council |
| ANU | Australian National University |
| ANZ | Air New Zealand |
| ANZ | Australia and New Zealand Banking Group |
| ANZAAS | Australian New Zealand Association for the Advancement of Science |
| ANZAM | Australian New Zealand Academy of Management |
| ANZCERTA | Australian New Zealand Closer Economic Relations Trade Agreement |
| ANZECP | ASEAN New Zealand Economic Cooperative Program |
| ANZIA | Associate of the New Zealand Institute of Architects |
| ANZIC | Associate of the New Zealand Institute of Chemists |
| ANZJMC | ASEAN New Zealand Joint Management Committee |
| ANZLA | Associate of the New Zealand Library Association |
| ANZSIC | Australia New Zealand Standard Industry Classification |
| ANZUS | Australia, New Zealand and United States |
| ANZAC | Australia, New Zealand Army Corps |
| AOFM | Australian Office of Financial Management |
| AOI | All Ordinaries Index (Australia) |
| AOL | America On Line |
| AOM | Australian Options Market |

| AON | All or none |
|---|---|
| AOP | Association of Persons (India) |
| AOPU | Asian Oceanic Postal Union |
| AOQC | Australian Organization for Quality Control |
| AOT | Approved Oil Trader Scheme (Singapore) |
| AOTS | Association for Overseas Technical Scholarships |
| AP | Associated Press |
| APAA | ASEAN Port Authorities Association |
| APABA | Asia Pacific Association of Business Administration (Taiwan) |
| APC | ASEAN Paris Committee |
| APC | Asian Pepper Community |
| APC | Australian Petroleum Company |
| APCA | Australian Payments Clearing Association |
| APCC | Asian and Pacific Coconut Community |
| APCOL | All Pakistan Confederation of Labour |
| APCOM | Agricultural Price Commission (Pakistan) |
| APCTT | Asian and Pacific Centre for Transfer of Technology |
| APCU | ASEAN Population Coordination Unit |
| APDAC | Asian and Pacific Development Administration Centre |
| APDC | Asian and Pacific Development Centre |
| APDI | Asian and Pacific Development Institute |
| APEC | Asia Pacific Economic Cooperation |
| APEI | Indonesian Association of Securities Underwriters |
| APF | Asia Pacific Foundation (Canada) |
| APF | Asian Packaging Federation |
| APFC | Asia Pacific Forestry Commission |
| APF | Asian Policy Forum |
| APFTU | All Pakistan Federation of Trade Unions |
| API | Air Pollution Index |
| APINDO | Asosiasi Pengusaha Indonesia |
| | (Employers Association of Indonesia) |
| APKINDO | Association of Indonesian Wood Panel Producers |
| APL | Administrative Punishment Law (China) |
| APL | Alliance of Progressive Labour (Philippines) |
| APM | Administered pricing mechanism |
| APMT | Asia Pacific Mobile Telecommunication satellite project |
| APO | Asian Productivity Organization |
| APP | Anti-Poverty Program |
| APP | ASEAN Population Program |
| APPEC | Asian Pacific Petroleum Export Conference |
| APPI | Asian Petroleum Price Index |
| APPI | International Association for the Promotion and Protection of Private Foreign Investments |
| APPTC | Asian Pacific Postal Training Centre |

| APPU | Asian Pacific Postal Union |
| APRA | Australian Prudential Regulation Authority |
| APRACA | Asian and Pacific Regional Agricultural Credit Association |
| APRIA | Asia Pacific Risk and Insurance Association |
| APRIL | Asia Pacific Resources International Ltd |
| APRO | Asia and Pacific Regional Office (of ICFTU) |
| APRTC | ASEAN Poultry Research and Training Centre |
| APRU | Association of Pacific Rim Universities |
| APSC | Australian Payments System Council |
| APSDEP | Asia and Pacific Skills Development Program |
| APSEB | Andhra Pradesh State Electricity Board (India) |
| APT | Asset Privatization Trust (Philippines) |
| APTC | Asia and Pacific Telecommunication Community |
| APTMA | All Pakistan Textile Mills Association |
| APTPA | Asia and Pacific Trade Promotion Association |
| APTU | Australian Postal and Telecommunications Union |
| APU | Asian Parliamentary Union |
| APU | Asian Payment Union |
| APWA | All Pakistan Women's Association |
| APWRCN | Asia and Pacific Women's Resource Collection Network |
| APWSS | Asian Pacific Weed Science Society |
| AQL | Acceptable quality level |
| AR | Account receivable |
| AR | Annual report |
| AR | Annual return |
| ARC | Applied Research Corporation |
| ARC | ASEAN Reinsurance Corporation |
| ARC | Asian Reinsurance Corporation |
| ARC | Asset Reconstruction Company (India) |
| ARC | Australian Research Council |
| ARCBC | ASEAN Regional Centre for Biodiversity Conservation |
| ARCSTC | ASEAN Russia Commission on Scientific and Technological Cooperation |
| ARDB | Agricultural Rural Development Bank (India) |
| ARDC | Agricultural Refinance Development Corporation (India) |
| ARDCMR | ASEAN Regional Development Centre for Mineral Resources |
| ARF | Additional Registration Fee (Singapore) |
| ARF | ASEAN Regional Forum |
| ARF | Asset Reconstruction Fund (India) |
| ARF-ISG | ASEAN Regional Forum Inter-session Supporting Group |
| ARIBA | Associate of the Royal Institute of British Architects |
| ARM | Additional resource mobilization |
| ARM | Adjustable rate mortgage |
| ARMM | Autonomous Region for Muslim Mindanao (Philippines) |
| ARO | Agency regional office |

| ARR | Administrative Reconsideration Regulations (China) |
|---|---|
| ARTCHINA | China National Arts and Crafts Import and Export Corporation |
| ARTEP | Asian Regional Team for Employment Promotion |
| ARTI | Agrarian Research and Training Institute (Sri Lanka) |
| ARU | Australian Railways Union |
| AS | Accounting standards |
| AS | American Standard |
| AS | Australian Standard |
| A/S | Aksjeselskap (Limited liability company in Norway) |
| A/S | Aktieselskab (Limited liability company in Denmark) |
| ASA | ASEAN Swap Arrangement |
| ASA | Association of Southeast Asia |
| ASA | Asia Society of America |
| ASA | Association of Southeast Asia |
| ASA | Australian Society of Accountants |
| ASAC | Asian Securities' Analysts Council |
| ASAC | Asian Standards Advisory Committee |
| ASAF | Asian Securities Analysts Federation |
| ASAIHL | Association of Southeast Asian Institutes of Higher Learning |
| ASAP | Association of Securities Analysts of the Philippines |
| ASAS | Advertising Standards Authority of Singapore |
| ASB | Accounting Standards Board |
| ASB | Amanah Saham Bumiputera (Indigenous Trust Shares) |
| ASC | Accounting Society of China |
| ASC | Accounting Standards Council (Philippines) |
| ASC | Agrarian Services Centre (Sri Lanka) |
| ASC | Approved Securities Company |
| ASC | ASEAN Standing Committee |
| ASC | Australian Securities Commission |
| ASCA | Association for Science Cooperation in Asia |
| ASCHN | ASEAN Sub-Committee on Health and Nutrition |
| ASCII | American Standard Code for Information Interchange |
| ASCLA | ASEAN Sub-Committee on Labour Affairs |
| ASCM | Association of Stockbroking Companies Malaysia |
| ASCO | Association of Securities Companies (Thailand) |
| ASCOE | ASEAN Sub-Committee on Education |
| ASCOPE | ASEAN Council on Petroleum |
| ASDF | ASEAN Social Development Fund |
| ASEI | Asuransi Ekspor Indonesia (Indonesian export insurance company) |
| ASEAN | Association of Southeast Asian Nations |
| ASEAN-CCI | ASEAN Chambers of Commerce and Industry |
| ASEAN-EUJCC | ASEAN-EU Joint Cooperative Committee |
| ASEAN-ISIS | ASEAN Institutes of Strategic and International Studies |
| ASEANTA | ASEAN Tourism Association |

| | |
|---|---|
| ASEAUK | Association of Southeast Asian Studies in the UK |
| ASEF | Asia-Europe Foundation |
| ASEM | Asia-Europe Meeting |
| ASEM-S&T | Asia-Europe Meeting – Science and Technology |
| ASEP | ASEAN Sub-regional Environment Program |
| ASF | ASEAN Science Fund |
| ASFR | Age specific fertility rate |
| ASI | Aeronautical Society of India |
| ASIA | Asian Securitization and Infrastructure Assurance |
| ASIAF | Asian Foundation |
| ASIC | Administration of the State Investment Corporation (China) |
| ASIC | Australian Securities and Investment Commission |
| ASKRINDO | Asuransi Kredit Indonesia (Indonesian credit insurance company) |
| ASL | ASEAN Supreme Fund Limited |
| ASMC | ASEAN Specialized Meteorological Centre |
| ASME | Association of Small and Medium Enterprises |
| ASOD | ASEAN Senior Officials on Drug Matters |
| ASOEN | ASEAN Senior Officials on the Environment |
| ASP | APEC Support Program |
| ASP | ASEAN-UNDP Sub-Regional Program |
| ASPA | Association of South Pacific Airlines |
| ASPAC | Asia and Pacific Area Council |
| ASPAC | Asian and Pacific Council |
| ASPAT | Asia-Pacific (International) Trade |
| ASPC | Auditing Standards and Practices Council (Philippines) |
| ASQP | ASEAN Standards and Quality Program |
| ASSARD | Asian Survey on Agrarian Reform and Rural Development |
| ASSET | Automated Trading System for the Stock Exchange of Thailand |
| ASSETS | Automated Self-Service Enquiry Terminals (Singapore) |
| ASSOCHAM | Associated Chamber of Commerce and Industry of India |
| AST | Automated screen trading system |
| ASTA | American Society of Travel Agents |
| A*STAR | Agency for Science, Technology and Research (Singapore) |
| ASTEC | Australian Science, Technology and Engineering Council |
| ASTEK | Asuransi Sosial Tenaga Kerja (Indonesia) (Social Insurance Scheme) |
| ASTINFO | Asian Scientific and Technological Information Network |
| ASTRO | International Association of State Trading Organizations of Developing Countries |
| ASX | Australian Stock Exchange |
| ASXD | ASX Derivatives Options Market |
| ASY | ASEAN Sub-Committee on Youth |
| ASYCUDA | Automated System for Customs Data (Nepal) |
| ATA | Admission Temporair/Temporary Admission |
| ATC | Agreement on Textile and Clothing (WTO) |

| | |
|---|---|
| ATC | Australian Tourist Commission |
| ATC | Authorized Trading Centre (Singapore) |
| ATEP | Asian Trade Expansion Program |
| ATF | ASEAN Tourism Forum |
| ATF | ASEM Trust Fund |
| ATH | ASEAN Telecom Holding Sendirian Berhad |
| ATI | Account Transfer Instruction |
| ATI | Association of Thai Industries |
| ATIC | ASEAN Trade and Investment Corporation |
| ATIMM | ASEAN Trade and Industry Ministers Meeting |
| ATIRI | Ahmedabad Textile Industry Research Institute (India) |
| ATM | Asynchronous Transfer Mode |
| ATM | Automated teller machine |
| ATN | Asian Telecommunications Network |
| ATO | Air Transportation Office (Philippines) |
| ATOMS | Automated Traffic Offence Management System (Singapore) |
| ATP | Approved training program |
| ATPC | Association of Tin Producing Countries |
| ATR | ASEAN Tourist Region |
| ATS | Alternative trading system |
| ATS | Automated Trading System HKFE |
| ATTC | ASEAN Timber Technology Centre |
| ATTS | Association of Taxation Technicians of Singapore |
| AUBC | Association of Universities of the British Commonwealth |
| AUC | Affiliated university college |
| AUD | Australian dollar |
| AUDMP | Asian Urban Disaster Mitigation Program |
| AULLA | Australasian Universities Language and Literature Association |
| AUMLA | Australasian Universities Modern Language Association |
| AUP | Australian United Press |
| AusAID | Australian Agency for International Development |
| AUSTCHAM | Australian Chamber of Commerce in Indonesia |
| AUSTRAC | Australian Transaction Reports and Analysis Centre |
| AUSTRED | Australian Red Cross |
| AusTrade | Australian Trade Commission |
| AUTA | Association of University Teachers of Accounting |
| AV | Ad valorem |
| AV | Added value |
| AVA | Agri-food and Veterinary Authority |
| AVA | Audio visual aid |
| AVL | Air Vanuatu Limited |
| AVM | Automated vending machine |
| AWA | Australian Workplace Agreement |
| AWARE | Asian Women Association for Research and Education |
| AWB | Airway bill |

| | |
|---|---|
| AWB | Australian Wheat Board |
| AWBC | Australian Wine and Brandy Corporation |
| AWF | Australian Wine Foundation |
| AWNL | Australian Women's National League |
| AWOL | Absent without leave |
| AWP | ASEAN Women's Program |
| AWRA | Australian Wool Realization Agency |
| AWRC | Australian Water Resources Council |
| AWRC | Australian Wool Research Commission |
| AWS | Annual Wage Supplement |
| AWSJ | Asian Wall Street Journal |
| AWU | Australian Workers' Union |
| AWWA | Asian Women's Welfare Association |
| AXSEZ | Almanac of the Xiamen Special Economic Zone (China) |
| B2B | Business to business |
| B2C | Business to consumer |
| BA | Banker's Acceptance |
| BA | British Airways |
| BAAC | Bank of Agriculture and Agricultural Cooperatives (Thailand) |
| BAAIC | Basic Agreement on ASEAN Industrial Complementation |
| BAAIJV | Basic Agreement on ASEAN Industrial Joint Ventures |
| BAC | Bioethics Advisory Committee |
| BAC | Budget and Administration Committee |
| BAcc | Bachelor of Accountancy |
| BACIEC | Beijing Arts and Crafts Import and Export Corporation |
| BACS | Bankers' Automatic Clearing Services Limited (Hong Kong) |
| BACSC | Beijing Arts and Crafts Service Centre |
| BAD | Bank Accounts Debits tax (Australia) |
| BADC | Bangladesh Agricultural Development Corporation |
| BAEC | Bangladesh Atomic Energy Commission |
| BAF | Business Angel Fund |
| BAFIA | Banking and Financial Institutions Act (Malaysia) |
| BAg | Bachelor of Agriculture |
| BAgEc | Bachelor of Agricultural Economics |
| BAgSc | Bachelor of Agricultural Sciences |
| PT Bahana | Indonesian venture capital company |
| BAI | Board of Audit and Inspection |
| BAI | Bureau of Animal Industry (Philippines) |
| BAIC | Bangladesh Agricultural Inputs Corporation |
| BAIC | Beijing Agricultural Industrial and Commercial Company |
| BAIC | Beijing Automotive Industry Corporation |
| BAIDCO | Bangladesh Agricultural Industrial Development Corporation |
| BAIEC | Beijing Automotive Import and Export Corporation |
| BAKSAL | Bangladesh Krishak Sramik Awami League |
| BAL | Basic Agrarian Law (Indonesia) |

| | |
|---|---|
| BAMC | Beijing United Automobile Motor Cycle Manufacturing Corporation |
| BAMTI | Beijing Aeronautical Manufacturing Technology Research Institute |
| BANI | Badan Arbitrase Nasional Indonesia (Indonesian National Arbitration Board) |
| Bao Viet | Vietnamese state-owned insurance company |
| BAP | Bankers Association of the Philippines |
| BAPA | Bangladesh Airline Pilots Association |
| BAPEDAL | Indonesian Environmental Impact Assessment Agency |
| BAPEKSTA | Import Duty Exemption and Drawback Scheme (Indonesia) |
| BAPEPAM | Badan Pengawas Pasar Modal (Indonesia) (Capital Market Supervisory Board) |
| BAPEPAM | Badan Pelaksana Pasar Modal (Indonesia) (Capital Market Executive Board) |
| BAPETI | Indonesian Commodity Exchange Executive Agency |
| Bapindo | Bank Pembangunan Indonesia (Indonesian Development Bank) |
| BAPPENAS | Badan Perencanaan Pembangunan Nasional (Indonesia) (National Development Planning Board) |
| BAPPEDA | Badan Perencanaan Pemenrintah Daerah (Indonesia) (Regional Planning Board) |
| BAppSc | Bachelor of Applied Science |
| BARC | Bhabha Atomic Research Centre (India) |
| BARC | Brunei Agricultural Research Centre |
| BArch | Bachelor of Architecture |
| BARD | Bangladesh Academy for Rural Development |
| BAS | Bureau of Agricultural Statistics (Philippines) |
| BASIC | Bank of Small Industries and Commerce (Bangladesh) |
| BASIC | Beginner's All-purpose Symbolic Instruction |
| BAST | Beijing Association for Science and Technology |
| BAT | British American Tobacco Company |
| BATAN | Badan Tenaga Atom Nasional (Indonesia) (National Atomic Commission) |
| BATI | Beijing Automation Technical Institute |
| BAU | Bangladesh Agricultural University |
| BAVIC | Beijing Audio and Video Industries Corporation |
| BAW | Beijing Automobile Works |
| BAWRA | British Australian Wool Realization Association |
| BB | Bangladesh Bank |
| BBA | Bachelor of Business Administration |
| BB&CI | Bombay, Baroda and Central India Railway |
| BBC | Banahaw Broadcasting Corporation (Philippines) |
| BBC | Bangkok Bank of Commerce |
| BBC | Brand-to-brand complementation |
| BBC | British Broadcasting Corporation |
| BBD | Bank Bumi Daya (Indonesia) |

| BBI | Beijing Broadcasting Institute |
| BBL | Bangkok Bank Limited |
| BBM | Bachelor of Business Management |
| BBMB | Bank Bumiputra Malaysia Berhad |
| BBN | Bea Balik Nama Kendaraan Bermotor (Indonesia) (Vehicle ownership tax) |
| BBS | Bangladesh Bureau of Statistics |
| BBS | Bhutan Broadcasting Service |
| BBSW | Bank Bill Swap reference rate (Australia) |
| BBus | Bachelor of Business |
| B/C date | Book close date |
| BCA | Bank Central Asia (Indonesia) |
| BCA | Benefit cost analysis |
| BCA | Building and Construction Authority (Singapore) |
| BCBS | Basle Committee on Banking Supervision |
| BCC | Beijing Conciliation Centre |
| BCC | Business Cooperation Contract (Vietnam) |
| BCCHK | Bank of Credit and Commerce Hong Kong Limited |
| BCCI | Bank of Credit and Commerce International |
| BCCI | Bhutan Chamber of Commerce and Industry |
| BCCS | Board of Commissioners of Currency of Singapore |
| BCDA | Bases Conversion Development Authority (Philippines) |
| BCEL | Banque pour le Commerce Exterrior Lao (Foreign Commercial Bank of Lao PDR) |
| BCGC | Bankers Association of the Philippines Credit and Guarantee Corporation |
| BCI | Bangladesh Chamber of Industries |
| BCIA | Beijing Capital International Airport |
| BCIC | Bangladesh Chemical Industries Corporation |
| BCIC | Bumiputra Commercial and Industrial Community (Malaysia) |
| BCIGC | Beijing Chemical Industries Group Import and Export Corporation |
| BCIQ | Bureau of Commodity Inspection and Quarantine (Taiwan) |
| BCIS | Bandaranaike Centre for International Studies (Sri Lanka) |
| BCL | Bougainville Copper Limited (Papua New Guinea) |
| BCNZ | Broadcasting Corporation of New Zealand |
| BCOFIEC | Beijing Cereals Oils and Foodstuffs Import and Export Corporation |
| BCom | Bachelor of Commerce |
| BCP | Business Collaboration Program |
| BCPIT | British Council for the Promotion of International Trade |
| BCSIR | Bangladesh Council of Science and Industrial Research |
| BCTCM | Beijing College of Traditional Chinese Medicine |
| BCTS | Beijing China Travel Service |
| BCV | Brussels Convention of Valuation |

| | |
|---|---|
| bd | Bank draft |
| BD | Brunei Darussalam |
| BDAS | Buildable Design Appraisal System |
| BDB | Bank Dagang Bali (Indonesia) |
| BDC | Beneficiary developing country |
| BDC | Bond Dealing Centre (Thailand) |
| BDFC | Bhutan Development Finance Corporation |
| BDG | Bangladesh Government |
| BDPT | Bureau of Domestic Trade Promotion |
| BDN | Bank Dagang Negara (Indonesia) |
| BDNI | Bank Dagang Nasional Indonesia |
| BDR | Bearer depository receipt |
| BDS | Bachelor of Dental Surgery |
| BDS | Business Development Scheme |
| BDT | Bureau of Domestic Trade (Philippines) |
| BDV | Brussels Definition of Value |
| BE | Bank of England |
| BE | Bonus ekspor (Indonesia) (export bonus) |
| BE | Break-even analysis |
| BE | Budget estimate |
| B/E | Bill of exchange |
| BEA | Bangladesh Economic Association |
| Bea Cukai | Customs Department (Indonesia) |
| BEAM | Business Excellence Action Mapping |
| BEBIC | Beijing Ever Bright Industrial Company |
| BEC | Beijing Exhibition Centre |
| BEcon | Bachelor of Economics |
| BECR | Bureau of External Cultural Relations (China) |
| BEd | Bachelor of Education |
| BEI | Beijing Economics Institute |
| BEII | Bank Ekspor Impor Indonesia |
| BEJ | Bursa Efek Jakarta (Jakarta Stock Exchange) |
| BEL | Bankers Equity Limited (Pakistan) |
| BEMP | Bonded Export Marketing Board of the Philippines |
| BENELUX | Belgium, Netherlands and Luxembourg |
| BEng | Bachelor of Engineering |
| BEPZ | Biyagama Export Processing Zone (Sri Lanka) |
| BEPZA | Bangladesh Export Processing Zones Authority |
| BERD | Business Expenditure on Research and Development |
| BERNAMA | Berita Nasional Malaysia |
| BERTS | Bangkok Elevated Road and Train System |
| BES | Bursa Efek Surabaya (Surabaya Stock Exchange) |
| BESC | Bangladesh Engineering and Shipping Corporation |
| BESF | Budget of Expenditure and Sources of Financing |
| BESS | Book Entry Settlement System |

| BETP | Bureau of Export Trade Promotion |
| BETRO | British External Trade Research Organization |
| BFCCI | Bangladesh Federation of Chamber of Commerce and Industry |
| BFCE | Banque Francaise du Commerce Exterieur |
| BFCPC | Bangladesh Fertiliser Chemical and Pharmaceutical Corporation |
| BFF | Bilateral Financial Facility |
| BEST | Basic Education for Skills Training |
| BFAD | Bureau of Food and Drugs (Philippines) |
| BFI | Board of Foreign Investment (Mongolia) |
| BFL | Brunei Fisheries Limit Act |
| BFP | Business Fusion Program |
| BFS | Board for Financial Supervision (India) |
| BFTV | Bank for Foreign Trade of Vietnam |
| BFTC | Beijing Foreign Trade Corporation |
| BG | Balanced growth |
| BG | Brigadier General |
| BGA | Ball grid array |
| BGMEA | Bangladesh Garments Manufacturers and Exporters Association |
| BHBFC | Bangladesh House Building Finance Corporation |
| BHC | Bank holding company |
| BHCA | Bank Holding Company Act (US) |
| BHF | Bharat Heavy Electric Co Ltd (India) |
| BHEARI | Beijing Household Electrical Appliance Research Institute |
| BHP | Broken Hill Proprietary Limited (Australia) |
| BHQ | Business headquarters |
| BHS | Bank Harapan Sentosa (Indonesia) |
| BHT | Baht (currency of Thailand) |
| BHU | Basic health unit |
| BI | Bank Indonesia |
| BI | Buy in |
| BI | Code for Royal Brunei Airlines |
| BIA | Bandaranaike International Airport (Sri Lanka) |
| BIBF | Bangkok International Banking Facility |
| BIC | Beijing International Club |
| BICL | Administrative Measures on Borrowing of International Commercial Loans (China) |
| BIDA | Batam Industrial Development Authority (Indonesia) |
| BIDC | Bangladesh Industrial Development Corporation |
| BIDC | Business and Investment Development Committee (Fiji) |
| BIDP | Bintan Integrated Development Project (Indonesia) |
| BIDS | Bangladesh Institute of Development Studies |
| BIDS | Bond Information Dissemination System (Malaysia) |
| BIDV | Bank for Investment and Development of Vietnam |
| BIE | Bintan Industrial Estate |

| | |
|---|---|
| BIF | Beijing International Fair |
| BIFB | Beijing International Finance Building |
| BIFR | Board for Industrial and Financial Reconstruction (India) |
| BII | Bank Internasional Indonesia |
| BII | Bio Informatics Institute (Singapore) |
| BIIA | Bangladesh Institute of Industrial Engineers |
| BIICT | Beijing Institute of Information and Control |
| BILA | Bureau of International Labour Affairs |
| BIM | Board of Industrial Management (Pakistan) |
| BIM | British Institute of Management |
| Biman | Bangladesh Airlines |
| BIMAS | Bimbingan Massal (Indonesia) (Mass guidance programme) |
| BIMB | Bank Islam Malaysia Berhad |
| BIMBO | Buy-in management buy-out |
| BIMP | Brunei, Indonesia, Malaysia and Philippines |
| BIMP-EAGA | Brunei, Indonesia, Malaysia and Philippines East ASEAN Growth Area |
| BINA | Brunei Industrial Development Authority |
| BIP | Batamindo Industrial Park |
| BIR | Bureau of Internal Revenue (Philippines) |
| BIRA | Bank Indonesia Raya |
| BIRD | Banque Internationale pour la Reconstruction et de Development (IBRD: International Bank for Reconstruction and Development) |
| BIS | Bank for International Settlements |
| BIS | Bureau of Import Services (Philippines) |
| BIS | Bureau of Indian Standards |
| BISD | Basic Instruments and Selected Documents |
| BIST-EC | Bangladesh India Sri Lanka Thailand – Economic Cooperation Forum |
| BITAC | Bangladesh Industrial Technical Assistance Centre |
| BITIC | Beijing International Trust and Investment Corporation |
| BITR | Bureau of International Trade Relations |
| BITS | Bank Interchange and Transfer System (Australia) |
| BIV | Banque de Indosuez Vanuatu |
| BIWTA | Bangladesh Inland Water Transport Authority |
| BIWTC | Bangladesh Inland Water Transport Corporation |
| BJACC | Beijing Arts and Crafts Corporation |
| BJEC | Bangladesh Jute Export Corporation |
| BJMC | Bangladesh Jute Mills Corporation |
| BJP | Bharatiya Janata Party (India) |
| BJPC | Beijing Petroleum Corporation |
| BKB | Bangladesh Krishi Bank |
| BKK | Badan Kredit Kecamatan (Indonesia) |
| BKPM | Badan Koordinasi Penanaman Modal (Indonesia) (Investment Coordinating Board) |

| | |
|---|---|
| BKPMD | Badan Koordinasi Penanaman Modal Daerah (Indonesia) (Regional Investment Coordinating Board) |
| BKTRN | Badan Koordinasi Tata Ruang Nasional (Indonesia) (National Spatial Coordination Agency) |
| BL | Bachelor of Law |
| B/L | Bill of lading |
| BLE | Board of Legal Education |
| BLISS | Bagon Lipunan Sites and Services (Philippines) |
| BLNG | Brunei LNG Sendirian Berhad |
| BLR | Base lending rate |
| BLS | Bureau of Labour Statistics (United States) |
| BLS | Bridging Loan Scheme (Singapore) |
| BLT | Build, lease and transfer |
| BMA | Bangkok Metropolitan Administration |
| BMA | Bangkok Metropolitan Area |
| BMA | Bureau of Monetary Affairs (Taiwan) |
| BMB | Bangkok Metropolitan Bank |
| BMC | Biro Maklumat Cek (Malaysia) |
| BMDC | Bangladesh Management Development Centre |
| BME | Benefit monitoring and evaluation |
| BMEDC | Bangladesh Mineral Exploration and Development Corporation |
| BMEIEC | Beijing Machinery and Equipment Import and Export Corporation |
| BMET | Bureau of Manpower Employment and Training (Bangladesh) |
| BMF | Bumiputera Malaysia Finance Berhad |
| BMGI | Bureau of Marine Geological Investigation (China) |
| BMI | Bank Mua'malat Indonesia |
| BMI | Business Monitor International |
| BMIB | Beijing Machinery Industry Bureau |
| BMIEC | Beijing Machinery Import and Export Corporation |
| BMP | Brunei Malaysia and Philippines |
| BMR | Balancing, modernization and replacement |
| BMR | Bangkok Metropolitan Region |
| BMRC | Biomedical Research Council (Singapore) |
| BMRDC | Bangkok Metropolitan Region Development Committee |
| BMRE | Balancing modernization, replacement and expansion |
| BMSC | Beijing Marine Shipping Company |
| BMTA | Bangkok Metropolitan Transport Authority |
| BMTA | Bangkok Mass Transit Authority |
| BMTRC | Beijing Mass Transit Rail Company |
| BMTRI | Beijing Machine Tool Research Institute |
| BMU | Beijing Medical University |
| BMW | Bersih, Manusiawi, Wibawa (Indonesia) (Clean, humanly, dignity) |
| BMW | Bonded manufacturing warehouse |

| | |
|---|---|
| BNA | Bureau of National Affairs (United States) |
| BNB | Bhutan National Bank |
| BND | Brunei national dollar |
| BNESAA | Bureau of Near Eastern and South Asian Affairs (US State Department) |
| BNI | Bank Negara Indonesia |
| BNM | Bank Negara Malaysia |
| BNP | Banque National de Paris |
| BNU | Beijing Normal University |
| BO | Build and operate |
| BOA | Bank of America |
| BOA | Bank of Asia (Thailand) |
| BOA | Based on approval |
| BOA | Board of Architects (Singapore) |
| BOAC | British Overseas Airways Corporation |
| BOB | Bank of Bhutan |
| BOB | Bureau of the Budget (United States) |
| BOC | Bureau of Customs (Philippines) |
| BOC | Bank of China |
| BOCOM | Bank of Communications (China) |
| BOE | Bank of England |
| BOFT | Board of Foreign Trade (Taiwan) |
| BOGA | Brunei Oil and Gas Authority |
| BOI | Board of Investment |
| BOJ | Bank of Japan |
| BOK | Bank of Korea |
| BOL | Bank of Lao PDR |
| BOL | Bill of lading |
| BOL | Build, operate and lease |
| BOLT | Bombay Stock Exchange On-Line Trading System |
| BOM | Bank of Mongolia |
| BOMAS | Business Opportunity and Management Advisory Service (Fiji) |
| BONY | Bank of New York |
| BONUS | Borrower's option for notes and underwriting standby |
| BOO | Build, own and operate |
| BOO | Build, operate and own |
| BOOT | Build, own, operate and transfer |
| BOP | Balance of payments |
| BOT | Bank of Thailand |
| BOT | Bank of Tokyo |
| BOT | Board of Trade |
| BOT | Build, operate and transfer |
| BOTABEK | Bogor, Tangerang, Bekasi (Indonesia) |
| BOY | Beginning of year |
| BP | British Petroleum Company |

| BPA | Bilateral Purchase Agreement |
|---|---|
| BPC | Bangladesh Petroleum Corporation |
| BPC | Bangladesh Parjatan (Tourism) Corporation |
| BPC | Budget Priorities Committee (Papua New Guinea) |
| BPCL | Bharat Petrochemicals Limited (India) |
| Bpd | Barrels per day |
| BPD | Bank Pembangunan Daerah (Indonesia) |
| BPDB | Bangladesh Power Development Board |
| BPEN | National Export Development Agency (Indonesia) |
| BPG | Best Practice Guide |
| BPHC | Beijing People's High Court |
| BPI | Bank of the Philippine Islands |
| BPIEC | Beijing Publication Import and Export Corporation |
| BPK | State Audit Board (Indonesia) |
| BPM | Bank Pertanian Malaysia |
| BPMB | Bank Pembangunan Malaysia Berhad |
| BPMG | Bureau of Petroleum and Marine Geology (China) |
| BPN | Land Agrarian Office (Indonesia) |
| BPNG | Bank of Papua New Guinea |
| BPPE | Bureau for Program Policy and Evaluation |
| BPPN | Badan Penyehatan Perhankan Nasional (Indonesia) (Indonesian Bank Restructuring Agency) |
| BPR | Bank Perkreditan Rakyat (Indonesia) (People's Lending Banks, rural banks) |
| BPS | Biro Pusat Statistik (Indonesia) (Central Bureau of Statistics) |
| bps | Bits per second |
| BPS | Bureau of Product Standards |
| BPTR | Best prevailing tariff rate |
| BPTTT | Bureau of Patents, Trademarks and Technology Transfer (Philippines) |
| BPULN | Badan Penyelesaian Utang dan Lelang Negara (Indonesia) (State Debt Recovery Agency) |
| BPWD | Bangladesh Public Works Department |
| BQA | Bilateral Quarantine Agreement (Vanuatu) |
| BQS | Bond Quotation System |
| BR | Bank receipt |
| BR | Beijing Review |
| BRA | Bougainville Revolutionary Army (Papua New Guinea) |
| BRAC | Bangladesh Rural Advancement Committee |
| BRBNMPL | Bharatiya Reserve Bank Note Mudran Private Limited (India) |
| BRDB | Bangladesh Rural Development Board |
| BRI | Bank Rakyat Indonesia |
| BRICI | Beijing Research Institute of Chemical Industries |
| BRC | Burma Railways Corporation |

| | |
|---|---|
| BRL | Bharat Refineries Limited (India) |
| BRM | Bank Rahardja Maksur (Indonesia) |
| BRRI | Beijing Radio Research Institute |
| BRT | Bougainville Royalty Trust (Papua New Guinea) |
| BS | British Standard |
| BS | Bureau of Standards (United States) |
| BSA | Bilateral Swap Arrangement |
| BSA | British Standard Association |
| BSB | Bangladesh Sericulture Board |
| BSB | Bangladesh Shilpa (Industrial) Bank |
| BSBL | Bangladesh Samabaya (Cooperative) Bank Limited |
| BSc | Bachelor of Science |
| BSC | Bangladesh Shipping Corporation |
| BSCIC | Bangladesh Small and Cottage Industries Corporation |
| BSDC | Bangkok Stock Dealing Centre |
| BSE | Beijing Securities Exchange |
| BSE | Bombay Stock Exchange |
| BSE | Bovine spongiform encephlopathy (mad cow disease) |
| BSEC | Bangladesh Steel and Engineering Corporation |
| BSES | Bombay Suburban Electricity Supply Limited (India) |
| BSF | Bangladesh Silk Foundation |
| BSFIC | Bangladesh Sugar and Food Industries Corporation |
| BSGC | Beijing Stone Group Corporation |
| BSI | Bangladesh Standards Institute |
| BSI | Batala Steel Corporation (India) |
| BSI | British Standards Institute |
| BSIC | Bangladesh Small Industries Corporation |
| BSKL | Bursar Saham Kuala Lumpur (Malaysia) |
| BSM | Brunei Shell Marketing Company Sdn Bhd |
| BSMBD | Bureau of Small and Medium Business Development |
| BSN | Bank Simpanan Nasional (Malaysia) |
| BSocSc | Bachelor of Social Science |
| BSP | Bangko Sentral ng Pilipinas (Central Bank of the Philippines) |
| BSP | Bank of South Pacific (Papua New Guinea) |
| BSP | Bonus share plan |
| BSP | Brunei Shell Petroleum Company Sendirian Berhad |
| BSPC | Brunei Shell Petroleum Company |
| BSPP | Burmese Socialist Program Party |
| BSRS | Bangladesh Shilpa Rin Sangstha (Industrial credit organization) |
| BSRTI | Bangladesh Sericulture Research and Training Institute |
| BSS | Bangladesh Sangbad Sangstha |
| BSS | Bittaheen Samabaya Samity Coop Society (Bangladesh) |

| BSS | Business start-up scheme |
| BSSL | Bureau of Standards of Sri Lanka |
| BST | Brunei Shell Tankers Sendirian Berhad |
| BSTI | Bangladesh Standards and Testing Institute |
| BT | Board of Trade |
| BT | Build and transfer |
| BT | Business tax |
| BT | Business Times (Singapore) |
| BTA | Bangladesh Transport Authority |
| BTA | Beijing Telecommunications Administration |
| BTA | Bilateral trade agreement |
| BTA | Board of Technical Assistance (UN) |
| BTC | Bangladesh Tobacco Company |
| BTC | Bankers Training Centre (Nepal) |
| BTC | Bhutan Tourism Corporation |
| BTC | Bioprocessing Technology Centre (Singapore) |
| BTCC | Beijing Tourist Car Company |
| BTCL | Bhutan Tourism Corporation Ltd |
| BTDC | Business and Trade Development Council |
| BTEC | Business and Technology Education Council |
| BTIC | Bangladesh Textile Industries Corporation |
| BTMA | Bangladesh Textile Mills Association |
| BTMC | Bangladesh Textile Mills Corporation |
| BTN | Bank Tabungan Negara (Indonesia) |
| BTN | Brussels Tariff Nomenclature |
| BTO | Beijing Telegraph Office |
| BTO | Build, transfer and own |
| BTR | Bureau of Tourism Research (Australia) |
| BTr | Bureau of Treasury |
| BTRCP | Bureau of Trade Regulation and Consumer Protection (Philippines) |
| BTS | Bangkok Transit System |
| BTS | Beijing Travel Service |
| BT-SRI | Business Times – Singapore Regional Index |
| BTT | Board of Trade of Thailand |
| BTTB | Bangladesh Telegraph and Telephone Board |
| BTTC | Beijing Travel and Tourism Corporation |
| BTUC | Bangladesh Trade Union Centre |
| BTUU | Bank Tabungan Untuk Umum (Indonesia) |
| BTV | Bangladesh Television |
| BUAJ | Bond Underwriters Association of Japan |
| BUCC | Beijing Urban Construction Corporation |
| BUDMP | Bangladesh Urban Disaster Mitigation Program |
| BUET | Bangladesh University of Engineering and Technology |
| BUILD | BOI's Unit of Industrial Linkage Development |

| | |
|---|---|
| BUIP | Bali Urban Infrastructure Project (Indonesia) |
| BUKOPIN | Bank Umum Koperasi Indonesia (Indonesian Cooperative Bank) |
| BULOG | Badan Urusan Logistik (Indonesia) (National Logistics Agency) |
| BUMN | Badan Usaha Milik Negara (Indonesia) (State-owned enterprise) |
| BUN | Bank Umum Nasional (Indonesia) |
| BUPLN | Badan Urusan Piutang dan Lelang Negara (Agency for State Receivables and Auctions) |
| BUPT | Beijing University of Post and Telecommunications |
| BUS | Bank Umum Servitia (Indonesia) |
| BV | Book value |
| BWCIE | Beijing Workers' Centre for International Exchange |
| BWDB | Bangladesh Water Development Board |
| BWDC | Bretton Woods Development Committee |
| BWI | Bretton Woods Institutions |
| BWK | Bank Windu Kencana (Indonesia) |
| BWTC | Beijing World Trade Centre |
| CA | Chartered Accountant |
| CA | Collective agreement |
| CA | Companies Act |
| CAA | Civil Aviation Authority |
| CAAC | Civil Aviation Administration of China |
| CAAIF | China Association for the Advancement of International Friendship |
| CAARC | Commonwealth Advisory Aeronautical Research Council |
| CAAS | China Academy of Agricultural Sciences |
| CAAS | Civil Aviation Authority of Singapore |
| CAB | China Association of Banks |
| CAB | Civil Aeronautics Board (United States) |
| CAB | Civil Aviation Bureau (Japan) |
| CAB | Commonwealth Agriculture Bureau |
| CABI | Chase Asia Bond Index |
| CABR | China Academy of Building Research |
| CABS | China National Animal Breeding Stock Import and Export Corporation |
| CAC | Collective Action Clause |
| CAC | Commissioner for Administrative Complaints (Hong Kong) |
| CACC | Central Agencies Coordinating Committee (Papua New Guinea) |
| CACCI | Confederation of Asia Pacific Chambers of Commerce and Industry |
| CACM | Central American Common Market |
| CACS | Capital adequacy, Asset quality, Compliance and System |
| CAD | Canadian dollar |

| | |
|---|---|
| CAD | Capital Adequacy Directive |
| CAD | Computer aided design |
| CAD | Current account deficit |
| CADC | China Aviation Development Corporation |
| CADI | Centro de Apoio ao Desenvolvimento Industrial (Macau) (Industrial Training and Development Centre) |
| CADTIC | China Agribusiness Development Trust and Investment Corp |
| CAE | College of Advanced Education |
| CAEFI | Chinese Association of Enterprises with Foreign Investment |
| CAFEA-ICC | Commission on Asian and Far Eastern Affairs (of the International Chamber of Commerce) |
| CAFI | Commercial Advisory Foundation in Indonesia |
| CAFIC | China Arab Finance and Investment Company |
| CAFIU | Chinese Association for International Understanding |
| CAFST | China Association of Foreign Service Trade |
| CAG | Comptroller and Auditor General (India) |
| CAGR | Compounded annual growth rate |
| CAHB | Commerce Asset Holding Berhad (Malaysia) |
| CAI | Computer aided instruction |
| CAIE | China Association of Industrial Economics |
| CAIEC | China National Automobile Import and Export Corporation |
| CAIEI | China American International Engineering Inc. |
| CAIEP | China Association for International Exchange of Personnel |
| CAIPDI | China Aviation Industry Planning and Design Institute |
| CAJEA | Council of All Japan Exporters Association |
| CAL | China Air Lines (Taiwan) |
| CALABARZON | Cavite, Laguna, Batangas, Rizal and Quezon |
| CALF | China International Engineering Corporation for Agriculture, Livestock and Fisheries |
| Call | Cum all |
| CAM | Cash acceptance machine |
| CAM | Computer aided manufacturing |
| CAMA | China National Construction and Agriculture Machinery Import and Export Corporation |
| CAMC | China National Agriculture Machinery Import and Export Corporation |
| CAMDC | Chinese American Machinery and Development Corporation |
| CAMEL | Capital adequacy, Asset quality, Management, Earnings, Liquidity |
| CAMELOT | Capital adequacy, Asset quality, Management, Earnings, Liquidity, Operations quality and Treasury management |
| CAMELS | Capital adequacy, Asset quality, Management, Earnings, Liquidity, and Sensitivity to market risk |
| CAMINCO | Cambodian National Insurance Company |
| CAMMS | Chinese Academy of Military Medical Sciences |

| | |
|---|---|
| CAMS | Chinese Academy of Medical Sciences |
| CAO | Contract and operate |
| CAO | Company Announcements Office (Australia) |
| CAOSC | China Aviation Oil Supply Corporation |
| CAP | Common Agricultural Policy |
| CAP | Consolidated appeal process |
| CAP | Consumers Association of Penang (Malaysia) |
| CAPA | Confederation of Asian and Pacific Accountants |
| CAPA | Confederation of ASEAN and Pacific Accountants |
| CAPCO | China American Petrochemical Corporation |
| CAPI | China Association for the Promotion of Investment |
| CAPM | Capital asset pricing model |
| CAPS | Capital augmented preferred shares |
| CAQC | Computer aided quality control |
| CAR | Capital Adequacy Ratio |
| CAR | Civil Aviation Regulations (United States) |
| CAR | Cordillera Administrative Region (Philippines) |
| CARE | Capital and reserve system (Philippines) |
| CARE | Centre for Applied Research in Education (Brunei) |
| CARL | Comprehensive Agrarian Reform Law (Philippines) |
| CARP | Comprehensive Agrarian Reform Program |
| CARSEL | Capital adequacy, Asset quality, Regulatory compliance, Strategies and stability, Earnings and Liquidity |
| CAS | China Academy of Sciences |
| CAS | China Association for Standardization |
| CAS | Civil Affairs Service (Myanmar) |
| CAS | Cost accounting standards |
| CASC | China Aviation Supplies Corporation |
| CASE | Consumers' Association of Singapore |
| CAST | China Association for Science and Technology |
| CAT | Centre for Advanced Technology (India) |
| CAT | Communication Authority of Thailand |
| CARE | Credit Analysis and Research Ltd (India) |
| CATA | Commonwealth Association of Tax Administrators |
| CATC | Commonwealth Air Transport Council |
| CATCM | China Academy of Traditional Chinese Medicine |
| CATI | Civil Aviation Training Institute |
| CATIC | China Agribusiness Trust and Investment Corporation |
| CATS | Computed Assisted Trading System |
| CATV | Community antenna television |
| CB | Central bank |
| CB | Conference Board (United States) |
| CBA | Central Bank Act (Malaysia) |
| CBA | Collective bargaining agent |

| CBA | Collective bargaining agreement |
| CBA | Commonwealth Bank of Australia |
| CBA | Cost benefit analysis |
| CBA | Currency Board Arrangement |
| CBAE | Commonwealth Bureau of Agricultural Economics |
| CB-BOL | Central Bank-Board of Liquidators (Philippines) |
| CBC | Central Bank of China (Taiwan) |
| CBC | Communications Bank of China |
| CBC | Construction Bank of China |
| CBCG | China Business Consultants Group |
| CBCI | Central Bank Certificate of Indebtedness (Philippines) |
| CBC | China Banking Corporation (Philippines) |
| CBD | Central Business District |
| CBDM | Community Based Disaster Management |
| CBDT | Central Board of Direct Taxes (India) |
| CBEC | Central Board of Excise and Customs (India) |
| CBFMP | Community Based Flood Mitigation and Preparedness Project |
| CBI | Central Bureau of Investigation (India) |
| CBI | Cum bonus issue |
| CBL | Cambodia Brewery Ltd |
| CBL | Commercial Bank Law |
| CBM | Central Bank of Myanmar |
| CBMC | China National Building Material and Equipment Import and Export Corporation |
| CBMW | Customs Bonded Manufacturing Warehouse (Philippines) |
| CBO | Collateralized Bond Obligation |
| CBO | Community-based organization |
| CBOA | Central Board of Approval (India) |
| CBOE | Chicago Board Options Exchange |
| CBOT | Chicago Board of Trade |
| CBP | Central Bank of the Philippines |
| CBP | Central Business Park |
| CBRSP | Committee on Banking Regulation and Supervisory Practices (Cooke Committee) |
| CBS | Central Bureau of Statistics (Nepal) |
| CBS | Columbia Broadcasting System (United States) |
| CBSI | Central Bank of Solomon Islands |
| CBSC | China Broadcasting Satellite Corporation |
| CBSL | Central Bank of Sri Lanka |
| CBT | Coin box telephone |
| CBTDC | China Building Technology Development Centre |
| CBU | Completely built up |
| CBV | Conseil des Bourses de Valeurs (France) |
| CC | Coastal city (China) |
| CC | Commercial Code (Japan) |

| | |
|---|---|
| CCA | China Consumers Association |
| CCAS | Committee of Concerned Asian Scholars |
| CCASS | Central Clearing and Settlement System (Hong Kong) |
| CCB | Central cooperative bank (India) |
| CCB | China Construction Bank |
| CCB | Coconut Cultivation Board (Sri Lanka) |
| CCBC | Canadian China Business Council |
| CCBCC | Coordinating Centre for Business Cooperation in China |
| CCC | Cargo Consolidation Centre |
| CCC | Ceylon Chamber of Commerce |
| CCC | Civil and Commercial Code |
| CCC | Commission of Counter Corruption (Thailand) |
| CCCA | Coordinating Committee on the Implementation of the CEPT for AFTA |
| CCCI | Chittagong Chamber of Commerce and Industries |
| CCCN | Customs Cooperation Council Nomenclature |
| CCCP | Cooperative Credit Purchasing Company (Japan) |
| CCDC | China Computer Development Corporation |
| CCDSI | Coordination Council for Development of Small Industry (Malaysia) |
| CCEA | Cabinet Committee on Economic Affairs (India) |
| CCFC | China Chemical Fibre Corporation |
| CCFF | Compensatory and Contingency Financing Facility |
| CCFI | Cabinet Committee on Foreign Investment (India) |
| CCH | Commercial Clearing House |
| CCHDP | China Canada Human Development Program |
| CCI | Chamber of Commerce and Industry |
| CCI | Consumer Confidence Index |
| CCI | Controller of Capital Issues (India) |
| CCIA | Central Carpet Industries Association (Nepal) |
| CCIB | China Commodity Inspection Bureau |
| CCIC | Chemical Construction Installation Company |
| CCIC | China Chamber of International Commerce |
| CCIC | China National Import and Export Commodities Inspection Corp |
| CCIEC | China National Chemicals Import and Export Corporation |
| CCIEC | China National Coal Import and Export Corporation |
| CCIET | China Commercial Corporation of International Economic and Technical Cooperation |
| CCL | Contingency Credit Line |
| CCMB | Centre for Cellular and Molecular Biology (India) |
| CCMRG | Commonwealth Committee on Mineral Resources and Geology |
| CCMRI | Central Coal Mining Research Institute (China) |
| CCO | Chief Compliance Officer |
| CCOEC | China National Corporation for Overseas Economic Cooperation |
| CCOIC | China Chamber of International Commerce |

| | |
|---|---|
| CCOP | Committee for Coordination of Joint Prospecting of Mineral Resources in the South Pacific Area |
| CCP | Chart Pattana Party (Thailand) |
| CCP | Communist Party of China |
| CCP | Comprehensive Contracts Policy |
| CCPAP | Coordinating Council for the Philippine Assistance Program |
| CCPI | Colombo Consumer Price Index (Sri Lanka) |
| CCPI | Composite Consumer Price Index |
| CCPIT | China Council for Promotion of International Trade |
| CCPS | Convertible cumulative preference share |
| CCRC | Committee on Commercial Relations with China (United States) |
| CCS | Central Cooperative Society (Myanmar) |
| CCS | Comprehensive consolidated supervision |
| CCS | Credit cooperative society |
| CCSD | Conference of Central Securities Depositories |
| CCSI | China Corporation of Shipbuilding Industry |
| CCTC | Canada-China Trade Council |
| CCTV | China Central Television |
| CCTV | Closed circuit television |
| CCUDC | China Coal Utilization and Development Corporation |
| CCV | Chamber of Commerce of Vanuatu |
| cd | Cum dividend |
| CD | Certificate of deposit |
| CD | China Daily |
| CD | Convertible debenture |
| CDA | Chittagong Development Authority (Bangladesh) |
| CDA | Coconut Development Authority (Sri Lanka) |
| CDA | Cooperative Development Authority (Philippines) |
| CDB | China Development Bank |
| CDB | Construction Development Board (Bhutan) |
| CDC | Clark Development Corporation (Philippines) |
| CDC | Commonwealth Development Corporation |
| CDC | Council for the Development of Cambodia |
| CDCP | Construction and Development Corporation of the Philippines |
| CDCXSEZ | Construction and Development Corporation of Xiamen Special Economic Zone |
| CDF | Cluster Development Fund |
| CDF | Comprehensive Development Framework |
| CDFC | Commonwealth Development Finance Company |
| CDI | Centre for Development Information (Sri Lanka) |
| CDI | CHESS Depository Interests |
| CDIC | Central Deposit Insurance Corporation |
| CDIS | Curriculum Development Institute of Singapore |
| CDO | Community development officer |

| | |
|---|---|
| CDP | Committee for Development Planning (UN) |
| CDP | Central Depository Private Limited |
| CDPPP | Centre for Development Planning, Projections and Policies (UN) |
| CDR | Court Dispute Resolution |
| CDRAC | Corporate Debt Restructuring Advisory Committee (Thailand) |
| CDRC | Consolidated Daily Report of Condition (Philippines) |
| CDRC | Corporate Debt Restructuring Committee (Malaysia) |
| CDRI | Cambodia Development Research Institute |
| CDS | Central Depository System |
| CDWP | Central Development Working Party (Pakistan) |
| CE | Cum entitlement |
| CEA | Central Electricity Authority |
| CEA | Central Environment Authority (Sri Lanka) |
| CEA | Central Executing Agency |
| CEA | China Eastern Airlines |
| CEA | Chinese Economic Area |
| CEB | Ceylon Electricity Board (Sri Lanka) |
| CEC | Chinese Economic Circle |
| CEC | Commodity Exchange Commission (United States) |
| CEC | Commonwealth Economic Committee |
| CEC | Cotton Export Corporation (Pakistan) |
| CECC | Commonwealth Economic Consultative Council |
| CECA | Comprehensive Economic Cooperation Agreement (Singapore) |
| CECO | Control of Exemption Clauses Ordinance (Hong Kong) |
| CEDA | Centre for Economic Development Administration (Nepal) |
| CEDEL | Centrale de Livraison de Valeurs Mobilieres |
| CEDLI | Committee on Efficient Distribution of Life Insurance |
| CEED | Cooperation Education for Enterprise Development |
| CEGAT | Customs, Excise and Gold Appelate Tribunal |
| CEHRD | Committee on Education and Human Resource Development (ASEAN) |
| CEIEC | China Electronics Import and Export Corporation |
| CEITIC | China Everbright International Trust and Investment Corp |
| CEM | Country Economic Memorandum |
| CEMA | China Enterprise Management Association |
| CEMA | Council for Economic Mutual Assistance |
| CEMTEX | Central Magnetic Tape Exchange |
| CENA | China Economic News Agency |
| CENPAC | Central Pacific Area |
| CENWOR | Centre for Women Research (Sri Lanka) |
| CEPD | Council for Economic Planning and Development (Taiwan) |
| CEPIN | Comissao Especial para a Politica Industria (Macau) (Special Advisory Committee on Industrial Policy) |
| CEPT | Common Effective Preferential Tariff Scheme |

| | |
|---|---|
| CEPZ | Chittagong Export Processing Zone |
| CEJNSA | Council of European and Japanese National Shipowners' Association |
| CEM | Country Economic Memorandum |
| CEO | Chief Executive Officer |
| CEPA | Cambodian Export Promotion Agency |
| CEPA | Consolidated Electric Power Asia |
| CEPT | Common Effective Preferential Tariff |
| CEPU | City Economic Planning Unit (Malaysia) |
| CEPZ | Cavite Export Processing Zone (Philippines) |
| CER | Australia-New Zealand Closer Economic Relations Trade Agreement |
| CERA | Cambridge Energy Research Associates |
| CERC | Central Electricity Regulatory Commission (India) |
| CERIS | Central Engineering Research Institute of Iron and Steel Industry (China) |
| CEROILFOOD | China National Cereals, Oils and Foodstuffs Import and Export Corporation |
| CERTAS | Certification Assistance Scheme (Singapore) |
| CES | Central Energy System (Mongolia) |
| CESC | Calcutta Electric Supply Corporation |
| CESI | Chinese Electronics Standardization Institute |
| CESTI | Centre for Science and Technology Information |
| CET | Centre for Entrepreneurship (Singapore) |
| CETRA | China External Trade Development Centre (Taiwan) |
| CETS | China Everbright Travel Service |
| CFA | Cash flow accounting |
| CFA | Chartered Financial Analyst |
| CFA | Commonwealth Forestry Association |
| CFA | Corporate Finance Association |
| CFA | Court of Final Appeal (Hong Kong) |
| CFC | Ceylon Fisheries Corporation (Sri Lanka) |
| CFC | Chemin de Fer du Cambodia (Cambodian Railway) |
| CFC | Chlorofluorocarbon |
| CFCC | China Film Co-production Corporation |
| CFECA | China Foreign Exchange Control Administration |
| CFETS | China Foreign Exchange Trading System |
| CFH | China Fund for the Handicapped |
| CFHC | Ceylon Fisheries Harbours Corporation (Sri Lanka) |
| CFIEP | Countryside Financial Institutions Enhancement Program (Philippines) |
| CFITDC | China Food Industry and Techniques Development Corp |
| CFM | Committee on Financial Markets (OECD) |
| CFO | Chief Financial Officer |

| | |
|---|---|
| CFP | Certified Financial Planner |
| CFR | Council on Foreign Relations |
| CFRI | Central Fuel Research Institute (India) |
| CFS | Committee on Financial System |
| CFS | Consumer Finance Survey (Sri Lanka) |
| CFSA | Consolidated Financial Supervision Agency (Korea) |
| CFSTD | China Foundation of Science and Technology for Development |
| CFT | Commodity Futures Test |
| CFTC | Commonwealth Fund for Technical Cooperation |
| CFZ | Commercial free zone |
| CFTC | Commodity Futures Trading Commission (United States) |
| CG | Consultative Group Meeting for Cambodia |
| CGA | Customs General Administration (China) |
| CGC | Corporate Governance Committee |
| CGC | Credit Guarantee Corporation |
| CGCC | Chinese General Chamber of Commerce (Hong Kong) |
| CGCI | China Gold Coin Corporation |
| CGE | Committee on Governance of the Exchanges |
| CGEC | China General Electric Corporation |
| CGFS | Committee on Global Financial System |
| CGM | Consultative Group Meeting |
| CGR | Ceylon Government Railways |
| CGS | Commonwealth Government Securities (Australia) |
| CGSO | Consumer Goods Safety Ordinance (Hong Kong) |
| CGT | Capital gains tax |
| CHAPS | Clearing House Automated Payment System |
| CHATS | Clearing House Automated Transfer System |
| CHC | Cargo handling company |
| CHED | Commission on Higher Education (Philippines) |
| CHESS | Clearing House Electronic Sub-register System |
| CHINAPACK | China National Import and Export Packaging Corporation |
| CHINASILK | China National Silk Import and Export Corporation |
| CHINATEX | China National Textile Import and Export Corporation |
| CHIPS | Clearing House Inter-bank Payment System |
| CHMC | China National Heavy Machinery Corporation |
| CHOGM | Commonwealth Heads of Government Meeting |
| CI | Certificate of indebtedness |
| CI | Commercial and Industrial Index |
| CI | Composite Index |
| CI | Cum interest |
| CIA | Cambodia International Airlines |
| CIA | Central Intelligence Agency (United States) |
| CIAC | Construction Industry Arbitration Commission |
| CIAP | Construction Industry Authority of the Philippines |
| CIAST | Centre for Instructor and Advanced Skills Training (Malaysia) |

| CIB | China Investment Bank |
| CIBI | Credit Information Bureau Inc (Philippines) |
| CICC | Coalition for an International Criminal Court |
| CIB | Cambodia Investment Board |
| CIB | China Investment Bank |
| CIBI | Credit Information Bureau Inc (Philippines) |
| CIC | China Insurance Company |
| CIC | Cotton Industries Corporation (Bangladesh) |
| CICEC | China International Culture Exchange Centre |
| CICETE | China International Centre for Economic and Technical Exchange |
| CICP | Cambodian Institute for Cooperation and Peace |
| CICPA | Chinese Institute of Certified Public Accountants |
| CICT | Committee of International Cooperative Trade |
| CID | Centre for Industrial Development (UN) |
| CIDA | Canadian International Development Agency |
| CIDB | Construction Industry Development Board (Singapore) |
| CIDP | Construction Industry Development Plan |
| CIEC | China International Exhibition Centre |
| CIEM | Central Institute for Economic Management (Vietnam) |
| CIETAC | China International Economic and Trade Arbitration Commission |
| CIETEC | China International Economic and Technical Exchange Centre |
| CIF | Cost, insurance and freight |
| CIFB | Central Institute of Finance and Banking (China) |
| CIFCI | Cost, insurance, freight, commission and interest |
| CII | Chartered Insurance Institute |
| CII | Confederation of Indian Industries |
| CII | Council of Islamic Ideology (Pakistan) |
| CIIA | Certified International Investment Analyst |
| CIIS | Customs Intelligence Investigation Service (Philippines) |
| CIM | Computer Integrated Manufacturing |
| CIMA | Chartered Institute of Management Accountants |
| CIMB | Commerce International Merchant Bankers Berhad (Malaysia) |
| CIME | Committee on International Investment and Multinational Enterprise (OECD) |
| CINTEC | Computer and Information Technology Council of Sri Lanka |
| CIO | Chief Information Officer |
| CIO | Chief Investment Officer |
| CIOB | Chartered Institute of Bankers |
| CIOS | Conseil Internationale de l'Organization Scientifique (World Council of Management) |
| CIP | Central issue price |
| CIP | Concordia Industrial Park (Macau) |
| CIPC | Central Investment Promotion Committee (Pakistan) |
| CIQ | Customs, immigration and quarantine |

| CIRAD | Cooperation Internationale en Recherche Agronomique pour le Development (International Cooperation Centre on Agrarian Research and Development) |
|---|---|
| CIRC | China Insurance Regulatory Commission |
| CIRDAP | Centre on Integrated Rural Development for Asia and the Pacific |
| CIRIEC | Centre Internationale de Recherches et l'Information sur l'Economie Collective |
| CIS | Chartered Industries of Singapore |
| CIS | Collective Investment Scheme (India) |
| CIS | Commonwealth of Independent States |
| CISA | Certified Investment and Securities Analyst (Thailand) |
| CISCO | Commercial and Industrial Security Corporation |
| CISG | Contracts for the International Sale of Goods (UN Convention) |
| CISIR | Ceylon Institute of Scientific and Industrial Research |
| CIT | Charter inclusive tour |
| CIT | Comptroller of Income Tax |
| CITB | Construction Industry Training Board |
| CITC | Construction Industry Training Centre |
| CITC | Cottage Industry Technology Centre (Philippines) |
| CITES | Convention on International Trade in Endangered Species of Wild Fauna and Flora |
| CITC | Cottage Industry Technology Centre |
| CITEM | Centre for International Trade Expositions and Missions |
| CITI | Clothing Industry Training Institute (Sri Lanka) |
| CITI | Construction Industry Training Institute |
| CITIC | China International Trust and Investment Corporation |
| CITREP | Critical IT Skills Resource Program |
| CITS | China International Travel Service |
| CITT | Measures on the Prohibition of Conducts of Collusion in the Invitation of Tenders and Tendering |
| CKD | Completely knocked-down |
| CLA | Corporate Law Authority (Pakistan) |
| CLA | Council of Labour Affairs (Taiwan) |
| CL&P | China Light and Power Company (Hong Kong) |
| CLARA | Centre for Labour Relations Assistance |
| CLB | Company Law Board (India) |
| CLF | Countryside Loan Fund (Philippines) |
| CLIC | China Life Insurance Company |
| CLM | Cambodia, Laos, Myanmar |
| CLM | Community Loan Mechanism |
| CLOB | Central Limit Order Book |
| CLRFC | Company Legislation and Regulatory Framework Committee |
| CLU | Chartered Life Underwriter |

| | |
|---|---|
| CLUST | Central Luzon and Southern Tagalog (Philippines) |
| CLV | Cambodia, Laos and Vietnam |
| CMA | Cash Management Account |
| CMA | Chinese Medical Association |
| CMAC | Cambodian Mine Action Centre |
| CMAC | China Maritime Arbitration Commission |
| CMAG | Commonwealth Ministerial Action Group |
| CMC | Cooperative Multimedia Centre (Australia) |
| CMD | Cubic metres per day |
| CMDA | Capital Markets Development Authority (Fiji) |
| CMDP | Capital Market Development Program (Pakistan) |
| CME | Chicago Mercantile Exchange |
| CME | Contractual Management Enterprise (China) |
| CMEA | Council for Mutual Economic Assistance |
| CMF | Centre for Micro Finance (Nepal) |
| CMI | Capital market intermediary |
| CMI | Census of Manufacturing Industries (Pakistan) |
| CMI | Chiang Mai Initiative |
| CMIE | Centre for Monitoring the Indian Economy |
| CMNP | PT Citra Marga Nusaphala Persada (Indonesia toll road operator company) |
| CMO | Collateralized Mortgage Obligation |
| CMP | Capital Markets Masterplan (Malaysia) |
| CMP | Common Minimum Program |
| CMPC | Capital Market Policy Council (Indonesia) |
| CMPP | PT Centris Multi Persada Pratama (Indonesian taxi company) |
| CMS | Capital Market Society of Indonesia |
| CMSC | Capital Market Strategic Committee (Malaysia) |
| CMT | Conseil des Marches Financiers (France) |
| CMU | Central Moneymarkets Unit (Hong Kong) |
| CMU | Ceylon Mercantile Union (Sri Lanka) |
| CNA | China Northern Airlines |
| CNAC | China National Aviation Company |
| CNAIC | China National Aviation Industry Corporation |
| CNAPS | China National Automatic Payment System |
| CNB | Central Narcotics Bureau (Singapore) |
| CNC | Ceylon National Congress |
| CNC | Computer numerical control |
| CNCIEC | China National Coal Import and Export Corporation |
| CNIECIC | China National Import and Export Commodities Inspection Corporation |
| CNMC | Cambodian National Mekong Committee |
| CNMV | Comision Nacional del Mercado de Valores (Spain) |
| CNN | Cable News Network |

| | |
|---|---|
| CNO | Crude coconut oil |
| CNRET | Centre for Natural Resources, Energy and Transport (UN) |
| CNS | China News Service |
| CNS | Chinese National Standards (Taiwan) |
| CNS | Continuous net settlement |
| CNSA | China National Space Agency |
| CNSIC | China National Space Industry Corporation |
| CO | Certificate of origin |
| COA | Certificate of Airworthiness |
| COA | Contract of Affreightment |
| COA | Council of Agriculture (Taiwan) |
| COB | Chip on board |
| COB | Commission des Operations de Bourse (France) |
| COC | Certificate of Competency |
| COC | Chamber of Commerce |
| COC | Coastal open city (China) |
| COCI | Committee on Culture and Information (ASEAN) |
| COD | Cash on delivery |
| COE | Certificate of Entitlement (Singapore) |
| COE | Collectively-owned enterprise (China) |
| COF | Chip on flex |
| COF | Committee on Finance (ASEAN) |
| COFAB | Committee on Finance and Banking (ASEAN) |
| COFACE | Compagnie Francaise pour l'Assurance de Commerce Exterieur |
| COFAF | Committee on Food Agriculture and Forestry (ASEAN) |
| COFED | Cooperatives Federation Limited |
| COFI | Committee on Fisheries (UN) |
| COFM | Council of Foreign Ministers (SAARC) |
| COI | Committee of Investment |
| COIME | Committee on Industry, Minerals and Energy (ASEAN) |
| COIT | Committee on International Trade |
| COJTC | Certified On-the-Job Training Centre |
| COL | Cost of living |
| COLA | Cost of living adjustment |
| COLA | Cost of living allowance |
| COLI | Cost of Living Index |
| COM | Commodity Options Market |
| COME | Committee on Minerals and Energy (ASEAN) |
| COMECON | Council for Mutual Economic Assistance |
| Comelec | Commission on Elections (Philippines) |
| COMEX | Commodity and Mercantile Exchange (New York) |
| COMMEX | Commodity Exchange of Malaysia |
| COMPASS | Composers and Authors Society of Singapore |
| COMPOL | National Computer Policy Committee (Sri Lanka) |
| COMSAT | Communication satellite |

| | |
|---|---|
| COMTTAC | Committee on Transport, Tourism and Communications (ASEAN) |
| CONCOR | Container Corporation of India Limited |
| CONFILO | Confederation of Filipino Organizations |
| CONSOB | Italian Securities Commission |
| COO | Chief Operating Officer |
| COP | Committee on Privatization (Philippines) |
| COP | Committee on Productivity (Singapore) |
| COPE | Committee on Public Enterprises (Sri Lanka) |
| COPE | Community Organizers of the Philippine Enterprise |
| CORES | Computed Assisted Order Routing and Execution System |
| COSCO | China Ocean Shipping Company |
| COSD | Committee on Social and Development (ASEAN) |
| COST | Committee on Science and Technology (ASEAN) |
| COTAC | Committee on Transport and Communications (ASEAN) |
| COTII | Committee on Trade, Industry and Investment (ASEAN) |
| COTT | Committee on Trade and Tourism (ASEAN) |
| COV | Committee for Overseas Vietnamese |
| COW | Contract of Work |
| CP | Charoen Pokphand (Thailand) |
| CP | Commercial paper |
| CP | Contract party |
| CP | Corporate paper |
| CPA | Cambodian Petroleum Authority |
| CPA | Cathay Pacific Airways |
| CPA | Certified Public Accountant |
| CPA | Chittagong Port Authority |
| CPA | Claims paying ability |
| CPA | Consumer Protection Act (Korea) |
| CPC | Ceylon Petroleum Corporation |
| CPC | Committee for Planning and Cooperation |
| CPC | Council for Public Corporation (Bangladesh) |
| CPC | Criminal Procedure Code (India) |
| CPCB | Central Pollution Control Board (India) |
| CPCN | Certificate of Public Convenience and Necessity (Philippines) |
| CPCPIT | Chinese People's Committee for the Promotion of International Trade |
| CPCWP | Chinese People's Committee for World Peace |
| CPD | Centre for Peace and Development (Cambodia) |
| CPE | Central public enterprise |
| CPE | Centrally planned economy |
| CPE | Code of professional ethics |
| CPSE | Central public sector enterprise |
| CPF | Central Provident Fund (Singapore) |
| CPFIS | CPF Investment Scheme |

| | |
|---|---|
| CPF PAGE | CPF Phone Answers on General Enquiries |
| CPF PAL | CPF Personal Auto Link |
| CPI | Characters per inch |
| CPI | Consumer Price Index |
| CPI-AL | Consumer Price Index for Agricultural Labourers |
| CPIB | Corrupt Practices Investigation Bureau (Singapore) |
| CPIFA | Chinese People's Institute of Foreign Affairs |
| CPI-IW | Consumer Price Index for Industrial Workers |
| CPIT | Committee for the Promotion of International Trade |
| CPI-UNME | Consumer Price Index for Urban, Non-Manual Employees |
| CPK | Communist Party of Kampuchea |
| CPKO | Crude palm kernel oil |
| CPL | Certified Professional Logistician program |
| CPM | Cost plus method |
| CPO | Central Planning Office (Papua New Guinea) |
| CPO | Conveyancing and Property Ordinance (Hong Kong) |
| CPO | Crude palm oil |
| CPOA | Cheques and Payments Order Act (Australia) |
| CPP | Chamber of Pawnbrokers of the Philippines |
| CPPCC | China People's Political Consultative Conference |
| CPRU | Construction Planning and Research Unit (Brunei) |
| CPS | Characters per second |
| CPS | Consumer price survey |
| CPTC | Chemical Process Technology Centre |
| CPTE | Council for Professional and Technical Education |
| CPU | Central processing unit |
| CPUOS | Committee on Peaceful Use of Outer Space (UN) |
| CPV | Communist Party of Vietnam |
| CQAHE | Committee for Quality Assurance in Higher Education (Australia) |
| CQS | Consolidated quotation system |
| CR | Riel (Cambodian currency) |
| Cr | Crore (India) 10 million |
| CRA | Community Reinvestment Act (United States) |
| CRA | Company Registration Authority (China) |
| CRA | Convertible Rupee Account (Sri Lanka) |
| CRA | Conzinc Riotinto of Australia Ltd |
| CRA | Country risk assessment |
| CRAFICARD | Committee to Review Arrangements for Institutional Credit for Agriculture and Rural Development (India) |
| CRAMEL | Capital adequacy, Resources, Asset quality, Management evaluation, Earnings and Liquidity |
| CRAR | Capital to risk-weighted asset ratio |
| CRB | Cooperative Rural Bank (Sri Lanka) |
| CRC | Car Repair Corporation (Mongolia) |
| CRC | Central Reinsurance Corporation (Taiwan) |

| CRC | Cooperative Research Centre (Australia) |
| CRC | Cost Review Committee (Singapore) |
| CRCE | Chicago Rice and Cotton Exchange |
| CRDB | Cambodian Rehabilitation and Development Board |
| CRDC | City of Rangoon Development Committee |
| CREST | Centre for Resource and Environmental Studies (Nepal) |
| CRI | Cum rights issue |
| CRISIL | Credit Rating Information Services of India Ltd |
| CRP | Commissioner of the Registration of Persons (Sri Lanka) |
| CRPS | Council of Retired Civil Servants (Nepal) |
| CRR | Cash reserve ratio |
| CRR | Cash reserve requirement |
| CRS | Contract Responsibility System (China) |
| CSA | Canadian Securities Administrators |
| CSA | Chinese Securities Association (Taiwan) |
| CSA | Currency swap agreement |
| CSB | Central Silk Board (India) |
| CSBSOE | Central Steering Board for State-owned Enterprises |
| CSC | Committee on Singapore's Competitiveness |
| CSC | Civil Service College (Singapore) |
| CSCE | China Zhengzhou Commodity Exchange |
| CSCE | Coffee, Sugar and Cocoa Exchange |
| CSD | Central Securities depository |
| CSD | Commission on Sustainable Development (UN) |
| CSD | Committee on Social Development (UN) |
| CSE | Chittagong Stock Exchange |
| CSE | Colombo Stock Exchange (Sri Lanka) |
| CSER | Regulations for Converting the Status of the Enterprises Owned By the Whole People (China) |
| CSEZ | Clark Special Economic Zone (Philippines) |
| CSFB | Credit Suisse First Boston |
| CSIE | Consolidated Statement of Income and Expense (Philippines) |
| CSIR | Council of Scientific and Industrial Research (India) |
| CSIRO | Commonwealth Scientific and Industrial Research Organization (Australia) |
| CSIS | Centre for Strategic and International Studies (Indonesia) |
| CSO | Central Statistical Organization (India) |
| CSO | Central Statistical Organization (Pakistan) |
| CSOC | Consolidated Statement of Condition (Philippines) |
| CSP | Comprehensive Shipping Policy (Hong Kong) |
| CSPI | Composite Share Price Index |
| CSRC | China Securities Regulatory Commission |
| CSS | Central Statistical Service |
| CSS | Centrally sponsored scheme |
| CSSD | China-Singapore Suzhou Development Company |

| CSSI | Cottage and Small Scale Industry (Sri Lanka) |
|------|----------------------------------------------|
| CSV | Cash surrender value (insurance) |
| CT | Chart Thai Party (Thailand) |
| CT | Consumption tax |
| CT&DC | Central Trading and Development Corporation |
| CTB | Ceylon Transport Board (Sri Lanka) |
| CTB | Chamber of Thrift Banks (Philippines) |
| CTC | Central Trust of China (Taiwan) |
| CTC | Centre for Transnational Corporations (UN) |
| CTC | Ceylon Tobacco Company (Sri Lanka) |
| CTC | Commodities Trading Commission |
| CTCB | Chinatrust Commercial Bank (Taiwan) |
| CTE | Committee on Trade and Environment (WTO) |
| CTI | Committee on Trade and Investment (APEC) |
| CTMA | Ceylon Textile Manufacturers Association |
| CTN | Cotton Exchange (New York) |
| CTO | Commodities Trading Ordinance (Hong Kong) |
| CTRP | Comprehensive Tax Reform Program (Philippines) |
| CTS | China Travel Service |
| CU | Customs union |
| CUF | CHESS Units of Foreign Securities |
| CUHK | Chinese University of Hong Kong |
| CULS | Convertible unsecured loan stock |
| CUNDP | Measures on the Prohibition of Conducts of Unfair Competition of Counterfeiting the Unique Names, Packaging and Decoration of Well Known Products |
| CUP | Comparable uncontrolled price |
| CUSFTA | Canada United State Free Trade Agreement |
| CV | Commanditaire Vennootschap Limited partnership (Indonesia) |
| CVC | Central Vigilance Commission (India) |
| CVC | Customs Valuation Code of GATT |
| CVD | Counterveiling duty |
| CVIC | China Venturetech Investment Corporation |
| CVP | Communist Party of Vietnam |
| CVT | Capital value tax |
| CWE | Cooperative Wholesale Establishment (Sri Lanka) |
| CWTC | China World Trade Centre |
| CXT | Common external tariff (EU) |
| D/A | Document against acceptance |
| DA | Department of Agriculture |
| DA | Depository Agent |
| DAC | Development Assistance Committee |
| DAI | Indonesian Insurance Council |
| Dana | Islamic-based unit trust |
| Danareksa | National Investment Trust (Indonesia) |

| DANIDA | Danish International Development Agency |
| DAP | Development Action Plan |
| DAPH | Department of Animal Production and Health (Sri Lanka) |
| DAR | Department of Agrarian Reform (Philippines) |
| DARE | Department of Agricultural Research and Education (India) |
| DAS | Department of Agrarian Services (Sri Lanka) |
| DAS | Department of Agriculture and Stock (Papua New Guinea) |
| DASC | Disclosure and Accounting Standards Committee |
| DATS | Derivatives Automated Trading System (Australia) |
| DB | Department of Budgeting |
| DB | Development bank |
| DBA | Doctor of Business Administration |
| DBAP | Development Bankers Association of the Philippines |
| DBCC | Department Budget Coordinating Commission |
| DBE | Department of Basic Education |
| DBJ | Development Bank of Japan |
| DBKL | Dewan Bandaraya Kuala Lumpur |
| | (Federal Territory Authority) |
| DBP | Development Bank of the Philippines |
| DBR | Disclosure-based regulation |
| DBS | Development Bank of Singapore |
| DBS | Department of Banking Supervision (India) |
| DBSI | Development Bank of Solomon Islands |
| DBU | Domestic banking unit |
| DBV | Development Bank of Vanuatu |
| DC | Developed country |
| DCB | District Decentralized Budget (Sri Lanka) |
| DCCI | Dhaka Chamber of Commerce and Industries |
| DCE | Dalian Commodity Exchange (China) |
| DCF | Discounted cash flow |
| DCI | Direct Credit Instruction |
| DCR | Duff and Phelps Credit Rating |
| DCS | Department of Census and Statistics (Sri Lanka) |
| DCS | Direct Clearing Service |
| DD | Designated dealer |
| DDC | Dairy Development Corporation (Nepal) |
| DDC | Dedicated data circuit |
| DDC | Divisional Development Council (Sri Lanka) |
| DDCP | Divisional Development Council Program (Sri Lanka) |
| DDD | Direct distance dialing |
| DDF | Digital Data Feed |
| DDI | Direct Debit Instruction |
| DDM | Dividend discount model |
| DDP | District Development Plan (Malaysia) |
| DDP | District Development Plan (Sri Lanka) |

| | |
|---|---|
| DEA | Designated external account |
| DEB | Dasar Ekonomi Baru (Malaysia) |
| | (New Economic Policy) |
| DECS | Department of Education, Culture and Sports |
| DEd | Doctor of Education |
| DEDO | Duty Drawback Office (Bangladesh) |
| DEEC | Duty Exemption Entitlement Certificate (India) |
| DEETYA | Department of Employment, Education, Training and Youth Affairs (Australia) |
| DEL | Direct exchange line |
| DEM | Deutschemark |
| DENR | Department of Environment and Natural Resources (Philippines) |
| DEPZ | Dhaka Export Processing Zone (Bangladesh) |
| DES | Department of Education and Science |
| DES | Department of Electrical Services |
| DES | Diamond Exchange of Singapore |
| DESA | Dhaka Electric Supply Authority (Bangladesh) |
| DF | Deficit financing |
| DFA | Department of Foreign Affairs |
| DFAT | Department of Foreign Affairs and Trade |
| DFC | Development finance company |
| DFCC | Development Finance Corporation of Ceylon |
| DFHI | Discount and Finance House of India Ltd |
| DFI | Development financial institution |
| DFI | Direct foreign investment |
| DFID | Department for International Development (United Kingdom) |
| DFPO | Dairy Farming Promotion Organization (Thailand) |
| DG | Director General |
| DGB | Directorate General of Budget (Indonesia) |
| DGCA | Directorate General of Civil Aviation (India) |
| DGCI&S | Directorate General of Commercial Intelligence and Statistics (India) |
| DGEU | Department of Government Electricity Undertakings (Sri Lanka) |
| DGFT | Directorate General of Foreign Trade (India) |
| DGMWR | Department of Geology, Mines and Water Resources (Vanuatu) |
| DGP | Development Guide Plan |
| DGPT | Directorate General of Posts and Telecommunications (Vietnam) |
| DHEC | Measures Concerning the Determination and Handling of Void Economic Contracts (China) |
| DHSHD | Department of Human Settlement and Housing Development (Myanmar) |
| DI-Aceh | Daerah Istimewa Aceh (Special province of Aceh, Indonesia) |
| DIC | Deposit Insurance Corporation |
| DICGC | Deposit Insurance and Credit Guarantee Corporation (India) |
| DID | Department of Industrial Development (India) |

| | |
|---|---|
| DII | Domestic Investment Initiative |
| DILG | Department of Interior and Local Government (Philippines) |
| DIMIA | Department of Immigration and Multicultural and Indigenous Affairs (Australia) |
| DIR | Department of Industrial Relations (Australia) |
| DIRP | District Integrated Rural Development Program (Sri Lanka) |
| DISC | Domestic International Sales Corporation |
| DIST | Department of Industry Science and Tourism |
| DIT | Department of Information Technology (India) |
| DITR | Department of Industry, Tourism and Resources |
| DITTB | Documentation, Information and Technology Transfer Bureau (Philippines) |
| DJIA | Dow Jones Industrial Average |
| DKB | Dai-Ichi Kangyo Bank (Japan) |
| DKI | Daerah Khusus Ibukota (Indonesia) (Capital City Special Region) |
| DKKKN | National Council for Occupational Safety and Health (Indonesia) |
| DKSPIA | Dewan Kerja Sama Pengusaha Indonesia Australia |
| DKT | Daehan Korea Trust |
| DLC | Documentary letter of credit |
| DLGCD | Department of Local Government and Community Development |
| DLKN | National Council for Work Training (Indonesia) |
| DLKN | National Wages Council (Indonesia) |
| DLO | District Land Office |
| DM | District Ministry (Sri Lanka) |
| DMA | Department of Monetary Affairs (Taiwan) |
| DMB | Deposit money bank |
| DMC | Developing member country (of ADB) |
| DMT | Dual mode terminal |
| DND | Department of National Defence (Philippines) |
| DNI | Daftar Negatif Investasi (Indonesia) (Negative Investment List) |
| DNRAEDM | Department of Natural Resources Assessment and Environmental Data Management (Cambodia) |
| DNS | Depository and Common Nominee System |
| DO | Delivery order |
| DOA | Department of Agriculture |
| DOCA | Department of Communications and the Arts (Australia) |
| DOE | Department of Education |
| DOE | Department of Electronics |
| DOE | Department of Environment |
| DOE | Deed of Establishment |
| DOE | Department of Energy |
| DOF | Department of Finance |

| | |
|---|---|
| DOG | Days of grace |
| DOH | Department of Highways |
| DOH | Department of Health |
| Doi moi | Renovation or renewal (Vietnam) |
| DOJ | Department of Justice |
| DOL | Department of Labour |
| DOL | Department of Livestock |
| DOLA | Department of Local Administration |
| DOLE | Department of Labour and Employment |
| DONE | Department of Non-formal Education |
| DORTS | Department of Mass Rapid Transit System |
| DOS | Department of State |
| DOSRI | Loans to directors, officers, stockholders and related interests (Philippines) |
| DOST | Department of Science and Technology |
| DOT | Department of Telecommunications |
| DOT | Department of Tourism |
| DOT | Department of Trade |
| DOT | Department of Transport |
| DOT | Department of the Treasury |
| DOT | Develop, operate and transfer |
| DOTC | Department of Transportation and Communications (Philippines) |
| DOVE | Department of Vocational Education |
| DP | Data processing |
| DP | Democrat Party (Thailand) |
| DP | Devisa perlangkap (Indonesia) (Complementary foreign exchange) |
| D/P | Document against payment |
| DPA | Dewan Pertimbangan Agung (Indonesia) (Supreme Advisory Council) |
| DPC | District Planning Committee (India) |
| DPE | Dewan Penunjang Ekspor (Indonesia) (Export Support Board) |
| DPEP | District Primary Education Program (India) |
| DPG | Directorate of Public Grievances (India) |
| DPIE | Department of Primary Industries and Energy |
| DPN | National Productivity Council (Indonesia) |
| DPP | Dewan Pengurus Pusat (Indonesia) (National Board) |
| DPLK | Financial institution pension fund (Indonesia) |
| DPPK | Employer pension fund (Indonesia) |
| DPR | Dewan Perwakilan Rakyat (Indonesia) (People's Representative Council) |
| DPRD | Dewan Perwakilan Rakyat Daerah (Indonesia) (Regional People's Representative Council) |
| DPRDI | Provincial House of Representatives (Indonesia) |
| DPRDII | District/Municipal House of Representatives (Indonesia) |

| | |
|---|---|
| DPRK | Democratic People's Republic of Korea |
| DPS | Dividend per share |
| DPWH | Department of Public Works and Highways |
| DR | Depository receipt |
| Dra | Doktoranda (Indonesian) (Female graduate) |
| DRAM | Dynamic random access memory (chips) |
| DRC | Division of Revenue and Customs (Bhutan) |
| DRP | Disaster Recovery Plan |
| DRP | Dividend Reinvestment Plan |
| DRS | Debt Report System (India) |
| Drs | Doktorandus (Indonesian) (Male graduate) |
| DRT | Debt Recovery Tribunal (India) |
| DSAS | Direct Selling Association of Singapore |
| DSB | Dispute Settlement Body |
| DSC | Defence Saving Certificate (Pakistan) |
| DSD | Department of Skills Development (Thailand) |
| DSE | Dhaka Stock Exchange (Bangladesh) |
| DSEC | Direccao dos Servicos de Estatistica e Censos (Statistics and Census Service, Macau) |
| DSI | Data Storage Institute (Singapore) |
| DSM | Department of Standards Malaysia |
| DSN | Dewan Standardiasi Nasional (Standardization Council of Indonesia) |
| DSO | Defence Science Organization |
| DSP | Dafta Skala Prioritas (Indonesia) (Investment Priorities List) |
| DSS | PT Dharmala Sakti Sejahtera (Indonesia) |
| DST | Daylight Saving Time |
| DST | Department of Science and Technology |
| DST | Documentary stamp tax (Philippines) |
| DSTA | Defence Science and Technology Agency |
| DSTO | Defence Science and Technology Organization (Australia) |
| DSU | Dispute Settlement Understanding |
| DSWD | Department of Social Welfare and Development |
| DTA | Domestic Tariff Area (India) |
| DTA | Double Taxation Agreement |
| DTAT | Double Taxation Avoidance Treaty (India) |
| DTB | Deutsche Terminborse |
| DTC | Defence Teaming Centre (Australia) |
| DTC | Deposit-taking company |
| DTC | Deposit-taking cooperative |
| DTCD | Directorate of Training and Career Development (Sri Lanka) |
| DTD | Double Taxation Deduction Scheme |
| DTF | Derivative Trading Facility |
| DTI | Department of Textile Industries |
| DTI | Department of Trade and Industry |

| | |
|---|---|
| DTI | Deposit-taking institution |
| DTIC | Department of Trade, Industry and Commerce (Vanuatu) |
| DTL | Demand and time liabilities |
| DTR | Daily Transaction Report |
| DTRI | Deposit-taking financial institution |
| DTROP | Drug Trafficking (Recovery of Proceeds) Ordinance (Hong Kong) |
| DTTDC | Delhi Tourism and Transportation Development Corporation |
| DUSB | Danaharta Urus Sendirian Berhad |
| DVEZ | Dinh Vu Economic Zone (Vietnam) |
| DvP | Delivery vs payment |
| DVP | Design Ventures Program |
| Dwt | Deadweight ton |
| EA | Employment Advocate (Australia) |
| EA | Exporters' Association (Macau) |
| EAAU | East Asia Analytical Unit |
| EAB | East Asia Commercial Joint Stock Bank |
| EABC | East ASEAN Business Council |
| EAC | East Asiatic Company |
| EAEC | East Asian Economic Caucus |
| EAEG | East Asian Economic Group |
| EAFC | East Asia Financial Crisis |
| EAGA | East ASEAN Growth Area |
| EAI | East Asian Institute |
| EAMF | East Asian Monetary Fund |
| EAMM | Europe Asia Ministerial Meeting |
| EAOSEF | East Asian and Oceanian Stock Exchanges Federation |
| E&P | Exploration and production |
| EAP | Early action plan |
| EAP-AP | Environmental Assessment Program of Asia and the Pacific |
| EAS | Employment Assurance Scheme (India) |
| EASDAQ | European Association of Securities Dealers Automated Quotations |
| EAT | Economic Advisory Team (Cambodia) |
| EBA | Exchange Banks' Association |
| EBC | Equitable Banking Corporation (Philippines) |
| ebi | Excluding bonus issue |
| EBMR | Extended Bangkok Metropolitan Region |
| EBRD | European Bank for Reconstruction and Development |
| EBS | Export Bonus Scheme (Pakistan) |
| EBTS | Electronic Bond Trading System (Taiwan) |
| EC | Economic Committee |
| EC | Electronic commerce |
| EC | Electoral Commission |
| EC | European Community |
| ECA | Environmentally critical area |
| ECA | Export credit agency |

| | |
|---|---|
| ECAFE | Economic Commission for Asia and Far East |
| ECB | European Central Bank |
| ECB | External commercial borrowing |
| ECC | Environmental Compliance Certificate |
| ECC | Export Credit Cell (Sri Lanka) |
| ECDG | Export Credit Guarantee Department (United Kingdom) |
| ECFIN | Institute for Economics and Financial Research (Indonesia) |
| ECGC | Export Credit Guarantee Corporation (India) |
| ECGD | Export Credit Guarantee Department |
| ECI | Export credit insurance |
| ECIC | Export credit insurance corporation |
| ECICS | Export Credit Insurance Corporation of Singapore |
| ECIIPS | European Community International Investment Partners Scheme |
| ECIL | Electronic Corporation of India |
| ECJ | European Court of Justice |
| ECL | Economic Contract Law (China) |
| ECM | Electronics contract manufacturer |
| ECM | European Common Market |
| ECM | Exchange control measure |
| ECNU | East China Normal University (Shanghai) |
| ECO | Economic Cooperation Organization |
| ECOTECH | Economic and technical cooperation |
| ECOZONE | Special Economic Zone (Philippines) |
| ECP | Environmentally critical project |
| ECR | Electronic cash register |
| ECR | export credit refinancing |
| ECRS | Export Credit Refinance Scheme |
| ECS | Electronic clearing service |
| ECS | Electronic clearing system |
| ECU | European Clearing Union |
| ECU | European Currency Unit |
| ED | Executive director |
| ED | Export declaration |
| E day | Exercise day |
| EDA | Economic Development Authority (South Australia) |
| EDA | Export Development Act (Philippines) |
| EDB | Economic Development Board |
| EDB | Energy Development Board (Philippines) |
| EDB | European Development Bank |
| EDC | Export Development Council (Philippines) |
| EDCB | Export Development Corporation of Bhutan |
| EDF | Entrepreneur Development Fund (Singapore) |
| EDI | Economic Development Institute |
| EDI | Electronic data interchange |
| EDL | Electricite du Laos (Electricity authority) |

| | |
|---|---|
| EDP | Electronic data processing |
| EDS | EAGA Development Strategy |
| EDS | Electronic data system |
| EDSA | Epifanio de los Santos Avenue |
| EDU | Enforcement Directorate Unit (Malaysia) |
| EE | Eastern Express |
| EEA | European Economic Area |
| EEC | European Economic Community |
| EEF | Exchange Equalization Fund (Thailand) |
| EEOC | Equal Employment Opportunity Commission (United States) |
| EEOITL | Economic Entity and Organization Income Tax Law (Mongolia) |
| EERI | Effective Exchange Rate Index |
| EEZ | Exclusive economic zone |
| EFAC | Exchange Fund Advisory Committee (Hong Kong) |
| EFF | Extended Fund Facility |
| EFI | Economics and Finance Institute (Cambodia) |
| EFIC | Export Finance Investment Corporation (Australia) |
| EFIL | Exchange Fund Investment Ltd (Hong Kong) |
| EFMD | European Foundation of Management Development |
| EFN | Exchange Fund Note |
| EFP | Equity Financing Program |
| EFP | Exchange of Futures for Physicals |
| EFS | Electronic filing system |
| EFS | Electronic financial services |
| EFS | Export Finance Scheme (Pakistan) |
| EFT | Electronic fund transfer |
| EFTA | European Free Trade Association |
| EFTA | European Free Trade Area |
| EFTPOS | Electronic fund transfer at point of sale |
| EFU | Eastern Federal Union (Pakistan) |
| EG | Experts group |
| EGAT | Electricity Generating Authority of Thailand |
| EGM | Experts group meeting |
| EGM | Extraordinary general meeting |
| EHTP | Electronic Hardware Technology Park (India) |
| EHS | Environment, health and safety |
| EIA | Environmental impact assessment |
| EIB | European Investment Bank |
| EIB | Export and Import Bank |
| EIC | East India Company |
| EIR | Earned income relief |
| EIRR | Economic internal rate of return |
| EIS | Environmental impact statement |
| EIS | Export Institute of Singapore |
| EIU | Economic Intelligence Unit |

| | |
|---|---|
| EJV | Equity joint venture |
| EKB | Expanded commercial bank (Philippines) |
| ELCOM | Electricity Commission (Papua New Guinea) |
| ELIPS | Economic Law and Improved Procurement System (Indonesia) |
| ELSS | Equity-Linked Savings Scheme (India) |
| EM | Emerging market |
| E-mail | Electronic mail |
| EMAS | Exchange Main Board Share Index (Malaysia) |
| EMB | Environmental Management Bureau |
| EMBA | Executive MBA program |
| EMBI | Emerging Market Bond Index |
| EMC | Export management company |
| EMCF | European Monetary Cooperation Fund |
| EMEAP | Executives' Meeting of East Asia and Pacific Central Banks |
| EMEF | Emerging Market Economy Forum |
| EMF | European Monetary Fund |
| EMR | Extended metropolitan region |
| EMS | East Malaysian states |
| EMS | European Monetary System |
| EMS | Environmental Management System |
| EMS | Electronic mail service |
| EMS | Express mail service |
| EMU | European Monetary Union |
| EMSIS | Electronic Mail Stock Information Service |
| EMT | Efficient market theory |
| EMU | European Monetary Union |
| ENDEC | Entrepreneurship Development Centre (Singapore) |
| ENEL | Italian electricity utility |
| ENV | Ministry of Environment (Singapore) |
| EO | Education Officer |
| EO | Executive Officer |
| EO | Executive Order |
| EOI | Eradication of illiteracy |
| EOI | Export-oriented industrialization |
| EON | Edaran Otomobil Nasional Ltd (Malaysia) |
| EOU | Export-oriented unit |
| EOY | End of year |
| EP | Employment Pass (Singapore) |
| EP | Export permit |
| EPA | Economic Planning Agency |
| EPA | Environmental Protection Agency (United States) |
| EPB | Environmental Protection Bureau |
| EPB | Export Promotion Board |
| EPB | Export Promotion Bureau |
| EPC | Employment Promotion Centre |

| | |
|---|---|
| EPC | Enterprise Promotion Centre Private Ltd |
| EPC | European Patent Convention |
| EPC | Export Promotion Council |
| EPCG | Export promotion capital goods |
| EPF | Employees' Provident Fund |
| EPF | Equity Participation Fund (Pakistan) |
| EPFC | Employees' Provident Fund Corporation (Nepal) |
| EPFO | Employees' Provident Fund Organization (India) |
| EPG | Eminent Persons Group |
| EPI | Electronic Payment Instruction |
| EPOC | ESCAP Pacific Operation Centre |
| EPP | Export Priority Plan |
| EPP | Export Promotion Program |
| EPR | Earnings price ratio |
| EPS | Earning per share |
| EPS | Easy Pay System |
| EPS | Electronic Payment for Shares (Singapore) |
| EPTE | Entrepot Produksi Tujuan Ekspor Zone (Indonesia) (Special export production zone) |
| EPTL | Enterprise des Posts et Telecommunications (Laos) |
| EPQ | Exchange price quotation |
| EPU | Economic Planning Unit |
| EPZ | Export processing zone |
| EPZA | Export Processing Zone Administration |
| EPZA | Export Processing Zone Authority |
| EQ | Emotional quotient |
| EQC | Environmental quality control |
| ERA | Effective rate of assistance |
| ERB | Energy Regulatory Board (Philippines) |
| ERC | Economic Research Centre |
| ERC | External Resources Division (Bangladesh) |
| ERF | Enterprise Rehabilitation Fund |
| ERI | European Roundtable of Industrialists |
| ERISA | Employee Retirement Income Securities Act (United States) |
| ERM | Exchange Rate Mechanism (Europe) |
| ERP | Electronic Road Pricing (Singapore) |
| ERP | Enterprise Resource Planning |
| ERP | Effective rate of production |
| ERP | Effective rate of protection |
| ERSO | Electronics Research and Service Organization (Sri Lanka) |
| ERTA | Expressway and Rapid Transit Authority of Thailand |
| ESA | Electronic share application |
| ESA | Exchange settlement account |
| ESAA | Electricity Supply Association of Australia |
| ESAF | Enhanced Structural Adjustment Facility (Laos) |

| | |
|---|---|
| ESAF | Enhanced Structural Fund Facility (Pakistan) |
| ESANZ | Economic Society of Australia and New Zealand |
| ESAP | Economic Stabilization Policy (Cambodia) |
| ESB | Export Support Board (Indonesia) |
| ESC | Economic and Social Council (UN) |
| ESCAP | Economic and Social Commission for Asia and Pacific |
| ESCB | European System of Central Banks |
| ESCL | Exchangeable Subordinated Capital Loan |
| ESCO | Educational Scientific and Cultural Organization (UN) |
| ESCO | Energy service company |
| ESDC | Entrepreneur Skills Development Centre (Malaysia) |
| ESDW | Equity share with detachable warrant |
| ESF | Early Stage Fund |
| ESF | Economic Support Fund (Philippines) |
| ESFTA | EFTA-Singapore Free Trade Agreement |
| ESI | Externally sourced investment |
| ESL | Employment Service Law (Taiwan) |
| ESOP | Employee Stock Option Plan |
| ESOP | Employee Stock Ownership Plan |
| ESOS | Employee share option scheme |
| ESP | Economic Stabilization Program (Philippines) |
| ESR | Exclusive sales representative |
| ESRC | Economic and Social Research Council (United Kingdom) |
| ET | Environmental technology |
| ETA | Estimated/expected time of arrival |
| ETA | Expressway and Transit Authority (Thailand) |
| ETC | Estimated time of completion |
| ETC | Export trading company |
| ETD | Estimated/expected time of delivery |
| ETD | Estimated/expected time of departure |
| ETDZ | Economic and Technological Development Zone |
| ETF | Employees' Trust Fund (Sri Lanka) |
| ETF | Exchange Traded Fund |
| ETO | Exchange Traded Options |
| ETO | Express Transportation Organization (Thailand) |
| ETRI | Electronics and Telecommunications Research Institute (Sri Lanka) |
| ETRS | Electronic Trade Related Services |
| ETSP | External Trade Shipment Policy |
| ETV | Educational television |
| EU | European Union |
| EUR | Euro (currency of EU) |
| EURAP | European Union Reintegration Assistance Program |
| EUROSEAS | European Association for South East Asian Studies |
| EVA | Economic value added |
| EVN | Electricity Vietnam |

| | |
|---|---|
| EVO | Evaluation Office |
| EVSL | Early Voluntary Sectoral Liberalization |
| EXIM | Export import |
| EXPONET | Export Assistance Network (Philippines) |
| EXPRESS | Exchange Price Reporting System (Malaysia) |
| Ew | Excluding warrants |
| EWC | East West Centre |
| EWC | East West Corridor |
| EWCTP | East West Corridor Transport Project |
| ex dv | Excluding dividend |
| EXIM | Bank Ekspor Impor Indonesia |
| EXIM | Export and Import Bank |
| F&B | Food and beverage |
| F&F | Furniture and fixtures |
| FA | Foreign aid |
| FAA | Federal Aviation Administration (United States) |
| FAA | Financial Advisors Act (Singapore) |
| FAI | Fertilizer Association of India |
| FAIR | Foundation for Advanced Information and Research (Japan) |
| FAMA | Federal Agricultural Marketing Authority (Malaysia) |
| FAME | Filipino Association of Mariner's Employment |
| FAME | Furnishing and Apparel Manufacturers Exchange (Philippines) |
| Fannie Mae | Federal National Mortgage Association (United States) |
| F&NPPD | Food and Nutrition Policy Planning Division (Sri Lanka) |
| FAO | Food and Agriculture Organization (UN) |
| FAO | Foreign Affairs Office |
| FAQ | Fair average quality |
| FAQ | Frequently asked questions |
| FAS | Free alongside ship |
| FASA | Federation of ASEAN Shipping Associations |
| FASA | Fellow of the Australian Society of Accountants |
| FASB | Financial Accounting Standards Board (United States) |
| FASC | Federation of ASEAN Shippers Council |
| FAST | Flexible Accelerated Security Transfer |
| FAST | Fully Automated Securities Trading (Taiwan) |
| FAST | Fully Automated System for Tendering (Malaysia) |
| FATA | Federally Administered Tribal Areas (Pakistan) |
| FATF | Financial Action Task Force (Hong Kong) |
| FAV | Fertilizer Association of Vietnam |
| FBC | Freight booking centre |
| FBCB | First Bangkok City Bank |
| FBCCI | Federation of Bangladesh Chambers of Commerce and Industries |
| FBDC | Fort Bonifacio Development Corporation (Philippines) |
| FBI | Federal Bureau of Investigation (United States) |
| FBIM | Fellow of British Institute of Management |

| FBR | Futures Broker's Representative |
| FBRL | Futures Broker's Representative Licence |
| FBSEA | Foreign Bank Supervision Enhancement Act (United States) |
| FBSI | Federasi Buruh Seluruh Indonesia (All Indonesian Labour Federation) |
| FBSO | Federal Banking Supervisory Office (Germany) |
| FC | Foreign currency |
| FCA | Fellow of the Institute of Chartered Accountants |
| FCA | Fishery Conservation Area (Vanuatu) |
| FCAG | Financial Centre Advisory Group |
| FCB | Food Corporation of Bhutan |
| FCBU | Foreign Currency Banking Unit |
| FCC | Federal Communications Commission (United States) |
| FCCB | Foreign currency convertible bond |
| FCCC | Framework Convention on Climate Change |
| FCCCI | First Commodities Clearing Corporation of India Ltd |
| FCD | Fully convertible debenture |
| FCDI | Forum for Comprehensive Development of Indochina |
| FCDU | Foreign Currency Deposit Unit |
| FCI | Factors Chain International |
| FCI | Food Corporation of India |
| FCIDC | Foreign Capital Inducement Deliberation Committee (Korea) |
| FCIE | First Cavite Industrial Estate (Philippines) |
| FCIL | Foreign Capital Investment Law (Korea) |
| FCMA | Fellow of Institute of Cost and Management Accountants |
| FCNR | Foreign Currency Non Resident account (India) |
| FCNR (B) | Foreign Currency Non Resident account (Bank) (India) |
| FCPA | Foreign Corrupt Practices Act (United States) |
| FD | Fixed deposit |
| FDA | Food and Drug Administration (United States) |
| FDB | Fiji Development Bank |
| FDC | Franchise Development Centre |
| FDI | Foreign direct investment |
| FDIC | Federal Deposit Insurance Corporation (United States) |
| FDIC | Industry and Commerce Development Fund (Macau) |
| FDICIA | FDIC Improvement Act (United States) |
| FDPP | Fund for Development and Planning and Projection (UN) |
| FDSC | Financial Disputes Settlement Committee (Korea) |
| FDSS | Fixed Delivery and Settlement System |
| FEA | Franchise Excellence Award |
| FEAC | Foreign Exchange Adjustment Centre (China) |
| FEALAC | Forum for East Asia Latin American Cooperation |
| FEAP | Far East and the Pacific |
| FEAS | Federation of Euro-Asian Stock Exchanges |
| FEB | Far East Bank (Philippines) |

| FEBC | Foreign Exchange Bearer Certificate |
| FEBTC | Far East Bank and Trust Company (Philippines) |
| FEC | Foreign exchange certificate |
| FECA | Foreign Exchange Control Act (Korea) |
| FECL | Foreign Economic Contract Law (China) |
| FECR | Foreign Exchange Control Regulations (Korea) |
| Fed | Federal Reserve Board (US) |
| FEDAI | Foreign Exchange Dealers Association of India |
| FEE | Foreign exchange earning |
| FEECS | Foreign Exchange Entitlement Certificate Scheme (Sri Lanka) |
| FEED | Front-end Engineering and Design |
| FEER | Far Eastern Economic Review |
| FEFC | Far East Freight Conference |
| FEITL | Foreign Enterprise Income Tax Law |
| FELCRA | Federal Land Consolidation and Rehabilitation Authority |
| FELDA | Federal Land Development Authority (Malaysia) |
| FELT | Fair, efficient, liquid and transparent |
| FEMA | Foreign Exchange Management Act (India) |
| FEMB | Foreign Exchange Management Board (Myanmar) |
| FENCO | Foundation of Canada Engineering Corporation |
| FEOF | Foreign Exchange Operation Fund |
| FEOP | Far East oil price |
| FEPZ | Falta Economic Processing Zone (India) |
| FERA | Foreign Exchange Regulation Act |
| FERET | Foreign Economic Relations and Trade |
| FESCO | Foreign Enterprises Service Corporation (China) |
| FETA | Foreign Exchange Transaction Act (Korea) |
| FETAC | Foreign Economic and Trade Arbitration Commission (China) |
| FETC | Foreign Exchange Transaction Centre |
| FETC | Foreign Exchange Trading Centre |
| FETTC | Foreign Economic and Technical Trading Company (China) |
| FEU | Forty-foot equivalent unit container |
| FEZ | Free export zone |
| FEZAO | Free Export Zone Administration Office (Korea) |
| FFA | South Pacific Forum Fisheries Agency |
| FFFI | Foreign funded financial institution (China) |
| FFHC | Foreign-funded holding company |
| FFHC | Freedom from Hunger Campaign (Sri Lanka) |
| FFI | Foreign financial institution |
| FFIEC | Federal Financial Institutions Examination Council |
| FFMA | Foreign funded medical institution (China) |
| FFTA | Foreign funded travel agency (China) |
| FFW | Federation of Free Workers (Philippines) |
| FGLID | Factories and General Labour Inspection Department (Myanmar) |
| FGSH | Federal Government Services Hospital (Pakistan) |

| | |
|---|---|
| FHFC | Federation of Hokkaido Fisheries Cooperatives (Japan) |
| FHC | Financial holding company |
| FHP | Family health program |
| FI | Fiji Islands |
| FIA | Fellow of the Institute of Actuaries |
| FIA | Foreign Investment Act (Philippines) |
| FIA | Foreign Investment Approval Status (Taiwan) |
| FIA | Futures Industry Act (Malaysia) |
| FIAC | Foreign Investment Advisory Committee (Sri Lanka) |
| FIAM | Fellow of the International Academy of Management |
| FIAPA | International Federation of Advertising Managers Associations |
| FIAS | Foreign Investment Advisory Service (Sri Lanka) |
| FIATA | International Federation of Freight Forwarders Associations |
| FIB | Federal Investment Bond (Pakistan) |
| FIB | Foreign Investment Board (Solomon Islands) |
| FIB | Fellow of the Institute of Bankers |
| FIBV | International Federation of Stock Exchanges (Federation Internationale des Bourses de Valueurs) |
| FIC | Foreign Investment Committee (Malaysia) |
| FIC | Foreign Investment Commission |
| FIC | Forest Industry Council (Papua New Guinea) |
| FICCI | Federation of Indian Chambers of Commerce and Industry |
| FICCI | Foreign Investors Chambers of Commerce and Industries (Bangladesh) |
| FICE | Foreign invested commercial enterprise (China) |
| FICCI | Federation of Indian Chambers of Commerce and Industry |
| FICE | Foreign-invested commercial enterprise |
| Ficorinvest | First Indonesia Finance and Investment Corp (Indonesia) |
| FICP | International Federation of Advertising Clubs |
| FICPI | International Federation of Industrial Property Attorney |
| FICAS | Federation of International Civil Servants Associations |
| FID | Financial institution duty (Australia) |
| FID | Foreign Investment Department |
| FIDA | Fibre Industry Development Authority (Philippines) |
| FIDEJ | International Federation of Newspaper Publishers |
| FIDF | Financial Institution Development Fund (Thailand) |
| FIDIC | International Federation of Consulting Engineers |
| FIE | Foreign invested enterprise (China) |
| FIEC | Fujian Investment Enterprise Corporation (China) |
| FIEO | Federation of Indian Export Organizations |
| FIES | Family Income and Expenditure Survey (Philippines) |
| FIET | International Federation of Commercial, Clerical, Professional and Technical Employees |
| FIFO | First in first out |
| FIFO | Fly in fly out |

| | |
|---|---|
| FIFS | First in first served |
| FIFTA | Foreign Investment and Foreign Trade Agency (Mongolia) |
| FII | Foreign institutional investor |
| FIICK | Foundation for International Industrial Cooperation of Korea |
| FIJ | Fasteners Institute of Japan |
| FIJSC | Foreign invested joint stock company (China) |
| FIL | Foreign Investment Law |
| FILO | First in last out |
| FILP | Fiscal Investment and Loan Program |
| FIMC | Foreign Investment Management Committee |
| FIMMDA | Fixed Income Money Market and Derivatives Association of India |
| FINA | Following items not available |
| FINBEL | France, Italy, Netherlands, Belgium, Luxembourg |
| Finconesia | Financial Corp of Indonesia |
| FINEX | Financial Executives Institute of the Philippines |
| FINEX | Financial Instrument Exchange (New York) |
| FINL | Foreign Investment Negative List (Philippines) |
| FINTECH | Filipinas Information Technology Services |
| FINTEL | Fiji International Telecommunications Ltd |
| FIO | Fixed interest offering (Australia) |
| FIO | Forest Industry Organization (Thailand) |
| FIPA | Foreign Investment Promotion Act (Korea) |
| FIPB | Foreign Investment Promotion Board (India) |
| FIPC | Foreign Investment Promotion Council (India) |
| FIPF | Financial Institution Pension Fund (Indonesia) |
| FIRB | Foreign Investment Review Board (Australia) |
| FIRE | Financial Institution Reform and Expansion (India) |
| FIRR | Financial internal rate of return |
| FISB | Foreign Investment Services Bureau (Maldives) |
| FISC | Financial Information Services Co Ltd (Taiwan) |
| FISC | Foreign Investment Service Centre (China) |
| FISE | Federation of Indian Stock Exchanges |
| FISH | First in still here |
| FISH | Financial Information Services Hub (Singapore) |
| FISO | Federal Insurance Supervisory Office (Germany) |
| FIT | Free of income tax |
| FIT | Free independent tour |
| FITA | Federation of International Trade Organizations |
| FIU | Financial intelligence unit |
| FIYTO | Federation of International Youth Travel Organizations |
| FKLI | KLSE Composite Index Futures |
| FKI | Federation of Korean Industries |
| FKTU | Federation of Korean Trade Unions |
| FLA | Free luggage allowance |
| FLP | Foreign Language Press (China) |

| FLPDA | Foreign Languages Publication and Distribution Administration (China) |
| FLR | Front line regulator |
| FLSRO | Front-line self-regulatory organization |
| FMA | Forestry Management Agreement |
| FMCG | Fast moving consumer goods |
| FMFB | Final Mine Feasibility Report (Bhutan) |
| FMM | Federation of Malaysian Manufacturers |
| FMD | Foot and mouth disease |
| FMO | Fish Marketing Organization (Thailand) |
| FMPRC | Foreign Ministry of the People's Republic of China |
| FMS | Financial Management Service |
| FMUTM | Federation of Malaysian Unit Trust Managers |
| FMV | Fair market value |
| FNBC | First National Bank of Chicago |
| FNCB | First National City Bank |
| FNCCI | Federation of Nepalese Chambers of Commerce and Industries |
| FNI | Fellow of National Institute of Sciences in India |
| FNZIM | Fellow of the New Zealand Institute of Management |
| FNZSA | Fellow of the New Zealand Society of Accountants |
| FNMA | Federal National Mortgage Association (United States) |
| FNPF | Fiji National Provident Fund |
| FOB | Free on board |
| FOC | Flag of convenience |
| FOC | Free of charge |
| FOC | Fund of Cambodia |
| FOGS | Functioning of the GATT system |
| FOI | For our information |
| FOI | Free of interest |
| FOK | Fill or kill |
| FOMC | Federal Open Market Committee (United States) |
| FONASBA | Federation of National Associations of Ship Brokers and Agents |
| FOP | Free on plane |
| FORES | Floor Order Routing and Execution System (Japan) |
| Forex | Foreign exchange |
| FOSCO | Foreign Service Corporation |
| FOX | London Futures and Options Exchange |
| FPC | Formosa Plastics Corporation |
| FPCCI | Federation of Pakistan Chambers of Commerce and Industry |
| FPI | Federation of Philippine Industries |
| FPI | Foreign private investment |
| FPLC | Federation of Public Listed Companies (Malaysia) |
| FPSO | Floating production, storage and offloading vessel |
| FRA | Financial Restructuring Authority (Thailand) |
| FRA | Forward Rate Agreement |

| FRAC | Financial Restructuring Advisory Committee (Thailand) |
| FRANDAS | Franchise Development Assistance Scheme |
| FRB | Federal Reserve Board (US) (The Fed) |
| FRC | Financial Reconstruction Commission (Japan) |
| FRC | Financial Reporting Council (Australia) |
| FRCD | Floating rate certificate of deposit |
| FRER | Financial Sector Restructuring for Economic Recovery (Thailand) |
| FRF | Financial Reporting Foundation |
| FRIM | Forest Research Institute of Malaysia |
| FRN | Floating rate note |
| FRR | Financial Resources Rules |
| FRRP | Foreign Researchers Recruitment Program |
| FRS | Federal Reserve System |
| FRS | Financial Review and Surveillance |
| FRSNZ | Fellow of the Royal Society of New Zealand |
| FSA | Farm Support Association (Vanuatu) |
| FSA | Financial Services Act (United Kingdom) |
| FSA | Financial Services Agency |
| FSA | Financial Supervisory Agency |
| FSAC | Financial Sector Advisory Council |
| FSAL | Financial Sector Adjustment Loan (World Bank) |
| FSAP | Financial Sector Assessment Program (IMF) |
| FSB | Fujian Statistical Bureau (China) |
| FSC | Federal Shariah Court (Pakistan) |
| FSC | Financial Supervisory Commission (Korea) |
| FSC | Foreign Sales Corporation |
| FCS | Fishermen's Cooperative Society (Sri Lanka) |
| FSDC | Financial Supervision and Control Department |
| FSDP | Full scale demonstration project |
| FSF | Financial Stability Forum |
| FSF | Financial support facility |
| FSF | Law on Foreign Securities Firms (Japan) |
| FSFRL | Far Seas Fisheries Research Laboratory |
| FSLA | Federal Savings and Loan Association (United States) |
| FSLIC | Federal Savings and Loan Insurance Corporation (United States) |
| FSOC | Financial Sector Outline Committee (Indonesia) |
| FSP | Financial System Planning Bureau (Japan) |
| FSP | Foundation for the Peoples of the South Pacific |
| FSPSI | Federasi SPSI (Indonesia) |
| FSR | Financial system reform |
| FSRG | Financial Sector Review Group |
| FSS | Financial Supervisory Service (Korea) |
| FSSA | Financial Sector Stability Assessment (IMF) |
| FSSO | Federal Securities Supervisory Office (Germany) |
| FT | Financial Times |

| | |
|---|---|
| FTA | Fair Trading Act (Australia) |
| FTA | Free trade agreement |
| FTA | Free trade area |
| FTA | Free trade association |
| FTA | Futures Trading Act |
| FTAA | Financial and Technical Assistance Agreement |
| FTAA | Free Trade Agreement of the Americas |
| FTAC | Foreign Trade Arbitration Commission |
| FTAS | Foreign Trade Agency System |
| FTB | Foreign Trade Bank (Cambodia) |
| FTB | Foreign Trade Bureau |
| FTC | Fair Trade Commission (Japan) |
| FTC | Fair Trade Commission (Taiwan) |
| FTC | Federal Trade Commission |
| FTC | Finance and Treasury Centre scheme |
| FTC | Foreign Trade Commission (United States) |
| FTC | Foreign Trade Corporation |
| FTC | Foreign trading company |
| FTC | Free Trade Commission |
| FTI | Federation of Thai Industries |
| FTIB | Fiji Trade and Investment Board |
| FTKL | Federal Territory Kuala Lumpur |
| FTL | Fair Trade Law (Taiwan) |
| FTL | Foreign Trade Law |
| FTP | Free trade port |
| FTR | Financial Transaction Report Act (Australia) |
| FT-SE | Financial Times–Stock Exchange (Footsie) Index |
| FTSC | Foreign Trade Service Corps |
| FTU | Federation of Trade Unions |
| FTZ | Free trade zone |
| FUNCINPEC | National United Front (Cambodia) |
| FUNDDAP | UN Trust Fund for Development Planning and Projection |
| FUNDWI | UN Fund for the Development of West Irian |
| FWB | First Women's Bank (Pakistan) |
| FWH | Flexible working hours |
| FWHF | Federation of World Health Foundations |
| FWS | Flexible wage system |
| FWT | Fair wear and tear |
| FX | Foreign exchange |
| FXRN | Fixed rate note |
| FXTN | Fixed Rate Treasury Note (Philippines) |
| FY | Financial year |
| FY | Fiscal year |
| FYI | For your information |
| FYP | Five-year plan |

| | |
|---|---|
| G5 | Group of Five nations |
| G7 | Group of Seven nations |
| G10 | Group of Ten nations |
| G20 | Group of Twenty nations |
| G22 | Group of Twenty-two nations |
| GA | Government Agent (Sri Lanka) |
| GAAP | Generally accepted accounting principles |
| GAAS | Generally accepted auditing standards |
| GAB | General Arrangement to Borrow |
| GAC | General Administration of Customs (China) |
| GAIL | Gas Authority of India Limited |
| GAMC | General Agreement on Multinational Companies |
| GAO | General Accounting Office (United States) |
| GAS | General Administration Service |
| GATS | General Agreement on Trade and Services |
| GATT | General Agreement on Tariffs and Trade |
| GAUN | General Assembly of United Nations |
| GAV | Gross annual value |
| GAVI | Global Alliance for Vaccines and Immunization |
| GB | Grameen Bank (Bangladesh) |
| GBA | Grameen Bank Approach |
| GBE | Government business enterprise (Australia) |
| GBHN | Garis-garis Besar Haluna Negara (Indonesia) (Guidelines of State Policy) |
| GBMR | Greater Bangkok Metropolitan Region |
| GBRT | Gross Business Receipts Tax (Taiwan) |
| GC | Global Company |
| GCEC | Greater Colombo Economic Commission |
| GCIO | Government Chief Information Officer |
| GCOP | Government Committee on Organization and Personnel |
| GCP | Ghee Corporation of Pakistan |
| GCPI | Greater Colombo Consumer Price Index |
| GCR | Global Competitiveness Report |
| GCT | Guangzhou Commerce and Trading Centre (China) |
| GCWM | General Conference of Weights and Measures |
| GDB | Guangdong Development Bank (China) |
| GDBTB | Guangdong Broadcasting and Television Bureau (China) |
| GDC | General Department of Customs (Vietnam) |
| GDCF | Gross domestic capital formation |
| GDFI | Gross domestic fixed investment |
| GDFTC | Guangdong Foreign Trade Corporation (China) |
| GDFTD | Guangdong Foreign Trade Development Corporation (China) |
| GDI | Gross domestic investment |
| GDNT | General Department of National Taxation (Mongolia) |
| GDP | General Development Plan |

GDP          Gross domestic product
GDR          General Department of Rubber (Vietnam)
GDR          General drawing right
GDR          German Democratic Republic
GDR          Global depository receipt
GDS          General Department of Statistics (Vietnam)
GDS          Gross domestic savings
GDSTC        Guangdong Science and Technology Commission (China)
GDT          General Department of Tourism (Vietnam)
GDTV         Guangdong Television (China)
GEC          General Electric Corporation
GEF          Global Environmental Fund (World Bank)
GEI          Government Employees' Insurance (Taiwan)
GEL          General Exception List
GEM          Global Entrepreneurship Monitor
GEM          Growth with Equity in Mindanao program (Philippines)
GEMS         Global Environmental Monitor System
GEMS         Government Electronic Mail System
GEPB         Guangxi Electric Power Bureau (China)
GEPF         Government Employees Provident Fund (Bhutan)
GERD         Government Expenditure on Research and Development
GES          Gold Exchange of Singapore
GES          Gold Exchange Standard
GES          Good Enterprise System
GFC          Government financial centre
GFCF         Gross fixed capital formation
GFEDC        Guangdong Foreign Economic Development Company (China)
GFI          General fixed investment
GFI          Government financial institution
GFISC        Guangdong Foreign Investment Service Centre (China)
GFSME        Guarantee Fund for Small and Medium Enterprises (Philippines)
GFTC         Guangdong Foreign Trade Corporation (China)
GFTIEC       Guangdong Foreign Trade Import and Export Corporation
             (China)
G-G          Government to government
GG           PT Gudang Garam (Indonesia)
GGLS         Group Guaranteed Lending and Savings Scheme
GGS          General Guarantee Scheme
GHB          Government Housing Bank
GIA          General Insurance Association (Singapore)
GIC          General Insurance Corporation (India)
GIC          Government Investment Corporation (Singapore)
GIC          Guaranteed investment certificate
GICOI        General Insurance Corporation of India
GIE          Gross income earned

| | |
|---|---|
| GIEC | Guangdong International Exhibition Centre (China) |
| GIETC | Guangdong International Economic and Technical Cooperation (China) |
| GIGO | Garbage in garbage out |
| GII | Government Investment Issue |
| GIO | Government Information Office (Taiwan) |
| GINSI | Importers Association of Indonesia |
| GIR | Gross international reserves |
| GIS | Genome Institute of Singapore |
| GITIC | Guangdong International Trust and Investment Company (China) |
| GIZ | General Industrial Zone |
| GKBI | Gabungan Koperasi Batik Indonesia (Indonesian Association of Batik Cooperatives) |
| GKN | National Partnership Movement (Indonesia) |
| GKO | Russian government securities |
| GLC | General line of credit |
| GLC | Government-linked company |
| GLO | Government Lottery Office (Thailand) |
| GLS | Government Land Sales program |
| GmbH | Gesellschaft mit beschrankter Haftung (private limited liability company in Germany) |
| GMC | Genetically modified crop |
| GMO | Genetically modified organism |
| GMB | Greater Mekong Basin |
| GMDSS | Global Maritime Distress and Safety System |
| GMI | German Malaysia Institute |
| GMPP | Geothermal Modular Power Program |
| GMS | General meeting of shareholders |
| GMS | Greater Mekong Sub-region |
| GMSBF | GMS Business Forum |
| GMT | Greenwich Mean Time |
| GMTB | Guangdong Maritime Transport Bureau (China) |
| GMU | Gajah Mada University (Indonesia) |
| GNC | Gross national consumption |
| GNE | Gross national expenditure |
| GNFS | Goods and non-factor services |
| GNG | Group on Negotiating Goods |
| GNI | Gross national income |
| GNMA | Government National Mortgage Association (US) (Ginnie Mae) |
| GNP | Gross national product |
| GNS | Group on Negotiating Services |
| GNS | Gross National Savings |
| GNSS | Global navigation satellite system |
| GNW | Gross national wealth |
| GNW | Gross national welfare |

| GO | Glass Organization (Thailand) |
| GOA | Government of Australia |
| GOB | Government of Bangladesh |
| GOB | Government of Brunei Darussalam |
| GOBU | Government owned business undertaking (Sri Lanka) |
| GOCC | Government owned and controlled corporation (Philippines) |
| GOI | Government of India |
| GOI | Government of Indonesia |
| GOJ | Government of Japan |
| Golkar | Golongan Karya ("functional groups" Indonesia) |
| GOM | Government of Malaysia |
| GOP | Government of Pakistan |
| GOP | Government of the Philippines |
| GPA | Government procurement agreement |
| GPA | Gross problematic asset |
| GPB | Government Price Board (Vietnam) |
| GPC | Government Pricing Commission (Vietnam) |
| GPC | Government Parliamentary Committee (Singapore) |
| GPCL | General Principles of Civil Law (China) |
| GPG | General public goods |
| GPM | Graduated payment mortgage |
| GPO | General Post Office |
| GPO | Government Pharmaceutical Organization (Thailand) |
| GPO | Government Printing Office |
| GPS | Generalized preferential system |
| GPS | Guaranteed Price Scheme (Sri Lanka) |
| GR | Green Revolution |
| GRC | Group Representative Constituency (Singapore) |
| GRDP | Gross regional domestic product |
| GRGI | PT Great River Garment Industries (Indonesia) |
| GRI | Government research institute |
| GRT | Gross receipts tax (Philippines) |
| GRT | Gross registered tonnage |
| GSA | General sales agent |
| GSA | General Services Administration (United States) |
| GSA | Government Shareholding Agency (Solomon Islands) |
| GSB | Government Savings Bank |
| GSD | Government securities dealer |
| GSDP | Gross state domestic product |
| GSIS | Government Service Insurance System (Philippines) |
| GSM | Global System for Mobile Communications |
| GSM | Government securities market |
| GSM | Gram per square metre |
| GSO | Government Statistical Office (Vietnam) |
| GSP | Generalized System of Preferences |

| | |
|---|---|
| GSP | Gross Social Product |
| GSP | Gross State Product |
| GST | General sales tax |
| GST | Goods and services tax |
| GSTPA | Global Straight Through Processing Association |
| GT | Growth triangle |
| GTC | General trading company |
| GTC | Good-till-cancelled order |
| GTC | Government Trade Commission |
| GTC | Government trading company (Vietnam) |
| GTC | Green Trade Company (Cambodia) |
| GTD | Good-till-date order |
| GTEB | Garments and Textile Export Board (Philippines) |
| GTH | Gifts, toys and houseware |
| GTP | Global Trader Scheme (Singapore) |
| GTP | Gogol Timber Project (Papua New Guinea) |
| GTS | General Telephone System |
| GTSM | GreTai Securities Market (Taiwan) |
| GTZ | German Agency for Technical Cooperation |
| GVA | Gross value added |
| GVAIO | Gross Value of Agriculture and Industrial Output |
| GVIO | Gross Value of Industrial Output |
| GWBA | Geelong Woolbrokers Association (Australia) |
| GWh | Gigawatt hour |
| GWRDC | Grapes and Wine Research and Development Corporation (Australia) |
| GZU-AF | Guangzhou Autumn Fair |
| GZU-SF | Guangzhou Spring Fair |
| 1-h | First half |
| 2-h | Second half |
| HACOVA | Hanoi Cultural Product Company |
| HACTL | Hong Kong Air Cargo Terminals Ltd |
| HAL | Hindustan Aeronautics Limited (India) |
| HARCOBANK | Haryana State Cooperative Apex Bank |
| H&S | Hospital and surgical insurance |
| Ha | Hectare |
| HBAMS | Hebei Academy of Medical Sciences (China) |
| HBFC | House Building Finance Corporation (Pakistan) |
| HBL | Habib Bank Ltd |
| HBL | Himalayan Bank Ltd (Nepal) |
| HBOAB | Hebei Oil Administration Bureau (China) |
| HBR | Harvard Business Review |
| HBS | Harvard Business School |
| HCI | Heavy and chemical industries |
| HCMC | Ho Chi Minh City |

| HCMC P&T | Ho Chi Minh City Post and Telecommunications |
| HCPEP | Hardcore Poor Eradication Program |
| HCS | Health Corporation of Singapore |
| HDB | Housing and Development Board (Singapore) |
| HDC | Home Development Centre (Sri Lanka) |
| HDFC | Home Development Finance Corporation (Sri Lanka) |
| HDFC | Housing Development Finance Corporation (India) |
| HDI | Human Development Index |
| HEC | Higher Education Council (Australia) |
| HECS | Higher Education Contribution Scheme (Australia) |
| HEPC | Handloom Export Promotion Council (India) |
| HEPR | Hunger Eradication and Poverty Reduction Program |
| HEPZA | Ho Chi Minh City Export Processing Zone Authority |
| HES | Household Expenditure Survey |
| HF | High frequency |
| HGB | Hak Guna Bangunan (Indonesia) (Right to build on the land) |
| HFC | Housing finance company |
| HGU | Hak Guna Usaha (Indonesia) (Right to conduct business on the land) |
| HIBOR | Hong Kong Interbank Offer Rate |
| HICB | Hong Kong Industrial and Commercial Bank Limited |
| HICO | Hyosung Industries Company (Korea) |
| HICOM | High Commission |
| HIECC | Ho Chi Minh City International Exhibition and Convention Centre |
| HIES | Household Income and Expenditure Survey (Pakistan) |
| HIETC | Hainan International Economic and Trade Centre (China) |
| HIGC | Home Insurance Guarantee Corporation (Philippines) |
| HIN | Holder Identification Number |
| HIP | Hubungan Industri Pancasila (Indonesia) (Pancasila Industrial Relations) |
| HIPC | Heavily indebted poor country |
| HISSBI | Himpunan Serikat Serikat Buruh Indonesia |
| HIT | Hong Kong International Terminals |
| HITC | Hanoi International Technology Centre |
| HITIC | Hainan International Trust and Investment Corp (China) |
| HIV | Human Immuno-deficiency Virus |
| HKAB | Hong Kong Association of Bankers |
| HKCC | Hong Kong Clearing Corporation |
| HKCMA | Hong Kong Capital Markets Association |
| HKD | Hong Kong dollar |
| HKECIC | Hong Kong Export Credit Insurance Corporation |
| HKELA | Hong Kong Equipment Leasing Association |
| HKFE | Hong Kong Futures Exchange |
| HKFGC | Hong Kong Futures Guarantee Corporation |

| | |
|---|---|
| HKFI | Hong Kong Federation of Industries |
| HKGCC | Hong Kong General Chamber of Commerce |
| HKH | Hindu Kush Himalayan region |
| HKIA | Hong Kong International Airport |
| HKICL | Hong Kong Interbank Clearing Ltd |
| HKIFA | Hong Kong Investment Funds Association |
| HKMA | Hong Kong Management Association |
| HKMA | Hong Kong Monetary Authority |
| HKMAO | Hong Kong and Macau Affairs Office |
| HKMC | Hong Kong Mortgage Corporation |
| HKS | Hong Kong Standard |
| HKSA | Hong Kong Society of Accountants |
| HKSAR | Hong Kong Special Administrative Region |
| HKSCC | Hong Kong Securities Clearing Company |
| HKSOA | Hong Kong Ship Owners' Association |
| HKTA | Hong Kong Tourist Association |
| HKTDC | Hong Kong Trade Development Council |
| HKTVB | Hong Kong Television and Broadcasting Company |
| HKU | Hong Kong University |
| HKUST | Hong Kong University of Science and Technology |
| HKUTA | Hong Kong Unit Trust Association |
| HLF | Himalayan Light Foundation (Nepal) |
| HLF | Hong Leong Finance Ltd |
| HLI | Highly leveraged institution |
| HLL | Hindustan Lever Limited (India) |
| HMDF | Home Mutual Development Fund (Philippines) |
| HMG | His/Her Majesty's Government |
| HMGN | His Majesty's Government of Nepal |
| HMIIC | Hongkong Macau International Investment Company |
| HMO | Health Maintenance Organization |
| HMS | PT Hanjaya Mandala Sampoerna (Indonesia) |
| HNB | Hatton National Bank (Sri Lanka) |
| HND | Higher National Diploma |
| HNW | High net worth |
| HO | Head office |
| HOD | Head of department |
| HOS | Home Ownership Scheme |
| HP | Hak Pakai (Indonesia) (Right to use the land) |
| HP | Hewlett Packard |
| HP | Hire purchase |
| HP | Horsepower |
| HPA | Hire Purchase Act |
| HPAE | High performing Asian economy |
| HPB | Health Promotion Board |
| HPCL | Hindustan Petrochemicals Limited (India) |

| | |
|---|---|
| HPH | Hak Pengusabaan Hutan (Indonesia) |
| | (Forest Exploitation Right or Concession) |
| HQ | Headquarters |
| HRA | House rent allowance |
| HRD | Human resource development |
| HRDC | Human Resources Development Council (Malaysia) |
| HRDF | Human Resources Development Fund (Malaysia) |
| HRDM | Human resource development and management |
| HRDS | Human Resource Development Service |
| HRIS | Human Resource Information System |
| HRM | Human resource management |
| HS | Harmonized System |
| HSB | Health Science Board (Singapore) |
| HSBC | Hongkong and Shanghai Banking Corporation |
| HSCCI | Hang Seng China-Affiliated Corporations Index |
| HSCEI | Hang Seng China Enterprises Index |
| HSD | Human Settlements Division |
| HSDC | Human Settlements Development Corporation (Philippines) |
| HSI | Hang Seng Index |
| HSIDC | Haryana State Industrial Development Corporation (India) |
| HSIP | Hsinchu Science-based Industrial Park (Taiwan) |
| HSN | Harmonized System of Nomenclature |
| HTP | High Technology Park |
| HTSUS | Harmonized Tariff Schedule of the United States |
| HTZ | High Technology Zone |
| HUDC | Housing and Urban Development Corporation (Singapore) |
| HUDCC | Housing and Urban Development Coordinating Council (Philippines) |
| HUF | Hindu Undivided Family (India) |
| HULRB | Housing and Land Use Regulatory Board (Philippines) |
| HWB | Heavy Water Board (India) |
| HWBC | Hanoi Water Business Company |
| HYV | High yielding variety (seed) |
| I-21 | Industry 21 |
| IA | Investment advisor |
| IA | India Airlines Ltd |
| IAA | Industrial Advancement Administration (Korea) |
| IAA | International Actuarial Association |
| IAA | International Advertising Association |
| IAAE | International Association of Agricultural Economists |
| IAAP | International Accepted Accounting Principles |
| IABA | International Association Aircraft Brokers and Agents |
| IABC | Indonesia Australia Business Council |
| IAC | Indian Airlines Corporation |
| IAC | Industrial Arbitration Court (Singapore) |

| IAC | Inter-agency Committee |
| IAC | International advisory committee |
| IAC | International Anti-counterfeiting Coalition |
| IACA | International Air Carriers Association |
| IACC | Indo American Chamber of Commerce |
| IACOMS | International Advisory Committee on Marine Sciences (UN) |
| IACP | Investment Advisory Centre of Pakistan |
| IACS | International Association of Classification Societies |
| IADB | Inter-American Development Bank |
| IADC | International Agriculture Development Centre (China) |
| IADP | Industry-wide Automation Development Program |
| IADS | International Association of Department Stores |
| IAE | Institute of Atomic Energy (China) |
| IAEA | Indian Adult Education Association |
| IAEA | International Atomic Energy Agency |
| IAEA | Institute of Asian Economic Affairs (Japan) |
| IAESTE | International Association for the Exchange of Students for Technical Experience |
| IAEVG | International Association for Education and Vocational Guidance |
| IAF | Indian Air Force |
| IAF | Industrial Adjustment Fund |
| IAF | International Aeronautical Federation |
| IAF | International Automobile Federation |
| IAG | International Auditing Guidelines |
| IAGLO | International Association of Government Labour Officials |
| IAI | Ikatan Akuntan Indonesia (Association of Indonesian Accountants) |
| IAI | Industrial Art Institute (Japan) |
| IAIABC | International Association of Industrial Accident Boards and Commissions |
| IAIB | International Association of Islamic Banks |
| IAIS | International Association of Insurance Supervisors |
| IAL | International Arbitration League |
| IAL | Investment Adviser Licence |
| IAM | Institute of Administrative Management (United Kingdom) |
| IAMCR | International Association for Mass Communication Research |
| IANC | International Airline Navigators Council |
| IAOPA | International Council of Aircraft Owners and Pilot Associations |
| IAP | Individual action plan |
| IAP | Indonesian Accounting Principles |
| IAP | International Advisory Panel |
| IAP | Internet Access Policy |
| IAPC | International Auditing Practices Committee |
| IAPCO | International Association of Professional Congress Organizers |
| IAPH | International Association of Ports and Harbours |

| IAPIP | International Association for the Protection of Industrial Property |
| IARC | Indian Agricultural Research Council |
| IARI | Indian Agricultural Research Institute |
| IARIW | International Association for Research in Income and Wealth |
| IAS | Indian Academy of Sciences |
| IAS | Indian Administrative Service |
| IAS | Innovator Assistance Scheme |
| IAS | International Accounting Standard |
| IAS | International Aircraft Standards |
| IAS | Investment Allowance Scheme |
| IASA | International Air Safety Association |
| IASB | International Accounting Standards Board |
| IASC | International Accounting Standards Committee |
| IASEA | Institute of Applied Social and Economic Research (Papua New Guinea) |
| IASLIC | Indian Association of Special Libraries and Information Centres |
| IASP | International Association of Scholarly Publishers |
| IASSIST | International Association for Social Science Information Service and Technology |
| IATA | International Air Transport Association |
| IATEP | Inter-ASEAN Technical Exchange Program |
| IAU | International Association of Universities |
| IAUP | International Association of University Presidents |
| IAWL | International Association for Water Law |
| IAWPRC | International Association for Water Pollution Research and Control |
| IBA | Indian Banks' Association |
| IBA | Industry Building Allowance (Malaysia) |
| IBA | Islamic Banking Act (Malaysia) |
| IBA | International Bankers Association |
| IBA | International Banking Act (United States) |
| IBAM | Institute of Business Administration and Management (Japan) |
| IBAS | International Bidding Assistance Scheme (Singapore) |
| IBB | Islamic Bank of Bangladesh |
| IBBM | Institut Bank-Bank Malaysia |
| IBBR | Inter-bank bid rate |
| IBC | International Beverages Company (Vietnam) |
| IBCFP | International Board of Standards and Practices of Certified Financial Planners |
| IBCL | Inter-bank call loan |
| IBDR | International Bank for Debt Redemption |
| IBE | Institute of Bioengineering |
| IBEC | International Bank for Economic Cooperation |
| IBF | Institute of Banking and Finance |
| IBF | International banking facility |

| | |
|---|---|
| IBF | International Booksellers Federation |
| IBG | Inter-bank GIRO |
| IBH-2000 | International Business Hub – 2000 Plan (Singapore) |
| IBI | Indonesian Banker Institute |
| IBIS | Inter Bank Information System |
| IBJ | Industrial Bank of Japan |
| IBK | Industrial Bank of Korea |
| IBM | International Business Machines |
| IBMP | International Brand Marketing Program |
| IBO | Inter-bank offer rate |
| IBP | International Business Park (Singapore) |
| IBRA | Indonesian Bank Restructuring Agency |
| IBRD | International Bank for Reconstruction and Development |
| IBRD | International Bank for Rural Development |
| IBRO | International Bank Research Organization |
| IBT | Industry-based training |
| IBWM | International Bureau of Weights and Measures |
| IC | Identity card |
| IC | Integrated circuit |
| IC | Insurance contract |
| IC | Investment Commission (Taiwan) |
| ICA | Industrial Coordination Act (Malaysia) |
| ICA | Institute of Chartered Accountants |
| ICA | International Cocoa Agreement |
| ICA | International Coffee Agreement |
| ICA | International Communications Association |
| ICA | International Congress of Accountants |
| ICA | International Cooperative Alliance |
| ICAA | Institute of Chartered Accountants in Australia |
| ICAC | Independent Commission Against Corruption (Hong Kong) |
| ICAC | International Civil Aviation Committee |
| ICAC | International Committee for Accounting Cooperation |
| ICAEW | Institute of Chartered Accountants in England and Wales |
| ICAF | Indochina Assistance Fund |
| ICAI | Institute of Chartered Accountants of India |
| ICAJ | Instrumentation Control Association of Japan |
| ICAN | Institute of Chartered Accountants of Nepal |
| ICAO | International Civil Aviation Organization |
| ICAR | Indian Council of Agricultural Research |
| ICAS | International Council of Aeronautical Sciences |
| ICAT | International Civil Aviation Treaty |
| ICB | Industrial Commercial Bank (Singapore) |
| ICB | Industrial Corporation of Bangladesh |
| ICB | International competitive bidding |
| ICB | Investment Corporation of Bangladesh |

| | |
|---|---|
| ICBC | Industrial and Commercial Bank of China |
| ICBC | Industrial and Commerce Bank of China (Taiwan) |
| ICBC | International Commercial Bank of China (Taiwan) |
| ICBL | International Campaign to Ban Landmines |
| ICBM | Inter-Continental Ballistic Missile |
| ICC | Indian Chamber of Commerce |
| ICC | Indian Copper Corporation |
| ICC | Indonesian Commercial Code |
| ICC | International Chamber of Commerce |
| ICC-CAPA | International Chamber of Commerce Commission on Asian and Pacific Affairs |
| ICC | International Coffee Council |
| ICC | International Criminal Court |
| ICC | Investment Coordination Committee |
| ICCA | International Council for Commercial Arbitration |
| ICCAP | International Coordinating Committee for the Accountancy Profession |
| ICCC | Independent Consumer and Competition Commission (Papua New Guinea) |
| ICCEC | Intergovernmental Council for Copper Exporting Countries |
| ICCH | International Commodities Clearing House |
| ICCO | International Cocoa Organization |
| ICCST | International Conference Centre for Science and Technology (China) |
| ICEB | Indonesian Commodity Exchange Board |
| ICEC | International Culture Exchange Centre (China) |
| ICES | Institute of Chemical and Engineering Sciences (Singapore) |
| ICETE | International Centre for Economic and Technical Exchanges (China) |
| ICF | International Compensation Fund |
| ICFA | Institute of Certified Financial Analysts |
| ICFC | Industrial and Commercial Finance Corporation |
| ICFP | Institute of Certified Financial Planners |
| ICFTU | International Confederation of Free Trade Unions |
| ICG | International Commission on Glass |
| ICGEB | International Centre for Genetic Engineering and Biotechnology |
| ICHDA | International Cooperative Housing Development Association |
| ICI | Imperial Chemical Industries Company |
| ICIA | International Credit Insurance Association |
| ICIB | Indian Commercial Information Bureau |
| ICICI | Industrial Credit and Investment Corporation of India |
| ICIF | International Cooperative Insurance Federation |
| ICIMOD | International Centre for Integrated Mountain Development (Nepal) |
| ICIS | Information Communications Institute of Singapore |

| | |
|---|---|
| ICITO | Interim Commission for the International Trade Organization |
| ICJ | International Court of Justice |
| ICL | International Computers Limited |
| ICL | International Container Line |
| ICLARM | International Centre for Living Aquatic Resources Development |
| ICM | International Currency Market |
| ICMA | Institute of Cost and Management Accountants |
| ICMF | Indian Cotton Mills Federation |
| ICO | International Coffee Organization |
| ICO-CA | International Coffee Organization – Certification Agency |
| ICO | International Commodity Organization |
| ICOP | International comparison of output and productivity |
| ICOR | Incremental Capital Output Ratio |
| ICOR | Industrial Capital Output Ratio |
| ICORC | International Committee on the Reconstruction of Cambodia |
| ICP | Indonesian crude price |
| ICP | Indonesian contractual price |
| ICP | International commodity price |
| ICP | Investment Corporation of Pakistan |
| ICPA | Institute of Certified Public Accountants |
| ICPA | International Cooperative Petroleum Association |
| ICPA | International Cotton Producers Association |
| ICPAS | Institute of Certified Public Accountants of Singapore |
| ICPC | International Cable Protection Committee |
| ICPCIC | International Committee for Promotion of Chinese Industrial Cooperation |
| ICPE | International Centre for Public Enterprises in Developing Countries |
| ICPIP | International Convention for the Protection of Industrial Property |
| ICPO | International Criminal Police Organization (INTERPOL) |
| ICORC | International Committee for Reconstruction in Cambodia |
| ICPUAE | International Conference on the Peaceful Use of Atomic Energy |
| ICQC | International Conference on Quality Control |
| ICR | Institute for Communications Research (Singapore) |
| ICRA | Investment and Credit Rating Agency of India |
| ICRB | International Cooperative Reinsurance Bureau |
| ICRC | International Committee of the Red Cross |
| ICRR | Incremental cash reserve ratio |
| ICS | Indian Chemical Society |
| ICS | Insurance Corporation of Singapore |
| ICS | International Chamber of Shipping |
| ICSC | International Communication Satellite Consortium |
| ICSI | Institute on Church and Social Issues |
| ICSID | International Centre for Settlement of Investment Disputes |
| ICSID | International Council of Societies of Industrial Design |

| ICSM | International Council for Scientific Management |
| ICT | Information and communication technology |
| ICTC | International Research, Consulting and Training Centre for Foreign Economic Relations (Vietnam) |
| ICTF | International Cocoa Traders Federation |
| ICU | Implementation and Coordination Unit (Malaysia) |
| ICVC | Indonesian Civil Code |
| ICW | International Council of Women |
| ID | Identity card |
| IDA | Infocomm Development Authority (Singapore) |
| IDA | International Development Association (World Bank) |
| IDB | Indian Development Bonds |
| IDB | Inter-dealer broker |
| IDB | Industrial Development Board |
| IDB | Industrial Development Bond |
| IDB | Industrial Development Bureau (Taiwan) |
| IDB | International Development Bank |
| IDB | Islamic Development Bank |
| IDBI | Industrial Development Bank of India |
| IDBP | Industrial Development Bank of Pakistan |
| IDC | Industrial Development Centre |
| IDC | Institutional development cell (India) |
| IDC | International Data Corp |
| IDD | International direct dial |
| IDEA | International Data Exchange Association |
| IDF | Indian Development Forum |
| IDFC | Indonesian Development Finance Company |
| IDFC | Infrastructure Development Finance Company (India) |
| IDG | International development goal |
| IDI | Industrial Development Incentives Act (Tonga) |
| IDIC | Industrial Development and Investment Commission (Taiwan) |
| IDLC | Industrial Development Leasing Company (Bangladesh) |
| IDP | Industrial development plan |
| IDP | International Development Program |
| IDR | Indonesian rupiah |
| IDR | Indonesian Depository Receipt |
| IDR | International depository receipt |
| IDRBT | Institute for Development and Research in Banking Technology |
| IDRC | International Development Research Centre |
| IDS | International dialing service |
| IE | Industrial estate |
| IE | International Enterprise (Singapore) |
| IEA | Indian Economic Association |
| IEA | Institute of Economic Affairs |
| IEA | International Economic Association |

| | |
|---|---|
| I-EAGA | Indonesia sub-region of EAGA |
| IEAT | Industrial Estate Authority of Thailand |
| IEC | International Electrotechnical Commission |
| IEC | International Exhibition City program (Singapore) |
| IECDF | International Economic Cooperation Development Fund (Taiwan) |
| IEDI | Industrial Enterprise Development Institute (Nepal) |
| IEE | Institution of Electrical Engineers |
| IEEE | Institute of Electrical and Electronics Engineers |
| IEFC | International Emergency Food Council |
| IEG | Investment Experts Group |
| IEM | Industrial Entrepreneurs Memorandum (India) |
| IEM | Instituto Emissor de Macau (Issuing Institute of Macau) |
| IEM | International express mail |
| IEOWP | Law on Industrial Enterprises Owned by the Whole People (China) |
| IEPA | International Economic Policy Association |
| IEPC | International Economic Policy Council |
| IEQ | Import Entitlement Quota (Sri Lanka) |
| IERA | International Employment Relations Association |
| IERDC | International Energy Research and Development Consortium |
| IESF | International Exchange Stabilization Fund |
| IET | Interest Equalization Tax (United States) |
| IFA | Independent financial advisor |
| IFA | International Finance Association |
| IFA | International Fiscal Association |
| IFAC | International Federation of Accountants |
| IFAD | International Fund for Agricultural Development |
| IFALPA | International Federation of Airline Pilots Associations |
| IFATCA | International Federation of Air Traffic Controllers Associations |
| IFAWPCA | International Federation of Asian and Western Pacific Contractors Associations |
| IFBPW | International Federation of Business and Professional Women |
| IFBS | Interest free banking scheme |
| IFC | International Finance Corporation |
| IFCB | Measures on the Issuance of Foreign Currency Bonds by Domestic Organizations (China) |
| IFCI | Industrial Finance Corporation of India |
| IFCT | Industrial Finance Corporation of Thailand |
| IFCTU | International Federation of Christian Trade Unions |
| IFDA | International Foundation for Development Alternatives |
| IFDAS | International Fairs Development Assistance Scheme |
| IFFCO | Indian Farmers Fertiliser Cooperative Ltd |
| IFFPA | International Federation of Film Producers Associations |
| IFG | International Factors Group |
| IFGA | International Federation of Grocers Associations |

| | |
|---|---|
| IFHP | International Federation for Housing and Planning |
| IFI | Indonesian Finance and Investment Co |
| IFI | International financial institution |
| IFIA | International Federation of Inventors Associations |
| IFIAC | International Financial Institution Advisory Commission |
| IFIAS | International Federation of Institutes of Advanced Study |
| IFIAT | International Federation of Independent Air Transport |
| IFICB | International Finance Investment and Commercial Bank (Bangladesh) |
| IFLA | International Federation of Library Associations |
| IFMA | Industrial Forest Management Agreement (Philippines) |
| IFMP | Institute of Fiscal and Monetary Policy (Japan) |
| IFORS | International Federation of Operations Research Societies |
| IFPRI | International Food Policy Research Institute |
| IFS | Indian Forest Service |
| IFS | International Financial Statistics (IMF) |
| IFS | International Foundation for Science |
| IFSE | International Federation of Stock Exchanges |
| IFSMC | International Federation of Small and Medium Companies |
| IFSMI | International Federation of Small and Medium Industries |
| IFSSO | International Federation of Social Science Organizations |
| IFSTAD | Islamic Federation for Science Technology and Development |
| IFTA | International Federation of Travel Agents |
| IFTA | International free trade area |
| IFTDO | International Federation of Training and Development Organizations |
| IFTS | Inter-bank Fund Transfer System |
| IFTUTW | International Federation of Trade Unions of Transport Workers |
| IFWFRI | Indian Fresh Water Fisheries Research Institute |
| IFWTO | International Federation of Women's Travel Organizations |
| IGA | International Grains Arrangement |
| IGAD | Inter Government Authority on Development |
| IGC | Inter Government Committee |
| IGCAR | Indira Gandhi Centre for Atomic Research (India) |
| IGCC | Inter Government Copyright Committee |
| IGDS | International Group of Department Stores |
| IGEG | Inter Government Experts Group |
| IGGI | Inter-governmental Group on Indonesia |
| IGIDR | Indira Gandhi Institute of Development Research (India) |
| IGO | Inter Government Organization |
| I-GT | Indonesia Growth Triangle Sub-region |
| IHA | International Hotel Association |
| IHA | Issuing House Association |
| IHAP | Investment Houses Association of the Philippines |
| IHC | International Help for Children |

| | |
|---|---|
| IHEP | Institute of High Energy Physics (China) |
| IHHSF | International Habitat and Human Settlements Foundation |
| IHL | Institute of Higher Learning |
| IHPC | Institute of High Performance Computing (Singapore) |
| IHS | International Humanitarian Service |
| IHT | International Herald Tribune |
| IIA | Insurance Intermediaries Act |
| IIAA | Information Industries Action Agenda (Australia) |
| IIAS | International Institute of Administrative Sciences |
| IIB | Inflation-indexed bond |
| IIB | International Investment Bank |
| IIBI | Industrial Investment Bank of India |
| IIC | Indian Investment Centre |
| IIC | Industrial Investment Credit |
| IICIA | Industrial Injury Compensation Insurance Act (Korea) |
| IIDC | Information Industries Development Centre (Australia) |
| IIE | International Institute of Economy |
| IIE | International Institute of Education |
| IIEA | International Institute of Environmental Affairs |
| IIED | International Institute for Environment and Development |
| IIF | Institute of International Finance |
| IIFT | Indian Institute of Foreign Trade |
| III | Institute for Information Industry (Sri Lanka) |
| IIIA | International Investment Insurance Association |
| IIIBE | International Institute of Islamic Banking and Economy |
| IILP | Inter-Institutional Linkages Program |
| IILS | International Institute for Labour Studies |
| IIM | Indian Institute of Metals |
| IIMARP | Institutional Investors, Mergers and Acquisitions, Research and Publication Department (India) |
| IIMD | International Institute for Management Development |
| IIMM | International Islamic Money Market |
| IIMM | Islamic Inter-bank Money Market |
| IIMT | International Institute for Management of Technology |
| IILP | Inter-Institutional Linkages Program |
| IIP | Index of Industrial Production |
| IIP | Indian Institute of Petroleum |
| IIPF | International Institute of Public Finance |
| IIPS | Institute for Industry Policy and Strategy (Vietnam) |
| IIPS | International Institute for Population Studies |
| IIR | Indian Infrastructure Report |
| IIRA | International Industrial Relations Association |
| IIRR | International Institute for Rural Reconstruction |
| IIS | Insurance Institute of Singapore |
| IISCO | Indian Iron and Steel Company |

| IISD | International Institute for Sustainable Development |
| IISE | International Institute of Social Economics |
| IISI | International Iron and Steel Institute |
| IISRP | International Institute of Synthetic Rubber Producers |
| IISS | International Institute for Strategic Studies |
| IIT | Indian Institute of Technology |
| IIT | International Investment Trust |
| IITA | International Institute of Tropical Agriculture |
| IITF | Indian International Trade Fair |
| IITMC | International Investment Trust Management Company |
| IIU | PT Inti Indorayon Utama (Indonesia) |
| IIU | International Islamic University (Malaysia) |
| IJIRA | Indian Jute Industries Research Association |
| IK | PT Indah Kiat (Indonesia) |
| IKAMA | Australian Alumni Association of Indonesia |
| IKM | Institut Vokasional Mara (Malaysia) (Mara Vocational Institute) |
| IKPN | Induk Koperasi Pergawai Negeri (Indonesia) (Civil Servants' Cooperative) |
| IKPI | Induk Koperasi Perikanan Indonesia (Indonesia) (Indonesian Fisheries Cooperative) |
| IKPPC | PT Indah Kiat Pulp and Paper Corporation (Indonesia) |
| IKTA | Izin Kerja Tenaga Asing (Indonesia) (work permit) |
| IL | Import licence |
| IL | Inclusion List |
| IL | International law |
| ILA | International Law Association |
| ILC | International Law Commission (UN) |
| ILC | Irrevocable letter of credit |
| ILO | International Labour Organization |
| ILP | Industrial Linkage Program (Malaysia) |
| ILP | Investment-linked insurance product |
| ILSSA | Institute of Labour Studies and Social Affairs |
| IMA | Indian Medical Association |
| IMA | Indian Military Academy |
| IMA | Institute of Management Accountants |
| IMA | Institute of Molecular Agrobiology (Singapore) |
| IMA | International Management Association |
| IMAR | Inner Mongolia Autonomous Region |
| IMAS | International Marine and Shipping Conference |
| IMAS | Investment Management Association of Singapore |
| IMB | Building Construction Licence (Indonesia) |
| IMC | Institute of Management Consultants |
| IMCB | Institute of Molecular and Cell Biology (Singapore) |
| IMCO | Inter-government Maritime Consultative Organization |

| IMD | Institute for Management Development |
| IME | Institute of Microelectronics (Singapore) |
| IMF | International Marketing Federation |
| IMF | International Monetary Fund |
| IMFC | International Monetary Financial Committee |
| IMFI | International Monetary Fund Institute |
| IMM | PT Indosat Multi Media (Indonesia) |
| IMM | International Monetary Market |
| IMMS | International Material Management Society |
| IMO | International Maritime Organization |
| IMO | International money order |
| IMP | Industrial Master Plan (Malaysia) |
| IMPA | International Maritime Pilots Association |
| IMPM | Institut Manajemen Prasetya Mulya (Indonesia) (Institute of Management) |
| IMR | Infant mortality rate |
| IMRE | Institute of Materials Research and Engineering (Singapore) |
| IMRO | Investment Management Regulatory Organization |
| IMS-GT | Indonesia Malaysia Singapore – Growth Triangle |
| IMT-GT | Indonesia Malaysia Thailand – Growth Triangle |
| IMTNAP | International Meteorological Telecommunication Network for Asia and the Pacific |
| INALUM | PT Indonesian Asahan Aluminum (aluminium producing company) |
| INAS | Improvement of National Accounts Statistics (Pakistan) |
| Incombank | Industrial and Commercial Bank of Vietnam |
| INCOTERMS | International Code of Trade Terms |
| Indosat | PT Indonesian Satellite Corporation |
| Indovest | Indonesian Investments International |
| INDRA | Indonesian Debt Restructuring Agency |
| INEN | Industry and energy |
| INFMMA | Indian Non-Ferrous Metals Manufacturers Association |
| INKOPAD | Induk Koperasi Angkatan Darat (Indonesia) (National Army Cooperative) |
| INKOPAL | Induk Koperasi Angkatan Laut (Indonesia) (National Navy Cooperative) |
| INKOPAU | Induk Koperasi Angkatan Udara (Indonesia) (National Air Force Cooperative) |
| INKOPPOL | Induk Koperasi Kepolisian (Indonesia) (National Police Cooperative) |
| INKOVERI | Induk Koperasi Veteran Republik Indonesia (National Veterans Cooperative) |
| INMARSAT | International Maritime Satellite Organization |
| INPADOC | International Patent Documentation Centre |
| INPFC | International North Pacific Fisheries Commission |
| Inpres | Instruksi Presiden (Indonesia) (Presidential decree) |

| | |
|---|---|
| INRA | International Natural Rubber Agreement |
| INRO | International Natural Rubber Organization |
| INS | Immigration and Naturalization Service (United States) |
| INSA | International Ship-owners Association |
| INSDOC | Indian National Scientific Documentation Centre |
| INSEAD | European Institute of Business Administration |
| INSET | In-service training (Malaysia) |
| INST | Institute of Nuclear Science and Technology (Vietnam) |
| INSTRIMPEX | China National Instruments Import and Export Corp |
| INTAN | National Institute of Public Administration (Malaysia) |
| INTELSAT | International Telecommunication Satellite Consortium |
| Intercallin | PT International Chemical Industry Company Ltd (Indonesia) |
| Intertanko | International Association of Independent Tanker Owners |
| INTLX | International telex |
| INTOSAI | International Organization of Supreme Audit Institutions |
| INTRACO | International Trading Company (Singapore) |
| INTRADE | International Trade Development Association |
| INTUC | Indian National Trade Union Congress |
| INTV | Institut National de Technologie du Vanuatu |
| I-O | Input-output |
| IOAAS | Institute of Acoustics Academia Sinica (China) |
| IOB | Indian Overseas Bank |
| IOB | Institute of Bankers |
| IOB | Insurance Ombudsman Bureau |
| IOBC | International offshore business centre |
| IOC | Immediate-or-cancel order |
| IOC | Indian Oil Corporation |
| IOC | International oil company |
| IOC | International Olympic Committee |
| IOC | International Organization of Coffee |
| IOCC | International Office of Cocoa and Chocolate |
| IOCC | International Options Clearing Corporation |
| IOCU | International Organization of Consumers Unions |
| IOD | Institute of Directors |
| IOE | Individually-owned enterprise (China) |
| IOE | International Organization of Employers |
| IOFC | Indian Ocean Fisheries Commission |
| IOFC | International offshore financial centre |
| IOI | International Ocean Institute |
| IOM | Index and options market |
| IOM | International Organization for Migration |
| IOMA | International Options Markets Association |
| IOMAC | Indian Ocean Marine Affairs Cooperation |
| IOOC | International Olive Oil Council |
| IORARC | Indian Ocean Rim Association for Regional Cooperation |

| IOS | International Organization for Standardization (ISO) |
| IOS | Investors Overseas Services |
| IOSCO | International Organization of Securities Commissions |
| IOSAI | International Organization of Supreme Audit Institutions |
| IOST | International Office of Social Tourism |
| IOU | I owe you |
| IP | Implementation plan |
| IP | Import permit |
| IP | Intellectual property |
| IPA | Indonesian Petroleum Association |
| IPA | Institute of Public Administration |
| IPA | Institute of Public Affairs |
| IPA | Integrated Program of Action |
| IPA | Investment Promotion Agency |
| IPA | Investment Promotion Authority (Papua New Guinea) |
| IPAM | Institute of Public Administration and Management (Singapore) |
| IPAP | Investment Protection Action Plan |
| IPB | Investment Promotion Board (Pakistan) |
| IPBC | Independent Public Business Corporation (Papua New Guinea) |
| IPBC | Inter-bank Participation Certificate (India) |
| IPBM | Institut Peniaga Bon Malaysia |
| IPC | Infrastructure project company |
| IPC | Investment Promotion Cell |
| IPC | International Patent Classification |
| IPC | International Petroleum Commission |
| IPCL | Indian Petrochemical Corporation Limited |
| IPCT | International Patent Cooperation Treaty |
| IPDC | Industrial Promotions and Development Company of Bangladesh |
| IPE | Institute of Political Economy (Philippines) |
| IPE | International Petroleum Exchange |
| IPEC | Independent petroleum exporting country |
| IPEC | International Program on the Elimination of Child Labour |
| IPEDA | Iuran Pembangunan Daerah (Indonesia) |
| IPEJ | Jakarta Securities Brokers Club (Indonesia) |
| IPF | International Pharmaceutical Federation |
| IPFC | Indo-Pacific Fisheries Council (UN) |
| IPI | Industrial Production Index |
| IPI | Institute of Patentees and Inventors |
| IPI | International Patent Institute |
| IPLC | International product life cycle |
| IPMA | International Primary Markets Association |
| IPMI | Institut Pengembangan Manajemen Indonesia (Indonesian Institute of Management Development) |
| IPO | Initial public offer |
| IPOS | Intellectual Property Office of Singapore |

| IPP | Independent power producer |
|-----|------|
| IPP | Investment Priorities Plan |
| IPP | Investment Promotion Plan |
| IPPM | Institut Pendidikan dan Pengembangan Manajemen (Indonesia) (Institute of Management Education and Development) |
| IPR | Institute of Plasma Research (India) |
| IPR | Intellectual property rights |
| IPRA | International Public Relations Association |
| IPRO | International Patent Research Office |
| IPS | Institute of Policy Studies (Singapore) |
| IPS | Institute of Policy Studies (Sri Lanka) |
| IPSA | International Passenger Ships Association |
| IPSFC | International Pacific Salmon Fisheries Commission |
| IPSITA | Interim Provisions on Stock Issuing and Trading Administration (China) |
| PSJ | Information Processing Society of Japan |
| IPTA | International Patent and Trademark Association |
| IPTN | Industri Pesawat Terbang Nusantara (Indonesia) (State-owned Nusantara Aircraft Industry) |
| IPU | Indek Pencemeran Udara (Malaysia) (Air pollution index) |
| IQ | Import quota |
| IQ | Intelligence quotient |
| Ir | Insinyur (Indonesian) (Engineering graduate) |
| IR | Investor relations |
| IRA | Insurance Regulatory Authority (India) |
| IRA | Interest rate agreement |
| IRA | Internal revenue allotment |
| IRAS | Inland Revenue Authority of Singapore |
| IRB | Industrial revenue bond |
| IRB | Inland Revenue Board of Malaysia |
| IRB | International Resources Bank |
| IRBI | Industrial Reconstruction Bank of India |
| IRC | Indian Road Congress |
| IRC | Internal Revenue Commission (Papua New Guinea) |
| IRC | International Red Cross |
| IRC | International revenue code |
| IRC | International Rice Commission |
| IRDA | Insurance Regulatory and Development Authority (India) |
| IRDC | International Rubber Development Committee |
| IRDP | Integrated Rural Development Program |
| IREF | International Real Estate Federation |
| IRJA | Irian Jaya/West Papua Province |
| IRMRA | Indian Rubber Manufacturers Research Association |
| IRO | International Relief Organization |
| IRR | Interest rate rules |

| IRR | Internal rate of return |
| IRRA | Industrial Relations Research Association |
| IRRDB | International Rubber Research and Development Board |
| IRRI | International Rice Research Institute |
| IRS | Interest rate swap |
| IRS | Interest rebate scheme (Sri Lanka) |
| IRS | Internal Revenue Service (United States) |
| IRSS | Indian Railway Standard Specification |
| ISA | International Seabed Authority |
| ISA | International Standardization Association |
| ISA | International Standards on Auditing |
| ISA | International Sugar Agreement |
| ISBI | International Savings Banks Institute |
| ISBN | International Standard Book Number |
| ISC | Industrial Services Centre (Nepal) |
| ISC | Insurance and Superannuation Commission |
| ISC | International Statistical Classification |
| ISC | International Sugar Council |
| ISCAS | Institute of Software of Chinese Academy of Science |
| ISCO | International Standard Classification of Occupations |
| ISCS | International Satellite Communication Society |
| ISD | Inspection and Supervision Department |
| ISD | Internal Security Department |
| ISD | Investment Services Directive (EU) |
| ISDA | International Swap and Derivatives Association |
| ISDB | Islam Development Bank |
| ISDN | Integrated Service Digital Network |
| ISE | Islamabad Stock Exchange (Pakistan) |
| ISEAS | Institute of Southeast Asian Studies |
| ISEC | International Securities and Exchange Commission |
| ISF | Improvement Services Fund (Malaysia) |
| ISF | International Shipping Federation |
| ISI | Indian Standards Institute |
| ISI | PT Indomobil Suzuki International (Indonesia) |
| ISI | International Statistical Institute |
| ISIC | International Standard Industrial Classification |
| ISIN | International Securities Identification Numbers |
| ISIS | Institute of Strategic and International Studies (Malaysia) |
| ISLLSS | International Society for Labour Law and Social Security |
| ISMA | International Securities Market Association |
| ISO | International Satellite Organization |
| ISO | International Standards Organization |
| ISO | International Sugar Organization |
| ISOCARP | International Society for City and Regional Planners |
| ISP | Internet service provider |

| ISQAP | Industrial Standards and Quality Assurance Program |
| ISQC | Indian Society for Quality Control |
| ISR | Indonesian Standard Rubber Company |
| ISRA | International Shipbuilding Research Association |
| ISRO | Indian Space Research Organization |
| ISS | Industrial standard specification |
| ISS | Institute of Systems Science (Singapore) |
| ISS | Institutional Settlement Service |
| ISSA | International Society of Securities Administrators |
| ISSC | International Shipping Service Centre (China) |
| ISSC | International Social Science Council |
| ISSCT | International Society for Sugar Cane Technologies |
| ISSN | International Standard Serial Number |
| ISTF | International Society of Tropical Foresters |
| ISTIC | Institute of Science and Technical Information of China |
| ISTIH | Institute of Science and Technical Information of Hunan (China) |
| ISTIS | Institute of Science and Technical Information of Shanghai (China) |
| IT | Information technology |
| IT2000 | Information Technology Plan 2000 |
| ITA | Indian Trust Act |
| ITA | Information Technology Agreement |
| ITA | International Textile Agreement |
| ITA | International Tin Agreement |
| ITA | International Trade Act (Korea) |
| ITA | International Trade Administration |
| ITA | Investment Tax Allowance |
| ITAF | Industrial Training Assistance Fund (Malaysia) |
| ITB | Industrial Training Board |
| ITB | Invitation to bid |
| ITC | Indian Tobacco Company |
| ITC | International Telecommunication Convention |
| ITC | International Tea Commission (UN) |
| ITC | International Tin Council |
| ITC | International Trade Charter |
| ITDC | Indian Tourist Development Corporation |
| ITDI | Industrial Technology Development Institute |
| ITE | Institute of Technical Education (Singapore) |
| ITE | International Telephone Exchange |
| ITEC | India Technical and Economic Cooperation |
| ITG | International Trade Group |
| ITGWU | Industrial Transport and General Workers' Union (Sri Lanka) |
| ITH | Income tax holiday |
| ITI | Indian Telephone Industries Ltd |
| ITI | Industrial Training Institute (Malaysia) |

| ITIC | International Trust and Investment Corporation |
| ITJ | International Telecommunication of Japan |
| ITL | Income Tax Law |
| ITLFE | Income Tax Law on Foreign Enterprises (China) |
| ITL | Ifira Trust Limited (Vanuatu) |
| ITLI | Income Tax Law on Individuals (China) |
| ITM | In the money |
| ITM | Institut Teknologi MARA (Malaysia) (MARA Institute of Technology) |
| ITM | International trade mark |
| ITMF | International Textile Manufacturers Federation |
| ITN | Independent Television News (Sri Lanka) |
| ITO | International Trade Organization |
| ITO | International Travel Organization |
| ITP | Information Technology Park (Bangalore) |
| ITPO | Indian Trade Promotion Organization |
| ITM | Integrated ticketing machine |
| ITRI | International Trade Research Institute |
| ITSA | Insolvency and Trustee Service Australia |
| ITT | Information technology and telecommunication |
| ITTO | International Tropical Timber Organization |
| ITU | International Telecommunication Union (UN) |
| IUAA | International Union of Advertisers Association |
| IUAI | International Union of Aviation Insurers |
| IUCAB | International Union of Commercial Agents and Brokers |
| IUCN | International Union for Conservation of Nature and Natural Resources |
| IUCP | Investment and Underwriting Corporation of Philippines |
| IUKL | Izin Usaha Ketenaga-Listrikan (Indonesia) (Permit for Electrical Power Business) |
| IUMI | International Union of Marine Insurance |
| IUOTO | International Union of Official Travel Organizations |
| IUT | Permanent Operating Licence (Indonesia) |
| IVB | Indovina Bank |
| IVR | Interactive voice response |
| IWT | Inland Water Transport (Myanmar) |
| IZ | Industrial zone |
| JAA | Japan Aeronautic Association |
| JAACE | Japan Association of Automatic Control Engineers |
| JABOTABEK | Jakarta, Bogor, Tanerang, Bekasi (Indonesia) |
| JACA | Japan Air Cleaning Association |
| JACCP | Japan-ASEAN Cooperation Promotion Program |
| JACRAN | Japanese Committee for Radio Aids to Navigation |
| JADF | Japan Air Defence Force |
| JAE | Japan Aero-Electronic Industry Company |

| | |
|---|---|
| JAL | Japan Airlines Ltd |
| JAEC | Japan Atomic Energy Commission |
| JAEIP | Japan Atomic Energy Insurance Pool |
| JAEP | Japan ASEAN Exchange Program |
| JAERI | Japan Atomic Energy Research Institute |
| JAF | Japan Automobile Federation |
| JAIDO | Japan International Development Organization |
| JAIF | Japan Atomic Industrial Forum |
| JAK | Jammu and Kashmir |
| JAL | Japan Airlines |
| JAMAIA | Japan Motor Articles Industry Association |
| Jamsostek | Employees' Social Security Scheme (Indonesia) |
| JAPCO | Japan Atomic Power Company |
| JAPEX | Japan Petroleum Exploration Company |
| JAPIA | Japan Auto Parts Industry Association |
| JAPIT | Japan Association for Promotion of International Trade |
| JARRP | Japan Association for Radiation Research on Polymers |
| JAS | Japan Agricultural Standard |
| JASDEC | Japan Securities Depository Centre |
| JASS | Japan Architectural Standard Specifications |
| JATI | Japan Association for Technical Information |
| JATS | Jakarta Automated Trading System |
| JBA | Japan Business Automation Company |
| JBIC | Japan Bank for International Cooperation |
| JBP | Japan Brazil Pulp Company |
| JBRI | Japan Bond Research Institute |
| JCA | Japan Container Association |
| JCB | Japan Credit Bureau |
| JCBM | Japanese Corporate Bond Market |
| JCC | Joint Consultative Committee |
| JCC | Joint Cooperation Committee |
| JCCI | Japanese Chamber of Commerce and Industry |
| JCCIF | Japanese Chamber of Commerce and Industry Foundation |
| JCE | Joint cooperative enterprise |
| JCEA | Japan Chemicals Exporters Association |
| JCED | Japan Committee for Economic Development |
| JCFA | Japan Chemical Fibres Association |
| JCFC | Japan Chemical Fibres Company |
| JCFIA | Japan Canned Food Inspection Association |
| JCG | Japan Credit Guarantee Company |
| JCI | Jakarta Composite Index |
| JCI | Japan Chemical Industrial Company |
| JCI | Jute Corporation of India |
| JCIA | Japan Chemicals Importers Association |
| JCIF | Japan Centre for International Finance |

| | |
|---|---|
| JCIS | Japan Camera Industrial Standard |
| JCL | Japan Confederation of Labour |
| JCM | Joint Consultative Meeting |
| JCT | Jaya Container Terminal (Sri Lanka) |
| JCTEA | Japan Cotton Textile Exporters Association |
| JCMRE | Joint Committee on Marine Resource Management |
| JCRA | Japan Credit Rating Agency |
| JDA | Japan Defence Agency |
| JDB | Japan Development Bank |
| JDR | Japanese depository receipt |
| JEAC | Japan Electric Association Code |
| JEAG | Japan Electric Association Guide |
| JEC | Japan Engineering Consultant Company |
| JEC | Japan Electrotechnical Committee |
| JECC | Japan Electronic Computer Company |
| JED | Japan Engineering Development Company |
| JEDB | Janatha Estate Development Board (Sri Lanka) |
| JEIA | Japan Electronic Industries Association |
| JEIA | Joint export and import agency |
| JEIC | Japan Electronic Instrument Company |
| JEIDA | Japan Electronic Industry Development Association |
| JEL | Japan Electric Lamp Manufacturers Association Standard |
| JEM | Japan Electrical Manufacturers Association Standard |
| JEMA | Japan Electrical Manufacturers Association |
| JEMC | Janak Education Materials Centre (Nepal) |
| JEOL | Japan Electron Optics Laboratory Company |
| JEPIA | Japan Electronic Parts Industries Association |
| JERC | Japan Economic Research Centre |
| JERI | Japan Economic Research Institute |
| JES | Japan Engineering Standards |
| JESC | Japan Electronic Standardisation Committee |
| JESRA | Japan Engineering Standards of Radiation Apparatus |
| JETCO | Joint Electronic Teller Services Company (Hong Kong) |
| JETDC | Jilin Province Economy and Trade Development Co (China) |
| JETRO | Japan External Trade Organization |
| JENGKA | Pahang North Development Corporation (Malaysia) |
| JFIF | Jardine Fleming Indonesia Fund |
| JFN | Jardine Fleming Nusantara Index (Indonesia) |
| JFNF | PT Jardine Fleming Nusantara Finance (Indonesia) |
| JFPR | Japan Fund for Poverty Reduction |
| JFRCA | Japan Fisheries Resources Conservation Association |
| JFSEO | Japan Federation of Small Enterprise Organization |
| JFTC | Japan Foreign Trade Council |
| JGB | Japan Government Bond |
| JGC | Japan Gasoline Company |

| JHS | Japan Heat Treatment Standard |
| JIB | Journal of the Institute of Bankers |
| JIBICO | Japan International Bank and Investment Company |
| JIBOR | Jakarta Interbank Offer Rate |
| JIBS | Journal of International Business Studies |
| JIC | Jakarta Investors Club |
| JICA | Japan International Cooperation Agency |
| JICPA | Japan Institute of Certified Public Accountant |
| JICST | Japan Information Centre for Science and Technology |
| JIDA | Japan Industrial Designers Association |
| JIDC | Japan Industrial Development Corporation |
| JIEE | Japan Institute of Electrical Engineers |
| JIH | PT Jakarta International Hotel |
| JIMA | Japan Industrial Management Association |
| JINAS | Jiangnan Shipyard (Shanghai, China) |
| JIOC | Japan Indonesia Oil Company |
| JIRA | Japan Industry Association of Radiation Apparatus |
| JIS | Japan Industrial Standard |
| JISC | Japan Industrial Standard Committee |
| JISEA | Japan Iron and Steel Exporters Association |
| JISF | Japan Iron and Steel Federation |
| JIT | Just in time |
| JITIC | Jilin International Trust and Investment Corp (China) |
| JITPA | Japan International Trade Promotion Association |
| JIVA | Japan Industrial Vehicles Association |
| JIVAS | Japan Industrial Vehicles Association Standard |
| JIWWA | Japan Industrial Work Water Association |
| JJDB | Jingji Daobao (China) (Economic Reporter) |
| JJFSC | Jin Jiang Foreign Service Company (China) |
| JJRB | Jingji Ribao (China) (Economic Daily) |
| JKR | Jabatan Kerja Raya (Malaysia) (Public Works Department) |
| JKSE | Jakarta Stock Exchange |
| JLG | Joint Liaison Group between China and Britain (Hong Kong) |
| JLPA | Japan Liquefied Petroleum Association |
| JMA | Japan Management Association |
| JMA | Japan Meteorological Agency |
| JMAS | Japan Precision Measuring Instrument Association Standard |
| JMC | Joint Management Committee |
| JMC | Jute Marketing Corporation (Pakistan) |
| JMEA | Japan Machinery Exporters Association |
| JMI | Jamnadas Madhavji International (India) |
| JMI | Japan Machinery and Metals Inspection Institute |
| JMM | Japan Merchant Marine |
| JMM | Joint Ministerial Meeting |
| JMRPA | Japan Marine Resources Protection Association |

| | |
|---|---|
| JMD | Japan Marine Standards |
| JMSDF | Japan Maritime Self Defence Force |
| JMSTC | Japan Marine Science and Technology Centre |
| JMTBA | Japan Machine Tool Builders Association |
| JMTTA | Japan Machine Tools Trade Association |
| JNCP | Jawaharlal Nehru Container Port (India) |
| JNOC | Japan National Oil Corporation |
| JNR | Japanese National Railway |
| JNTA | Japan National Tourist Association |
| JOCV | Japan Overseas Cooperation Volunteer |
| JODC | Japan Oil Development Company |
| JODC | Japan Overseas Development Corporation |
| JOHS | Japan Oil Hydraulic Standard |
| JOM | Japan Offshore Market |
| JPA | Japan Pneumatics Association |
| JPA | Johor Port Authority (Malaysia) |
| JPAS | Japan Pneumatics Association Standards |
| JPBCC | Japan Pakistan Business Cooperation Committee |
| JPC | Japan Patent Classification |
| JPC | Joint Planning Committee |
| JPDC | Japan Petroleum Development Corporation |
| JPEPB | Jiangsu Provincial Electric Power Bureau (China) |
| JPI | Japan Petroleum Institute |
| JPMC | Joint Planning and Management Committee |
| JP | Justice of the Peace |
| JPPH | Jabatan Penilaian dan Pengurusan Harta Benda (Malaysia) (Valuation and Property Management Department) |
| JPS | Japan Painting Standard |
| JPS | Social Safety Network Program (Indonesia) |
| JPY | Japanese yen |
| JSA | Japan Ship-owners Association |
| JSA | Japan Standards Association |
| JSAC | Jute Sector Adjustment Credit (Bangladesh) |
| JSAE | Japan Society of Automotive Engineering |
| JSAS | Japan Safety Appliances Association Standard |
| JSB | Joint stock bank (Vietnam) |
| JSCC | Japan Securities Clearing Corporation |
| JSDA | Japan Securities Dealers Association |
| JSDF | Japan Self Defence Forces |
| JSDF | Japan Social Development Fund |
| JSEA | Japan Ship Exporters Association |
| JSG | Joint Study Group |
| JSIA | Japan Software Industry Association |
| JSID | Japan Society for International Development |
| JSIST | Japan Singapore Institute of Software Technology |

| JSQS | Japan Shipbuilding Quality Standard |
| JSR | Japan Synthetic Rubber Company |
| JSSA | Japan Stainless Steel Association |
| JSSF | Japan Society of Scientific Fisheries |
| JSTC | Joint Science and Technology Committee |
| JSW | Japan Steel Works Company |
| JSX | Jakarta Stock Exchange |
| JTA | Joint traffic agreement |
| JTB | Jabatan Telekom Brunei |
| JTC | Jurong Town Corporation (Singapore) |
| JTCI | JTC International (Singapore) |
| JTCJP | Joint Trading Corporation of Jiangsu Province (China) |
| JTIA | Japan Textiles Imports Association |
| JTM | Jabatan Telecom Malaysia |
| JUB | Amount of circulating money (Indonesian acronym) |
| JUSE | Japanese Union of Scientists and Engineers |
| JV | Joint venture |
| JVC | Joint venture company |
| JVPC | Japan Vietnam Petroleum Company |
| JWIF | Japan Wool Products Inspection Institute Foundation |
| JWWA | Japan Water Works Association |
| JXEC | Jiangxi Provincial Economic Commission (China) |
| KABC | Korea Audit Bureau of Circulation |
| KAC | Kawasaki Aircraft Company (Japan) |
| KADA | Kemubu Agricultural Development Authority (Malaysia) |
| KADIN | Kamar Dagang dan Industri Indonesia (Indonesian Chamber of Commerce and Industry) |
| KAFTZ | Kandala Free Trade Zone (India) |
| KAIGIN | Nihon Kaihatsu Ginko (Japan) |
| KAIST | Korea Advanced Institute of Science and Technology |
| KAIT | Korea Academy of Industrial Technology |
| KAL | Korean Air Lines |
| KAMCO | Korea Asset Management Company |
| KANUPP | Karachi Nuclear Power Plant |
| KATS | KLOFFE Automated Trading System (Malaysia) |
| KB | Commercial bank (Philippines) |
| KBE | Knowledge-based economy |
| KBI | Key budget inclusion |
| Kbs | Kilobits per second |
| KBS | Korean Broadcasting System |
| KCAB | Korea Commercial Arbitration Board |
| KCCI | Korea Chamber of Commerce and Industry |
| KCNA | Korean Central News Agency |
| KCRC | Kowloon Canton Railways Corporation |
| KCT | Kelang Container Terminal Berhad (Malaysia) |

| | |
|---|---|
| KCTU | Korea Confederation of Trade Unions |
| KD | Knocked down |
| KDA | Khulna Development Authority (Bangladesh) |
| KDB | Korean Development Bank |
| KDD | Kokusai Denshin Denwa (Japan) |
| KDEI | PT Kliring Deposit Efek Indonesia |
| | (Indonesian Securities Clearing and Depository Corporation) |
| KDFC | Korea Development Finance Corporation |
| KDI | Korean Development Institute |
| KDIC | Korea Deposit Insurance Corporation |
| KDLC | Korea Development Leasing Company |
| KEB | Korea Exchange Bank |
| KEC | Kanagawa Electric Company (Japan) |
| KEC | Kokusai Electric Company (Japan) |
| KECT | Korea Emerging Companies Trust |
| KEDA | Kedah State Regional Development Authority (Malaysia) |
| KEDO | Korea Peninsula Energy Development Organization |
| KEF | Korea Employers Federation |
| KEI | Korea Economic Institute |
| KEI | Kokusai Electronic Industry Company |
| KEPCO | Kansai Electric Power Company (Japan) |
| KEPCO | Korea Electric Power Corporation |
| Kepres | Keputusan Presiden (Indonesia) (Presidential decision) |
| KEJORA | Johor Tenggara State Development Corporation (Malaysia) |
| KEPZ | Karachi Export Processing Zone |
| KEPZ | Katunayake Export Processing Zone (Sri Lanka) |
| KEPZ | Kaohsiung Export Processing Zone (Taiwan) |
| KEPZA | Kaohsiung Export Processing Zone Administration |
| KERI | Korea Economic Research Institute |
| KESC | Karachi Electric Supply Corporation |
| KESEDAR | South Kelantan State Development Corporation (Malaysia) |
| KEW | Kawaguchi Electric Works Company (Japan) |
| KEXIM | Korea Export Import Bank |
| KFB | Korea Federation of Banks |
| KFB | Korea First Bank |
| KFSB | Korea Federation of Small Business |
| KFTA | Korea Foreign Trade Association |
| KFTC | Korea Financial Telecommunications and Clearings Institution |
| KG | Kanematsu Gosho Ltd (Japan) |
| KGE | Knowledge-driven global economy |
| KgEPZ | Koggala Export Processing Zone (Sri Lanka) |
| KHB | Korea Housing Bank |
| KHI | Kawasaki Heavy Industries (Japan) |
| KHIC | Korea Heavy Industries Corporation |
| KHIDI | Kunming Hydroelectric Investigation and Design Institute (China) |

| | |
|---|---|
| KIC | Korea Investment Corporation |
| KICA | Korea International Cooperation Agency |
| KIDC | Korea Industry Development Corporation |
| KIEP | Korea Institute for International Economic Policy |
| KIET | Korea Institute for Industrial Economics and Trade |
| KIF | Korea Institute of Finance |
| KIHSA | Korean Institute of Health and Social Affairs |
| KIK | Kredit Investasi Kecil (Indonesia) (Small investment loan) |
| KILC | Korea Industrial Leasing Company |
| KIPF | Korea Institute of Public Finance |
| KIPO | Korea Industrial Property Office |
| KISC | Korea Investment Services Centre |
| KIT | Korea International Trust |
| KITI | Korea Institution of Trade Inspection |
| KITIC | Kanghua International Trust and Investment Corp (China) |
| KK | Kabushiki Kaisha (Japan) (Limited liability company) |
| KKB | Kesepakatan Kerja Bersama (Indonesia) (Collective labour agreement) |
| KKIP | Kota Kinabalu Industrial Park (Malaysia) |
| KKMB | Komplek Kewangan Malaysia Berhad |
| KKU | Khon Kaen University (Thailand) |
| KKUD | Kredit Kepada Koperasi Unit Desa (Indonesia) (Credit to Rural Unit Cooperatives) |
| KLACH | Kuala Lumpur Automatic Clearing House |
| KLBI | Bank Indonesia Liquidity Credit |
| KLCC | Kuala Lumpur City Centre |
| KLCCH | Kuala Lumpur Commodity Clearing House |
| KLCE | Kuala Lumpur Commodity Exchange |
| KLCI | Kuala Lumpur Stock Exchange Composite Index |
| KLH | Ministry of Population and the Environment (Indonesia) |
| KLI | Korea Life Insurance |
| KLIA | Kuala Lumpur International Airport |
| KLIBOR | Kuala Lumpur interbank offer rate |
| KLM | Koninklijke Luchtvaart Mastszhappij (Netherlands) |
| KLOFFE | Kuala Lumpur Options and Financial Futures Exchange |
| KLSE | Kuala Lumpur Stock Exchange |
| KLSE LINK | KLSE Listing Information Network |
| KMKP | Kredit Modal Kerja (Indonesia) (Permanent working capital loan) |
| KMO | Kobe Marine Observatory |
| KMRI | Kunming Metallurgy Research Institute (China) |
| KMT | Kuomintang (Nationalist Party) |
| KMU | Kilusang Mayo Uno (Philippine trade union) |
| KNP | Korean Netizen Profile |
| KNTC | Korea National Tourism Corporation |

| KOAMI | Korea Association of Machinery Industry |
| KOBACO | Korea Broadcasting Advertising Corporation |
| KOCO | Korea Oil Corporation |
| KODC | Korea Overseas Development Corporation |
| KOEX | Korea Exhibition Centre |
| KOGIN | Nihon Kogyo Ginko (Japan) |
| KOPEC | Korea National Committee for Pacific Economic Cooperation |
| Kopemkei | Koperasi Pemodal Pemodal Kecil Indonesia (Small Investors Cooperative of Indonesia) |
| KOPIE | Korea Official Pool of International Economists |
| KORPRI | Korps Pegawai Republik Indonesia (Indonesian Civil Servants Corps) |
| KOSCOM | Korea Securities Computer Corporation |
| KOSDAQ | Korea Securities Dealers' Association Automated Quotation |
| KOSPI | Korea Composite Stock Price Index |
| Kostrad | Army Strategic Command (Indonesia) |
| KOTRA | Korea Trade Promotion Corporation |
| Kp | Kip |
| KPA | Key production area |
| KPC | Korea Productivity Centre |
| KPEI | Indonesian Stock Clearing and Guarantee Corporation |
| KPH | Kilometre per hour |
| KPR | Housing credit provided by Indonesian banks |
| KRA | Key rural area |
| KRB | Korea Reconstruction Bank |
| KRDL | Kent Ridge Digital Labs (Singapore) |
| KRW | Korean won |
| KS | Korean Standard |
| KSC | Kansai Steel Corporation (Japan) |
| KSC | Korea Steel Chemical Corporation |
| KSCT | Korea Small Companies Trust |
| KSDA | Korea Securities Dealers Association |
| KSDC | Korea Securities Depository Corporation |
| KSE | Karachi Stock Exchange |
| KSE | Korea Stock Exchange |
| KSEI | Indonesian Stock Central Custodian Corporation |
| KSFC | Korea Securities Finance Corporation |
| KSL | Kobe Steel Ltd (Japan) |
| KSO | "Joint operating scheme" in telecommunications (Indonesia) |
| KSS | Krishi Smabaya Samity (Bangladesh) (Farmers' Cooperative Society) |
| KSTDC | Karnataka State Tourism Development Corporation (India) |
| KT | Korea Trust |
| KT | Korea Telecom |
| KTB | Krung Thai Bank |

| | |
|---|---|
| KTDB | Kinh Te Va Du Bao (Vietnam) (Economy and Forecasting Review) |
| KTI | Kanematsu Trading Indonesia |
| KTM | Kretapi Tanah Melayu (Malaysian Railway) |
| KTT | Krung Thai Thanakit PCL |
| KUD | Kooperasa Unit Desa (Indonesia) (Village cooperative unit) |
| KUK | Kredit Usaha Kecil (Indonesia) (Small scale credit program) |
| KUKMI | Indonesian Small and Medium Business Association |
| KULBER | KLSE Bernama Real-time Information Services |
| Kupedes | Kredit Umum Pedesaan (Indonesia) (General purpose village loan) |
| KUT | Kredit Usaha Tani (Indonesia) (General lending scheme for farmers) |
| KV | Kilovolt |
| KVID | Khadi and Village Industries Board (India) |
| KW | Kilowatt |
| KWh | Kilowatt hour |
| Kye | Kye market (a rotating credit club in Korea) |
| LA | Letter of authority |
| LA | Licensed Accountant (Malaysia) |
| LAB | Local area bank |
| LABOR | Labuan interbank offer rate |
| LAF | Liquidity Adjustment Facility |
| LAN | Local Area Network |
| Lao PDR | Lao People's Democratic Republic |
| LAR | Liquidity assets requirement ratio |
| LARGE | Legal Adjustments and Reforms for Globalizing the Economy (India) |
| LAS | Leasing Association of Singapore |
| LAUA | Lloyd's Aviation Underwriters Association |
| LAW | Liquidity Adjustment Window |
| LBO | Leveraged buy-out |
| LBP | Land Bank of the Philippines |
| LBS | Lead Bank Scheme (India) |
| LBS | London Business School |
| LC | Letter of credit |
| LCBO | Large complex banking organization |
| LCC | London Chamber of Commerce |
| LCCI | London Chamber of Commerce Institute |
| LCE | London Commodity Exchange |
| LCE | Lower Certificate of Examination |
| LCD | Liquid crystal display |
| LCF | Liquidity conversion factor |
| LCP | Loan classification and provisioning |
| LCP | Low cost production |
| LDA | Less developed area |

| | |
|---|---|
| LDAL | Labour Disputes Adjustment Law (Korea) |
| LDC | Less developed country |
| LDC | Least developed country |
| LDC | Local development council |
| LDI | Local direct investment |
| LDIP | Local Development Investment Program |
| LDO | Land Development Ordinance (Sri Lanka) |
| LDO | Liquor Distillery Organization (Thailand) |
| LDP | Liberal Democratic Party (Japan) |
| LDP | Local development plan |
| LDR | Loan deposit ratio |
| LDR | London depository receipt |
| LDTC | Licensed deposit taking company |
| LEAP | Local Enterprise Accounting Program (Singapore) |
| Leaprodexim | Vietnam National Leather and Footwear Corporation |
| LECO | Lanka Electricity Company (Sri Lanka) |
| LECP | Local Enterprise Computerization Program (Singapore) |
| LECP | Local Enterprise E-Commerce Program (Singapore) |
| LEFS | Local Enterprise Finance Scheme (Singapore) |
| Lemhannas | National Resilience Institute (Indonesia) |
| LEPO | Low Exercise Price Option (Australia) |
| LERMS | Liberalized Exchange Rate Management System (India) |
| LESCO | Lao Employment Services Company |
| LETAS | Local Enterprise Technical Assistance Scheme |
| LEUC | Local Enterprise Upgrading Centre |
| LFAR | Long form accountant's report |
| LFAR | Long form audit report |
| LFETO | Leveraged Foreign Exchange Trading Ordinance (Hong Kong) |
| LFHPT | Loan Fund for Hawkers and Petty Traders |
| LFI | Law on Foreign Investment |
| LFPR | Labour force participation rate |
| LFS | Labour Force Survey |
| LFTC | Liaoning Foreign Trade Corporation (China) |
| LG | Letter of guarantee |
| LG | Local government |
| LGC | Local Government Council |
| LGFM | London Grain Futures Market |
| LGS | Liquid and government securities |
| LGS | Liquid assets and government securities |
| LGC | Local government code |
| LGP | Local government plan |
| LGU | Local government unit |
| LHS | Left hand side |
| LIA | Life Insurance Association (Singapore) |
| LIAC | Local Investment Appraisal Committee (Sri Lanka) |

| LIAM | Life Insurance Association of Malaysia |
| LIBID | London Interbank Bid Rate |
| LIBOR | London Interbank Offer Rate |
| LIC | Life Insurance Company (India) |
| LICOI | Life Insurance Corporation of India |
| LIDAS | Licensing Development Assistance Scheme (Singapore) |
| LIFE | Local Initiative Facility for the Urban Environment |
| LIFE | London International Futures Exchange |
| LIFFE | London International Financial Futures Exchange |
| LIFFOE | London International Financial Futures and Options Exchange |
| LIFO | Last in first out |
| LIIP | Laguna International Industrial Park (Philippines) |
| LILAMA | Vietnam Machinery Erection Corporation |
| LILO | Last in last out |
| LIMA | Langkawi International Maritime and Aerospace Exhibition |
| LIOFC | Labuan International Offshore Financial Centre |
| LIP | Life insurance policy |
| LIPCO | Lao Investment Promotion Company |
| LIPI | Indonesian Council of Sciences (or Indonesian Institute of Science) |
| LIT | Laboratories for Information Technology (Singapore) |
| LITTT | Luoyang Institute of Tracking and Telecommunications Technology (China) |
| LIUP | Local Industry Upgrading Program (Singapore) |
| LKP | Clearing and guarantee institution (Indonesia) |
| LKPM | Report on Domestic and Foreign Capital Investment Activities (Indonesia) |
| LKPP | Clearing, Settlement and Depository Institution (Indonesia) |
| LLB | Bachelor of Law |
| LLCA | Limited Liability Company Act (Japan) |
| LLD | Doctor of Law |
| LLDA | Laguna Lake Development Authority (Philippines) |
| LLG | Local Level Government |
| LLL (L3) | Legal lending limit |
| LLL | Life-long learning |
| LLR | Lender of last resort |
| LMB | Lands Management Bureau (Philippines) |
| LMCL | Labour Management Council Law (Korea) |
| LMH | Liquidity management house |
| LMI | Local market instrument |
| LMIS | Labour market information system |
| LMLC | Lakas Manggagawa Labour Centre (Philippines) |
| LME | London Metal Exchange |
| LMFM | London Meat Futures Exchange |
| LMI | Labour market information |

| | |
|---|---|
| LMK | Lembaga Musyawarah Kota (Indonesia) (City Consensus Agency) |
| LMM | Locally manufactured machinery |
| LMP | Labour market policy |
| LMR | Labour management relations |
| LMW | Licensed Manufacturing Warehouse (Malaysia) |
| LNCD | Long-term negotiable certificate of deposit |
| LNG | Liquefied natural gas |
| LOA | Leave of absence |
| LOBATA | Labuan Offshore Business Activity Tax Act |
| LOC | Letter of credit |
| LOFSA | Labuan Offshore Financial Services Authority |
| LOGODEV | Local Government Development Foundation (Philippines) |
| LOI | Letter of instruction |
| LOI | Letter of intent |
| LOLPA | Labuan Offshore Limited Partnership Act |
| LOLR | Lender of last resort |
| Lonsum | London Sumatra Indonesia (Plantation company in Indonesia) |
| LOS | Letter of support |
| LOST | Law of the Sea Treaty |
| LOSIA | Labuan Offshore Securities Industry Act |
| LOTA | Labuan Offshore Trust Act |
| Loteco | Long Binh Techno Park Development Company (Vietnam) |
| LPG | Liquefied petroleum gas |
| LPM | Lines per minute |
| LPP | Settlement and custody institution (Indonesia) |
| LPSM | Self-help development institution (Indonesia) |
| LR | Lloyd's Register (Shipping) |
| LRC | Law Reform Commission of Hong Kong |
| LRC | Land Reform Commission (Sri Lanka) |
| LRO | Licensing and Regulation Office |
| LRO | Local representative office |
| LRP | Long range planning |
| LRSC | Land Reform Savings Corporation (Nepal) |
| LRT | Light Rail Transit |
| LRTA | Light Rail Transit Authority (Philippines) |
| LSE | Lahore Stock Exchange (Pakistan) |
| LSE | London School of Economics |
| LSE | London Stock Exchange |
| LSFO | Low sulphur fuel oil |
| LSL | Labour Standards Law (Korea) |
| LSL | Labour Standards Law (Taiwan) |
| LSR | Loan-to-security ratio |
| LSRS | Law Source Retrieving System (Taiwan) |
| LTA | Land Transport Authority (Singapore) |

| | |
|---|---|
| LTAB | Transaction statement (stock exchange) (Indonesia) |
| LTCA | Labuan Trust Companies Act |
| LTCB | Long Term Credit Bank (Japan) |
| LTCM | Long Term Capital Management |
| LTFRB | Land Transportation Franchising and Regulatory Board (Philippines) |
| LTO | Long term operation |
| LTOM | London Traded Options Market |
| LTP | Long term plan |
| LTPC | Lao Trade Promotion Centre |
| LTPLR | Long term prime lending rate |
| LTSB | London Trustee Savings Bank |
| LTVR | Loan-to-value ratio |
| LUA | Life Underwriters' Association (Singapore) |
| LUAEE | Loosely United ASEAN Economic Entity |
| LUMO | Land Use Mapping Office (Cambodia) |
| LURC | Land Use Rights Certificate (Vietnam) |
| LURO | Land Use Rights Owner (Vietnam) |
| LUTH | Lembaga Urusan dan Tabung Haji |
| LWUA | Local Waterworks Utilities Administration (Philippines) |
| M1 | Mobile One (Singapore) |
| M21 | Manpower 21 (Singapore) |
| M2000 | Manufacturing 2000 (Singapore) |
| MA | Memorandum of Association |
| MA | Monetary Authority (Hong Kong) |
| MA | Moving average |
| M&A | Mergers and acquisitions |
| MAA | Malaysian Assurance Alliance Berhad |
| MAATS | Modern Australian Apprenticeship and Traineeship System |
| MABEC | Malaysia Bloomberg E-Commerce |
| MAC | Myanmar Accountancy Council |
| MACC | Malaysian American Chamber of Commerce |
| MACD | Moving Average Convergence-Divergence |
| MACHIMPEX | China National Machinery Import and Export Corporation |
| MACPA | Malaysian Association of Certified Public Accountant |
| MADA | Muda Agricultural Development Authority (Malaysia) |
| MADR | Ministry of Agricultural Development and Research (Sri Lanka) |
| MAEI | Malaysian American Electronics Industries Association |
| MAF | Mekong ASEAN Fund |
| MAF | Ministry of Agriculture and Forestry |
| MAFF | Ministry of Agriculture Fisheries and Food |
| MAFI | Ministry of Agriculture and Food Industry |
| MAI | Market for Alternative Investment |
| MAI | Multilateral Agreement on Investment |
| MAIHR | Member of the Australian Institute of Human Relations |

| | |
|---|---|
| MAINS | Maritime Information Systems |
| MAJUIKAN | Fisheries Development Authority (Malaysia) |
| MAMPU | Malaysian Administrative Modernization and Management Planning Unit |
| MANCOM | Management committee |
| MAP | Military Assistance Program |
| MAPA | Manila Action Plan for APEC |
| MAPI | Member of the Australian Planning Institute |
| MAPI | Mitsubishi Atomic Power Industries Ltd (Japan) |
| MAR | Market average rate |
| MARA | Majlis Amanah Rakyat (Malaysia) (Council of Trust for Indigenous People) |
| MARC | Malaysian Rating Corporation Berhad |
| MARCAP | Market capitalization |
| MARD | Ministry of Agriculture and Rural Development |
| MARDB | Myanmar Agricultural and Rural Development Bank |
| MARDI | Malaysian Agriculture Research and Development Institute |
| MARINA | Maritime Industry Authority (Philippines) |
| MARO | Municipal Action Reform Officer (Bangladesh) |
| MARPOL | International Convention for the Prevention of Pollution from Ships |
| MART | Money Market Association of the Philippines |
| MARTRADE | Malaysian External Trade Development Corporation |
| MAS | Malaysian Airline System |
| MAS | Monetary Authority of Singapore |
| MAS | Myanmar Agricultural Services |
| MASB | Malaysian Accounting Standards Board |
| MASET | Malaysian Airlines System Electronic Ticketing |
| Mass ATI | Mass Account Transfer Instruction |
| MASTIC | Malaysian Science and Technology Information Centre |
| MAT | Minimum Alternative Tax (India) |
| MANTRA | Man-made Textile Research Association (India) |
| MATRADE | Malaysian External Trade Development Corporation |
| MAV | Minimum access volume |
| Maybank | Malayan Banking Berhad |
| MB | Metropolitan Bank (Philippines) |
| MB | Monetary Board (Philippines) |
| MB | Monetary Board (Korea) |
| MBA | Master of Business Administration |
| MBA | Military Bases Agreement (Philippines) |
| MBA | Mutual Benefit Association (Philippines) |
| MBC | Manila Broadcasting Corporation (Philippines) |
| MBC | Munhwa Broadcasting Corporation (Korea) |
| MBDA | Mongolian Business Development Agency |
| MBI | Management buy-in |

| | |
|---|---|
| MBIM | Member of the British Institute of Management |
| MBM | Master of Business Management |
| MBO | Management buy-out |
| MBS | Mainichi Broadcasting System (Japan) |
| MBS | Mortgage-backed securities |
| Mbs | Megabits per second |
| MBSB | Malaysia Building Society Berhad |
| MBSRP | Mekong Basin Sub-Regional Program |
| MBTC | Metropolitan Bank and Trust Company (Philippines) |
| MC | Mekong Committee |
| MC | Member company |
| MC | Ministerial conference |
| MC | Ministry of Communications |
| MC | Ministry of Construction |
| MCA | Malaysian Chinese Association |
| MCA | Mongolian Companies Association |
| MCAT | Mongolian Civil Air Transport |
| MCB | Malaysian Coconut Board |
| MCB | Minimum cash balance |
| MCB | Muslim Commercial Bank (Pakistan) |
| MCCI | Metropolitan Chamber of Commerce and Industries (Bangladesh) |
| MCCI | Mongolian Chamber of Commerce and Industry |
| MCCM | Malay Chamber of Commerce Malaysia |
| MCCRRP | Manila Cavite Coastal Road and Reclamation Project |
| MCD | Malaysian Central Depository |
| MCDS | Ministry of Community Development and Sports |
| MCEI | Marketing Communication Executives International |
| MCFS | Modified Carry Forward System |
| MCH | Maternity and child health |
| MCI | Ministry of Commerce and Industry |
| MCI | Monetary conditions index (New Zealand) |
| MCI | Multiple currency intervention |
| MCIT | Minimum Corporate Income Tax (Philippines) |
| MCIT | Ministry of Communication and Information Technology |
| MCL | Melbourne City Link |
| M Com | Master of Commerce |
| MCOT | Mass Communication Organization of Thailand |
| MD | Managing director |
| MDB | Multilateral development bank |
| MDC | Multimedia Development Corporation (Malaysia) |
| MDCH | Malaysian Derivatives Clearing House Berhad |
| MDP | Multi-Disciplinary Professional Practice |
| MDFP | Mindanao Development Framework Plan (Philippines) |
| MDT | Mobile Data Terminal |
| MEA | Malaysian Economic Association |

| | |
|---|---|
| MEA | Metropolitan Electricity Authority (Thailand) |
| MEA | Multilateral Environmental Agreement |
| M-EAGA | Malaysian sub-region of EAGA |
| MEAF | Ministry of Economic Affairs and Finance |
| MEB | Myanmar Economic Bank |
| MEC | Marginal efficiency of capital |
| MECIB | Malaysian Export Credit Insurance Berhad |
| M Ed | Master in Education |
| MEDC | Mindanao Economic Development Council |
| MEDCo | Mindanao Economic Development Council (Philippines) |
| MEDEC | Malaysian Entrepreneurial Development Centre |
| MEDEP | Micro Enterprise Development Program (Nepal) |
| MECIB | Malaysian Export Credit Insurance Berhad |
| MECO | Manila Electric Company (Philippines) |
| MEER | Ministry of External Economic Relations |
| MEF | Ministry of Economy and Finance (Cambodia) |
| MEFP | Memorandum of Economic and Financial Policies (Cambodia) |
| MEFR | Macro-Economic and Financial Report (Cambodia) |
| MEGS | Maharashtra Employment Guarantee Scheme |
| MEHEC | China National Medicine and Health Products Import and Export Corporation |
| MEI | Matsushita Electric Industries |
| MEIP | Metropolitan Environmental Improvement Program (World Bank) |
| MEIC | Myanmar Export and Import Corporation |
| MELCO | Mitsubishi Electric Corporation |
| MENDAKI | Council for the Development of the Muslim Community (Singapore) |
| MEPE | Myanmar Electric Power Enterprise |
| MEPF | Ministry of Economy, Planning and Finance |
| MEPS | Malaysian Electronic Payment System |
| MEPS | MAS Electronic Payment System |
| MEPZ | Mactan Export Process Zone (Philippines) |
| MEPZ | Madras Export Processing Zone (India) |
| MER | Management Expense Ratio |
| MERALCO | Manila Electric Company |
| MERC | Chicago Mercantile Exchange |
| Merincorp | Merchant Investment Corporation (Indonesia) |
| MESDAQ | Malaysian Exchange of Securities Dealing and Automated Quotation |
| MESEAM | Medium and Small Enterprises Association of Malaysia |
| METC | Military Electronics Telecommunications Corporation |
| MEY | Maximum economic yield |
| MF | Ministry of Finance |
| MFA | Ministry of Foreign Affairs |

| MFA | Multi Fibre Agreement |
| MFAIC | Ministry of Foreign Affairs and International Cooperation (Cambodia) |
| MFC | Multi-finance Corporation |
| MFI | Malaysia France Institute |
| MFI | Multilateral framework on investment |
| MFL | Madras Fertilizers Limited |
| MFN | Most Favoured Nation |
| MFP | Ministry of Finance and Planning |
| MFSC | Multi function securities company |
| MFSL | Myanmar Five Star Line |
| MFT | Ministry of Foreign Trade |
| MFTB | Myanmar Foreign Trade Bank |
| MFW | Marine Federation of the World |
| MGB | Mines and Geo-Sciences Bureau (Philippines) |
| MGBI | PT Matsushita Gobel Battery Industry (Indonesia) |
| MGMR | Ministry of Geology and Mineral Resources |
| MGS | Malaysian Government Securities |
| MGS | Multimedia Super Corridor Research and Development Grant Scheme |
| M-GT | Malaysia Growth Triangle sub-region |
| MHA | Ministry of Home Affairs |
| MHI | Mitsubishi Heavy Industries |
| MHPI | Malaysian Housing Price Index |
| MHRA | Ministry of Home and Religious Affairs |
| MHS | Ministry of Human Settlements |
| MHT | Manufacturers Hanover Trust |
| MHT | Ministry of Hotels and Tourism |
| MHW | Ministry of Health and Welfare |
| MHz | Mega-hertz |
| MI | Mekong Institute |
| MI | Minority interest |
| MIA | Malaysian Institute of Accountants |
| MIA | Missing in action |
| MIAT | Mongolian Airlines |
| MIB | Malayu Islam Beraya (Brunei) (Malay Islamic Monarchy) |
| MIC | Malaysian Indian Congress |
| MIC | Middle income country |
| MIC | Myanmar Investment Commission |
| MICB | Myanmar Investment and Commercial Bank |
| MICCI | Malaysian International Chamber of Commerce and Industry |
| MICE | Meetings, incentives, conventions and exhibitions |
| MICG | Malaysian Institute of Corporate Governance |
| MICR | Magnetic Ink Character Recognition |
| MID | Ministry of Industrial Development (Sri Lanka) |

| | |
|---|---|
| MIDA | Malaysian Industrial Development Authority |
| MIDAS | Market and Investment Development Assistance Scheme |
| MIDF | Malaysian Industrial Development Finance Berhad |
| MIDFCCS | MIDF Consultancy and Corporate Services Sendirian Berhad |
| MIDFIH | MIDF Investment Holdings Sendirian Berhad |
| MIDI | Muslim International Development Inc |
| MIEC | China Metallurgical Import and Export Corporation |
| MIEL | Malaysian Industrial Estate Limited |
| MIER | Malaysian Institute of Economic Research |
| MIF | Myanmar Investment Fund |
| MIFC | Mutual International Finance Corp (Indonesia) |
| MIFE | Manila International Futures Exchange |
| MIFO | Malaysian Institute of Futures and Options |
| MIGA | Multilateral Investment Guarantee Agency |
| MII | Ministry of Information Industry |
| Mij | Maatschappij (Business partnership, Netherlands) |
| MILCO | Milk Industries of Lanka Co. (Sri Lanka) |
| Miliar | billion (Indonesia) |
| MIM | Malaysian Institute of Management |
| MIM | Mount Isa Mines (Papua New Guinea) |
| MIMB | Malaysian International Merchant Bankers |
| MINDECO | Mine and Metals International Enterprises Development Corporation (China) |
| MINDEF | Ministry of Defence (Singapore) |
| MINEXPORT | Vietnam National Minerals Export Import Corporation |
| MINLAW | Ministry of Law (Singapore) |
| MISC | Malaysian International Shipping Corporation |
| MISDRI | Ma'anshan Iron Steel Design Research Institute (China) |
| MISH | Market Information Survey of Households (India) |
| MISU | Market Intelligence and Surveillance Unit (India) |
| MIT | Madras Institute of Technology (India) |
| MITA | Malaysian Income Tax Act |
| MITA | Ministry of Information and the Arts (Singapore) |
| MITI | Ministry of Industry, Trade and Investment |
| MITI | Ministry of International Trade and Industry |
| MITTA | Malaysia Indonesia Thailand Travel Association |
| MJ | Ministry of Justice |
| MJBC | Mongolian Japan Business Club |
| MJDS | Multi-jurisdictional disclosure system |
| MKK | Mitsubishi Kakoki Kaisha Ltd |
| MkSE | Makati Stock Exchange |
| MLA | Minimum liquid asset |
| MLA | Monetary Law Act |
| MLCF | Medium and Long Term Credit Fund |
| MLLD | Ministry of Lands and Land Development |

| | |
|---|---|
| MLLE | Maximum Limit of Loan Extension |
| MLMUPC | Ministry of Land Management, Urban Planning and Construction |
| MLR | Minimum lending rate |
| MLR | Minimum liquidity requirement |
| MLSW | Ministry of Labour and Social Welfare |
| MM | Magister Manajemen (Indonesia) (Master in Management degree) |
| MM | Master of Management |
| MM | Metro Manila |
| MMA | Maldives Monetary Authority |
| MMA | Metro Manila Authority |
| MMA | Metropolitan Manila Area |
| MMA | Myanmar Mines Authorities |
| MMAI | PT Multi Media Asia Indonesia |
| MMBI | Ministry of Machine Building Industry |
| MMC | Malaysian Mining Corporation |
| MMC | Metropolitan Manila Commission |
| MMC | Money market certificate |
| MME | Malaysian Monetary Exchange |
| MMEI | Ministry of Machinery and Electronics Industry |
| MMF | Man-made fibre |
| MMI | Ministry of Machinery Industry |
| MMI | Ministry of Metallurgical Industry |
| MMinute | Metro Manila Infrastructure Utilities and Engineering |
| MMMA | Mines and Minerals Management Act (Bhutan) |
| MMMF | Money Market Mutual Fund (India) |
| MMO | Money market operations |
| MMR | Maternal mortality rate |
| MMTA | Malaysian Motor Traders Association |
| MMTC | Mineral and Metals Trading Corporation (India) |
| MNB | Multinational bank |
| MNC | Multinational Corporation |
| MND | Ministry of National Development |
| MNE | Multinational enterprise |
| MNI | Malaysian National Insurance Sendirian Berhad |
| MNLF | Moro National Liberation Front |
| MNPED | Ministry of National Planning and Economic Development |
| MNRB | Malaysian National Reinsurance Berhad |
| MNT | Mongolian tugrik (currency) |
| MNZIE | Member of the New Zealand Institute of Engineers |
| MO | Marketing organization |
| MO | Medical Officer |
| MO | Money order |
| MOA | Memorandum of agreement |
| MOA | Ministry of Agriculture |

| | |
|---|---|
| MOAC | Ministry of Agriculture and Cooperatives |
| MOC | Ministry of Commerce |
| MOC | Ministry of Communication |
| MOC | Ministry of Construction |
| MOCI | Ministry of Culture and Information |
| MOD | Ministry of Development |
| MOD | Ministry of Overseas Development |
| MODVAT | Modified Value Added Tax (India) |
| MOE | Ministry of Education |
| MOE | Ministry of Energy |
| MOEA | Ministry of Economic Affairs |
| MOEF | Ministry of Environment and Forests |
| MOET | Ministry of Education and Training |
| MOEYS | Ministry of Education, Youth and Sports |
| MOF | Ministry of Finance |
| MOF | Ministry of Food |
| MOF | Marketing Organization for Farmers (Thailand) |
| MOF | Multiple option facility |
| MOFE | Ministry of Finance and Economy |
| MOFERT | Ministry of Foreign Economic Relations and Trade |
| MOFF | Multiple options funding facility |
| MOFT | Ministry of Foreign Trade |
| MOFTEC | Ministry of Foreign Trade and Economic Cooperation |
| MOG | Ministry of Geology and Mineral Resources |
| MOGE | Myanmar Oil and Gas Enterprise |
| MOH | Malaysian Oriental Holding Ltd |
| MOH | Ministry of Health |
| MOHA | Ministry of Home Affairs |
| MOHI | Ministry of Heavy Industries |
| MOHLG | Ministry of Housing and Local Government |
| MOHWF | Ministry of Health and Family Welfare |
| MOI | Ministry of Industries |
| MOI | Ministry of Information |
| MOI | Ministry of Interior |
| MOI | Mobil Oil Indonesia Ltd |
| MOJ | Ministry of Justice |
| MOL | Ministry of Labour |
| MOL | Mitsui OSK Lines |
| MOLISA | Ministry of Labour, War Invalids and Social Affairs |
| MOLSS | Ministry of Labour and Social Security |
| MOM | Ministry of Manpower |
| MOMP | Ministry of Marine Products |
| MOND | Ministry of National Defence |
| MOP | Margin of preference |
| MOP | Ministry of Petroleum |

| | |
|---|---|
| MOPI | Mobil Oil Philippines Incorporated |
| MOPT | Ministry of Posts and Telecommunication |
| MOR | Manual of Regulations |
| MOR | Ministry of Railways |
| MORC | Memorandum of Regulatory Cooperation |
| MORI | Market Opinion and Research International |
| MOSS | Model Occupational Skills Standards |
| MOST | Ministry of Science and Technology |
| MOSTE | Ministry of Science, Technology and Environment |
| MOT | Ministry of Trade |
| MOT | Ministry of Transport |
| MOTC | Ministry of Transport and Communications |
| MOU | Memorandum of understanding |
| MOU | Monetary Operations Unit (Sri Lanka) |
| MP | Macau pataca (Macau currency, divided into 100 avos) |
| MP | Member of Parliament |
| MPA | Master of Public Administration degree |
| MPA | Maritime and Port Authority of Singapore |
| MPA | Mongla Port Authority (Bangladesh) |
| MPA | Myanmar Port Authority |
| MPBF | Maximum permissible bank finance |
| MPC | Metropolitan Planning Committee (India) |
| MPC | Mongolian Petroleum Company |
| MPC | Multi-purpose card |
| MPDF | Mekong Project Development Facility |
| MPEDA | Marine Products Export Development Authority (India) |
| MPF | Mandatory Provident Fund |
| MPI | Macro prudential indicator |
| MPI | Ministry of Petroleum Industry |
| MPI | Ministry of Planning and Investment |
| MPI | Ministry of Plan Implementation |
| MTIP | Medium Term Investment Program |
| MPO | Menghitung Pajak Orang (Withholding tax) |
| MPOPC | Malaysian Palm Oil Promotion Council |
| MPR | Majelis Permusyawaratan Rakyat (Indonesia) (People's Consultative Assembly) |
| MPR | Mongolian People's Republic |
| MPRP | Mongolian People's Revolutionary Party |
| MPS | Marginal propensity to save |
| MPS | Million instructions per second |
| MPS | Material product system |
| MPS | Ministry of Public Security |
| MPT | Ministry of Posts and Telecommunications |
| MPTDGP | Directorate General of Posts of MPT |
| MPTDGT | Directorate General of Telecommunications of MPT |

| MPV | Multi-purpose vehicle |
|---|---|
| MR | Ministry of Railways |
| MRA | Mutual recognition agreement |
| MRCB | Malaysian Resources Corporation Berhad |
| MRDC | Malaysian Rubber Development Corporation |
| MRC | Mekong River Commission |
| MRCP | Member of the Royal College of Physicians |
| MRCS | Member of the Royal College of Surgeons |
| MRDC | Malaysian Rubber Development Corporation |
| MRDC | Mineral Resources Development Corporation (Papua New Guinea) |
| MRE | Malaysian Rubber Exchange |
| MRf | Rufiyaa (curreny of Maldives) |
| MRR | Manila Reference Rate |
| MRRDB | Malaysian Rubber Research and Development Board |
| MRSF | Mineral Resources Stabilization Fund (Papua New Guinea) |
| MRSM | Malaysian abbreviation for Mara Junior Science Colleges |
| MRT | Mass Rapid Transit |
| MRTA | Metropolitan Rapid Transit Authority |
| MRTC | Mass Rapid Transit Corporation (Singapore) |
| MRTP | Monopolies and Restrictive Trade Practices Act (India) |
| MRTP | Mortgage Reducing Term Policy |
| MRTPC | Monopolies and Restrictive Trade Practices Commission (India) |
| MSA | Maritime Safety Agency (Japan) |
| MSAR | Macau Special Administration Region |
| MSB | Malaysian Savings Bond |
| MSB | Monetary Stabilization Bond |
| MSc | Master of Science |
| MSC | Multimedia Super Corridor (Malaysia) |
| MSCI | Morgan Stanley Capital International |
| MSCI HK | Morgan Stanley Capital International Hong Kong Index |
| MSCII | Morgan Stanley Capital Investment Index |
| MSDF | Maritime Self Defence Force (Japan) |
| MSE | Manila Stock Exchange |
| MSEC | Myanmar Securities Exchange Centre |
| MSG | Melanesian Spearhead Group |
| MSG | Monosodium glutamate |
| MSHI | Mitsubishi Singapore Heavy Industries Ltd |
| MSL | Melanesian Shipping Line |
| MSLE | Myanmar Small Loans Enterprise |
| MSocSc | Master of Social Science |
| MSP | Market service provider |
| MSP | Minimum support price |
| MSR | Malaysian Standard Rubber |
| MSRS | Malaysian Share Registration Services Sendirian Berhad |

| | |
|---|---|
| MSS | Mahila Smabaya Samity (Bangladesh) (Women's Cooperative Society) |
| MSY | Maximum sustainable yield |
| MT | Mail transfer |
| MTA | Mong Tai Army (Myanmar) |
| MTA | Mongolian Telecommunication Authority |
| MTA | Multilateral trade agreement |
| MTACS | Malaysian Trade Allocation and Confirmation System |
| MTBC | Mitsui Trust and Banking Corporation |
| MTC | Malaysian Tobacco Company |
| MTC | Minimum terms and conditions |
| MTC | Mongolian Telecommunication Company |
| MTCA | Ministry of Transport and Civil Aviation |
| MTCF | Multilateral Technical Cooperation Fund |
| MTDB | Maldives Tourism Promotion Board |
| MTDC | Malaysian Technology Development Corporation |
| MTE | Myanmar Timber Enterprise |
| MTFA | Medium Term Financial Assistance facility |
| MTI | Ministry of Textile Industry |
| MTI | Ministry of Trade and Industry |
| MTL | Macau Telecommunications Ltd |
| MTN | Medium term note |
| MTN | Multilateral trade negotiation |
| MTNL | Mahanagar Telephone Nigam Limited (India) |
| MTO | Multilateral Trade Organization |
| Mtoe | Million tonnes of oil equivalent |
| MTP | Marine Transport Department |
| MTP | Medium term plan |
| MTPB | Malaysian Tourism Promotion Board |
| MTPDP | Medium Term Philippine Development Plan |
| MTPIP | Medium Term Philippine Investment Plan |
| MTPLR | Medium term prime lending rate |
| MTR | Mass Transit Railway |
| MTRC | Mass Transit Railway Corporation |
| MTUC | Malaysian Trades Union Congress |
| MUC | Major urban centre |
| MUI | Malayan United Industries Berhad |
| MUIS | Majlis Ugama Islam Singapura |
| MULTICOR | Multinational Finance Corporation (Indonesia) |
| MUNAS | National Congress (Indonesia) |
| MUSPIDA | Musyawarah Pimpinan Daerah (Indonesia) (Consortium of Regional Leaders) |
| MUST | Manpower Upgrading for Science and Technology (Singapore) |
| MVA | Market value added |
| MVA | Manufacturing value added |

| | |
|---|---|
| MVC | Monthly variable component (Singapore) |
| MVIL | Motor Vehicles Insurance Limited (Papua New Guinea) |
| Mvpd | Motor vehicles per day |
| Mw | Megawatt |
| MW | Ministry of Works |
| MWA | Metropolitan Waterworks Authority (Thailand) |
| Mwh | Megawatt hour |
| MWREP | Ministry of Water Resources and Electric Power |
| MWSS | Metropolitan Waterworks and Sewerage System (Philippines) |
| MYR | Malaysian ringgit |
| NA | National Assembly |
| NA | National Association |
| NAA | National Auditing Agency (Cambodia) |
| NAA | National Auditing Authority (Cambodia) |
| NAB | National Accreditation Board (Malaysia) |
| NAB | National Australia Bank |
| NAB | New Arrangement to Borrow |
| NABARD | National Bank for Agricultural and Rural Development (India) |
| NABL | Nepal Arab Bank Ltd |
| NAC | National Archives of Cambodia |
| NAC | National Arts Council (Singapore) |
| NACC | National Agricultural Coordination Committee (Pakistan) |
| NACC | Nigeria ASEAN Chamber of Commerce |
| NACC | Non-Aligned Countries Conference |
| NACCS | National Automatic Cheque Clearing System (Malaysia) |
| NACD | National Authority for Combating Drugs (Cambodia) |
| NACE | National Advisory Council for the Elderly (Singapore) |
| NACESTID | National Centre for Scientific and Technological Information and Documentation (Vietnam) |
| NACF | National Agricultural Cooperative Federation (Korea) |
| NACL | Nippon Aviotronics Co Ltd |
| NACLI | National Community Leadership Institute (Singapore) |
| NADC | Northern Agricultural Development Corporation (Australia) |
| NADRA | National Database and Registration Authority (Pakistan) |
| NAFA | Nanyang Academy of Fine Arts (Singapore) |
| NAFED | National Agency for Export Development (Indonesia) |
| NAFED | National Agricultural Cooperative Marketing Federation of India |
| NAFTA | New Zealand Australia Free Trade Area |
| NAFTA | North American Free Trade Agreement |
| NAFTA | North Atlantic Free Trade Area |
| NAIA | Ninoy Aquino International Airport |
| NAIC | National Association of Insurance Companies (China) |
| NAITA | National Apprenticeship and Industrial Training Agency (Sri Lanka) |
| NAL | National Aeronautical Laboratory (Japan) |

| | |
|---|---|
| NAL | National Aerospace Laboratories (India) |
| NALIS | National Land Information System (Malaysia) |
| NAM | Non-Aligned Movement |
| NAMARCO | National Marketing Corporation (Philippines) |
| NAMC | Nanchang Aircraft Manufacturing Corporation (China) |
| NANEAP | North Africa, Near East, Asia and Pacific |
| NAP | National Agricultural Policy (Malaysia) |
| NAP | New Aspiration Party (Thailand) |
| NAPCO | New Airport Projects Coordination Office (Hong Kong) |
| NAPOCOR | National Power Corporation (Philippines) |
| NARA | National Aquatic Resources Agency (Sri Lanka) |
| NARASA | Natural Resources, Energy and Science Authority of Sri Lanka |
| NARC | Nepal Agricultural Research Council |
| NAREA | National Agricultural Research and Extension Agenda (Philippines) |
| NARPRA | Natural Rubber Producers Research Association |
| NARI | Nanjing Automation Research Institute (China) |
| NARI | National Agricultural Research Initiative (Australia) |
| NARIC | National Rice and Corn Corporation (Philippines) |
| NAS | National Account Statistics |
| NAS | National Apprenticeship Scheme (Malaysia) |
| NASA | National Aeronautics and Space Administration (United States) |
| NASD | National Association of Securities Dealers (United States) |
| NASDA | National Space Development Agency (Japan) |
| NASDAQ | National Association of Securities Dealers Automated Quotations (United States) |
| NATA | National Association of Testing Authorities (Australia) |
| NATAS | National Association of Travel Agents Singapore |
| NATO | North Atlantic Treaty Organization |
| NatWest | NatWest Australia Bank |
| NAV | Net asset value |
| NBC | Nanyang Commercial Bank (Hong Kong) |
| NBC | National Bank of Cambodia |
| NBC | National Broadcasting Commission (Papua New Guinea) |
| NBC | Net bank credit |
| NBCT | North Butterworth Container Terminal |
| NBEET | National Board of Employment, Education and Training (Australia) |
| NBFC | Non-bank finance company |
| NBFI | Non-bank financial institution |
| NBFI | Non-bank financial intermediary |
| NBFTI | Non-bank financial thrift institution |
| NBER | National Bureau of Economic Research |
| NBL | Nepal Bank Ltd |
| NBMC | National Bond Market Committee (Malaysia) |

| | |
|---|---|
| NBP | National Bank of Pakistan |
| NBR | National Board of Revenue (Bangladesh) |
| NBS | National Bureau of Standards (United States) |
| NBS | National Bureau of Standards (Taiwan) |
| NBSI | National Bank of Solomon Islands |
| NBSM | National Bureau of Surveying and Mapping (China) |
| NBV | National Bank of Vanuatu |
| NCADA | National Council Against Drug Abuse (Singapore) |
| NCAER | National Council of Applied Economic Research (India) |
| NCAP | National Centre for Agricultural Economics and Policy Research (India) |
| NCB | National Computer Board (Singapore) |
| NCB | Nationalized commercial bank |
| NCB | Net clearing balance |
| NCB | Nippon Credit Bank |
| NCBS | National Centre for Biological Sciences (India) |
| NCC | National Clearing Centre (India) |
| NCC | National Coordination Committee (Pakistan) |
| NCC | Nepal Chamber of Commerce |
| NCCC | National Credit Consultative Council (Pakistan) |
| NCCI | National chamber of commerce and industry |
| NCCIM | National Chamber of Commerce and Industry of Malaysia |
| NCCT | Non-cooperative country and territory |
| NCD | National Capital District (Papua New Guinea) |
| NCD | Negotiable certificate of deposit |
| NCD | No claim discount (insurance) |
| NCD | Non-convertible debenture |
| NCDA | National Centre for Development Studies (Papua New Guinea) |
| NCDC | National Capital District Commission (Papua New Guinea) |
| NCDC | National Cooperative Development Corporation (India) |
| NCEA | National Committee for Environmental Affairs (Myanmar) |
| NCERT | National Council of Education Research and Training (India) |
| NCG | Net Credit to Government (Sri Lanka) |
| NCGUB | National Coalition Government of the Union of Burma |
| NCHE | National Council of Higher Education (Sri Lanka) |
| NCI | North China Institute of Computing Technology |
| NCL | New Company Law (Indonesia) |
| NCM | New Capital Market |
| NCM | Non-Clearing Member or Non-Clearing Options Trading Member |
| NCMB | National Conciliation and Mediation Board (Philippines) |
| NCMC | North Colombo Medical College |
| NCMEDI | North China Municipal Engineering Design Institute |
| NCMP | Non-constituency Member of Parliament (Singapore) |
| NCMR | National Committee on Mineral Resources (China) |
| NCNA | New China News Agency |

| | |
|---|---|
| NCOCI | National Committee on Culture and Information (Cambodia) |
| NCOTC | Nanjing Changjiang Oil Transportation Corp (China) |
| NCPA | North China Power Administration |
| NCPC | North China Pharmaceutical Corporation |
| NCPG | North China Power Group |
| NCR | National Capital Region (Philippines) |
| NCRCS | New Comprehensive Rural Credit Scheme (Sri Lanka) |
| NCS | National Co-insurance Scheme (Pakistan) |
| NCSC | National Companies and Securities Commission (Australia) |
| NCSRD | National Council for Scientific Research and Development (Malaysia) |
| NCSS | National Council for Social Services (Singapore) |
| NCTI | National Council for Trade and Investment (India) |
| NCUA | National Credit Union Administration (China) |
| ND | National debt |
| NDA | Net domestic assets |
| NDB | National Development Bank (Sri Lanka) |
| NDC | National defined contribution |
| NDC | National Design Centre (Sri Lanka) |
| NDC | National Development Committee |
| NDC | National Development Company (Philippines) |
| NDC | National Development Council (India) |
| NDD | National direct dialing |
| NDDB | National Diary Development Board (India) |
| NDF | Non-deliverable foreign exchange forward |
| NDFC | National Development Finance Corporation (Pakistan) |
| NDRP | National Debt Retirement Program (Pakistan) |
| NDP | National Development Plan |
| NDP | National Development Policy (Malaysia) |
| NDTL | Net demand and time liabilities |
| NEA | National Electrification Administration (Philippines) |
| NEA | National Energy Administration (Thailand) |
| NEA | National Environment Agency (Vietnam) |
| NEA | Nepal Electricity Authority |
| NEAC | National Economic Action Council (Malaysia) |
| NEACD | North East Asia Cooperation Dialogue |
| NEAEF | North East Asian Economic Forum |
| NEAP | National environmental action plan |
| NEAT | National Exchange for Automated Trading system (India) |
| NEB | National Electricity Board (Malaysia) |
| NEB | National Environment Board (Thailand) |
| NEC | National Economic Council (Pakistan) |
| NEC | National Education Council (Sri Lanka) |
| NEC | National Executive Council (Papua New Guinea) |
| NEC | Nepal Electricity Corporation |

| | |
|---|---|
| NEC | New Economic Policy |
| NEC | Nippon Electric Company |
| NECC | National Economic Consultative Council |
| NECC | National Electronic Commerce Committee |
| NED | Non-executive director |
| NEDA | National Economic Development Authority (Philippines) |
| NEDCOL | National Economic Development Corporation (Thailand) |
| NEDfi | North Eastern Development Finance Corporation (India) |
| NEER | Nominal effective exchange rate |
| NEGPF | North East General Pharmacy Factory (China) |
| NEIB | Nantong Electronic Industry Bureau (China) |
| NEIEC | Nanjing Electronics Import and Export Corporation (China) |
| NELP | New Exploration Licensing Policy (India) |
| NEM | New Economic Mechanism (Laos) |
| NEMS | National Exchange Market System |
| NEP | New Economic Policy (Malaysia) |
| NEPA | National Environment Protection Administration (China) |
| NEPC | National Energy Policy Committee (Laos) |
| NEPC | National Energy Policy Council (Thailand) |
| NEPRA | National Electric Power Regulatory Authority (Pakistan) |
| NEPSE | Nepal Stock Exchange |
| NEPZ | Noida Export Processing Zone (India) |
| NERD | National Engineering Research and Development Centre (Sri Lanka) |
| NERI | National Economic Research Institute (China) |
| NERP | National Economic Recovery Plan (Malaysia) |
| NESDB | National Economic and Social Development Board (Thailand) |
| NET | Nippon Educational Television |
| NETRACO | National Export Trading Corporation (Philippines) |
| NETRC | National Educational Testing and Research Centre (Philippines) |
| NETS | National Electronic Trading System (China) |
| NETS | Network for Electronic Transfers (Singapore) |
| NEU | National Economics University (Vietnam) |
| NFA | National Fisheries Authority (Papua New Guinea) |
| NFA | National Futures Association (United States) |
| NFA | National Food Authority (Philippines) |
| NFA | Net Foreign Assets |
| NFA | National Futures Association (Taiwan) |
| NFB | New financial business |
| NFB | Nippon Fudosan Bank |
| NFC | National Fertilizer Corporation (Pakistan) |
| NFC | National Finance Commission (Pakistan) |
| NFC | National Fisheries College (Papua New Guinea) |
| NFCAP | National Forest and Conservation Action Program (Papua New Guinea) |

| | |
|---|---|
| NFCD | Non-resident Foreign Currency Deposit |
| NFDC | National Fertilizer Development Centre (Pakistan) |
| NFE | Non-formal education |
| NFETC | Nanjing Foreign Economic Relations and Trade Corp (China) |
| NFFC | National Federation of Fisheries Cooperatives (Korea) |
| NFHS | National Family Health Survey (India) |
| NFL | National Federation of Labour (Philippines) |
| NFL | National Fertilizers Ltd (India) |
| NFP | National forestry policy |
| NFRD | National Framework for Regional Development |
| NFS | Non-farm sector |
| NGA | Non-government agency |
| NGCF | National Ginseng Cooperative Federation (Korea) |
| NGF | National Guarantee Fund (Australia) |
| NGO | Non-governmental organization |
| NGSM | National Graduate School of Management (Australia) |
| NHA | National Highway Authority (India) |
| NHA | National Housing Authority |
| NHB | National Housing Bank (India) |
| NHC | National Housing Commission (Papua New Guinea) |
| NHC | National Housing Corporation (Vanuatu) |
| NHC (LTO) | National Housing Credit (Long term operation) (India) |
| NHDA | National Housing Development Authority (Sri Lanka) |
| NHEOC | Nanhai East Oil Corporation (China) |
| NHI | National Health Insurance (Taiwan) |
| NHK | Nippon Hoso Kyokai |
| | (Japan Public Broadcasting Company) |
| NHMFC | National Home Mortgage Finance Corporation (Philippines) |
| NHRI | Nanjing Hydraulic Research Institute (China) |
| NHS | National Health Service (United Kingdom) |
| NHWOC | Nanhai West Oil Corporation (China) |
| NI Tour | National and International Tourist Bureau of Indonesia |
| NI | PT Nomura Indonesia |
| NIA | National Insurance Academy (India) |
| NIAM | Nederlands Indonesische Aordolic Maatschappij |
| NIAS | Nordic Institute of Asian Studies |
| NIB | Nordic Investment Bank |
| NIBM | National Institute of Bank Management (India) |
| NIBM | National Institute of Business Management (Sri Lanka) |
| NIBOR | New York interbank offer rate |
| NIBT | Net income before tax |
| NIC | National Insurance Corporation (Nepal) |
| NIC | National Insurance Corporation (Pakistan) |
| NIC | Neft Import Concern (Mongolia) |
| NIC | New industrializing country |

| | |
|---|---|
| NIC | Nepal Industrial and Commercial Bank Ltd |
| NICA | Nepal Incentive and Convention Association |
| NICL | National Insurance Corporation Limited (India) |
| NIC (LTO) | National Industrial Credit (Long term operations) (India) |
| NICVD | National Institute of Cardiovascular Disease (Pakistan) |
| NID | Negotiable Instrument of Deposit |
| NIDA | National Information Communications Technology Development Authority (Cambodia) |
| NIDA | National Institute of Development Administration (Thailand) |
| NIDA | National Investment Development Authority (Papua New Guinea) |
| NIDC | National Investment and Development Corp (Philippines) |
| NIDC | Nepal Industrial Development Corporation |
| NIDCI | National Industrial Development Corporation of India |
| NIDL | New International Division of Labour |
| NIE | National Institute of Education (Singapore) |
| NIE | New Industrializing Economy |
| NIECER | NIE Centre for Educational Research (Singapore) |
| NIEM | National Institute of Education Management (Malaysia) |
| NIEO | New International Economic Order |
| NIF | New investment fund |
| NIF | Nomura International Finance (Japan) |
| NIF | Note issuing facility |
| NIFM | National Institute of Financial Management (India) |
| NIFT | National Institute of Fisheries Training (Sri Lanka) |
| NIH | National Institute of Health |
| NIIS | National Information Industries Strategy (Australia) |
| Nikkei | Nihon Keizai Shimbun |
| NIL | Negotiable Instruments Law (China) |
| NIM | National Institute of Metrology (China) |
| NIM | New issue market |
| NIM | Net interest margin |
| NIMTC | National Industrial Manpower Training Council |
| NIP | New Industrial Policy (India) |
| NIPAS | National Integrated Protected Areas System Act (Philippines) |
| NIPFP | National Institute of Public Finance and Policy (India) |
| NIPH | National Institute of Public Health (Cambodia) |
| NIPM | National Institute of Plantation Management (Sri Lanka) |
| NIPS | National Investment Priorities Schedule (Papua New Guinea) |
| NIRC | National Industrial Relations Commission (Pakistan) |
| NIS | National innovation system |
| NIS | National Institute of Statistics (Cambodia) |
| NIS | National Investment Scheme (Papua New Guinea) |
| NISCO | Northern Islands Stevedoring Company Limited (Vanuatu) |
| NISI | National Institute of Sciences of India |
| NISP | PT Bank Nilai Inti Sari Penyimpan (Indonesia) |

| NIST | National Institute of Standards and Technology |
| NISTADS | National Institute of Science, Technology and Development Studies (India) |
| NISTPAS | National Institute for Science and Technology Policy and Strategy Studies (Vietnam) |
| NIT | National Investment Trust (Pakistan) |
| NITC | National Information Technology Council (Malaysia) |
| NITE | National Institute of Technical Education (Sri Lanka) |
| NITIC | Nanjing International Trust and Investment Corp (China) |
| NITSC | National IT Standards Committee (Singapore) |
| NITVET | National Institute for Technical Vocational and Education Training (Philippines) |
| NIURP | National Institute of Urban and Regional Planning (Vietnam) |
| NIV | New improved variety |
| NIZ | National Industrial Zone (Pakistan) |
| NJAU | Nanjing Agricultural University (China) |
| NJI | New Jubilee Insurance (Pakistan) |
| NJPA | Nanjing Port Authority (China) |
| NKDT | National Kommunity Development Trust (Vanuatu) |
| NKF | National Kidney Foundation (Singapore) |
| NKK | Nippon Kangyo Kakumaru |
| NLA | National Land Agency (Indonesia) |
| NLAC | National Labour Advisory Council (Sri Lanka) |
| NLC | National Listing Committee (Australia) |
| NLCF | National Livestock Cooperative Federation (Korea) |
| NLD | National League for Democracy (Myanmar) |
| NLDB | National Livestock Development Board (Sri Lanka) |
| NLRA | National Labour Relations Act (United States) |
| NLRC | National Labour Relations Commission (Philippines) |
| NLV | National Library of Vietnam |
| NMA | Nepal Mountaineering Association |
| NMB | National Milk Board (Sri Lanka) |
| NMDC | National Minerals Development Corp (India) |
| NMIEC | National Non-ferrous Metal Import and Export Company (China) |
| NMP | Net material product |
| NMP | Nominated Member of Parliament (Singapore) |
| NMRB | National Mutual Royal Bank (Australia) |
| NMTP | National Metropolitan Transit Committee (Thailand) |
| NMYC | National Manpower and Youth Council (Philippines) |
| NNE | Net national expenditure |
| NNI | Net national income |
| NNP | Net national product |
| NNPT | Nuclear Non-Proliferation Treaty |
| NNW | Net national welfare |
| NOC | No objection certificate |

| | |
|---|---|
| NODC | National Oceanographic Data Centre |
| NOF | Net-owned fund |
| NOI | Net operating income |
| NOL | Neptune Orient Line (Singapore) |
| NOP | National Opinion Poll |
| NOPAR | National Office of Personnel and Administrative Reform (Maldives) |
| NORAD | Norwegian Agency for International Development |
| NORINCO | North Industries Corporation (China) |
| NORPAC | North Pacific Area |
| NOSODECO | North Sumatra Oil Development Corporation (Indonesia) |
| NOSS | National Occupational Skills Standards |
| NOW | Negotiable order of withdrawal account |
| NP | Net profit |
| NPA | National Packaging Association (Australia) |
| NPA | National Pipeline Authority (Australia) |
| NPAC | National Poverty Alleviation Committee |
| NPAP | National Poverty Alleviation Program |
| NPAT | Net profit after tax |
| NPB | National Productivity Board (Singapore) |
| NPBT | Net profit before tax |
| NPC | National People's Congress (China) |
| NPC | National Petroleum Corp (Thailand) |
| NPC | National Planning Commission |
| NPC | National Power Corporation (Philippines) |
| NPC | National Productivity Centre (Malaysia) |
| NPCIL | Nuclear Power Corporation of India Limited |
| NPD | National Parks Division (Thailand) |
| NPD | Nuclear Power Department |
| NPEDC | National Productivity and Economic Development Centre (Nepal) |
| NPF | National Provident Fund (Solomon Islands) |
| NPF | National Provident Fund (Papua New Guinea) |
| NPFDB | National Population and Family Development Board (Malaysia) |
| NPFP | National Physical Framework Plan |
| NPI | Nuclear Power Institute (China) |
| NPIMS | National Public Investment Management System (Cambodia) |
| NPKC | National Peace Keeping Council (Thailand) |
| NPL | Non-performing asset |
| NPL | Non-performing loan |
| NPM | Northern Peninsula Malaysia |
| NPO | National productivity organization |
| NPRC | National Pensions Research Centre (Korea) |
| NPRD | National Program to Rehabilitate and Develop Cambodia |
| NPSO | National Planning and Statistics Office (Vanuatu) |
| NPV | Net present value |

| | |
|---|---|
| NPWP | Taxpayer Registration Number (Indonesia) |
| NRB | Nepal Rashtra Bank |
| NRC | National research coordinator |
| NRC | National Rural Credit (India) |
| NRC (LTO) | National Rural Credit (Long term operations) (India) |
| NRCC | Nanjing Radio Corporation, China |
| NRCPS | Non-redeemable convertible preference shares |
| NRCPSS | Non-redeemable convertible cumulative preference share |
| NRCSTD | National Research Centre for Science and Technology for Development (China) |
| NRDB | Natural Rubber Development Board |
| NRDC | National Reconciliation and Development Council |
| NRE | Non-Resident External |
| NRFC | Non-Resident Foreign Currency account (Sri Lanka) |
| NRI | Nomura Research Institute (Japan) |
| NRI | Non-repatriable investment |
| NRI | Non-resident Indian |
| NRIET | Nanjing Research Institute of Electronics Technology (China) |
| NRNR | Non-Resident Non-Repatriable (India) |
| NRP | Nominal rate of protection |
| NRS | New Remuneration Scheme (Malaysia) |
| NRSA | National Remote Sensing Agency (India) |
| NS | National Service |
| NSman | National Serviceman (Singapore) |
| NSC | National Steel Corporation (Philippines) |
| NSC | National Science Centre (Malaysia) |
| NSC | National Science Council (Taiwan) |
| NSC | National Securities Commission (Vietnam) |
| NSC | National Shipping Corporation (Pakistan) |
| NSCB | National Statistical Coordination Board (Philippines) |
| NSCC | National Securities Clearing Corporation |
| NSCCL | National Securities Clearing Corporation Ltd (India) |
| NSDL | National Securities Depository Ltd (India) |
| NSDP | Net state domestic product |
| NSE | Nagoya Stock Exchange |
| NSE | National Stock Exchange (India) |
| NSE | Non-state enterprise |
| NSE | North-South Expressway (Malaysia) |
| NSF | National Science Foundation (United States) |
| NSFC | National Natural Science Foundation of China |
| NSIC | National Small Industries Corporation (India) |
| NSO | National Savings Organization (Pakistan) |
| NSO | National Statistics Office (Thailand) |
| NSO | National Statistical Office (Mongolia) |
| NSREP | Nanchang Shuguang Rare Earth Plant (China) |

| | |
|---|---|
| NSRF | National Self Reliance Fund (Pakistan) |
| NSRS | National Skills Recognition System (Malaysia) |
| NSS | National Sample Survey (India) |
| NSSF | National Small Savings Fund (India) |
| NSSO | National Sample Survey Organization (India) |
| NSTB | National Science and Technology Board (Singapore) |
| NSTP | New Straits Times Press Berhad (Malaysia) |
| NSTP-2000 | National Science and Technology Plan 2000 (Singapore) |
| NSTP-2005 | National Science and Technology Plan 2005 (Singapore) |
| NSTPCC | National Science and Technology Planning Coordinating Committee (Sri Lanka) |
| NSTS | National securities trading system |
| NSW | New South Wales |
| NT | New Taiwan Dollar |
| NT | Northern Territory (Australia) |
| NT | Nota transaksi (Indonesia) (Stock exchange transaction note) |
| NT&SA | National Trust and Savings Association (United States) |
| NTA | National Tourism Administration (China) |
| NTA | Net tangible asset |
| NTB | Nakornthon Bank (Thailand) |
| NTB | National training board |
| NTB | Nepal Tourism Board |
| NTB | Non-tariff barrier |
| NTC | National Telecommunications Commission (Philippines) |
| NTC | National Tariff Commission (Pakistan) |
| NTC | National Transport Board (Sri Lanka) |
| NTC | Nepal Telecommunications Corporation |
| NTD | New Taiwan dollar |
| NTDC | National Transmission and Distribution Company |
| NTDC | Nepal Tea Development Corporation |
| NTDP | National Telecommunications Development Plan (Philippines) |
| NTFP | Non-timber forest product |
| NTM | Non-tariff measure |
| NTO | National tourism organization |
| NTO | National Tourism Office (Vanuatu) |
| NTP | National Technology Plan (Singapore) |
| NTP | National Telecom Policy (India) |
| NTP | National Telecommunication Policy (Malaysia) |
| NTPC | National Thermal Power Corporation (India) |
| NTRC | National Tax Research Centre (Philippines) |
| NTRC | National Taxation Reform Commission (Pakistan) |
| NTT | Nippon Telegraph and Telephone |
| NTU | Nanyang Technological University (Singapore) |
| NTU | National Taiwan University |

| | |
|---|---|
| NTU | Northern Territory University (Australia) |
| NTUC | National Trades Union Congress (Singapore) |
| NTV | Nippon Television Network |
| NUC | National Unification Commission (Philippines) |
| NUH | National University Hospital (Singapore) |
| NUS | National University of Singapore |
| NV | Naamloze Vennotschap (Limited liability company in Belgium, Netherlands) |
| NV | Nominal value |
| NVDR | Non-Voting Depository Receipt (Thailand) |
| NVI | National Valuation Institute |
| NVL | Navigation Vanua Limited |
| NVOCC | Non-vessel owning common carrier |
| NVP | National Vision Policy (Malaysia) |
| NVTC | National Vocational Training Council (Malaysia) |
| NWC | National Wages Council |
| NWFP | North West Frontier Province (Pakistan) |
| NWR | North Western Railway (Pakistan) |
| NWRB | National Water Resources Board (Philippines) |
| NWSDB | National Water Supply and Drainage Board (Sri Lanka) |
| NYCE | New York Cocoa Exchange |
| NYCE | New York Commodity Exchange |
| NYCE | New York Cotton Exchange |
| NYCSCE | New York Coffee, Sugar and Cocoa Exchange |
| NYFE | New York Futures Exchange |
| NYK | Nippon Yusen Kaisha Line |
| NYMEX | New York Mercantile Exchange |
| NYPC | National Youth Pioneer Corps (Malaysia) |
| NYSCO | National Youth Service Cooperative Organization (Sri Lanka) |
| NYSC | National Youth Services Council (Sri Lanka) |
| NYSE | New York Stock Exchange |
| NZAS | New Zealand Association of Scientists |
| NZBC | New Zealand Broadcasting Corporation |
| NZCER | New Zealand Council for Educational Research |
| NZCSD | New Zealand Central Securities Depository |
| NZDA | New Zealand Department of Agriculture |
| NZDCS | New Zealand Department of Census and Statistics |
| NZDLS | New Zealand Department of Lands and Survey |
| NZDMO | New Zealand Debt Management Office |
| NZDSIR | New Zealand Department of Science and Industrial Research |
| NZEI | New Zealand Electronics Institute |
| NZFIB | New Zealand Fishing Industry Board |
| NZFL | New Zealand Federation of Labour |
| NZFOE | New Zealand Futures and Options Exchange |
| NZIER | New Zealand Institute of Economic Research |

| | |
|---|---|
| NZFP | New Zealand Forest Products Limited |
| NZFRI | New Zealand Forest Research Institute |
| NZFS | New Zealand Forest Service |
| NZIC | New Zealand Institute of Chemistry |
| NZIE | New Zealand Institution of Engineers |
| NZIM | New Zealand Institute of Management |
| NZLA | New Zealand Library Association |
| NZMN | New Zealand Merchant Navy |
| NZMS | New Zealand Meteorological Service |
| NZNAC | New Zealand National Airways Corporation |
| NZNCOR | New Zealand National Committee on Oceanic Research |
| NZOI | New Zealand Oceanographic Institute |
| NZPA | New Zealand Press Association |
| NZPE | New Zealand Petroleum Exploration Limited |
| NZPO | New Zealand Post Office |
| NZS | New Zealand Standard |
| NZSA | New Zealand Statistical Association |
| NZSC | New Zealand Shipping Company |
| NZSI | New Zealand Standard Institute |
| NZSS | New Zealand Standard Specification |
| NZUSA | New Zealand University Students Association |
| NZVA | New Zealand Veterinary Association |
| NZWB | New Zealand Wool Board |
| O&M | Operation and maintenance |
| OA | Open account |
| OAA | Orient Airlines Association |
| OAEC | Organization for Asian Economic Cooperation |
| OAG | Office of Auditor General |
| OALOS | Office for Ocean Affairs and Law of the Sea |
| OANA | Organization of Asian News Agencies |
| OBA | Offshore Banking Act (Malaysia) |
| OBEC | Organization of Banana Exporting Countries |
| OB/OS | Over-bought/over-sold Index |
| OBR | Overnight borrowing rate |
| OBS | Office of Bank Supervision (Korea) |
| OBSA | Off balance sheet activities |
| OBU | Offshore Banking Unit |
| O/C | Officer in charge |
| OCA | Offshore Companies Act (Malaysia) |
| OCB | Overseas Corporate Body (India) |
| OCBC | Overseas-Chinese Banking Corporation (Singapore) |
| OCC | Office of the Controller of Currency |
| OCC | Oil Coordination Committee (India) |
| OCC | Options Clearing Company Private Limited (Singapore) |
| OCC | Options Clearing Corporation |

| | |
|---|---|
| OCCI | Overseas Construction Council of India |
| OCH | Options Clearing House (Australia) |
| OCL | Overseas Containers Limited |
| OCM | Olympic Council of Malaysia |
| OCOI | Operating cost on operating income |
| OCR | Ordinary capital resources |
| OCR | Optical character recognition |
| OCW | Overseas contract worker |
| OD | Overdraft |
| ODA | Official development assistance |
| ODA | Organization of Development of Asia |
| ODA | Overseas Development Assistance |
| ODC | Overseas Development Council |
| ODR | Official discount rate |
| OEA | Office of Employment Advocate (Australia) |
| OEA | Overall external assistance |
| OECD | Organization for Economic Cooperation and Development |
| OECD | Organization for European Cooperation and Development |
| OECD-NEA | OECD Nuclear Energy Agency |
| OECF | Overseas Economic Cooperation Fund (Japan) |
| OEEC | Organization for European Economic Cooperation |
| OEIC | Open-ended Investment Company |
| OEL | Orient Express Lines |
| OEM | Original equipment manufacturer |
| OESP | Office of Evaluation of Strategic Planning |
| OEZ | Open Economic Zone |
| OFC | Offshore financial centre |
| OFC | Optical fibre cable |
| OFCL | On-shore foreign currency loan |
| Off-JT | Off-the-job training |
| OFW | Overseas Filipino Worker |
| OGDC | Oil and Gas Development Corporation |
| OGL | Open General Licence |
| OHG | Offene Handelsgesellschaft (Business partnership, Austria) |
| OHMS | On Her Majesty's Service |
| OHQ | Operational Headquarters |
| OHS | Occupational health and safety |
| OIA | Offshore Insurance Act (Malaysia) |
| OIC | Omnibus Investments Code (Philippines) |
| OIC | Organization of Islamic Conference |
| OICL | Oriental Insurance Company Limited (India) |
| OIL | Oil India Ltd |
| OIPA | International Organization for the Protection of Works of Art |
| OIRT | International Radio and Television Organization |

| OISCA | Organization Industrial Spiritual Cultural Advancement International |
| OJT | On-the-job training |
| OLA | Office of Legal Affairs (Bhutan) |
| OLS | Ordinary Least Squares |
| OLTT | On-line teller terminal |
| OM | Open market |
| OMA | Orderly marketing arrangement |
| OMC | Open Market Committee (Bank Indonesia) |
| OME | Osaka Mercantile Exchange |
| OMF | Output Monitoring Framework |
| OMO | Open market operations |
| OMV | Open market value |
| ONGC | Oil and Natural Gas Commission (India) |
| ONO | Or nearest offer |
| OOCL | Orient Overseas Container Line |
| OOO | Out of order |
| OOP | Office of Operational Planning |
| OP | Office of the President (Philippines) |
| OPA | Oil pool account |
| OPC | Oil producing country |
| OPE | Office of Project Evaluation |
| OPEC | Organization of Petroleum Exporting Countries |
| OPIC | Overseas Private Investment Corporation |
| OPL | Outer port limit |
| OPM | Other people's money |
| OPP1 | First Outline Perspective Plan (Malaysia) |
| OPP2 | Second Outline Perspective Plan (Malaysia) |
| OPP3 | Third Outline Perspective Plan (Malaysia) |
| OPPS | Outline Perspective Plan for Sabah |
| OPSF | Oil Price Stabilization Fund |
| OPTAD | Organization of Pacific Trade and Development |
| OPR | Office of Policy Research |
| OPRC | International Convention for Oil Pollution Preparedness Response and Cooperation |
| OPT | Operasi Pasar Terbuka (Indonesia) (Open market operation) |
| ORBA | Orde Baru (Indonesia) (New Order Government) |
| ORCD | Organization for Regional Cooperation and Development |
| ORSA | Operations Research Society of America |
| ORSO | Occupational Retirement Schemes Ordinance |
| OSA | Official Secrets Act |
| OSA | One-stop agency |
| OSAC | One-Stop Action Centre |
| OSC | Office of Special Concerns |

| | |
|---|---|
| OSCO | Organized and Serious Crimes Ordinance (Hong Kong) |
| OSE | Office of State Enterprises (Thailand) |
| OSE | Osaka Securities Exchange |
| OSE | Osaka Stock Exchange |
| OSEC | Office of the Secretary |
| OSEC | Organization of Sand Exporting Countries |
| OSFI | Office of Superintendent of Financial Institutions (Canada) |
| OSH | Occupational safety and health |
| OSHA | Occupational Safety and Health Administration (United States) |
| OSJ | Oceanographical Society of Japan |
| OSMOS | Off-site Monitoring System |
| OSROK | Office of Supply of the Republic of Korea |
| OTB | Overseas Trust Bank |
| OTC | Office of the Textiles Commissioner (India) |
| OTC | Organization for Trade Cooperation (UN) |
| OTC | Over-the-counter |
| OTC | Overseas Trade Corporation (United Kingdom) |
| OTCEI | Over-the-Counter Exchange of India |
| OTC-FIS | Over-the-Counter Fixed Income Service |
| OTCILS | Ong Teng Cheong Institute of Labour Studies (Singapore) |
| OTCA | Overseas Technical Cooperation Agency (Japan) |
| OTH | Over the horizon (radar) |
| OTM | Out of the money |
| OTML | Ok Tedi Mining Limited (Papua New Guinea) |
| OTS | Off the shelf |
| OTS | Office of Thrift Supervision (United States) |
| OTTV | Overall thermal transfer value |
| OUB | Overseas Union Bank (Singapore) |
| OUP | Oxford University Press |
| OURD | Overseas Uranium Resources Development Co (Japan) |
| OWIU | Oil Workers International Union |
| OXFAM | Oxford Committee for Famine Relief (United Kingdom) |
| OY | Optimum yield |
| Oy | Osakeyhtiot (Limited liability company, Finland) |
| P3DN | Peningkatan Pendayagunaan Produksi Dalam Negeri (Junior Minister for the Promotion of the Use of Domestically Produced Goods) |
| P3GI | Research Centre of Indonesian Sugarcane Plantations |
| P4BM | Pusat Pengelolaan Pembebasan dan Pengembalian Bea Masuk (Indonesia) (Centre for the Administration of Duty Exemptions and Drawbacks) |
| P4D | Panitya Penyelesaihand Perburuhan Daerah (Indonesia) (Regional Committee for Settlement of Labour Disputes) |

| | |
|---|---|
| P4P | Panitya Penyelesaian Perselisihand Perburuhan Pusat (Indonesia) (Central Committee for Settlement of Labour Disputes) |
| P&A | Purchase and acquisition |
| P&L | Profit and loss |
| P&O | Peninsular and Oriental Steam Navigation Company |
| PA | People's Alliance (Sri Lanka) |
| PA | Personal assistant |
| PA | Power of attorney |
| PA | Presidential Assistant |
| PA | Principal assistant |
| PA | Public accountant |
| PAA | Provisional Airport Authority |
| PAB | Philippine Amanah Bank |
| PAC | Public Accounts Committee (India) |
| PACC | Presidential Anti-Crime Commission (Philippines) |
| PACO | Pakistan Automobile Corporation |
| PACRA | Pakistan Credit Rating Agency |
| PACS | Primary agricultural credit society (India) |
| PADC | Pakistan Agriculture Development Corporation |
| PACT | Philippines American Cooperation Talks |
| PAEC | Pakistan Atomic Energy Commission |
| PAEC | Philippine Atomic Energy Commission |
| PAFC | Philippine Association of Finance Companies |
| PAFIE | Pacific Asian Federation of Industrial Engineering |
| PAFTAD | Pacific Trade and Development Conference |
| PAIC | Ping Ann Insurance Company |
| Pakfeb | Paket Februari (Indonesia) (February reform package) |
| Pakdes | Paket Desember (Indonesia) (December reform package) |
| Pakmei | Paket Mei (Indonesia) (May reform package) |
| PAKSA-Lupa | National Union of the Urban Poor for Urban Land Reform (Philippines) |
| PAKSI | Pakistan Standards Institute |
| Pakto | Paket Oktober (Indonesia) (October reform package) |
| PAL | Philippine Air Lines |
| PAMCOR | Philippine Automotive Manufacturing Corporation |
| PAMI | Pacific Asian Management Institute (Hawaii) |
| PAN | Permanent account number |
| Pancasila | Five principles of the State (Indonesia) |
| PANY | Port Authority of New York |
| PAP | People's Action Party (Singapore) |
| PASBDI | Philippine Association of Securities Brokers and Dealers Incorporated |
| PASLA | Pan Asian Securities Lending Association |
| PAR | Peking Adjustment Rules |

| | |
|---|---|
| PAR | Prime asset ratio |
| PARC | Pakistan Agriculture Research Council |
| PAS | Performance Agreement System |
| PAS | Philippine Association of Securities |
| PASAR | Philippine Associated Smelting and Refining Corporation |
| PASMIC | Pakistan Steel Mills Corporation |
| PAT | Port Authority of Thailand |
| PATA | Pacific Area Travel Association |
| PATA | Pacific Asia Travel Association |
| PATC | Philippine Aerial Taxi Company |
| PATCRA | Papua New Guinea and Australia Trade and Commercial Relations Agreement |
| PATO | Pacific and Asian Treaty Organization |
| PATOC | Pacific Area Telecommunication Operations Centre |
| PAX | Passenger |
| PAYE | Pay as you earn |
| PAYE | Pay as you enter |
| PAYG | Pay as you go |
| PAYIC | Pay in cash |
| PAYS | Pay as you see |
| PBAC | Prequalification, Bids and Awards Committee (Philippines) |
| PBB | Property tax (Indonesia) |
| PBC | Pakistan Banking Council |
| PBC | Pakistan Broadcasting Corporation |
| PBC/PBOC | People's Bank of China |
| PBC | Philippine Banking Corporation |
| PBCL | Law on the People's Bank of China |
| PB Com | Philippine Bank of Communications |
| PBCT | Padang Besar Container Terminal (Malaysia) |
| PBD | Piawan Brunei Darussalam |
| PBEC | Pacific Basic Economic Council |
| PBECCC | Pacific Basic Economic Council Cooperation Committee |
| PBIT | Profit before interest and tax |
| PBME | Project Benefit Monitoring and Evaluation |
| PBT | Profit before tax |
| PBVC | Price to book value ratio |
| PCA | Philippine Coconut Authority |
| PCA | Philippines Constructors Association |
| PCA | Prompt corrective action |
| PCAB | Philippines Constructors Accreditation Board |
| PCARDB | Primary cooperative agricultural and development bank (India) |
| PCB | Primary cooperative bank (India) |
| PCB | Printed circuit board |
| PCB | Measures on the Prohibition of Commercial Bribery (China) |
| PCBC | People's Construction Bank of China |

| | |
|---|---|
| PCCI | Philippine Chamber of Commerce and Industry |
| PCCCI | Philippine Commercial Credit Card Inc |
| PCD | Partly convertible debenture |
| PCD | Philippine Central Depository Incorporated |
| PCE | Personal consumption expenditure |
| PCFR | Price to cash flow ratio |
| PCGG | Presidential Commission on Good Government (Philippines) |
| PCI | Participating credit institution (Sri Lanka) |
| PCI | Per capital income |
| PCI | Philippine Composite Index |
| PCIA | Philippine Cement Industry Authority |
| PCIB | Philippine Commercial and Industrial Bank |
| PCIB | Philippine Commercial and International Bank |
| PCIC | Philippine Crop Insurance Corporation |
| PCICC | Pacific Insurance Company of China |
| PCL | Public company limited |
| PCN | Personal Communications Network |
| PCO | Public calling office |
| PCP | Presidential Commission on Privatization (Sri Lanka) |
| PCP | Project completion report |
| PCRW | Production Credit for Rural Women (Nepal) |
| PCS | Provisional Clearing Statement |
| PCSE | Pacific Coast Stock Exchange (United States) |
| PCSIR | Pakistan Council for Scientific and Industrial Research |
| PCSP | Permanent Commission of the Conference on the Use and Conservation of the Marine Resources of the South Pacific |
| PCT | Patent Cooperation Treaty |
| PCUP | Presidential Commission for the Urban Poor |
| PD | Persahaan Dagang (Indonesia) (Trading company) |
| PD | Presidential Decree (Philippines) |
| PD | Primary dealer |
| PDA | Personal digital assistant |
| PDAM | Regional Drinking Water Company (Indonesia) |
| PDB | Power Development Board (Bangladesh) |
| PDB | Private Development Bank (Philippines) |
| PDB | Pudong Development Bank (China) |
| PDC | Philippine Dockyard Corporation |
| PDC | Provincial Development Corporation (Papua New Guinea) |
| PDCB | Philippine Domestic Construction Foundation |
| PDCP | Private Development Corporation of the Philippines |
| PDDCP | Product Development and Design Centre of the Philippines |
| PDFCI | Private Development Finance Company of Indonesia |
| PDI | Partai Demokrasi Indonesia (Indonesian Democratic Party) |
| PDIC | Philippine Deposit Insurance Corporation |
| PDM | People's Democratic Movement (Papua New Guinea) |

| | |
|---|---|
| PDMP | Pambansang Diwa Ng Manggagawang Pilipino (Philippine trade union) |
| PDO | Public Debt Office (India) |
| PDOS | Pre-departure Orientation Seminar (Philippines) |
| PDP | Participatory Development Program |
| PDP | Phalang Dharma Party (Thailand) |
| PDP | Planters Development Bank (Philippines) |
| PDR | People's Democratic Republic (Laos) |
| PDRCI | Philippine Dispute Resolution Centre Incorporated |
| PDS | Payment delivery system |
| PDS | Philippine Dealing System |
| PDS | Philippine Debt Securities market |
| PDS | Private debt securities |
| PDS | Public distribution system |
| PE | Permanent establishment |
| PE | Price earning ratio |
| PE | Public enterprise |
| PEA | Provincial Electricity Authority (Thailand) |
| PEA | Public Estate Authority (Philippines) |
| P-EAGA | Philippines Sub-region of EAGA |
| PEBT | Pemberitahuan ekspor barang tertentu (Indonesia) (Certificate of export for special products) |
| PEC | Philippine Environmental Code |
| PEC | Project and Equipment Corporation of India |
| PECC | Pacific Economic Cooperation Council |
| PECV | Profit Earning Capacity Value |
| PEDP | Philippine Export Development Plan |
| PEFINDO | PT Peringkat Efek Indonesia (Indonesia's securities rating agency) |
| PEFLGC | Philippine Export and Foreign Loan Guarantee Corporation |
| PEKSI | Persatuan Eksportir Indonesia |
| PEL | Pacific Eagle Lines |
| PELGC | Philippine Foreign Loan Guaranty Corp |
| Pelita | Pengembangan lima tahun (Indonesia) (Five-year Development Program) |
| PEN | Privatization exchangeable note |
| EOE | Pakistan Edible Oil Corporation |
| PEP | Personal Equity Plan |
| PEP | Philippine Environmental Policy |
| PEP | Public Expenditure Program |
| PEPCO | Pakistan Electric Power Company |
| PEPT | Philippine Educational Placement Test |
| Perbanas | Perhimpunan Bank-Bank Umum Nasional Swasta (Indonesia) |
| PERC | Political and Economic Risk Consultancy |
| PERC | Public Enterprise Reform Committee (Sri Lanka) |

| | |
|---|---|
| PERDA | Penang State Development Corporation (Malaysia) |
| Perjan | Perusahaan Jawatan (Indonesia) (Government agency) |
| PERMINDO | Perusahaan Minjak Indonesia |
| PERNAS | Perbadanan Nasional Berhad (Malaysia) |
| PERT | Program Evaluation Review Technique |
| PERTAMINA | Perusahaan Pertambangan Minyak dan Gas Bumi Negera (Indonesian state-owned petroleum and natural gas company) |
| Perum | Perusahaan Umum (Indonesia) (public corporation) |
| Perum PKK | Perusahaan Umum Pengembangan Keuangan Koperasi (Indonesia) |
| Perumka | Perum Kreta Api (Indonesian state railway company) |
| PERUMKA | Perhubungan Umum Kereta Api (Department of Public Railways, Indonesia) |
| PERUMTEL | Perum Telekomunikasi (Indonesia) |
| PET | Pre-employment training |
| PETROBANGLA | Bangladesh Oil, Gas and Minerals Corporation |
| Petrolimex | National Petroleum Import Export Corporation |
| PETRONAS | Petrolium Nasional Berhad (Malaysia) |
| PETROVIETNAM | Vietnam Oil and Gas Corporation |
| PEZA | Philippine Economic Zone Authority |
| PF | Provident fund |
| PFA | Press Foundation of Asia |
| PFEL | Pacific Far East Line (United States) |
| PFP | Personal financial planning |
| PFP | Public Framework Paper |
| PGS | Principal Guarantee Scheme |
| PHBK | Bank and Self-help Group Link Project (Indonesia) |
| PHC | Public health care |
| PhD | Doctor of Philosophy |
| PHEIA | Private Higher Educational Institutions Act (Malaysia) |
| PHHC | People's Homesite and Housing Corporation (Philippines) |
| PHI | Public Health Inspector |
| PHILACOR | Philippine Appliance Corporation |
| PHILCEMCOR | Philippine Cement Manufacturers Corporation |
| PHILCITE | Philippine Centre for International Trade and Exhibition |
| PHILCOM | Philippine Global Communications Inc |
| Philea | Philippine Industrial Estate Association |
| PHILNABANK | Philippine National Bank |
| PHILPHOS | Philippine Phosphate Fertilizer Corporation |
| PHILREX | Philippine Real Estate Exchange |
| PHILSLA | Philippine League of Savings and Loan Associations |
| PHINMA | Philippine Investment Management Corporation |
| PHIVIDEC | Philippine Veterans' Investment Development Corporation |
| PHM | Public Health Midwife |
| PHN | Public Health Nurse |

| PHP | Philippine peso |
| PIA | Pakistan International Airline |
| PIA | PHIVIDEC Industrial Authority (Philippines) |
| PIA | Promotion of Investment Act (Malaysia) |
| PIA | Provincial income account |
| PIACC | Pacific Islands Association of Chamber of Commerce |
| PIAM | Persatuan Insuran Am Malaysia |
| PIB | Public investment budgeting |
| PIC | Pacific island country |
| PIC | Pakistan Insurance Corporation |
| PIC | Prior-informed-consent system |
| PIC | Property insurance contract |
| PICA | Private Investment Company for Asia |
| PICC | People's Insurance Company of China |
| PICIC | Pakistan Industrial Credit and Investment Corporation |
| PICPA | Philippine Institute of Certified Public Accountants |
| PIDC | Pakistan Industrial Development Corporation |
| PIE | People's Industrial Enterprise (Philippines) |
| PIE | PHIVIDEC Industrial Estate (Philippines) |
| PIFRA | Project for Improvement to Financial Reporting and Auditing (Pakistan) |
| PIIF | Pakistan International Industries Fair |
| PIL | Pacific International Lines |
| PIL | Public Investment List |
| PILTEL | Pilipino Telephone Corporation |
| PIMC | Public Investment and Management Company (Sri Lanka) |
| PIN | Personal identification number |
| PIN | Public Information Notice |
| PINSTECH | Pakistan Institute of Nuclear Science and Technology |
| PINZ | Plastics Institute of New Zealand |
| PIO | Protection of Investors Ordinance (Hong Kong) |
| PIOSA | Pan Indian Ocean Science Association |
| PIP | Public Investment Program |
| PIR | Perusahan Inti Rakyat (Indonesia) (Smallholder enterprise) |
| PIR | Pancasila Industrial Relations (Indonesia) |
| PIRMA | People's Initiative for Reform, Modernization and Action (Philippines) |
| PISC | Petroleum Import and Supply Company (Mongolia) |
| PISO | Public Information Services Office |
| PIT | Personal income tax |
| PITAC | Pakistan Industrial Technical Assistance Centre |
| PITC | Philippine International Trading Corporation |
| PITF | Pacific International Trade Fair |
| PITO | Private Investment and Trade Opportunity |
| PJB | PT Pembangkit Listrik Jawa Bali (Indonesia) |

| PJEC | Pakistan Jute Export Corporation |
| PJP-II | Second Long Term Development Plan (Indonesia) |
| PJVU | Privatization and Joint Venture Unit (Malaysia) |
| PKO | Palm kernel oil |
| PKI | Partai Komunis Indonesia (Indonesian Communist Party) |
| PKM | Proyek Kredit Mikro (Indonesia) (Micro Credit Project) |
| PKNS | Perbadanan Kemajuan Negeri Selangor (Malaysia) (Selangor State Development Corporation) |
| PKT | Proyek Kemitraan Terpadu (Indonesia) (Integrated Partnership Program) |
| PKUK | Holder of the Authority for Electric Power Business (Indonesia) |
| PLA | Paddy Lands Act (Sri Lanka) |
| PLA | Patent licence agreement |
| PLA | People's Liberation Army (China) |
| PLA | Personal Ledger Account |
| PLA | Port of London Authority |
| PLATO | Programmed Logic for Automated Teaching Operation |
| PLC | Public limited company |
| PLDT | Philippine Long Distance Telephone Company |
| PLF | Plant load factor |
| PLI | Poverty Line Index |
| PLIC | Personal insurance contract |
| PLMO | Property Loan Management Organization (Thailand) |
| PLN | Perum Listrik Negara (Indonesia) (State-owned electric company) |
| PLR | Prime lending rate |
| PLS | Profit and loss sharing |
| PLUS | Projek Lebuhraya Utara-Selatan (Malaysia) |
| PM | Prime Minister |
| PMA | Pakistan Medical Association |
| PMA | Penanaman Modal Asing (Indonesia) (Foreign investment company) |
| PMB | Paddy Marketing Board (Sri Lanka) |
| PMC | Post Ministerial Conference (ASEAN) |
| PMDC | Pakistan Mineral Development Corporation |
| PMDC | Punjab Mineral Development Corporation |
| PME | Plant, machinery and equipment |
| PMDN | Penanaman Modal Dalam Negeri (Indonesia) (Domestic investment company) |
| PMO | Postal money order |
| PMO | Prime Minister's Office |
| PMO | Project Management Office |
| PMP | Privatization Master Plan (Malaysia) |
| PMS | Portfolio management scheme (India) |
| PMS | Poverty Monitoring Survey |
| PMS | Project Monitoring System |

| | |
|---|---|
| PMSEIC | Prime Minister's Science, Engineering and Innovation Council (Australia) |
| PMVD | Local venture capital company (Indonesia) |
| PN | Perusahaan Negara (Indonesia) (State corporation) |
| PNB | Permodalan Nasional Berhad (Malaysia) |
| PNB | Philippine National Bank |
| PNB | Punjab National Bank |
| PNCC | Philippine National Construction Corporation |
| PNCP | Philippine National Centre of Petroleum |
| PNG | Pakistan National Guard |
| PNG | Papua New Guinea |
| PNGBC | Papua New Guinea Banking Corporation |
| PNGDB | Papua New Guinea Development Bank |
| PNGDF | Papua New Guinea Defence Force |
| PNI | Partai Nasional Indonesia |
| PNO | Pakistan National Oil Corporation |
| PNOC | Philippine National Oil Commission |
| PNOC | Philippine National Oil Company |
| PNP | Philippine National Police |
| PNR | Philippine National Railway |
| PNS | Philippine National Standards |
| PNS | Philippine News Service |
| PNSC | Pakistan National Shipping Corporation |
| PNSL | Perbadanan Nasional Shipping Line Berhad (Malaysia) |
| PNTR | Permanent Normal Trade Relations |
| PO | Payment order |
| PO | People's organization |
| PO | Post office |
| PO | Postal order |
| PO | Presidential Order |
| PO | Public officer |
| PO | Purchase order |
| POA | Pacific Ocean Area |
| POC | Pakistan Oilfields Corporation |
| POC | Patent Office of China |
| POCB | Philippine Overseas Construction Board |
| PODC | Philippine Oil Development Corporation |
| POE | Port of entry |
| POE | Privately-owned enterprise |
| POEA | Philippine Overseas Employment Administration |
| POFI | Portfolio and other foreign investments |
| POGEI | Philippine Oil and Geothermal Energy Incorporated |
| POL | Petroleum, oil and lubricant product |
| POMSoX | Port Moresby Stock Exchange (Papua New Guinea) |
| POPRC | Patent Office of the People's Republic of China |

| | |
|---|---|
| POR | Payable on receipt |
| PORIM | Palm Oil Research Institute of Malaysia |
| PORLA | Palm Oil Registration and Licensing Authority (Malaysia) |
| POS | Point of sale |
| POSB | Post Office Savings Bank (Singapore) |
| POSCO | Pohang Steel Corporation (Korea) |
| POST | Pacific Ocean Security Treaty |
| POTC | Philippine Overseas Telecommunication Corporation |
| POW | Prisoner of war |
| POWERGRID | Power Grid Corporation of India |
| PP | Perusahaan Persaorangan (Indonesia) (Sole proprietorship) |
| PP | Private placement |
| PPA | Pakistan Press Association |
| PPA | Philippine Ports Authority |
| PPA | Power purchase agreement |
| PPA | Protocol of Provisional Agreement |
| PPAF | Pakistan Poverty Alleviation Fund |
| PPAW | Provision for Productive Asset write-off |
| PPBS | Planning, Programming and Budgeting System |
| PPC | Philippine Petroleum Corporation |
| PPC | Punjab Provincial Cooperative Bank |
| PPCC | Phnom Penh Chamber of Commerce (Cambodia) |
| PPD | Policy and Planning Division |
| PPD | Primary Production Department |
| PPE | Project Performance Evaluation |
| PPFC | People's Pearl and Fishery Corporation (Myanmar) |
| PPFC | Philippine Phosphate Fertilizer Corporation |
| PPH | Pajak Penghasilan (Income tax) |
| PPH | Ownership notification form used in stock exchange (Indonesia) |
| PPI | Pakistan Packaging Institute |
| PPI | Pakistan Press International |
| PPI | Producer Price Index |
| PPL | Partnership Pacific Ltd (Australia) |
| PPL | Philippine President Lines |
| PPM | Process and production method |
| PPO | Partially paid ordinary shares |
| PPP | Pakistan Peoples Party |
| PPP | Partai Persatuan Pembangunan (Indonesia) (United Development Party) |
| PPP | Policy, program and plan |
| PPP | Purchasing power parity |
| PPPRF | Pan Pacific Public Relations Federation |
| PPS | Pension Payment System |
| PPUE | Perserikatan Perdagangan Uang dan Efek-Efek (Indonesia) (Association of Money and Securities Trading) |

| | |
|---|---|
| PPUE | Stock Exchange Dealers' Union (Indonesia) |
| PPUK | Proyek Pengembangan Usaha Kechil (Indonesia) (Small Enterprise Development Project) |
| PQLI | Physical Quality of Life Index |
| PR | Permanent resident |
| PR | Proportional Representative |
| PRA | Petroleum Refinery of Australia |
| PRA | Philippine Retirement Authority |
| PRAB | Provisional Regulation on the Administration of Banks (China) |
| PRBD | People's Republic of Bangladesh |
| PRC | People's Republic of China |
| PRC | Professional Regulations Commission (Philippines) |
| PREIT | Provisional Regulation on Enterprise Income Tax (China) |
| PRESS | Payments Registration and Electronic Settlement System (Australia) |
| PRGF | Poverty Reduction and Growth Fund (India) |
| PRI | Pacific Resources Incorporated (Australia) |
| Pribumi | Indigenous Indonesian |
| PRO | Public Relations Office |
| PROBE | Public Report on Basic Education in India |
| PROKASIH | Clean Water Program in Indonesia |
| PROLUS | Program Latihan yang diluluskan (Malaysia) (Approved Training Scheme) |
| PROOC | Pearl River Oil Operation Company (China) |
| PROPER | Program for Pollution Control, Evaluation and Rating (Indonesia) |
| PROTON | Perusahaan Otomobil Nasional Berhad (Malaysia) |
| PRS | Pakistan Revenue Service |
| PRSP | Poverty reduction strategy papers |
| PRT | People-mover Rapid Transit |
| PS | Permanent Secretary |
| PS | Product standard |
| PS | Public servant |
| PS | Public service |
| PSA | Pacific Science Association (United States) |
| PSA | Port of Singapore Authority |
| PSA | Prices Surveillance Authority (Australia) |
| PSA | Public Servants Association (Papua New Guinea) |
| PSB | Philippine Savings Bank |
| PSB | Philippines Shippers Bureau |
| PSB | Productivity and Standards Board (Singapore) |
| PSB | Public sector bank |
| PSB | Public Security Bureau (China) |
| PSBR | Public Sector Borrowing Requirement |
| PSC | Pakistan Shipping Corporation |
| PSC | Pasig Steel Corporation (Philippines) |

| | |
|---|---|
| PSC | Philippine Shippers Council |
| PSC | Production sharing contract |
| PSC | Public Service Commission |
| PSD | Public Service Department |
| PSD | Public Service Division |
| PSDC | Penang Skill Development Centre |
| PSDN | Public Switched Data Network |
| PSDN | Public Switched Digital Network |
| PSDP | Public Sector Development Plan (Pakistan) |
| PSDW | Preference shares with detachable warrant |
| PSE | Pacific Stock Exchange |
| PSE | Philippine Stock Exchange |
| PSE | Public sector enterprise |
| PSEFI | PSE Foundation Incorporated (Philippines) |
| PSEI | Parallel Stock Exchange of Indonesia |
| PSI | Pakistan Standards Institute |
| PSI | Pollutants Standards Index |
| PSI | Pre-shipment inspection |
| PSI | Private sector initiative |
| PSIC | Philippine Standard Industrial Classification |
| PSMFC | Pacific States Marine Fisheries Commission (United States) |
| PSO | Private sector organization |
| PSP | PT Putra Saridaya Persada (Indonesia) |
| PSQC | Philippine Society for Quality Control |
| PSR | Price to sales ratio |
| PSRAG | Public Sector Reform Advisory Group (Papua New Guinea) |
| PSRMU | Public Sector Reform Management Unit (Papua New Guinea) |
| PSRP | Canada China Public Sector Reform Program |
| PSS | Postal Savings System (Taiwan) |
| PST | Pacific Standard Time (United States) |
| PST | Pakistan Standard Time |
| PSU | Public sector undertaking |
| PT | Perseroan Terbatas (Indonesia) (Limited liability company) |
| PT | Preferential tariff |
| PTA | Pakistan Tea Association |
| PTA | Pakistan Telecommunication Authority |
| PTA | Policy target agreement |
| PTA | Preferential Trading Arrangement (ASEAN) |
| PT&T | Philippine Telegraph and Telephone Company |
| PTC | Pacific Telecommunication Council |
| PTC | Pacific Tuna Conference |
| PTC | Pakistan Television Corporation |
| PTC | Pakistan Trading Corporation |
| PTC | Postal and Telecommunication Corporation (Papua New Guinea) |
| PTCL | Pakistan Telecommunication Company Limited |

| | |
|---|---|
| PTDC | Pakistan Tourism Development Corporation |
| PTI | Press Trust of India |
| PTIC | Posts and Telecommunication Industry Corporation (China) |
| PTL | Pakistan Tours Limited |
| PTLR | Prime term lending rate |
| PTM | PT Timar Putra Nasional (Indonesia) |
| PTN | PT Perusahaan Listrik Negara (Indonesia) |
| PTO | Please turn over |
| PTP | PT Perkebunan (Indonesia) (State-owned plantation) |
| PTP | Port Tanjung Pelapas (Malaysia) |
| PTQ | Preferential Tariff Quota (ASEAN) |
| PTS | Philippine Trade Standard |
| PTS | Proprietary trading system |
| PTT | Petroleum Authority of Thailand |
| PTTC | Philippines Trade Training Centre |
| PTV | Pakistan Television |
| Pty Ltd | Proprietary Limited |
| PUB | Public Utilities Board (Singapore) |
| PUB | Public utility bus |
| PUK | Perwakilan Unit Kerja (Indonesia) (Enterprise work unit) |
| PUT | People's Unit Trust (Papua New Guinea) |
| PV | Present value |
| PVC | polyvinyl chloride |
| PVF | Port Vila Fisheries Limited (Vanuatu) |
| PVO | Private volunteer organization |
| PvP | Payment versus payment |
| PWA | Provincial Waterworks Authority (Thailand) |
| PWC | Preliminary Working Committee (of the Preparatory Committee of the Hong Kong Administrative Region) |
| PWD | Public Works Department (Singapore) |
| PWI | Indonesian Journalists Association |
| PWO | Public Warehouse Organization (Thailand) |
| PWP | People's Works Program (Pakistan) |
| Q&A | Question and answer |
| QAL | Queensland Alumina Limited (Australia) |
| QANTAS | Queensland and Northern Territory Aerial Services |
| QC | Quality control |
| QC | Queen's Counsel |
| QDEDC | Qingdao Economic Development Corporation (China) |
| QCC | Quality control circle |
| QFB | Qualified Full Bank |
| QFD | Quasi fiscal deficit |
| QFII | Qualified Foreign Institutional Investor |
| QFRI | Queensland Fishery Research Institute (Australia) |
| QHDHA | Qinhuangdao Harbour Administration (China) |

| | |
|---|---|
| QIB | Qualified institutional buyer |
| QLFS | Quarterly Labour Force Survey |
| QR | Quantitative restriction |
| QRST | Quality assurance, Rational use, Self-sufficiency and Threat |
| QUT | Queensland University of Technology (Australia) |
| R&D | Research and development |
| RA | Registered Accountant (Malaysia) |
| RA | Reinvestment Allowance (Malaysia) |
| RAAF | Royal Australian Air Force |
| RAAMC | Royal Australian Army Medical Corps |
| RAANS | Royal Australian Army Nursing Service |
| RAB | Regional arrangement to borrow |
| RAC | Royal Air Cambodge |
| RAC | Royal Automobile Club (United Kingdom) |
| RACA | Royal Automobile Club of Australia |
| RACFIU | Regulation and Admission Criteria of Foreign Insurance Undertakings (China) |
| RACI | Royal Australian Chemical Institute |
| RACP | Royal Australasian College of Physicians |
| RACS | Royal Australasian College of Surgeons |
| RACV | Royal Automobile Club of Victoria (Australia) |
| RADD | Real aggregate domestic demand |
| RADR | Restricted American Depository Receipt |
| RAE | Royal Australian Engineers |
| RAGA | Royal Australian Garrison Artillery |
| RAHS | Royal Australian Historical Society |
| RAIA | Royal Australian Institute of Architects |
| RAIC | Regional Agri-industrial Centre (Philippines) |
| RAIN | Registrars' Association of India |
| RAM | Rating Agency Malaysia Berhad |
| RAME | Royal Australian Mechanical Engineers |
| RANC | Royal Australian Naval College |
| RANR | Royal Australian Naval Reserve |
| RANVR | Royal Australian Naval Volunteer Reserve |
| RAOU | Royal Australian Ornithologists Union |
| RAR | Royal Australian Rifles |
| RAS | Royal Asiatic Society |
| RAS | Rubber Association of Singapore |
| RATE | Risk assessment, tools of supervision and evaluation |
| RB | Rural bank |
| RBA | Reserve Bank of Australia |
| RBA | Royal Brunei Airlines |
| RBAP | Rural Bankers Association of the Philippines |
| RBB | Rastriya Banijya Bank (Nepal) |
| RBC | Risk-based capital |

| RBI | Reserve Bank of India |
|---|---|
| RBITS | Reserve Bank Information and Transfer System (Australia) |
| RBNZ | Reserve Bank of New Zealand |
| RBOI | Regional Board of Investment (Philippines) |
| RBP | Restricted business practices |
| RBRP | Rural Bank Rehabilitation Program (Philippines) |
| RB&STC | Rural Banking and Staff Training College (Sri Lanka) |
| RBV | Reserve Bank of Vanuatu |
| RCA | Radio Corporation of America |
| RCB | Registry of Companies and Businesses (Singapore) |
| RCB | Resolution and collection bank |
| RCBC | Rizal Commercial Banking Corporation (Philippines) |
| RCC | Rural credit cooperative |
| RCCPS | Redeemable convertible cumulative preference share |
| RCF | Revolving credit facility |
| RCFS | Revised Carry Forward System |
| RCGP | Royal College of General Practitioners |
| RCP | Reduced cut policy |
| RCPI | Radio Communication of the Philippines |
| RCPS | Redeemable cumulative preference share |
| RCTFC | Risk Capital and Technology Finance Corporation (India) |
| RCTI | PT Rajawali Citra Televisi Indonesia |
| RDA | Road Development Authority (Sri Lanka) |
| RDB | Regional development bank |
| RDC | Regional Development Council |
| RDFC | Regional Development Finance Corporation (Pakistan) |
| RDIP | Regional Development Investment Program |
| RDL | Regional Division of Labour |
| RDNS | Regional Directorate of National Savings (Pakistan) |
| RDP | Regional Development Plan |
| RDPC | Rangoon Division People's Council |
| RDL | Royal Drug Limited (Nepal) |
| RDS | Rural Development Society (Sri Lanka) |
| RE | Retained earnings |
| REB | Rural Electrification Board (Bangladesh) |
| RECSAM | Regional Centre for Science and Mathematics (Malaysia) |
| REDAS | Real Estate Developers' Association of Singapore |
| REDP | Rural Energy Development Program (Nepal) |
| REE | Refrigeration and Electrical Engineering Corporation (Vietnam) |
| REER | Real effective exchange rate |
| REERI | Real Effective Exchange Rate Index |
| REIT | Real estate investment trust |
| Reksadana | Pension mutual funds (Indonesia) |
| RELC | Regional Language Centre (Singapore) |
| RENSTRA | Strategic Plan of Bank Indonesia |

| REO | Rubber Estate Organization (Thailand) |
| Repelita | Rencana pengembangan lima tahun (Indonesia) (Five-year plan) |
| Repo | Repurchase agreement |
| RETA | Regional Technical Assistance |
| RER | Real exchange rate |
| RFA | Regional Financial Arrangement |
| RFC | Resident Foreign Currency Account (Sri Lanka) |
| RFNRE | Revolving Fund for Natural Resources Exploration (UN) |
| RFP | Request for proposal |
| RFP | Rural finance project |
| RFQ | Request for quote |
| RGC | Royal Government of Cambodia |
| RGNP | Regional gross national product |
| RGOB | Royal Government of Bhutan |
| RGSA | Royal Geographical Society of Australasia |
| RHB | Rashid Hussain Berhad (Malaysia) |
| RHC | Rural health centre |
| RHS | Right hand side |
| RHQ | Regional Headquarters |
| RI | Republic of Indonesia |
| RIA | Regional integration arrangement |
| RIB | Resurgent India Bond |
| RIC | Reinsurance contract |
| RICB | Royal Insurance Corporation of Bhutan |
| RIDA | Rural Industrial Development Authority (Malaysia) |
| RIDF | Rural Infrastructure Development Fund (India) |
| RIDU | Rural Infrastructure Development Union |
| RIIAM | Research Institute of Investment Analysts Malaysia |
| RIL | Reliance Industries Limited (India) |
| RINPO | Research Institute of Nuclear Power Operation (China) |
| RIP | Rural Improvement Program (Papua New Guinea) |
| RISDA | Rubber Industry Smallholders Development Authority (Malaysia) |
| RISM | Research Institute of Survey and Mapping (China) |
| RITST | Research Institute for Technological and Scientific Transportation |
| RITT | Research Institute of Telecommunication Transmission (China) |
| RKT | Annual work plan (Indonesia) |
| RKUB | Rajshahi Krishi Unnayan Bank (Bangladesh) |
| RLB | Restricted licence bank |
| RM | Reserve money |
| RM | Ringgit (Malaysian currency) |
| RMA | Royal Monetary Authority (Bhutan) |
| RMA | Rubber Manufacturers Association |
| RMAI | Radio Manufacturers Association of India |
| RMB | Renminbi (Chinese currency) |
| RMIT | Royal Melbourne Institute of Technology |

| | |
|---|---|
| RMRB | Renmin Ribao (People's Daily) (China) |
| RNAC | Royal Nepal Airlines Corporation |
| RNBC | Residuary non-banking company (India) |
| RNK | Radio National of Kampuchea |
| RNNFC | Resident Non-National Foreign Currency Account (Sri Lanka) |
| RNZA | Royal New Zealand Army |
| RNZAF | Royal New Zealand Air Force |
| RNZAS | Royal New Zealand Astronomical Society |
| RNZN | Royal New Zealand Navy |
| RO | Regional office |
| ROA | Return on assets |
| ROC | Registrar of Companies |
| ROC | Registry of Companies |
| ROCE | Return on capital employed |
| ROE | Return on equity |
| ROI | Return on investment |
| ROCA | Risk management, Operational control, Compliance and Asset quality |
| ROCE | Return on capital employed |
| ROIC | Return on invested capital |
| ROK | Republic of Korea |
| ROL | Refurbish, operate and lease |
| ROM | Rehabilitate, operate and maintain |
| RONAST | Royal Nepal Academy of Science and Technology |
| ROO | Rehabilitate, own and operate |
| ROO | Rules of Origin |
| ROPUMS | Regulations on the Prohibition against the Underground Money Shops (Taiwan) |
| RORO | Roll-on roll-off |
| ROSC | Report on Observance of Standards and Codes (IMF) |
| ROSCA | Rotating Savings and Credit Association (Nepal) |
| ROSE | ROC Over-the-counter Securities Exchange |
| ROT | Rehabilitate, operate and transfer |
| ROVR | Repatriation Opportunities for Vietnamese Returnees |
| Rp | Indonesian rupiah |
| RP | Republic of the Philippines |
| R/P | Repurchase agreement |
| RPB | Recognized professional body |
| RPC | Regional Plantation Companies (Sri Lanka) |
| RPCC | Royal Pacific Capital Corporation |
| RPCCE | Real Per Capita Consumption Expenditure |
| RPDO | Regional Planning and Development Office |
| RPI | Retail Price Index |
| RPTKA | Rencana Penggunaan Tenaga Kerja Asing (Indonesia) (Foreign Manpower Plan) |

| | |
|---|---|
| RRB | Regional Rural Bank (India) |
| RRDB | Regional Rural Development Bank (Sri Lanka) |
| RRDI | Rice Research Development Institute (Sri Lanka) |
| RRF | Reverse Repurchase Facility |
| RRI | Radio Republik Indonesia |
| RRI | Rubber Research Institute (Sri Lanka) |
| RRIM | Rubber Research Institute of Malaysia |
| RR/P | Reverse repurchase agreement |
| RRP | Recommended retail price |
| RSA | Risk-focused supervisory assessment |
| RSCC | Rollover spot currency contract |
| RSE | Research scientist and engineer |
| RSI | Relative Strength Indicator |
| RSNZ | Royal Society of New Zealand |
| RSS | Regulated short selling |
| RSTP | Rural Skills Training Program (Vanuatu) |
| RTA | Reciprocal trade agreement |
| RTA | Retail transaction account (Australia) |
| RTAF | Royal Thai Air Force |
| RTC | Rural training centre |
| RTD | Research and Technological Development |
| RTG | Royal Thai Government |
| RTGS | Real Time Gross Settlement System |
| RTIO | Regional Trade and Industry Office (Bhutan) |
| RTM | Registered trade mark |
| RTN | Royal Thai Navy |
| RTP | Regional Training Program |
| RTS | Radio and Television of Singapore |
| RTS | Reserve Tranche System (Sri Lanka) |
| RTW | Ready to wear |
| RUF | Revolving Underwriting Facility |
| Rukan | House-cum-office (Indonesia) |
| Ruko | House-cum-shop (Indonesia) |
| RVF | Regional Venture Funds Incentive |
| RWCR | Risk weighted capital ratio |
| RZ | Restricted Zone |
| S21 | Singapore 21 |
| SA | Sociedad Anonima (Limited liability company in Mexico, Spain) |
| SA | Societe Anonyme (SA) (Limited liability company in France, Luxembourg, Switzerland) |
| SA | South Australia |
| SA | Sustainability assessment |
| SAA | Securities Analysts Association (Thailand) |
| SAA | Standards Association of Australia |
| SAA | State Archives Administration (China) |

| | |
|---|---|
| SAARC | South Asia Association for Regional Cooperation |
| SAAS | Shanghai Academy of Agricultural Sciences (China) |
| SAAST | Sanyo Association for Advancement of Science and Technology |
| SABINCO | Saudi-Bangladesh Industrial and Agricultural Investment Company |
| SABMI | State Administration for Building Materials Industry (China) |
| SAC | Scientific Advisory Committee (UN) |
| SAC | Security and Administration Committee (Myanmar) |
| SAC | Singapore Accreditation Council |
| SAC | Structural Adjustment Credits (Laos) |
| SAC | Syariah Advisory Council (Malaysia) |
| SACCO | Savings and Credit Cooperative (Nepal) |
| SACEOS | Singapore Association of Convention and Exhibition Organizers and Suppliers |
| SACFM | South Australian Centre For Manufacturing |
| SACM | State Administration of Chinese Medicine (China) |
| SACP | Special Agricultural Credit Program (Bangladesh) |
| SACP | State Administration of Commodity Prices (China) |
| SADF | South Asia Development Fund |
| SAEC | State Administration of Exchange Control (China) |
| SAEI | Sumitomo Atomic Energy Industries (Japan) |
| SAF | Singapore Armed Forces |
| SAF | Structural Adjustment Facility (Laos) |
| SAFCON | International Conference on Safety of Life at Sea |
| S&FA | Shipping and forwarding agent |
| SAFE | State Administration of Foreign Exchange (China) |
| SAFE | Statute for the Administration of Foreign Currency (Taiwan) |
| SAFEC | State Administration for Foreign Exchange Control (China) |
| SAFTA | South American Free Trade Area |
| SAFTA | South Asia Free Trade Area |
| SAIC | SAARC Agricultural Information Centre |
| SAIC | State Administration for Industry and Commerce (China) |
| SAIC | State Agricultural Investment Company (China) |
| SAIECI | State Administration of Import and Export Commodity |
| SAIL | Steel Authority of India |
| SAL | Structural Adjustment Loan |
| S&LA | Savings and Loan Association |
| SALT | Strategic Arms Limitation Talk |
| SAM | Self-service Automated Machine |
| SAM | Society for the Advancement of Management |
| SAMA-SAMA | Samahan ng Maralita Para sa Makatarungang Peninirahan (Philippines) (Solidarity of the Poor for Just Housing) |
| SAMB | Shanghai Agricultural Machinery Bureau (China) |
| SAMC | Shenyang Aircraft Manufacturing Company (China) |

| SAMCO | Saigon Motors Company |
|---|---|
| SAN | Shared ATM Network |
| SANZ | Standards Association of New Zealand |
| S&P | Standard and Poor's |
| SAP | Social Action Program |
| SAP | Social Action Party (Thailand) |
| SAP | Standard accounting procedure |
| SAPAP | South Asia Poverty Alleviation Program |
| SAPTA | South Asian Preferential Trading Agreement |
| SAR | Special Administrative Region |
| SARDI | South Australian Research and Development Institute |
| SARFT | State Administration of Radio Film and Television (China) |
| SARP | Standards and Recommended Practices (UN) |
| SARS | Severe Acute Respiratory Syndrome |
| SASMIRA | Silk and Artificial Silk Mills Research Association (India) |
| SAS | Singapore Accounting Standards |
| SASMIRA | Silk and Art Silk Mills Research Association (India) |
| SAST | Shanghai Association of Science and Technology (China) |
| S&T | Science and technology |
| SAT | Scholastic Aptitude Test |
| SAT | Sports Authority of Thailand |
| SATC | South Australian Tourism Commission |
| SATCM | State Administration of Traditional Chinese Medicine (China) |
| Satelindo | PT Satelit Palapa Indonesia |
| SATF | South Asia Task Force |
| SATS | Singapore Airport Terminal Services |
| SAVECRED | Save the Children through Credit program (Sri Lanka) |
| SAVEC | SAARC Audio Visual Exchange Committee |
| SAYE | Save As You Earn |
| SBA | Shanghai Bureau of Aeronautics (China) |
| SBA | Singapore Broadcasting Authority |
| SBA | Small Business Administration (United States) |
| SBAP | Savings Bankers Association of the Philippines |
| SBBMI | State Bureau of Building Materials Industry (China) |
| SBC | Securities brokerage company |
| SBC | Singapore Broadcasting Corporation |
| SBC | Stock-broking company |
| SBC | Strategic business centre |
| SBDC | Small Business Development Centre (Malaysia) |
| SBF | Singapore Business Federation |
| SBF | Subic Bay Freeport (Philippines) |
| SBFC | Small Business Finance Corporation (Pakistan) |
| SBGFC | Small Business Guarantee and Finance Corporation (Philippines) |
| SBI | Sertifikat Bank Indonesia (Bank Indonesia Certificate) |
| SBI | State Bank of India |

| | |
|---|---|
| SBICAP | SBI Capital Markets Ltd (India) |
| SBL | Securities borrowing and lending |
| SBL | Single borrower's limit |
| SBLA | Securities borrowing and lending agreement |
| SBLP | Serikat Buruh Lapangan Pekergaan (Industrial sector union) |
| SBM | State Bureau of Metrology (China) |
| SBMA | Subic Bay Metropolitan Authority (Philippines) |
| SBP | State Bank of Pakistan |
| SBPU | Surat Berhaga Pasar Uang (Indonesia) (Money market securities) |
| SBS | Seoul Broadcasting System (Korea) |
| SBS | Singapore Bus Services Limited |
| SBSA | State Bank of South Australia |
| SBSC | State Bureau of Surveying and Cartography (China) |
| SBSI | Serikat Buruh Sajahtera Indonesia (Indonesian Prosperous Workers' Union) |
| SBSM | Shanghai Bureau of Standardization and Metrology (China) |
| SBTC | Sino-British Trade Council |
| SBTS | State Bureau of Technical Supervision (China) |
| SBU | Small business unit |
| SBU | Strategic business unit |
| SBV | State Bank of Vietnam |
| SC | Securities Commission |
| SC | Standing committee |
| SC | State Council (China) |
| SCAC | Shanghai Culture and Arts Centre (China) |
| SCAC | Sichuan Aviation Corporation (China) |
| SCAE | Singapore Changi Airport Enterprise |
| SCAL | Singapore Contractors Association Limited |
| SCANS | Securities Clearing Automated Network Services |
| SCAP | Singapore Code of Advertising Practice |
| SCAPS | Share and Care Apostolate for Poor Settlers (Philippines) |
| SCARDB | State cooperative and agricultural rural development bank (India) |
| SCB | Scheduled commercial bank (India) |
| SCB | Shanghai Cultural Bureau (China) |
| SCB | Standard Chartered Bank |
| SCB | State Cooperative Bank (India) |
| SCC | Sabah Credit Corporation |
| SCCCI | Singapore Chinese Chamber of Commerce and Industry |
| SCCI | SAARC Chamber of Commerce and Industry |
| SCCI | State Committee for Cooperation and Investment (Vietnam) |
| SCCP | Securities Clearing Corporation of the Philippines |
| SCCP | State Cement Corporation of Pakistan |
| SCDF | Singapore Civil Defence Force |
| SCEC | Sichuan Province Construction and Engineering Corp (China) |
| SCEC | State Committee for Environmental Control (Mongolia) |

| | |
|---|---|
| S-CECF | Spring Chinese Export Commodities Fair |
| SCEJ | Society of Chemical Engineers of Japan |
| SCEPA | Sichuan Electric Power Administration (China) |
| SCF | Special Cooperation Fund |
| SCF | Standard cubic feet |
| SCGT | South China Growth Triangle |
| SCH | Securities Clearing House |
| SCHA | Singapore Clearing House Association |
| SCI | Shipping Corporation of India |
| SCI | Singapore College of Insurance |
| SCI | Singapore Confederation of Industries |
| SCI | Small and cottage industry |
| SCIB | Shanghai Chemical Industry Bureau (China) |
| SCIB | Siam City Bank |
| SCIC | State Communications Investment Corporation (China) |
| SCICI | Shipping Credit and Investment Company of India |
| SCIRD | Sub-Committee on Science and Technology, Infrastructure and Resources Development (ASEAN) |
| SCJ | Science Council of Japan |
| SCMP | South China Morning Post (Hong Kong) |
| SCNPC | Standing Committee of the National People's Congress (China) |
| SCNPO | State Council Nuclear Power Office (China) |
| SCO | Special Communication Organization (Pakistan) |
| SCOPE | Scientific Committee on Problems of the Environment |
| SCORE | Singapore Corporation of Rehabilitative Enterprise |
| SCOT | Sub-Committee on Tourism (ASEAN) |
| SCPC | State Chemical Products Corporation (India) |
| SCPC | State Commission of Price Control (China) |
| SCRA | Securities Contracts Regulation Act (India) |
| SCRCC | Soil Conservation and Rivers Control Council (New Zealand) |
| SCRES | State Commission for Restructuring the Economic System (China) |
| SCSC | Shanghai Changjiang Shipping Corporation (China) |
| SCSC | State Council Securities Committee (China) |
| SCSHHP | South China Sea Headquarters for Petroleum Prospecting (China) |
| SCSI | Shanghai Corporation of Shipbuilding Industry (China) |
| SCSPC | State Council Securities Policy Commission (China) |
| SCSR | State Commission of Structural Reform (China) |
| SCST | Scheduled Caste and Scheduled Tribe (India) |
| SCT | Small Claims Tribunal |
| SCUBA | Self-Contained Underwater Breathing Apparatus |
| SCV | Singapore Cable Vision |
| SCX | Sub-contract Exchange scheme (Malaysia) |
| SD | Satellite dealer (India) |
| SD | Sustainable development |
| SDA | Sarhad Development Authority (Pakistan) |

| | |
|---|---|
| SDB | Shenzhen Development Bank (China) |
| SDB | State Development Bank (China) |
| SDC | SAARC Documentation Centre |
| SDC | Sentosa Development Corporation (Singapore) |
| SDC | Share Depository Centre (Thailand) |
| SDDS | Special Data Dissemination Standards (Hong Kong) |
| SDEC | Shandong Economic Committee (China) |
| SDF | Skills Development Fund |
| SDN | System development network |
| Sdn Bhd | Sendirian Berhad |
| SDO | State Development Office |
| SDP | Strategic Development Plan |
| SDPC | State Development and Planning Commission (China) |
| SDR | Special Drawing Right |
| SE | Sertifikat Ekspor (Export certificate) |
| SE | Stock exchange |
| SEA | Securities Exchange Act (United States) |
| SEA | Southeast Asia |
| SEA | Strategic Environmental Assessment |
| SEACEN | South East Asian Central Banks |
| SEACORP | Southeast Asia Development Corporation |
| SEADB | Southeast Asia Development Bank |
| SEAFDEC | Southeast Asian Fisheries Development Centre |
| SEAISI | Southeast Asian Iron and Steel Institute |
| SEAMEO | Southeast Asian Ministers of Education Organization |
| SEAMEO BIOTROP | SEAMEO Regional Centre for Tropical Biology |
| SEAMEO CHAT | SEAMEO Regional Centre for History and Tradition |
| SEAMEO INNOTECH | SEAMEO Regional Centre for Educational Innovation and Technology |
| SEAMEO RECSAM | SEAMEO Regional Centre for Education in Science and Mathematics |
| SEAMEO RELC | SEAMEO Regional Language Centre |
| SEAMEO RETRAC | SEAMEO Regional Training Centre |
| SEAMEO RIHED | SEAMEO Regional Centre for Higher Education and Development |
| SEAMEO SEAMOLEC | SEAMEO Regional Open Learning Centre |
| SEAMEO SEARCA | SEAMEO Regional Centre for Graduate Study and Research in Agriculture |
| SEAMEO SPAFA | SEAMEO Regional Centre for Archaeology and Fine Arts |
| SEAMEO TROPMED | SEAMEO Tropical Medicine and Public Health Network |
| SEAMEO VOCTECH | SEAMEO Regional Centre for Vocational and Technical Education |
| SEAMS | Southeast Asian Mathematical Society |
| SEANWFZ | Southeast Asian Nuclear Weapon Free Zone |
| SEANZA | Southeast Asia, New Zealand and Australia |

| | |
|---|---|
| SEAP | Southeast Asia and the Pacific |
| SEAP | Southeast Asian Peninsula |
| SEAPCENTRE | Southeast Asian Program Centre for Trade, Investment and Tourism |
| SEAPDC | Southeast Asia Petroleum Development Corporation |
| SEAPEX | Southeast Asia Petroleum Exploration Group |
| SEAPFA | Southeast Asia, the Pacific and the Far East |
| SEAQ | Stock Exchange Automated Quotation |
| SEAQI | SEAQ for International Equities (United Kingdom) |
| SEARCA | Southeast Asia Regional Centre for Graduate Study and Research in Agriculture |
| SEARCH | Singapore Employment Advisory and Recruitment Channel |
| SEARI | Shanghai Electrical Apparatus Research Institute (China) |
| SEARP | Southeast Asian Regional Program |
| SEATAC | Southeast Asian Agency for Regional Transport and Communication Development |
| SEATAG | Southeast Asian Trade Advisory Group |
| SEATE | Southeast Asian Transitional Economies |
| SEATELCOM | Southeast Asian Telecommunication System |
| SEATI | Shanghai Electrical Apparatus Technology Institute (China) |
| SEATO | Southeast Asia Treaty Organization |
| SEATRDC | Southeast Asia Tin Research and Development Centre |
| SEATS | Stock Exchange Automated Trading System (Australia) |
| SEATS | Stock Exchange Alternative Trading Service (United Kingdom) |
| SEAVI | Southeast Asia Venture Investment |
| SEB | State Electricity Board (India) |
| SEBI | Securities and Exchange Board of India |
| SEC | Securities and Exchange Commission |
| SEC | Securities Exchange Centre (Nepal) |
| SEC | State Engineering Corporation (Pakistan) |
| SEC | Supreme Economic Council (Australia) |
| SECC | SAARC Economic Cooperation Conference |
| SECRI | Shanghai Electrical Cable Research Institute (China) |
| SEDC | Sarawak Economic Development Corporation (Malaysia) |
| SEDC | State Economic Development Corporation |
| SEDC | State Education Commission (China) |
| SEDP | Socio-economic Development Plan (Cambodia) |
| SEE | State Economic Enterprise (Myanmar) |
| SEEC | Stock Exchange Executive Council (China) |
| SEEDS | Startup Enterprise Development Scheme (Singapore) |
| SEEPZ | Santa Cruz Electronics Export Processing Zone |
| SEF | Straits Exchange Foundation |
| SEHK | Stock Exchange of Hong Kong |
| SEIC | State Economic Information Centre (China) |
| SEIC | State Energy Investment Corporation (China) |

| SEIS | Stock Exchange Information Services Limited |
| SEL | Securities and Exchange Law |
| SEM | Single European Market |
| SEMS | Stock Exchange of Malaysia and Singapore |
| SEO | Subsequent equity offering |
| SEOCH | SEHK Options Clearing House |
| SEOM | Senior Economic Officials Meeting |
| SEPA | Southeast Pacific Area |
| SEPC | State Enterprise Policy Commission (Thailand) |
| SEPZ | Special Economic Promotion Zone |
| SERC | Science and Engineering Research Council (Singapore) |
| SERC | State Enterprise Reform Commission (Thailand) |
| SERI | Samsung Economic Research Institute |
| SERTS | SCANS Electronic Registration and Transfer Service |
| SES | Self Employment Scheme (Pakistan) |
| SES | Social economic survey |
| SES | Stock Exchange of Singapore |
| SESC | Securities and Exchange Surveillance Commission (Japan) |
| SESDAQ | SES Dealing and Automated Quotation System |
| SESKOAD | Army's Staff and Command College (Indonesia) |
| SET | Secure electronic transaction |
| SET | Stock Exchange of Thailand |
| SETC | State Economic and Trade Commission (China) |
| SETRI | Shanghai Electric Tool Research Institute (China) |
| SEWA | Self-employed Women's Association |
| SEZ | Special Economic Zone |
| SEZDC | Shenzen Special Economic Zone Development Corporation |
| SFA | Syndicated Facility Agreement |
| SFAO | Shanghai Foreign Affairs Office (China) |
| SFAR | Short form accountant's report |
| SFAS | Statements of Financial Accounting Standards (Philippines) |
| SFC | Securities and Futures Commission |
| SFC | State financial corporation (India) |
| SFCCI | Singapore Federation of Chambers of Commerce and Industry |
| SFCI | Singapore Federation of Computer Industry |
| SFCL | Shanghai Foxboro Company Limited |
| SFDA | Special Fund for Development Assistance (UN) |
| SFDP | Small Farmers' Development Program (Nepal) |
| SFE | Shanghai Futures Exchange (SFE) |
| SFE | Sydney Futures Exchange |
| SFDP | Small Farmers' Development Program (Bangladesh) |
| SFETC | Shanghai Foreign Exchange Transaction Centre |
| SFI | Securities and Futures Institute (Taiwan) |
| SFI | Sugar Factories Incorporated (Thailand) |
| SFIC | Shanghai Federation of Industry and Commerce |

| | |
|---|---|
| SFIDvD | Simultaneous Final and Irrevocable Delivery versus Payment |
| SFLEP | Shanghai Foreign Language Education Press |
| SFLLDC | Special Fund for Land Locked Developing Countries (UN) |
| SFRP | SAARC Fund for Regional Projects |
| SFTC | Shandong Foreign Trade Corporation (China) |
| SFTC | Shanghai Foreign Trade Corporation (China) |
| SFTC | Sichuan Foreign Trade Corporation (China) |
| SG | Shipping guarantee |
| SGB | Specialized government bank |
| SGC | Superannuation Guarantee Charge (Australia) |
| SGD | Singapore dollar |
| SGH | State Great Hural (Mongolia) |
| SGIEC | Shanghai Garments Import and Export Corporation (China) |
| SGL | Societa a Garanzia Limitata (private limited liability company in Switzerland) |
| SGL | Subsidiary general ledger (India) |
| SGMEC | Shou Gang Machinery Equipment Corporation (China) |
| SGNIC | Singapore Network Information Centre |
| SGQPC | Shanghai Gaoqiao Petroleum Corporation (China) |
| SGS | Singapore Government Securities |
| SGTDC | Sichuan Global Technological Development Corp (China) |
| SGV | SyCip Gorres Velayo and Company (Philippines) |
| SGX | Singapore Exchange |
| SGX-DC | Singapore Exchange Derivatives Clearing |
| SGX-DT | Singapore Exchange Derivatives Trading |
| SGX-ETS | Singapore Exchange Electronic Trading System |
| SGX-ST | Singapore Exchange Securities Trading |
| SH | Sarjana Hukum (Indonesian) (Law graduate) |
| SHAC | Shougang Heavy Automotive Corporation (China) |
| SHACO | Shanghai Harbour Container Corporation (China) |
| SHANTRA | Shanghai Foreign Trade Corporation (China) |
| SHANTRADE | Shandong Foreign Trade Corporation (China) |
| SFTC | Sichuan Foreign Trade Corporation (China) |
| SHB | Shanghai Harbour Board (China) |
| SHB | Sheng Heng Bank (Macau) |
| SHCC | Shanghai Harbour Construction Corporation (China) |
| SHCIL | Stock Holding Corporation of India Limited |
| SHD | Sustainable Human Development |
| SHE | Safety, health and environment |
| SHG | Self-help group |
| SHHOC | South Huanghai Oil Corporation (China) |
| SHIFT | System for Handling Inter-bank Fund Transfer |
| SHLDTO | Shanghai Long Distance Telecommunication Office (China) |
| SHMI | Small and Household Manufacturing Industries (Pakistan) |
| SHMP | Shenyang Heavy Machinery Plant (China) |

| | |
|---|---|
| SHRD | SAARC Human Resources Development Centre |
| SHRI | Singapore Human Resources Institute |
| SHSE | Shanghai Securities Exchange |
| SHZ | Shenzhen Securities Exchange |
| SHTEX | Shanghai Textiles Import and Export Corporation (China) |
| SHUDC | Shanghai Hongqiao United Development Corporation (China) |
| SI | Settlement instruction |
| SIA | Secretariat for Industrial Approvals (India) |
| SIA | Securities Industry Act (Malaysia) |
| SIA | Singapore Airlines |
| SIABE | Sistem Informasi Agroindustri Berbasis Ekspor (Indonesia) (Export Oriented Agroindustry Information System) |
| SIAH | Shanghai International Airport Hotel (China) |
| SIAP | Statistical Institute for Asia and the Pacific |
| SIAS | Scandinavian Institute of Asian Studies |
| SIAS | Securities Investors Association of Singapore |
| SIB | Securities Investment Board (United Kingdom) |
| SIB | Sistem Informasi Baseline Economic Survey (Indonesia) (Information System for Baseline Economic Survey) |
| SIBA | Singapore Insurance Brokers Association |
| SIBAS | Shanghai Institute of Biochemistry Academia Sinica |
| SIBC | Solomon Islands Broadcasting Corporation |
| SIBOR | Singapore Inter Bank Offer Rate |
| SIC | Securities Industry Council |
| SIC | Standard industrial classification |
| SICA | Sick Industrial Companies Act (India) |
| SICC | Shanghai Investment Consulting Corporation |
| SICC | Singapore Island Country Club |
| SICC | Singapore International Chamber of Commerce |
| SICCI | Singapore Indian Chamber of Commerce and Industry |
| SICDA | Securities Industry (Central Depository) Act |
| SICO | Scientific Instrument Company (India) |
| SICOM | Singapore Commodity Exchange |
| SICOF | State Investment Corporation of Forestry (China) |
| SICT | Shanghai Institute of Computing Technology (China) |
| SID | Singapore Institute of Directors |
| SID | Society for International Development (United States) |
| SIDA | Swedish International Development Agency |
| SIDBI | Small Industries Development Bank of India |
| SIDC | Small Industries Development Corporation (Nepal) |
| SIDC | State Industrial Development Corporation |
| SIEA | Solomon Islands Electricity Authority |
| SIEC | Shenzhen International Exhibition Centre (China) |
| SIERA | Share Investment External Rupee Account (Sri Lanka) |
| SIF | Shanghai Industrial Foundation (China) |

| | |
|---|---|
| SIF | Singapore International Foundation |
| SIFA | Singapore International Franchise Association |
| SIFC | Short-term Investment and Finance Company |
| SIFC | Small Industries Finance Corporation (Thailand) |
| SIFN | Statute for Investment by Foreign Nationals (Taiwan) |
| SIFO | Small Industries Finance Office (Thailand) |
| SIIC | State Industrial Investment Corporation (India) |
| SIJORI | Singapore, Johor, Riau (Growth Triangle) |
| SIL | Special import licence |
| SILCO | Shanghai International Leasing Corporation |
| SI-LMUK | Sistem Informasi Pola Perbiayan/Lending Model Usaha Kechil (Indonesia) (Lending Model Information System) |
| SIM | Singapore Institute of Management |
| SIM | Standards Institute of Malaysia |
| SIMAJ | Scientific Instrument Manufacturers Association of Japan |
| SIMEX | Singapore International Monetary Exchange |
| SIMPEDES | Simpanan Pedesaan (Indonesia) (Rural savings scheme) |
| SIMTC | Shanghai Industrial Management Training Centre |
| SINDA | Singapore Indian Development Association |
| SingCERT | Singapore Computer Emergency Response Team |
| SingCham | Singapore Chamber of Commerce and Industry |
| SINERGY | Singapore Initiative in New Energy Technology |
| SingTel | Singapore Telecom |
| SINOCHART | China National Chartering Corporation |
| SINOCHEM | China National Chemicals Import and Export Corporation |
| Sino-Latin | China National Latin America Trading Corporation |
| SINOPEC | China National Petrochemical Corporation |
| SINOPET | China Petrochemical Corporation |
| SINOTECHMART | China Technology Market Management and Promotion Centre |
| SINOTRAN | China National Foreign Trade Transportation Corporation |
| SIOC | Shanghai Institute of Organic Chemistry |
| SIOC | Statute for Investment by Overseas Chinese (Taiwan) |
| SIOFM | Shanghai Institute of Optics and Fine Mechanics |
| SIOFT | Shanghai Institute of Foreign Trade |
| SIP | Social Investment Program |
| SIP | State Investment Plan (Laos) |
| SIP | Suzhou Industrial Park |
| SIPA | Water Supply Licence (Indonesia) |
| SIPFI | Securities Investors Protection Fund Incorporated (Philippines) |
| SI-PMK | Sistem Informasi–Prosedur Memperoleh Kredit (Indonesia) (Information System for Credit Procedure) |
| SIPRI | Stockholm International Peace Research Institute |

| | |
|---|---|
| SIPTOC | State Industries Promotion Corporation of Tamil Nadu (India) |
| SI-PUK | Sistem Informasi–Terpadu Pengembangan Usaha Kechil (Indonesia) (Integrated Information System for Small Enterprise Development) |
| SIR | Singapore Immigration and Registration |
| SIRIM | Standard and Industrial Research Institute of Malaysia |
| SIRV | Special Investor's Resident Visa (Philippines) |
| SISCO | Shanghai International Securities Company |
| SISCO | Southern Iron and Steel Company (India) |
| SITA | Solomon Islands Tourist Authority |
| SITA | Students International Travel Association |
| SITC | Securities investment trust company |
| SITC | Shanghai International Tendering Company |
| SITC | Shanghai International Trade Centre |
| SITC | Standard International Trade Classification |
| SITCA | Securities Investment Trust and Consulting Association (Taiwan) |
| SITCO | Shanghai Investment and Trust Corporation |
| SITDC | Shantou International Trade Development Corporation (China) |
| SITDDEC | South Investment, Trade and Development Data Exchange Centre |
| SITDRAC | Singapore IT Dispute Resolution Advisory Committee |
| SITE | Securities investment and trust enterprise (Taiwan) |
| SITE | Sind Industrial and Trading Estates (Pakistan) |
| SITEC | Shanghai International Technology Import and Export Corporation |
| SITIC | Shanxi International Trust and Investment Corporation (China) |
| SITIC | Shenyang International Trust and Investment Corporation (China) |
| SITRA | South India Textile Research Association |
| SITSC | Shantou International Trust Service Corporation (China) |
| SITTDEC | South Investment Trade and Technology Data Exchange Centre |
| SITV | Singapore International Television |
| SIU | Statute for Promotion of Industrial Upgrading (Taiwan) |
| SIUPD | Shanghai Institute of Urban Planning and Design |
| SJAC | Society of Japanese Aerospace Companies |
| SJAC | Society of Japanese Aircraft Constructors |
| SKAPI | Standar Khusus Akuntansi Perbankan Indonesia (Special Standard for Application of Banking Accounting in Indonesia) |
| SKD | Semi knocked-down |
| SKEJ | Jakarta Electronic Clearing System |
| SKM | Malaysian Skill Certificate |
| SL | Sensitive List |
| SLA | Savings and Loan Association |
| SLACH | Sri Lanka Automated Clearing House |

| SLAS | Sri Lanka Administrative Service |
| SLBC | Sri Lanka Broadcasting Corporation |
| SLBDC | Sri Lanka Business Development Centre |
| SLBFE | Sri Lanka Bureau of Foreign Employment |
| SLCTB | Sri Lanka Central Transport Board |
| SLDB | State Land Development Bank (India) |
| SLECIC | Sri Lanka Export Credit Insurance Corporation |
| SLFP | Sri Lanka Freedom Party |
| SLFP | Sri Lanka Freedom Party |
| SLFSP | Sri Lanka Freedom Socialist Party |
| SLI | Small local investor |
| SLI | State-level institution (India) |
| SLIC | State Life Insurance Corporation (Pakistan) |
| SLICM | Sri Lanka Institute of Cooperative Management |
| SLIDA | Sri Lanka Institute of Development Administration |
| SLIDC | Sri Lanka Industrial Development Company |
| SLIIC | State-level Inter-institutional Committee (India) |
| SLIM | Solvency, liquidity, income and management |
| SLIPS | Sri Lanka Interbank Payment System |
| SLISES | Sri Lanka Institute of Social and Economic Studies |
| SLORC | State Law and Order Restoration Council (Myanmar) |
| SLPA | Sri Lanka Ports Authority |
| SLR | Sri Lanka Railway |
| SLR | Statutory liquidity ratio |
| SLS | Special Loan Scheme |
| SLSB | Sri Lanka Standards Board |
| SLSC | Sri Lanka Sugar Corporation |
| SLSI | Sri Lanka Standards Institute |
| SLSPC | Sri Lanka State Plantations Corporation |
| SLT | Sri Lanka Telecom |
| SLTB | Sri Lanka Tea Board |
| SMAP | Small and Medium Enterprise Assistance Project (Sri Lanka) |
| SMATS | Stock Market Automated Trading System |
| SMB | Savings and mortgage bank (Philippines) |
| SMC | Secondary Mortgage Corporation |
| SMC | San Miguel Corporation (Philippines) |
| SMC | Shanghai Metro Corporation |
| SMCFSL | Small Medium Company Formation Support Law (Korea) |
| SMDRI | Shanghai Metallurgical Design Research Institute |
| SME | Small and medium enterprise |
| SMEDA | Small and Medium Enterprises Development Authority (Pakistan) |
| SMEDC | Small and Medium Enterprise Development Council |
| SMEIA | Shanghai Mechanical and Electrical Industries Administration |
| SMEPN | Shanghai Municipal Electric Power Bureau |
| SMERI | Shanghai Marine Equipment Research Institute |

| | |
|---|---|
| SMERT | Shanghai Municipal Foreign Economic Relations and Trade Commission |
| SMF | Secondary Mortgage Facility |
| SMFD | Measures on the Collection of Statistics and Monitoring of Foreign Debts (China) |
| SMG | Shanghai Municipal Government |
| SMGC | Shanghai Municipal Gas Company |
| SMH | Sydney Morning Herald (Australia) |
| SMI | Small and medium industry |
| SMIB | Small and Medium Industry Bank (Korea) |
| SMIB | State Mortgage and Investment Bank (Sri Lanka) |
| SMIDEC | Small and Medium Industries Development Corp (Malaysia) |
| SMIEC | Shanghai Machinery Import and Export Corporation |
| SMILE | Singapore Myanmar Investment and Leisure Enterprise |
| SMILE | Small and Micro Industries Leader and Entrepreneur Promotion Project (Sri Lanka) |
| SMM | Secondary Mortgage Market |
| SMMB | Shenyang Municipal Metallurgical Bureau (China) |
| SMO | State Management Organization (Laos) |
| SMP | Second Malaysia Plan (1970–75) |
| SMR | Standard Malaysian rubber |
| SMRC | SAARC Meteorological Research Centre |
| SMRT | Singapore MRT Limited |
| SMT | Surface mount technology |
| SMTC | Shenyang Materials Trade Centre (China) |
| SMU | Singapore Management University |
| SNA | System of National Accounts |
| SNAC | State Nationalities Affairs Commission (China) |
| SNAP | Sarawak National Party (Malaysia) |
| SNCD | Short-term negotiable certificate of deposit |
| SNEF | Singapore National Employers Federation |
| SNGPL | Sui Northern Gas Pipeline Limited (Pakistan) |
| SNIF | Standby note issuance facility |
| SNITS | Simplified Net income Taxation Scheme (Philippines) |
| SNOC | Singapore National Olympic Council |
| SNS | Singapore Network Services |
| SNU | Seoul National University (Korea) |
| SO | Securities Ordinance (Hong Kong) |
| SOC | Social overhead capital |
| SOCB | State-owned commercial bank |
| SOCOG | Sydney Organizing Committee for the Olympic Games |
| SOE | State-owned enterprise |
| SOES | Small Order Entry System/Small Order Execution System (United States) |
| SOGO | Sale of Goods Ordinance (Hong Kong) |

| SOHO | Small home office |
|---|---|
| SOHYO | General Council of Japan Labour Unions |
| SOLAIR | School of Labour and Industrial Relations (University of the Philippines) |
| SOLAIR | Solomon Islands Airways Limited |
| SOLAS | International Convention for the Safety of Life at Sea |
| SOM | School of Management |
| SOM | Senior Officials Meeting (ASEAN) |
| SOMTC | Senior Officials Meeting on Transnational Crime |
| S-ONE | Securities One (Thailand) |
| SOOSC | Shanghai Offshore Oil Service Corporation |
| SOPAC | Committee for Coordination of Joint Prospecting of Mineral Resources in the South Pacific Area |
| SOPAC | South Pacific News Service Limited |
| SOSA | Strength of Support Assessment |
| SOSITO | Supply of Services (Implied Terms) Ordinance (Hong Kong) |
| SOTUS | Share Ownership Top-Up Scheme (Singapore) |
| SP | Singapore Power |
| SpA | Societa per Aziono (Limited liability company, Italy) |
| SPA | Shanghai Patent Agency |
| SPA | Sichuan Petroleum Administration (China) |
| SPA | Sichuan Planning Authority (China) |
| SPAB | Shanghai Pharmaceutical Administration Bureau |
| SPAC | State Pharmaceutical Administration of China |
| SPARC | Society for Promotion of Area Residence Centres |
| SPARTECA | South Pacific Regional Trade and Economic Cooperation Agreement |
| SPC | Saigon Postal Corporation (Vietnam) |
| SPC | South Pacific Commission |
| SPC | South Pacific country |
| SPC | Special purpose company |
| SPC | State Pharmaceutical Corporation (Sri Lanka) |
| SPC | State Planning Commission |
| SPC | State Planning Committee |
| SPC | State Property Committee (Mongolia) |
| SPDC | State Peace Development Council (Myanmar) |
| SPE | State public enterprise |
| SPEC | South Pacific Bureau for Economic Cooperation |
| SPERI | Shanghai Power Equipment Research Institute |
| SPF | South Pacific Forum |
| SPFC | South Pacific Fishing Company Limited (Vanuatu) |
| SPFFP | South Pacific Fruit Fly Project |
| SPI | Stock Price Index |
| SPIC | Shanghai Pharmaceutical Industry Corporation |

| | |
|---|---|
| SPIDI | Shanghai Pharmaceutical Industry Design Institute |
| SPKUI | Sistem Penunjang Keputusan Untuk Investasi (Indonesia) (Decision Support System for the Financial Aspect of Lending Model) |
| SPM | Supplementary Payments Mechanism |
| SPM | Sijil Pelajaran Malaysia |
| SPMS | School of Postgraduate Management Studies |
| SPN | Secured premium note |
| SPOCC | South Pacific Organizations Coordinating Committee |
| SPP | Social protection policy |
| SPP | Small power producer |
| SPPP | Surat Pemberitahuan Persetujuan Presiden (Indonesia) (Letter of Presidential Approval) |
| SPPBS | Synchronized Planning Programming and Budgeting System |
| SPREP | South Pacific Regional Environment Program |
| SPRINTER | Singapore Press Release on the Internet |
| SPSB | Shanghai Public Security Bureau |
| SPSE | South Pacific Stock Exchange |
| SPSI | Serikat Pekerja Seluruh Indonesia (All Indonesian Workers' Union) |
| SPSP | Surat Persetujuan Sementara (Indonesia) (Provisional Letter of Approval) |
| SPSS | Statistical Package for Social Sciences |
| SPT | Special permit to transfer |
| SPTC | South Pacific Trade Commission |
| SPTF | Skim Perbankeru Tanpu Faedah (Malaysia) (Interest free banking scheme) |
| SPTP | Serikat Pekerja Tingkat Perusahaan (Indonesia) (Enterprise union) |
| SPTS | Saigon Post and Telecommunications Services |
| SPUG | Small Power Utilities Group (Philippines) |
| SPV | Special purpose vehicle |
| SPZ | Special Promotion Zone |
| SQ | Sociedad por Quota (Private limited liability company, Portugal) |
| SRA | Sugar Regulatory Administration (Philippines) |
| SRAJ | Shipbuilding Research Association of Japan |
| SRB | Self-regulating banking |
| SRD | Statutory reserve deposit |
| SRF | Supplemental Reserve Facility |
| SRI | Society of Rubber Industry (Japan) |
| SRI | Sugar Cane Research Institute (Sri Lanka) |
| SRICI | Shanghai Research Institute of Chemical Industry |
| SRIS | Society of Rubber Industry Standard (Japan) |
| SRL | Sociedad a Responsabilidad Limitada (private limited liability company in Mexico and Spain) |

| | |
|---|---|
| SRL | Societe a Responsabilite Limitee (private limited liability company in France and Luxembourg) |
| SRMIC | State Raw Material Investment Corporation (China) |
| SRN | Security-holder Reference Number (Australia) |
| SRO | Self-regulatory organization |
| SRO | Statutory Regulatory Order (Bangladesh) |
| SRP | Sijil Rendah Pelajaran (Malaysia) |
| SRQ | Strategic Response Quotient |
| SRR | Statutory reserve ratio |
| SRR | Statutory reserve requirement |
| SRRP | Smallholder Rubber Rehabilitation Project (Sri Lanka) |
| SRS | Supplementary Retirement Scheme |
| SRT | State Railways of Thailand |
| SSA | Singapore Shipping Association |
| SSAP | Statement of Standard Accounting Practice |
| SSB | Shari'ah Supervisory Board (Indonesia) |
| SSB | State Statistical Bureau (China) |
| SSC | State Securities Commission (Vietnam) |
| SSE | Secretariat of State for Environment (Cambodia) |
| SSE | Shanghai Shipping Exchange |
| SSED | Small Scale Enterprises Division (Malaysia) |
| SSHI | Social Science and Human Studies Institute (Vietnam) |
| SSP | Special service provider |
| SSPP | Shan State Progress Party (Myanmar) |
| SSRI | Shanghai Silk Research Institute |
| SSRI | Singapore Securities Research Institute |
| SSRI | Social Science Research Institute (United States) |
| SSS | Staff Suggestion Scheme |
| SSS | Social Security System (Philippines) |
| SSSRI | Shanghai Ship and Shipping Research Institute |
| SSTEC | Shanghai Centre for Scientific and Technological Exchange with Foreign Countries |
| SSX | Surabaya Stock Exchange |
| ST | Singapore Telecom |
| ST | Singapore Technologies |
| STA | Science and Technology Agency (Japan) |
| STACRES | Standing Committee on Research and Statistics (UN) |
| STADA | Singapore Training and Development Association |
| STAND | Science and Technology Agenda for National Development (Philippines) |
| STAP | Special Technical Assistance Program |
| STAQS | Securities Trading Automated Quotation System (China) |
| STAR | Sistem Transit Aliran Ringan (Malaysia) |
| START | Strategic Arms Reduction Talk |

| | |
|---|---|
| STASCo | Shell International Trading and Shipping Company |
| STB | Singapore Tourism Board |
| STBM | Secondary Treasury Bill Market (Sri Lanka) |
| STC | Shanghai Transit Company |
| STC | State Science and Technology Commission (China) |
| STC | State Trading Corporation (India) |
| STC | Statute for Technical Cooperation (Taiwan) |
| StCB | State cooperative bank (India) |
| STCB | State Trading Corporation of Bhutan |
| STCI | Securities Trading Corporation of India |
| STCS | Science and Technology Commission of Shanghai |
| STCW | Standards of Training, Certification and Watch-keeping Convention |
| STD | Subscriber trunk dialing |
| STE | State trading enterprise |
| Stelco | State Electric Company (Maldives) |
| STEP | Singapore Thailand Enhanced Program |
| STET | Submission through electronic transmission |
| STFB | State Bank Treasury Federal Bond (Pakistan) |
| STFC | Short term finance company |
| STI | Science, technology and innovation |
| STI | IMF-Singapore Regional Training Institute |
| STI | Straits Times Index |
| STIB | Shanghai Textile Industry Bureau |
| STIB | Shanxi Textile Industry Bureau |
| STIC | Science and Technology Information Centre (Taiwan) |
| STIC | Shanghai Trust and Investment Corporation (China) |
| STIC | Singapore Technologies Industrial Corporation |
| STICERD | Suntory Toyota International Centre for Economics and Related Disciplines |
| STIDC | Scientific and Technical Information and Documentation Committee |
| STIEC | Shanghai Toys Import and Export Corporation |
| STK | Satuan Tugas Khusus (Indonesia) (Bad debt workout team) |
| STM | Skeloh Tinggi Manajemen (Indonesia) (Management college) |
| STMB | Syarikat Telekom Malaysia Berhad |
| STMS | Short-term monetary support facility |
| STMY-GS | Short-term yielding government securities |
| STN | Shalimar Television Network (Pakistan) |
| STO | State Trading Organization (Maldives) |
| STOL | Short take-off and landing |
| STP | Short-term plan |
| STP | Software Technology Park (India) |
| STPLR | Short-term prime lending rate |
| STPM | Sijil Tinggi Pelajaran Malaysia |

| | |
|---|---|
| STR | Special Trade Representative (United States) |
| STRI | Shanghai Textile Research Institute |
| STRIPS | Separate Trade Registered Interest and Principal Strategy |
| STS | Ship-to-ship operations |
| STSI | Securities trading service institution |
| SUAR | Sinkiang Uighur Autonomous Region (China) |
| SUBC | Singapore–United States Business Council |
| SULSEL | South Celebes/Sulawesi Province |
| SULTENG | Central Celebes/Sulawesi Province |
| SVC | Stored value card |
| SVCP | Measures on the Administration and Supervision of the Verification and Cancellation of Payment of Foreign Exchange for Imports (China) |
| SVP | Standard valuation practice |
| SVWAC | Shanghai Volkswagen Automotive Corporation |
| SWAPU | South and West Asia Postal Union |
| SWCEPA | Southwest China Electric Power Administration |
| SWCIE | Shanghai Workers' Centre for International Exchange |
| SWDCAP | Social Welfare and Development Centre for Asia and the Pacific |
| SWIFT | Society for Worldwide Inter-bank Financial Telecommunications |
| SYFAO | Shenyang Foreign Affairs Office (China) |
| SYNDP | Six-Year National Development Plan (Taiwan) |
| SYSTCO | Sydney Steel Corporation (Australia) |
| SYTTA | Shenyang Travel and Tourism Administration (China) |
| SZN | Shenzhen |
| SZOPAD | Special Zone of Peace and Development |
| SZSE | Shenzhen Securities Exchange |
| T+3 | Three market days from trade date |
| T+7 | Seven calendar days from trade date |
| T21 | Technopreneurship 21 (Singapore) |
| TA | Technical assistance |
| TA | Timber Authority (Papua New Guinea) |
| TAA | Technical Assistance Administration (UN) |
| TAA | Technical assistance agreement |
| TAB | Tariff Advisory Board |
| TAB | Tourism Authority of Bhutan |
| TAB | Treasury Adjustable Rate Bond (Australia) |
| TABANAS | Tabungan Nasional (Indonesia) (Nationwide Saving Program) |
| TAC | Thailand Acrylic Company |
| TAC | Total adjusted capital |
| TAC | Treaty of Amity and Cooperation |
| T&D | Training and development |
| T&D | Transmission and distribution |
| TAF | Targeted Assistance Fund |
| TAF | Temporary Advance Facility |

| | |
|---|---|
| TAFE | Technical and Further Education (Australia) |
| TAFI | Total assets of financial institution |
| TAFIPS | Total assets of financial institution plus securities |
| TAFTA | Transalantic Free Trade Agreement |
| TAG | Technical Advisory Group |
| TAGP | Trans-ASEAN Gas Pipeline |
| TAIC | Tokyo Atomic Industry Consortium |
| TAIEX | Taiwan Stock Exchange |
| TAIFEX | Taiwan Futures Exchange |
| TAIMEX | Taiwan International Mercantile Exchange |
| TAM | PT Toyota Astra Motor (Indonesia) |
| TAMADES | Tabungan Masyarakat Pedesaan (Indonesia) (Village Savings Program) |
| TAR | Tunku Abdul Raham College (Malaysia) |
| TAS | Telecommunication Authority of Singapore |
| TASEAP | Thailand Australia Science and Engineering Assistance Program |
| TAUN | Technical Assistance of United Nations |
| TB | Treasury bill |
| TB | Thrift bank |
| TBA | Thai Bankers' Association |
| TBA | To be announced |
| TBD | To be determined |
| TBS | Tokyo Broadcasting System |
| TBT | Technical barriers to trade |
| TBTF | Too big to fail |
| TC | Traveller's cheque |
| TCB | The Chinese Bank (Taiwan) |
| TCB | Trade Corporation of Bangladesh |
| TCC | Textiles Consultative Committee (Macau) |
| TCC | Thai Chamber of Commerce |
| TCC | Transport and Communication Commission (UN) |
| TCCP | Tariff and Customs Code of the Philippines |
| TCDC | Special Unit for Technical Cooperation Among Developing Countries |
| TCE | Tokyo Commodities Exchange |
| TCF | Textiles, clothing and footwear |
| TCH | Tokyo Clearing House |
| TECHIMPORT | China National Technical Import and Export Corp |
| TCL | Technology Contract Law (China) |
| TCM | Traditional Chinese Medicine |
| TCOC | Taiwan Chamber of Commerce |
| TCP | Technical Cooperation Program |
| TCP | Trading Corporation of Pakistan |
| TCS | Trade Capture System |
| TCTP | Third Country Training Program (Singapore) |

| | |
|---|---|
| TDA | Trade Development Authority (India) |
| TD&T | Tan Duc Vocational Training School (Vietnam) |
| TDB | Technology Development Board (India) |
| TDB | Thai Danu Bank |
| TDB | Tonga Development Bank |
| TDB | Trade Development Board (Singapore) |
| TDC | Tourist Development Corporation (Malaysia) |
| TDC | Township Trade Dispute Committee (Myanmar) |
| TDICI | Technology Development and Information Company of India |
| TDMC | Tourism Development Management Committee (Myanmar) |
| TDP | Technical Development Plan |
| TDP | Company registration number (Indonesia) |
| TDRI | Thailand Development Research Institute |
| TDS | Tax deducted at source |
| TDZ | Trade Development Zone |
| TEC | Tata Electric Company |
| TECHNONET | Asian Network for Industrial Technology Information and Extension |
| TEDA | Tianjin Economic Technological Development Area (China) |
| TEDA | Tumen Economic Development Area |
| TEL | Temporary Exclusion List |
| TELCO | Tata Engineering and Locomotive Company (India) |
| Telco | Telecommmunication company |
| Teleseara | PT Telekomindo Selular Mitra Raya (Indonesia) (Cellular phone operator) |
| Telkom | PT Telekomunikasi (Indonesia) (State-owned telecommunication company) |
| TEMF | Templeton Emerging Markets Fund |
| TEPTC | Tianjin Environment Protection Technology Centre (China) |
| TESDA | Technical Skills Development Authority |
| TESDA | Technical Education and Skills Development Authority (Philippines) |
| TEU | Twenty-foot equivalent unit container |
| TEWA | Termination of Employment of Workmen Act (Sri Lanka) |
| TFB | Tai Fung Bank (Macau) |
| TFB | Thai Farmers Bank |
| TFC | Term finance certificate |
| TFC | Tourism Forecasting Council (Australia) |
| TFCI | Tourism Finance Corporation of India |
| TFCN | Treaty of Friendship Commerce and Navigation |
| TFP | Total factor productivity |
| TFS | Trade finance system |
| TG | Thai Airways International |
| Tg | Tugrik (currency of Mongolia) |
| TGE | Tokyo Grain Exchange |

| | |
|---|---|
| TGF | Trade Guarantee Fund (Philippines) |
| T-GT | Thailand Growth Triangle sub-region |
| THAI | Thai Airways International |
| THB | Thai baht |
| THW | Toxic and hazardous waste |
| TIBOR | Taipei Inter-bank Offer Rate |
| TIBOR | Tokyo Inter-bank Offer Rate |
| TIC | Tipya Insurance Company Limited |
| TIC | Trust and Investment Corporation |
| TICCI | Technical Information Centre for Chemical Industry (India) |
| TIE | Taiwan Invested Enterprises (China) |
| TIER | Taiwan Institute of Economic Research |
| TIFFE | Tokyo International Financial Futures Exchange |
| TIGER | Taiwan Innovative Growing Enterpreneurs Board |
| TILF | Trade and investment liberalization and facilitation |
| TILM | Trade, investment and labour mobility |
| TIMEX | China National Timber Import and Export Corporation |
| TIMS | The Institute of Management Science (United States) |
| TIMS | Theoretical Intermarket Margin System |
| TIN | Tax Identifier Number (Pakistan) |
| TIPP | Trade and Investment Promotion Program |
| TIS | Trade Insurance System |
| TISCO | Tata Iron and Steel Company (India) |
| TISCO | Thai Investment and Securities Corporation |
| TISCO | Tianjin Iron and Steel Corporation (China) |
| TITIC | Tianjin International Trust and Investment Corp (China) |
| TJEDC | Tianjin Economic Development Corporation (China) |
| TJIM | Tianjin International Market |
| TK | Taka (Bangladesh currency) |
| TKB | Taiyo Kobe Bank (Japan) |
| TLA | Timber license agreement |
| TLC | Transfer loan certificate |
| TLF | Thailand Locker Fund |
| TLI | Transfer loan instrument |
| TLO | Township Labour Office (Myanmar) |
| TLRC | Technology and Livelihood Research Centre (Philippines) |
| TM | Trademark |
| TMB | Thai Military Bank |
| TMEETB | Tianjin Machinery and Electrical Equipment Tendering Bureau (China) |
| TMIC | Thai Maize Import Company |
| TMNC | Thai Maritime Navigation Company |
| TMO | Telegraphic money order |
| TMO | Trademark Office |
| TMP | Tourism Master Plan (Vanuatu) |

| | |
|---|---|
| TNB | Tenaga Nasional Berhad (Malaysia) |
| TNC | Transnational corporation |
| TNI | Tata Niaga Impor (Approved Importers System) |
| TNPCB | Tamil Nadu Pollution Control Board (India) |
| TNSW | Tourism New South Wales (Australia) |
| TO | Tanning Organization (Thailand) |
| TOAP | Trust Officers Association of the Philippines |
| TOB | Take over bid |
| TOCOM | Tokyo Industrial Products Exchange |
| TOE | Ton of oil equivalent |
| TOEFL | Test of English as a Foreign Language |
| TOFE | Tableau des Operations Financieres de l'Etat |
| TOKOM | Tokyo Commodity Exchange |
| TOPIC | Teletext Output of Price Information by Computer (United Kingdom) |
| TOPIX | Tokyo Stock Price Index |
| TOPS | Traded Options System (Hong Kong) |
| TOR | Terms of reference |
| TORAY | Toyo Rayon Company (Japan) |
| TORC | Thailand Oil Refining Company |
| TOSHIBA | Tokyo Shibaura Electric Company |
| TOT | Telephone Organization of Thailand |
| TOT | Terms of trade |
| TOT | Transfer, operate and transfer |
| TPA | Trade Practice Act (Australia) |
| TPAC | Trade Policy Advisory Council (Australia) |
| TPB | Tea Promotion Bureau (Sri Lanka) |
| TPC | Trade Promotion Centre (Nepal) |
| TPCC | Tianjin Petrochemical Corporation (China) |
| TPF | Teachers Provident Fund (Malaysia) |
| TPFC | Trans Pacific Freight Conference |
| TPI | Thai Petrochemical Industry Company |
| TPI | Televisi Pendidikan Indonesia (Private television station) |
| TPKP | Corporate employee housing savings scheme (Indonesia) |
| TPM | Technology Park Malaysia |
| TPN | PT Timor Putra Nasional (Indonesia) |
| TPNG | Territory of Papua New Guinea |
| TPKP | Corporate employee housing savings scheme (Indonesia) |
| TPRB | Trade Policy Review Body (WTO) |
| TPRM | Trade Policy Review Mechanism |
| TQB | Textile Quota Board (Sri Lanka) |
| TQC | Total quality control |
| TQM | Total quality management |
| TR | Trust receipt |
| TRAD | Tea Rehabilitation and Development Program (Sri Lanka) |

| | |
|---|---|
| TRAI | Telecom Regulatory Authority of India |
| TRB | Toll Regulatory Board (Philippines) |
| TRC | Thai Rice Company |
| TRC | Taiwan Ratings Corporation |
| TRC | Tax Reform Committee (India) |
| TRCO | Transportation and communications |
| TREZ | Tumen River Economic Zone |
| TRI | Tea Research Institute (Sri Lanka) |
| TRIM | Trade Related Investment Measure |
| TRIPS | Trade Related Intellectual Property Rights |
| TRIS | Thai Rating and Information Services |
| TRM | Trade and related matters |
| TRQ | Tariff rate quota |
| TRT | Thai Rak Thai Party |
| TRUF | Transferable revolving underwriting facility |
| TSA | Tasmania State Archives (Australia) |
| TSA | Time series analysis |
| TSB | Trustee Savings Bank (United Kingdom) |
| TSBA | Trustee Savings Banks Association (United Kingdom) |
| TSCD | Taiwan Securities Central Depository Co Limited |
| TSD | Thailand Securities Depository |
| TSDA | Taipei Securities Dealers Association |
| TSE | Taiwan Stock Exchange |
| TSE | Tokyo Stock Exchange |
| TSF | Technical service fee |
| TSHDA | Tea Small Holding Development Authority (Sri Lanka) |
| TSI | Thailand Securities Institute |
| TSIPA | Tainan Science-based Industrial Park (Taiwan) |
| TSITAS | Taipei Securities Investment Trust and Advisory Association |
| TSK | Tokyo Senpaku Kaisha Line |
| TSMC | Taiwan Semiconductor Manufacturing Company |
| TSR | Transferable subscription rights |
| TSTEC | Tianjin Scientific and Technical Exchange with Foreign Countries (China) |
| TT | Telegraphic transfer |
| TTA | Tianjin Tourism Administration (China) |
| TTAT | Thai Telephone and Telecommunications |
| TTB | Asian Highway Transport Technical Bureau |
| TTEC | Thai Technical and Economic Cooperation Office |
| TTM | Thailand Tobacco Monopoly |
| TTO | Thai Textile Organization |
| TTR | Technology Transfer Registry (Philippines) |
| TTSI | Textile Training and Services Institute (Sri Lanka) |
| TTZ | Tan Thuan Export Processing Zone (Vietnam) |
| TUC | Trades Union Congress (United Kingdom) |

| | |
|---|---|
| TUCP | Trade Union Congress of the Philippines |
| TUF | Tokyo University of Fisheries |
| TUIAPPW | Trade Union International of Agriculture, Forestry and Plantation Worker |
| TUIMWE | Trade Union International of Miners and Workers in Energy |
| TVA | Tennessee Valley Authority (United States) |
| TVE | Township and village enterprise (China) |
| TVIE | Township and village industrial enterprise (China) |
| TVK | National Television of Kampuchea |
| TVL | Telecom Vanuatu Limited |
| TVRI | Televisi Republik Indonesia (State-owned television) |
| TWARO | Textile Workers' Asian Regional Organization |
| TWh | Terrawatt-hour |
| TWG | Technical working group |
| TWI | Trade-weighted Index |
| TWI | Training within industry |
| TWSC | Township Workers' Supervisory Committee (Myanmar) |
| TWTC | Taipei World Trade Centre |
| UAB | United Asian Bank |
| UASC | United Arab Shipping Company |
| UATI | Union of International Engineering Organizations |
| UAW | United Automobile Workers (United States) |
| UB | United Bank Ltd (Pakistan) |
| UB | Union of Burma |
| UBA | Union of Burma Airways |
| UBARI | Union of Burma Applied Research Institute |
| UBB | Union Bank of Bangkok |
| UBC | Unit business cost |
| UBC | University of British Columbia (Canada) |
| UBD | University of Brunei Darussalam |
| UBEC | Union of Banana Exporting Countries |
| UBI | United Bank of India |
| UBL | United Bank Limited (Pakistan) |
| UBP | Union Bank of the Philippines |
| UBS | Union Bank of Switzerland |
| UBS | Union of Burma Standard |
| UCC | Uniform Commercial Code |
| UCC | Universal Copyright Convention |
| UCC | Urban credit cooperative (China) |
| UCCA | Upazila Central Cooperative Association (Bangladesh) |
| UCCC | Uniform Consumer Credit Code (Australia) |
| UCIL | Union Carbide India Ltd |
| UCIL | Uranium Corporation of India Limited |
| UCLA | University of California at Los Angeles |
| UCO | Unconscionable Contracts Ordinance (Hong Kong) |

| | |
|---|---|
| UCP | Uniform Customs and Practice for Documentary Credits |
| UCPB | United Coconut Planters' Bank (Philippines) |
| UCQ | University of Central Queensland (Australia) |
| UCSTM | University College of Science and Technology Malaysia |
| UDA | Urban Development Authority (Malaysia) |
| UDC | Under-developed country |
| UDESCO | Urban Development Service Company (Vietnam) |
| UDHA | Urban Development and Housing Act (Philippines) |
| UEM | United Engineers (Malaysia) Berhad |
| UF | United Front |
| UGC | University Grants Commission |
| UI | University of Indonesia |
| UIA | Universiti Islam Antarabangsa (Malaysia) (International Islamic University) |
| UIBE | University of International Business and Economics (China) |
| UIC | Underground investment company (Taiwan) |
| UIC | United Industrial Corporation (Singapore) |
| UIEO | Union of International Engineering Organizations |
| UIEOA | International Union for Oriental and Asian Studies |
| UiTM | Universiti Teknologi MARA (Malaysia) |
| UKM | Universiti Kebangsaan Malaysia |
| ULC | Unit labour cost |
| ULC | United Leasing Company (Bangladesh) |
| ULCC | Ultra large crude carrier |
| ULF | United Left Front (Sri Lanka) |
| UM | University of Malaya/Universiti Malaya |
| UMAST | Upper Mekong Associated Survey Team |
| UMBC | United Malayan Banking Corporation |
| UMIST | University of Manchester Institute of Science and Technology |
| UMM | Universiti Multimedia Malaysia |
| UMS | Universiti Malaysia Sabah |
| UMNO | United Malays National Organization (Malaysia) |
| UMPAP | Urban Management Program for Asia and the Pacific (UN) |
| UN | United Nations |
| UNA | United Nations Association |
| UNAA | United Nations Association of Australia |
| UNAEC | UN Atomic Energy Commission |
| UNAECC | UN Atomic Energy Control Commission |
| UNAPEC | UN Action Program for Economic Cooperation |
| UNARCO | UN Narcotics Commission |
| UNB | United Nations Bookshop |
| UNBTAO | UN Bureau of Technical Assistance Operations |
| UNC | United Nations Charter |
| UNCA | United Nations Correspondents Association |
| UNCC | United Nations Cartographic Commission |

| | |
|---|---|
| UNCDF | UN Capital Development Fund |
| UNCDPPP | UN Centre for Development Planning, Projections and Policies |
| UNCED | UN Conference on Environment and Development |
| UNCHE | UN Conference on Human Environment |
| UNCHS | UN Centre for Human Settlements |
| UNCIO | UN Conference on International Organizations |
| UNCIP | UN Commission for India and Pakistan |
| UNCITRAL | UN Commission on International Trade Law |
| UNCLS | UN Conference on Law of the Sea |
| UNCPPP | UN Centre for Projection, Planning and Policy |
| UNCPUSO | UN Committee on Peaceful Use of Outer Space |
| UNCRC | UN Convention on the Rights of the Child |
| UNCSD | UN Committee on Sustainable Development |
| UNCSTD | UN Centre on Science and Technology for Development |
| UNCTAD | UN Conference on Trade and Development |
| UNCTC | UN Centre for Transnational Corporations |
| UNCTC | UN Commission on Transnational Corporations |
| UNDC | UN Development Corporation |
| UNDC | UN Disarmament Commission |
| UNDCP | UN Drug Control Program |
| UNDDSMS | UN Department of Development Support and Management Services |
| UNDOF | UN Disengagement Observation Force |
| UNDP | UN Development Program |
| UNDPKO | UN Department of Peacekeeping Operations |
| UNDRO | UN Disaster Relief Office |
| UNDTCD | UN Department of Technical Cooperation for Development |
| UNE | University of New England (Australia) |
| UNECA | UN Economic Commission for Asia |
| UNEDA | UN Economic Development Administration |
| UNEF | UN Environment Fund |
| UNEP | UN Environment Program |
| UNEPTA | UN Expanded Program for Technical Assistance |
| UNESCO | UN Education, Scientific and Cultural Organization |
| UNETAS | UN Emergency Technical Aid Service |
| UNFAO | UN Food and Agriculture Organization |
| UNFB | UN Film Board |
| UNFDAC | UN Fund for Drug Abuse Control |
| UNFPA | UN Fund for Population Activities |
| UNFSSTD | UN Financing System for Science and Technology for Development |
| UNFSTD | UN Fund for Science and Technology for Development |
| UNHCHR | UN High Commission for Human Rights |
| UNHCR | UN High Commission for Refugees |
| UNHHSF | UN Habitat and Human Settlements Foundation |

| | |
|---|---|
| UNI | United News of India |
| Unibank | United City Bank (Indonesia) |
| UNICEF | UN Children's Fund |
| UNIDF | UN Industrial Development Fund |
| UNIDO | UN Industrial Development Organization |
| UNIDROIT | International Institute for the Unification of Private Law |
| UNIFEM | UN Fund for Women |
| UNIMAS | Universiti Malaysia Sarawak |
| UNIO | UN Information Organization |
| UNIS | UN Information Service |
| UNIS | UN International School |
| UNISCAT | UN Expert Committee on Application of Science and Technology |
| UNISIST | Universal System for Information on Science and Technology |
| UNITAR | UN Institute for Training and Research |
| UNITAR | Universiti Tun Abdul Razak (Malaysia) |
| UNITEM | Universiti Terbuka Malaysia (Open University) |
| UNITES | UN Information Technology Service |
| UNJSPB | UN Joint Staff Pension Board |
| UNKRA | UN Korea Reconstruction Agency |
| UNMAC | UN Mixed Armistice Commission |
| UNMOGIP | UN Military Observer Group in India and Pakistan |
| UNO | United Nations Organization |
| UNOCHA | UN Office for Coordination of Humanitarian Assistance |
| UNOPS | UN Office for Project Services |
| UNP | United National Party (Sri Lanka) |
| UNPA | UN Postal Administration |
| UNPC | UN Population Commission |
| UNPOC | UN Peace Observation Commission |
| UNREF | UN Refugee Emergence Fund |
| UNRF | UN Revolving Fund |
| UNRFNRE | UN Revolving Fund for Natural Resources Exploration |
| UNROB | United Nations Relief Operations in Bangladesh |
| UNRISD | UN Research Institute for Social Development |
| UNRRA | UN Relief and Rehabilitation Administration |
| UNRWA | UN Relief and Works Agency |
| UNSA | UN Special Account |
| UNSAC | UN Scientific Advisory Committee |
| UNSC | UN Security Council |
| UNSC | UN Social Commission |
| UNSCC | UN Standards Coordination Committee |
| UNSCEAR | UN Scientific Committee on the Effects of Atomic Radiation |
| UNSCR | UN Security Council Resolution |
| UNSD | UN Statistics Division |
| UNSF | UN Special Fund for Economic Development |
| UNSG | UN Secretary General |

| | |
|---|---|
| UNSO | UN Statistical Office |
| UNSR | UN Space Registry |
| UNSW | University of New South Wales (Australia) |
| UNTA | UN Technical Assistance |
| UNTAA | UN Technical Assistance Administration |
| UNTAB | UN Technical Assistance Board |
| UNTAC | UN Transitional Authority in Cambodia |
| UNTAM | UN Technical Assistance Mission |
| UNTAO | UN Technical Assistance Operations |
| UNTAP | UN Technical Assistance Program |
| UNTC | UN Trusteeship Council |
| UNTCOK | UN Temporary Commission on Korea |
| UNTDB | UN Trade and Development Board |
| UNTEA | UN Temporary Executive Authority |
| UNTFDPP | UN Trust Fund for Development Planning and Projections |
| UNTT | UN Trust Territory |
| UNV | UN Volunteers |
| UNWCC | UN War Crimes Commission |
| UOB | United Overseas Bank (Singapore) |
| UP | Uttar Pradesh (India) |
| UP | University of the Philippines |
| UPC | UNESCO Publication Centre |
| UPC | Uniform Practice Code |
| UPC | Universal Products Code |
| UPE | Universalization of Primary Education |
| UPEIK | Unit Perancangan Ekonomi Ibu Kota (Malaysia) (City Economic Planning Unit) |
| UPI | United Press International |
| UPI | United Press of India |
| UPL | United Philippine Lines |
| UPL | International Institute for the Unification of Private Law |
| UPM | Universiti Putra Malaysia (formerly Universiti Pertanian Malaysia) |
| UPNG | University of Papua New Guinea |
| UPOU | University of the Philippines Open University |
| UPOV | International Union for the Protection of New Varieties of Plant |
| UPS | Uninterrupted power supply |
| UPSEB | Uttar Pradesh State Electricity Board (India) |
| UPUK | Small Business Development Unit (Indonesia) |
| UR | Uruguay Round |
| URA | Urban Redevelopment Authority (Singapore) |
| URBANICOM | International Association on Town Planning and Distribution |
| URC | Uniform Rules for Collections |
| USAEC | US Atomic Energy Commission |
| US-AEP | US-Asia Environment Partnership |

| | |
|---|---|
| USAF | US Air Force |
| USAFFE | US Air Force in the Far East |
| USAID | US Agency for International Development |
| USBC | US Bureau of the Census |
| USBS | US Bureau of Standards |
| USCG | US Coast Guard |
| USCPFA | US-China Peoples' Friendship Association |
| USCSC | US Civil Service Commission |
| USD | US dollar |
| USDA | US Development Agency |
| US-EPA | US Environmental Protection Agency |
| USIA | US Information Agency |
| USIS | US Information Service |
| USITC | US International Trade Commission |
| US-JTC | US-Japan Trade Council |
| USM | Unlisted securities market |
| USM | Universiti Sains Malaysia |
| USMC | US Marine Corps |
| USN | US Navy |
| USP | University of the South Pacific |
| USQ | University of Southern Queensland (Australia) |
| USSR | Union of Soviet Socialist Republics |
| USTDA | US Trade and Development Agency |
| USTR | US Trade Representative |
| USUN | US Mission to the United Nations |
| USWB | US Weather Bureau |
| UT | Union Territories (India) |
| UT | Unit trust |
| UTB | Unit Trust of Bhutan |
| UTI | United Trust of India |
| UTM | Universiti Teknologi Malaysia |
| UTS | Unified Trading System (Philippines) |
| UTS | University of Technology in Sydney |
| UUG | Nuisance Act Permit (Indonesia) |
| UUM | Universiti Utara Malaysia |
| UWA | University of Western Australia |
| UWCCB | United World Chinese Commercial Bank (Taiwan) |
| VA | Value added |
| VA | Veterans' Administration (United States) |
| VACC | Vietnam American Chamber of Commerce |
| VACM | Vietnam Association of Cigarette Manufacturers |
| VACO | Vietnam Auditing Company |
| VAID | Village Agricultural and Industrial Development (Pakistan) |
| VALENTE | ASEAN Energy Database, Valorization of Energy Technology |
| VAN | Value Added Network |

| | |
|---|---|
| VANAIR | Vanuatu Internal Air Services Limited |
| VANGO | Vanuatu Association of NGOs |
| VAR | Vector auto regression |
| VAR | Value at risk model |
| VARNET | Vietnam Academic Research and Education Network |
| VAS | Value added services |
| VASCO | Vietnam Air Service Company |
| VASP | Vanuatu Agricultural Security Project |
| VAT | Value added tax |
| VAVYP | Vietnamese American Volunteer Youth Project |
| VBA | Vietnam Bank of Agriculture |
| VBARD | Vietnam Bank for Agriculture and Rural Development |
| VBTC | Vanuatu Broadcasting and Television Corporation |
| VBL | Vanuatu Brewing Limited |
| VC | Venture capital |
| VC | Vice Chancellor |
| VCA | Vietnam Computer Association |
| VCC | Vietnam Cement Corporation |
| VCCI | Vietnam Chamber of Commerce and Industry |
| VCIE | Venture Capital Investment Enterprise (Taiwan) |
| VCMB | Vanuatu Commodities Marketing Board |
| VCP | Voluntary Cooperation Program |
| VCR | Video cassette recorder |
| VCSBL | Vanuatu Cooperative Savings Bank Limited |
| VCU | Vanuatu Credit Union |
| VDC | Vietnam Datacommunication Corporation |
| VDIC | Vietnam Development Information Centre |
| VDIS | Voluntary Disclosure Income Scheme (India) |
| VDP | Vendor Development Program (Malaysia) |
| VDU | Visual display unit |
| VEAM | Vietnam Engineering and Agriculture Machinery Corporation |
| VEDF | Village Economic Development Fund (Papua New Guinea) |
| VEFAC | Vietnam Exhibition and Trade Fair Centre |
| VEIC | Vietnam Electronics and Informatics Corporation |
| VER | Voluntary export restraint |
| VET | Vocational Education and Training |
| VFCR | Voluntary Foreign Currency Restriction |
| VFF | Vietnam Fatherland Front |
| VFHA | Vanuatu Family Health Association |
| VFI | Vanuatu Fishing Investments Ltd |
| VFSC | Vanuatu Financial Services Commission |
| VFSP | Vanuatu Fisheries Development Project |
| VHF | Very high frequency |
| VHW | Voluntary health worker |
| VIA | Vietnam International Assurance Company |

| VIAC | Vietnam International Arbitration Centre |
| VIAS | Vietnam Investment Advisory Service |
| VICOFA | Vietnam Cocoa and Coffee Association |
| VIDAMCO | Vietnam Daewoo Motor Company |
| Vietcochamber | Chamber of Commerce and Industry of Vietnam |
| Vietcombank | Bank for Foreign Trade Bank of Vietnam |
| Vietindebank | Bank for Investment and Development of Vietnam |
| Viglacera | Vietnam Corporation of Ceramics and Construction Glass |
| VILC | Vietnam International Leasing Company |
| VIMPEX | China National Vehicle Import and Export Corporation |
| Vinacafe | Vietnam National Coffee Corporation |
| Vinachem | Vietnam Chemical Corporation |
| Vinacoal | Vietnam National Coal Company |
| Vinafor | Vietnam Forestry Product Company |
| Vinalines | Vietnam National Maritime Corporation |
| Vinamarine | Vietnam National Maritime Bureau |
| Vinamilk | Vietnam National Milk Company |
| Vinapco | Vietnam Air Petrol Co. |
| Vinapico | Vietnam National Alcohol, Beer and Beverage Corporation |
| Vinaplat | Vietnam Plastic Imports and Exports |
| Vinare | Vietnamese Reinsurance Company |
| Vinashin | Vietnam Shipbuilding Industry Corporation |
| Vinataba | Vietnam National Tobacco Corporation |
| Vinataxi | A joint venture taxi company |
| Vinatex | Vietnam National Textile and Garment Corporation |
| Vinatom | Vietnam Atomic Energy Commission |
| VIR | Village Irrigation Rehabilitation (Sri Lanka) |
| VISS | Venture Investment Support for Start-ups (Singapore) |
| VISTA | Vietnam Information Network for Science and Technology Advance (VISTA Network) |
| VJA | Vietnamese Journalist Association |
| VLC | Very large carrier |
| VLCC | Very large crude carrier |
| VLD | Vanuatu Livestock Development Limited |
| VLSS | Vietnam Living Standards Survey |
| VMI | Vietnam Management Initiative |
| VMLC | Vanuatu Meat and Livestock Corporation |
| VMS | Vietnam Mobile Service |
| VMY | Visit Malaysia Year |
| VMY | Visit Myanmar Year |
| VNA | Vietnam Airlines |
| VNA | Vietnamese News Agency |
| VNAPIEC | Vietnam National Agricultural Produce Import Export Corporation |
| VNAT | Vietnam National Administration of Tourism |

| | |
|---|---|
| VNCS | Vanuatu National Council of Women |
| VND | Vietnamese dong (currency) |
| VNGDPT | Vietnam General Department of Post and Telecommunications |
| VNPF | Vanuatu National Provident Fund |
| VNPT | Vietnam Posts and Telecommunications Corporation |
| VOC | Vereenigde Oost-Indische Compagnie (Dutch East India Company) |
| VOCTEC | Vocational and technical education |
| VOSCO | Vietnam Ocean Shipping Company |
| VOV | Voice of Vietnam |
| VPC | Vanuatu Postal Corporation |
| VPS | Vietnam Postal Services |
| VPSD | Valuation and Property Services Department |
| VQC | Veterinary Quarantine Clearance |
| VRA | Voluntary Restraint Agreement |
| VRM | Variable rate mortgage |
| VRU | Voice Response Unit |
| VRU | Vietnam Railway Union |
| VSAT | Very small aperture terminal |
| VSC | Vietnam Steel Corporation |
| VSIP | Vietnam Singapore Industrial Park |
| VSNL | Videsh Sanchar Nigam Limited (India) |
| VSPA | Victoria Scallop Processors Association (Australia) |
| VSSC | Vietnam Scientific Shipbuilding Corporation |
| VSTF | Very short term financing facility |
| VSTTC | Vietnam Singapore Technical Training Centre |
| VTA | Vietnam Tourism Administration |
| VTE | Vocational and technical education |
| VTGC | Vietnam Textile and Garment Corporation |
| VTR | Video tape recorder |
| VTV | National Vietnam Television |
| VUEIE | Vietnam Union of Electronic and Informatic Enterprises |
| VWO | Voluntary Welfare Organization |
| WA | Western Australia |
| WAACC | Western Australia Automobile Chamber of Commerce |
| WAAP | World Association for Animal Production |
| WACA | World Airline Clubs Association |
| WACAE | Western Australia College of Advanced Education |
| WACC | Weighted average cost of capital |
| WAFD | Western Australia Fisheries Department |
| WAIT | Western Australia Institute of Technology |
| WAITRO | World Association of Industrial and Technological Research Organizations |
| WAPDA | Water and Power Development Authority (Pakistan) |
| WAPT | West Australia Petroleum Proprietary Limited |

| | |
|---|---|
| WASA | Water and Sewerage Authority (Bangladesh) |
| WAST | Western Australia Standard Time |
| WATA | World Association of Travel Agencies |
| WAY | World Assembly of Youth |
| WB | World Bank |
| WBCSD | World Business Council for Sustainable Development |
| WBG | World Bank Group |
| WCCU | World Council of Credit Unions |
| WCL | World Confederation of Labour |
| WCM | World Council of Management |
| WCN | World Conservation Union |
| WCPG | World Coffee Producers' Group |
| WCPS | World Confederation of Productivity Science |
| WDM | Wholesale debt market |
| WDRC | World Data Referral Centre |
| WEC | World Energy Council |
| wef | With effect from |
| WEF | World Economic Forum |
| WEFA | Wharton Econometric Forecasting Associates Incorporated |
| WEPZA | World Export Processing Zones Association |
| WEI | World Environment Institute |
| WERC | World Environment and Resources Council |
| WFAFW | World Federation of Agriculture and Food Workers |
| WFC | World Finance Corporation |
| WFC | World Food Council |
| WFDFI | World Federation of Development Financial Institutions |
| WFED | World Federation of Engineering Organizations |
| WFETT | Wuxi Foreign Economic and Technical Trade Corporation (China) |
| WFF | World Food Fund |
| WFFTH | World Federation of Workers in Food Tobacco and Hotel Industries |
| WFO | World Food Council |
| WFOE | Wholly foreign-owned enterprise |
| WFP | World Food Program |
| WFS | World Futures Society |
| WFSW | World Federation of Scientific Workers |
| WFTU | World Federation of Trade Unions |
| WFUNA | World Federation of United Nations Associations |
| WG | Working Group |
| WGC | World Gold Council |
| WGEC-CLM | Working Group on Economic Development in Cambodia, Laos and Myanmar |
| WHO | World Health Organization |
| WIA | Wireless Institute of Australia |
| WIC | Work Improvement Circle |

| WIDER | World Institute for Development Economics Research |
| WIEL | Wholly Individual-owned Enterprise Law |
| WIP | Work in progress |
| WinSCORE | Broker Front-End System (Malaysia) |
| WIPO | World Intellectual Property Organization |
| WIR | World Investment Report |
| WIRA | Wool Industries Research Association |
| WISCO | Wuhan Iron and Steel Corporation (China) |
| WISDRI | Wuhan Iron and Steel Design and Research Institute (China) |
| WMA | Ways and Means Advance (India) |
| WMC | Western Mining Corporation (Australia) |
| WMC | World Meteorological Centre |
| WMO | World Meteorological Organization |
| WMRI | Wuhan Metallurgical Research Institute (China) |
| w/o | Without |
| WOMAN | World Organization of Mothers of All Nations |
| WOO | World Oceanic Organization |
| WOS | Wholly-owned subsidiary |
| WP | Work Permit |
| WPCF | Water Pollution Control Federation |
| WPI | Wholesale Price Index |
| WPI | World Patents Index |
| WPSA | World Poultry Science Association |
| WRA | Workplace Relations Act (Australia) |
| WRI | World Resources Institute |
| WRONZ | Wool Research Organization of New Zealand |
| Wrt | Warrant |
| WSB | Wage Stabilization Board |
| WSC | World Summit for Children |
| WSIP | Wuxi Singapore Industrial Park |
| WSPA | World Society for the Protection of Animals |
| WSRO | World Sugar Research Organization |
| WTA | Willing to accept |
| WTA | World Transport Agency |
| WTAA | World Trade Alliance Association |
| WTAO | World Touring and Automobile Organization |
| WTC | World Trade Centre |
| WTC | World Trade Committee |
| WTCA | World Trade Centres Association |
| WTCC | World Trade Centres Club |
| WTCM | Macau World Trade Centre Limited |
| WTI | World Trade Institute |
| WTO | World Tobacco Organization |
| WTO | World Tourism Organization |
| WTO | World Trade Organization |

| WTP | Willing to pay |
| WTRC | Wool Textile Research Council |
| WTTC | World Travel and Tourism Council |
| WUA | Water Users' Association (India) |
| WULTUO | World Union of Liberal Trade Union Organizations |
| WV | World Vision |
| WVA | Wages as share of value added |
| WVA | World Veterinary Association |
| WWC | World Water Council |
| WWF | World Wide Fund for Nature |
| WWF | World Wildlife Fund |
| WWMO | Waste Water Management Organization (Thailand) |
| WWW | World Wide Web |
| WXITC | Wuxi Investment and Trust Corporation (China) |
| xa | Excluding all |
| xall | Excluding all |
| xbi | Excluding bonus issue |
| xd | Excluding dividend |
| xe | Excluding entitlement |
| XITIC | Xiamen International Trust and Investment Corporation (China) |
| XMEIC | Xiamen Economic Information Centre (China) |
| XMRB | Xiamen Ribao (China) (Xiamen Daily) |
| XNA | Xinhua News Agency (China) |
| xo | Excluding offer |
| xp | Excluding partial redemption |
| xri | Excluding rights issue |
| XSB | Xiamen Statistical Bureau (China) |
| XSEZ | Xiamen Special Economic Zone (China) |
| XUDC | Xiamen SEZ United Development Company Ltd |
| xw | Excluding warrant |
| YA | Year of assessment |
| YAB | Yang Amat Berhomat (The Most Honourable) (Prime Minister, Deputy Prime Minister and Chief Minister) |
| YAVC | Yamaichi Asia Venture Capital |
| YB | Yang Berhomat (The Honourable) (Members of Parliament) |
| YCDC | Yangon City Development Committee (Myanmar) |
| YES | Yield Enhancement Structure |
| YIPS | Youth Investment Promotion Society (Pakistan) |
| YITAC | Yunnan International Technology Advancement Corporation (China) |
| YLBHI | Indonesian Institute of Legal Aid |
| YLKI | Indonesian Foundation for Consumer Protection |
| YMEC | Yunnan Machinery and Equipment Import and Export Corporation (China) |
| YOB | Year of birth |

| YOY | Year-on-year |
| YPIEC | Yunnan Provincial Import and Export Corporation (China) |
| YPPM | Yayasan Pendidikan dan Pengembangan Manajemen (Management Education and Development Foundation) |
| YRI | Yamaichi Research Institute |
| YTB | Yasuda Trust and Bank Company (Japan) |
| YTC | Yield to call |
| YTM | Yield to maturity |
| ZBB | Zero-base budget |
| ZCFIC | Zhejiang Chemical Fibres Industrial Corporation (China) |
| ZDP | Zero defect program |
| ZEDC | Zhejiang Economic Development Corporation (China) |
| ZEG | Zero economic growth |
| ZENGYOREN | Japanese National Federation of Fishery Cooperatives |
| ZFTC | Zhejiang Foreign Trade Corporation (China) |
| ZIA | Zamboanga International Airport (Philippines) |
| ZIA | Zia International Airport (Bangladesh) |
| ZIP | Zonal Improvement Program |
| ZITDC | Zhonghua International Technology Development Corporation (China) |
| ZITIC | Zhejiang International Trust and Investment Corporation (China) |
| ZNCD | Zero-coupon negotiable certificate of deposit |
| ZOPAD | Zone of Peace and Development |
| ZOPFAN | Zone of Peace, Freedom and Neutrality (ASEAN) |
| ZOTO | Zone One Tondo Organization (Philippines) |
| ZPG | Zero population growth |
| ZPO | Zoological Park Organization (Thailand) |

# REFERENCES

### General

ASEAN Secretariat (1998) *Compendium of Investment Policies and Measures in ASEAN Countries*, ASEAN Secretariat Jakarta.

Barouski, W. A. and Beutel, M. M. (1999) *The Supervisory Impact of Technology on South East Asian Banking*, South East Asian Central Banks (SEACEN) Research & Training Centre, Kuala Lumpur.

Courtis, Neil (ed.) (1999) *How Countries Supervise Their Banks, Insurers and Securities Markets*, Central Banking Publication Ltd, London.

De Brouwer, G. and Pupphavesa, W. (eds.) (1999) *Asia Pacific Financial Deregulation*, Routledge, London.

Dobson, W. and Hufbauer, G. C. (2001) *World Capital Markets*, Institute for International Finance, Washington, D.C.

Euromoney Publications (1996) *International Capital Markets: A Guide for Asian Business*, Asia Law & Practice Ltd, Hong Kong.

Findlay, C. and Garnaut, R. (eds.) (1986) *Political Economy of Manufacturing Protection: Experiences of ASEAN and Australia*, Allen and Unwin, Sydney.

Johnson, H. J. (1997) *Banking in Asia*, Lafferty Publications, Dublin.

Kao, Kim Hourn and Kaplan, J. A. (eds.) (2000) *The Greater Mekong Subregion and ASEAN*, Cambodian Institute for Cooperation and Peace, Phnom Penh, Cambodia.

Kim, Yoon Hyung & Wang, Yunjong (eds.) (2001) *Regional Financial Arrangements in East Asia*, Korea Institute for International Economic Policy, Seoul.

Sampson, G. P. (ed.) (2001) *The Role of World Trade Organisation in Global Governance*, United Nations University Press, Tokyo.

Scott, H. S. and Wellons, P. A. (1996) *Financing Capital Market Intermediaries in East and Southeast Asia*, Kluwer Law International, The Hague.

Steil, B. (ed.) (1994) *International Financial Market Regulation*, Wiley, Chichester.

Tan, Chwee Huat (2000) *Financial Sourcebook for Southeast Asia and Hong Kong*, Singapore University Press, Singapore.

Tan, Khee Giap & Chen, Kang (2001) "Financial cooperation and coordination in East Asia: an ASEAN perspective", in Kim, Yoon Hyung & Wang, Yunjong (eds.) (2001) *Regional Financial Arrangements in East Asia*, Korea Institute for International Economic Policy, Seoul, pp. 307–320.

Thant, Myo and Tang, Min (eds.) (1996) *Indonesia Malaysia Thailand Growth Triangle: Theory to Practice*, Asian Development Bank, Manila.

Wong, T. C. and Singh, Mohan (eds.) (1999) *Development and Challenge: Southeast Asia in the New Millennium*, Times Academic Press, Singapore.

World Trade Organization (1996) *Trade Policy Review: Sri Lanka 1995*, World Trade Organization Secretariat, Geneva.


### Australia

Batten, J. and Rouse, J. (2002) "Australia", in Batten, J. and Fetherston, T. A. (2002) *Asia-Pacific Fixed Income Markets*, Wiley, Singapore, pp. 23–50.

Euromoney Publications (1996) *International Capital Markets: A Guide for Asian Business*, Asia Law & Practice Ltd, Hong Kong.

ISI Publications (1996) *The Practitioner's Guide to the Listing Rules of the Australian Stock Exchange*, ISI Publications, Hong Kong.

Weerasooria, W. (1996) *Banking Law and the Financial System in Australia*, Butterworths, Sydney.


### Cambodia

Kao, Kim Hourn and Kaplan, J. A. (2000) *The Greater Mekong Subregion and ASEAN*, Cambodian Institute for Cooperation and Peace, Phnom Penh.

Trade & Development Board (1999), *Post Mission Report on Cambodia*, Singapore.


### China

Batten, J. (2002) "China", in Batten, J. and Fetherston, T. A. (2002) *Asia-Pacific Fixed Income Markets*, Wiley, Singapore.

Chen, B, Dietrich, J.K. and Fang, Y. (eds.) (2000) *Financial Market Reform in China: Progress, Problems, and Prospects*, Westview, Boulder.

Corne, P. H. (1997) *Foreign Investment in China: the Administrative Legal System*, Hong Kong University Press, Hong Kong.

Hu, Yebi (1993) *China's Capital Market*, Chinese University Press, Hong Kong.

Luo, Qi (2001) *China's Industrial Reform and Open-door Policy 1980–1997: A Case Study from Xiamen*, Ashgate, Hampshire, England.

Norton, J. J., Cheng, C. J. and Fletcher, I. (eds.) (1994) *International Banking Operations and Practices: Current Developments*, Graham & Trotman, London.

_____ (1994) *International Banking Regulation and Supervision: Change and Transformation in the 1990s*, Graham & Trotman, London.

Norton, J. J., Li, C. J. and Huang, Yangxin (eds.) (2000) *Financial Regulation in the Greater China Area: Mainland China, Taiwan and Hong Kong SAR*, Kluwer Law International, The Hague.

Wan, Timothy H. (1999) *Development of Banking Law in the Greater China Area: PRC and Taiwan*, Kluwer Law International, The Hague.

Wang, Guiguo and Wei, Zhenying (eds.) (1996) *Legal Developments in China: Market Economy and Law*, Sweet & Maxwell, Hong Kong.

World Trade Press (1994) *China Business: the Portable Encyclopedia for Doing Business with China*, World Trade Press, San Rafael, California.

Yu, Guanghua and Gu, Minkang (2001) *Law Affecting Business Transactions in the PRC*, Kluwer Law International, The Hague.

Zhou, Zhongfei (2001) *Chinese Banking Law and Foreign Financial Institutions*, Kluwer Law International, The Hague.

## Fiji

Asian and Pacific Development Centre (1993) *Fiji: Country Profile*, Asian and Pacific Development Centre, Kuala Lumpur.

Peak Marwick (1986) *Investment in Fiji*, Suva.

**Hong Kong**

Hong Kong Monetary Authority (1997) *Prudential Supervision in Hong Kong*, Hong Kong.

Hong Kong Institute of Banker (1998) *Hong Kong Banking System and Practice*, 4th ed, Hong Kong Institute of Bankers, Hong Kong.

Wang, Guiguo and Wei, Zhenying (eds.) (1996) *Legal Developments in China: Market Economy and Law*, Sweet and Maxwell, Hong Kong.

**Indonesia**

Asia Law & Practice Ltd (1996) *Indonesia Investment Manual*, Asia Law & Practice Ltd, Hong Kong.

Business International (1990) *Indonesia: Investment Perceptions and Potential*, Business International Asia Pacific, Hong Kong.

Chia, R., Marzuki Usman, Suyanto Gondokusumo and Wong Kwei Cheong (1992) *Globalisation of the Jakarta Stock Exchange*, Prentice Hall, Singapore.

**Japan**

Fabozzi, F. J. (1990) *The Japanese Bond Markets*, Probus Publishing Co., Chicago.

Hall, M. J. B. (1998) *Financial Reform in Japan*, Edward Elgar, Chelterham, UK.

Isaacs, J. (1990) *Japanese Equities Market*, Euromoney Publications, London.

Isaacs, J. and Ejiri, Takashi (1990) *Japanese Securities Market*, Euromoney Publications, London.

Suzuki, Y. (ed.) (1987) *Japanese Financial System*, Clarendon Press, Oxford.

**Korea**

Barouski, W.A. and Beutel, M.M. (1999) *Supervisory Impact of Technology on South East Asian Banking*, South East Asian Central Banks (SEACEN) Research & Training Centre, Kuala Lumpur.

Euh, Yoon-Dae and Baker, J. C. (1990) *Korean Banking System and Foreign Influence*, Routledge, New York.

Kim, Yoon Hyung & Wang, Yunjong (eds.) (2001) *Regional Financial Arrangements in East Asia*, Korea Institute for International Economic Policy, Seoul.

Kwon, O. Y. and Shephard, W. (eds.) (2001) *Korea's Economic Prospects*, Edward Elgar, Cheltenham, UK.

Nam, Sang-Woo (1995) "Korea's financial markets and policies", in Shahid N. Zahid, *Financial Sector Development in Asia: Country Studies*, Asian Development Bank, Manila, pp. 1–79.

World Trade Press (1994) *Korea Business: Portable Encyclopedia for Doing Business With Korea*, World Trade Press, San Rafael, California.

Young Shim (2000), *Korean Banking Regulation and Supervision: Crisis and Reform*, Kluwer Law International, The Hague.

**Laos**

Anderson, Kym (1999) *Lao: Economic Reform and WTO Accession*, Centre for International Economic Studies, University of Adelaide and Institute of Southeast Asian Studies, Singapore.

Bourdet, Y. (2000) *The Economics of Transition in Laos*, Edward Elgar, Cheltenham, UK.

Brahm, L. J. (1992) *Banking and Finance in Indochina*, Woodhead-Faulker, Hemel Hempstead, Hertfordshire, UK.

Brahm, L. J. and Macpherson, N. T. (1991) *Investment in the Lao People's Democratic Republic*, Longman, Hong Kong.

Khamsay Souphanouvong (1995) "Developments in the banking and finance industry — how can foreign investors capitalise on the opportunities in the emerging markets: the case of People's Democratic Republic of Laos", Paper presented at the Conference on Banking & Finance in Indochina and Myanmar, 30–31 March 1995, Bangkok, Thailand.

Sunshine, Russell (1995) *Managing Foreign Investment: Lessons From Laos*, Honolulu, Hawaii, East-West Centre, 1995.

United Nations Industrial Development Organisation (1994) *Lao People's Democratic Republic — Industrial Transition*, Industrial Development Reviews Unit, UNIDO, Vienna, Austria.

484     DICTIONARY OF ASIA PACIFIC BUSINESS TERMS

Varit Lekprasert (1995), "Banking operations: what you should know about the People's Democratic Republic of Laos", Paper presented at the Conference on Banking & Finance in Indochina and Myanmar, 30–31 March 1995, Bangkok, Thailand.


## Macau

Hongkong & Shanghai Banking Corporation (1992) *Business Profile Series: Macau*, 5th ed., Hongkong & Shanghai Banking Corporation, Hong Kong.

Sit, V.F.S., Cremer, R.D. and Wong, S.L. (1991) *Entrepreneurs and Enterprises in Macau*, Hong Kong University Press, Hong Kong.


## Malaysia

Low Chee Keong (ed.) (2000) *Financial Markets in Malaysia*, Malayan Law Journal Sdn Bhd, Kuala Lumpur.

Moha Asri Abdullah (1999) *Small and Medium Enterprises in Malaysia*, Ashgate, Aldershot, England.

Okposin, S.B., Abdul Halim Abdul Hamid and Ong, Hway Boon (1999) *The Changing Phases of Malaysian Economy*, ASEAN Academic Press, London.


## Mongolia

Asian Development Bank (1992) *Mongolia: A Centrally Planned Economy in Transition*, Oxford University Press, New York.

Organisation for Economic Cooperation and Development (2000) *Investment Guide for Mongolia*, OECD, Paris.


## Myanmar

Trade Development Board (1996) *Market Research Report: Myanmar*, Trade Development Board, Singapore.


## Nepal

Asian Productivity Organization (2001) *Public Sector Productivity Enhancement: Strategies, Programs and Critical Factors*, Asian Productivity Organization, Tokyo.

Chowdhury, A.H.M.N. and Garcia, M. C. (1993) *Rural Institutional Finance in Bangladesh and Nepal: Review and Agenda for Reforms*, Asian Development Bank, Manila.

James, W. and Quibria, M.G. (1988) *Improving Domestic Resource Mobilisation Through Financial Development*, Asian Development Bank.

Regmi, Mahesh C. (1972) *A Study on Nepali Economic History 1768–1846*, Adroit Publishers, Delhi.

Rehnstrom, J. (2000) *Development Cooperation in Practice: the UN Volunteers in Nepal*, United Nations University Press, New York.

Singh, Nagendra K. (1997) *Nepalese Economy and India*, Ammol Publications, New Delhi.


## New Zealand

Wilson, P. and Batten, J. (2002) "New Zealand", in Batten, J. and Fetherston, T. A. (2002) *Asia-Pacific Fixed Income Markets*, Wiley, Singapore, pp. 253–72.

Weerasooria, W. (ed.) (1999) *Perspectives on Banking, Finance and Credit Law*, Prospect Media Pty Ltd, St Leonard, NSW, Australia.

Williams, J. J. and Marshall, R. (1999) *Business Opportunities in Australia*, Prentice Hall, Singapore.


## Papua New Guinea

World Bank (1978) *Papua New Guinea: Its Economic Situation and Prospects for Development*, World Bank, Washington, D.C.

Asian and Pacific Development Centre (1987) *Business and Investment Environment in South Pacific (Fiji, PNG, Solomon Islands, Tonga, Vanuatu)*, Asian and Pacific Development Centre, Kuala Lumpur and South Pacific Bureau for Economic Cooperation, Suva, Fiji.


## Pakistan

Dobson, W. and Hufbauer, G.C. (2001) *World Capital Markets*, Institute for International Finance, Washington, D.C.

Endo, Tadashi (1998) *Indian Securities Market: A Guide For Foreign and Domestic Investors*, Vision Books, New Delhi.

Haque, Nadeem Ul and Shahid Kardar (1995) "Development of the financial sector of Pakistan", in Shalid N. Zahid (ed.) (1995) *Financial Sector Development in Asia: Country Studies*, Asian Development Bank, Manila, pp. 471–90.

Khawaja Amjad Saeed (1999) *Economy of Pakistan*, Institute of Business Management, Lahore.

United Nations Industrial Development Organisation (1990) *Pakistan: Towards Industrial Liberalisation and Revitalisation*, United Nations Industrial Development Organisation, Vienna.

**Philippines**

Kirk, Donald (1999) *Business Guide to the Philippines*, Butterworth Heinemann Asia, Singapore.

Lamberte, M. B., and Llanto, G.M. (1995) "A study of financial sector policies: the Philippine case", in Shalid N. Zahid (ed.) (1995) *Financial Sector Development in Asia: Country Studies*, Asian Development Bank, Manila, pp. 235–301.

Mahal Kong Pilipinas Inc (1993) *Investor's Guide to the Philippines 1993/94*, Manila.

Parlade, C.V. (1997) *Foreign Direct Investment in the Philippines*, Sweet & Maxwell, Hong Kong.

Euromoney Publications (1997) *Philippines Investment Manual*, Asia Law and Practice Publishing Ltd, Hong Kong.

Tan Teck Meng *et al.* (1996) *Business Opportunities in the Philippines*, Prentice Hall, Singapore.

**Singapore**

Monetary Authority of Singapore, annual reports, various years.

Tan, Chwee Huat (1999) *Financial Markets and Institutions in Singapore*, 10th ed., Singapore University Press, Singapore.

Tan, Chwee Huat (2002) *Singapore Financial & Business Sourcebook*, Singapore University Press, Singapore.

## Solomon Islands

Asian and Pacific Development Centre (1987) *Business and Investment Environment in South Pacific (Fiji, PNG, Solomon Islands, Tonga, Vanuatu)*, Asian and Pacific Development Centre, Kuala Lumpur and South Pacific Bureau for Economic Cooperation, Suva, Fiji.

## Sri Lanka

Asian and Pacific Development Centre (1993) *Sri Lanka: Country Profile*, Vol. 1 and 2, Asian and Pacific Development Centre, Kuala Lumpur.

Central Bank of Sri Lanka (1998) *Economic Progress of Independent Sri Lanka, 1948–1998*, Central Bank of Sri Lanka, Colombo.

Jackson, Paul (2002) *Business Development in Asia and Africa: the Role of Government Agencies*, Palgrave, Houndmills, UK.

Karunatilake, H. N. S. (2000) *Fifty Years of Central Banking in Sri Lanka 1950–2000* Centre for Demographic and Socio Economic Studies, Sri Lanka.

Wignaraja, Ganeshan (1998) *Trade Liberalisation in Sri Lanka*, Macmillan Press, London.

Williams, Tushara (1999) *The Impact of Credit on Small and Medium Scale Industries in Sri Lanka*, Institute of Policy Studies, Colombo.

Gunitilaka, Ramani (1999) *Labour Legislation and Female Employment in Sri Lanka's Manufacturing Sector*, Institute of Policy Studies, Colombo.

World Trade Organization (1996) *Trade Policy Review: Sri Lanka 1995*, World Trade Organization Secretariat, Geneva.

## Taiwan

KPMG Peat Marwick (1993) *Banking in Taiwan*, KPMG Peat Marwick, Taipei.

Securities and Futures Institute (1997) *Taiwan Securities & Future Markets 1997*, Securities and Futures Institute, Taipei.

Wan, Timothy Haosen (1999) *Development of Banking Law in the Greater China Area: PRC and Taiwan*, Kluwer Law International, The Hague.

World Trade Press (1994) *Taiwan Business: Portable Encyclopedia for Doing Business With Taiwan*, World Trade Press, San Rafael, California.

## Tonga

Asian and Pacific Development Centre (1987) *Business and Investment Environment in South Pacific (Fiji, PNG, Solomon Islands, Tonga, Vanuatu)*, Asian and Pacific Development Centre, Kuala Lumpur and South Pacific Bureau for Economic Cooperation. Suva, Fiji.

## Vanuatu

Asian Development Bank (undated) *Vanuatu: Economic Performance, Policy and Reform Issues*, Pacific Studies Series.

Asian and Pacific Development Centre (1987) *Business and Investment Environment in South Pacific (Fiji, PNG, Solomon Islands, Tonga, Vanuatu)*. Asian and Pacific Development Centre, Kuala Lumpur and South Pacific Bureau for Economic Cooperation, Suva, Fiji.

## Vietnam

Nguyen Duc Thao and Pham Dinh Thuong (1994) *Viet Nam — Banking System and its Payment Modalities*, Statistical Publishing House, Hanoi.

Roman, Lisa (1999) *Institutions in Transition: Vietnamese State Bank Reform*, Kluwer, Boston.

Burke, F. (2000) *Guide to Banking and Finance Law in Vietnam*, Baker & McKenzie.